HOW TO LEGALIZE DRUGS

HOW TO LEGALIZE DRUGS

Edited by

JEFFERSON M. FISH, PH.D.

JASON ARONSON INC.
Northvale, New Jersey
London

Production Editor: Elaine Lindenblatt

This book was set in 10 pt. Goudy Old Style and printed and bound by Book-mart Press, Inc. of North Bergen, New Jersey.

Library of Congress Cataloging-in-Publication Data

How to legalize drugs / edited by Jefferson M. Fish.
    p. cm.
    Includes bibliographical references and index.
    ISBN 0-7657-0151-0 (alk. paper)
    1. Drug legalization—United States. 2. Drug abuse—United
States. 3. Narcotics, Control of—United States. 4. Narcotic laws-
-United States. I. Fish, Jefferson M.
    HV5825.H69 1998
    362.29'0973—dc21   97-40745

Printed in the United States of America on acid-free paper. For information and catalog write to Jason Aronson Inc., 230 Livingston Street, Northvale, New Jersey 07647-1726. Or visit our website: http://www.aronson.com

To the victims of drug prohibition

Contents

Preface

Increasing numbers of people have become convinced that the policy of drug prohibition has failed, just as alcohol prohibition failed earlier in the century. The question now, as it was then, is What to do? It is an important question, deserving serious consideration from multiple perspectives, so that informed people can take remedial action.

This is not a book about whether or not to legalize drugs. Those who need further convincing might start by reading *Licit and Illicit Drugs* by Edward Brecher and the editors of *Consumer Reports* (1972) or Ethan Nadelmann's article "Drug Prohibition in the United States" in *Science* (1989). More recently, Steven Duke and Albert Gross's *America's Longest War* (1994) and Dan Baum's *Smoke and Mirrors* (1996) show how the United States, by ever more vigorously pursuing a counterproductive policy, has managed to create for itself an unprecedented drug, crime, corruption, civil liberties, AIDS, and foreign policy disaster.

Many chapters in this book do refer to the appalling consequences of our current policy as they make the case for more desirable alternatives. But the book takes the position that the debate over whether to end drug prohibition has already been resolved in the affirmative. It is time to move on to the next question.

As the title states, this is a book about how to legalize drugs. That is, it considers ways of limiting and/or ending the involvement of the criminal justice system in people's use of psychoactive substances. For at least some substances at some dosage levels in some quantities, as well as for substance-related paraphernalia, the government should simply leave responsible adults alone. This book discusses, from multiple perspectives, a variety of proposals for achieving this end.

There are two main approaches to ending drug prohibition, reflecting differing American values; both are amply represented here. One is the public health or harm reduction or cost-benefit approach, which implements the American value of pragmatism. It looks at the social science and biomedical evidence regarding the effects of each drug, attempts to weigh the positive and negative consequences of various courses of action, and proposes policies with the best overall mix of outcomes. Public health approaches to drug legalization emphasize harm reduction (e.g., preventing the spread of disease, maintaining the health of drug users, and guaranteeing drug purity) and controlling in various ways the quantities available for individual purchase, dosage levels, and other aspects of drugs and their use, as well as drug advertising. Public health strategies often involve taxing currently illicit substances (as well as alcohol and tobacco)—possibly in rough relation to their harmfulness (Grinspoon 1990)—and usually dedicate tax revenues to the treatment and prevention of drug-related problems. Such strategies aim to minimize the negative effects of psychoactive substances while holding regulation to a level that will keep the black market as small as possible.

The other—libertarian or rights-based—approach to legalizing drugs can be seen to implement the American value of individualism. It views the private behavior of adults as none of the government's business, and aims at maximizing individual freedom. Whether the issue is consensual heterosexual or homosexual activity, masturbation, contraception, abortion, suicide, or using psychoactive substances, the position of libertarians is the same: people should be free to do in private whatever they want with their own bodies, as long as they don't injure others in some quite direct way.

Libertarians argue that along with freedom comes responsibility for the consequences of one's actions. The great majority of those who use currently illegal substances recreationally can do so with no ill effects, and they should be allowed to do so in peace. The small minority who use those substances in ways that others view as self-destructive should also be allowed to do so as long as they do not injure others—and if they do, they should be punished for their crimes just like anyone else.

Opponents of drug prohibition have long recognized that the great majority of social ills attributed to drugs are actually the result of the war on drugs—and specifically of the colossal black market created by prohibitionist policy.

The black market causes crime by driving drug prices through the roof, so that some miserable and socially marginalized consumers who seek solace in illicit substances steal or prostitute themselves to finance purchases. Drug prohibition defines crime into existence by criminalizing otherwise normal market transactions. The black market created by prohibition produces bystander deaths from turf battles, and kills drug users with unpredictable dosage levels and impurities and with AIDS and other diseases spread by clandestine drug-taking practices.

By allocating limited resources to fight the war on drugs, government increases crime in several other ways. Violent crime and property crime increase because resources are diverted from combating them to jailing drug offenders; those who commit crimes of violence return to the streets early to make room in overcrowded prisons for drug offenders serving mandatory minimum sentences. In addition, while putting a rapist or murderer in jail decreases the number of rapes and murders and makes society safer, putting a drug dealer in jail has the opposite effect. Because of the black market, jailed drug dealers are replaced by others who take their place, thereby increasing the total number of such people. And when drug dealers get out of prison, after years of training to develop their worst potential, they return to poor neighborhoods to make them even more unsafe (Blumstein 1993, 1995).

Because smugglers need to pack as much of their illicit substances into as small a space as possible, the black market pushes people to use higher, and therefore more dangerous, dosage levels. Just as Prohibition promoted a transition from safe low-dosage alcohol (beer) to high-dosage alcohol (whiskey) of unpredictable safety, drug prohibition has promoted a transition from low-dosage coca (coca tea or the original Coca-Cola) to powdered cocaine to crack. Because marijuana is bulky and aromatic, it is easy to detect and therefore to seize. This drives up the black market price of marijuana relative to that of cocaine and heroin, creating an economic incentive for more people to use "hard" drugs over "soft" drugs.

Black market money corrupts American lawyers, judges, police, and politicians; overseas it has distorted and undermined entire economies and corrupted and destabilized entire governments. The black market responds to severe adult criminal penalties by recruiting poor children at high wages. This results in increases in drug experimentation and abuse among children (from sampling their product), youth crime, dangerous schools, and deaths of children working for or caught in the crossfire of the black market. Drug prohibition spreads AIDS because clean needles are not freely available. And the ever-expanding black market created by drug prohibition leads to ever more draconian attempts to control it. These controls have led to the "drug exception to the Bill of Rights," in which all basic rights and freedoms, from private property to life itself (in erroneous drug raids), have been suspended in a self-defeating war on drugs. Ubiquitously and inevitably, as the war on drugs has escalated, the black market has grown in size, power, and corrosiveness—leading for calls to further intensify the war and making matters ever worse.

Advocates of both public health and libertarian approaches recognize that the black market-generating effects of prohibition must be reversed by a black market-destroying strategy of legalization. But they deal with the issue in different ways.

Public health approaches emphasize a regulated market, building on and adapting to each substance the kinds of strategies used to control tobacco and alcohol. Libertarian approaches advocate a free market (for adults), requiring only guarantees of purity, and truth in labeling and advertising—and they advocate a free market in tobacco, alcohol, and prescription drugs as well. Libertarians believe that the free market, individual preferences, and nongovernmental social pressures will do at least as well as a regulated market in controlling drug use while having the added benefit of keeping government out of areas of personal preference. Advocates of public health approaches remain skeptical to varying degrees and in varying ways about the adequacy of an unfettered free market as an alternative to the prohibition of psychoactive substances.

The end of Prohibition did not lead to a single, uniform legalization of alcohol. Rather, states and local governments became the laboratories for policy experimentation envisioned by the Constitution, and some areas of the country remain dry to this day. Similarly, one likely scenario for the end of drug prohibition—terminating the federal government's oppressive role—would encourage a diversity of approaches, implementing different mixes of public health and libertarian rationales, as different parts of the country attempt to develop the forms of legalization (or continued restrictions) that suit them best.

Drug prohibition has caused many deaths. It has ruined the lives or harmed the careers of numerous people, whose only crime was the crime of pleasure, or curiosity, or yielding to peer pressure. It has ravaged the communities of our inner cities and of Third World countries, undermined our democratic institutions, and wreaked havoc with our foreign policy.

Drug prohibition has encouraged the expression of repugnant forms of social scapegoating by cloaking base deeds in the garments of moral outrage. It has legitimized racist attacks on minority groups by demonizing them—from Chinese opium smokers to African-American crack users. At the individual level, drug hysteria has made it seem normal, and even praiseworthy, to jail recreational drug users, confiscate their property, and destroy their lives. Meanwhile, the similarly popular destruction of problem drug users amounts to a state-enforced policy of kicking people when they're down.

In a few decades, when the nightmare of our current drug policy has receded to a bad memory, people will ask themselves—as many do now about Prohibition or segregation—How could we have done that? How could we have destroyed so many lives, and brought so much misery, by so miguided a use of the power of the state? I hope this book will bring comfort to those who have suffered needlessly, and will help bring that future to us a bit sooner.

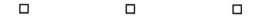

How to Legalize Drugs is written for concerned citizens—especially those uncomfortable with our present policy who haven't yet thought through legalization—as well as for health professionals, social scientists, legislators, and jurists. It aims at helping individuals work out for themselves how best to go about legalizing drugs, to decide which evidence and/or lines of argument they find most compelling.

The book, in two parts of twelve chapters each, helps in two ways. Part I, "Understanding the Problem," consists of theoretical and philosophical, cultural, and social science analyses and findings that shed light on drugs, prohibition, and legalization. Part II, "Approaches to Legalization," discusses general considerations relevant to legalization, and then presents a variety of suggestions and models, from the most limited to the most sweeping, with their accompanying rationales. These proposals can be pondered in light of the background presentations in Part I.

In order for the book to provide adequate breadth of coverage, I have included chapters from leading scholars and practitioners in a wide variety of fields: anthropology, communications, economics, education, history, law (a law professor, a Federal District Court judge, policy analysts, and practicing attorneys, as well as five scholars in three other fields who also hold law degrees), philosophy, political science, psychiatry, psychology, and sociology.

In my introductions to Parts I and II I have attempted to summarize some of the central points of each chapter, as well as to indicate how the various chapters fit into the overall organization of the book. In a few instances I have discussed, reacted to, or amplified ideas raised by the authors in ways different from or that go beyond the authors' presentations. Where I have introduced my own commentary, I have tried to make clear that I was doing so.

The chapters are quite variable in length, in part because I emphasized to the authors that I was interested in quality rather than quantity—"whatever it takes to do the job" was my message.

Editing such a wide-ranging volume has been a fascinating intellectual experience, but it also revealed a minor technical difficulty: each discipline has its own stylistic practices, especially with regard to text-related notes and the listing of references. Because any given chapter will most likely be cited, and its references consulted, primarily by those in the author's (or authors') field, I made the editorial decision to allow authors to generally follow their own discipline's stylistic practices—and I have included a list of references cited in this preface as well. In some cases the in-text references as well as the endnotes have been recast in the publisher's style. There are a few other minor inconsistencies; for example, the spelling *marijuana* is used by all chapter authors but one, who prefers *marihuana*. In apologizing to readers for this lack of editorial standardization, I take heart in Oscar Wilde's observation, "Consistency is the last refuge of the unimaginative," but hasten to add that consistency remains a virtue of the internal logic of each chapter.

It has been a privilege to edit this book, and to work with so many dedicated colleagues from so many different fields to bring the project to fruition. I want to take this opportunity to express to them my gratitude and admiration not only for their professional competence, but for their personal courage in working for long overdue but belligerently resisted policy changes. Their chapters are what the First Amendment is all about. Their contributions are good citizenship in action.

For decades the federal government—the President, the Congress, and the courts—as well as state governments, both political parties, and a wide array of extragovernmental forces have combined to stifle the expression of a simple truth: *drug prohibition, and its instrument of oppression, the war on drugs, makes the drug problem worse rather than better by creating a gigantic black market; America has the world's worst drug problem because America has the world's worst drug policy.*

At present, increasing numbers of thoughtful people see our counterproductive policy for the failure that it is, but few are willing to run the risk of acting on their beliefs. Editing this book has brought home to me the ways in which the war on drugs has stifled freedom of expression. A couple of potential chapter authors declined to participate because they were concerned about the consequences they might have to suffer by being associated with a book entitled *How to Legalize Drugs*. One chapter author, who had planned to remain anonymous, courageously decided at the last minute to put his name on his work and live with whatever the future brings. Another chapter author (Bart Majoor), who has been trying to practice the kind of harm reduction in the United States that is common in the Netherlands, wound up getting arrested in the hallway of an apartment building where he had gone to meet a needle exchange client. Fortunately, I have tenure and am in the latter part of my career, so that, while I do not anticipate any unpleasant surprises, any that may await me as a result of editing and contributing to the book should be limited in severity and duration.

On a more positive note, after rereading this manuscript one last time, I have a feeling of pride about what we have accomplished together. Let us hope that this work will help shift the public debate from whether to legalize drugs to how best to go about doing so.

REFERENCES

Baum, D. (1996). *Smoke and Mirrors: The War on Drugs and the Politics of Failure*. Boston: Little, Brown.

Blumstein, A. (1993). Making rationality relevant—the American Society of Criminology 1992 presidential address. *Criminology* 31(1):1–16.

————— (1995). Crime and punishment in the United States over 20 years: a failure of deterrence and incapacitation? In *Integrating Crime Prevention Strategies: Propensity and Opportunity*, ed. P. H. Wikstrom, R. V. Clarke, and J. McCord, pp. 123–140. Stockholm, Sweden: Swedish National Council for Crime Prevention.

Brecher, E. (1972). *Licit and Illicit Drugs: The Consumers Union Report on Narcotics, Stimulants, Depressants, Inhalants, Hallucinogens, and Marijuana—Including Caffeine, Nicotine, and Alcohol*. Boston: Little, Brown.

Duke, S. B., and Gross, A. C. (1994). *America's Longest War: Rethinking Our Tragic Crusade against Drugs*. New York: Putnam.

Grinspoon, L. (1990). The harmfulness tax: a proposal for regulation and taxation of drugs. *North Carolina Journal of International Law and Commercial Regulation* 15(3):505–510.

Nadelmann, E. (1989). Drug prohibition in the United States: costs, consequences, and alternatives. *Science* 245:939–947.

Acknowledgments

The author of a book usually devotes some space to thank those whose assistance made the work a better one, but this is an edited book, so the contributions of chapter authors *are* the book. Hence, I must begin by expressing once again my gratitude to them for joining me in this project. They are all extremely busy people, and they put up with my frequent inquiries, reminders, and feedback with remarkably good humor. My apologies go out to the many people I do not know whose competing needs must have been put on hold so that chapter authors could do their part for this book.

Research reductions in my teaching load at St. John's University have provided me with some badly needed time to work on this and other contemporaneous projects, and my research assistant, Yale Tockerman, was also of help.

I have benefited from the advice of others at all stages of the project, and most of their names appear below under various rubrics, but responsibility for the book's overall organization and conception, for better or worse, remains with me. As an editor, I have attempted to help authors to say better what they wanted to say, or to deal with matters they might not have included in an initial draft, but I have attempted not to interfere with their messages. Thus I have deliberately included chapters that disagree with one another, or with me, or that formulate issues differently from the way I would. The point of this book is to encourage debate throughout the country over how to legalize drugs, and I have tried to do so between its covers as well.

I am a member of the board of directors of Partnership for Responsible Drug Information (PRDI), an organization aimed at encouraging informed discussion of drug policy issues. (I should mention that PRDI does not sponsor legalization or any other specific drug policy. Its purpose is to stimulate thought, analysis, and public discussion of alternatives to our current drug policy.) I would like to thank three other members of the board of directors who contributed chapters to this book: Mary Cleveland, Stanley Neustadter, and Eric Sterling. In addition, PRDI was of help as an information resource for this project.

I am grateful to those friends and colleagues from various disciplines who commented on my parts of the book, or on the entire manuscript, or reviewed one or more chapters, including Charles Adler, Frank Brady, Young Back Choi, Robert Ghiradella, Jeremy Haritos, Jeffrey Long, Jeffrey Nevid, Dolores Newton, Alice Powers, David Sprintzen, Igor Tomic, and Lynn Zimmer.

A number of contributors gave helpful feedback on or reviewed one another's work (including my own) and I would like to thank Richard Evans, Stanley Neustadter, Rodney Skager, and Eric Sterling for this additional participation in the project. While the authors of individual chapters have acknowledged those whose input enriched their work, I would like to make clear my appreciation for their assistance as well.

Finally, I would like to thank Michael Moskowitz, my publisher at Jason Aronson Inc., for his encouragement of this controversial project.

It was difficult for me not to dedicate this book to my wife, Dolores Newton, and my daughter, Krekamey Fish. Their support and encouragement have, as always, made the burden lighter and the journey more interesting; they remain my beloved and lifelong traveling companions.

Jefferson M. Fish

Contributors

Luis Barrios, Ph.D., a clinical psychologist and Episcopalian priest, is Associate Professor in the Puerto Rican Studies Department of John Jay College of Criminal Justice of the City University of New York.

Joel H. Brown, Ph.D., M.S.W., an education and evaluation researcher, is the Director of Educational Research Consultants in Berkeley, California.

Ted Galen Carpenter, Ph.D., a diplomatic historian, is Vice President for Defense and Foreign Policy Studies at the Cato Institute in Washington, DC.

Michael C. Clatts, Ph.D., an anthropologist, is Principal Investigator in the Institute for AIDS Research of the National Development Research Institutes, Inc., in New York City.

Mary M. Cleveland, Ph.D., an economist, is a member of the Board of Directors of the Schalkenbach Foundation and of the Partnership for Responsible Drug Information in New York City.

Richard Curtis, Ph.D., is Associate Professor of Anthropology at the John Jay College of Criminal Justice of the City University of New York.

Steven B. Duke, LL.M., teaches criminal law and holds the Chair of Law of Science and Technology at Yale Law School in New Haven, Connecticut.

Richard M. Evans, J.D., is Executive Director of the Voluntary Committee of Lawyers and practices law in Northampton, Massachusetts.

Jefferson M. Fish, Ph.D., is Professor and former Chair of the Department of Psychology at St. John's University in New York City.

Robert S. Gable, J.D., Ph.D., a specialist in forensic psychology and behavior therapy, is Professor of Psychology at the Claremont Graduate University in Claremont, California, where he previously served as Director of the Institute for Applied Social and Policy Research.

Toni M. Gallo, B.A., is an ethnographer in the Institute for AIDS Research of the National Development Research Institutes, Inc., in New York City.

Kelvin Alexander Gray, B.A., a political activist and member of the Board of Directors of the American Civil Liberties Union, is completing his Ph.D. in political science at the American University.

Lester Grinspoon, M.D., is Associate Professor of Psychiatry at Harvard Medical School.

Albert C. Gross, J.D., practices family law in San Diego County, California.

Edward A. Harris, J.D., Ph.D. (philosophy), practices as a commercial litigator in New York City and is on the Board of Managers of the Voluntary Committee of Lawyers.

Douglas N. Husak, J.D., Ph.D., is Professor of Philosophy and Law at Rutgers University in New Jersey.

Lee M. Kochems, M.A., who is completing his Ph.D. in anthropology at the University of Chicago, is an ethnographer in the Institute for AIDS Research of the National Development Research Institutes, Inc., in New York City.

Harry G. Levine, Ph.D., is Professor in the Department of Sociology of Queens College and the Graduate Center of the City University of New

York and is Director of the Drug Research Group at the Michael Harrington Center for Democratic Values and Social Change at Queens College.

Pellegrino A. Luciano, M.A., a Ph.D. student in anthropology at the City University of New York, is an ethnographer in the Institute for AIDS Research of the National Development Research Institutes, Inc., in New York City.

Drs. Bart Majoor, who was trained as a psychologist in the Netherlands, is Deputy Director of St. Ann's Corner of Harm Reduction in New York City and Chair of the Substance Users Work Group of the HIV Prevention Planning Group of the New York City Department of Health.

Jerry Mandel, Ph.D., is a sociologist in Berkeley, California.

Ethan A. Nadelmann, J.D., Ph.D. (political science), is Director of the Lindesmith Center in New York City.

Stanley Neustadter, LL.B., a private practitioner in New York City concentrating in criminal appeals, is Adjunct Professor of Law at both Brooklyn Law School and the Cardozo School of Law, and is on the Board of Managers of the Voluntary Committee of Lawyers.

James Ostrowski, J.D., is Adjunct Scholar at the Ludwig von Mises Institute in Auburn, Alabama, Chair of the Human Rights Committee of the Erie County, New York Bar Association, and a trial and appellate attorney in Buffalo, New York.

Craig Reinarman, Ph.D., is Professor and former Chair of the Department of Sociology of the University of California at Santa Cruz.

Rodney Skager, Ph.D., a teacher and researcher in adolescent development, drug education, and drug policy, is Professor Emeritus in the Graduate School of Education and Information Science of the University of California at Los Angeles and Contributing Editor to *Prevention File*.

Jo L. Sotheran, M.A., who is completing her Ph.D. in sociology at Rutgers University, is Co-investigator in the Institute for AIDS Research of the National Development Research Institutes, Inc., in New York City.

Eric E. Sterling, J.D., is President of the Criminal Justice Policy Foundation, Coordinator of the National Drug Strategy Network, and Editor-in-Chief of the *National Drug Strategy Network News Briefs* in Washington, DC.

Robert W. Sweet, LL.B., former Deputy Mayor of New York City and former Assistant U.S. Attorney, is U.S. District Judge for the Southern District of New York.

Mark Thornton, Ph.D. (economics), is Alford Professor of Political Economy at the Ludwig von Mises Institute, Auburn University, in Auburn, Alabama.

Richard E. Vatz, Ph.D., a rhetorician, is Professor in the Department of Mass Communication/Communication Studies at Towson University in Towson, Maryland, and Associate Psychology Editor of USA *Today Magazine.*

Lee S. Weinberg, J.D., Ph.D., an attorney and political scientist, is Associate Professor of Public and International Affairs at the Graduate School of Public and International Affairs at the University of Pittsburgh and Associate Psychology Editor of USA *Today Magazine.*

PART I

UNDERSTANDING THE PROBLEM

Introduction

The first half of this book, "Understanding the Problem," explores the insight that drug prohibition is counterproductive because of the drug war- and black market-related problems it creates, and discusses issues involved in making matters better. This discussion paves the way for the second half, which considers specific alternatives to our current policy.

Understanding the problem is a complex undertaking, in part because the war on drugs has affected so many areas of everyday life. It is also complex in part because decades of drug war propaganda have equated critical thinking with "being soft on drugs." The stifling of critical thinking has allowed false prohibitionist assertions to flourish, among which are: all drugs are the same; all use equals abuse; licit drugs are different in kind from and less dangerous than illicit drugs; giving people truthful information about drugs will only stimulate their use. Thus it is important to disseminate evidence and logic to persuade a skeptical public. Finally, the complexity stems in part from the multidisciplinary nature of a problem that requires multiple perspectives and differing kinds of information from a variety of specialties to understand it.

While the first half of this book is not an exhaustive presentation, its twelve chapters, arranged in three sections of four, provide readers with a wide-ranging view of issues related to drugs and drug policy, all of which bear on or have clear implications for legalization.

Section IA, "Theoretical and Philosophical Analyses," aims at clarifying a variety of complex issues bearing on legalization.

In Chapter 1, I explain five methodological errors that are well known to social and behavioral scientists, but not necessarily to the public at large. These errors often appear in discussions of drug policy, and are used to justify faulty conclusions with unfortunate social consequences.

In Chapter 2, Douglas N. Husak explores the philosophical bases of the two main rationales for drug policy reform: the public health or harm reduction or cost-benefit approach, and the rights-based or libertarian approach. While the author makes clear his preference for the rights-based approach to legalization, he presents a thorough explication of both approaches.

A strength of the public health approach is that, by devising a different policy for each substance based on scientific knowledge, it should be possible to minimize health and social problems. A weakness of the approach is that its very pragmatism leaves it open to the vagaries of political and social trends, since the means for minimizing harm vary over time, as do judgments about what constitutes a problem and how serious a problem is. Furthermore, in times of economic adversity, political upheaval, or ethnic conflict, the "public health" label could be used as a pretext for scapegoating minority groups, as "public safety" is being used now and as "mental health" is also being used to mistreat social deviants.

A strength of the rights-based approach is that, by guaranteeing the rights of individual adults, those who make unpopular choices would have a better chance of being protected even when the political climate is hostile. I thought it might be useful to include a list of rights—most of which are enshrined in the Constitution—that have been ignored on a massive scale in what has come to be known as "the drug exception to the Bill of Rights." I should mention, though—to paraphrase the Ninth Amendment—that the enumeration in the following list of certain rights shall not be construed to deny or disparage others retained by the people that are infringed by drug prohibition:

> The right to freedom of speech (e.g., for physicians to recommend marijuana or other controlled substances)
>
> The right to freedom of religion (e.g., for Native American peyote rituals)
>
> The right to privacy (e.g., so that one's liquor cabinet and medicine cabinet are not the government's business, no matter what intoxicating substances they contain)

The right to control over one's own body (e.g., to take adequate pain medication or other psychoactive substances)

The right to equal protection of the law (e.g., so that penalties for possession of crack cocaine used by inner city blacks are not 100 times as severe as for powdered cocaine used by suburban whites)

The right to protection against illegal searches and seizures (e.g., so that neither the government nor employers can investigate the contents of one's bladder)

The right not to be deprived of life, liberty, or property without due process (e.g., not to be harmed, jailed, or have one's property destroyed in drug sweeps; not to be jailed because the government misclassifies the properties of psychoactive substances; not to be jailed because the government defines "selling drugs" to include sharing a marijuana cigarette with another person at a party)

The right not to be deprived of one's property without just compensation (e.g., having one's house confiscated if drugs are found in it)

The right not to be forced to incriminate oneself (e.g., by mandatory breath or blood samples)

The right not to suffer cruel and unusual punishment (e.g., a life sentence for possession of a single marijuana cigarette, under "three strikes and you're out" laws)

The right not to be tried twice for the same crime (e.g., trying people in a federal court who have already been found not guilty of drug charges in a state court, and vice versa)

A weakness of the rights-based approach is that the policy that gives individuals the most freedom to choose might not wind up with as good a mix of outcomes for society as a whole as would be produced by the more limited freedom of public health approaches.

Chapter 2 also examines claims that drug use is immoral, and finds them to be unsupported assertions and thus an inadequate basis for drug policy. We must ask ourselves whether it is the legacy of our industrial society, founded on the work ethic and Puritanism, that people who indulge in aimless pleasure are viewed as immoral simply because they are not spending their time producing and consuming economically significant quantities of goods and services.

In Chapter 3, Richard E. Vatz and Lee S. Weinberg subject the debate over the legal status of drugs to a rhetorical analysis. Those waging the drug war use "scenic rhetoric," in which the causes of behavior are viewed as external to the individual. They have been able to portray drug taking as an involuntary act, thereby requiring the power of the state to protect people from themselves. Those opposed to drug prohibition would need to convince the public with "agent rhetoric," in which individuals are viewed as choosing their actions freely. The authors do not see this change as particularly likely, at least in the short run (for what it is worth, I am more optimistic than they). In addition, the chapter points out that the public would have to come to recognize that many of the ill effects currently attributed to drugs are really the result of drug prohibition and the black market it creates.

In Chapter 4, I explore the concepts of continuous and discontinuous change as applied to the war on drugs. While many advocates of drug legalization (including several chapter authors) are pessimistic about the possibilities for change, I suggest that they are making the implicit assumption that change must come about gradually. Instead, I argue, sudden, qualitative, discontinuous change may be a more appropriate model to apply to the complex interactive system of which drug prohibition is a part. We have recently seen discontinuous change in the collapse of the Soviet Union after decades of the Cold War, and earlier in the century we saw it in the end of alcohol prohibition.

Although the stated intent of drug prohibition is to stop drug abuse, its actual impact is on occasional use. Occasional users are intimidated by severe penalties, while nothing will prevent abusers from getting drugs, as is evident from their widespread availability in prisons.

Even when it comes to severe abuse, the drug warriors' causal arrows are pointed in the wrong direction. Although they claim that drugs push people to marginalized existences and crime, it is the socially marginalized who seek consolation from their misery in drugs, while criminals use illegal substances as part of a pattern of defying society's rules. They claim that fear of criminal penalties will help abusers by giving them an incentive to stay off drugs, but in fact such penalties make their already miserable lives significantly worse. Finally, although they claim that prohibition aims at ridding poor minority communities of the scourge of drugs, the war on drugs has actually turned such communities into mini police states, putting grossly disproportionate percentages of their inhabitants behind bars and financing the "prison industrial complex" with funds that are desperately needed for schools and medical and social services. If this weren't bad enough, drug prohibition also spreads AIDS, hepatitis, tuberculosis, and other diseases by deliberately preventing appropriate public health measures, and thus is responsible for death and disease on a massive scale.

The four chapters in Section IB, "Cultural Analyses," examine the effects of prohibition on drug abusers and minority groups (African-Americans and Latinos). Some of the vivid accounts in this section are disturbing, but readers who brace themselves and take advantage of this rare opportunity to examine and reflect on the world of drug abuse among socially marginalized people and members of minority groups will be rewarded by an understanding of the severe social costs imposed by our counterproductive policy. Some passages reflect understandable outrage at our current policies (and are consequently written in the rhetoric of political action); others encourage hope by showing the positive effects of treating people more humanely in our own country as well as of alternative policies that exist abroad.

In Chapter 5, Michael C. Clatts, Jo L. Sotheran, Pellegrino A. Luciano, Toni M. Gallo, and Lee M. Kochems bring the anthropological method of participant observation to bear on studying the actual injection behavior of abusers at high risk for HIV infection. As is evident from the authors' precise descriptions, injecting oneself with a drug is a complicated process that must be followed rigorously if health risks are to be avoided.

Drug prohibition, by artificially raising prices out of all proportion to market levels, creates economic incentives for people to use higher dosages as a result of smugglers cramming the maximum quantity of an illicit substance into the smallest possible container. It also creates economic incentives for people to use riskier methods of administration so as to get the maximum high from the minimum amount purchased (e.g., injecting is riskier than smoking). In this sense, prohibitionist policies, which are aimed at making drug taking risky, succeed in their goal—at the expense of the nation's health. The authors make it obvious from their case examples that the dangers created by a climate of illegality lead injecting drug users, including participants in needle exchange programs, to take many risks, thereby endangering themselves and others.

In Chapter 6, Luis Barrios and Richard Curtis focus on Puerto Ricans as they shed light on the larger issue of the effects of the drug war on Latinos in the United States as well as on Puerto Rico as representative of Latin America and the Caribbean. The chapter raises the issue of discrimination against Latinos by the criminal justice system, a matter dealt with in greater detail as regards African-Americans at the end of this section in Chapter 8, and relates it to foreign policy issues, dealt with in the next section in Chapter 11.

Latin Americans suffer the multiple insults of discriminatory drug policy in the United States (with higher rates of arrest, incarceration, and disease), destabilizing of governments and distorting of economies throughout the region (through a militarized foreign drug policy), and simultaneous covert acceptance of drug trafficking when it suits American foreign policy objectives. It is easy for Latinos to view our government as one that makes Latin-American drug dealers fabulously rich by creating black markets, looks the other way as they smuggle drugs into our ghettos (e.g., in exchange for their helping to fight the Contras in Nicaragua), and then incarcerates those Latinos who use them. Finally, a disturbing and illuminating case study illustrates both the devastation of crime and drugs in a poor Puerto Rican family and the way in which humane childrearing—as opposed to police crackdowns—offers hope for the future.

In Chapter 7, Bart Majoor discusses drug policy in the Netherlands, an ethnically diverse country whose dominant northern European culture is not that different from our own. The Dutch have approached the drug problem in a strikingly different way from us, however, and with much better results. By explaining Dutch humanitarian and pragmatic values, the author enables American readers to understand not only the substance of the country's harm reduction policies, but also how they relate to the tolerant attitudes of its people. (The Netherlands is not a country where slogans like "Zero Tolerance" have great appeal.)

Recognizing that some people will always abuse drugs, the Dutch have tried to find ways to minimize the amount of abuse (e.g., by allowing less dangerous substances to be available as alternatives to more dangerous ones) as well as to minimize AIDS and other drug-related health problems. The Dutch harm reduction policy is aimed at normalizing marginalized groups and at offering a variety of levels and kinds of treatment to drug abusers. Those who deal with abusers are trained to approach them with a client-centered attitude of service to consumers, and they are part of a network with links to education, job training, health care, and other social services. Majoor presents statistics indicating that the Dutch approach is cost-effective not only in the amount of money spent but also in lower rates of drug use, drug abuse, AIDS, and other relevant behaviors.

Given Majoor's statistics, I would like to digress briefly to explore further why it is that Americans so doggedly persist in an extremely expensive but counterproductive drug policy. Perhaps it fulfills other functions that justify the cost. One function discussed throughout Section IB is racism: the war on drugs legitimates the attack on minority groups by providing the pretext that drugs, rather than African-Americans or Latinos, are the enemy. But another related function might be public entertainment, like the public executions of our past, or ancient Romans throwing undesirables to the lions before cheering crowds. Crime documentaries are popular on television, and allow viewers to follow real police as they break down the doors to real people's houses and arrest them for drug possession. If politics is about providing bread and circuses for the masses, then "fighting drugs" may provide the kind of exciting entertainment that citizens are willing to pay for with votes and taxes.

In any event, the same Dutch pragmatism that has moved toward normalization of the problem of substance use and public health approaches to its management has been confronted by severe foreign policy pressures. With international drug policy dominated by the American war on drugs, and with integration into the European Economic Community as a top priority, the

Dutch have begun to consider pulling back from policies that are working well. They are finding themselves forced to explore more repressive drug policies as a possible price for other national priorities. If the United States were to reverse course and pursue a hands-off policy toward Dutch experimentation in drug policy, we might learn a lot from their expanded efforts. That is, at no cost to American taxpayers, we would be able to learn from successful innovations in the Netherlands (or Australia, or other countries). On an international scale, this would be similar to our taking the federal government out of drug policy and seeing what works best in the laboratories of the fifty states.

Section IB concludes with a call to action that also provides a transition to the beginning of Section IC. The author, Kevin Alexander Gray, is a political activist who has devoted his career to the African-American cause. Chapter 8 takes up the case of his community and, in an appeal for political action, he documents the disastrous effects of the war on drugs on African-Americans and sounds the call for an antiwar movement.

Blacks use illicit substances at about the same rate as whites, but are treated more severely at every stage of the criminal justice system, from being stopped to being arrested to being tried to being convicted to receiving more severe sentences. The forms of illegal drugs preferred by blacks are penalized more heavily than those preferred by whites. Blacks suffer more from AIDS and other preventable drug-related diseases. Poor urban black families disintegrate when parents are convicted of drug offenses and are taken to rural prisons to provide jobs for poor white guards. Demonizing drugs and associating them with African-Americans provides a socially acceptable way for whites to dehumanize blacks and justify turning their neighborhoods into war zones. And they are no safer outside their neighborhoods, with discrimination excused as being directed at drugs rather than skin color. "DWB"—Driving While Black—is the motor vehicle violation justified by "police profiles." An expensive car suggests the well-dressed driver is a drug dealer; a jalopy suggests the poorly-attired driver is an addict. And the drug war zone in inner cities chases away legitimate businesses and encourages inhabitants to participate in the black market, while drug legalization would, over time, create the possibility for new businesses and an influx of jobs.

Section IC, "Social Science Analyses," looks at drug prohibition from the perspectives of history, foreign policy, and drug education, draws inferences concerning the impact of our current drug policy, and suggests possible alternatives.

In Chapter 9, Jerry Mandel examines the beginning of the war on drugs in the middle of the last century, with a tax only on opium prepared for smoking. He provides readers with one déjà vu experience after another as he details the way the war was waged to punish a despised minority group (the Chinese), how it created a black market complete with smugglers and criminals, made users switch from smoking to injecting, corrupted government officials, and generally made matters much worse. In addition, the chapter presents evidence of a natural quasi-experiment in what psychologists call an "A-B-A-B reversal design." That is, an initial condition A (legal opium) is followed by an intervention B (punitive taxation or criminal penalties) that is then reversed (return to A) and reinstated (return to B). The fact that matters got worse after B, then better after A, and then worse again after B suggests that it is the war on drugs itself, not other factors, that is responsible for the disastrous results.

In Chapter 10, Harry G. Levine and Craig Reinarman examine alcohol policy before, during, and after Prohibition, and present much the same story. For example, just before Prohibition Americans were getting twice as much of their alcohol from beer as from hard liquor. After Prohibition that proportion was gradually restored. During Prohibition, however, drinkers got two to three times as much of their alcohol from hard liquor as from beer. Not only were the dosage levels higher, but many people died or were injured from contaminated alcohol or other unregulated substances sold as alcohol. And, of course, we're all familiar with the massive scale of crime and corruption caused by Prohibition. The authors argue that post-Prohibition government regulation of alcohol has worked well and can serve as a model for the way other substances can be regulated following the end of drug prohibition. In examining various drug policy issues for which the alcohol experience can serve as a model, the authors suggest the kinds of public health measures that might be undertaken as alternatives.

In Chapter 11, Ted Galen Carpenter reviews America's efforts around the globe to stem the flow of illegal drugs, and shows how they have been just as counterproductive abroad as they have been at home. Prohibition abroad imposes our values on cultures that may view psychoactive substances differently; it spreads black markets, crime, corruption, and drug abuse to friendly countries who are less stable than we, thereby undermining our allies even as it fails to stem the flow of drugs. Americans have recently become aware of the danger our drug policy poses to Mexico, with whom we share a long and problematic border, and to the stability of its government. The author presents an interesting discussion of the dislocations, challenges, and opportunities that a reversal of U.S. policy in the direction of drug legalization would create in the international arena; and he makes clear his support for international drug legalization despite the problems that can be anticipated.

In Chapter 12, Rodney Skager and Joel H. Brown examine drug education in the United States. They show how current drug education practices, both "humanitarian" and "hard line," have been based on unsupported myths, ignoring relevant research findings, and have therefore—sadly but not surprisingly—been a multibillion dollar failure. In addition, they repeat the theme we have seen in several other chapters: punishment marginalizes drug users and thereby makes it more difficult to change their behavior. In contrast to current policies, the authors offer an educational approach based on harm reduction and explain why they see it as more promising.

Policymakers have thus far refused to recognize that the great majority of substance use by adolescents (perhaps unfortunately, but in any event whether we like it or not) is best understood as normal behavior. That is, just as the transition from childhood to adulthood involves trying out new friendships, intimate relationships, hobbies, aesthetic experiences, and developing new intellectual and vocational interests, adolescents also experiment with psychoactive substances.

In the great majority of cases, this learning of adult behavior through trial and error, observation of others, and the exchange of information works well. It is the form of socialization developed by our culture, which stresses individualistic values and learning from one's own mistakes. But a few friendships end in violence; a few intimate relationships end in venereal disease, or pregnancy, or violence; a few hobbies lead to crime; the intellectual development of a few gets sidetracked in illiteracy; the vocational development of a few ends in unemployment; and the drug experimentation of a few ends in drug abuse. The small proportion of casualties from drug experimentation is similar to and representative of the other developmental mishaps that await a minority of adolescents, and occurs for the same reasons. Thus it is not surprising—though it flies in the face of current drug education dogma—that research reveals that adolescents who experiment with substances are in better psychological shape than both abstainers and heavy users.

Given this understanding, it is easy to see what kind of drug education offers the best prospects. It would provide the kind of factual and developmentally relevant information that would help students to make their own best choices on their trial-and-error path to adulthood. It would not treat all illegal substances as the same, but would clarify differences among them. It would not label all use as abuse, but would help students to distinguish between the two. And it would offer treatment to teen abusers rather than throwing them out of school.

With these twelve chapters as background, the reader should have a solid basis for evaluating the merits of the varied approaches to legalization discussed in Part II.

Section IA
Theoretical and
Philosophical Analyses

1

Methodological Considerations and Drug Prohibition

Jefferson M. Fish

Many false beliefs about drugs and erroneous inferences about the dangers of legalization result from a few well-known methodological errors. Fallacious conclusions that do not take into account the effects of selection bias (Cook and Campbell 1979) or base rates (Meehl and Rosen 1955), that are based on reified concepts, or that refuse to consider probabilistic predictions or cost-benefit analyses are often used to justify bad policy. This chapter briefly explains these methodological considerations and their relevance to drug legalization.

SELECTION BIAS

Have you ever sneezed when you were with a lot of people, and "discovered" to your amazement that you were in the midst of a flu epidemic? One person says that she is just getting over a cold, another has an uncle who has been in bed for a week with the flu, and someone else's friend has just called with a cough and sniffles to postpone a get-together, These instances are not sufficient to conclude that a flu epidemic is raging, and the making of such an inaccurate inference can be seen as an instance of selection bias.

Selection bias is the term experimenters use for the way in which the nonrandom selection of subjects for different treatment groups can produce inaccurate or biased results. The concept can easily be extended outside the laboratory to understand many social phenomena in which people inaccurately assume they are observing the behavior of a random sample of others. (In a related methodological problem, the observer may even evoke unusual behavior in others. For example, overseas tourists may mistakenly assume that those around them are displaying culturally typical behavior, when it is the tourists' unusual presence that is leading the "natives" to act in unusual ways [Fish 1996].)

In the case of the "flu epidemic," those who said they were sick, or knew others who were, did not constitute a random sample of the people around you. Their comments were made in response to your sneeze—in the terms of this chapter, they were "selected" by your sneeze. To gather evidence about the possibility of an epidemic, you might begin by asking everyone present— not just those who speak up—whether they know anyone with a cold or the flu, to see how large the proportion really is. You might try to find out how representative of people in your region the group itself is (in terms of age, education, gender, ethnicity, socioeconomic status, and so forth). You might even try to reassemble them on the same date the following year and compare numbers.

The point is that each of us lives in a particular social world that is not representative of the larger society, and our behavior itself evokes responses from a nonrandom sample of others. For this reason we have to exercise caution, and engage in critical thinking, when we draw inferences about apparent social patterns we see around us.

People who act in uncommon, unpopular, deviant, or stigmatized ways draw attention to themselves (like someone sneezing) and create an opportunity for inaccurate generalizations. Where social stereotypes or prejudices already exist, selection bias provides an easy way to confirm them.

Consider the example of homosexuality—never a popular form of behavior, and until recently considered a mental illness. When psychiatry finally removed it from the list of mental disorders, many therapists rebelled. "How can you say that homosexuality is normal? I have treated many homosexuals, and they all had psychological problems."

The therapists were telling the truth, but they were not engaging in critical thinking. The people they see in therapy are self-selected for having psychological problems. The same reasoning would lead to the conclusion that heterosexuality is abnormal, since all their heterosexual clients also have psychological problems. However, since the therapists presumably did not come from a wide enough social circle to have had contact with well-adjusted homosexuals, their provincial life experience gave them no reason to question conventional stereotypes.

Once one begins to think in terms of selection bias, it is easy to locate many examples. Matchmakers have a more positive view of marriage than divorce lawyers because the two occupations select different client groups. Matchmakers are surrounded by people who want to get married and divorce lawyers are in constant contact with those who want to get divorced.

Thus it is not surprising that many law enforcement officials, judges, and others who work with addicts and drug-related criminals should have a negative view of drugs and oppose legalization. It is not surprising, but it is not any more defensible intellectually than the position of therapists who viewed homosexuality as a mental illness because of their lack of experience with well-adjusted homosexuals. Those involved in drug enforcement might equally well conclude (and, sadly, some of them do) that poor people or members of minority groups are criminals because the only poor people or members of minority groups they know are in trouble with the law. They do not, however, conclude that all men are criminals because they are at least cosmopolitan enough to be acquainted with many men who are not.

People involved in drug enforcement often see the worst of the worst, and develop a biased view of reality because of the unrepresentative social world in which they work. They are not in contact with the huge majority of those experimenting with drug use, or who are casual, occasional, recreational users. The distortion of their view of drugs and drug use—which has become the official version of reality—can be seen by comparing it to the view of alcohol of those working in a Skid Row mission. They see people who have a glass of wine with dinner several times a week as beginning on the slippery slope toward alcoholism, degradation, and death, though moderate drinkers would be appalled at being viewed in this way. Yet it is not unusual to hear, "I started as a social drinker," in the Skid Row mission.

This is selection bias, pure and simple. Those in a Skid Row mission are not a random sample of all drinkers and addicts in the criminal justice system are not a random sample of illicit drug users. Most people who drink do so occasionally or in moderation, and for a variety of reasons. These include the intrinsic pleasure of intoxication as well as its purported enhancing effect on other activities (sex, TV sports), participation in a social event (cocktail parties, wine and cheese receptions), or religious activity (the Mass, Passover seder), self-medication (after getting fired, or at the end of a relationship), and health promotion (moderate drinking reduces the risk for heart attacks). In the same way, most people who use illicit drugs do so occasionally or in moderation, and for the most diverse reasons.

Failure to think critically in terms of selection bias has led to the invention of statistically indefensible concepts like "gateway drugs." Thus some who would acknowledge that marijuana is not dangerous still argue that it should remain illegal because it leads to the use of substances that are. They base their view on stories of addicts who, like the Skid Row alcoholics, describe their experimentation with marijuana as the first step on the road to cocaine or heroin addiction. If, instead of addicts, they had interviewed college honors students, they might have reached the equally erroneous conclusion that weekend marijuana use relaxes people and leads to greater overall achievement.

In addition to exaggerating the dangerousness of drugs, selection bias has also been used to exaggerate the effectiveness of drug treatment. Alcoholics Anonymous and other drug treatment programs sometimes claim high rates of success for "all people who complete the program." Here, instead of interviewing addicts about their history of drug use and falsely claiming it to be typical, one interviews ex-addicts about their history of recovery and falsely claims it to be typical. High dropout rates are common in such programs, so a large percentage of a small proportion winds up as not very much. The relevant response to such assertions of effectiveness is, "What is the rate of success for all people who enter the program?" In addition, one would want to know how representative the people in the program are of alcoholics-in-general or addicts-in-general.

Thinking in terms of selection bias does not mean that all drugs are the same or that no treatment works. It does remind us, though, that when a claim is made in this emotionally charged field, it should be evaluated in part on the representativeness of the sample on which it is based.

REIFICATION OF CONCEPTS

We live in a world not just of things, but of socially constructed meanings. Different cultures, at different times and in different places, invent different concepts to organize their world and to make communication possible about matters of common interest. Even when it comes to objects in nature, cultures differ in the concepts they invent. For example, English speakers consider almonds, cashew nuts, and peanuts to be examples of *nuts*, a category that does not exist in Portuguese and that does not correspond to the way botanists would classify these edible parts of different plants. Cultures invent new concepts when circumstances demand—*cyberspace* is a recent example.

Culturally invented concepts differ in the decree to which they correspond to observable phenomena. *Ghosts* and *unicorns* are familiar concepts in our culture, though evidence that they refer to observable phenomena is hard to come by. Many Americans' actions are governed by these concepts (avoiding graveyards at night or painting pictures of unicorns) just as they are by the concept of *nuts*, in contrast to the behavior of people from cultures with none of the three concepts. And the actual behavior of people in the real world has real consequences for them and others, regardless of whether they are acting in terms of observable phenomena. Real people have been put to death for *witchcraft*, despite the lack of scientific evidence for the concept.

Reification of a concept is a fallacious process of treating a concept as a thing, and when people act with reference to reified concepts undesirable consequences often result. Unfortunately, the field of drug prohibition is rife with reified concepts that have led to untold mischief. Some of these are *drugs* (as opposed, for example, to *food*), *gateway drugs*, and *codependency*. One could easily write a chapter, or even a book, about such concepts; those who are interested in exploring the matter further would do well to consult the relevant works of Thomas Szasz (1974, 1992).

For the purposes of this chapter, I will briefly explore the reified concept of *addiction*, since it is the cornerstone on which other reifications, misguided thinking, and counterproductive policy are built. The following is the supposed phenomenon in nature that is described by the concept of addiction.

> Certain potent substances exist, called drugs. Drugs that are not medicine are evil because they have the power to destroy the lives of upstanding individuals. These substances, for reasons rooted in human biology, give people such overwhelming pleasure, or so effectively blot out their misery, that they crave and use more and more. Because the substances are irresistible, society must make them illegal, but individuals hooked on drugs will pay any price and risk any danger to get them. Thus they descend into poverty, prostitution, and crime on the antisocial and self-destructive road to an early death.

In reading this dramatic narrative, certain features are evident. There is the emphasis on the substance itself, rather than on the person who uses it, the circumstances under which it is used, or other individual, social, or cultural factors. The substance is viewed as evil, and thus becomes an enemy that society can declare war on. Furthermore, addiction is understood as a unitary and repetitive phenomenon, so that a variety of substances can be lumped together as *drugs*, all of which cause addiction. Finally, by shifting the emphasis from an objective description of people and their behavior to a moral crusade against drugs and addiction, one is relieved of responsibility for discovering what happens to whom in the domain of substance use under differing social policies.

It is important to recognize that people can be found who behave like the addicts just described, but this is not adequate evidence that the concept of addiction describes a natural phenomenon. We have seen from the discussion of selection bias how easy it is to make such mistakes. For example, we could invent the "Sherlock Holmes syndrome," which describes people who take cocaine, play a musical instrument, and are interested in criminology. We could then look around us and find people who suffer from the syndrome, as well as borderline cases who sing or are interested in the sociology of deviance. But we would be deluding ourselves if we thought that the Sherlock Holmes syndrome really existed, and doing damage if we based social policy on this reified concept.

In other words, reification goes beyond the description of behavior (cocaine + musical instrument + criminology) to the creation of an entity, like a disease ("The poor man is suffering from Sherlock Holmes syndrome"). Once a concept has been reified, it can be used for fallacious explanations (e.g., "He takes cocaine because he has Sherlock Holmes syndrome") and as a basis for social policy (e.g., ban the sale of musical instruments as Sherlock Holmes syndrome-related paraphernalia).

Like the Sherlock Holmes syndrome, the concept of addiction as it is understood by the general public and by too many legal and health professionals does not describe the ways in which people use drugs. We have long known, as Brecher (1972) indicates, that the effects of a licit or illicit drug depend on "who is taking the drug, in what dosage, by what route of administration, and under what circumstance" (p. xi). The effects of "set and setting"—the drug taker's learned expectations of the effects of the drug and the social circumstances under which he or she takes it—are of central importance (Zinberg 1984). At low dosages, drug effects are often indistinguishable from placebo effects, and given the irregular supplies of black markets, low dosages are not uncommon. Furthermore, there is wide variation among individuals in their patterns of drug use, as well as great variation over time in the drug-taking behavior of any given individual.

It is true that different drugs have different physiological effects (though these vary from person to person), and may have characteristic withdrawal syndromes (which also vary among people), but these physiological aspects do not bear a strong relationship to the social behavior that is the object of drug policy. All of the supposed equations associated with the concept of addiction—(a) pleasurable or pain-reducing subjective effects of a drug = (b) behavioral evidence of intoxication = (c) need for increasing dosage, or tolerance = (d) intensity and duration of withdrawal symptoms = (e) difficulty in quitting use of the drug—are known to be inaccurate. These five indices vary separately from one another, and form different patterns for different drugs (as do other indices); they also vary among different users. In discussing heroin, for example, Peele (1990) points out that "a substantial number of patients who report potent addictive symptoms have taken little or no heroin, while regularly maintained narcotics users often express feeble or inconsistent withdrawal" (p. 206).

Since patterns of drug use do not conform to our concept of addiction, one might ask how the concept arose. Not surprisingly, Peele (1990) and Levine (1978) find the answer in history. They discuss the evolution of the concept of addiction and show how it was shaped by social forces (the religiously inspired temperance movement and Alcoholics Anonymous; government institutions like Harry Anslinger's Federal Bureau of Narcotics) rather than by scientific data. Hence, attempts to understand the complexities of drug usage show the concept of addiction to be a misleading reification, and attempts to understand the concept of addiction lead us to historical forces unrelated to scientific accuracy.

(Since there are people with significant problems in living associated with drug usage, it is sometimes necessary, in order to communicate, to refer to them as a group despite their diversity. One can use the term *addict* as shorthand to refer to those who repeatedly take high levels of psychoactive substances despite what observers view as significant negative consequences to themselves or others. But when such terms are used for convenience [e.g., in the next section], it is important to make sure that they are not reified.)

When drug policy is based on reified concepts like addiction, it is bound to have unfortunate consequences. If we want to make the world a better place, we have to base our actions on reality as we find it, rather than on concepts that we treat as real. If we want to improve our current drug policy, we should base our thinking on observable evidence and logic rather than on reified concepts that reflect current social prejudices.

BASE RATES

Consider the following "proof" that marijuana is a slow-acting poison:

1. Everyone who smoked marijuana before 1875 is dead.
2. Over 99 percent of those who smoked marijuana between 1875 and 1900 are dead.
3. Over 90 percent of those who smoked marijuana between 1900 and 1925 are dead.
4. As the date of first smoking marijuana gets closer to the present, the number of resulting deaths decreases, because, for increasing numbers of people, too little time has elapsed for the slow-acting poison to take its toll.

Statisticians would say that this "proof" is fallacious because it does not take base rates into account. The base rate is defined as the percentage of the target condition in the parent population. In this case the target condition is *death* and the first parent population is *all people alive before 1875*. Thus the base rate is 100 percent. As the number of deaths among those who smoked marijuana does not exceed the base rate, one cannot infer that marijuana contributed to their deaths. In a similar way, the death rate among those who smoked marijuana does not exceed the base rate for the general population during the periods 1875 to 1900, 1900 to 1925, or subsequently.

Base rates can be used to evaluate the effectiveness of doing something to people, such as treating or jailing them, to prevent them from becoming addicts. They can also be used to evaluate the effectiveness of the judicial system by examining the ratio of those unjustly convicted to those justly convicted.

Suppose we thought it would be a good idea to make drug addiction a crime so that we could send addicts to jail where they would cease using drugs, and so that they would remain drug-free after release from fear of reincarceration. (This is a dubious premise, since drugs are widely available in prison, and it ignores the ethical issue of punishing individuals for something they do to themselves rather than to others. I should mention in passing that some people make the claim that addicts harm others, such as family members, not only by assaulting or robbing them, which are quite separate crimes, but also by making them feel bad. This kind of logic would criminalize someone who broke up with an unwilling girlfriend or boyfriend, or a teacher who made a student feel bad by giving a failing grade. In any event, the rationale of criminalizing addiction does lie behind much current drug policy, such as making it illegal to possess certain psychoactive substances, so it is worth considering.)

Let us further suppose that we did not want to send nonaddicts to jail, even if they did occasionally use illicit drugs. This is because jailing them is costly to taxpayers, harmful to the nonaddicts, and takes up jail space better occupied by violent criminals. A problem then arises. How can the courts differentiate between addicts, who should be sent to jail, and nonaddicts, who should not?

Table 1-1 illustrates the hypothetical situation of courts unable to differentiate between addicts (however defined) and nonaddicts. Out of 200 cases, half are known to be addicts and half are known not to be. Since the courts cannot tell the difference, fifty of the 100 addicts are correctly identified and fifty are misidentified as nonaddicts. Similarly, fifty of the 100 nonaddicts are correctly identified but fifty are misidentified as addicts. The courts correctly convict fifty addicts at the expense of sending fifty nonaddicts to jail.

Table 1-1. Courts Unable to Differentiate between Addicts and Nonaddicts

Conviction	Addict	Nonaddict	Number of Cases
Certain Knowledge			
Addict	50	50	100
Nonaddict	50	50	100
Number of Cases	100	100	200

Table 1-2 illustrates the hypothetical situation of courts that are able to differentiate reasonably well between addicts and nonaddicts. Despite crowded calendars and limited resources, they are able to make correct decisions 70 percent of the time. Once again, 200 cases are presented. Half are known to be addicts and half are not. Since the courts are 70 percent effective, seventy of the 100 addicts are correctly identified and thirty are misidentified as nonaddicts. Similarly, seventy of the 100 nonaddicts are correctly identified but thirty are misidentified as addicts. The courts correctly convict seventy addicts at the expense of sending thirty nonaddicts to jail.

Table 1-2. Courts 70 Percent Accurate in Differentiating between Addicts and Nonaddicts

Conviction	Addict	Nonaddict	Number of Cases
Certain Knowledge			
Addict	70	30	100
Nonaddict	30	70	100
Number of Cases	100	100	200

In a system where, to guarantee individual liberties, it is supposed to be preferable to free ten guilty people rather than send one innocent person to prison, this is not an outstanding record. Nevertheless, the balance is positive, and people who view drugs as a terrible menace might say that the lessening of the "justice ratio" from 10:1 to 7:3 is defensible.

In the real world, however, addicts and nonaddicts do not come in groups of equal sizes. Addicts are a small proportion of those who use illicit drugs, say 5 percent though the actual figure is lower. (They do, of course, use a disproportionate amount of the illegal drugs. One rule of thumb is that 80 percent of the drugs are used by 20 percent of the users. This is a ratio of 16:1 in the consumption rates between the top fifth and bottom fifth of users, and the behavior of most of the top fifth would not meet any conceivable definition of addiction.)

Table 1-3 illustrates what happens when courts that are 70 percent effective attempt to convict addicts from a population with a base rate of 95 percent nonaddicts. The courts correctly convict seven of the ten addicts, while misidentifying three as nonaddicts. They are similarly accurate in identifying 133 of the 190 nonaddicts, while inaccurately convicting the remaining fifty-seven.

Table 1-3. Courts 70 Percent Accurate in Differentiating between Addicts and Nonaddicts with a Base Rate of 95 Percent Nonaddicts

Conviction	Addict	Nonaddict	Number of Cases
Certain Knowledge			
Addict	7	3	10
Nonaddict	57	133	190
Number of Cases	64	136	200

Let us examine more closely the results of applying this 70 percent accurate legal procedure to the population under discussion. Sixty-four people go to jail, of whom only seven are addicts. This is an "injustice ratio" of more than 8:1! That is, by applying a 70 percent valid legal procedure to detect a condition that occurs only 5 percent of the time, one winds up making more than eight wrong decisions for every correct one.

In contrast, by rejecting the valid legal procedure and making decisions based on base rates alone, one can be accurate 95 percent of the time. This can be verified by looking at the last column of Table 1-3. By consulting no evidence and applying no procedure whatsoever, one could declare all 200 people to be nonaddicts. This classification is correct in 190 of the cases and incorrect in only ten. (It might be mentioned in passing that this 95 percent accuracy implies a policy of not jailing addicts.) To restate the contrast, by using a 70 percent valid procedure one makes wrong decisions 8:1 over right ones, and by using base rates one makes correct decisions 19:1 over wrong ones. The discrepancy between the two is in excess of 150:1.

This is an indefensibly unjust result. When the effectiveness of the procedure that one is using does not exceed the base rate, bad outcomes are bound to occur. While our incarceration rate is the highest in the world, Table 1-4 indicates that there is ample room for things to get much worse. If 70,000,000 Americans have used an illegal substance at least once, and if 5 percent of them are addicts, a Zero Tolerance policy avidly enforced could lead to the imprisonment of tens of million of additional people, the overwhelming majority of whom would have been convicted unjustly.

Table 1–4. Courts 70 Percent Accurate in Differentiating between Addicts and Nonaddicts with a Base Rate of 95 Percent Nonaddicts among All Americans

Conviction	Addict	Nonaddict	Number of Cases
Certain Knowledge			
Addict	2,450,000	1,050,000	3,500,000
Nonaddict	46,550,000	19,950,000	66,500,000
Number of Cases	49,000,000	21,000,000	70,000,000

In addition, when a policy creates so much room to be applied unjustly, there is an opportunity for it to be used in a discriminatory manner. Unfortunately, it is clear that such discrimination is taking place. Using U.S. government statistics, Mauer (1996) reported that African-Americans represent 12 percent of the U.S. population, 13 percent of drug users, 35 percent of arrests for drug possession, 55 percent of convictions for drug possession, and 74 percent of prison sentences for drug possession. Such unjust applications are ethically indefensible and socially divisive, and they undermine respect for and the integrity of our criminal justice system.

Whatever one thinks of illicit drugs, a consideration of base rates makes one wonder whether the undesirable results of drug prohibition, like the undesirable results of alcohol prohibition before it, make a change of policy worth considering.

PREDICTIONS ARE PROBABILISTIC

Some people say, "Unless you can assure me that drug legalization won't make us a nation of addicts, I can't support it." While the reified term *addiction* was discussed above, and other difficulties with the statement are discussed in the next section, I would like to focus on its demand for certainty. A moment's reflection tells us that nothing in life is certain. Even though the sun has risen every day, we cannot be certain that it will rise tomorrow. The fallacy in the demand for certainty is that of a false dichotomy—the implication that one must choose between total certainty and total uncertainty.

In other words, when people say, "We cannot know with certainty what will happen following drug legalization," and even, "Evidence from nineteenth-century America or from other countries today can't give us that certainty," they are really saying, "I refuse to think about this matter." The trouble with refusing to consider alternatives without certainty is that such a position constitutes an ideological support for the status quo, no matter how bad it may be, simply because it is conceivable that an alternative might be worse.

Instead of demanding certainty, one can and should seek probabilities. That is, we can ask, "Based on evidence and reason, what are the most likely consequences of various approaches to legalization?" This is in contrast to asking, based on fear and prejudice, "What are the most awful consequences imaginable?" since improbable worst-case scenarios will lead us (and indeed have led us) to policies that are counterproductive because they are divorced from reality.

What are some of the kinds of predictions that would emerge from such analyses? In very general terms, they are ones like the following. I list these four predictions, along with suggestions of the evidence supporting them, to illustrate the difference between reasonable predictions and the demand for certainty that cannot, in principle, be met.

1. *No matter what drugs are legalized in what ways, tobacco and alcohol will remain by far our severest problems.*

   In the case of tobacco, this prediction is made because people find it so difficult to stop using nicotine—it is approximately as difficult to give up as heroin—and because smoking is so deadly (over 400,000 deaths per year in this country). In addition, cigarettes are popular because the mind-altering effects of nicotine are subtle, allowing people to work, drive, operate machinery, and carry on social relationships without noticeable impairment.

   While a much smaller percentage of those who use alcohol have difficulty stopping, the population of users is so huge that even a small percentage of abusers is a very large number of people. Furthermore, alcohol does affect coordination and judgment. Unfortunately, people using alcohol are often not aware of these effects and manage to conceal them from others (e.g., "He knows how to hold his booze"). For these reasons among others, alcohol remains extremely popular, even though it is associated with well over 100,000 deaths per year. In the nineteenth century, when opiates, cocaine, and marijuana were all legal and available, the prohibition movement was directed at alcohol rather than other substances. It was obvious at the time that the numbers of people affected and the scale of the associated psychological, social, and physical misery were much greater than the negative effects seen with other substances. Under any system of legalization, this will likely continue to be the case.

   In contrast, opiates and cocaine are each associated with only a few thousand deaths per year. Both substances interfere with people's ongoing work and social lives, thereby imposing real costs on their users and making the substances less attractive. While excessive use of alcohol creates similar problems, people find it easier to moderate their consumption of alcohol than of opiates and cocaine. Thus, if these substances became legal, the demand for them among occasional users of psychoactive substances would probably not be great. Furthermore, those who did want to try opiates or cocaine would probably experiment with low dosages so as to minimize the associated risks.

Marijuana is probably the only illegal substance whose use would increase significantly following legalization, because it enables occasional users to become intoxicated with so few disadvantages. Marijuana has never caused a death from overdose, and this positive feature would likely continue after legalization.

The interaction of the legal use of marijuana with the legal use of alcohol is likely to produce a variety of positive and negative public health effects. Many who might otherwise use alcohol would be likely to use marijuana instead. This decrement should ultimately result in a saving of life among those who would otherwise go on to use alcohol heavily. This health benefit might be partially undercut by a slight increase in accidents among those using alcohol and marijuana simultaneously over those using alcohol alone, as well as by accidents among marijuana users. Furthermore, although low use of alcohol may confer some health benefits, marijuana smoke is more carcinogenic than tobacco smoke. On the other hand, marijuana is used in very small amounts in comparison to tobacco, and people find it much easier to stop using. Therefore, the increase in cancer mortality from marijuana legalization is likely to be slight. Nevertheless, since the carcinogens in both marijuana and tobacco are different from the nicotine and THC that people seek from these plants, legalization will provide yet another argument for developing safer ways to smoke. Finally, since marijuana stays in the body longer than alcohol, there is an incentive for users to hold down consumption (e.g., so that an intoxicated evening won't interfere with work performance the next day).

2. *There will not be much change in the numbers of severe drug abusers under any system of legalization.*

This prediction is based on the relatively stable numbers of such people over extended periods of time and differing legal sanctions. Unfortunately, there will always be a small percentage of individuals who will be chronic alcoholics or abusers of other drugs, just as there will always be some psychotics, criminals, and other social misfits. This state of affairs appears to be unavoidable. We can experiment with social policies to minimize severe substance abuse and to minimize the harm severe abusers do to themselves and others (e.g., by making clean needles available to prevent the spread of AIDS), but attempts to stamp it out by force are doomed to failure, as we have reconfirmed decade after decade, ad absurdum and ad nauseam.

On the other hand, the way of life of this relatively small population is so clearly stigmatized that ending drug prohibition would be unlikely to contribute substantially to their numbers. Although long-term expectations are for no major change in severe abuse, there might be an initial increase following legalization. Still, our experience—in the last century when everything was legal as well as following the end of Prohibition—gives no reason to worry that these numbers would exceed the current range of fluctuations as fads in substance abuse wax and wane over time.

3. *Experimentation by occasional users will increase.*

In contrast to severe abuse, occasional experimentation should increase. This is because the main effect of prohibition is not on severe abusers, who make sure they get their substances one way or another, but on occasional users. Adults who hold down jobs and are raising families might have a drink or two in the evening, but would not risk drinking heavily, or trying an illegal substance, because the potential negative consequences for them are too great. Once prohibited substances become legal, they might experiment with them in the same prudent way.

4. *Dosage levels for occasional users will decrease.*

The economics of the black market lead producers to concentrate as much of an illegal substance as possible in as small a space as possible. This is another way of saying that the black market encourages high dosage levels, dosages that interfere more with people's lives and that are associated with more negative consequences. As Chapter 10 describes in detail, Prohibition changed us from a nation of beer drinkers to whiskey drinkers, but after the end of Prohibition, we gradually drifted back to beer with its lower-dosage level of alcohol. More specifically, because alcohol is legal, a range of dosage levels is available for all preferences, from beer to wine to cocktails to straight whiskey. Only a small proportion of people prefer the highest levels of alcohol, while the largest proportion prefer the lowest levels. Similarly, only a small proportion of those who drink do so to excess, while the great majority do so in limited quantities.

Drug prohibition has similarly led to the progression from opium to morphine to heroin, from coca to powdered cocaine to crack cocaine, and to the creation and use of marijuana with higher THC levels. Making any prohibited substance legal, even if a wide range of dosage levels is permitted, should lead to the kind of preference for lower dosages that we see with alcohol. Because occasional users are committed to their work, families, and social relationships, they seek occasional mild intoxication. They do not want intense intoxication, with all its attendant problems, from currently illegal substances any more than they want to get drunk from alcohol, even though they have plenty available in their liquor cabinets.

These four probabilistic predictions can be seen as an alternative to the unfulfillable demand for certainty that is sometimes used to justify the status quo.

COST-BENEFIT ANALYSES

As indicated above, people sometimes argue against drug legalization by saying that it would lead to an increase in the use of drugs. This argument is an example of the more general one, "Maintain (or change) policy X because to do otherwise will have undesirable consequences." (There are other ways to discuss the argument, but they are not relevant to the purposes of this chapter, and they appear elsewhere in the book.)

It is amazing that such arguments continue to be made, but it is worth pointing out their shortcomings. *All policies have undesirable consequences.* They also have desirable consequences. The problem in comparing a proposed new policy with the current one is to consider the relative costs and benefits of each, in both economic and social terms, to arrive at an overall decision as to which is best.

There are two kinds of errors that one might make: an erroneous rejection of current policy in favor of a proposed alternative, and an erroneous continuation of current policy in lieu of the alternative. Table 1-5 illustrates the way in which the desirable and undesirable consequences have to be weighed for both current policy and a proposed alternative policy.

Table 1–5. Desirable and Undesirable Consequences of Current and Alternative Policies

	Current Policy	Alternative Policy
Desirable Consequences	a	m, n, o, p, q, r, s, t, u, v
Undesirable Consequences	b, c, d, e, f, g h, i, j, k, l	w, x, y, z

For example, we might want to compare current marijuana policy to an alternative policy of making the drug legal for adults, and regulating it much as we do alcohol and tobacco. In this case, Table 1-5 might be interpreted as follows:

Desirable consequences of current policy
   a. shows society's disapproval for using marijuana
Undesirable consequences of current policy
   b. promotes the growth of a huge black market
   c. causes deaths, injury, and property loss from marijuana-related crime
   d. legalizes injuring (occasionally killing), property confiscation, and jailing of many users who are no danger to anyone
   e. creates huge marijuana-related economic costs of prisons and the legal process
   f. increases dependency of local law enforcement on federal funding and forfeiture income
   g. infringes civil rights by antimarijuana drug war legislation
   h. corrupts police and politicians with marijuana-related money
   i. releases violent prisoners early to make space for marijuana-related prisoners serving mandatory minimum sentences
   j. encourages loss of respect for government and the legal system
   k. promulgates false information about the effects of marijuana, leading to loss of respect for drug education (and probably to increased use as well)
   l. increases physical suffering and disability from many conditions because physicians cannot prescribe and patients cannot use marijuana
Desirable consequences of alternative policy
   m. makes marijuana available to treat many medical conditions
   n. destroys the black market for marijuana, decreasing crime, including innocent bystander injuries and deaths from turf war battles
   o. increases long-term economic potential for poor areas as a result of diminished crime
   p. decreases alcohol-related disease and accidents from those who use marijuana instead
   q. ends property loss, injury, and death from mistaken marijuana-related law enforcement action
   r. eliminates marijuana-related crime, enabling police to devote more resources to violent crime
   s. decreases corruption among police and politicians
   t. decreases cost of law enforcement
   u. ends jail crowding; available space adequate to contain violent criminals
   v. increases respect for government and the legal system
Undesirable consequences of alternative policy
   w. decreases number of prisoners and jailers, which will increase unemployment
   x. creates short-term financial losses in poor areas as a result of the loss of black market income

y. eliminates use by government of forfeited marijuana-related assets
z. increases (possibly) accidents and lung cancer (if marijuana smoking increases)

This enumeration of the desirable and undesirable consequences of current marijuana policy and an alternative policy is not necessarily complete or indisputable. For example, it omits a discussion of taxation and the use for such revenues (e.g., to pay for drug education and drug treatment). But it does illustrate the use of cost-benefit analyses in considering policy alternatives.

In summary then, an understanding of selection bias, reification of concepts, base rates, probabilistic predictions, and cost-benefit analyses is helpful in making informed judgments about drug policy.

REFERENCES

Brecher, E. (1972). *Licit and Illicit Drugs*. Boston: Little, Brown.

Cook, T. D., and Campbell, D. T. (1979). *Quasi-Experimentation: Design and Analysis Issues for Field Settings*. Boston: Houghton Mifflin.

Fish, J. M. (1996). *Culture and Therapy: An Integrative Approach*. Northvale, NJ: Jason Aronson.

Levine, H. G. (1978). The discovery of addiction: changing conceptions of habitual drunkenness in America. *Journal of Studies on Alcohol* 39:143–174.

Mauer, M. (1996). The drug war's unequal justice. *Drug Policy Letter* 28:11–13.

Meehl, P. E., and Rosen, A. (1955). Antecedent probability and the efficiency of psychometric signs, patterns, or cutting scores. *Psychological Bulletin* 52:194–216.

Peele, S. (1990). Addiction as a cultural concept. In *Psychology: Perspectives and Practice*, ed. S. M. Pfafflin, J. A. Sechzer, J. M. Fish, and R. L. Thompson, pp. 205–220 (Annals, Vol. 602). New York: New York Academy of Sciences.

Szasz, T. S. (1974). *Ceremonial Chemistry: The Ritual Persecution of Drugs, Addicts, and Pushers*. New York: Anchor/Doubleday.

––––––– (1992). *Our Right to Drugs: The Case for a Free Market*. New York: Praeger.

Zinberg, N. E. (1984). *Drug, Set, and Setting: The Basis for Controlled Intoxicant Use*. New Haven, CT: Yale University Press.

2

Two Rationales for Drug Policy: How They Shape the Content of Reform

Douglas N. Husak

INTRODUCTION

Those many commentators who have long proposed a fundamental rethinking of our nation's drug policy have become impatient for the debate to proceed to the next level. Their impatience is understandable. Many thoughtful critics have found the arguments against the status quo to be compelling—and frustratingly repetitive. Every week an academic from one discipline or another discovers anew that the "war on drugs" has been a disaster. Each successive book recites all-too-familiar arguments about the failures of what might be called our *criminal justice* drug policy. According to this policy, the best way to deal with those drugs used largely for recreational purposes—in particular, marijuana, cocaine, and heroin—is by severely punishing persons who use them.[1]

Even those commentators who have not been wholly persuaded by these arguments are anxious to see the controversy move in a different direction. To some theorists, the case in favor of fundamental change cannot be decisive in the absence of a blueprint for reform. These more cautious critics withhold judgment about our criminal justice policy until a detailed description of a new strategy for dealing with drugs becomes available for evaluation. Although deeply skeptical of the status quo, these commentators know it is naive to suppose that "things can't get much worse."

Why do most theorists decline the invitation to provide the specifics of a better drug policy? Many explanations are possible, apart from the obvious fact that attacking a proposal is always easier than defending a solution. This chapter is an attempt to account for this state of affairs by contrasting two distinct bases for dissatisfaction with contemporary drug policy. Many persons who are unified in their opposition to the status quo divide in their reasons to oppose it. The shape of an ideal drug policy cannot be specified without a relatively clear idea of why our criminal justice approach is so deficient.

The two bases for opposition to our criminal justice drug policy might be called the *harm reduction* perspective and the *rights-based* perspective. Although these two perspectives are logically compatible, and in many ways complementary, this chapter highlights the respects in which they are in tension with one another and concludes by contrasting their implications for drug policy reform. I will argue that no one should profess to be able to describe more than the barest outlines of an ideal drug policy without choosing between a harm reduction and a rights-based perspective. The details of a new drug policy depend not only on which of the two perspectives is adopted, but also on further subdivisions and refinements within each perspective. Careful reflection about the deficiencies of our criminal justice drug policy is required before the debate can be taken to the next level and the details of a preferable strategy can be described.

THE HARM REDUCTION PERSPECTIVE

In this Section I will describe the harm reduction perspective to drug policy reform. Because I tend to favor the competing rights-based perspective, discussed later in this chapter, I focus here largely on what I take to be the difficulties with the harm reduction approach. Of course, harm reduction theorists do not speak with a single voice. In particular, they disagree with one another about matters of fact, about how harm is best reduced. In this text, however, I explore theoretical rather than empirical problems within this perspective.

Many commentators have concluded that our criminal justice drug policy "does not work." Our policy is alleged not to work because it is largely ineffective in reducing either the supply or the demand for drugs, and no realistic measures to significantly improve our efforts are on the horizon. In addition, our policy is alleged not to work because it is counterproductive in myriad ways. I will not recount the several respects in which our criminal justice drug policy is counterproductive.[2] These reasons are familiar to any-one who is not a novice to the drug policy debates.

What would it mean for a policy to "work"? According to this perspec-tive, the best drug policy would minimize harm. This reply opens all aspects of drug policy to reexamination; it makes no presuppositions about which kind of policy will emerge as optimal. Contrary to the accusations of some of its opponents, harm reduction is not a disguise for a drug decriminaliza-tion agenda.[3] Admittedly, many theorists are persuaded that harm will be minimized by repealing criminal penalties designed to deter drug use.[4] But deterrence might be a component of the most effective approach; some de-fenders of the status quo are prepared to defend our criminal justice policy on harm reduction grounds.[5] In any event, the question of what policy "works" is contingent, dependent on careful research and a dispassionate assessment of various alternatives.

Perhaps the greatest virtue of the harm reduction perspective is that its ultimate objective seems beyond serious reproach. As Ethan Nadelmann asks, "Who, in their right mind, could oppose the notion of reducing harm?"[6] Perhaps the alleged consensus about the proper goal of drug policy accounts for the wide ideological diversity of persons who have joined in the call for fundamental reform on harm reduction grounds. Both liberals and conserva-tives should welcome a drug policy that "works."

Theorists who advocate a harm reduction perspective should be well aware, however, that their objective is not really so platitudinous. A harm reduction perspective is incompatible with what might be called *legal moral-ism*.[7] According to the legal moralist, the criminal law should punish immoral behavior, apart from any harm that such conduct might cause. Legal moral-ism provides the theoretical foundation for many defenses of our criminal justice drug policy. Former "drug czar" William Bennett states: "The simple fact is that drug use is wrong. And the moral argument, in the end, is the most compelling argument."[8] The reigning czar, Barry McCaffrey, echoes this sentiment in the context of defending the disparate treatment of licit and illicit drugs. He writes: "The reason drugs are wrong and dangerous is not that they're illegal but that they're destructive of a person's physical, emo-tional and moral strength—and also of their families. That central assertion also applies to alcohol. Nicotine may be more of a health problem, but these other drugs are dangerous because they pull you apart physically and emo-tionally."[9] Many commentators join political appointees in invoking legal moralism to support a punitive approach to drug policy. James Q. Wilson writes:

> If we believe—as I do—that dependency on certain mind-altering drugs
> is a moral issue, and that their illegality rests in part on their immoral-

ity, then legalizing them undercuts, if it does not eliminate altogether, the moral message. That message is at the root of the distinction we now make between nicotine and cocaine. Both are highly addictive; both have harmful physical effects. But we treat the two drugs differently, not simply because nicotine is so widely used as to be beyond the reach of effective prohibition, but because its use does not destroy the user's essential humanity. Tobacco shortens one's life, cocaine debases it. Nicotine alters one's habits, cocaine alters one's soul.[10]

Moral judgments against drug use are expressed again and again. Even those commentators who are ambivalent about our existing drug policy and cautiously defend various reforms admit to moral reservations about illegal drug use. John Kaplan confesses that "I cannot escape the feeling that drug use, aside from any harm it does, is somehow wrong."[11]

How do theorists who adopt a harm reduction perspective respond to these legal moralists? They cannot easily incorporate the supposed wrongfulness of drug use into their harm reduction calculus. The alleged immorality of drug use is not simply another kind of harm—"moral harm"—to be included along with physical, psychological, and economic harm. The concept of "moral harm" is rejected by most harm reduction theorists as incoherent.[12] Some harm reduction theorists are explicit in regarding allegations about the immorality of drug use as irrelevant to their framework.[13] The fact that the harm reduction perspective aspires to moral neutrality about drug use is yet another reason its defenders find this approach so appealing. In an era in which many persons profess skepticism about moral discourse and believe normative controversies to be irresolvable, a perspective that claims not to depend on moral judgments, but only on reducing harm, seems enlightened and progressive.

In what follows, I will raise a number of difficulties that surface in the reply that harm reduction theorists offer to the legal moralists. I do not insist that any of the problems I discuss is fatal to the harm reduction perspective, so that all talk of harm reduction should be abandoned. I have no interest in dividing drug reformers against one another; thus far they have presented a fairly unified front against a common enemy: our criminal justice policy. Perhaps the difficulties I examine should be construed as invitations for further conceptual work on the part of those theorists who embrace a harm reduction perspective. Commentators who have refined this perspective have done an enormous service in identifying several respects in which our criminal justice drug policy is ineffective and counterproductive. In addition, they are pledged to improving drug policy, and have pointed out several practical steps that would help to do so.[14] I am prepared to concede that a harm reduction perspective may ultimately prove the more successful in stimulating drug policy reform in the court of public opinion. Nonetheless, I believe that the questions I raise indicate some of the relative merits of a rights-based perspective—even though this approach faces considerable problems of its own.[15]

I have already mentioned the central difficulty. Legal moralists who defend our criminal justice drug policy by alleging that much drug use is wrongful—apart from its harmful consequences—cannot be expected to subscribe to a perspective that purports to avoid the moral dimension of drug use as too controversial or otherwise irrelevant in shaping policy. From their point of view, any methodology that fails to acknowledge the wrongfulness of drug use misses the crucial point and ignores the primary rationale that drug policy should be designed to serve. Many retributivists believe that the punishment of wrongdoers is intrinsically good, even if the institutions that apprehend and convict these wrongdoers are inefficient.[16] Harm reduction critics of our criminal justice drug policy may disagree with this judgment. They should not, however, beg the question by applying a criterion to choose between competing drug policies that assumes that moral judgments play no proper role in the decision.

Allegations about the immorality of drug use should not be dismissed as anachronistic, unscientific, or irrelevant. These allegations must be addressed directly; persons who insist that illicit drug use is wrongful are owed a reply. A philosopher would *like* to respond to their *arguments*. Unfortunately, arguments for the alleged immorality of drug use are almost never produced; this judgment is typically put forward as a kind of brute moral fact or uncontrovertible moral intuition.[17] In the absence of an argument for this judgment, it is hard to know how a reply should be structured. When commentators do not defend their views, conflicts of moral intuitions are nearly impossible to resolve. Still, I believe it is necessary to offer *some* response to the legal moralists, even if I cannot critique an argument they are unable or unwilling to provide.

One matter is clear: allegations about the wrongfulness of drug use should not be ignored simply because they are moral judgments. I suspect that many harm reduction theorists are disingenuous if they claim to regard moral judgments as irrelevant to the formation of public policy. Commentators would be unwilling to put aside their moral views if asked to choose between competing policies about which they hold strong opinions of their own. Take any example about which there exists a social consensus about the immorality of conduct. Suppose we agree that domestic violence is wrong. Imagine that some clever theorist argued in favor of a policy to minimize the harm of domestic violence that dispensed with the use of criminal punishment. After all, it is always a contingent matter whether the best policy for reducing the harm caused by persons who batter their spouses will include the imposition of the criminal sanction. How should these arguments be received? Few of us would be prepared to entertain these arguments seriously. We would be reluctant to allow spouse-batterers to escape their just desserts simply because we became convinced that less harm would be caused by a nonpunitive approach.

Consider also the converse phenomenon. Take any example about which there exists a social consensus that conduct is morally permissible. Suppose we agree that watching television is not wrongful. Imagine that some clever theorist argued in favor of a policy to minimize the harm of watching television that included the use of criminal punishment. After all, it is always a contingent matter whether the best policy for dealing with the harms caused by television will include the imposition of the criminal sanction. Again, few of us would be prepared to entertain these arguments seriously. We would be unwilling to punish persons who watch television simply because we became convinced that less harm would be caused by a criminal justice approach. I conclude that if we really believe that a given kind of conduct is wrongful—or firmly hold it to be morally permissible—we would not be happy to embrace a methodology that regarded the moral status of that conduct to be irrelevant to the formation of public policy. Legal moralists have a point when they respond that the supposed moral neutrality of the harm reduction perspective is not a virtue that any reasonable person should welcome.

But can the harm reduction perspective really maintain moral neutrality? I think not. My skepticism arises from attempting to understand the nature of "harm" that these reformers propose to minimize. What is harm? Theorists are likely to respond by reciting a list of uncontroversial examples of the negative consequences of our criminal justice drug policy: overcrowded prisons, violence by drug dealers defending turf, emergency medical treatment by persons ingesting contaminated drugs, and the like. But I am not simply asking for examples, or for a list of harms. In inquiring what harm *is*, I am asking what *makes* something a harm. In virtue of what property or properties does something qualify for inclusion on the list?

One cannot simply identify a given consequence as a harm in the same way that he or she can identify a person's shoe size or height. Smokers who die premature deaths help to keep the Social Security fund solvent. Are their early deaths a harm? The problem is not simply the existence of contested, borderline examples. The problem is that no *empirical* test can answer this kind of question. Without making judgments about which consequences we want or don't want, the contrast between the harmless and the harmful cannot be drawn. And which consequences should we not want? We should not want those consequences that are bad. A "harm," I think, is any consequence that is bad. It is what some philosophers and economists call "disutility." "Bad," of course, is not a morally neutral concept. If I am correct, harm is not a morally neutral concept either.[18] Perhaps the moral content of harm is not widely recognized because we tend to think of moral questions as controversial, and there is nothing controversial about judgments such as "drug-related killings of children to protect turf are bad." But a moral judgment is not transformed into something other than a moral judgment simply because its truth is so evident. Not all moral questions are intractable; some moral judgments are obviously true.

The realization that harm is a moral concept casts the harm reduction perspective in a new and different light. The harm reduction approach to drug policy, no less than that of the legal moralist, depends on moral judgments. The harm reduction perspective does not offer a morally neutral alternative to the enforcement of morality. At best, it simply proposes a different version of the morality to be enforced.[19]

Further evidence that the harm reduction perspective incorporates a moral point of view is easily provided. Harm reduction theorists divide over a number of issues that cannot be resolved empirically. I will mention two such issues. First, is harm to users to be given the same status as harm to nonusers? On the one hand, it is difficult to treat harms to users differently from harms to nonusers. The death of a smoker from lung cancer and the death of a nonsmoker as a result of secondary, side-stream smoke each count as a fatality caused by tobacco. If our objective is to reduce harm, shouldn't we strive equally hard to prevent each death? On the other hand, it is difficult to treat harms to users comparably to harms to nonusers, and few harm reduction theorists are prepared to do so. After indicating that "drug use is viewed as neither right or wrong in itself," one prominent defender of a harm reduction perspective continues: "Rather, drug use is evaluated in terms of harm to others, and, to some extent, harm suffered by users. The latter is regrettable, but acceptable if it arises from 'informed choice.' "[20]

According to this train of thought, not all harms are alike. Some kinds of harm—those arising from "informed choice"—are "acceptable." No theorist who adopts this stance can pretend that his approach is morally neutral. Any basis for concluding that some harms "don't count" in the harm reduction calculus is almost certain to be derived from a theory that presupposes some conception of the autonomy of agents. Unlike harms to others, self-inflicted harms caused through informed choice are exempted because they are the product of autonomous choice. Needless to say, any defense of this conclusion—an account of the nature and importance of autonomy—involves moral reasoning.[21]

Consider a second moral issue that divides theorists in the harm reduction camp. Notice that the goal of harm reduction seems curiously incomplete. Consider two policies, A and B. Suppose that policy A produces less harm than policy B. Is policy A therefore preferable? Almost certainly not.

In order to choose between A and B, we need to know not only which policy minimizes harm, but also which policy maximizes benefits. A moral argument is needed to show why harms should count, but benefits should not. Most harm reduction theorists would probably agree that the best drug policy would not simply minimize harm, but would do so while maximizing benefits. If "harm" is equated with "cost," the best drug policy achieves the most favorable ratio of benefits to costs.[22]

Two problems arise if the focus is shifted away from the simple goal of harm reduction toward the more complex goal of achieving the most favorable ratio of benefits to costs (or harms). The first problem is to identify the benefits to be balanced against the harms or costs; the second is to balance them. Neither problem can be solved without making moral judgments.

Begin with the benefits to be balanced against the harms or costs of drug use. What is the nature of these benefits? If I am correct that harm is a moral concept—equivalent to anything bad—it should come as no surprise that benefit is a moral concept as well—equivalent to anything good. And what is good about drug use? Much has been said and written about the harms of drug use—and, from harm reduction theorists, about the harms of prohibiting drug use—but a discussion of the benefits of drug use is conspicuously absent in the cost-benefit literature. Some commentators, to be sure, have emphasized the artistic creativity, spiritual enlightenment, and consciousness expansion that drug use may produce.[23] These effects should not be dismissed as unimportant. Such benefits do not, however, capture the motivation behind most recreational drug use. The explanation of why many persons consume drugs is no more mysterious than the explanation of why many persons consume so much fat or sugar: they enjoy the experience. The main benefit persons obtain is pleasure or euphoria, the "high" of drug use.

Does pleasure count as a benefit in the cost-benefit calculus? An affirmative answer seems obvious; to demand a defense of the significance of pleasure is odd.[24] Yet there is a puzzling reluctance among commentators to mention pleasure as the main benefit of drug use.[25] Despite occasional allegations that Americans are puritanical, we do not really regard pleasure per se as objectionable or suspicious; we engage in all kinds of activities that are important to us solely (or at least primarily) because of the pleasure we derive from them. Although there is some nutritional value in potato chips, almost no one devours them for that reason. Eye–hand coordination is developed by video games, but few play them to gain that skill. These activities are popular because they are almost purely recreational—they are pursued for fun. No one could afford to ignore the superior taste of ice cream relative to wheat germ if asked to prepare a cost-benefit analysis of these foods. Licit recreational drugs such as alcohol would fail a cost-benefit test if the pleasure of intoxication were omitted from consideration. Like the pleasure derived from eating, playing video games, or from any other activity, the pleasure of illicit drug use must be included in the cost-benefit calculus, unless there is some basis for disqualifying it.[26] But any basis for claiming that not all pleasures count equally has the same status as the foregoing claim that not all harms count equally. The rationale for differentiating between kinds of pleasures in a cost-benefit analysis, for alleging that some pleasures are good and other pleasures are bad, must be moral in nature.

The second problem in attempts to achieve the most favorable ratio of costs and benefits is to justify a decision about how the various factors should be weighed and balanced. Even if all the costs and benefits of various drug policies could be predicted with reasonable accuracy, there is simply no common denominator by which it is possible to decide whether the costs outweigh the benefits or vice versa. The balancing metaphor suggests the existence of a common denominator, or a common currency, in which all costs and benefits can be expressed. Unfortunately, no such common denominator is available. One theorist will judge that the costs of a given activity outweigh its benefits; another will reach the opposite conclusion. He will judge that the pleasure of a drug high (or of a jelly doughnut) outweighs the health risks that such activities create. The point is not simply that there is no way to decide who is correct: many empirical disagreements seem quite intractable. Instead, the point is that the disagreement is moral rather than factual. Here again, the tendency of theorists who subscribe to a cost-benefit analysis to depict themselves as empirical and scientific is inaccurate. Like those who employ a perspective they typically resist, they too are engaged in moral debate.

With this conclusion in mind, return again to Nadelmann's rhetorical question: "Who, in their right mind, could oppose the notion of reducing harm?" He asks this question, of course, in the context of identifying the best drug policy, and perhaps a harm reduction perspective is supposed to apply *only* to drug policy. Yet confining a harm reduction approach to drug policy seems suspiciously ad hoc. Of course, theorists who aspire to the improvement of society must begin somewhere, and I sympathize with those who believe that the greatest payoffs will occur by overhauling our drug policy. Still, in principle, Nadelmann's rhetorical question could be raised in any other context. Is it equally sensible—no more or no less—to implement a harm reduction perspective to *any* issue whatever? After all, harm reduction seems just as viable when applied to educational policy, defense policy, or anything else about which we may want a policy. For example, Americans do not eat as well as we might. Who in his right mind could oppose harm reduction when formulating food policy? Americans do not read as much as we might. Why not pursue a harm reduction approach to reading policy?

Something seems to have gone wrong here. There are some matters about which it seems inappropriate to implement a "policy," even if harm reduction strategies should be applied to those matters for which a policy is desirable. No one talks about the need for harm reduction in designing a "speech policy," not because no harms are caused by speech, or because nothing could possibly be done to reduce them. A harm reduction perspective should not be applied to a controversy about whether a given speaker should be tolerated or persecuted because it seems clear that *rights* are at stake in matters of speech. When rights are implicated, the very suggestion that controversies should be decided by reference to a policy seems misguided. Harm reduction or cost-benefit analyses are largely beside the point when rights are at stake. I am concerned that the assumption that drug policy should be formulated on harm reduction grounds implicitly presupposes that no rights are implicated by drug use.

Are rights at stake in drug use? I now turn to this question.

THE RIGHTS-BASED PERSPECTIVE

I believe that the rights-based perspective to drug policy reform has several advantages over the competing harm reduction perspective, even though it has received far less attention.[27] In particular, it provides a better response to those legal moralists who support our criminal justice drug policy. Still, this perspective faces considerable problems of its own, which I will attempt to resolve as best I can.

According to the rights-based perspective, drug policy, like any other policy, must respect moral rights. These rights constrain what can be done in the name of policy. Our criminal justice approach is defective because it infringes the moral rights of drug users. Many commentators who endorse a harm reduction perspective also believe that moral rights are violated by the status quo. Yet the two perspectives are clearly different, and in some respects are in tension with each another.[28]

Recall that the harm reduction perspective dealt with the moral dimension of drug use by applying a methodology that dismissed such issues as unimportant.[29] By contrast, the rights-based perspective offers a cogent reply to the legal moralists. One can concede that drug use might be wrongful while still believing it to be protected by a moral right. The supposition that rights can apply to and protect wrongful conduct is familiar to our thinking about rights.[30] Consider just a few examples. No one supposes that privacy rights protect only morally innocent activities. Most people concede the immorality of Nazi politics or racist speech while still believing that these activities are protected by moral rights. To be sure, moral rights do not confer an absolute immunity on persons to engage in immoral conduct, a point to which I will return.[31] The supposition that recreational drug use is protected by a right does not entail that consequentialist considerations are utterly irrelevant to the resolution of issues about drug use. Still, moral rights can and do offer some degree of protection to wrongful behavior.

I faulted harm reduction theorists for adopting positions on normative issues while purporting to moral neutrality. Recall that the very distinction between the harmful and the harmless cannot be drawn without a willingness to make moral judgments. Moreover, harm reduction theorists cannot explain why harm to oneself should count less than harm to others without recourse to moral reasoning. Since a rights-based perspective has no aspirations to moral neutrality, it seems capable of solving problems that embarrassed the harm reduction perspective. In any theory of rights, for example, persons enjoy a much broader freedom to harm themselves than to harm others.

Nonetheless, some theorists who endorse a cost-benefit (or harm reduction) perspective on drug policy have expressed skepticism about the cogency of a rights approach. Kaplan concedes that "many people speak of the individual's right to do what he wishes with his own body, his right to harm himself, or his right to eat, drink, or otherwise ingest what he pleases." But, he continues, "the problem with such 'rights' is that they are all assertions. They do not carry any argument with them."[32]

It is not entirely clear what would satisfy Kaplan's demand that defenders of a rights-based perspective produce an "argument." I construe his complaint as follows. No one should simply *allege* that persons have a moral right to eat, drink, or otherwise ingest what they please. A theorist who defends our criminal justice drug policy will not concede that these rights exist. As I have indicated, legal moralists believe that drug use is wrongful, and that drug offenders should be punished for that reason alone. But I have also noted that they have not *argued* for this position. Both sides seem equally guilty of begging the question against their opponents; each reports moral intuitions the other rejects. The only hope of making progress in this standoff is to produce an argument. Commentators who defend a rights-based perspective must provide a plausible argument in favor of the existence of a moral right to use drugs that is infringed by our criminal justice policy.

How might one defend the existence of such a moral right? The best strategy would be to provide a comprehensive theory of moral rights, and to show that a right to use drugs is among those particular rights countenanced by the theory. I will not pursue this very ambitious strategy here, although I welcome attempts to do so.[33] Moral philosophers have struggled for centuries to provide an adequate theory of rights, and I have no confidence that I will succeed where they have failed. A general theory of moral rights would be just as controversial as the existence of any particular right—such as a right to use drugs—that might be derived from it.

In the absence of a comprehensive theory of rights, how might one proceed in reforming drug policy from a rights-based perspective? One alternative is to rely on analogies. If there are any recreational activities one believes to be protected by a moral right, he or she must explain why recreational drug use is not similarly protected.[34] But even if two recreational activities are similar in all relevant respects, this strategy is still vulnerable to a difficulty that plagues all analogical reasoning. Someone may simply deny that moral rights protect *any* recreational activity.[35]

In what follows, I pursue a third strategy. I will inquire whether a right to use drugs might be derived from some other, more general right, the existence of which is likely to be accepted by all parties to the debate. Many arguments that proceed in the name of rights have followed this strategy. They have not posited new rights, which are always rejected as "odd, frightening, or laughable,"[36] but have expanded the scope of existing rights. Consider, for example, the controversy about flag burning. No one who believes that criminal laws are justified in order to prevent flag burning is likely to change his mind by a commentator who retorts that persons have a right to burn the flag. The existence of such a right must be the conclusion of an argument, not its premise. A cogent defense of a right to burn the flag would derive this particular right from a more general right, the existence of which is likely to be accepted on both sides of the controversy. In the case of flag burning, of course, that right is freedom of speech. Once a general right to freedom of speech is invoked, debates about flag burning move to a new level, where the hope of progress becomes more realistic. Opponents of flag burning are far more likely to allege that the general right to freedom of speech does not apply to or protect the specific activity of flag burning than to reject that general right altogether.

What more general moral rights might be infringed by proscriptions of drug use? This question raises the greatest single challenge to the rights-based perspective on drug policy reform. Of course, the zealous enforcement of our criminal justice drug policy has jeopardized familiar and easily identifiable rights.[37] But the legal moralists who defend our criminal justice policy can apologize for the frequent abuses in law enforcement without surrendering their basic contention that drug use is wrongful. Do drug prohibitions per se infringe rights? If so, which rights?

The supposed need to answer this question by reference to a right, the existence of which is acknowledged by all parties to the debate, may seem too stringent. A right becomes well known not simply because we are confident of its existence, but because it has been threatened so frequently as to attract our attention and vigilance. Some rights are less familiar because they have been infringed so rarely that they are taken for granted. Everyone is aware that states have often sought to interfere with freedom of speech, and civil libertarians are quick to sound the alarm when any such interferences are proposed. Apart from interference with food *additives*, modern Western states have not, to my knowledge, sought to interfere with our decisions about what foods we eat.[38] Thus a "right to eat whatever foods we like" sounds unfamiliar and controversial. If the state really did endeavor to interfere with our decisions about the foods we eat, I would anticipate howls of protest at least as loud as those that greet attempts to interfere with rights that are much more well known, such as our right to freedom of speech.

Still, my argument will not depend on controversial and unfamiliar rights, such as an alleged right to eat whatever foods we like. Which general rights that are presumed to exist by a broad social consensus can serve as candidates from which a right to use drugs might be derived? The Constitution provides the best source of such rights. I assume that most of the rights included in the Bill of Rights have both a legal as well as a moral status. Although some moral rights may not be included in the Constitution, the advantages of deriving a right to use drugs from some constitutional source are clear. Despite contemporary skepticism and disagreement about moral issues, few people seem prepared to reject the very existence of a right that is protected by our Constitution.

The two most obvious candidates from which to derive a moral right to use drugs are the general rights of equal protection and privacy.[39] How should we decide whether either of these rights apply to and protect drug use? I answer this question by invoking the general theory of interpretation defended by Ronald Dworkin.[40] As Dworkin notes, rights are described with varying degrees of generality or specificity. The rights to equal protection and privacy are very abstract, and no abstract right can be applied to concrete cases "except by assigning some overall *point* or *purpose* [to it]."[41] One must decide whether the point or purpose of the rights to equal protection or privacy is promoted or frustrated by applying these rights to drug use.

These questions have already been litigated, of course; courts have had ample opportunity to decide whether drug proscriptions infringe the rights of equal protection or privacy. A number of constitutional challenges to our criminal justice drug policy have been brought, and it is instructive to examine how courts have responded. Almost all of these constitutional challenges have failed, although a few have succeeded. It is important to assess the reasons that courts have given when forced to decide whether the rights to equal protection or privacy are infringed by drug proscriptions. Thus I briefly examine some recent (but not *too* recent) constitutional history in perhaps the two leading cases in which the rights of drug users were litigated. I will conclude that the rights of equal protection and privacy provide a plausible basis from which a right to use drugs might be derived.

In *Ravin v. State*,[42] the constitutionality of Alaska's marijuana prohibition was challenged. The defendant alleged that this statute violated both his right to equal protection and his right of privacy under the federal and

State of Alaska constitutions. Five years later, in *NORML v. Bell*,[43] a similar challenge was brought to that part of the Federal Controlled Substances Act that prohibited the private possession and use of marijuana. Although neither court held that drug proscriptions violated a right to equal protection, Ravin, unlike NORML, prevailed on the privacy issue.

I begin by assessing the equal protection arguments. Both the litigants in *Ravin* and *NORML* alleged that marijuana proscriptions were underinclusive as well as overinclusive. Marijuana proscriptions were alleged to be underinclusive because the statutes failed to attach comparable punishments to the use of relevantly similar substances, most notably tobacco and alcohol. The intuitive force behind this argument is easy to appreciate. How is it fair for the state to prohibit the drugs preferred by some persons but not those preferred by other persons? Unless there is good reason to believe that the drugs permitted are less dangerous than those prohibited, this discrimination would seem to deny persons the equal protection of the laws. The statute was also alleged to be overinclusive on the ground that the use of marijuana was punished as severely as the use of relevantly dissimilar substances, most notably cocaine and heroin.

Neither court was persuaded by these allegations. To succeed in a challenge based on underinclusiveness, a plaintiff must show that a statutory classification is "clearly wrong, a display of arbitrary power, not an exercise in judgment."[44] Almost no challenge can sustain such a heavy burden of proof. Legislatures are granted wide latitude in attacking social ills "one step at a time." A statutory prohibition should not be overturned simply because the legislation did not cover every evil that might conceivably have been addressed. The fact that alcohol and tobacco may have adverse affects on health that resemble those of marijuana does not necessitate that these substances must be regulated by the same statutory scheme that applies to marijuana.

The *NORML* court had more difficulty disposing of the allegation that marijuana proscriptions were overinclusive. The plaintiffs contended that marijuana does not satisfy the criteria for placement on Schedule I, that part of the Controlled Substances Act that regulates the most dangerous drugs. The court responded that Congress was warranted in punishing the use and possession of marijuana as severely as the use and possession of more harmful substances. Congress had a rational basis for rejecting attempts to impose less severe punishments for marijuana possession, "fearing that such action would create the impression that marijuana use was acceptable."[45] The court expressed reservations about whether marijuana satisfied the criteria for placement on Schedule I. Still, when correctly interpreted, these criteria were said to be satisfied. In what may be the most confusing aspect of the court's reasoning,[46] these statutory criteria were construed not as "dispositive"—that is, as necessary conditions—but as mere "guides in determining the schedule to which a drug belongs."[47] Thus the constitutional challenge based on the overinclusiveness of the statute fared no better than the challenge based on its underinclusiveness.

I admit that courts are ill equipped to upset whole statutory schemes on the ground that allegedly similar substances are treated dissimilarly. In light of medical uncertainty and disagreement, judges should tend to defer to good-faith legislative judgments about whether different drugs merit comparable treatment. Thus the courts may have resolved correctly the equal protection issues in *Ravin* and *NORML*.[48] Just because courts should be reluctant to second-guess legislators, however, does not mean that legislators acted correctly in the first place. The prior decision to prohibit some drugs while allowing others does not appear to reflect an impartial (although controversial) judgment about their relative dangers.[49] As I have indicated, drug czars have tended to resort to legal moralism to defend the distinctions between licit and illicit substances.[50] The use of some drugs but not others is alleged to be wrongful. This basis for distinguishing among various drugs poses a genuine threat to equal protection. May the state prohibit the drugs preferred by some persons while allowing the drugs preferred by other persons because the preferences of the former class are alleged to be immoral? I do not insist that moral reasons can never be invoked on behalf of a legislative discrimination. But unless these moral reasons are produced and evaluated, one comes to suspect that the state is simply using its raw power to discriminate against some persons because it disapproves of their preferences, and thus would seem to deny them the equal protection of the laws.

Next, consider the privacy issue. Here *Ravin*'s constitutional challenge, unlike *NORML*'s, ultimately prevailed. Why did the courts reach different results on very similar allegations? Several answers might be given.[51] Most important, the *Ravin* court was prepared to struggle to formulate a general conception of the right of privacy to determine whether the use of marijuana might be protected by it. The court characterized privacy as "a right of personal autonomy in relation to choices affecting an individual's personal life"[52] and, even more generally, as a "right to be let alone."[53] On the basis of these conceptions, the court concluded that "this right of privacy would encompass the possession and ingestion of substances such as marijuana in a purely personal, non-commercial context."[54]

How do the foregoing conceptions of privacy differ from that articulated in *NORML*? Remarkably, no answer can be given, since the *NORML* court failed to articulate any conception of privacy at all. It simply claimed that the right of privacy was limited to those matters to which the Supreme Court had previously applied it. Subsequent cases have followed this trend. Courts have been reluctant to apply the right of privacy to issues of personal autonomy other than those involving marriage, reproduction, and the family.[55] One can only guess why such matters are unique in meriting protection by the right of privacy.

The most difficult challenge confronting attempts to show that the right of privacy protects drug use is to defend a general conception of privacy that applies to this activity.[56] If either of the conceptions formulated in *Ravin* are accepted—if privacy is construed either as a "right to be let alone" or a "right of personal autonomy in relation to choices affecting an individual's personal life"—its application to drug use seems relatively clear. This challenge must also be confronted by those theorists who believe that the right of privacy does not protect drug use. Their task is to formulate a general conception of privacy that protects such activities as the use of contraceptives, but does not apply to drug use. The court in *NORML* evaded this challenge.

Why did the *Ravin* court bother to articulate a general conception of privacy at all? The need to characterize this right, and to do so broadly, was necessary to enable the court to make sense of some of its own precedents. In *Breese v. Smith*, "one of the most significant decisions [in which] this court has dealt with the concept of privacy," Alaska had found a school hair length regulation to be unconstitutional.[57] The *NORML* court's failure to provide a general conception of privacy makes it impossible to decide whether such matters as hair length would receive any degree of constitutional protection.[58]

The *Ravin* court found that the right of privacy applied to decisions about both marijuana use and hair length. But the court did not deem the right to use marijuana to be a fundamental constitutional right, even though the court had found the liberty interest in *Breese* to be fundamental. "Hairstyle," the court said, "is a highly personal matter involving the individual and his body."[59] Why did the court not reach the same conclusion about marijuana use? Isn't it too a "highly personal matter involving the individual and his body"? The court answered: "Few would believe they have been deprived of something of critical importance if deprived of marijuana, though they would if stripped of control over their personal appearance."[60] This answer was quoted with approval in *NORML*.[61]

This basis for contrasting the degree of protection offered to hair length in *Breese* from that offered to marijuana use in *Ravin* is deficient. First, no empirical data are cited to support the court's conjecture about what "few would believe." Persons who smoke marijuana might feel just as strongly about their preference as persons who violate the school ordinance governing hair length. Moreover, it is unclear that the degree of protection offered by the right of privacy should depend on the numbers of persons who have or lack the relevant beliefs. Third and most significant, the question is rigged to enable the court to justify its answer. I concede that more persons would be outraged if "stripped of control over their personal appearance" than if "deprived of marijuana." But the terms of the comparison are flawed and misleading.

The first part of the comparison is very general and the second is very specific. Imagine how the question would have been answered if the first part of the comparison were very specific and the second were very general. How would persons feel if "stripped of control over what they are allowed to put into their bodies" relative to a "deprivation of shoulder-length hair"? Clearly, the outcome of such a determination would be very different. To be meaningful and unbiased, the examples to be compared must invoke the same level of generality. On that basis it is hard to decide whether persons care more about control over what they are permitted to put into their bodies than about control over their personal appearance. I see no reason to regard either matter as more important, basic, or fundamental than the other.

The case in favor of extending the rights of equal protection or privacy to protect drug use is plausible but inconclusive. Perhaps drug use might receive some degree of protection from rights seldom thought applicable to it. Consider, for example, Thomas Scanlon's well-known basis for protecting freedom of speech.[62] Scanlon attempts to ground the right of free speech in a conception of autonomy. The persons whose autonomy Scanlon endeavors to protect by treating speech as a right are not the speakers themselves, but rather the members of the potential audience to whom that speech would be addressed. According to Scanlon, infringements of speech deny these persons the "grounds for making an independent judgment" about the view suppressed.[63] No autonomous person would grant the state the power to restrict information in order to protect him or her from whatever harm the suppressed speech might cause.

Dworkin's subsequent defense of freedom of speech is similar. Like Scanlon, he rejects all instrumentalist accounts that regard free speech as important because it contributes to some other value, like the discovery of truth. Instead, freedom of speech is said to be an essential and constitutive feature of a just political society. Any such society must treat all its sane adult members as responsible moral agents, as equal participants in shaping the moral environment in which they live. The state insults its citizens, and treats them as less than responsible agents, when it decrees that they cannot be trusted to hear speech that might lead them to dangerous or offensive convictions. Individuals retain their dignity only when they insist that no one, not even a majority of their fellow citizens, may withhold an opinion from them on the ground that they cannot be trusted to hear and consider it.[64] Dworkin continues: "It is obviously inconsistent with respecting citizens as responsible moral agents to dictate what they can read on the basis of some official judgment about what will improve or destroy their characters."[65]

Like nearly all defenders of freedom of speech,[66] Dworkin extends his rationale to protect materials he detests. Disrespect for persons as responsible moral agents is exhibited even when the materials censored are disgust-

ing and loathsome. Dworkin defends freedom of speech for Nazis and racists, although he is clearly repelled by their message. He also defends freedom of speech for distributors and readers of pornography, even though he
regards their materials as "grotesquely offensive" and "insulting, not only to
women but to men as well."[67] Clearly, support for freedom of speech is distinct from support for the content of the speech itself.

I am not especially concerned with assessing the general adequacy of
these accounts. My point is that these rationales, if accepted, protect more
than mere speech; they seem equally applicable to many kinds of activities
that neither Scanlon nor Dworkin had in mind. Drug use is among these
activities. Suppose we alter the foregoing quotation from Dworkin in one
simple respect: substitute "what drug they can use" for "what they can read."
The revised passage is: "It is obviously inconsistent with respecting citizens
as responsible moral agents to dictate what drug they can use on the basis of
some official judgment about what will improve or destroy their characters."
This new claim is responsive to the rationale of the legal moralist for proscribing drug use. Recall that the legal moralist neither defends drug prohibitions by arguing that illicit drug use is harmful to the rights of *others* nor
favors the proscription of illicit drugs because they are harmful to health.
Harm is not of central concern to the legal moralist at all. Instead, illicit
drugs are proscribed (or "censored") because they are alleged to destroy the
moral character of persons who use them.

It is hard to see why anyone who agrees with Dworkin's original quotation will disagree with the version I have substituted for it. If the original
is true and the revision false, less disrespect for persons as responsible agents
must be shown by proscriptions of drug use than by censorship of materials.
I suspect that any tendency to believe that less disrespect is exhibited by drug
proscriptions than by censorship is due to a failure to recall that Dworkin's
rationale is explicitly designed to protect behavior he believes to be despicable. It may be tempting to suppose that persons are shown greater disrespect when prohibited from listening to a politician than when barred from
injecting heroin. But is it equally sensible to suppose that persons are shown
greater disrespect when prohibited from reading sadomasochistic pornography than when barred from smoking marijuana? The true test of respect is
whether it is exhibited even when persons engage in behavior that is not
condoned or admired. No one is tempted to censor beliefs or opinions of
which he approves. As I have indicated, this familiar feature of moral rights—
that they allow persons to make less than optimal choices—provides the rights-
based perspective with a better response to the legal moralist than the harm
reduction perspective.

Return now to Scanlon's closely related defense of freedom of speech.
Recall that he resists all infringements of speech because they deny persons
the "grounds for making independent judgments" about the view suppressed.

This rationale, like Dworkin's, can be applied to many behaviors that are not instances of speech. Suppose that someone wants to make an "independent judgment" about whether cherry pie tastes better than chocolate pie. Under what conditions is he or she best able to make an "independent judgment" about this matter? Protecting his or her freedom to read and speak about this matter is clearly less valuable than protecting the freedom to actually taste the pies. Only then is judgment truly "independent." Thus Scanlon's account would seemingly condemn an interference with an act of eating, or, by parity of reasoning, with an act of drug use. A person is unable to make an independent judgment about whether he or she prefers cocaine to alcohol unless he is free to try these substances. The women who drinks alcohol and wonders what she might be missing must be content to satisfy her curiosity by relying on second-hand accounts of cocaine use. Legal moralists would deny her the freedom to reach an independent judgment about this matter because they fear she would exercise this freedom to her moral detriment.

I hope not to be misunderstood. I am not suggesting that there is no conceivable rationale for prohibiting drug use. I am only responding to the legal moralist. My response attempts to bring drug use within the scope of some familiar right, and I have suggested that the rationale for protecting freedom of speech may also provide some degree of protection to drug use. I am not arguing that the concept of speech is so elastic that it can be stretched to include drug use. My point is not that drug use is speech, but that some of the most plausible theories of the point or purpose of the right of free speech—theories of why speech should be entitled to protection—can be extended with little strain to protect drug use as well. Most important, the application of these rights-based rationales does not require that protected conduct be morally innocent. The legal moralist basis for prohibiting drug use fails for the same reason as the legal moralist basis for infringing other rights.

I conclude that plausible interpretations of either the right of equal protection or the right of privacy—or even the rationale for freedom of speech—can be applied to offer some degree of protection to drug use. Perhaps other moral rights are implicated as well. If I am correct, the legal moralist has been answered, and the greatest obstacle in defending a rights-based perspective to drug policy reform has been overcome.

THE DIFFERING POLICY IMPLICATIONS
OF THE TWO PERSPECTIVES

The shape of an ideal drug policy that improves on our criminal justice approach cannot be described in any detail without deciding which of the two foregoing rationales for reform should be accepted. A policy that implements a harm reduction perspective and seeks to maximize the ratio of benefits to costs will differ substantially from a policy that is geared to respect moral rights. The specifics of a new drug policy depend not only on which of the two perspectives is embraced, but on further subdivisions and refinements within each perspective. In briefly supporting these claims in this final section, I am especially concerned with identifying a few specific issues on which a harm reduction and a rights-based perspective are likely to disagree. Of course, my efforts take only the smallest step in pointing the direction of drug policy reform. All I can hope to accomplish is to provide some of the reasons why a blueprint for change has been so hard to produce.

Which variables affect the shape of a drug policy designed to implement a harm reduction perspective? Changing circumstances are the most important such factors. A policy that minimizes harm today might not continue to do so tomorrow. The ratio of costs to benefits is in a state of flux as newer and more effective means to reduce the harms of drugs become available. For example, harm reduction theorists frequently despair of our prospects of reducing the supply of drugs from drug-producing countries. But a breakthrough might radically change this assessment. Suppose, for example, that coca-eating moths could be unleashed in the Andes, devouring much of the world's supply of coca. I do not pretend that this particular "technological fix" is especially realistic. My point is that any such innovation would radically alter the balance of costs and benefits of drug policy.

Apart from changing circumstances and technological innovations, the details of drug policy will be influenced by the answers that harm reduction theorists provide to two of the questions I raised above. I asked, first, whether the harm reduction calculus treats the harm that drug users do to themselves on a par with the harm that drug users do to others. If each kind of harm is comparable, theorists who implement a harm reduction perspective will have a great deal of harm to try to reduce. After all, most of the harm caused by drugs is suffered by users themselves, so policy makers have a greater incentive to decrease this harm by curtailing use. Thus they are more likely to regard abstinence from drugs as an ideal. Perhaps this ideal is unrealistic to attain, so harm reduction strategies must aim lower. But abstinence remains an ideal nonetheless, and the policy maker must always be willing to consider measures that would help to transform this ideal into a reality.

Suppose, on the other hand, that self-inflicted harms are exempted from the harm reduction calculus when they are the product of autonomous choice. By this simple stroke of the accountant's pen, the amount of harm caused by drugs is drastically reduced. According to this school of thought, abstinence is less clearly an ideal to which drug policy should aspire. Harm reduction theorists should concentrate only on reducing those harms that drug users cause to others. Since self-inflicted harms are important only when they are not the product of autonomous choice, harm reduction theorists should endeavor to create the conditions under which drug use is autonomous.

I can think of at least three reasons why some instances of drug use might be regarded as nonautonomous. First, since adolescents are typically believed to lack the capacity for autonomous choice, harm reduction theorists should adopt strategies to decrease drug use among adolescents. Second, since false beliefs are generally thought to undermine autonomous choice, harm reduction theorists should devote substantial resources to drug education. Finally, since addiction might render drug use nonautonomous, harm reduction theorists should favor whatever programs have been shown to help addicts.[68] Of course, these reasons provide no basis to conclude that *all* drug use is nonautonomous. Once an informed adult uses drugs autonomously, any detrimental consequences his acts create for himself are unimportant from a harm reduction perspective. Thus measures to reduce drug use per se become much less appealing.

I also asked whether pleasure counts as a benefit on the cost-benefit calculus. If pleasure is not included, little can be said in favor of drug use that could possibly outweigh all that can be said against it. Again, abstinence becomes an attractive ideal. Suppose, on the other hand, that pleasure counts in the cost-benefit calculus, and therefore must be weighed against harm. If so, entirely new issues become relevant. Abstinence would be undesirable, since it would sacrifice all the benefits that can be gained from drug use.

Once pleasure is included in the calculus, there are two very different strategies for improving the cost-benefit ratio of drug use. This ratio can be improved not only by making drugs less harmful, but also by making them more pleasurable. This option is largely unexplored in the harm reduction literature. But cost-benefit theorists who include pleasure in their calculus should be enthusiastic about proposals to create new and more exhilarating drugs. Here the possibilities quickly strain the imagination.[69] Even without producing entirely new substances, measures to increase the pleasure of existing drugs are not so hard to imagine. Perhaps the simplest strategies would involve improving the delivery systems by which drugs are consumed. Although harm reduction theorists have said a lot about how to increase the safety of delivery systems, they have said little about how to make these systems more pleasurable. Consider just two suggestions. First, the discomfort caused by needles may be the greatest barrier to more widespread heroin use. If so, harm reduction theorists who take their pleasure seriously should applaud the recent trend of first-time users to smoke rather than to inject heroin.[70] Second, the greater use of filters and water pipes should decrease the irritation to the lungs and throat caused by smoking marijuana. Needless to say, defenders of our criminal justice policy will be appalled at the prospects of making drug use more pleasurable.

If it is difficult to specify the characteristics of a drug policy that implements a cost-benefit, harm reduction perspective, the details of a drug policy designed to respect moral rights are only slightly clearer. Which variables affect the shape of a drug policy designed to implement a rights-based perspective? I mention only two such factors. The first is the nature of the general right from which a right to use drugs is derived. Suppose that drug proscriptions are thought to infringe a right of privacy. If so, the details of drug policy will depend on how the distinction between the public and the private is drawn. A policy would be expected to attach great significance to the place at which drugs are used. For example, a right of privacy might protect conduct in the home that is unprotected elsewhere.[71] Recall that the right to consume marijuana upheld in *Ravin* was restricted to the home.[72]

Suppose, however, that drug proscriptions are thought to infringe a right to equal protection. If so, a comprehensive rethinking of all drugs, legal and illegal, is required. After all, unjust discrimination among the preferences of drug users can be remedied in either of two ways. First, drugs currently classified as illicit—marijuana, cocaine, and heroin—might be subjected to lesser restrictions. Alternatively, drugs not currently classified as illicit—tobacco and alcohol—might be subjected to greater restrictions. Commentators who propose a fundamental change in our criminal justice drug policy tend to favor the former alternative. Until recently, the latter option seemed unthinkable. At this time, however, the political process seems destined to bring tobacco under the supervision of the Food and Drug Administration. Other commentators have predicted "new, extensive regulation of the liquor industry."[73] The important point is that either means to produce a uniform system of drug regulation respects the right to equal protection that is allegedly infringed by our criminal justice policy.

I am devoting somewhat more attention to the second variable that affects the shape of a rights-based drug policy. The details of this policy will be influenced by the nature of the considerations that are regarded as sufficient to override whatever right is infringed by proscriptions of drug use. It is one thing to say that a right is infringed by drug prohibitions, and quite another to say that the right that is infringed is absolute.[74] An absolute right, as I understand it, is not subject to being overridden by more stringent moral considerations. I doubt that any moral right is absolute.[75] But even if I am mistaken, and some rights *are* absolute, it is hardly plausible to include the right to use drugs among those few absolute rights that may exist. Surely there can be good reasons to override whatever moral rights are infringed by recreational drug use. The consequences of drug use might provide such a reason. Contrary to the claims of some libertarians, consequentialist considerations may justify drug prohibitions after all, even if such prohibitions infringe the moral rights of drug users.[76]

Theorists unequivocally committed to drug decriminalization are unlikely to be thankful for this result. What is the practical difference, they will ask, between saying that no right is infringed by our criminal justice drug policy, and saying that the right that is infringed is overridden by more stringent moral considerations? In fact, the difference between these two statements is important. A higher standard must be satisfied to justify overriding a right than to prohibit an activity that is not protected by a right in the first place. Simple utilitarian considerations—the outcome of a cost-benefit analysis—can justify prohibiting an activity that is unprotected by a right. When a right is involved, however, mere utilitarian considerations are insufficient to justify the infringement.[77] If utilitarian reasons are inadequate, what considerations *are* sufficiently weighty to override a right to use drugs? Providing a theory of the conditions under which rights may be overridden is yet another major challenge confronting defenders of a rights-based perspective. Not only must the theorists show that a right applies to and protects drug use, they must also decide whether this right may be infringed by whatever objectives drug prohibitions are designed to achieve. Once we have settled on a rationale for the prohibition of a particular drug, the next question is whether that rationale is sufficient to justify the infringement of a right.

This task is daunting. No standard theory of the conditions under which rights may be overridden is widely accepted. Fortunately, we are not totally dependent on philosophical speculation for help in answering this question. Justifiable infringements of the rights that drug prohibitions might infringe—equal protection, privacy, or the rationale for freedom of speech—have been developed over time by constitutional lawyers. The "clear and present danger" test, for example, was devised to identify a circumstance under which the right of free speech could be infringed. But few of the familiar reasons for punishing drug users fall within any of the established justifications for infringing rights.

Consider, for example, William Bennett's rationale for punishing casual users in the war on drugs. Bennett insists that the "non-addicted casual" drug user "remains a grave issue of national concern," even though such a person "is likely to have a still-intact family, social and work life" and "to 'enjoy' his drug for the pleasure it offers." Nonetheless, Bennett argues, the casual drug user should be punished severely, because he is "much more willing and able to proselytize his drug use—by action or example—among his remaining non-user peers, friends, and acquaintances. A non-addict's drug use, in other words, is highly contagious."[78] Whatever one might think about this rationale if rights were not involved, it is clearly inadequate to justify the infringement of a right. In no other context is a right overridden on the ground that its exercise might induce other persons to exercise their rights as well. Many other rationales for drug prohibitions fare no better. For example, in no other context is a right overridden on the ground that its exercise might set a bad example for adolescents.[79]

Let me tentatively advance a strong hypothesis about the nature of the moral considerations that suffice to override a moral right: only the violation of a competing, more stringent right can justify the infringement of a right. I will not attempt to defend this hypothesis here. But if it is accepted, many familiar rationales for drug prohibitions will fail to justify infringing the rights of drug users. Consider, for example, James Q. Wilson's allegations that drug users tend not to be "healthy people, productive workers, good parents, reliable neighbors, [or] attentive students."[80] Suppose these allegations are true, although they seldom are supported by empirical evidence. But if they *are* true, the social disutility of drug use is clearly established. Mere utilitarian considerations, however, are insufficient to justify the infringement of a right. According to my tentative hypothesis, these allegations provide a good reason to infringe the rights of drug users only if the behaviors Wilson describes violate some competing, more stringent right. A comprehensive theory of rights would be needed to demonstrate that these behaviors do *not* violate any rights. Even in the absence of such a comprehensive theory, however, the inadequacy of these allegations is apparent. Apart from the context of drug use, no one believes that anyone possesses a right to mandate that persons be healthy, that workers be productive, that parents be good, that neighbors be reliable, or that students be attentive. If such rights did indeed exist, many of our social practices would have to be drastically revised. Any activities that tended to make persons less reliable, for example, would become eligible for proscription on the ground that they violate the rights of their neighbors. Thus I conclude that a rights-based perspective, when supplemented by my hypothesis about how rights may be overridden, will reject these allegations as a good reason to infringe moral rights. These reasons fail to justify our criminal justice drug policy.

Is my hypothesis too strong? Is the violation of a competing, more stringent right always needed to justify the infringement of a right? Perhaps not. My greatest reservation about this hypothesis is that it seemingly excludes all paternalistic reasons for proscribing drug use. Many commentators, hostile to paternalism, undoubtedly regard this feature of a rights-based perspective as an advantage. I am less confident, however. Suppose that some substance actually had the extreme effects described by sensationalistic media campaigns designed to deter drug use. Imagine, for example, that a given drug did to the brain what a frying pan does to an egg. I would be reluctant to allow such a drug to be available for use. Yet I am unable to identify a competing right that would justify infringing the rights of persons to use this imaginary drug. Thus the rights-based perspective, when combined with my strong hypothesis about how rights may be overridden, would not justify criminal sanctions. This consideration indicates that my hypothesis about how rights may be overridden might be too strong. Fortunately, no existing drug used for recreational purposes remotely satisfies this horrible description.[81] Thus I will not further explore my reservations about the strength of my hypothesis about how rights may be overridden.

In any event, not all rationales for drug prohibitions will fail this stringent test. Surely one can imagine a drug that is sufficiently threatening to the rights of others that no reasonable person would want to allow it to be used. Fiction provides the least controversial examples of drugs that should be prohibited on this ground. Dr. Jekyll took a substance that transformed him into the evil Mr. Hyde. Would anyone doubt that the state has authority to proscribe a substance that actually turned persons into homicidal monsters?[82] Any right to use a given drug would surely be overridden by the competing right that innocent persons not be endangered by crazed villains. Such extreme cases are clear, and demonstrate that a rights-based perspective can be sensitive to consequentialist considerations and need not allow persons to use any conceivable drug that might ever be created. But less extreme cases raise hard questions. How great a risk of harm to the rights of others must a drug create before the state has good reason to prohibit it?[83]

A policy designed to respect moral rights has additional implications for reform. Theorists who defend a harm reduction perspective often endorse a medical model that emphasizes treatment and makes drugs available by prescription. This "medicalization" alternative is defended as a progressive measure that produces less harm than our criminal justice approach.[84] But if persons have a right to use drugs, to propose that drugs be available by prescription so that users can be treated rather than punished is only a marginal improvement. The pursuit of pleasure hardly seems like a disease or illness. Persons who want to use drugs for recreational purposes would have no more access to the substances of their choice under a medical model than under a criminal justice approach. Anyone who circumvents the prescription system to obtain drugs for recreational purposes would still be subject to criminal sanctions. Although a medical model might be recommended from a harm reduction perspective, it is hard to see how it would respect a right to use drugs.

I will conclude by briefly commenting on the single matter that is perhaps more likely than any other to divide harm reduction theorists from those who defend drug policy reform from a rights-based perspective. Harm reduction theorists are especially sensitive to an accusation that inevitably is brought by commentators who support our criminal justice drug policy. Any relaxation of criminal prohibitions, it is said, is bound to trigger a massive explosion in the number of drug users.[85] Harm reduction theorists can hardly ignore this accusation, or pretend that it is irrelevant. Their responses are varied.

Most reply that the impact of their recommendations on the incidence of drug use is far less clear than their critics suppose. Others promise that the benefits of harm reduction will more than compensate for any costs incurred by the increased numbers of drug users. Still others admit to uncertainty about whether drug users should be punished if a harm reduction perspective were implemented. They do not categorically reject the imposition of criminal sanctions as a deterrent. Even casual drug users might be imprisoned as part of the most effective strategy to reduce the incidence of drug abuse.[86] Perhaps some breakthrough in law enforcement will render a criminal justice approach more viable than harm reduction theorists are inclined to believe. After all, the question of whether harm is minimized by retaining criminal penalties is contingent, to be decided by further study.

Commentators who believe that rights are infringed by our criminal justice approach are not so ambivalent about punishing drug users. A rights-based perspective offers much greater protection to drug users because its application to policy does not depend on whether a given strategy happens to "work." Persons who endorse this perspective are likely to favor the punishment of drug users only when they consume a drug that creates a substantial and unjustifiable risk to the rights of others. Most importantly for the point at hand, there is far less reason to worry about how the implementation of a rights-based policy will affect the number of drug users or the quantity of drugs they consume. No one believes that the question of whether the act of burning the flag is protected by a right depends on how the answer will affect the incidence of flag burning. Nor does anyone believe that the question of whether a right to burn the flag may be overridden depends on how the answer will affect the number of flag-burners. If persons have a right to burn the flag—or to use drugs—dire predictions about how the lack of deterrence will increase the number of persons who engage in these behaviors seem immaterial. The supposition that decriminalization will lead to a dramatic growth in drug use, even if true, will not justify infringements of the right to use drugs. If our criminal justice approach infringes moral rights, as I have suggested, the punishment of drug users is objectionable, even if the absence of criminal sanctions increases the incidence of drug use.

I hope to avoid misunderstanding. Predictions about how various reforms will affect the number of drug users are not totally irrelevant to the formation of all aspects of drug policy. According to the rights-based perspective I favor, these predictions are irrelevant only to the issue of whether drug users should be *punished*. But criminal punishment is not the only means by which society may protect itself from the disutility that would result from an explosion of drug use. Defenders of a rights-based perspective are pro-choice and pro-rights, not pro-drug. Thus they may support any number of devices to discourage drug use short of criminal punishment.[87] These devices might include taxes, tort liability for injuries caused by drug users, zoning and licensing restrictions, drug education programs, prohibitions of advertising, and the like.[88] A society may *not*, however, resort to punishment. If drug use is protected by a right, the fear that too many persons might join someone who exercises his right is simply not a good reason to infringe and override his right.

CONCLUSION

I have been especially concerned in this chapter to contrast two rationales for critiquing our criminal justice drug policy dwelling on the several respects in which they are complementary. If these rationales are as different as I have suggested, it is relatively easy to understand why the details of an ideal drug policy are so hard to provide. A policy designed to respect moral rights is likely to differ fundamentally from a policy designed to achieve the optimal ratio of costs and benefits. In particular, theorists who embrace these perspectives are able to offer different responses to the legal moralist as well as to those who fear that a radical rethinking of our criminal justice policy will greatly increase the incidence of drug use. I believe that the responses to these concerns provided by rights-based theorists are preferable to those offered by harm reduction theorists. For these reasons, among others, I tend to favor drug policy reform on the former basis. But I want to close on a more conciliatory note. The disagreements between a rights-based and a harm reduction perspective on drug policy reform are far less important than their agreement that our criminal justice policy is indefensible.

ENDNOTES

1. Two qualifications are needed. First, of course, the criminal justice system plays a much more modest role in governing the recreational use of many other drugs, primarily tobacco and alcohol. For convenience, however, I will refer to our present drug policy as reflecting a criminal justice orientation. Second, I should not be misunderstood to say that our approach relies *exclusively* on punishment. Considerable amounts of money are expended on drug education and treatment. Still, by any measure, our approach to drugs is mostly punitive. In case there is any doubt, see Margaret Spencer: "Sentencing Drug Offenders: The Incarceration Addiction," 40 *Villanova Law Rev.* 335 (1996).

2. The best summary is Ethan Nadelmann: "Drug Prohibition in the United States: Costs, Consequences, and Alternatives," 245 *Science* (1989), p. 939. More recent and detailed accounts of the respects in which our criminal justice drug policy is ineffective and counterproductive appear frequently.

3. "The relationship between the 'harm reduction' approach and the notion of drug legalization remains ambiguous." Ethan Nadelmann: "Progressive Legalizers, Progressive Prohibitionists and the Reduction of Drug-Related Harm," in Nick Heather, Alex Wodak, Ethan Nadelmann,

and Pat O'Hare, eds.: *Psychoactive Drugs & Harm Reduction: From Faith to Science* (London: Whurr Publishers, 1993), pp. 34, 36.

4. Some theorists who adopt a harm reduction perspective actually define their methodology to underscore their reservations about the desirability of deterring use. According to one commentator, "[T]he most logical definition of [harm reduction] is those policies and programs which are designed to reduce the adverse consequences of mood altering substances without necessarily reducing their consumption." See Alex Wodak: "Harm Reduction: Australia as a Case Study," *Bulletin of the New York Academy of Medicine* (1995), pp. 339, 340.

5. One theorist concludes that "a rational, hard-nosed prohibitionist could profitably employ the harm reduction platform, as I suspect many are beginning to realise." Stephen Mugford: "Harm Reduction: Does It Lead Where Its Proponents Imagine?" in Heather et al., op. cit. Note 3, pp. 21, 24. For a similar point of view, see also Geoffrey Pearson: "Drugs and Criminal Justice: A Harm Reduction Perspective," in P. A. O'Hare, R. Newcombe, A. Matthews, E. C. Buning, and E. Drucker, eds.: *The Reduction of Drug-Related Harm* (New York: Routledge, 1992), p. 15.

6. Nadelmann: Op. cit. Note 3, p. 37.

7. For a description of legal moralism, *see* Joel Feinberg: *Harm to Others* (New York: Oxford University Press, 1984), p. 12.

8. William Bennett: "The Plea to Legalize Drugs Is a Siren Call to Surrender," in Michael Lyman and Gary Potter, eds.: *Drugs in Society* (Cincinnati: Anderson Pub. Co., 1991), p. 339.

9. William Raspberry: "Prevention and the Powers of Persuasion," in *Washington Post National Weekly Edition* (July 15–21, 1996), p. 29.

10. James Q. Wilson: "Against the Legalization of Drugs," in James Inciardi and Karen McElrath, eds.: *The American Drug Scene* (Los Angeles: Roxbury Pub. Co., 1995), pp. 336, 342.

11. John Kaplan: *Marijuana: The New Prohibition* (New York: World Pub. Co., 1970), p. xi.

12. See Feinberg: Op. cit. Note 7, pp. 65–70.

13. "Drug use is viewed as neither right nor wrong in itself. Rather, drug use is evaluated in terms of harm." Mugford: Op. cit. Note 5. Comparable claims are made by other harm reduction theorists. One writes: "The true champion of harm reduction is not necessarily anti-drugs; nor necessarily pro-drugs. . . . A pre-determined position on drug use as intrinsically 'bad' or 'good' has no meaning in this context." John Strang: "Drug Use and Harm Reduction: Responding to the Challenge," in Heather, et al., op. cit. Note 3, p. 3.

14. The specific measure that is perhaps the most easily defended on harm reduction grounds is a needle exchange program to retard the spread of AIDS.

15. *See* section, "The Rights-Based Perspective," this chapter.

16. For a powerful defense of this retributivist position, see Michael Moore: "The Moral Worth of Retribution," in Ferdinand Schoeman, ed.: *Responsibility, Character, and the Emotions* (Cambridge: Cambridge University Press, 1989), p. 179.

17. The most respectable arguments for the immorality of illicit drug use invoke a conception of virtue or human excellence. Apart from other difficulties, these arguments provide an inadequate basis for criminal policy. For further discussion, *see* Douglas Husak: *Drugs and Rights* (New York: Cambridge University Press, 1992), pp. 64–68.

18. To be sure, some harm reduction theorists do not drape themselves in the cloak of moral neutrality; they admit that "deciding whether particular consequences of drug use are harms, benefits, or of neutral value, depends on the morals and values of the decision maker(s)." Russell Newcombe: "The Reduction of Drug-Related Harm: A Conceptual Framework for Theory, Practice and Research," in O'Hare, et al., eds.: Op. cit. Note 5, pp. 1, 3.

19. For further discussion *see* Douglas Husak: *Philosophy of Criminal Law* (Totowa, NJ: Rowman & Littlefield, 1987), pp. 224–248.

20. Mugford: Op. cit. Note 5, p. 21.

21. For a thoughtful discussion, *see* Gerald Dworkin: *The Nature and Practice of Autonomy* (Cambridge: Cambridge University Press, 1988).

22. Kaplan maintains that the case for or against drug decriminalization "boils down to a careful weighing of the costs of criminalizing each drug against the public-health costs we would expect if that drug were to become legally available." Presumably, he would evaluate policy a! ternatives other than decriminalization by the very same standard. See John Kaplan: "Taking Drugs Seriously," 92 *The Public Interest* (1988), pp. 32, 37.

23. Perhaps the best defense is provided in Andrew Weil: *The Natural Mind* (Boston: Houghton Mifflin Co., 2d. ed., 1986).

24. For an interesting discussion, *see* Henry Clark: *Altering Behavior: The Ethics of Controlled Experience* (London: Sage Publications, 1987), pp. 64–77 and pp. 178–1812.

25. Mugford, op. cit. Note 5, p. 28, is an exception. He writes: "Where illicit drug use is concerned, there is currently only one kind of benefit that can be counted—pleasure—which is difficult to defend in the sober, rational discourse that harm reduction would like to be."

26. See the discussion in Sheridan Hough: "The Moral Mirror of Pleasure: Considerations about the Recreational Use of Drugs" in Steven Luper-Foy and Curtis Brown, eds.: *Drugs, Morality, and the Law* (New York: Garland Pub. Co., 1994), p. 153.

27. To date, most of the work on a rights-based perspective on drug policy reform has been undertaken by libertarians. Where are the liberals? Is all they can say against the massive incarceration of drug offenders that this policy is ineffective and counterproductive? Moral and political philosophers—indeed, philosophers generally—have been strangely silent in the drug policy debate. Perhaps their silence accounts for the relative popularity of a harm reduction perspective, which tends to be favored by social scientists.

28. Some theorists explicitly subordinate rights to policy. See John Strang: "Drug Use and Harm Reduction: Responding to the Challenge," in Heather et al.: op. cit. Note 3, pp. 15–16: "From the pure harm reduction perspective, the support of the personal freedom of one or other group of drug users should be determined solely by the extent to which one or other course of action can be shown to result in an overall reduction of harm accrued."

29. *See* "The Harm Reduction Perspective," this chapter.

30. *See* Jeremy Waldron: "A Right to Do Wrong," 92 *Ethics* (1981), p. 21.

31. *See* "The Differing Policy Implications of the Two Perspectives," this chapter.

32. John Kaplan: *The Hardest Drug: Heroin and Public Policy* (Chicago: University of Chicago Press, 1983), p. 103.

33. *See* David Richards: "Book Review" in *Ethics* (1994), p. 645. Richards criticizes my unwillingness to provide a foundation for the moral rights I allege to be infringed by proscriptions of recreational drug use. I acknowledge this deficiency, and appreciate his efforts to supply the needed foundation.

34. I relied on analogical reasoning throughout much of op. cit. Note 17.

35. Richards seems to defend this response. *See* op. cit. Note 32, p. 647. Courts tend to be unwilling to afford protection to activities deemed "recreational." *See NORML v. Bell*, 488 F.Supp. 123 (1980).

36. See Chris Stone: "Should Trees Have Standing?" 45 *Southern California Law Review* (1972), pp. 450, 455.

37. For one discussion, *see* Stephen Wisotsky: "Crackdown: The Emerging 'Drug Exception' to the Bill of Rights," 38 *Hastings Law Journal* (1987), p. 889.

38. Noninterference with food should not be taken for granted. *See* Alan Hunt: *Governance of the Consuming Passions: A History of Sumptuary Law* (New York: St. Martin's Press, 1996).

39. I do not discuss the libertarian attempt to derive a right to use drugs from a general right to property. According to some libertarians, "producing, trading in, and using drugs are property rights." Thomas Szasz: *Our Right to Drugs* (New York: Praeger Pub. Co., 1992), p. 2.

40. This theory is described and defended in Ronald Dworkin: *Law's Empire* (Cambridge: Harvard University Press, 1986).

41. Ronald Dworkin: *Freedom's Law* (Cambridge: Harvard University Press, 1996), p. 199.

42. 537 P.2d 494 (Alaska 1975).

43. 488 F.Supp. 123 (1980).

44. *Id.*, p. 137.

45. *Id.*, p. 139.

46. For a more detailed discussion, *see* Husak: op. cit. Note 17, pp. 27–37.

47. Op. cit. Note 42, p. 140.

48. I fail to understand, however, why a more stringent test is not applied whenever the state enacts criminal legislation that can result in lengthy terms of imprisonment. Liberty is a fundamental interest that should be subject to deprivation only by a compelling state interest. *See* Sherry Colb: "Freedom from Incarceration: Why Is This Right Different from All Other Rights?" 69 *New York University Law Review* (1994), p. 781.

49. *See* David Musto: *The American Disease: Origins of Narcotics Control* (New York: Oxford University Press, exp.ed., 1987), p. 260.

50. *See* "The Harm Reduction Perspective," this chapter.

51. Two considerations other than the factor I discuss help to explain the different judgments. First, *Ravin* was decided under the Alaska state constitution, which contains an enumerated right of privacy, as well as under the federal Constitution, which does not. States may construe their own constitutions to provide broader protection to individual rights than that afforded by the federal government. Second, the State of Alaska applied a different standard to test the constitutionality of governmental action that abridges a defendant's liberty. The NORML court assessed this statutory interference with liberty under the "rational basis" test and had no difficulty finding the government's interest in prohibiting marijuana to be rational. The *Ravin* court, however, invoked a more demanding test: it asked whether the means chosen bear a "substantial relationship" to whatever governmental interest is properly served by restricting the use of marijuana. This standard is much harder to satisfy than the rational basis test.

52. *Id.*, p. 500.

53. *Id.*, p. 500.

54. *Id.*, p. 504.

55. The domain of unenumerated personal liberty now includes the right to marry, to choose a marital partner, to define family relationships, to procreate, to rear and educate one's children, to determine one's sexual relationships, to prevent conception, to terminate a pregnancy, and to seek medical treatment and care. *See* Edward Keynes: *Liberty, Property, and Privacy: Toward a Jurisprudence of Substantive Due Process* (University Park: Pennsylvania State University Press, 1996), p. 158.

56. *See* Norbert Gilmore: "Drug Use and Human Rights: Privacy, Vulnerability, Disability, and Human Rights Infringements," 356 *Journal of Contemporary Health Law and Policy* (1996), p. 355.

57. 501 P.2d 159 (Alaska 1972).

58. A regulation limiting the hair length of policemen was upheld in *Kelly v. Johnson*, 425 U.S. 238 (1976).

59. Op. cit. Note 41, p. 502.

60. *Id.*, p. 502.

61. Op. cit. Note 42, p. 133. Perhaps I should say that this answer was misquoted in NORML, since a crucial part of the quotation is missing. The court quotes *Ravin* as saying that "few would believe they have been deprived of something of critical importance if deprived of marijuana." The court deletes the remainder of the sentence: ". . . though they would if stripped of control over their personal appearance." It is easy to see why the second half of this sentence was deleted from the quotation. According to the conception of privacy applied in NORML, privacy has no more application to personal appearance in general or to hair length in particular than to drug use.

62. Thomas Scanlon: "A Theory of Freedom of Expression," in Ronald Dworkin, ed.: *The Philosophy of Law* (New York: Oxford University Press, 1977), p. 153.

63. *Id.*, p. 164.

64. Dworkin: Op. cit. Note 40, p. 200.

65. *Id.*, pp. 207-208.

66. But not all. Many defenses of freedom of speech are not designed to offer protection to all categories of speech. Some defenses, for example, apply only to political speech. *See* Frank Michelman: "Conceptions of Democracy in American Constitutional Argument: The Case of Pornography Regulation," 56 *Tennessee Law Review* (1989), p. 303.

67. Op. cit. Note 40, p. 218.

68. For a recent discussion see James Inciardi, Duane McBride, and James Rivers: *Drug Control and the Courts* (London: Sage Publications, 1996).

69. *See* the discussion in Clark: op. cit. Note 23.

70. *See* J. Strange, M. Gossop, P. Griffiths, and B. Powis: "First Use of Heroin: Changes in Route of Administration over Time," 304 *British Medical Journal* (1992), p. 1222.

71. The most important case in favor of this proposition is *Stanley v. Georgia*, 394 U.S. 557 (1969).

72. This restriction was not due solely to the fact that the decision was reached on privacy grounds, but also because drug use outside the home posed more of a threat to important state interests such as highway safety.

73. Aaron and David Musto: "Temperance and Prohibition in America," in Mark Moore and Dean Gerstein, eds.: *Alcohol and Public Policy: Beyond the Shadow of Prohibition* (Washington: National Academy Press, 1981), pp. 127, 176.

74. Thus I have spoken of drug proscriptions as *infringing* rather than as *violating* rights. I adopt that terminology according to which rights-violations, as opposed to rights-infringements, are always wrongful. *See* Judith Thomson: "Some Ruminations about Rights," 19 *Arizona Law Review* (1977), p. 45.

75. *See* Alan Gewirth: "Are There Any Absolute Rights?" 31 *Philosophical Quarterly* (1981), p. 1.

76. Thomas Szasz is not among those libertarians who believe that rights are absolute and can never be overridden by the social consequences of exercising them. He writes: "I recognize a need for limiting the free market in drugs. . . . The legitimate place for that limit, however, is where free access to a particular product presents a 'clear and present danger' to the safety and security of *others.*" Szasz: Op. cit. Note 39, p. 7.

77. The metaphor of rights as trumps is developed in Ronald Dworkin: *Taking Rights Seriously* (Cambridge: Harvard University Press, 1977).

78. Office of the National Drug Control Policy: *National Drug Control Strategy* (Washington, D.C., 1989), p. 11.

79. *See* the thoughtful discussion of drug policy for adolescents in Franklin Zimring and Gordon Hawkins: *The Search for Rational Drug Control* (Cambridge: Cambridge University Press, 1992), pp. 115-136.

80. James Q. Wilson: "Drugs and Crime," in Michael Tonry and James Q. Wilson, eds.: *Drugs and Crime* (Chicago: University of Chicago Press, 1990), pp. 521, 524.

81. It is hard to believe that the harm risked by users of any existing drug is greater than the harm a user would suffer by imprisonment. Thus the interests of users cannot justify the proscription of any existing drug. Criminal paternalism can be justified, if at all, only when punishments are not severe. For further discussion of this point, see Stephen Nathanson: "Should Drug Crimes Be Punished?" in Luper-Foy and Brown: Op. cit. Note 25, p. 243.

82. Some libertarians actually have doubts. *See* Walter Block: "Drug Prohibition: A Legal and Economic Analysis," in Luper-Foy and Brown: Op. cit. Note 25, p. 199.

83. I discuss some of these matters further in Douglas Husak: "The Nature and Justifiability of Nonconsummate Offenses," 37 *Arizona Law Review* 151 (1995).

84. *See*, for example, Eva Bertram, Morris Blachman, Kenneth Sharpe, and Peter Andreas: *Drug War Politics: The Price of Denial* (Berkeley: University of California Press, 1996).

85. *See*, for example, Mark Moore: "Drugs: Getting a Fix on the Problem and the Solution," 8 *Yale Law & Policy Review* (1990), p. 701.

86. *See* Mugford: Op. cit. Note 5.

87. Some ingenious proposals are discussed in Chester Mitchell: *The Drug Solution* (Ottawa: Carleton University Press, 1990).

88. Of course, commentators who endorse a rights-based perspective will support these devices only if they do not infringe rights. I have not commented on whether and to what extent bans on drug advertising, for example, respect moral rights.

3

Rhetorical Dimensions of Decriminalization

Richard E. Vatz, Lee S. Weinberg

The University of Michigan's Institute for Social Research (1995, cited in Thomas 1995) reports that after a decline in the late 1980s, teenagers have shown a steady increase in drug use throughout the 1990s. While an assortment of problems collectively referred to under the generic name "drug abuse" appear to have proliferated, the concern of the public grows, but opposition to most proposals for decriminalization remains steady. The term *decriminalization* is used here, as opposed to *legalization*, because the latter implies that the state would be conferring approval on the use of currently prohibited drugs, whereas the former carries no such implication (Szasz 1992). As we use the term, decriminalization means more than replacing the penalty of prison with that of fines. Fines and prison terms constitute punishment for criminal behavior, and decriminalization means the elimination of both types of punishment. In the current context it means that the use of at least some drugs would no longer constitute violation of the criminal law. Some researchers maintain that there is no meaningful distinction to be made (Duke and Gross 1993), but we find the difference between the absence of punishment for an act and the conferring of approval for an act to be significant.

It is assumed as a given in this chapter that the central claims of the decriminalization advocates are at least partially true: the war against drugs may contribute significantly to the ongoing social disintegration in the United

States; those who believe in individual rights and responsibilities may reasonably, if not definitively, oppose drug prohibition for adults; and the prohibition of drugs and the concomitant expenses involved in interdiction and other aspects of the war on drugs are costly and minimally effective in preventing drug use or the crime associated with it. In addition, as Steven Duke (1996) persuasively asserts, "the 'drug war' is responsible for at least half of our serious crime" (p. 47) and, as Randy E. Barnett points out, "every enforcement effort consumes scarce resources" (Barnett 1994, p. 2596). Finally, there is Barnett's critical message that criminalization is like antibiotics: neither should be overused. To do so, as Duke and Gross (1993) observe, "undermines, rather than strengthens, our morals and our fidelity to criminal law" (quoted in Barnett 1994, p. 2625).

The proposals for reforming America's drug laws range from limited ones, such as the recent California initiative to permit the medical use of marijuana, to dramatic ones that would essentially create an unrestricted free-market economy for the production, sale, and use of drugs. While we recognize the failures of current drug policies, we are not advocating any of the particular versions of reform offered in this volume. Instead, given that there is a substantial argument for some type of decriminalization of the use of drugs, we are recognizing that for this argument to become a politically acceptable position would require substantial rhetorical adjustments in the ways in which we define and talk about drugs—in short, the rhetoric of drugs.

The following analysis defines rhetoric as Aristotle did: discovering the available means of persuasion. As applied to the controversy surrounding proposals to decriminalize drugs in America, a rhetorical analysis therefore seeks to identify how language and argument are employed to create public perceptions regarding the rights and responsibilities of drug users, both in terms of their drug consumption and their conduct subsequent to consumption. The identification and analysis of the rhetorical location of individual responsibility in taking and/or distributing drugs and the identification and analysis of the metaphors and images (termed *fantasies*) that support current drug policy constitute the "rhetoric of drugs."

In order to effect an end to the current drug "war" (itself a rhetorical construction or "fantasy"), it will be necessary to change the rhetoric surrounding the "war." This includes altering the rhetoric of responsibility location, changing the fantasies that the public has about drug use, and offering an alternative paradigm for defining drug-related issues and drug policy.

RHETORIC OF LOCATING RESPONSIBILITY

Kenneth Burke (1969), the preeminent rhetorical theoretician of this century, speaks of "scenic" and "agent" descriptions of reality, with the former implying motives and causes external to the individual, while the latter descriptions imply motives and causes within the individual. Thus "scenic" descriptions always imply "motion" (rather than "action") caused by external factors such as mental illness, bad upbringing, or evil companions over which the individual has no control and which mitigate personal responsibility. "Agent" descriptions always imply "action," or behaviors freely chosen as a result of intrinsic factors such as people being evil or good, or having sinister or noble intentions. In contrast to "scenic" descriptions, therefore, "agent" descriptions require that one assume personal responsibility for one's own behavior. Taken to their logical extremes, this analysis would lead to what we term the *ultraliberal* and *ultraconservative* positions. The former would hold that nobody is responsible for anything (some circumstance is ultimately to be blamed for all misconduct), while the latter would argue that there are no situations (even the presence of real brain disease or even what is legally described as duress) that should mitigate responsibility for misconduct.

Burke (1969) writes, "One may deflect attention from scenic matters by situating the motives of an act in the agent . . . or conversely, one may deflect attention from the criticism of personal motives by deriving an act or attitude not from the traits of the agent, but from the nature of the situation" (p. 17). Thus, for Burke, if one is under attack for behaving a certain way, he can first deny having engaged in the behavior. If the behavior is undeniable, and the person wishes to escape responsibility, he must depict it as a consequence of forces beyond his control, thus transforming himself into a victim rather than a perpetrator. This rhetorical process is a variant of the rhetorical transformation of rapist into a victim wherein he is seen as doing no more than simply following irresistible urges. Note that this argument blurs the distinction between *urges* over which the rapist may well have no control and the *acting on* such urges over which the rapist does have control. Indeed, failure to distinguish urges (which one cannot control) from behaviors in response to urges (which one can control) is the source of rhetorical confusion in a wide range of areas of misconduct, criminal and noncriminal alike.

Most of the conventional communications regarding drug use rely almost exclusively on the use of scenic language and are inconsistent and muddled. For example, drug use or abuse is generally seen as a disease or an irresistible urge that strikes some people and from which they can escape only by undergoing some type of therapy. Almost all of the popular cultural references to drug use define it as scenic; that is, either an involuntary taking of chemicals or an inability to stop ingesting them once one has started using them. It is typical, for example, to read of those who ingest drugs as "victims" who had no choice but to use drugs and involuntarily suffer their physical and behavioral effects (Szasz 1992).

Note the convolutions that underlie the current view: if drug users are defined as "victims" of a disease, it makes no more sense to punish them for "possession" of drugs than it would to punish someone for possession of a virus. But it would make sense in this view to punish those who "sell" or "distribute" drugs because it would be like punishing those who deliberately spread (distribute) the virus to members of the public. This position in turn is confused because the public generally defines the *decision* to take drugs, rather than mere possession of the drugs, as the "disease" that the users have "contracted." If one takes the opposing view and defines such drug users as engaging in freely chosen behavior, it then would make good sense to punish them—but only if one could make the very difficult case that it is the role of government to punish behavior that is self-indulgent and, in our view, unproductive and foolish. From this perspective, of course, it would no longer make sense to punish those who "sell" and "distribute," because the product they are selling would constitute just another of many temptations to the buyers on which to waste their time and money.

POSSIBLE CHANGES IN CURRENT SCENIC PERSPECTIVES

Indeed, the assumptions that the current erroneous perspective implies may be undergoing a slight change. Along with the general conservative changes in America, including those that led to the Republican revolution in 1995 and the moving toward the center-right by President Clinton to cement his successful reelection in 1996, there are hints throughout American society that point to a growing acceptance of the view that drug taking constitutes primarily volitional acts. Perhaps this reflects a new willingness to recognize the above-mentioned distinction: that the urge to take drugs to chemically produce a sense of euphoria and the actual taking of such drugs are simply two different things. In fact, the central character in a recent movie is portrayed taking drugs by choice, a classic Burkean agent perspective (Hunter 1996). Nonetheless, the American public typically still maintains that drugs are the most "critical" single contributing factor to crime in America. In fact, 94 percent of the public see drugs as "critical" or "very important" in causing crime (Newport and Saad 1993).

As long as the taking of drugs continues to be defined as an involuntary act (see *DSM-IV* 1994), the public will never be convinced to support decriminalization, nor to believe that extralegal rewards and punishments might well result in a reduction in drug use.

FANTASIES OF DRUG USE

Ernest Bormann, another prominent rhetorical theorist, uses what he has called "fantasy theme analysis" to explain the process by which the public comes to share a common interpretation of an event or series of events

(Bormann 1972). A fantasy theme may be defined as the accepted or consensual meaning of particular acts or events. For example, an American soldier fighting in Vietnam may have believed that his involvement in the war represented his helping his country "stand up to Communism." This fantasy theme, then, gives real meaning to his reality. Fantasy theme analysis involves the identification of the dominant fantasy themes regarding behavior, drug use in this case, and the dissemination of those themes to an ever-expanding audience, as well as conjecture as to what sort of rhetorical strategies would be necessary to replace the dominant interpretation with an alternative vision or fantasy theme.

The relevant fantasies that the public holds of drug use and, in particular, addiction, are all scenic. As witnessed in the squabble over 1996 Republican nominee Bob Dole's argument that cigarettes may not be addictive for all people, there was a flurry of incredulity over this heresy. Yet *addiction* is not a precise medical term, and the evidence shows at a minimum that millions of people do give up smoking. So if by addiction it is meant that the substance cannot be forsworn, it is manifestly evident that cigarettes are not addictive; that is, more simply, if by addictive one means that one cannot stop taking the chemical, then cigarettes are not addictive. On the other hand, one would have to be disingenuous to argue that there is no difficulty in giving up a chemical to which one has become habituated.

The rhetorical location of responsibility is linked to the dominant fantasy of drug use: that use itself is a disease. This fantasy would have to be replaced with the alternative fantasy that human behavior is freely chosen if American public opposition to the prohibition of drugs is to change. Psychiatrist Thomas Szasz has been the leading proponent of demolishing the disease metaphor for understanding why people take drugs. As he states (1992), "We do not blame the [overeating] of fat persons on the people who sell them food, but we do blame the drug habits of addicts on the people who sell them drugs" (p. 12). Moreover, he argues, "[B]ehavior, even if it is actually or potentially injurious or self-injurious, is not a disease, and no behavior should be regulated by sanctions called 'treatment'" (p. 18).

Similar to fantasies are factual misperceptions. For example, many persons believe that all currently illegal drugs are dangerous, independent of whether they are contaminated due to their being illegal and beyond government purity regulations. The public believes that many nontoxic drugs are life threatening, yet they simply are not. Marijuana, for example, has never caused a death, but how does one persuade the public to adopt a more accurate view of the pharmacological reality? (There is already some indication that teenaged Americans, at least, are no longer mystified by the frightening depictions of marijuana use in the media [O'Harrow and Wee 1996].) Moreover, and more significant, drugs are often depicted as a cause of crime, despite the obvious fact that "drugs do not—indeed, cannot—cause crime" (Szasz 1992, p. 22). Drug-related crime is obviously more closely tied to the high cost of obtaining drugs and to the criminal black market than to the chemical effects of the drugs themselves. The misperception that drugs are inherently dangerous would have to be changed to focus on the fact that it is largely their illegality that makes them dangerous (Duke and Gross 1993). Only when this dominant perception is changed so that it is the illegality itself that is defined as the danger will the public ever come to accept decriminalization.

RHETORICAL CREATION OF REALITY

Rhetorical study investigates the choice of what situations to make salient and the struggle for interpretations of those situations (Vatz 1973).

Currently, reportage of drug-related crime emphasizes drugs—as opposed to their illegality—as the source of the crime and a multitude of related consequences. Typical of this perspective is the media "take" that finds "addiction" to be the cause of the crime associated with the trafficking in illegal drugs (Gup 1996). Newspaper analyses of such crime and its victims almost never recognize the importance of the illegality of drugs in bringing about the mayhem associated with illegal drug use. If print and electronic media focused on what the illegality of drugs does to the cost of the drugs as well as the means of obtaining them, they could well change the perception of the general public so that the focus of anger would be on the laws as opposed to the drugs themselves.

None of this would require a redefinition of the wisdom or desirability of taking drugs. In fact, current media messages counseling averseness to drugs are not inconsistent with decriminalization, and may, in fact, have a salutary effect on the public's deciding not to take drugs for recreational purposes. In fact, the public could and likely would continue to see the use of drugs as unwise even if they were legal. Illegality per se actually seems to play a very small role in the choice of nondrug users not to use drugs. One recent survey (that allowed multiple responses) shows that, when adolescents who do not take drugs are asked to explain that choice, approximately one quarter said that the drug lifestyle was the reason. Three quarters reported that they believed that marijuana use would hurt their grades, and one fifth said that they feared mental or physical harm would result from taking drugs (Lewin 1995). Decriminalizing drugs would not be likely to change any of their views. This is one reason to speculate that decriminalizing drugs would not lead to a precipitous rise in their use.

Media messages regarding the effects of drugs have been marked by inconsistency. There has been a reported boom, for example, in the sales of Ritalin (methylphenidate), a significant cerebral stimulant, as a "therapy" for the psychiatric "disease" of attention deficit disorder. The message conveyed by the widespread prescribing of Ritalin could hardly be more mixed to young-sters: drugs are dangerous, and, simultaneously, they are a major, nondan-gerous, and salutary aid now being used by upward of two million children in America (ABC 1996). There does appear to be a slow, if belated, realiza-tion of the danger of promiscuous prescribing of this drug (Vatz and Wein-berg 1996).

The problems caused by drug taking and the problems caused by the illegality of drugs are consistently muddled. Many Americans appear to be-lieve that drugs cause no harm if they are given the imprimatur of a licensed physician. For example, Elvis Presley was said to be sincere in his belief that he could not be addicted since his drugs had come from a physician. In another example, years ago, after he had been shot in an abortive assassina-tion plot by Arthur Bremer, former Alabama governor George Wallace was asked by a journalist whether he was taking any "drugs" for his pain. Ruffled a bit, Wallace responded, "No, I'm not; now I am, of course, taking some *medication*."

Thus one of the major changes that will have to occur before the de-criminalization of drugs can become public policy is a transformative rhe-torical change: the public must come to recognize that many of the current problems with drugs are largely a result of their being illegal.

It should be noted that to articulate the rhetorical changes necessary to permit drug decriminalization to become public policy is not to be con-fused with approval of taking psychoactive drugs. Neither of this chapter's authors for example, uses such drugs, and neither supports casual use of drugs or other drug use for entertainment purposes.

The support for decriminalization emanates, at least partially, from a desire to lower crime rates by making such drugs legally available and thereby eliminating the criminal element in drug commerce. Elite media and politi-cal leaders focusing on illegality as the source of the intransigent problems of drugs might encourage a public rhetoric conducive to the decriminaliza-tion of drugs. Without such leadership, change is highly unlikely.

DEFINITIONS OF PUBLIC ISSUES AND PUBLIC POLICY

There appears to be no end to the availability of drugs. Whereas surveys indicate that drug use ebbs and flows, the most recent surveys show that both use and fear of soft and hard drugs are on the rise (Lewin 1995).

Part of the problem is that American adults see drugs as the irresistible scourge facing our generation. In fact, there is a wide disparity between the perceptions adults have of drugs and the perceptions that children have, especially of their availability, if not their power. In a study on the perceptions of the problems of drugs conducted by the Center on Addiction and Substance Abuse at Columbia University (Lewin 1995), it was found, similar to the adult population, that 32 percent of 12- to 17-year-olds named drugs as the biggest concern facing their generation, more than double the number who cited crime, the second largest concern. On the other hand, while 82 percent of adults believed heroin and cocaine were easily obtainable, only 30 percent of the adolescents held this view. Adults and adolescents thus share the view that drugs pose a major threat, but disagree as to their availability. Support for decriminalization is more likely to be a function of perceptions of danger than perceptions of availability. In view of these findings, therefore, rhetoricians of change face a daunting task.

Like most other issues on the public agenda, the outcome of the debate over decriminalizing drugs depends in large part on who wins the rhetorical battle of naming, defining, and infusing meaning into the events and behaviors at the heart of the drug debate. Our analysis, in sum, suggests that the following specific rhetorical battles must be won in the court of public opinion by those promoting decriminalization before serious reform can be achieved:

- Drug involvement (either using or selling) as well other more traditional criminal conduct must be defined primarily as agent behavior, which would enable the public to believe that using drugs is a voluntary choice to engage in a voluntary behavior. Some of the changes must come from the media. Instead of the current nonjudgmental locutions most often heard, such as, "The accused had a problem with drugs," media depictions will have to employ more judgmental language, such as, "In addition, the accused ingested a large amount of drugs." In addition, the concept of "correlation" as used in academic and popular writing will have to be clearly distinguished from the concept of "cause"; thus the ongoing literature on genes and alcoholism should emphasize that no behavior is caused by the genes and tissues that people inherit from their parents. In short, the implication that genes are destiny will have to be replaced with an emphasis on personal responsibility and choice. For a specific application, a drunk driver would be portrayed as unable to display the coordination necessary for handling a car, but quite able to choose whether to drive that car (Lester 1989).
- The concepts of desiring to engage in behavior and engaging in that behavior must be separated, which would enable the public to believe that the urge to take drugs is not irresistible. When C. Everett Koop ruled that smoking is "addictive" (Okie 1988), newspapers should have indicated that "addiction" is not a medical term and

merely describes the feelings (and, perhaps, physiological consequences) of cessation, not an irresistible imperative to continue smoking. The millions who have quit would provide sufficient evidence
of this distinction.

- Drug taking and criminal behavior following the ingestion of drugs
  must be separated, which would enable the public to believe that
  people commit crimes because they choose to rather than because
  they have taken drugs and that these criminal behaviors are the
  proper ones to be punished.
- The traditional emphasis on the role of criminal law in protecting
  the public from being harmed by others must regain its primacy. This
  would enable the public to support either a free market in drugs,
  wherein people would be free to be as self-indulgent as they like and
  pay whatever physical price may be involved, or, at least, a controlled
  market in drugs, wherein medical personnel could distribute drugs
  to those who have made the choice to be heavy users.

These latter two battles will not be easily won because the dominant
public perception—fueled by what may be well-motivated efforts to promote
alcohol and drug rehabilitation programs for those who abuse illicit drugs,
and by arguments of aggressive defense lawyers—continues to define such substance abuse as somewhat of a mitigating or exculpatory factor in criminal
behavior. Alcohol and drug rehabilitation programs are often statutorily
commingled with criminal penalties; rehabilitation is seen as an alternative
to punishment. Countering this perception would require that medical personnel, legislators, political leaders, and judges join prosecutors in a concerted
effort to persuade the public (and therefore juries in criminal cases) that those
who violate the criminal law have done so by choice and that that choice
must be punished. This effort might involve legislative changes that reduce
or eliminate alternatives to incarceration, sentencing guideline changes, and
increasingly harsh criticism of those who engage in crime while under the
influence of drugs and alcohol. Perhaps the most important—and least likely—
step that would move the public to understand that drugs don't "cause" crime
would be for the leadership of medical and mental health organizations to
change their emphasis from how to help abusers as an alternative to punishing criminal conduct to how to help abusers *while* punishing criminal conduct to the same extent as it punishes nonabusers. This could be comparable, in some respects, to the "guilty but mentally ill" plea that reaffirms the
primacy of a person's responsibility for his/her actions, but offers some help
to those who wish to change.

Our analysis suggests that the dominance of scenic rhetoric, combined
with a set of public fantasies and perceptions that fail to differentiate the

impact of drugs from the impact of their illegality, makes it unlikely that the policy of prohibiting drug use will change in the near future. The rhetorical transformations that must precede decriminalization currently lack credible powerful advocates—even in the current conservative political context—and this situation is also unlikely to change in the short run. However, the rhetorical foundations of the drug debate must be dramatically altered if the current unsuccessful drug war is ever to be replaced by any of the versions of decriminalization offered in this volume.

REFERENCES

ABC (1996). *World News Tonight with Peter Jennings*, July 16.

Barnett, R. E. (1994). Bad trip: drug prohibition and the weakness of public policy. *Yale Law Journal* 103:2593–2630.

Bormann, E. G. (1972). Fantasy and rhetorical vision: the rhetorical vision of social reality. *Quarterly Journal of Speech* 58:396–407.

Burke, K. (1969). *A Grammar of Motives*. Berkeley, CA: University of California Press.

Department of Health and Human Services (1995). National Survey Results on Drug Use from The Monitoring the Future Study 1975–1994. University of Michigan.

Diagnostic and Statistical Manual of Mental Disorders (DSM-IV) (1994). 4th ed. Washington, DC: American Psychiatric Association.

Duke, S., and Gross, A. C. (1993). *America's Longest War: Rethinking Our Tragic Crusade against Drugs*. New York: Putnam.

Gup, T. (1996). Evil twins: the deadly alliance of drugs and crime. *Cosmopolitan*, July 1, pp. 180–184.

Hunter, S. (1996). Film's makers say drugs are a choice, a bad choice. *Baltimore Sun*, July 26, p. E1.

Lester, D. (1989). The heritability of alcoholism: science and policy. *Drugs and Society* 3:29–68.

Lewin, T. (1995). Adolescents say drugs are biggest worry. *New York Times*, July 18, p. A8.

Newport, F., and Saad, L. (1993). Drugs seen as root cause of crime in the U.S. *Gallup Poll Monthly*, October, p. 33.

O'Harrow, R., and Wee, E. L. (1996). Marijuana users' air of defiance. *Washington Post*, August 3, p. 1.

Okie, S. (1988). Smoking addictive, Koop confirms. *Washington Post*, May 17, pp. 1, 6.

Szasz, T. (1992). *Our Right to Drugs: The Case for a Free Market*. New York: Praeger.

Thomas, P. (1995). Teens use more drugs, worry less about consequences. *Washington Post*, December 16, p. 1.

Vatz, R. E. (1973). The myth of the rhetorical situation. *Philosophy and Rhetoric* 6:154–161.

Vatz, R. E., and Weinberg, L. S. (1996). Better late than never. *Forbes MediaCritic* 3:91–93.

The war on drugs is lost (1996). *National Review* 48:34–48.

4

Discontinuous Change and the War on Drugs

Jefferson M. Fish

Although many people view the war on drugs as a failure, the conventional wisdom is that, if and when change comes, it will be slight and gradual. The reasoning behind this point of view stresses the wide array of political, legal, medical, religious, educational, economic, and other forces allied against change; the many, often powerful, institutions and individuals with a stake in drug prohibition; and the apparent widespread public support for and long history of punitive policies. In brief, the argument for gradual change is that, since nothing has happened for a long time, and because the forces arrayed against change continue to be formidable, the most that can be hoped for is a gradual chipping away at the status quo.

The argument for gradual change is based on the implicit assumption that there is only one kind of change, continuous change. A metaphor for gradual, continuous change would be that of grains of sand being added one at a time so that an anthill eventually becomes a mountain. While the mountain may look qualitatively different from the anthill, the process of achieving it was a gradual, quantitative one. In the case of drug policy reform, the assumption that change must be gradual would correspond to convincing one citizen at a time or one legislator at a time, or to amending a particular law so as to weaken it a bit, or otherwise to making minor changes that might, over an extended period, eventually accumulate enough to constitute a qualitative improvement.

There is, however, another kind of change, discontinuous change*, and I would argue that it provides a more likely model for the way in which real, qualitative, drug policy reform will come. A metaphor for discontinuous change would be the changing visual patterns in a kaleidoscope. As one gradually rotates a kaleidoscope, the pattern produced by light reflecting off the bits of colored glass remains the same. Eventually a threshold is reached, and any further rotation leads to an unpredictable reorganization of the shards and a qualitatively different visual pattern. No pattern ever merges gradually into its successor.

Discontinuous change takes place in complex systems in which multiple forces interact in complicated ways over time so that minor random events may be swept up by multiple feedback mechanisms and rapidly magnified and transformed in startling ways. In chaos theory (Gleick 1987), for example, this is referred to as "sensitivity to initial conditions," or more popularly as "the butterfly effect." The meteorological notion is that the flapping of the wings of a butterfly on one continent can be picked up by the swirling forces of nature and transformed into a hurricane on another.

Thinking in terms of discontinuous change has already become widespread in the physical and biological sciences, and is beginning to take hold in the social and behavioral sciences as well (Fish 1992). For example, Darwin's original theory of evolution, involving gradual speciation over great expanses of time, has been modified to the new view of punctuated equilibria (Eldredge 1985). This view is that new species evolve rapidly (in geological terms) and then remain stable for much longer. These periods of rapid growth, or "punctuations" (for example, following the rapid extinction of the dinosaurs that probably occurred after a comet struck the earth), constitute a kind of discontinuous change that is similar to the new view of the evolution of science itself. Instead of seeing the development of science as a gradual process in which one bit of knowledge is piled on another, it is now thought that long periods of "normal science" are periodically punctuated by "revolutions" (Kuhn 1970) in which basic assumptive paradigms are overthrown and replaced by new ones, which then usher in their own era of "normal science." To take a final example from anthropology, rubbish theory (Thompson 1979) studies the way in which everyday objects—from thimbles to houses—gradually lose their value until they become worthless ("rubbish") for an extended

---

*I am using the terms *continuous* and *discontinuous* informally as approximate equivalents for *gradual and quantitative* and *sudden and qualitative*, respectively. Since matter is made up mostly of space, all change is discontinuous in the mathematical sense, just as grains of sand (in the anthill to mountain metaphor) are distinct from one another.

period of time. Then, unexpectedly, some of them take on great and increasing value as antiques.

In all these cases, from meteorology to evolution to the history of science to the value of everyday objects, an understanding of dynamic processes in complex systems has challenged traditional views of gradual change and shown the usefulness of models of discontinuous change.

A key element to consider in understanding discontinuous change is the rapid and unpredictable nature of what takes place during the punctuation, or discontinuity, between the old steady state of a system and the new one. During long periods of continuity, perturbations and disruptions in the system get damped down by homeostatic feedback. As the saying goes, "The more things change, the more they stay the same." However, during a period of discontinuous change, anything can happen. Minor, random, and accidental events can get magnified, reacted to, and unexpectedly set off escalating processes of change in unpredicted directions.

Consider the example of the Cold War. For four decades nothing changed; then, as if the kaleidoscope had been rotated that extra millimeter, Soviet Communism collapsed, and world politics went from depressingly boring to unpredictably turbulent. Thirty years ago, if one had asked what a map of Eurasia would look like a decade or two later, the answer would have been, "The same." Following the breakup of the Soviet Union, the answer to that question became, "Who knows?"

The important point to understand is that world politics is in a punctuation right now, and anything can happen. George Bush's mistake in proclaiming a "new world order" had to do with his not considering the element of time. He recognized that there had been a previous world order and that it would be succeeded by another one, but he did not appreciate the necessary period of unpredictability in between. Some have aptly dubbed the current state of affairs the "new world disorder," but they too err in viewing it as the successor pattern to the previous one rather than as a transition period between the old pattern and the unpredictable new one that will eventually emerge.

One other point to remember about discontinuous change is the notion of threshold conditions beyond which homeostatic mechanisms are overcome and change takes place. These conditions constitute the limit beyond which the kaleidoscope pattern shifts or the snowball of change starts rolling downhill and becomes an avalanche. The arms race of the Cold War is an example of what is known in systems theory as a "symmetrical escalation." This is a tit-for-tat series of "I'll see you and raise you one" or "Anything you can do I can do better." While it had appeared that there was no end to the amount of overkill the two superpowers were building, or to the treasure they would squander on it, a limit was in fact reached. Beyond this limit the process of armament was reversed and that of disarmament began to accelerate. (It is interesting to note how the breakup of the Soviet Union has created unexpected problems for the unexpected process of disarmament. Because the Ukraine became a separate state, the armaments that were built up in a two-party escalation had to be undone in a three-party deescalation. This is just another example of the unpredictability introduced during a period of discontinuous change.)

In the area of drugs and drug policy, it is clear that we are dealing with a complex sociopoliticoeconomic system involving many people and institutions and huge amounts of money, and which pervades American society and has extensive linkages throughout the world. Furthermore, drugs that have long been illegal were legal in the last century, so there is nothing inevitable about the current state of affairs. Hence, it is reasonable to argue that drug policy exists in the kind of system in which discontinuous change occurs, and that the decades of stability are more reflective of homeostatic processes within the system than of any inherent unchangeableness in drug policy.

For these reasons I would argue that *when change does come to drug policy, it is likely to be sudden and dramatic.* In addition, such change is likely to include a chaotic period during which it will be all but impossible to predict the new pattern that drug policy will settle into. During this period unimportant, random, or otherwise unforeseen events could well nudge drug policy into unexpected directions, following which an acceleration of change in the new direction could develop rapidly. Those formulating policy during this turbulence will need to engage in an ongoing process of hypothesis testing and self-correction, as rapidly changing conditions and unpredicted consequences lead to frequent midcourse corrections.

The plausibility of this scenario, and the desirability of formulating the best alternative to our current failed policy, means that the following four issues, discussed briefly below, deserve serious consideration.

1. What strategies are likely to provoke discontinuous change in drug policy?
2. What can be done to increase the likelihood of the formulation of effective policy during the turbulent "punctuation" of discontinuous change?
3. Are there any special opportunities that will arise or unique issues that are likely to need attention during the process of discontinuous change?
4. Are any special kinds of planning suggested by a model of discontinuous change that might not otherwise be considered?

Like the arms race, the war on drugs has involved a version of symmetrical escalation between the purveyors of illegal drugs and the drug warriors. When the police get more firepower, the drug lords escalate their armaments. Greater ingenuity in tracking illegal funds is met by improved methods of hiding them. Stiffer sentences for adult drug dealers lead to the recruitment of children who are not subject to those penalties. Successful drug busts lead both to the creation of even more sources of supply and to the production of drugs in more concentrated forms (so that more of the illegal ingredient can be packed into less volume).

As with the arms race, the devastating effects of this symmetrical escalation are becoming increasingly obvious to all except the escalators—more participants and bystanders killed in shootouts, more drug money with its insidious effects on commerce and politics, more children lured into a life of crime and drugs, and more people abusing higher doses of drugs. (The disastrous effects of this escalation serve as a warning of the dangers of militarizing the drug war. It is one thing for drug money to corrupt a police force—the peril of corrupting armies that have nuclear weapons need not be spelled out.)

The real question is how bad things have to get before the symmetrical escalation passes a critical threshold and leads to discontinuous change. An honest answer is, "Only time will tell." Nevertheless, it is reasonable to speculate that we are quite near that point. Little has been achieved in reducing either supply or demand by the greatly increased drug war expenditures of the Bush and Clinton administrations; with national policy focused on reducing the deficit, rethinking drug policy offers the possibility of substantial savings. We will never know whether the Reagan escalation in military expenditures (including "Star Wars") provoked Gorbachev to reverse the arms race and move toward disarmament or whether he would have done so anyway. Still, the likelihood that federal budgets will have to reduce expenditures on the drug war suggests that a similar threshold will soon be reached. The logic seems inescapable: if "more" didn't produce desired results, then "less" in pursuit of the same policy surely won't. And if huge expenditures are being poured into an acknowledged losing proposition, then a major change in policy would seem to be inevitable.

If we are approaching the threshold where discontinuous change is possible, then what are some of the policies that might provoke it? In general, the most reasonable strategy would be to introduce a small change that will snowball. This is in contradistinction to a small change that will accumulate with other small changes to produce gradual, or first-order, change. Some theorists refer to the kind of small change that provokes systemic reorganization, or second-order change, as a "difference that makes a difference." To some extent, trial and error is necessary: depending on whether or not the change snowballs, it can be viewed with hindsight as a difference that did or did not make a difference. In general, though, a small change in the rules of the game is more likely to lead to systemic reorganization than is a small change in the application of the rules.

(An additional benefit of starting with a small change is that it could reassure public fears of the unknown. Assuming that reformers are correct that crime will diminish and a drug plague won't materialize—because the public has more common sense than drug warriors give it credit for—further change could be undertaken with greater confidence. Naturally, if the drug warriors' worst fears should be realized, the policy could be reversed. On the other hand, they might well discover to their amazement that, for example, legalizing marijuana would lead to a shift away from the more dangerous use of alcohol, with a corresponding drop over time in deaths from alcohol-related diseases. Drug reformers would expect to see an initial increase in experimentation out of curiosity about previously forbidden fruit, as occurred with the legalization of pornography in Scandinavia, but would anticipate that, as in Scandinavia, it would drop off quickly with the knowledge of continuing availability. Meanwhile, a ban on advertising could prevent the artificial stimulation of demand. A similar ban on advertising of tobacco and alcohol, the two most dangerous drugs, could also prove quite beneficial, as could an end to government support for growing tobacco. In general, a public health strategy aimed at legalizing drugs [perhaps only in relatively low dosages for at least some of them] so as to avoid the disastrous effects of the war on drugs while discouraging drug use and offering treatment for abusers [paid for by drug taxes] seems the most likely course of action. Exactly what form such a plan might take, and what process might be needed to achieve it, is still unclear and subject to the vagaries of discontinuous change.)

I will give two examples of policies that, though starting small, might well snowball. I am sure that experts in various fields can dream up many others if they distinguish between continuous and discontinuous change when they do their brainstorming.

One such policy would be to invoke federalism, reduce the role of the federal government in drug enforcement, and let the states be laboratories for drug policy. "The war on drugs has failed," the argument would go, "so let the states try fifty different approaches, and we can adopt what works." Then, if even one state makes a significant move in the direction of legalization, the hoped-for drop in violent crime and criminal justice expenses could lead to a spread of the strategy. (One unknown about this approach is that such a state could become a magnet for drug activity. This would doubtless produce many unanticipated positive and negative effects, possibly leading nearby states to imitate or retaliate against their neighbor's new policy. But that is just the point: discontinuous change produces unpredictable results, and continual responsiveness to changing conditions would be essential during the period of systemic reorganization.)

Another policy would be to legalize marijuana. "We can no longer afford the war on drugs," it could be asserted; "we'll have to limit ourselves to a war on hard drugs." A scaled-down drug war could then be financed—along with drug treatment and abuse prevention programs—in significant measure through taxes on marijuana. Once again, the diminution in violent crime and lack of the feared disastrous increase in drug abuse, along with the economic savings over current policy, could lead to further moves away from the current punitive direction.

If discontinuous change does occur, then rapidly changing conditions—possibly differing among the fifty states and interacting with one another in complex and unpredictable ways—could lead to urgent demands for new laws. Such demands might well be made with great emotional intensity amid the uncertainty of systemic reorganization. Such circumstances are hardly a suitable crucible in which to forge wise policy. For this reason it is desirable to make use of the time we have now to consider in detail a wide array of policy options. In this way proposals can be taken off the shelf promptly when needed during a period of rapid change, and one of the aims of this book is to stimulate thinking about such issues. The more proposals that can be accumulated and studied now, the more likely it is that some of them will be put to good use when they are needed.

Assuming that discontinuous change does occur, and that some kind of drug legalization does come about over a relatively brief period of time, a number of consequences appear likely and would present unique opportunities during the chaotic period of change. Legalization would doubtless create disarray in the black market for drugs; this would offer an unprecedented opportunity for attacking organized crime and seizing many billions of dollars of assets.

Historians can provide useful insights by looking more intensively at the period of discontinuous change immediately following the repeal of Prohibition so that we can avoid repeating the mistakes of the past. And economists can suggest ways to prevent drug fortunes from escaping detection as the market collapses. Perhaps we can prevent illegal drug kingpins from becoming legal drug moguls the way bootleggers became distillers after Prohibition. It makes more sense to take advantage of their scramble to protect their collapsing empires as an opportunity to gain evidence, punish them for their violent and other prosecutable crimes, and confiscate their assets. (This would provide a refreshing contrast to the "Zero Tolerance" policy of confiscating the assets of ordinary citizens who, though otherwise upstanding members of the community, experiment with illegal drugs or use them recreationally.

[Another problem with "Zero Tolerance" and its slogan of "Just say no" is that it falsely equates all drug use with abuse. In fact, there is a continuum of drug use, and use by any individual can vary quite widely over time. More reasonable slogans are "Moderation in all things," "Be careful," "Soyez sage," and "Caveat emptor".])

The obvious course of action following legalization would be to immediately reap the benefits by cutting law enforcement expenditures. However, recognizing the importance of the dimension of time to understanding discontinuous change could allow us to follow a less intuitive but more productive path. That is, we could delay or moderate those cuts for several years while shifting resources to attack the weakened structure of organized crime. (For example, we could time a change in the physical appearance of our currency to coincide with the legalization of drugs. This change would force illegal cash out of hiding in order to be traded for new bills by the deadline.) If the war on drugs built up organized crime by creating a huge black market, it is only reasonable to make use of legalization to undo as much of the damage as possible.

Meanwhile, many other kinds of planning can be useful in cushioning the end of the war on drugs. The emptying out of prison cells should create unemployment among both prisoners and jailers, and ultimately throughout law enforcement, while the collapse of the black market in drugs should lead to similar unemployment in the parallel economy. The drop in violent crime should also hurt the crime prevention industry, from burglar alarms to guns to guards and guard dogs. On the other hand, all kinds of economic activity that were deterred by the fear of crime should increase. Thinking about such issues now could allow for a more informed navigating of the white waters of change when it comes.

The range of issues addressed in this chapter merely scratches the surface of those meriting attention, but it does call attention to the different kinds of thinking about drug policy and strategies for action that arise from conceptualizing the field in terms of discontinuous change.

REFERENCES

Eldredge, N. (1985). *Time Frames: The Rethinking of Darwinian Evolution and the Theory of Punctuated Equilibria*. New York: Simon & Schuster.

Fish, J. M. (1992). Discontinuous change. *Behavior and Social Issues* 2(1):59–70.

Gleick, J. (1987). *Chaos: Making a New Science*. New York: Viking Penguin.

Kuhn, T. S. (1970). *The Structure of Scientific Revolutions*. 2nd ed. Chicago: University of Chicago Press.

Thompson, M. (1979). *Rubbish Theory: The Creation and Destruction of Value*. New York: Oxford University Press.

Section IB
Cultural Analyses

5

The Impact of Drug Paraphernalia Laws on HIV Risk among Persons Who Inject Illegal Drugs: Implications for Public Policy

Michael C. Clatts, Jo L. Sotheran,
Pellegrino A. Luciano, Toni M. Gallo,
Lee M. Kochems

INTRODUCTION

Much of the public policy debate about the use of illegal drugs such as heroin and cocaine, including debates over the merits of legalizing or decriminalizing these kinds of substances, has been framed in terms of moral and political abstractions. Amidst all the polemic, however, there is often relatively little consideration of how illicit drugs are actually used and how existing policies currently contribute to the ways in which drugs are used. In the light of emerging epidemiological trends, of particular concern in public health policy is the impact of drug policies on risk behaviors that have been implicated in the spread of HIV infection. Acquired immunodeficiency syndrome (AIDS) was first noted among drug injectors in New York City in 1981 and subsequently shown to result from human immunodeficiency virus (HIV) transmission in the course of "sharing" drug injection equipment, including syringes and other paraphernalia that are part and parcel of the way illegal

We acknowledge helpful commentary from Beatrice J. Krauss. This research was supported by the National Institute on Drug Abuse #DA 09522. The views expressed do not necessarily reflect the views of NIDA or of the institutions by which the authors are employed.

drugs are prepared and administered. Today, the circulation and serial reuse of infected drug injection equipment is the single most significant factor in the spread of HIV infection in drug injector populations in North and South America, Europe, and Southeast Asia (Marmor et al. 1987, Stimpson 1995). Moreover, much of the heterosexual and perinatal spread of HIV infection in these areas is also attributable to injection risks. New York City has nearly 90,000 reported cases of AIDS, over a third of which are associated with injection-mediated risk (NYCDOH 1996). These injection-mediated types of transmission include not only infection directly from drug injection, but also infection from sex with an injector in the case of heterosexual transmission, and mother–infant transmission (from an HIV-infected mother who acquired the infection either from her own drug injection or from sex with an injector) in the case of perinatal transmission.

While the advent of AIDS has brought increased awareness of the health risks among drug users, there is, nevertheless, relatively little discussion in policy debate of the actual techniques of drug administration, particularly injection of illegal drugs. Although high-risk injection behaviors have been widely studied, information about risk behavior among injecting drug users (IDUs) is generally limited to self-reported survey data and has focused primarily on individual determinants of risk behavior, with relatively limited attention to ecological and situational factors that shape the circumstances in which drugs are used and that may limit drug users' efforts to engage in risk reduction. In an effort to better inform the debate, this chapter has three basic objectives.

1. We describe the interrelated processes by which illicit drugs are obtained, prepared, and administered in a socially, economically, and culturally diverse neighborhood in New York City.
2. We show that drug acquisition, preparation, and injection practices may be viewed, in part at least, as an adaptation to a policy environment that restricts and penalizes the use of drug substances and drug injection paraphernalia.
3. We demonstrate that this adaptation to the policy and enforcement environment exacerbates risk for a number of poor health outcomes that are associated with high-risk injection practices, notably HIV infection.

We should note two things before proceeding: first, our focus is not on the health risks of chronic drug use itself, but rather on the health risks of injection as a method or route of drug administration (particularly risk for HIV infection). Second, we hasten to point out that not all drugs and drug users are alike. Our work can present a preliminary set of examples of points to be considered in an analysis of the relationship of the legal status of certain drugs (chiefly heroin and cocaine) to the ways they are administered and the risks posed, but we would not wish to generalize these observations to other drugs or forms of administration or to all types of drug users. Heroin, cocaine, and methamphetamine, for example, have very different pharmacological properties and are used by different groups and in different ways. Unfortunately, much of the existing debate about drug use has been framed by broad generalizations about the nature of drugs and drug users, often in the service of particular political goals. As yet the debate has included relatively little substantive attention to the fact that drugs and drug users are different and consequently that the constellation of risks, benefits, and consequences of illegal status may vary considerably among drugs and across types of drug users. The aim of this chapter then is to advance the present debate through presentation of a series of ethnographic descriptions aimed at demonstrating variation in drug use patterns and their possible implications for drug policy.

RESEARCH SETTING AND METHODS

The geographic area from which the data presented in this chapter are drawn is known as the Lower East Side, a large neighborhood located east of Greenwich Village in the lower Manhattan area of New York City. Culturally and economically diverse, the community consists of a mix of first-, second-, and third-generation immigrants, primarily of Latino, Eastern European, and Caribbean descent. It also contains a growing population of homeless squatters, most of whom are white. There are a number of relatively affluent streets in the area, but it is predominantly a lower-income district (including several high-rise public housing complexes and homeless shelters), and has long been known as a neighborhood with a high concentration of drug sales and use.

The ethnographic observations described in this chapter were conducted as part of a research study to describe and evaluate the potential HIV transmission risks of particular ways in which drugs are prepared, divided, and injected. A major goal of the study is to describe precisely the range of injection practices, including social situations and physical settings in which they occur. The dominant research method used for this aspect of the study is "participant observation." In this method, which is the centerpiece of traditional anthropological methods, the ethnographer spends extended periods of time with the study population so as to observe the full range of behaviors and activities as they occur (compare Adler 1990, Agar 1990).

The goal of participant observation in this study is to discern the interrelationship between various parts of the drug acquisition and injection process and the "natural" social and physical settings in which these activities occur rather than to rely simply on injectors' self-reported descriptions of these behaviors and settings, as is the case in most HIV research among IDUs. An extended "ethnographic presence" in injection settings is essential to achieve the degree of trust and acceptance necessary to acquire reliable and complete observational data. The methodological goal is for the ethnographers to become so immersed in the daily life of the community that their presence becomes part of the setting itself, such that they will be able to observe drug injectors' activities in a manner that minimizes the degree to which their presence influences the behaviors being observed. In terms of both theory and method, the central concept in anthropology of cultural *relativism* is an important dimension of this kind of research. Cultural relativism implies a "perspective that respects and recognizes as legitimate cultural values, beliefs, customs, and lifestyles that are different from your own" (Brooks 1994, p. 790). Consistent with the emphasis on validity that underpins most ethnographic research, the methodological tenet holds that cultural patterns are meaningful on their own terms and have their own "logic." The methodological implication is that to understand these meanings and logic in a manner that is not biased by the ethnographer's own values, the ethnographer must suspend judgment about a wide variety of behaviors in order to acquire an understanding of the way that participants in a particular social arena view themselves and one another. Particularly in studying highly stigmatized behaviors, this methodological posture is fundamental to the goals of both gaining access to particular kinds of "hidden populations" as well as to that of building the kind of rapport that is essential to acquiring truthful information.

In tandem with participant observation, the study is using various kinds of semistructured ethnographic interviews among the injectors whose behavior has been observed. Open-ended life history interviews focus on the injector's life experience, including details about early family life, relationships with parents and siblings, school, and employment. Attention is given to early drug use, initiation into drug injection, history of drug use over the life course, experience in drug treatment, and current drug use practices, including daily or routine practices of drug acquisition and injection. In addition to providing useful information, this kind of open-ended interview provides a substantial basis for building rapport with the interviewee. Moreover, use of this kind of approach also provides a rich background to the "lived" history of the community under study, information that may be important in understanding how particular patterns of behavior have developed and how the cultural meanings of these practices became established. Additional questions on characteristics of drug injection situations allow us to examine the influence of the social (the injection group)—and the situational (drug acquisition and preparation)—setting. Since recruitment for the ethnographic interviews derives from observed injection scenes, the resulting data set is highly detailed and cohesive, thus strengthening our capacity to interpret the observational data.

RESULTS

As part of this research project, over 150 injections were observed in natural settings to document the specific technical processes involved so as to examine their risk for transmission of HIV infection (Clatts 1996). The ethnographers had opportunities to observe how injectors made money for, searched out, and purchased drugs; acquired paraphernalia; prepared the drugs; and injected them. Previous work from this project has documented the importance of physical settings for certain kinds of injection risks (Clatts et al. 1996). The descriptions in this chapter will illustrate injection in three different kinds of settings, and are presented to show how the illegal status of drugs (and consequent fear of law enforcement) has affected the actual practices of injectors, with possible health consequences for the injectors and others.

Outsiders to the world of illegal drugs rarely appreciate the complexity of the drug injection process—both the types of equipment required and the amount of technique involved in acquiring, preparing, and injecting drugs. Each step in the process is at least partly shaped by the fact that drugs and/or some paraphernalia are illegal. Before outlining the elements of the injection process, we begin with a review of the legal status of drugs and paraphernalia. All the items usually involved are legal in everyday (nondrug-related) use and in fact are commonly available household objects, with two exceptions. One is the drugs themselves—as we will see, a great deal of time and energy revolves around seeking out and actually acquiring drugs. The other is syringes. New York is one of a handful of states—largely clustered in the northeastern United States—that restrict both sale of syringes without a prescription and the actual possession of syringes. (There are limited exceptions for participants in recognized syringe exchanges.) It is perhaps not accidental that most of the AIDS cases associated with drug injection in the U.S. are also geographically clustered in states in the Northeast corridor. (For a survey of these topics, see Normand et al. 1995.)

Injection itself is a multistep process, thus subject to considerable variation. In New York the most popular injected drugs are heroin and cocaine; they are sometimes injected in combination or in quick succession. The general drug preparation and injection process is as follows. Drugs (in powder or solid form) are dissolved with water in a small vessel ("cooker"). Typically a bottle cap or in some cases a spoon will be used for this purpose. Heat ("cooking") from a match or cigarette lighter is sometimes applied to speed the dissolving process and attempt to eliminate impurities. Then the solution is drawn into the syringe, usually through a small filter ("cotton") designed to cleanse the solution of potentially dangerous impurities. If two or more injectors are preparing drugs together, several techniques known as "frontloading" and "backloading" may be used to measure and divide the solution among them (compare Jose et al. 1993). Then the user must find a usable vein (a difficult step for those whose veins have collapsed from repeated injection), insert the needle correctly, check to see that a vein has in fact been found by pulling back on the syringe and drawing blood ("registering"), and then proceed to actually inject. Injectors sometimes rinse syringes with water before and/or after injection for a variety of reasons. Current guidelines formulated by federal public health agencies also recommend extended rinsing of syringes (first with household bleach for disinfection, then rerinsing with new water to remove bleach residue) and cleansing of the injection site with alcohol swabs to avoid introducing bacteria resident on the skin into the bloodstream. There are potential health risks in all of these steps. The probability of poor health outcomes from them is multiplied by the frequency of injection. While some drug injectors inject only rarely, some may inject as many as eight to ten times in a single day.

Omissions or errors in syringe and injection hygiene may have several health consequences. HIV infection is the best known, but it may also lead to increased risk for several opportunistic infections (such as tuberculosis) that are particularly prevalent among HIV-infected persons who use drugs. Other injection-related risks include transmission of hepatitis B and C (both blood-borne infections), endocarditis (dangerous infections of the heart valves), possible embolisms, cellulitis and skin abscesses, and collapsed veins. The illegal status of drugs poses an additional set of risks to all those who use them, whether by injection or by other means (sniffing or snorting, for example). Contaminated drugs, or errors in calculating drug dosage, can lead to frightening and potentially fatal overdoses.

Further, many drug injectors carry out their injection under the threat or actual influence of heroin withdrawal symptoms. Withdrawal is a dreaded process among heroin injectors (see Connors 1992b). A longtime user will experience withdrawal if heroin is not administered two or more times during a day. Omissions or errors in syringe and injection hygiene and technique are more likely when the injector is threatened with or experiencing withdrawal symptoms.

In short, anything that affects the acquisition and use of drugs and injection paraphernalia or the process of injection has some potential to contribute to health-related injection risks. We present extracts from three field-note narratives describing actual observations of injections in different kinds of settings and among different kinds of injectors to illustrate some of the possible risks and how the illegal status of drugs has contributed to them.

Our first example is culled from ethnographic field notes concerning a woman we'll call "Crystal," a commercial sex worker encountered on a local "stroll" (area where sex workers solicit clients). Names in all examples are pseudonyms, and some identifying details have been altered.

EXAMPLE ONE

I met Crystal on the "stroll" at about 11:45 A.M. Crystal was feeling "sick" (heroin withdrawal symptoms) and needed money for "dope" (heroin). Her usual means of supporting her habit is through commercial sex work. This morning she came to the stroll in the hopes of finding a quick "date" (client) but her withdrawal symptoms were making her too impatient to wait for one—she said she needed to "get straight." We left the stroll at noon and she headed to a "coke spot" (place where cocaine is sold) several blocks away. The coke spot, a "bodega" (small grocery store), was her regular coke locale so she knew "copping" (buying drugs) would be a sure thing there. The problem for her was finding the dope! On our way to the bodega Crystal began voicing her frustrations about her daughter (who was currently missing) and began to cry. As we walked we talked about the significance of family. Crystal, who is homeless and destitute, said, "A group of us hang out in this one place, we're like family we take care of each other and watch out for the cops when we shoot up."

We got to the coke spot and Crystal paused in front of the bodega. She made her purchase and in a couple of minutes came out and began her search for dope. We walked about a half mile to a known dope location. It was a building on a side street near the housing projects. There was a group of men hanging out around the area; some were clearly acting as "lookouts" (individuals paid by drug dealers to watch for possible police interdiction). Crystal said that the tenants in the building complained about the drug addicts so the owner changed the lock on the door, thus preventing potential buyers from entering. Now the drug users had to wait outside for someone to exit in order to get inside to the apartment that deals heroin.

After a few minutes elapsed with no sign of the dealer, the drug users began congregating out front; they seemed very nervous. They walked back and forth looking for indications of the police. Crystal and a number of other users started talking among themselves and asking what was going on. They approached an old man whom they recognized to be a lookout and asked him where the dealer was. The old man just shrugged his shoulders and said nothing. He then pointed to a blue van about a block away. The users looked over and began to voice their concerns out loud. One young man said, "I think they're cops, there's an awful lot people in the van." The van disappeared down another street and one user believed they were coming around to their direction. The small crowd of users began scattering in fear. Crystal was frustrated. Suddenly the blue van pulled up to our street and four young men jumped out. It seemed as if everybody froze for an instant; Crystal fixed her gaze in the direction of the van. After a tense moment everyone breathed a sigh of relief and Crystal said, "They're not the cops."

In the interim, an older man walked cautiously in our direction. Two users recognized him as a dealer and followed closely behind asking for some dope. The dealer was agitated because of the attention he was attracting so when Crystal asked him for a "bag" (of heroin) he snapped at her and said, "You'all just need to leave me alone 'cause you're starting to piss me off." The dealer tried to walk inconspicuously to a small, desolate street with a row of users tracing his steps. Crystal caught up to him and made her buy.

Crystal came back and introduced me to the dealer. All three of us walked in the same direction for a while. The dealer was a clean-cut older man who said he had just retired and needed extra income. He told us he was extremely worried about getting arrested, that he had never been arrested and it would devastate his family should it happen. Crystal told him she had been waiting for the other dealer from the building for a while and was very happy that he came along. Now that Crystal had her dope she had to find a place to inject.

Somewhere in midblock Crystal selected a stoop and sat on the top step. She opened up her shoulderbag and pulled a towel to the opening, placing her drug paraphernalia inside the towel to conceal it from public view. While Crystal arranged her equipment, a woman abruptly came out the front door and startled her. Crystal quickly stood up in an attempt to cover what she was doing, but she dropped her paraphernalia on the steps of the stoop. The woman looked but said nothing and walked away. Crystal gathered her stuff and started to prepare her shot. She grabbed the bottle cap she uses as a cooker and rinsed it with water from her water bottle. She then pulled out a syringe and filled it with water. Crystal threw a piece of cotton into the cooker and stealthily opened her dope package under the cloak of her handbag. She put the heroin into the cooker, squirted the water on top, and stirred the contents into a solution. As Crystal prepared her shot, pedestrians passed by and peered over at her. She finished drawing the heroin into the syringe just as a man approached the stoop to enter the house. Crystal quickly threw her syringe into her handbag, deciding it was better to go to the parked car in front of the house. She set her paraphernalia on the hood of the car and took out the dope-filled syringe and her bag of coke. She hastily placed some of the coke into the cooker. People passed and stared and Crystal became even more visibly flustered. Suddenly a postman arrived to deliver mail to the house nearby. Crystal cringed, her face wrinkling as if she were going to cry; "You see what I gotta go through?" she said. She was upset over the constant interruptions and complained about how difficult it is to inject because of the stigma. Finally she grabbed an opportune moment and rapidly injected into her arm. As people approached she shot up, and swiftly pulled the syringe out, spilling blood down her arm. She then lunged for the first article she could grab from her bag to wipe herself; it was her glove.

After a few minutes Crystal wanted to shoot again. She pulled out the coke and a syringe, but was startled when another mailman passed us: "These damn mailmen are all over the place." Once again she put the coke into the cooker, drew water into the syringe, and squirted it on the coke. Again she mixed it and drew it up in her syringe. Again she injected, but the gazing pedestrians made her nervous and she had trouble finding a vein. In an angry voice she said: "Drugs don't take you down, but the fact that it's illegal—that's a problem." Crystal tried hard to inject but the distractions would not allow her to finish, so she pulled the syringe with the remaining contents out of her arm and wiped the blood away. After waiting a few minutes she decided to try again. This time she ventured down the basement stairs outside the building but under the stoop. Now she was hidden from public view. She grabbed a clean syringe, prepared the remainder of the coke, quickly found a vein and injected. She put the syringe back into her bag, sighed, and said, "You see? When I have a little privacy it's so much easier." After two hours and forty-five minutes from the moment I had met her on the stroll, she finally accomplished her task of getting high.

This first example illustrates the role of "dopesickness" in risk behavior. A steady, high-frequency heroin injector (who often injects cocaine as well), Crystal has begun to feel the effects of heroin withdrawal symptoms, which will only worsen if she does not inject very soon; this discomfort is exacerbated by her difficulty in finding a supply of the heroin she so desperately seeks, a difficulty directly related to the need for dealers to conceal their activity from law enforcement. Finally, Crystal is desperate enough to inject out in the open, and as a result is constantly distracted by the possibility of detection and apprehension. The need for speed can result in a number of kinds of errors and short-cuts in injection technique and hygiene, as it did in this case. To mention only two, Crystal did not heat her drug solution, nor did she clean the skin surfaces.

Our second example is taken from ethnographic field notes involving "Luis," a man in his mid-thirties. In contrast to Crystal, he has a "home" of sorts, and his injection shows some of the results of privacy, relative lack of withdrawal symptoms, and being somewhat buffered from anxiety about enforcement.

EXAMPLE TWO

Luis has been a drug user for the past eighteen years. He began injecting drugs in his teens. He has lived in the "Goddess" Hotel for three years, since his last release from prison. It is one of a number of hotels in this part of the community that has remained a hotel for a primarily indigent population. A refuge for the lost and abandoned of the city, the male residents include the formerly homeless; hard-to-house clients of social services; and assorted alcoholics, parolees, "parole jumpers," and others who choose such a place as a refuge because of other illegal activities like heavy drug use or "being in hiding" for some criminal activity. Some residents have made it "home" for as long as twenty years, living in six- by five-foot "rooms" (cubicles enclosed by six- or seven-foot-high plasterboard topped with chicken wire, with a single bare light bulb and a padlock on the outside of the door). Luis painted and repaired his "home"—the room that he occupies and that he also uses to inject his drugs, always alone (except when I was invited to observe), with his own paraphernalia. His drug of choice was heroin, which he injects only a few times a week.

As part of a loose network of heroin injectors, he was supplied through a twenty-year user (who injected ten or more times per day) who pooled money from a group of users (often increasing it through "cons") and copped from a large local supplier, distributing the "stuff" to those who had contributed to the pool.

Luis always injected in his room where he kept a complete supply of paraphernalia. The main advantage was "privacy, because I prefer to inject by myself . . . at home." He would leave the door open while he prepared to inject. When he began to tie off (to find a vein), he closed the door.

The paraphernalia Luis used was carefully packaged in his room. His syringes were obtained from a nearby needle exchange program and kept in a plastic bag. After a syringe had been used for one injection, Luis's rule was to remove the piece of tape that he had wrapped around the top of the syringe's barrel when he initially acquired the supply. He produced a syringe out of the plastic bag that had tape around it, meaning that he had not used it previously.

He used a cooker that he also reported was from the needle exchange. It's the same cooker that he often used, and the cotton was already in it. Both had been used for at least one injection before this. He said that he's the only one that has used the cooker and the cotton because he injects alone, like almost everyone in the hotel. His water bottle was a small clear glass jar that previously held some sort of prescription medication or vitamin. It already had water in it, but preceding this injection and every other injection I observed, he rinsed and filled it with cold water from the tap, something not available to injectors without residences.

Typically, these materials would be laid out on the bed in full view of a passerby: drug use (all types) was common enough in this environment that it was generally ignored. He carefully cut the tape and unfolded the waxed paper of the bag, shaping it into a funnel, then poured the drugs into the cooker with the cotton. Afterward, he "sniffed" (inhaled) whatever remained in the paper, then used a wet finger to collect the residue and taste it. He "always did this to check the quality."

Taking a new syringe, he removed the cap, placed it on the bed, took the water bottle, and drew up water that he squirted gently into the cooker, tilting it slightly so that the force of the water did not dislodge or scatter any of the heroin. He then turned the cooker slightly to make sure all of the drug was part of the solution.

There was no special preparation of the injection site. Luis did not use an alcohol wipe, although he did have them available. Although he has lots of veins, they appeared to be collapsed in his arms (a frequent problem among persons who inject drugs). He noted that he was going to inject in his arm this time, but that he often injected in his thigh. He removed his lighter from his pants pocket, held it to the cooker, and cooked the solution for a few seconds.

Luis picked up the belt and tied off his left arm just below the elbow, wrapping it around and pulling it tight. He picked up the syringe with his right hand, cooker with his left, and drew the solution into the syringe. He moved the cotton ball around to make sure all the solution was there, then pressed the needle gently on the cotton to make sure that he had gotten all the solution (tapped once so no bubbles were present). He replaced the cooker on the bed.

Selecting a vein in his lower arm, he inserted the syringe. "Got a hit" (into a vein, rather than muscle), which he said, was of concern to him.

It registered slightly and then he registered again, drawing an additional amount of blood into the syringe. He was fairly certain that he had gotten a hit. To show me, he again drew back the plunger to demonstrate that it had registered. The vacuum in the plunger was apparent as it "steamed up," but at that point no additional blood entered the syringe. He had "lost it" (the vein). He continued to manipulate the syringe with his right hand for about twenty-five seconds. He mentioned that he wanted to make sure that he was in a vein, which is why he allowed a substantial amount of blood "to fill the barrel," and "I want to make sure that I don't inject any air bubbles." When the syringe had filled just over halfway, he became a bit frustrated; approximately thirty-five to forty seconds had elapsed since he had hit his arm. He was not certain that he had a hit.

At that point, after confirming that the door was closed, he removed the syringe, still filled with the blood/drug solution, from his arm, dropped the belt from his arm while holding the syringe in his mouth, and dropped his pants. Locating a vein in the upper part of his right thigh, he inserted the syringe, holding his leg above the insertion point with his left hand, again not preparing the injection site. He drew back the plunger, which immediately filled with blood. Convinced he had a solid hit, he slowly injected the blood/drug solution, then removed the syringe, licking its tip. Picking up a nearby towel, he wiped the injection point on his arm and thigh and began vigorously to scratch his thigh at the site of the injection.

He said he "felt that immediately" and described "a good feeling." His speech pattern slowed and he began talking to himself. His whole manner of movement slowed as he began to "nod" (a sleeplike state as heroin takes effect). Taking the water bottle, he drew up a full syringe of water, using his teeth to pull the plunger, and injected it onto the floor. After repeating the rinsing twice, he recapped the syringe and leaned forward on the bed into a full long nod. A few minutes later, managing to pull himself up, he removed the tape from the syringe, placed it back into the plastic bag, and sealed it. He put the cooker, syringes, and other paraphernalia on the cabinet by his bed, not their usual place. Face down, he hit the mattress.

This example of Luis's injection, not unlike others in the hotel, took place in private, with no sharing of paraphernalia or drug solution. The hotel environment actually contributed to safer injection practices by providing a relatively private facility that shielded him from police scrutiny and interruption. In contrast to Crystal, he can pause to check quality (and thus overdose potential) and the absence of air bubbles. Ready access to drugs

and drug injection equipment embedded him to exercise the common preference among drug injectors for private rather than multiperson injecting, and
he risked arrest only while copping or carrying (often long distances).

Luis can take his time about injection and maintain his own set of paraphernalia because he has little fear of interruption or of apprehension by law
enforcement. He has a somewhat private space in which to inject out of sight,
and as most of the hotel residents are willing to ignore others' drug use, the
risks from neighbors are small and the possible stigma minimal. The major
"copping" risk is taken by the user who buys for the group rather than by
Luis. Luis obtains sterile syringes legally through a syringe exchange. In addition, due to his participation in a drug treatment program, Luis does not
use heroin very often, and thus is unlikely to experience the "dopesickness"
(itself linked to the artificial scarcity of drugs, attributable to their illegal status)
so conducive to potentially unsafe behavior. It remains only to note that the
pharmacological effects of the heroin may affect risk. The deep "nod" hin-
ders his ability to concentrate on some aspects of hygiene, and—as seen in
the next example—can be a source of potentially dangerous confusion.

Our third example is that of "Vera" and her friend "Marie." This example,
despite the privacy of the environment and the relatively hidden nature of the
injector herself, throws into relief the kinds of things that can happen to injectors who experience withdrawal symptoms but still fear stigma and law enforcement.

EXAMPLE THREE

Vera, an intravenous drug user in her early thirties, makes her living
as a full time commercial sex worker. She has been "homeless" for the
past seven years. Vera is considered an important resource on the streets
by various people, helping with drug accessibility, working for drug
sellers by experimenting with drugs to test potency, and mapping police activity. Her income varies from day to day, but in comparison
with many of her co-workers, she is "successful," which promotes her
keen sense of independence and confidence. Vera seems to look out
for the well-being of the other "girls" (sex workers), yet she feels
dead-ended in her self-defined addiction and her lifestyle and really sees
no way of changing.

Marie, in her mid-thirties, is a self-defined heroin "sniffer" (someone
who administers drugs intranasally), although she allows a select few
to inject her. She has never been homeless, and has always managed
to maintain formal jobs, like waitressing. Marie depends on others to

assist her in finding where and when to "cop" and a person to inject her. She is very fearful of police.

I was invited to Marie's apartment by Vera, with whom I had had consistent contact for six months. On this afternoon, as part of our normal practice, we were "hanging out" and she invited me to walk to "a friend's" apartment. When we reached the fourth floor, Vera knocked on the door, and Marie, whom I had met a few weeks earlier, opened the door naked; she had been in the bath. Vera apologized and Marie recognized me and invited us both in. Marie had "overslept" (missed her first heroin dose of the day and was feeling pressured by the onset of withdrawal symptoms) and was waiting on a phone call from a "house connect" (drug purchase at an apartment, arranged by phone) to get her "straight" (alleviation of withdrawal symptoms) before she went to work as a waitress.

The apartment in which we found ourselves belonged to Marie's boyfriend, who does not know that Marie gets high. The boyfriend believes that Marie sleeps on the Lower East Side because her work and her friends are more accessible. Marie admits that she stays there because of proximity to drugs, but tells the boyfriend that it is the convenience of being close to her job.

It occurred to me that Vera wanted to see Marie not only to use the bathroom facilities to wash up: this was the infamous "friend with the house connect" she had so often mentioned in the past. Today, Marie was visibly nervous because the phone call was late and her anxiety was increasing by the minute. She was depending on this call to get straight before work because if she did not, she could not work. If she did not work, she would not have money to get straight—a vicious cycle.

The much needed phone connect did not materialize. Vera at this point attempted to encourage Marie to cop dope at a popular street "dope spot" not too far from the apartment. Vera was positive the spot was open for business, and if anyone knew the schedule of every dope spot in the vicinity, it was Vera. Marie was concerned that it would not be open and was worried that because of the time of day, the spot's supply would be almost gone and she needed to buy six bags of heroin.

They were successful in copping. Vera had only $5 when they set out to cop, but managed to get one "dime bag ($10)" for herself. Either the bag was from Marie in exchange for Vera's services, or merely a gift between friends. Marie did buy six bags as she was suffering from withdrawal. She mentioned that the sixth would last her until the morning.

Vera was clearly in charge of the paraphernalia and preparation even though the space and the majority of the dope belonged to Marie. Vera began to lay out her syringes and other paraphernalia on the kitchen table: a bag of cotton swabs the size of Q-Tip heads from the needle exchange place, cookers in the form of soda bottle caps, and syringes.

Marie retrieved a spoon from the kitchen wall for Vera to cook up Marie's share of the drugs. Marie, in the meantime, counted the money that her boyfriend had brought her before she copped. Vera divided the set of "works" (cooker, cotton, and syringe) between her and Marie. I asked Marie why she had told me she was a sniffer the last time I met her. She answered emphatically: "I really hate needles, and I never hit [inject] myself, but if there is someone who I trust to hit me like Vera, then I use intravenously, but I am a sniffer."

Vera prepared Marie's shot first, placing a dime bag of dope in the spoon and adding tap water from the bottle supplied by the needle exchange place. She then added a cotton swab from her needle exchange bag and heated the solution for a few seconds with a lighter. She placed the lighter on the table, examined the solution, stabbed the cotton with the tip of the needle, and drew up the solution with her thumb and middle finger. Taking her time, she released the solution back into the spoon twice, until she was satisfied that she had completely squeezed any remaining solution out of the cotton. She then asked Marie to take a seat. Marie wiped her arm with an alcohol pad and closed her eyes tightly while Vera injected the solution into her left arm, the middle portion of which vaguely revealed the small "track" marks (formed by repeated injection) forming on the arm of this sniffer.

Vera then prepared her own shot in another syringe, using a different piece of cotton and cooker. She added faucet water to the heroin and heated the solution with the lighter for a few seconds. She seemed to have an easier time drawing the solution out of the cooker, and did not seem to be as meticulous about drying the cotton completely. She tapped her syringe, made sure there were no air bubbles, and injected herself in her left arm. She did not clean the site. It took her about one and a half minutes of poking and pulling to find a vein.

Vera began to nod immediately following the shot. Marie said she felt straight, but nothing like Vera was feeling. She wanted to do another bag. She asked if Vera was all right enough to hit her again or if she (Marie) should just sniff the bag. As she nodded, Vera said, "No, I'm fine. I have low blood pressure. That's why it affects me so fast." Marie was visibly anxious because she had to leave for work and wanted to guarantee that she was set for the night. Marie begged, "Please, Vera, if you are going to do this, please do it now. I cannot be late for work."

Vera picked up her own syringe and cap first. Then she nodded. When she came out of her nod the third time, she still had not capped the syringe and Marie asked her to please hurry. Vera took the syringe in her hand and drew up some water from the bottle and added another bag of dope to the spoon with the old piece of cotton. Marie looked down and asked: "Why is the dope pink?" Both of them seemed not to realize that it contained blood. Vera looked for a moment, then jumped up and ran to the window apologizing.

There had been a mistake. Vera explained that while she was holding her syringe in her hand getting ready to cap it, she nodded and forgot that it was her own syringe and proceeded to use it to draw up and prepare the shot in Marie's cooker. Marie began to cry.

Vera insisted on buying the wasted bag from Marie, but Marie replied, "No, it was not your fault." Vera seemed to feel extraordinarily guilty and begged to repay her, "Please, Marie, take the offer when I have the money to do it. I feel terrible, it was just a mistake."

Vera began preparations anew by taking another one of Marie's syringes, which she had placed in a paper bag and hidden. She washed the spoon in the sink with water from and tap and used the same water in the bottle to draw up the necessary amount. She heated the solution, drew it up into the brand-new syringe, and injected Marie in the same arm. The time elapsed from preparation to injection time was just over two minutes. As the dope was part of Marie's stash, Vera promised to get her a replacement bag on the way to work or later on that evening. On the way out of the building Vera said they should meet later.

Stigma and criminalization of drugs have made Marie vulnerable in several ways. She cannot use drugs at her job, so she is under considerable pressure to complete the drug administration before she leaves for work. In addition, Marie's "oversleeping" has rendered her dopesick and hurried. Because of her difficulty in locating drugs, Marie is in a hurry and her difficulties in acquiring drugs in this case have made her dependent on Vera for locating a purchase. This means that Marie cannot minimize some of the health risks by injecting alone. Instead, she injects with Vera, which presents an opportunity for confusion of paraphernalia. Last but not least, the stigma and fear of law enforcement have limited Marie's opportunities to learn injection techniques, let alone those that can minimize some of the health consequences of injection, so she is again dependent on Vera to inject her.

This example illustrates the accidents that can happen even in a protected, private location to someone who has a supply of clean paraphernalia, when acquiring drugs becomes difficult because of their scarcity and dopesickness sets in. Note the contrast to Luis. Insulated from both the effects of dopesickness (he has a relatively low level of heroin use, and thus does not feel the deprivation as much) and risks of apprehension and stigma (someone else takes most of the risks of copping, and the hotel provides a private environment for injection), he carries out his injection alone, carefully, and with a minimum of health-related risk from injection.

DISCUSSION

These case histories exemplify some of the ways in which the legal situation seems to have contributed to actually or potentially unsafe injection practices. First, and perhaps most important, the illicit status of the drugs has contributed to their *scarcity*, with important consequences. As with most consumer products, scarcity tends to drive up costs. For the drug user, especially the relatively frequent user, the price of an adequate supply can quickly exceed the ability to finance it. The prices paid for individual "doses" described above ranged from $10 to $20. Few pharmaceutical drugs approach those costs per dose, and many users inject several times a day. Drug users often become involved in a variety of illegal and/or harmful activities in order to earn enough to support their habits. Common sources of cash among drug users include shoplifting, mugging, theft, panhandling, low-level drug dealing, and (as in the cases of Vera and Crystal) commercial sex work. Some of these—especially commercial sex work—carry health risks of their own quite apart from injection. While none of these activities would completely disappear if drug supplies were legal (and consequently cheaper), drug users would have less need to resort to them.

In addition, like any sought-after consumer product, drugs are not always easy to find. Drug sales are the subject of greater criminal sanction than is drug use. Dealers, always under considerable police pressure, must be cautious about being too visible and obvious (often changing location or time of sales), and about selling to strangers. As we saw in the cases of Marie and Crystal, learning about and finding suppliers consumes a great deal of time and energy, and users cannot always find a reliable source.

Finally, the illegal status of these drugs results in drug users having to obtain them from street sources where the drugs are not subject to any quality control. Sources of illegal drugs operate so as to maximize profit. Because they function outside the law, they are not subject to any standards of cleanliness, potency, and consistency. In fact, the potency of drugs available on the streets may vary considerably, often by as much as 35 percent in immediately contiguous drug-selling spots. Wide variations in potency result in higher risks for drug overdoses, particularly among new (relatively inexperienced) users and users who inject alone. Indeed, fear of overdose is one of the reasons that some drug injectors shoot up together, a fact that as described here often involves other kinds of risk in the course of the injection process itself. Marie and Crystal both took some risk of overdose in buying heroin from sources other than those they normally use and are accustomed to. Every year New York City sees a few deaths resulting from a batch of heroin that has, unknown to the users, much higher than the usual potency. Conversely, variation in potency also increases the risk for unanticipated bouts of withdrawal if the drugs are not potent enough for the user, often resulting in a frantic effort to obtain additional drugs. This panic-driven process is frequently associated with greater likelihood of drug sharing, sex-for-drugs trading, injection with strangers who have drugs, injection in unsafe places, needle sharing, and generally poor injection technique and hygiene. Again, Luis is the only injector in our examples who, not driven by the onset of withdrawal, can carry out his own rudimentary potency check before injecting.

Wide variation in consistency also poses a number of risks inherent to the injection process itself. Typically, heroin is "cut" (by the packager) with various kinds of sedatives that mimic the calming nature of heroin and other opiates, and make the mixture seem to contain more heroin than it really does. Similarly, drugs like cocaine are frequently cut with stimulants such as "speed" (amphetamines). In addition, however, these and other drugs purchased on the streets are cut with various adulterants that over time result in long-term damage to veins and muscle tissues, damage informally and are collectively known on the streets as "abscesses." The acute deterioration of veins that is commonplace among long-term injectors of adulterated street drugs makes the injection process all the more difficult and risky since it often necessitates multiple injection attempts (such as Luis's) in an effort to find a usable vein. At the very least this leads to multiple punctures, often with the assistance of another injector. As we have seen in the case of Vera and Marie, such circumstances are even more likely to involve injection risk.

There are several other practical, health-related consequences of the illegal status of injected drugs. First, scarcity and expense of drugs result in frequent struggles with withdrawal symptoms, which drug users fear greatly (see Connors 1992a,b). This is a major contributor to risk behavior, as many injectors themselves readily admit. Drug users go to some length not to waste their scarce drug supplies, even when not "dopesick," but more so when they are. This concern with waste lies beneath many of the techniques used to prepare and measure drugs for injection. There are, unfortunately, health risks associated with some of these techniques, as they often involve common use of syringes or auxiliary paraphernalia.

Second, fear of interruption or apprehension while injecting illicit drugs contributes to the techniques used to administer them. Even users who are not in withdrawal are concerned about keeping or carrying quantities of drugs and/or paraphernalia because of the risks of apprehension. Purchase and administration are closely connected. The imperative to inject shortly after purchase often contributes to the use of whatever setting is close and convenient, regardless of its suitability for injection (Neaigus et al. 1992, Ouellet et al. 1991). Settings such as the stoop used by Crystal are not optimum environments for injection hygiene. A further consequence of needing to inject quickly is anxiety and distraction, as in the case of Vera and Marie. Under such circumstances it is not difficult to confuse paraphernalia, or to take shortcuts in preparation.

Third, while the topic is itself too lengthy to pursue here (for surveys, see Normand et al. 1995), it is noteworthy that the criminalization of drugs has been the driving force behind the criminalization of the syringes with which to administer them. The states that criminalize syringes are those with the largest populations of drug injectors and, not incidentally, are also the states with the largest concentration of drug injectors infected with HIV. This relative scarcity of syringes is the source of much sharing of syringes, the major HIV infection risk among injection drug users. In the three examples described here, the injectors have access to sterile syringes and thus were able to avoid the significant HIV risk entailed in using the same syringe as another injector, but the outcomes might have been quite different if sterile syringes had not been available. Indeed, syringe sharing was historically a commonplace practice among drug injectors in New York City, declining sharply after the advent and proliferation of community-based syringe exchange programs (Clatts et al. 1994, Des Jarlais et al. 1994).

Last, the illegal status of drug use creates stigma and isolation that are themselves major barriers to changing injection and other drug-related health risks. Participation in health, educational, or social service programs presents risks to drug users precisely because it may reveal their participation in an illegal activity. Detection or admission of their drug use may carry actual legal sanctions, making users reluctant to come forward for services, including the health-related services that could reduce the consequences of drug use to both the user and others. (Such sanctions include loss of employment, loss of some government benefits, and removal of children by child welfare authorities, to name only a few.) At best, the stigma that is linked to the illegal status of drugs often contributes to negative attitudes, neglect, and substandard treatment from providers of services. Even programs designed specifically for drug users and their particular needs and lifestyle, and catering solely to drug users, assume that the user is willing to accept the stigmatized label of drug user in order to access the services. The requirement to adopt this label can be a major barrier for some drug users, especially those who are still trying to conceal their drug use. The need to be secretive about illegal drug acquisition and use often means being secretive about drug administration as well. In a highly stigmatized atmosphere such as this, not only will users not come forward themselves, but educational and behavioral interventions designed to locate them cannot always reach the people who would benefit most (Clatts et al. 1997). Thus, paradoxically, the illegal status of drugs not only contributes to health risks associated with their consumption, but is actually a major barrier to overcoming some of those health risks.

CONCLUSION

Criminalization of drugs and injection paraphernalia constrain injectors' capacity to engage in safer injection practices in a variety of ways. This is particularly the case among homeless injectors and others who use public settings in which to inject and are thus are at greatest risk of detection and apprehension. Women and new injectors are also at particular risk because they have greater difficulty negotiating the environments in which illegal drugs are acquired and used, a fact that often makes them dependent upon others to acquire drugs for them and/or help them inject, which exacerbates their risk for exposure to HIV (Inciardi and Page 1991, Mandell et al. 1994, Sotheran et al. 1994).

Drug laws, the degree and manner of their enforcement, and paraphernalia laws that restrict the availability of sterile injection equipment all play parts in encouraging high-risk injection practices. While the impact on injection practices and their associated health outcomes is just one aspect to be considered in any discussion of possible consequences of changing the legal status of any or all drugs, we should note that there are already some possible ways to decrease the risk of injection.

In particular, decriminalization of injection paraphernalia and broader access to sterile injection equipment can play a major part in reducing HIV risk. Possible mechanisms for providing such equipment include pharmacy sale, street outreach workers, and syringe exchange programs. Where such policies have been enacted (Groseclose et al. 1995, Heimer et al. 1993, Lurie and Reingold 1993, Normand et al. 1995, Valleroy et al. 1995, Watters et al. 1994), they have not been associated with increased drug use and have been shown to have a positive effect on reducing injection-related harm.

REFERENCES

Adler, P. (1990). Ethnographic research on hidden populations: penetrating the drug world. In *The Collection and Interpretation of Data from Hidden Populations*. NIDA Monograph 90:96–112.

Agar, M. H. (1990). *The Professional Stranger: An Informal Introduction to Ethnography*. New York: Academic Press.

Brooks, C. R. (1994). Using ethnography in the evaluation of drug prevention and intervention programs. *International Journal of the Addictions* 29(6):789–801.

Clatts, M. C. (1996). *Theoretical foundations for inter-disciplinary research in the study of injection related HIV risk: applications of ethnography in public health.* Paper presented at National Institutes of Health, Bethesda, MD, September.

Clatts, M. C., Davis, W. R., Bresnahan, M., et al. (1997). The harm reduction model: an alternative approach to AIDS outreach and prevention among street youth in New York City. In *Harm Reduction: New Direction for Drug Policies and Programs*, pp. 393–409. Toronto: University of Toronto Press.

Clatts, M. C., Davis, W. R., Deren, S., et al. (1994). AIDS risk behavior among drug injectors in New York City: critical gaps in prevention policy. In *Global AIDS Policy*, ed. D. Feldman, pp. 215–235. Westport, CT: Bergin and Garvey.

Clatts, M. C., Sotheran, J. L., Luciano, P., et al. (1996). *Ecological factors in high risk drug injection: implications for prevention policy.* Paper presented at the annual meeting of the American Public Health Association, New York City, November.

Connors, M. M. (1992a). Stories of pain and the problem of AIDS prevention: injection drug withdrawal and its effect on risk behavior. *Medical Anthropology Quarterly* 8(1):47–68.

———— (1992b). Risk perception, risk taking, and risk management among intravenous drug users: implications for AIDS prevention. *Social Science and Medicine* 34(6):591–601.

Des Jarlais, D. C., Friedman, S. R., Sotheran, J. L., et al. (1994). Continuity and change within an HIV epidemic: injecting drug users in New York City, 1984 through 1992. *Journal of the American Medical Association* 271(2):121–127.

Groseclose, S. L., Weinstein, B., Jones, B. T., et al. (1995). Impact of increased legal access to needles and syringes on practices of injecting-drug users and police officers—Connecticut, 1992–1993. *Journal of Acquired Immune Deficiency Syndromes and Human Retrovirology* 10:82–89.

Heimer, R., Kaplan, E. H., Khoshnood, K., et al. (1993). Needle exchange decreases the prevalence of HIV-1 proviral DNA in returned syringes in New Haven, Connecticut. *American Journal of Medicine* 95(2):214–220.

Inciardi, J. A., and Page, J. B. (1991). Drug sharing among intravenous drug users. *AIDS* 5(6):772–773.

Jose, B., Friedman, S. R., Neaigus, A., et al. (1993). Syringe-mediated drug sharing (backloading): a new risk factor for HIV among injecting drug users. *AIDS* 7:1653–1660.

Lurie, P., and Reingold, A. L. (1993). *The Public Health Impact of Needle Exchange Programs in the United States and Abroad: Summary, Conclusions and Recommendations.* Atlanta, GA: U.S. Public Health Service, Centers for Disease Control and Prevention.

Mandell, W., Vlahov, D., Latkin, C., et al. (1994). Correlates of needle sharing among injection drug users. *American Journal of Public Health* 84(6):920–923.

Marmor, M., Des Jarlais, D. C., Cohen, H., et al. (1987). Risk factors for infection with human immunodeficiency virus among intravenous drug abusers in New York City. *AIDS* 1(1):39–44.

Neaigus, A., Friedman, S. R., Curtis, R., et al. (1992). The emergence of outside injection settings as sites for potential HIV transmission in New York City. VIII International Conference on AIDS, Amsterdam, July.

New York City Department of Health, Office of AIDS Surveillance (1996). AIDS New York City: AIDS surveillance update, October.

Normand, J., Vlahov, D., and Moses, L. E., eds. (1995). *Preventing HIV Transmission: The Role of Sterile Needles and Bleach.* Panel on Needle Exchange and Bleach Distribution Programs, National Research Council and Institute of Medicine. Washington, DC: National Academy Press.

Ouellet, L. J., Jimenez, A. D., Johnson, W. A., and Wiebel, W. W. (1991). Shooting galleries and HIV disease: variations in places for injecting illicit drugs. *Crime & Delinquency* 37(1):64–85.

Sotheran, J. L., Friedman, S. R., Winston, J., et al. (1994). Gender and Sources of Sterile Syringes among IDUs in NYC, 1990-1993. American Public Health Association, Washington, DC, October 30-November 3.

Stimpson, G. (1995). *The health and social costs of drug injecting: the challenge to developing countries.* Paper presented at the Sixth International Conference on the Reduction of Drug Related Harm, Florence, Italy, March 26-30.

Valleroy, L. A., Weinstein, B., Jones, T. S., et al. (1995). Impact of increased legal access to needles and syringes on community pharmacies' needle and syringe sales—Connecticut, 1992-1993. *Journal of Acquired Immune Deficiency Syndromes and Human Retrovirology* 10:73-81.

Watters, J. K., Estilo, M. J., Clark, G. L., and Lorvick, J. (1994). Syringe and needle exchange as HIV/AIDS prevention for injection drug users. *Journal of American Medical Association* 271(2):115-120.

6

The Impact of the War on Drugs on Puerto Ricans: A Lost Generation

Luis Barrios, Richard Curtis

INTRODUCTION

Public opinion polls and many social scientists in the United States often contend that the public identifies illegal drugs as the number one social problem (Korzenny et al. 1990). The marketing of this issue by the government has been extremely effective and the public often seems ready to support any kind of intervention, including those that undermine hard-won civil rights. Fanning public hysteria via expensive propaganda campaigns, the government asserts that the drug problem so threatens national interests that real domestic crises in areas like education, housing, immigration, health, unemployment, welfare, race, class, and gender relations can be justifiably overlooked. While few would argue that drug abuse can have detrimental social outcomes—for example, by undermining health, costing taxpayers increased revenue, or leading to productivity losses for business (Benoit 1989)—the problem of illegal drugs has evoked a collective panic and many are ready to embrace desperate mea-

The authors acknowledge the valuable assistance of Rose Lindenmeyer, Kimberly Collica, and Janice Zummo at the John Jay College of Criminal Justice in collecting and interpreting the data and preparing the manuscript for publication.

sures to eradicate the problem. The allocation of federal drug enforcement funds has more than tripled since 1981, from less than 1 billion per year to about 3 billion dollars (Nadelmann 1988). Illegal drugs clearly command a disproportionate amount of governmental attention and money.

Many policy makers, health professionals, and social scientists react to illegal drugs as a criminal justice problem rather than one of public health (Nadelmann 1989). The criminalization of specific drugs is not unique to the twentieth century, but the transformation of particular events (drug taking) into "problem behaviors" has been conditioned by social, cultural, political, and economic factors unique to this century (Kappeler et al. 1996), and this has had a profound impact on particular segments of the population, especially the poor and racial/ethnic minorities.

This chapter examines the impact of the criminalization of drugs on Latinos and Latinas.[1] The first section provides an overview of the Latino community in the United States in general, and in Puerto Rico and New York City in particular.[2] The following section reviews the war on drugs as waged by the United States, especially in Latin America and the Caribbean, and the hypocritical ways in which the war has often been compromised by other foreign policy objectives. To further elucidate the manner in which the war on drugs has impacted Latinos, a case study from research conducted in New York City and Puerto Rico is presented. In the concluding section, the colonial status of Puerto Rico is explored to help the reader understand why problems such as violence, AIDS, and extraordinarily high rates of incarceration persist there. The authors also discuss the potential impact that an end to the war on drugs and the implementation of some style of drug legalization might have on the everyday lives of Puerto Ricans.

THE LATINO COMMUNITY AND DRUGS

Official statistics reveal that in 1995 Latinos were 9 percent of the total population of the United States (SAMSA 1996). The fastest-growing immigrant group in the country, they will be the second largest ethnic group in the nation after African-Americans by the year 2000. Latinos have long occupied the bottom rungs of the economic ladder in the United States; in 1994 the poverty rate among Latinos was about 29 percent, more than three times the rate among non-Latino whites (9 percent) (Institute for Puerto Rican Policy 1994, Kasarda 1992). In Puerto Rico the situation is even grimmer, with more

---

[1]For the purpose of stylistic presentation, the authors will subsequently use *Latino* throughout this chapter to indicate both males and females.

[2]Though our focus is on the problems that Puerto Ricans have faced as a result of their experiences with the war on drugs, other Latinos have suffered similar fates.

than half of the families falling below the federal poverty level (Cordero-Guzmán 1996).

Though Puerto Ricans live in cities throughout the United States, the majority of Puerto Rican immigrants live in New York City. Puerto Rico and New York City have a unique relationship that can be traced to post-World War II economic development programs (Cordero-Guzmán 1996, Phillips 1990). Following the implementation of "Operation Bootstrap" in 1947, which ensured Puerto Rico's economic and political dependence on the United States, a pattern of circular migration to the United States began in earnest. More than 75,000 Puerto Ricans migrated in 1953 alone, and through the 1960s more than a half million Puerto Ricans came to the United States—to New York City in particular—in search of jobs and a better life (Bonilla and Campos 1986). But the good life was hard to find (Bourgois 1989, Sullivan 1989). In 1994 the official unemployment rate of Latinos in the United States appeared to be "merely" double that of European Americans (12 percent versus 6 percent, respectively), but given the far greater participation of Latinos in the undocumented, informal sector of the economy, their unemployment rates have been grossly underestimated, particularly in the large metropolitan centers where most Latinos live (Mollenkopf and Castells 1991, Scharff 1987). The level of educational attainment for Latinos, a variable that is easier to report more accurately, has also been disproportionate, with about 47 percent of Latinos versus 85 percent of European Americans graduating from high school. Despite their relatively low level of high school achievement in comparison with the dominant group, however, Latinos are clearly taking advantage of education as a foundation for upward social mobility.

For the last 30 years, Puerto Rico has been the poorest "state," with an unemployment rate of 16.7 percent (Negociado de Estadísticas del Trabajo 1995). Officially, there are approximately 197,000 Puerto Ricans looking for work; however, more than 1.3 million unemployed people over the age of 16 are uncounted by such measures (Cordero-Guzmán 1996). Crime in the Latino community, and in Puerto Rico in particular, has been another enduring legacy of poverty, unemployment, lack of education, and drug prohibition. The murder rate in Puerto Rico in 1994 (27.5 per 100,000) was the highest in the western hemisphere and more than three times the average of the United States (9 per 100,000) (Nevares-Muñiz 1996). In 1995 nearly three quarters (73 percent) of all murders in Puerto Rico were classified by police as "drug-related" (Nevares-Muñiz 1996).

Drug-use patterns among Latinos show a remarkable congruence with overall trends in the United States, with alcohol and cigarettes consumed far more than all the illegal drugs combined. Among illegal drugs, marijuana has been the most popular drug, followed by powdered cocaine, hallucinogens, inhalants, stimulants, tranquilizers, crack, and heroin (SAMSA 1996). But while Latinos do not use drugs in ways or amounts that are different from those of other U.S. citizens, the number of murders in Puerto Rico suggests that they clearly have different outcomes as a result of their involvements with drugs. For example, Latinos are incarcerated at extraordinarily high rates, clearly an outcome of a greater number of arrests for illegal drugs in Latino neighborhoods and the unequal treatment they receive at the hands of the criminal justice system. Since the height of the "crack epidemic," federal guidelines have imposed mandatory sentences for crack offenses (a drug often sold in inner-city Latino neighborhoods) that were ten times longer than those for similar amounts of powdered cocaine (a drug more often sold by European Americans that can easily be converted into crack in a matter of minutes). In New York State, Latinos and African-Americans account for 93 percent of all persons incarcerated for drug-related offenses, and Latinos make up fully 32 percent of all inmates (Latino Commission on AIDS 1995).

Epidemiological studies of drug prevalence in Puerto Rico find considerable variation, with some researchers reporting that only 2.4 percent of the population "use and abuse" illegal drugs (García and Colón 1989) while others report rates as high as 8.2 percent of the population (Canino et al. 1993). It is perhaps significant to note that the latter study used only readily available data and did not take into consideration homeless, incarcerated, noninstitutionalized, and other people (e.g., the upper class) who often escape official scrutiny. Overlooking incarcerated people was especially unfortunate, since recent data from the Administración de Corrección (1994) revealed that approximately 70 percent of people sent to prison in 1994 were using illegal drugs and anecdotal evidence suggests that upon discharge from prison even higher percentages use them.

The incarceration of large numbers of young people is a tragedy that affects more than simply those who are locked up; it reverberates through the lives of families and neighborhoods. Family dysfunction and intergenerational strife are among the many unintended consequences of high rates of incarceration (Moore 1995). When men who are already disadvantaged in the legitimate job market are arrested and removed from households for long periods of time (especially given the mandatory minimum sentences that dominate legal systems throughout the United States), already fragile families are further weakened and welfare dependence is increased. Another outcome of the war on drugs has been the growth and proliferation of gangs in prison and neighborhood settings (Curtis and Hamid in press). In New York and Puerto Rico, criminal justice personnel are alarmed because the reliance on prisons in the war on drugs, rather than discouraging or restricting drug use, drug distribution, or crime, had instead facilitated social movement among the prisoners and permitted them to disburse and augment their economic, cultural, and/or political power. In New York City the Latin Kings/Queens have been singled out for special surveillance, and police believe that this street organization is an ultraviolent, supercriminal gang (Curtis

and Hamid in press). In Puerto Rico, Ñetas have been of particular interest
to branches of law enforcement.

Many researchers have documented the connection between law enforcement initiatives and public health (Curtis et al. 1995, Grund et al. 1992,
Wallace 1989). In the current period, the war on drugs has acted as a catalyst to the AIDS epidemic (Bearak 1992, Curtis et al. 1995). AIDS is the leading
cause of death among Latinos in the United States aged 25–44, and more
than half of those deaths are injection-related. The AIDS death rate for
Latinos aged 25-44 is more than double that of European Americans in the
same age group (Ortíz-Torres 1994). In New York State, though Latinos
constitute 32 percent of the inmate population, they account for more than
52 percent of all inmates with HIV/AIDS (Latino Commission on AIDS
1995). Researchers have estimated that the rate of HIV seroprevalence among
injecting drug users in the San Juan, Puerto Rico, area is as high as 45 percent and still rising (Colón 1994), while rates of HIV infection among Latino
injectors in New York City are well below 40 percent and dropping (Des Jarlais
et al. 1994). The unique status of Puerto Rico vis-á-vis the United States is
reflected in the alarming fact that people who live both on the island of Puerto
Rico and in the United States—circular migrants—have a much higher incidence of injection-related AIDS than do other Latino groups living in the
United States (Lindesmith Health Emergency Report 1997).

To understand the impact the war on drugs has had on Puerto Ricans
and other Latinos, it is necessary to explore how the battle has been fought
in both international and domestic arenas.

THE WAR ON DRUGS: LATIN AMERICAN
AND CARIBBEAN EXPERIENCE

The relationship of the United States to Latin America and the Caribbean
has been characterized as one of neocolonialism (Fitzpatrick 1980, Hamid
1997a,b, Horowitz 1983, Johnson 1980). Superficially, this type of relationship is often presented as a humanitarian gesture: the United States helping
its less fortunate neighbors to the south. But the extension of "foreign aid"
to these countries has not been to help them achieve self-sufficiency and self-
determination; it is a means by which the United States has exerted economic and political control over them and extended the reach of global
markets and capitalist enterprise. Recent debates about the "certification" or
"decertification" of countries in the war on drugs is a good example of this
process at work (Bertram and Sharpe 1997).

The war on drugs as defined by the United States requires that cooperative countries use a variety of means to stop the flow of illegal drugs. In
addition to using their own internal resources, such as the army, the judiciary, and economic sanctions, these countries are forced to accept "assis-

tance" from the United States in the form of troops, equipment, technical assistance, and materials (like herbicides) to curtail the production and distribution of illegal drugs (Conklin 1997, Dudley 1997, Press 1997). Countries that refuse the "offer that cannot be refused" are pressured in myriad ways to comply or are blackballed by the "international community" that dances to the U.S.-dictated tune. Ironically, successful drug trafficking on an international level requires political protection on the same level (Marshall 1992), and one of the most critical sources of such institutional protection for the drug trade has been the Central Intelligence Agency (McCoy 1991, Scott 1992). For example, when a top Mexican drug trafficker was arrested in 1975, he testified that "he was a CIA protegee, trained at Fort Jackson as a partisan in the secret war against Castro's Cuba. In return for helping the CIA move weapons to certain groups in Central America, he asserted, the Agency facilitated his movement of heroin and other drugs" (Marshall 1992, p. 198).

The willingness of the United States to abandon the war on drugs in the pursuit of foreign policy objectives suggests that many officials recognized, at some level, the sham it had become. For example, in the 1980s, 20 to 50 percent of the cocaine coming into the United States flowed through Honduras, a passage that was facilitated by an army with close connections to officials in Washington and to the Contras fighting the socialist government of Nicaragua (Scott 1992). The Contra drug connection was empowered by the National Security Act of 1947, which authorized government actions outside normal Congressional review and outside the rule of law. Only later, in the 1989 Kerry Report, did the U.S. Senate Committee on Foreign Relations investigate the connection between the Honduran army, the Contras in Nicaragua, and the flow of cocaine into the United States. Even then, however, few were punished and no new restrictions were placed on covert CIA operations. Latin America was not the first site of U.S. government involvement in increasing the supply of illegal drugs, but recent actions by the United States in several Latin American countries have left a profound impression on local populations. Since the 1980s, Puerto Rico has been an international crossroads for drug trafficking—the Caribbean's drug-smuggling hub (Navarro 1995)—and as such, has been witness to both international and domestic anti-drug strategies.

THE WAR ON DRUGS IN THE UNITED STATES AND PUERTO RICO

The war on drugs in the United States is often traced to the passage of the Harrison Act in 1914, and even earlier in several individual states (Musto 1987). In the late 1920s and '30s the drug war heated up as federal bureaucracies headed by such people as Eliot Ness, Harry Anslinger, and J. Edgar Hoover grew in size and reputation (McWilliams 1990, 1992). In the 1950s, as drug distribution and use became more associated with inner-city urban life and racial and ethnic minorities, a series of draconian laws were enacted that sought to legislate the problem away while simultaneously meting out lengthy prison terms for users and distributors alike. By the 1960s, a period of great experimentation with drugs, the primary responsibility for waging the war on drugs shifted from federal to state and local bodies (Chaisson 1988, Kelling and Moore 1988, Kleiman and Smith 1990).

For New York and other large cities in the United States, the 1960s were also a period of tremendous social, demographic, and economic change. Bustling, viable neighborhoods that thrived on stable manufacturing jobs were replaced by shuttered factories and block after block of abandoned buildings and empty lots. Lacking significant economic opportunity and entering an urban terrain where neighborhood conditions and controls were crumbling, many newcomers found themselves pulled into the orbit of drugs as distributors and/or users (Curtis and Maher 1992, Scharff 1987). As the heroin epidemic that began in 1964 swept across New York City, many new Latino immigrants found themselves well positioned to take over a role that had been largely given up by their predecessors (Preble and Casey 1969). Throughout the 1950s and early 1960s, neighborhood beat cops had kept local-level drug distribution and consumption in check, but when the Knapp Commission of 1968 was convened and police corruption made headlines across the nation, the police took a hands-off policy and concentrated the majority of their antidrug efforts on arresting "Mr. Big" (Kelling and Moore 1988, Kleiman and Smith 1990). This policy of malign neglect allowed drug distribution organizations to build empires in radically transformed neighborhoods that were characterized by their vacuum of political and economic power (Curtis and Maher 1992). From the mid-1960s to the late-1970s, illegal drug distribution in New York City progressed through a series of increasingly complex organizational "stages": from a scene where relatively chaotic freelancers hawked product on the streets, the market evolved to one where family businesses began to exert their dominance over entire blocks.

The street-level drug businesses that were prominent in New York City throughout the 1970s and '80s operated on a two-tiered system much like the economies described in segmented labor market theory: a core of "good" jobs existed for a privileged few while the majority were consigned to low-wage, high-risk, dead-end jobs. Whereas managers could advance through the ranks and enjoy some degree of site mobility, street-level workers found it difficult to advance to the managerial level or decide where they would work. Career options for street-level workers were severely restricted, and by the mid-1980s, when the size and audacity of these organizations fattened by crack sales began to draw the attention of police and policy makers, street-level workers were the frequent casualties of a reinvigorated war on drugs (Sviridoff et al. 1992, Zimmer 1987) Battered by repeated police interventions and struggling in a stagnant market, by the early 1990s, street-level drug markets that had been spread throughout New York City began to contract into a few drug supermarkets. These supermarkets were generally found in neighborhoods where street-level markets had long histories, usually those where heroin had been the dominant drug. For the most part these were Latino neighborhoods. One outcome of this concentration of drug markets into fewer neighborhoods was that the blatancy and visibility of the market brought increased pressure from various branches of law enforcement. For example, between 1988 and 1992, 8,168 arrests were made in Bushwick by the Police Department's Narcotics Divisions (Curtis et al. 1995).

In Puerto Rico, due to its colonial status, the war on drugs generally followed in the footsteps of strategies and tactics applied in the United States. Even though drug markets in the 1960s and '70s were largely confined to the *"caseríos"* (projects or public housing) and operated by residents who lived there, between 1968 and 1974 the government of Puerto Rico created bureaucracies to address the problem and enacted a series of strict laws (similar to the Rockefeller laws in New York) that increased sentences for possessing, trafficking, or selling illegal drugs. In the mid-1980s, as the appetite for smokable cocaine ballooned in the United States, the drug scene in Puerto Rico was fatefully affected. Drug trafficking expanded throughout the island, no longer confined to the *caseríos* or controlled by their residents, and Puerto Ricans too became major consumers of cocaine. The island also became a major transit point for drugs headed for the United States, preferred by major traffickers because "it is geographically convenient to both South and North America, and, because of its commonwealth status, once a drug shipment is in Puerto Rico customs inspections are no longer a factor" (Navarro 1995).

The war on drugs in Puerto Rico that began in the late 1960s kept local markets in turmoil by keeping distributors and users circulating between neighborhoods and jail, and the infusion of cocaine dollars in the 1980s further destabilized the situation by providing opportunities for new organizations to vie for control of local and international markets. As competition between upstart distributors grew, so did the rates of violence and homicide. By the early 1990s, after the number of homicides had doubled in less than five years, the government adopted dramatic measures to regain control of the situation and in 1993 deployed the National Guard to more than seventy housing projects and communities where they arrested thousands of distributors and users. The first target of this experimental intervention (a trial balloon closely watched in the United States) was Nemesio Canales, a notorious housing project where drug distribution had been entrenched since the 1950s. While the government and media trumpeted the success of their drive against out-of-control drug markets, and overshadowed the damage done to abrogated civil rights, evidence suggests that the problem was simply displaced to other neighborhoods and cities in Puerto Rico. For example, in Manati, a small town located thirty minutes from San Juan, homicides went from two in 1992 to twenty-seven in 1994 after distributors moved there to escape pressures that had been applied in the capital (Navarro 1995).

Puerto Ricans, having witnessed how the war on drugs is waged in international and domestic domains, have long been among its most prominent and tragic victims. This is a powerful impetus to initiate new strategies based on humanistic and realistic alternatives, such as harm reduction and drug legalization rather than further mobilization of an ineffective war on drugs. While the statistical information and broad historical accounts cited above give some indication of the impact the war on drugs has had on individual Puerto Ricans, their families, and their culture, it cannot convey the entire scope of the indelible legacy that it has left on the Puerto Rican people. But after having their neighborhoods occupied by armed soldiers, their young people interred in maximum security prisons or gunned down in internecine disputes, their health compromised by ignorance and neglect, and their economy battered by the economic whirlwind of international drug trafficking, Puerto Ricans would clearly benefit from a truce or armistice in the war on drugs.

To illustrate the complexity and depth of the injury, a case study of the Santurce family is presented below.[3] Its members were observed and repeatedly interviewed in Puerto Rico and New York over the last decade. To gain an accurate account of significant events and milestones in their lives, interviews were often triangulated and discrepancies discussed with individual members. A full account of the family cannot be provided in the limited space available here. Instead, highlights (or rather "lowlights") of members' involvements with drug markets, drug use, and the war on drugs are briefly detailed. Already pushed to the precipice of abject poverty and struggling to survive in a system heavily weighted against them, the Santurce family was chosen to illustrate how the difficult everyday lives of Puerto Ricans were further made miserable by the war on drugs.

CASE STUDY: THE SANTURCE FAMILY

The Santurce household was one filled with violence, turmoil, abuse, and dysfunction. When Don Esteban and Doña María got married in 1950, he brought three children from a previous marriage: Papo born in 1948, Chiquin in 1949, and William in 1950. The couple eventually had six

---

[3]The names of all family members are fictitious.

children themselves: Carlos in 1951, Wiso in 1952, Cheo in 1953, Bertin in 1959, Evelyn in 1961, and Samuel in 1967. Don Esteban was illiterate and had never found legitimate, mainstream employment. Living on his own since age 6, he supported himself by doing odd jobs for prostitutes, drug dealers, and *bancas* (gambling houses). He was also an alcoholic and a gambler, and during the time that he lived with his wife, Doña María, he often physically abused her in front of the children. For about ten years, in the 1950s and '60s, he worked for his brother-in-law and later for his youngest brother, helping them run their drug business. His responsibility in the business was to supply heroin and marijuana to twenty or thirty dealers who sold on local corners.

In the 1950s the Santurce family lived in one of the most notorious *caseríos* (public housing projects) in Hato Rey, Puerto Rico. The Nemesio Canales was an experimental, self-contained *caserío* of approximately 100 buildings surrounded by two major highways, the National Guard, the Police Department, and a large shopping mall. With only a single access road in and out, it was extremely isolated and without social services, and quickly became mired in poverty, crime, violence, and drug abuse. To escape the worsening situation in Nemesio Canales and a police crackdown in the neighborhood, the Santurce family moved to New York City's Lower East Side in 1960 and lived there for a little more than two years. Near the end of 1962, Don Esteban's brother started a new drug business in Puerto Rico and Don Esteban was called back to be part of this project. In 1963 the family returned to Puerto Rico and shortly thereafter moved into a smaller, more secure *caserío* in San Juan, San Juan Bautista. Though this neighborhood was considered to be better than Nemesio Canales, it had many similar problems, including a nearby public park that was a visible center for drug sales. For the children of the Santurce household, and many others, to get to school, church, or the store they had to cross the park. The park was also a favored meeting place and the Santurce children would meet in the park whenever they could to "hang out" among friends and observe the action. To make matters worse, Puerto Rico's first methadone maintenance program opened near the park, drawing hundreds of heroin users from throughout the area.

As the children grew, they too became part of the drug business. Papo and Chiquin were the first two to be initiated into it. Their responsibility was to help their father keep the various *puntos* (drug-selling spots) supplied. William, Carlos, Wiso, and Cheo got involved in the mid-1960s. Don Esteban was always strict about his children's involvement in the business, and told them, "Don't tell your mother about what we are doing. You distribute this shit, but I don't want to see any of you using it because I'll kill you." On several occasions, when he saw his sons hanging out in the streets, he beat them because he suspected they were using drugs.

Don Esteban was a well-known figure in the community and among local police. In 1968 he and his brother were arrested. Don Esteban began an eight-year sentence for drug trafficking and his brother got twenty-five years in federal prison in California for importing drugs into Puerto Rico. Three weeks after Don Esteban was incarcerated, Doña María filed for divorce. With her husband absent, she was forced into the job market, leaving the children with no adult supervision at home. She supported the family by finding off-the-books employment: cleaning houses, selling cooked food, and doing laundry for families in wealthy communities. She made enough money to supply only the barest of essentials, and paid the price with the loss of control over her family. She refused to discipline the children as her husband had, and turned to the church for psychological, spiritual, and emotional support. Despite her strong faith, the economic and social situation never improved, but got progressively worse.

Lacking adult supervision and role models, the Santurce children began to find their own way in the neighborhood and on the streets. Five of the eight brothers continued to work in the drug business, but because their father and uncle no longer controlled the drug supply, they were forced to participate in much riskier endeavors, selling drugs at the *puntos* rather than supplying them. Selling drugs at a *punto* was dangerous, and the children were compelled to carry weapons to protect themselves and others who sold drugs with them. Working full-time at various *puntos*, the five brothers eventually dropped out of school, starting smoking marijuana and, later, using (injecting) heroin. As their heroin habits increased and their superiors began to mistrust them, the brothers' responsibilities in the drug business decreased. Unable to support their habits and lifestyles by distributing drugs, they eventually began to break into cars and apartments and to rob tourists in San Juan. In less than four years (between 1968 and 1972), six of the boys (Papo, Chiquin, William, Carlos, Cheo, and Bertin) had become injecting drug users and notorious delinquents in the criminal justice system. Some of them went to juvenile hall and most of them later to jail.

The family's stability was further undermined by the constant migration of the children between San Juan and New York City. Their migration was rooted in soured drug transactions, escape from homicide charges, or to avoid the repercussions of stealing. Space does not permit a full account of the children's lives and how they impacted upon the extended family. A brief description of the outcome of each person's involvement with drugs is summarized below. Because we concentrate exclusively on this facet of their lives, there is the danger that readers will understand the Santurce children only through the narrow dimensions of drugs and criminality without appreciating the complexity of their social lives, but to illuminate the impact of drug prohibition and the war on drugs on Puerto Ricans, this concentration is necessary.

DON ESTEBAN

Now 83 years old and supported by public assistance, he lives by himself in a *caserío* in Villa Palmera, San Juan, Puerto Rico.

DOÑA MARÍA

Now 65, she never remarried and currently lives in her *caserío* apartment supported by social security benefits.

PAPO

Papo spent most of his life in prison in Puerto Rico; unlike most of his siblings, he never came to New York. His first arrest—for stealing, at age 14 (1962)—resulted in his being sent to juvenile hall. His next two arrests, for selling drugs at a *punto*, occurred at ages 17 and 20, and he was sent to prison at La Princesa and Oso Blanco, respectively. It was in prison, at age 22, that Papo began using (injecting) heroin; upon release he became a total street junkie, living in parks and cars. Arrested for stealing in 1975, he was sent back to Oso Blanco for another three years. Released in 1978, Papo returned to the same lifestyle on the streets, disconnected from family and friends. In 1980 he was shot three times in the back after taking a $5 bag of heroin from a seller's hand. He died on the spot at the age of 32.

Papo had two common-law wives, and had fathered one child with each of them: one boy and one girl. Both children met fates similar to their father's. Papo's son died of a heroin overdose in 1982 when he was 13 years old. His daughter was found dead of gun shots in a parking lot in 1986 when she was 14 years old, after she and her boyfriend stole drugs from a dealer.

CHIQUIN

Chiquin's first arrest, for selling marijuana to tourists in El Condado, was in 1968 when he was 18 years old. He received a strict sentence of four years and was sent to Oso Blanco prison. (At this time in Puerto Rico, any crime related to marijuana was punished severely, especially when it occurred in the tourist section.) Upon his release, Chiquin started selling drugs (heroin, cocaine, and marijuana) at a *punto* and was arrested in 1975 after he shot someone who owed him money. Sentenced to fifteen years in Oso Blanco, he served six years and was released on probation in 1981. Upon his release, Chiquin's wife refused to allow him back in the home, so he lived alone and went back to selling heroin at a *punto*. By 1983 his drug habit had escalated to the point where he could no longer take care of business and he started stealing to support his drug use. When his youngest daughter was born in 1983, Chiquin went to get her birth certificate and was shot six times in the chest by two dealers from whom he had stolen two bags of heroin ($10 worth). He died immediately at the age of 34.

After they split up, Chiquin's wife was hospitalized for LSD-induced psychosis. Their three children, two girls and a boy, were remanded to foster care and were never reintegrated back into the family. Family members see them occasionally and report that each has become an injecting drug user, preferring "speedballs" (a mixture of heroin and cocaine).

WILLIAM

William had a nasty, confrontational attitude toward people, and his first arrest, at the age of 15, was for assault. In 1971, at the age of 20, he was arrested by undercover police for using and selling drugs (heroin, cocaine, and marijuana) at a *punto* and sentenced to two years at La Princesa. In 1973 he was released on probation and opened a tire-repair shop. For a short period he used neither heroin nor cocaine (using only marijuana), nor did he sell any. Eventually, however, William began to supplement his income by selling heroin from the shop; in 1975 he was arrested for it and served five years in Oso Blanco. Upon release in 1980, William came to New York where he lived with his brothers in El Barrio and became a heavy heroin user. To support his habit, he began working for drug organizations in the neighborhood and was arrested in 1986 at 116th Street and Lexington Avenue, by undercover agents who followed him after he took delivery of a supply of drugs. After serving one year on Rikers Island, he was released on parole and fled to Puerto Rico, where he moved back in with his wife. In 1988 he was arrested for selling heroin at a *punto* after the other suspects had fled the scene. Evidence (guns and drugs) left at the scene was pinned on William, and he was sentenced to five years, which he served at Oso Blanco and Humacao prisons. After developing AIDS while in prison in 1991, he was released to a Christian residential rehabilitation program where he died in 1992, at the age of 42.

William's wife had died of AIDS two years earlier, in 1990. She was an injecting drug user who shared injection equipment with other users and had had unprotected sex with her husband. After his wife died, their three daughters (9, 10, and 11 at the time) were placed in foster care and were never reintegrated back into the family. Like Chiquin's children, all three of them were initiated into drug use while they were in foster care; at the present time their drug of choice is injected speedballs.

CARLOS

Carlos's first arrest came at the age of 14, for assaulting another youth in a drug-related altercation. Sent to juvenile detention in Hato Rey and then to Mayaguez, Carlos became very aggressive and violent, and his drug use (marijuana, heroin, and cocaine) escalated. He escaped from juvenile hall when he was 16 (1971) and fled to El Barrio, East Harlem, in New York City. Soon after, Carlos was selling drugs for organizations based near Lexington Avenue and 116th Street, but was quickly arrested and imprisoned in Sing-Sing for two years. Returning to El Barrio in 1973, he killed two people who he thought had informed on him and then fled to his mother's home in Puerto Rico. Carlos began selling drugs with his brothers again and within a year was arrested at one of the *puntos* for selling heroin. To avoid going to prison, Carlos enrolled in several drug-rehabilitation programs, including Hogar Crea, a private program where many offenders went to avoid prison sentences. When he dropped out of the program, Carlos was incarcerated at La Princesa and Oso Blanco, where he spent the next two years continuing to inject drugs with impunity. In 1977 Carlos was briefly hospitalized in a psychiatric facility, diagnosed with paranoid schizophrenia. After returning to New York in 1978, he was spotted by relatives of the two men he had killed five years earlier. They put Carlos in a car, took him to St. Ann's Avenue and 138th Street in the South Bronx, and shot him twice in the head. Carlos survived, but spent ten months in Lincoln Hospital undergoing intense physical rehabilitation. He eventually returned to El Barrio where he continued to live, using and selling drugs, until 1984, when he returned to Puerto Rico because his health had deteriorated. Hospitalized with full-blown AIDS in 1985, he died in Puerto Rico at the age of 35.

Unlike most of his siblings, Carlos never married and had no children.

CHEO

Cheo's first arrest, for stealing and fighting at age 15 (1968), resulted in his being sent to juvenile detention in Hato Rey. After five months he escaped from the facility and returned to the streets where he started selling drugs at a *punto* with his brothers. At the age of 17 he was asleep in his mother's apartment when he was arrested for selling drugs by undercover narcotics detectives. He served eighteen months at La Princesa before he was released on parole. Violating the conditions of his parole, Cheo fled to El Barrio in New York City where he stayed with his brothers and worked for a Puerto Rican drug-selling organization. At age 24 (1972) he was arrested by undercover police who caught him with a gun, heroin, and cocaine in a briefcase. After serving three years at an upstate prison, Cheo's parole officer in 1975 recommended him for a job working in a parking lot at a hospital in the Bronx. Cheo was abstinent from cocaine and heroin for two years (smoking only marijuana), but supplemented his wages by selling heroin as a freelancer from the parking lot. In 1980 a competitor in the drug business set him up. As he came out of the subway, corrupt undercover police arrested him and subsequently testified that he was apprehended with weapons and drugs. Cheo served six years at two different upstate prisons and returned to El Barrio in 1986. He avoided selling drugs for about a year and was only using cocaine and marijuana when he began to smoke crack. Unable to find employment even with drug distributors, he collected refundable bottles in the street and broke into cars and apartments to survive until he was arrested for burglary in 1988 and served two years at Riker's Island. When he was released in 1990, Cheo was rehired at his previous job at the parking lot, but it was with the explicit understanding he would again sell drugs as part of his work. After a domestic dispute with his wife in 1996, he was arrested for possession of cocaine and sent to prison. Shortly after, his wife "divorced" him.

Cheo and his common-law wife had begun their relationship when he was 16 and she was 18 years old. Both had used drugs and eventually became injectors. Cheo is "sick," but refuses to take an HIV test. His ex-wife's serostatus is unknown. Their only child, a son, was born in 1972 in Puerto Rico.

BERTIN

Unlike his brothers, Bertin was never arrested as a juvenile and was never arrested in Puerto Rico. He started using drugs (marijuana, and later injecting speedballs) when he was 15 years old (1975), and was selling drugs in the family business when he was 16. Bertin was somewhat protected by the close associations he developed with several police officials who employed him to obtain stolen merchandise. They also used Bertin to resell drugs they had seized from dealers they had arrested. In addition to these services, Bertin furnished cash to them when they asked him for it.

In 1983, to avoid arrest and retaliation after he shot a competitor for control of a *punto*, Bertin came to El Barrio in New York City. Like his brothers, he began to sell marijuana, cocaine, and heroin in El Barrio, but also worked as a freelance distributor in Central Park. Always well dressed, not standing in one spot too long, and using a bicycle to conduct business, Bertin managed to avoid being arrested in the park. But his luck ran out in 1985 when he was arrested by undercover police officers after picking up heroin in El Barrio. Because this was his first arrest, Bertin received probation with the stipulation that he find legitimate employment. He managed to convince the superintendent of his apartment building to tell his probation officer that he was working there, but he continued to sell drugs.

Bertin's next arrest, in 1989 at age 30, was at the Puerto Rican Day parade on 5th Avenue in Manhattan. He was intoxicated when he was arrested for selling cocaine, crack cocaine, and marijuana to revelers at the parade. Sentenced to six years in prison, Bertin was released on parole in 1990 after being diagnosed with AIDS. Family members believed that Bertin's release was not so much an act of compassion on behalf of the Department of Corrections, but rather a way of the lowering the alarming number and rate of AIDS deaths in New York State prisons. Bertin returned to Puerto Rico in 1990 and was hospitalized immediately. He died six months later in the hospital.

Bertin had a common-law wife but no children. She was also an injecting drug user and was diagnosed with AIDS in 1990. Family members subsequently lost contact with her and do not know whether she is still alive.

EVELYN

Evelyn never sold drugs in Puerto Rico, nor was she ever arrested there. She had three common-law husbands whose main occupation was selling drugs (marijuana, cocaine, and heroin), and each smoked marijuana and sniffed cocaine. Evelyn primarily smoked marijuana, but she experimented with sniffing cocaine and heroin. Unlike many of her siblings, she never injected drugs. In 1993 Evelyn moved with her four children to Lynn, Massachusetts, where she and her children began selling drugs to support themselves. In 1996 she suffered a cocaine-induced stroke that destroyed most of her brain, and she is currently an in-patient at a brain rehabilitation center. She cannot talk, see, move her hands, or walk, and can hear only a little through her right ear. After her accident her children were placed with her grandmother in Hato Rey, Puerto Rico. All four children, ranging in age from 14 to 20, are currently both using and selling drugs (cocaine and crack cocaine). The two oldest children are also on probation in Puerto Rico for drug sales.

SAMUEL

Samuel started smoking marijuana when he was about 13 years old, in 1980. At 14 he started sniffing heroin; three years later he started skin popping cocaine and heroin, progressing to intravenous use almost immediately. To support his habit, Samuel sold heroin and cocaine as a freelancer, and stole from cars and homes. As his habit increased, he started robbing people and even physically attacking them, targeting tourists in the Condado area of San Juan. Samuel was arrested several times for assault, larceny, and robbery, but managed to avoid prison each time by admitting himself into drug-rehabilitation programs. In 1983, at age 16, Samuel's first incarceration was for fighting and stealing and he was placed in a juvenile facility.

Samuel was the only one of his siblings who didn't sell at a *punto*; he worked for Cubans transporting cocaine in Puerto Rico and occasionally to New York, starting out as a bodyguard/hitman. Samuel used the profits from his criminal activities to support his habit and his family. This income, along with his other siblings' economic gains from drug selling, was very much needed by the family; for this reason, his mother found it very difficult to chastise Samuel, or any of her other children, for their activities.

In 1984, at the age of 17, Samuel was convicted of possession of cocaine and heroin. He was first sent to Oso Blanco and later to Humacao Prison and served six years. While in Humacao, Samuel was a key figure in the prison's drug business. Paying off the guards, he was let out once a week to go to the neighborhood, buy drugs, and bring them back to prison. He did this until he became ill with AIDS in 1990. Family members were angry because he had exhibited symptoms for eight months before medical staff diagnosed his condition; then, despite being terminally ill, he was not released so that he could die with dignity at home. Two weeks before he died in 1990, at the age of 23, Samuel was finally sent to a hospital. All of Samuel's closest friends from the community who were with him in prison, along with his brother, Bertin, died in the same year from AIDS.

Samuel had two common-law wives and had one child from each, a boy and a girl. Both of his former spouses remarried after ending their relationships with Samuel. One now lives in Los Angeles, one lives in upstate New York. Neither of his former wives ever used drugs, nor did his children. Samuel's son is now 11 years old and his daughter is 8. Both live with their mothers, their stepfathers, and their siblings. They maintain no relationship with their father's family.

WISO

The only child who did not become a direct victim of the war on drugs was Wiso. Although he was involved with his father's drug business as a boy, Wiso did not continue distributing drugs when his father went to prison. At the age of 12 he became involved with a minister from the neighborhood United Methodist Church. He continued to attend school even though he was socially isolated and extremely aggressive. At age 14, after hitting a teacher with a chair, he was psychologically evaluated and diagnosed as mentally retarded, instead of as an emotionally disturbed child (e.g., post-traumatic stress disorder). School authorities recommended Wiso's placement in a vocational institution because they felt he did not have the capacity to continue in regular classes. However, the minister and his mother decided that Wiso would live with the minister. Doña María was grateful for the opportunity that this represented and often said, "At least I am going to save one." The minister's household was a middle-class environment in which the parents and their four children often talked about going to college and embarking on professional careers. Wiso stayed with the family until he was 18 years old, and started college in 1969, eventually completing a doctorate in clinical psychology. He later went to a seminary and became an Anglican (Episcopalian) priest. Currently living in the United States and working as an Anglican priest and as a psychologist, Wiso has three children. His two oldest children live in Puerto Rico. One is in college, the other is in high school, anticipating going to college there. His 9-year-old son lives with him.

DISCUSSION

Of the nine Santurce siblings, only three remain alive today. Two of the brothers, Papo and Chiquin, died from drug-related violence. Four—William, Carlos, Bertin, and Samuel—succumbed to drug-injection-related AIDS. At present Cheo is in prison in upstate New York. A total of fifty years in prison has been served by the Santurce siblings. Evelyn, the only sister, remains alive, but is virtually brain-dead. Only Wiso, whose good fortune allowed him to escape the environment that claimed his siblings, remains drug- and arrest-free. As the only child to have escaped the ravages of the war on drugs, his case is important in that it demonstrates that the problems people have associated with illegal drugs are not the outcome of genetic, ethnic, or cultural differences, but rather the product of a system in which the cards are unfairly stacked.

The Santurce family was in many ways typical of many Puerto Rican families in the 1950s and '60s: separated from rural life, but without the opportunity or skills to compete for the few good jobs in the modern, capitalist sector of the economy. Through family cohesion, barter, exchange, and reliance on income generated through jobs in the informal sector, many were able to cobble together an uncertain existence on the fringe between these two worlds. In other regions of the global economy, informal-sector activities have sometimes provided a relatively stable economic environment, and have even provided the foundation for capitalist development (Schneider et al. 1972), but consumer tastes in the United States have dictated that the most lucrative opportunity in the informal sector in Puerto Rico is found in trafficking illegal drugs. While participation in the drug economy has enriched a few individuals and families, like the Santurces, the majority have posted significant losses in a contest whose odds are weighted heavily against them. The war on drugs has resulted in unprecedented family and neighborhood disruption and violence (Curtis and Hamid in press, Moore 1995, Wallace and Wallace 1989), more victimization, high rates of arrest (Moore 1995), unfair and inconsistent treatment from the criminal justice system (Nadelmann 1988), disproportionately harsh sentences, unnecessary drug overdoses, and public health crises by contributing to the spread of AIDS and other pathogens (Bearak 1992, Curtis et al. 1995, Grund et al. 1992).

The war on drugs has also devastated the extended families of the Santurce household. Death by AIDS or divorce has been the result of their unions. Among the eighteen children of the Santurce siblings, two died of drug-related violence at a young age. Eleven of them have used and/or sold drugs. The five children who remain relatively unscathed by the war on drugs were lucky enough to have been raised in middle-class environments, far removed from the skirmishes that claimed their elders.

Among Puerto Rican families, the Santurces may be atypical in the number of members annihilated under the current system of drug prohibition, but their case resonates with many of the problems that have affected Puerto Ricans on the island and in New York. Clearly, many of the problems the family suffered were not of their own making. The lack of significant economic opportunity in Puerto Rico and New York City ensured that family members would survive only through participation in the informal sector of the economy. Especially in Puerto Rico, where *caserios* were constructed in such a way as to enclose and isolate populations, the ability to find legitimate employment was virtually impossible. In this environment daily survival for the Santurce family meant earning money by doing odd jobs for sex workers, drug dealers, and *bancas*. As the most lucrative and consistent source of employment in the area, drug distribution proved irrestible to most of the Santurce brothers and they were pulled into drug distribution and use with disastrous results. The involvement of family members in this lifestyle was not entirely a matter of individual choice. As other drug researchers have noted, the same interests "that shape conditions of working-class life are also significant in shaping conditions of illegal drug use" (Waterston 1993, p. 242). The physical and social isolation experienced by Puerto Ricans living in *caserios* may tempt observers to interpret their behavior as being governed by a different set of rules than those followed by the mainstream, but there is no *"caserio* culture" (or *culture of poverty*, to use Oscar Lewis's term) and it would be a grave mistake to imagine that these neighborhoods function in isolation or opposition to the larger system of which they are part. To make sense of the outcomes observed in the *caserios*, and the Santurce family in particular, we cannot rely on antiquated psychological concepts like pathological, dysfunctional, deviant, borderline, irresponsible, criminal, sick, or psychotic personalities. Rather, *caserio* residents need to be seen as actors in a wider (international) arena who are responsive to economic inequality, class conflict, political power, and the hegemony of cultural forms (Morgan 1983, Perlman 1976). They also react viscerally to the "indirect violence" visited upon them by a capitalist system that chokes off economic empowerment and promotes poverty and social inequality (Salmi 1993).

Puerto Rico, like many countries in the third world, has gone through a period of rapid modernization without significant economic development (Barrios 1997a, Schneider et al. 1972). By this we mean that Puerto Ricans are increasingly exposed to consumer goods that they are encouraged to buy (in the many shopping malls that proliferate there), but have not been given the economic means to support this style of spending. Economic development strategies like Operation Bootstrap proved beneficial to the United States, but did little for the majority of Puerto Ricans. Indeed, while denying the Puerto Rican people genuine economic development, it brought them into the ever-expanding world of homogenized consumerism where cultural differences are rendered insignificant (Giddens 1991). Traditional Puerto Rican values that emphasized "family loyalties, personal relationships, individual dignity and respect" (Fitzpatrick 1980, p. 48) have been cast aside as obsolete and unworthy of modern life. The cultural crisis this has brought has led many Puerto Ricans to have second thoughts about the processes of modernization that have been forced upon them, and many are beginning to resist the encroachment of a uniform capitalist culture through their reinvention and/or reinvigoration of Puerto Rican nationalism. For many Puerto Rican men denied an opportunity to advance economically, the ability to survive and create an identity independent of mainstream society has been a source of pride. The "defiant *jíbaro*," the *caserío* hustler, and the Spanish Harlem crack dealer have all existed out of necessity and as forms of resistance to U.S. domination. According to Bourgois (1995):

> They refused to succumb to elite society's denigration under Spanish and U.S. colonialism. The hyper-urban reconstruction of a hip-hop version of the rural jíbaro represents the triumph of a newly constituted Puerto Rican cultural assertion among the most marginalized members of the Puerto Rican diaspora. The tragedy is that the material base for this determined search for cultural respect is confined to the street economy. [p. 326]

While in the process of making themselves and constructing identities that clashed with mainstream society, these Puerto Ricans lacked insight into their own social position. Samuel Santurce, for example, often said, "Gringos know how to do things better." This was a generalization he used in referring to employment, medical care, housing, and so on. He believed the system tended to work better in the United States than in Puerto Rico and maintained: "I don't know what the hell we're gonna do without the Gringos in Puerto Rico. They give us *cupones* [food stamps], they protect us from Castro. . . ." To Samuel, the enemy was not the United States, which structured the conditions of his everyday life—if anything, they represented an ideal for him—the enemies for him were the other drug dealers in the neighborhood. Like the colonized described by Fanon (1961), the aggressiveness that permeates everyday life is not directed at the colonizer, but rather is transformed into self-aggression and collective self-destruction. As Maldonado-Denis (1961) has noted:

> Colonialism is not merely a system based upon the economic exploitation and the political domination of one nation over another. It is also—and this is vital to its existence—an instrument of cultural penetration and psychological aggression. [p. 13]

Considering the character of colonialism helps us solve the mystery of how the crime rate in Puerto Rico—especially for violent crime—continues to increase, while crime in the United States, particularly in New York City, has dropped to unprecedented lows in the last several years (Krauss 1997). While it is argued that the war on drugs acts to increase rather than decrease violence (Barrios 1997b, Curtis and Hamid in Press), this premise does not account for the huge statistical discrepancy between New York City and Puerto Rico. Both regions have deployed similar tactics in waging their wars against illegal drugs. To understand why Puerto Rico surpasses every city in the United States in such unenviable categories as violent crime, murder, AIDS deaths, and overdoses, it is necessary to look beyond the obvious (and even not so obvious) explanations and examine the one feature that differentiates Puerto Rico from other places: its unique colonial status. There is an urgent need for further qualitative and quantitative research into the relationship between capitalist development colonialism, and the war on drugs as it impacts upon the Puerto Rican people.

Colonialism, of course, is not the only, or even the primary reason why Puerto Rico is plagued with drug-related violence. Ultimately, in a system of drug prohibition, violence is the only recourse that distributors have to ensure that market transactions occur as expected. But drug markets are not equally violent and those that are highly regulated and regimented typically exhibit less violence than those that are frequently disrupted by market forces or law enforcement initiatives (Curtis and Hamid in press, Reuter and Kleiman 1986). As illustrated by the Santurce family case study, Puerto Rico has clearly experienced tremendous dislocation of drug markets during the last decade; much of the violence the island has experienced has been an outcome of those changes. Further complicating the problem of drug-related violence has been the pattern of cyclical migration that has discouraged the local resolution of disputes, and has instead brought New York's unresolved problems to Puerto Rico and Puerto Rico's problems to New York. The manner in which cyclical migration contributes to the perpetuation of violence was clearly seen in the examples of Carlos and Bertin Santurce, who fled to New York and Puerto Rico following their involvements in violent episodes.

The violence associated with illegal drugs is not always an outcome of drug distributors or users committing reciprocated acts of revenge. Law enforcement agencies are also notorious for using excessive force (often against innocent people) in waging the war on drugs. But the war is not always waged by assault teams with high-powered rifles and bulletproof vests; sometimes the war proceeds by omission rather than commission (Salmi 1993). By selectively neglecting drug distribution and consumption when it benefits them to do so, law enforcement agencies have an impact on drug markets and abet processes that undermine families and neighborhoods. In the last few decades police officers who worked every day in Puerto Rico's caseríos were well aware of which residents were involved with illegal drugs, and in March 1996 hundreds were arrested when seventy-four caseríos were overrun by the National Guard and

police, an occupying army with a $25-million annual budget. Prior to this all-
out assault, the police were able to effectively control local populations through
the selective application of their authority and choosing to ignore or arrest
people at their discretion.

Many researchers have suggested that drug distributors and users perform a valuable role in maintaining the status quo by providing "symbolic
images of deviance and decadence" (Waterston 1993, p. 242) that serve to pit
different sectors of a population against each other. In Puerto Rico there is
little doubt that drug market participants have been demonized in such a way
that attention is drawn away from other social problems. The demonization
of drug users in Puerto Rico was facilitated by the fact that, at one time, much
of the problem was confined to *caseríos*, conveniently tucked away from public scrutiny. Yet the social problems associated with drugs were never exclusive to the *caseríos* and the explosion of AIDS cases in Puerto Rico in recent
years has made the problem impossible to overlook any longer, if for no other
reason than the enormous amount of money it will cost the state to address
it.

Today Puerto Rico stands at a crossroads. The country must choose
between waging a U.S.-style war on drugs (which has thus far held disastrous
consequences for Puerto Ricans) or using their political will to fashion a local
solution to the problem. Many Puerto Ricans are deeply cynical about the
current U.S.-led war on drugs. On the one hand, they see that huge and ever-
increasing commitments of money are spent on law enforcement personnel and
equipment, underscoring the U.S. government's dedication to the war. On the
other hand, the regularity with which covert government operatives under-
write and support known drug producers and traffickers is in direct conflict
with U.S. policy objectives. One conclusion is hypocrisy: the United States is
interested in waging a war on drugs only when it suits the country's interests,
but is perfectly willing to suspend the war to achieve other foreign policy
objectives. Illegal drugs are a crisis only when it is politically expedient for them
to be so.

The fact that some drugs (e.g., marijuana and heroin) are illegal while
others enjoy governmental protections (e.g., tobacco and alcohol) is an outcome of political economy, not pharmacology or sound scientific reasoning
(Musto 1987). One hundred years ago in the United States, when the temperance movement was gaining steam, alcohol was the object of scorn by genteel
men and women who would relax at the end of a day of protest by sipping on
opium-based elixirs (Inciardi 1986). Today alcohol is served in the White House
and opiate users are widely thought to be the scourge of the earth. But the
rationale for criminalizing some drugs while protecting others is coming under increasing scrutiny by a scientific community and general public that has
grown tired of the never-ending war on drugs (Benoit 1989, McCoy and Block

1992, Nadelmann 1989, Trebach 1993). Tobacco and alcohol are implicated in the deaths of more than 520,000 U.S. citizens per year (Nadelmann 1989), yet all the illegal drugs combined account for merely 3,600 drug-related deaths, and the majority of these deaths "occur not as a result of the drug used but as a result of drug laws" (Kappeler et al. 1996, p. 3). Still, any suggestion that drug laws need to be reformed is met with great consternation and fury on the part of public officials and law enforcement personnel. Police officials have built vast empires in waging this war that cannot be won, and their interests are clearly to spend more rather than less money in the ongoing campaign. Politicians, too, find the war on drugs to be expedient since it allows them to strike a noble pose as defenders of the public good while ignoring larger problems like poverty, racism, and violent crime. Clearly though, the war on drugs has been an unmitigated failure—particularly for Puerto Ricans—and it is time for genuine public debate on reforming the current system of drug prohibition.

In our view, it is time that the Latino community and the Puerto Rican community in particular (in Puerto Rico and the United States) open an earnest debate on alternatives to the disastrous system of drug prohibition, a dialogue that must seriously consider controlled legalization as an alternative. Encouraging steps toward drug legalization, which often include the principles of harm reduction and have few negative social consequences, have been tried elsewhere (Barrios 1997b, Colón 1994, Inciardi and McElrath 1995, Nadelmann 1988, Nevares-Muñiz 1996, Santiago-Negrón 1993). We envision a system in which Puerto Ricans will discard the legacy of violence and death associated with black market drug trafficking, find themselves able to proudly earn and save money, reduce the levels of crime and victimization associated with illegal drugs, avoid repeated and prolonged contact with police and the criminal justice system, restore civil liberties abrogated in the war on drugs, and find moderation in their use of all drugs without the risks of accidental overdose or disease. If steps are not soon taken to reach these goals, the sacrifice of an entire generation to the war on drugs will remain meaningless.

REFERENCES

Administración de Corrección (1994). *Perfil de la Población Total Sentenciada al 30 de Junio de 1994.* Gobierno de Puerto Rico.

Barrios, L. (1997a). *Seditious conspiracy: the struggle for political independence and the criminalization of Puerto Rican Independentistas.* Paper presented at the New York State Political Association, 51st Annual Conference. John Jay College of Criminal Justice. New York, April.

——— (1997b). The war on drugs: the fuel for violence in our urban cities. Paper presented at the conference on Violence and the Criminal Justice System. Inter American University of Puerto Rico, San Juan, Puerto Rico, February.

Bearak, B. (1992). In war on drugs, battle against AIDS falls behind. *Los Angeles Times*, September 28, p. 1.

Benoit, E. (1989). The case for legalization. *Financial World.* October 3, pp. 32–35.

Bertram, E., and Sharpe, K. (1997). The drug war's phony fix: why certification doesn't work. *The Nation*, April 28, pp. 18–22.

Bonilla, F., and Campos, R. (1986). *Industry and Idleness*. Centro de Estudios Puertorriqueño. New York: Hunter College, City University of New York.

Bourgois, P. (1989). In search of Horatio Alger: culture and ideology in the crack economy. *Contemporary Drug Problems* 16:619–649.

———— (1995). *In Search of Respect: Selling Crack in El Barrio*. New York: Cambridge University Press.

Canino, G., Anthony, J., Freeman, D., et al. (1993). Drug abuse in Puerto Rico. *American Journal of Public Health* 83(2).

Chaisson, M. R. (1988). *Street-Level Drug Enforcement: Examining the Issues*. Washington, DC: National Institute of Justice.

Colón, H. M. (1994). Recomendaciones Para la Prevención de la Epidemia de VIH Entre Usuarios de Drogas en Puerto Rico. *Centro de Estudios Puertorriqueños, Bulletin*, vol. VI, Nos. 1 & 2. New York: Hunter College, City University of New York.

Conklin, M. (1997). Terror stalks a Colombian town. *The Progressive*, February, pp. 23–25.

Cordero-Guzmán, H. R. (1996). Some contradictions of dependent development in Puerto Rico in the context of global economy. Unpublished paper. Centro de Estudios Puertorriqueños. New York: Hunter College, City University of New York.

Curtis, R., Friedman S. R., Neaigus, A., et al. (1995). Street-level drug markets: network structure and HIV risk. *Social Networks* 17:229–249.

Curtis, R., and Hamid, A. (in press). State-sponsored violence in New York City and indigenous attempts to contain it: the mediating role of the third crown (Sgt. at Arms) of the Latin Kings. Forthcoming in National Institute on Drug Abuse monograph.

Curtis, R., and Maher, L. (1992). Highly structured crack markets in the southside of Williamsburg, Brooklyn. Paper prepared for publication under contract with the Social Science Research Council and the Guggenheim Foundation Working Group on the Ecology of Crime and Drugs Nationwide.

Des Jarlais, D. C., Friedman, S. R., Sotheran, J. L., et al. (1994). Continuity and change within an HIV epidemic: injecting drug users in New York City, 1984 through 1987. *Journal of the American Medical Association* 271(2):121–127.

Dudley, S. (1997). U.S. interests stoke the violence in Colombia. *The Progressive*, February, pp. 26–27.

Fanon, F. (1961). *Los Condenados de la Tierra*. México: Fondo de Cultura Económica.

Fitzpatrick, J. (1980). *Puerto Rican Americans: The Meaning of Migration to the Mainland*. Englewood Cliffs, NJ: Prentice-Hall.

García, M., and Colón, H. (1989). Estimación de la Extención del Abuso de Drogas en Puerto Rico. San Juan, Puerto Rico: Instituto de Investigaciones, Departmento de Servicios Contra la Adicción.

Giddens, A. (1991). *Modernity and Self-Identity*. Stanford, CA: Stanford University Press.

Grund, J.-P., Stern, L., Caplan, C., et al. (1992). Drug use contexts and HIV consequences: the effect of drug policy on patterns of everyday drug use in Rotterdam and the Bronx. *British Journal of the Addictions* 87:381–392.

Hamid, A. (in press a). *The Political Economy of Drugs, Part 1: Ganja and the Rastafarians in San Fernando, Trinidad—A Precapitalist Mode of Production*. New York: Guilford Press (forthcoming).

———— (in press b). *The Political Economy of Drugs, Part 2: The Cocaine Smoking Epidemic of 1981–1991 in New York City's Low-Income Neighborhoods*. New York: Guilford Press (forthcoming).

Horowitz, R. (1983). *Honor and the American Dream: Culture and Identity in a Chicano Community*. New Brunswick, NJ: Rutgers University Press.

Inciardi, J. A. (1986). *The War on Drugs: Heroin, Cocaine and Public Policy*. Palo Alto, CA: Mayfield.

Inciardi, J. A., and McElrath, K. (1995). Policy. In *The American Drug Scene: An Anthology*, pp. 319–321. Los Angeles CA: Roxbury.

Institute for Puerto Rican Policy (1994). *Puerto Rico and Other Latinos in the United States*. March 1993. No. 16, June. New York, NY.

Johnson R. (1980). *Ruerto Rico: Commonwealth or Colony?* New York: Praeger.

Kappeler, V. E., Blumberg, M., and Potter, G. W. (1996). The social construction of crime myths. In *The Mythology of Crime and Criminal Justice*, 2nd ed., pp. 1–29. Prospect Heights, IL: Waveland.

Kasarda, J. D. (1992). The severely distressed in economically transforming cities. In *Drugs, Crime and Social Isolation: Barriers to Urban Opportunity*, ed. A. D. Harrell and G. E. Peterson. Washington, DC: Urban Institute Press.

Kelling, G., and Moore, M. (1988). The evolving strategy of policing. In *Perspectives on Policing*. November. Washington, DC: National Institute of Justice and the John F. Kennedy School of Government, Harvard University.

Kleiman, M., and Smith, K. (1990). State and local drug enforcement: in search of a strategy. In *Crime and Justice: A Review of Research*, vol. 13, ed. M. Tonry and N. Morris, pp. 197–229. Chicago: University of Chicago Press.

Korzenny, F., McClure J., and Rzyttki, B. (1990). Ethnicity, communication and drugs. *The Journal of Drug Issues* 20(1):87–98.

Krauss, C. (1997). Data show crime rates are still falling in New York. *New York Times*, July 3, p. A1.

Latino Commission on AIDS (1995). *Latino Prisoners with HIV/AIDS in New York State Prisons*, Part One. New York, NY.

Lindesmith Health Emergency Report (1997). *Health Emergency: The Spread of Drug-Related AIDS among African Americans and Latinos*. March 31, New York, NY.

Maldonado-Denis, M. (1961). *Puerto Rico: Una Interpretación Histórica Social*. México: Ediciones Siglo XXI.

Marshall, J. (1992). CIA assets and the rise of the Guadalajara connection. In *War on Drugs: Studies in the Failure of U.S. Narcotic Policy*, ed. A. W. McCoy and A. W. Block, pp. 197–208. San Francisco: Westview.

McCoy, A. W. (1991). *The Politics of Heroin: CIA Complicity in the Global Drug Trade*. New York: Lawrence Hill.

McCoy, A. W., and Block, A. (1992). *War on Drugs: Studies in the Failure of U.S. Narcotic Policy*. San Francisco, CA: Westview.

McWilliams, J. C. (1990). *The Protectors: Harry J. Anslinger and the Federal Bureau of Narcotics, 1930–1962*. Newark, DE: University of Delaware Press.

——— (1992). Through the past darkly: the politics and policies of America's drug war. In *Drug Control Policy: Essays in Historical and Comparative Perspective*, ed. W. O. Walker III, pp. 5–41. University Park, PA: Pennsylvania State University Press.

Mollenkopf, J. H., and Castells, M. (1991). *Dual City: Restructuring New York*. New York: Russell Sage Foundation.

Moore, J. (1995). *Bearing the Burden: How Incarceration Policies Weaken Inner-City Communities*. New York: Vera Institute of Justice.

Morgan, P. (1983). The political economy of drugs and alcohol: an introduction. *Journal of Drug Issues*, Winter, pp. 1–7.

Musto, D. F. (1987). *The American Disease: Origins of Narcotic Control*. New Haven, CT: Yale University Press.

Nadelmann, E. (1988). The case for legalization. *Public Interest* 92, Summer, pp. 3–31.

——— (1989). Drug prohibition in the United States: costs, consequences, and alternatives. *Science* 245, September, pp. 939–947.

Navarro, M. (1995). Drug traffic leaves Puerto Rico reeling. *New York Times News Service*. http://www.latinolink.com/prdrug.html.

Negociado de Estadísticas del Trabajo (1995). *Empleo y Desempleo en Puerto Rico*. January. San Juan: Departmento del Trabajo.

Nevares-Muñiz, D. (1996). *El Crimen en Puerto Rico: Tapando el Cielo con la Mano*. Hato Rey, PR: Instituto para el Desarrollo del Derecho, Inc.

Ortíz-Torres, B. (1994). The politics of AIDS research and the Latino community. *Centro de Estudios Puertorriqueños Bulletin*, vol. VI, Nos. 1 & 2, pp. 108–114. New York: Hunter College, City University of New York.

Perlman, J. (1976). *The Myth of Marginality: Urban Poverty and Politics in Rio de Janeiro*. Berkeley, CA: University of California Press.

Phillips, K. P. (1990). *The Politics of Rich and Poor: Wealth and the American Electorate in the Reagan Aftermath*. New York: Random House.

Preble, E., and Casey, J. (1969). Taking care of business: the heroin user's life on the streets. *International Journal of the Addictions* 4:1–24.

Press, E. (1997). Clinton pushes military aid: human-rights abusers lap it up. *The Progressive*. February, pp. 20–22.

Reuter, P., and Kleiman, M. (1986). Risks and prices: an economic analysis of drug enforcement. In *Crime and Justice: An Annual Review, vol. 7*, ed. M. Tonry and N. Morris, pp. 289–340. Chicago: University of Chicago Press.

Salmi, J. (1993). *Violence and Democratic Society: New Approaches to Human Rights*. UK: Biddles Ltd., Guilford.

Santiago-Negrón, S. (1993). Alternativas al Modelo Prohibicionista en el Tratamiento do la Adicción a Drogas. *Ciencia de la Conducta* 8(1–2):7–38. San Juan, PR: Revista del Centro Caribeño de Estudios Postgraduados.

Scharff, J. (1987). The underground economy of a poor neighborhood. In *Cities of the United States: Studies in Urban Anthropology*, ed. L. Mullings, pp. 213–232. New York: Columbia University Press.

Schneider, J., Schneider, P., and Hansen, E. (1972). Modernization and development: the role of regional elites. *Comparative Studies in Society and History* 3:328–350.

Scott, P. D. (1992). Honduras, the Contra support networks, and cocaine: how the U.S. government has augmented America's drug crisis. In *War on Drugs: Studies in the Failure of U.S. Narcotic Policy*, ed. A. W. McCoy and A. W. Block, pp. 125–176. San Francisco: Westview.

Substance Abuse and Mental Health Services Administration (SAMSA) (1996). *National Household Survey on Drug Abuse: Population Estimates, 1995*. Rockville, MD: U.S. Department of Health and Human Services.

Sullivan, M. (1989). *Getting Paid: Youth Crime and Work in the Inner City*. Ithaca, NY: Cornell University Press.

Sviridoff, M., Sadd, S., Curtis, R., and Grinc, R. (1992). *The Neighborhood Effects of New York City's Tactical Narcotics Team on Three Brooklyn Precincts*. New York: Vera Institute of Justice.

Trebach, A. (1993). The case for a Soviet solution. In *Legalize It?: Debating American Drug Policy*, ed. A. Trebach and J. A. Inciardi, pp. 23–40. Washington, DC: American University Press.

Wallace, R., and Wallace, D. (1989). *Origins of Public Health Collapse in New York City: The Dynamics of "Planned Shrinkage," Contagious Urban Decay and Social Disintegration*. New York: PISCS.

Waterston, A. (1993). *Street Addicts in the Political Economy*. Philadelphia: Temple University Press.

Zimmer, L. (1987). *Operation pressure point: the disruption of street-level drug trade on New York's Lower East Side*. New York: Center for Research in Crime and Justice at New York University School of Law.

7

Drug Policy in the Netherlands: Waiting for a Change

Bart Majoor

The mildest suggestion for change is a death-threat to some status quo . . .

—RICHARD BACH, 1988

The Netherlands and the international community are waiting for a change: a more liberal international consensus on drug policy. During the past twenty-five years, the Netherlands worked with a less repressive drug policy and was quite successful. Now the boundaries of experimentation have been reached. These boundaries are created by the international treaties on drug policy that strive for a drugfree world to be achieved by a prohibitive policy. The extremely negative results of prohibitive drug policy on all relevant criteria gives rise to expectations of change toward a more humane and cost-effective drug policy in the world community.

Dutch drug policy has its origins in a problem-solving tradition that effectively combines humanitarian values with pragmatic goals. The roots of Dutch drug policy cannot be understood without considering some aspects of the Dutch culture and its expression in the sociopolitical climate. This chapter discusses these roots of policy in the Netherlands with an emphasis on the changes in policy during the 1970s and the development and results

I am grateful to the team at St. Ann's Corner of Harm Reduction in the South Bronx for their teachings, and for allowing me the time to write this chapter. I thank Erik Fromberg for his inspiration, and am very grateful to Joyce Rivera for her enormous effort in helping shape this work.

of Dutch drug policy over the last two decades. Some major differences in the context and approach to drug use in the Netherlands and the United States are discussed in the last section of the chapter.

CHARACTERISTICS OF THE SOCIOCULTURAL HISTORY

The origins of a typically Dutch value system were becoming apparent in the sixteenth century, the "Golden Age" of the Netherlands. Separation of church and state kept a balance between the rigidity of the Calvinistic clergy and Dutch mercantilism. As a small nation of origin with ambitions on the level of global trade, the Dutch value system can be characterized as idealistic and humanitarian, yet utilitarian and pluralistic at the same time (Kaplan et al. 1996). This value system was served through continuous dialogue among several social forces. As the gateway to Europe, and one of the most prosperous trading nations in the world, the seventeenth century Republic of the United Netherlands absorbed many different cultures, religions, and traditions, and became a refuge for repressed minorities from all over Europe. The integration of this flow of capital and human resources required an evolving consciousness of need (pragmatism) served by tolerance (in its humanitarian aspect).

Dutch tolerance in the field of drug policy shows the same integration of pragmatism and humanitarian values. Effectiveness in terms of those two criteria requires consensus, an important characteristic of our problem-solving tradition. When there are so many different demands, you need to strive for consensus or you will destroy your materialistic and idealistic prosperity. The ability to be conscious of your individual interests, while being prepared to formulate and adapt to a collective goal, is typical of Dutch thinking. Because it is perceived that this approach will bring the optimal profit, Dutch policies are the politics of coalition, compromise, and consensus.

The collective Dutch value system has been characterized historically by a respect for individual freedom and social welfare. At present these core values remain dominant in regulating Dutch society. They have laid the foundation for a relatively "open" society with the capability of experimenting with different social potentials to find the most effective compromise (De Swaan 1988). In an often slow process of careful data collection and negotiations about the different points of view around the table, the "stretch space" for the solution is created. Until that moment in the problem-solving process, we need only to know, express, and take care of the "self." The better I am able to explain my position, the more will my position be represented in the solution. A crucial stage of this social problem-solving process is the next step, when the "other" comes in. The "self" knows that it has to listen to the opinion of the "other." Although this will eventually water down the splendid wine of my "self" opinions and interests, we—as a group—know it is inevitable. No one is really satisfied with the compromise, but a sense of respect and pragmatism is shared. Recently, the Dutch approach to policy development has been characterized as enlightened pragmatism (Moisi 1997).

Dutch society is making the shift from a "materialist" to a "postmaterialist" value orientation (Inglehart 1981, Kaplan et al. 1996). This means that the priority in policy values is gradually shifting from the *maintenance of national order* to *freedom of expression.* The basic value priorities of Western publics have been shifting from giving top priority to physical sustenance and safety toward heavier emphasis on belonging, self-expression, and quality of life. This shift has been traced to the unprecedented levels of economic and physical security that prevailed during the postwar era (Inglehart 1971). As the state guarantees basic security for its citizens, policy solutions aimed at controlling for individual safety are incrementally replaced by a focus on the integration of the interests and objectives of both the "self" and the "other." Postmaterialists have an internalized sense of security, and therefore can operate in a less self-centered manner. Abraham Maslow's (1954) theory of a need hierarchy underlying human motivation is a complementary concept in this context: only when an experience of basic security is internalized will a person be able to move toward more social value priorities.

CONCEPTION OF THE DRUG POLICY

The first Opium Laws of 1919 and 1928 are the only examples of laws that were not the result of a consensus of the Dutch population on how to address a social problem. They were the result of severe pressure by the United States to impose their perceptions of drug use on the rest of the world, as they actually succeeded in doing by the Single Convention in 1961 that was also signed by the Dutch government (Silvis 1982).

These laws and international treaties all passed in silence to the general public. As the Netherlands did not have a social drug problem at the time, the Dutch society did not realize that an international framework that would interfere with our usual approach to social problem solving in the future had been created. The space for experimenting was thus limited before the experiments would begin. Our own systematic approach to the drug problem is also limited by the other Dutch instinct to keep the balance with the international community that differs so deeply in their attitude to the drug problem. This remains a big problem for further development of Dutch drug policy.

Before 1960 the Netherlands hardly knew recreational use of drugs. Drug use was individualized, hidden, and well managed. The few users obtained their drugs mostly via medical channels. Until 1960 it was the general opinion in policy discussions regarding drug use that drug users were patients who should be approached in a medical fashion. One can say that the conditions for a medical social policy regarding drug use were present already in the first half of this century. Between 1920 and 1960 this policy had the explicit objectives of *preventing* a repressive approach and the marginalizing of drug users. The fact that the Netherlands did not have a drug problem during those years was partly the result of this policy (De Kort 1995).

During the 1960s the recreational use of drugs like cannabis, LSD, and amphetamines increased considerably. This nonmedical drug use by adolescents and young adults happened within a subcultural framework of resistance against the existing values of mainstream society. The first policy response to the rapid spread of drug use was still a conventionally repressive one, but on the waves of the antiauthoritarian movement, the societal criticism of a repressive government became very strong by the end of the decade. This resulted in a societal and political movement in favor of decriminalization that influenced the creation of a new drug policy in an important way.

In the beginning of the 1970s, when the "flower power" subculture grew rapidly and even became a small political force in the traditionally liberal city of Amsterdam and an increasing number of young people experimented with illegal drugs, it was obvious to the authorities that something had to be done. The sociopolitical dialogue on drug policy at the time was centered on two main issues. First, the general question posed was whether the possession of drugs should be prosecuted at all. This was a big issue, especially regarding cannabis, whose health risks were considered relatively limited. Second, most researchers, experts, and politicians considered the criminal approach to drug use wrong. They argued that it made no sense to lock up young people because they used drugs. There were other ways to prevent drug use, like education and care (Wever 1995).

In line with Dutch tradition, the government decided to set up a committee to amass expert advice on drug policy (the Baan Committee). Another such committee was set up simultaneously as a private initiative of the National Institute for Mental Health (the Hulsman Committee). At this juncture drug policy was approached in the traditional Dutch way. Insofar as drug policy was not perceived as a social problem, the laws and international treaties established earlier could pass in silence without the normal social dialogue between different groups and opinions. When drug use was considered a social problem, the traditional reaction was evoked immediately: set up committees to facilitate the airing of opinions and come to an informed conclusion (read compromise) about what is the most effective policy. The government's Baan Committee represented the "ruling powers," but from the "ruled" (the Hulsman Committee) came the same reaction. In this case the reaction of the citizenry was represented in a response by the mental health field, thus asserting the main perception of problematic drug use as medical/psychiatric, not delinquent.

Both committees published their final reports in 1971, and both largely agreed on the conclusion. They advised strongly for decriminalization of the use of drugs, especially cannabis (Baan Committee Report 1972, Hulsman Committee Report 1971).

Comparable committees set up simultaneously in Canada (the Le Dain Committee) and the United States (the Shafer Committee) reached similar conclusions, but in contrast these reports disappeared into oblivion, having been negated by their inquiring governments. The Dutch Ministerial Council discussed the Baan Report and at first the majority voted for complete legalization of cannabis. Only under heavy pressure by the departments of foreign and economic affairs was this not realized. Their argument not to legalize completely was rooted in international concerns because the Netherlands already had an isolated position with regard to the Israeli–Arab conflict (it was at the time of the first oil crisis), and we could not afford an isolated position on one more subject. Legalization of cannabis would bring further isolation because of our international obligations in the context of the Single Convention of 1961 that the Dutch government did not want to violate (Fromberg and Majoor 1993, Wever 1995).

The dilemma: Should we prosecute drug users, or decriminalize drug use? What is the better approach? This situation provides us with a clear example of the Dutch problem-solving tradition. The way the drug problem is approached reflects the combination of humanitarian values (i.e., decriminalization, education, care, respect for individual freedom of expression) and pragmatism (i.e., differentiate between soft and hard drugs; locking up kids because they use drugs does not work; focus law enforcement efforts on international drug trade). The Baan Committee report, and the government's acceptance of its findings, reflect how consensus, and the striving for consensus, has achieved institutionalization. The failure to support complete legalization of cannabis had a pragmatic basis around which there was consensus: the Dutch cannot isolate themselves from the international community because of their economic dependency on international trade. We see how sensitive Dutch (drug) policy is to geopolitical and foreign policy objectives. What we wanted as a society in itself could not be realized because of the limitations of geopolitical interests.

The first time the Dutch society dealt with the sociopolitical problem of drug use consciously, the inner social consensus was stretched. The Dutch instinct to create national consensus was overruled by the instinct not to create international dissonance. This prevented the Dutch from fully developing their experimental drug policy right at the start of the 1970s. When the country was ready for a next step in its development, the international community would hinder that step, and the Dutch government would comply.

In 1973, as a compromise between national and international interests, the government decided that cannabis would be defined as a drug whose use was considered an acceptable risk, a "soft" drug as opposed to the other drugs, labeled "hard" drugs, whose use was at that time considered an unacceptable risk. According to the then new narcotic law, the maximum penalties for trade in cannabis were significantly lower than for hard drugs. Moreover, the possession of cannabis for personal use became a misdemeanor. The amount to be considered for personal use was placed at 30 grams, not by law, but by a directive of the prosecutor general. This proposal finally became law in 1976, but the government's proposal of the law in 1973 presaged the end of the first phase of our policy regarding cannabis: the phase of criminalization by prohibition. Since 1976, no one has been prosecuted for simple possession of cannabis for personal use.

From 1973 on, Dutch drug policy has had two axes of development: one regarding the soft drug cannabis, and one regarding hard drugs (Fromberg and Majoor 1993). The separation of drug markets has proved to be a very successful approach in creating the conditions for developing an acculturation process around a substance (i.e., cannabis) that allows people to find their own rules in managing substance use in a meaningful way. The impetus has been to find an effective way to integrate a new drug without too much harm being done. Only in a regulated sociocultural space will the dialogue between the autonomy of the individual and the collective responsibilities find its balance.

BUREAUCRATIZATION OF CONSENSUS: NORMALIZATION

Even before the changes in the 1976 Opium Law were definite, the Dutch government decided to form the Inter-Governmental Steering Group for Drug Policy. The directive of this group of top executives of the different relevant federal departments (i.e., the Departments of Health and Welfare, Justice, Foreign Affairs, and Internal Affairs) was to develop and implement the new drug policy. In characteristic manner, this ongoing consensus committee has as its mission the shaping of the different interests of the various departments into a well-balanced national and international policy response. The striving for consensus had become bureaucratized.

Because of the prevailing perception that prevention and care, not repression via law enforcement, should be the answers to the social drug problem, the minister of health became the responsible and coordinating executive regarding our national drug policy, and it was this ministry that presided over the Inter-Governmental Steering Group.

The normalization of drug use was the main objective for the new drug policy that was immediately operationalized within the bureaucracy. This also meant that the workers for the government became the "enlightened" actors in terms of striving for the policy objective of normalization. Innovation, then, became a true concern for the public servants who dealt with the drug problem. This creative vacuum established the real space for experimentation and differentiation of the concept of harm reduction. Grass roots organizations met an unexpected ally in the government, and flourished as never before.

During the 1970s, heroin became a popular drug, especially among immigrants from Surinam and the Dutch Antilles. This occurred in the context of other social difficulties. In the bigger cities there was a concentration of problems around housing, unemployment, and assimilation in general. An extensive research program on the lifestyle of heroin users resulted in a typology of heroin users in Dutch society, and gave more empirical insight into this new social phenomenon called "the drug problem" (Janssen and Swierstra 1982, Swierstra et al. 1986). Conclusions showed that participation in a drug subculture, like the one around heroin, can be a normal reaction—or coping strategy—for certain groups in society. Moreover, the economic trade in drugs was a societal reality with all the interests of the individuals and communities involved. Interesting alternatives to the economic imperatives were not available, making many individuals choose a career in dealing drugs (Wever 1995).

The development of the hard drug problem in the Netherlands along with the institutional focus on prevention and care paved the way for an approach based on an important singular social insight for developing an effective drug policy: the nature of addictive behavior teaches us not to focus on the drugs and drug use itself, but always to see it in the perspective of other psychological and social phenomena (Zinberg 1984).

While the punishing, repressive idea of government gradually withdrew into the shade of a more social and integrating approach to government, the space was created to start building an extensive social safety net in Dutch society. During the 1960s and 1970s a system of health care and social security was created that has not been replicated elsewhere (De Kort 1995, Wever 1995, 1996). Every citizen has access to health care, social welfare money, the educational system, and the rapidly growing network of care and support agencies. The true insight of the normalizing policy was that it was not specific for problematic drug users, but for every marginalized group in society. When the marginalization of any group is a threat to the national community, it pays off in terms of humanitarian values *and* cost-effectiveness to invest prudently in the most vulnerable parts of the societal system.

Dutch drug policy is rooted in the realization that *any* social problem (poverty, racism, unemployment, illegal drugs, homosexuality) is a problem because society marginalizes certain groups by its written and unwritten rules. It is based on the notion that drug use as a social problem is just one of the symptoms of social marginalization of certain groups. It recognizes the fact that the function of hard drug use for consumers can be one of coping, as a form of self-medication. Drug use on a social level then becomes just one of the many faces of society. That face will not go away, yet it is not something to focus on any more, or less, than all the other related problems. Illegal drug use becomes a social phenomenon that can be *normalized*—in the sense of *integrated*—in our collective endeavors, and shrunk to individual proportions.

DEVELOPMENT OF THE DRUG SERVICE PROVISION: PREVENTION, CURE, AND CARE

If a society does not choose to use repression and marginalization as a strategy toward a social problem, it has to be prepared to respond in another way. *Normalization* is the name of the other policy response. It requires that "supposedly collective problems [be] demystified and socially redefined as primarily individual problems" (Wever 1996, p. 64). To guide marginalized people back into society, you need to show them how, and support them in every effective way possible. The social support system of mental health and specialized addiction services was expected to create that effective response, although initially it found it was not ready for the "new world" of care that was defined by the needs of drug users who came for assistance.

The traditional medical-psychiatric approach to the individual client did not work for a majority of drug users who came for help. Although at the end of the '60s the existing Medical Consultation Bureaus for Alcohol (MCA) renamed themselves the Bureaus for Consultation on Alcohol and Drugs (CAD) as an expression of their willingness to apply their competence on alcohol as well drugs, they were not prepared for the very different demands of drug users who came for help.

Although drug clients said they wanted to become abstinent, it soon became clear that they came for something else. They did not want to stop their habit. They wanted a temporary shelter from the "hit-and-run" life outside. They often were exhausted from living their lives in the drug scene. Because the treatment system was still very much focused on living an abstinent life, drug clients—who were soon called *junkies*—developed an inventive set of behaviors to get what they wanted (Fromberg and Majoor 1993). And so a new syndrome was born: the "junkie syndrome" that describes the lying, cheating, and stealing of drug-dependent clients, the games addicts play. The junkie syndrome compared the behavior of these clients with those of people in German concentration camps. In this view, behavior is singularly directed at one goal: obtaining what is crucial for survival, that is, drugs, or money to buy drugs. Any person they meet is seen in that light. Everyone is an instrument to reach that goal whether it is a dealer, an old lady with a fat purse, or a worker at the drug clinic (Noorlander 1985, Van Epen 1984). With those clients the "cure" (= abstinence-directed) way of thinking that helpers held had to be replaced by a more flexible "care" (= not just abstinence-directed) approach. On the level of drug care provision, the balance between humanitarian and pragmatic values again had to be operationalized. Once innovation of the traditional care system became a policy objective, a death threat was announced to the status quo.

Out of the framework of general youth care, an innovative approach had already come into development. It was influenced by the fact that within the subculture a strong tendency existed to care for each other. The subculture rejected the official caregivers, the CADs, if only because they considered all nonmedical drug use as abuse, and the abuser as a patient. For the subculture drug use was normal. If somebody experienced bad drug effects, he or she should be helped by kind caring. This was epitomized by the effects of LSD. It was this combination of self-help organized by the subculture and their recognition by the municipal authorities that created the "alternate drug care." Authorities recognized the failure of the traditional approach of the CADs and they supported the alternatives.

Community-based social rehabilitation as an approach to drug users became in the early '70s a substantive part of the drug policy in the Netherlands. The central goal of the government with this policy was the reduction of drug-related harm: to reduce the risks of drug taking for the user, his direct environment, and society as a whole. These risks were not restricted to the properties of the drug involved, but were also dependent on the reasons why drugs are used, the nature of the social group in which they are used, and the circumstances in which the use of drugs takes place (Majoor 1990). In the past three decades, based on these premises, a pragmatic approach to drug users who seek help has been developed.

In the 1980s the fields of drug care (i.e., harm reduction and social rehabilitation) and cure (i.e., drug treatment) remained quite separated in their methodological approach to drug users and in many ways did not cooperate. Only in the 1990s did the integration of their development, and a tuning into each other, take place. Balancing their opposite positions, the medical-psychiatric approach and the harm reduction/social rehabilitation approach needed to find their identity in separation. From both sides there was resistance about recognizing and using each other's approach. In the late '90s this stage of identification and separation is gradually being replaced by the stages of recognition and integration. Regional circuits of drug agencies are developed in which the client can choose an individual care or cure trail based on their needs and supported by a case manager. This is the process of "vertical linking" between service providers from all over the continuum of service provision for drug users (NRV 1994).

The next step seems to be that the united addiction care system will start building more bridges to the general care system. In the 1980s addiction care as a sector worked isolated from other relevant sectors. Normalization means that public services are able to handle the needs of drug users too. Knowledge and skills in dealing with addiction problems should not be isolated in a categorized addiction sector. This expertise should be available to other sectors that deal with substance users on a regular basis, for example health care, mental health care, the educational system, law enforcement, the prison system, and employment agencies. This horizontal linking between different sectors of society is very important to the creation of an effective and humanitarian balance in supporting drug users. This process is now taking place in the Netherlands. The government supports and stimulates this horizontal linking in the context of the quality of addiction care (NRV 1994).

CRIMINALITY AND AIDS: FURTHER NORMALIZATION

In the early 1980s a state-funded study was published wherein the authors made a social analysis of the hard drug scene in the Netherlands resulting in a typology of heroin users (Janssen and Swierstra 1982, Swierstra et al. 1986). The study showed in detail how criminalization and medicalization marginalized people who use illegal drugs. The Inter-Governmental Steering Group on Drug Policy, headed by the minister of health, used this study to extend and deepen its policy of normalization. In 1986 this decisive political platform published its drug policy in a paper called "Drug Policy in Motion, toward a Normalizing of the Drug Problem" (ISAD 1985) in which the steering group concluded that most of the drug problem is caused by drug policy itself and that care policy is directed primarily at taking care of the negative consequences of the worldwide illegality of those drugs. Thus they plead for normalization of the social drug problem by viewing it as no different from the many other social problems that we face (Engelsman 1986, 1989). In other words, stop the social overreaction to illegal drugs and let us perceive them in the context of the Dutch sociocultural picture.

Normalization also means that you hold criminal drug users responsible for their criminal behavior, as we do with any other citizen. Because the illegality of the drugs creates high prices on the black market, Dutch society chose to create a differentiated social support system to stop marginalization and deterioration of drug users. That is the big impulse for government-funded low-threshold support programs, including wide-scale methadone maintenance provision, needle exchange, and social rehabilitation programs.

Two main social problems that occurred during the 1980s have a clear relationship with the drug problem and further development of Dutch drug policy. First, the criminality that was perceived as related to illegal drug use was on the rise and, for the first time, the prison system was confronted with a drug-using population. Second, the AIDS epidemic amply demonstrated that intravenous drug users were a high risk group for contracting HIV. These two arguments, from the law enforcement side and from the public health perspective, resulted in greater harmonization of law enforcement and care interventions. The existing possibilities for a joint approach between law enforcement and the care approach are more extensively utilized (i.e., drugfree wings in prison, voluntary treatment as an alternative to incarceration). From here on, the law enforcement interests start to weigh heavier in the making of drug policy decisions.

Effective implementation of a harm-reducing drug policy took place on a regional/local level. The objective of the Dutch authorities was to create an effective balance among the three main policy instruments in the drug field, law enforcement, health care, and social rehabilitation. Regional/local policymakers have the best information on what specific factors create the drug problem in a certain city or region. It is at the level of local/regional government, especially the big cities, that the lead in experimenting with and implementing Dutch drug policy has been taken so far. By the end of the 1980s, this aspect was emphasized by the decision of the government to decentralize the still-existing federal power to implement drug policy at the level of regional authorities.

THE 1990S: INTERNATIONAL PRESSURE MOUNTS

One could say that the 1990s is the decade during which Dutch drug policy must withstand its international test. In the Netherlands the consensus on drug policy stands firm and is reported in several policy papers of the government that have been accepted by both Houses of Parliament ("Drugs and Nuisance" [Ministry of Health, Welfare and Sport 1993], "Continuity and Change" [Ministry of Foreign Affairs et al. 1995]).

The relative "splendid isolation" of our drug policy on the international stage cannot be maintained, however. In the first place, there is the public nuisance caused mainly by drug tourists who come to the Netherlands to buy their drugs. Others come to stay because they are users and decide to live in a more user-friendly country. The consequence of drug tourism is an excessive demand on the existing infrastructure (i.e., coffee shops, the hard drug dealer system, methadone programs, care services, and law enforcement capacity). This results in a public nuisance concentrated especially in the big cities (Amsterdam, Rotterdam) and in smaller towns along the border with

Germany and Belgium. Besides drug tourism, the other cause for public nuisance is the criminal and antisocial behavior of a small group of long-term hard drug users in big cities.

In the second place, there is the bigger context of the development of Europe toward the European Union that asks for harmonizing of policies on various subjects. Drug policy is now on the political agenda and Dutch drug policy has become the ugly duckling of the international community. Although several countries are sympathetic to the Dutch approach to illegal drug use, they may not vote in favor of a more liberal drug policy in the international arena. They may perceive too little benefit and too high a risk. The Netherlands, therefore, may experience isolation in the European dialogue on the subject.

RESULTS OF DUTCH DRUG POLICY

What are the main effects of Dutch drug policy since the 1970s? What has been accomplished in twenty-five years?

THE SEPARATION OF CONSUMER MARKETS OF SOFT AND HARD DRUGS

> Dutch policy on the use of cannabis is based on the assumption that people are more likely to make the transition from soft to hard drugs as a result of social factors than because of physiological ones. If young adults wish to use soft drugs—and experience has shown that many do—the Netherlands believes that it is better that they should do so in a setting in which they are not exposed to the criminal subculture surrounding hard drugs. Tolerating relatively easy access to quantities of soft drugs for personal use is intended to keep the consumer markets for soft and hard drugs separate, thus creating a social barrier to the transition from soft to hard drugs. . . . [Ministry of Foreign Affairs et al. 1995]

With the introduction of bona fide house dealers in youth clubs in the 1970s and the establishment of coffee shops in the 1980s, the infrastructure was created for the sale of cannabis for personal use. The judicial authorities tolerated this with a basic rational set of rules to protect the boundaries of the drug policy: no advertising, no sale of hard drugs, no nuisance, no sale to people under the age of 18, and no sale of more than 30 grams per transaction, per person. The number of cannabis users in the Netherlands increased somewhat between 1984 and 1994. This is a trend observed elsewhere in Europe and the United States (Cohen 1996, De Zwart and Mensink 1996).

The total number of people in the Netherlands who incidentally or regularly use cannabis is estimated to be around 675,000, or 5 percent of the total population (De Zwart and Mensink 1996). Only 0.3 percent of the cannabis users develop dependent behavior and seek professional assistance (Spruit 1997). The extent of cannabis use, and the patterns of use in the Netherlands, differ very little from other countries. Cannabis use is determined primarily by fashions in international youth culture and other autonomous developments, such as levels of long-term youth unemployment. After twenty years of this cannabis policy, the conclusion is that the separation of consumer markets for soft and hard drugs has shown practical value. The only aspect of the Dutch cannabis policy that was changed is the recent lowering of the maximum amount sold from 30 to 5 grams per transaction (Ministry of Foreign Affairs et al. 1995). This policy change is mainly to control the nuisance caused by drug tourists in the coffee shops near the border. Residents of some municipalities have complained about the attraction of large numbers of noisy visitors. In part this is the same kind of nuisance that is caused by catering establishments in general. An important factor causing the nuisance around coffee shops, though, is the demand on the coffee shop infrastructure by foreigners. On weekends, two thirds of coffee shop turnover in many municipalities is accounted for by drug tourists (Korf et al. 1993). By lowering the maximum amount of cannabis to be sold per transaction from 30 to 5 grams, the government hopes to discourage foreign buyers from making the trip to a Dutch coffee shop.

Epidemiological data show that the majority of the cannabis-using population does not use hard drugs. Of those that have ever used cannabis, only a few have also ever used heroin or cocaine. Even fewer of the recent cannabis users also recently used either heroin or cocaine. The data clearly indicate that there is hardly any progression to hard drug use (Cohen and Sas 1996, De Zwart et al. 1993, Fromberg 1993, Kuipers et al. 1993). The Dutch cannabis experiment shows no statistical support for the hypothesis of cannabis as a gateway drug.

What is established in the Netherlands, though, is that the consumer markets of soft and hard drugs are separated by a "cultural wall" (Fromberg 1993). The integration or acculturation of cannabis use in Dutch society is more or less accomplished. In this sense Dutch drug policy has been successful in normalizing the use of cannabis in the Netherlands. It allowed experimenting users of cannabis to find their own rules in managing the substance.

Several studies also shed light on the social function of the coffee shop where cannabis is for sale (De Loor 1993, Maalste 1995). It creates a social meeting point—like a bar—for otherwise marginalized groups. Coffee shops serve this important integrative objective in many communities. Different ethnic groups in the present youth culture create their own coffee shop around the cultural needs of their group. In fact, you see as much differentiation in coffee shops as in bars. They promote community group cohesion. As part of the social infrastructure, coffee shops keep certain groups socially integrated that would otherwise be marginalized.

MDMA AND OTHER DESIGNER DRUGS

In the 1990s the normalizing drug policy was challenged when methylenedioximethamphetamine (MDMA), popularly known as Ecstasy or XTC, was introduced to consumers. After an initial period of legality, MDMA was brought under the Opium Law in 1988. The Netherlands could not extend its normalizing experiment because of international pressure and its own, then limited, views on socially integrated, nonmedical drug use. MDMA was required to be scheduled under the Opium Law of 1976 as a hard drug as the law did not provide the option of scheduling new drugs as soft. The experts and the government in the 1970s were unable to imagine drugs other than cannabis as "soft" (Fromberg 1990). Clearly, also on the expert and policy level, a certain process of adaptation has to take place and that takes time. MDMA may have been the perfect opportunity to extend the social experiment to prove that carefully regulated incorporation of a drug will minimize any harmful effects on the individual consumer and on society at large.

The growing public notion is that MDMA is a soft drug, although some extra precautions are taken because not enough is known of its long-term effects. The Netherlands has been able to monitor the trends in designer drugs closely, and to intervene when necessary, by offering, for example, drug analyses and pill testing in public places, warning campaigns in the case of bad pills, first-aid personnel trained for the specific needs of consumers, flyers on safe use and the dangers of specific drugs, and local policy scenarios for large-scale parties (De Loor 1992, Ministry of Health, Welfare, and Sport 1995). The users, party organizers, and professional health workers, even several policymakers, police officers, and the judicial representatives, perceived and treated MDMA as a soft drug. The contradictory treatment of MDMA as a soft drug, even while it was defined by law as a hard drug, had the effect of blurring the formerly sharp distinction in the public mind between hard and soft drugs.

Now we see the MDMA story develop into a repeat of a known sequence of events: use and availability of the drug increase sharply as organized crime starts to draw on its infrastructure for MDMA production and sale. Amphetamine laboratories start producing the now illegal MDMA. The necessary laboratory equipment is already there. They just need other ingredients that are not hard to purchase. The profits from producing MDMA are much larger than those from the production of amphetamines. Another

well-known effect of making a substance illegal is that quality control becomes impossible. Consumers cannot know what they are buying on the
streets or at parties (De Loor 1989). Amphetamines, ketamine, other designer drugs like MDA (methylenedioxiamphetamine) and MDEA (methylene-
dioxiethylamphetamine), and many other substances are sold under the same
popular name XTC. This creates extremely unsafe circumstances for consumers that can be controlled only partially by prevention strategies.

The popularity of the drug grew as if it were legal, and MDMA consumers suddenly were shopping in the hard drug market. In terms of the
modern steppingstone theory, psychosocial factors like "all my friends use
it" and "availability of the drug and easy access to other drugs" are the reasons for moving on to harder drugs; yet the MDMA policy caused harm
because it failed to provide protection in separating the consumer markets
of hard and soft drugs, as was carefully crafted two decades earlier for cannabis (Fromberg 1993).

The Department of Health did invest in a number of very experimental and successful secondary prevention strategies for MDMA users that
stretched the inner consensus. They tried to reduce the harm of making
MDMA illegal by funding secondary prevention strategies like drug analyses
at rave parties. Drug analysis here means that partygoers can go to a little
stand at the party and have their pills tested to see what they have actually
bought. The testing device is, of course, not very specific, but can distinguish between main groups of known substances. When a pill cannot be
identified, it is taken to a laboratory and the consumer is advised to buy
another one. In this way the authorities closely monitor the trends on the
MDMA market (Fromberg and Jansen 1993). When a pill turns out to be
dangerous, a carefully directed warning campaign for potential users is immediately carried out. More of these strategies were developed out of the innovative prevention concept of "service" (De Loor 1990, Visser 1994).

The service approach to prevention states that to prevent drug-related
harm one has to approach the consumer in an attitude of service. When you
provide information, materials, and services the consumer really needs, the
majority will show responsible behavior and develop their own safe rules for
drug taking. This is client-centered prevention. Basic to the service approach
is the assumption that drug users are responsible consumers once they have
the right information and materials. The only way to really reduce drug-related harm is to make it possible for the consumer to opt in favor of responsible drug taking. Within the restrictions of prohibition, a limited adaptation
regarding MDMA could take place. The decisive factor in the effectiveness
of harm reduction measures is the clarity about reasonable boundaries of safety
(information and materials) combined with the experience of some freedom
of choice by the consumer (responsibility). All this is harm reduction: noth-

ing more than a traditional public health precept of not letting the best be the enemy of the good (Wodak 1992). It is better to work toward reachable goals than to be trapped in the frustrating struggle with unattainable goals.

CARE AND PREVENTION: NORMALIZATION INSTITUTIONALIZED

A continuum of drug care and prevention services was created on local and regional levels in the early 1990s. The part of the continuum called *cure/ treatment* has become less dominant as the harm reduction/nonabstinence aspects have been emphasized. We can say that the public health objectives of Dutch drug policy were earlier operationalized with the creation of a national training and education program for workers in the harm reduction field (Majoor 1994b). Out of this training program, in 1988, grew the national union and clearinghouse for agencies and workers in this field (Penning et al. 1988).

Thus, in the 1990s, the field of harm reduction was professionalized and fully integrated into the care spectrum. Respectful cooperation and even integration of care and cure services for drug users became possible. Clients could smoothly be referred to and from agencies at very different parts of the drug care continuum (Majoor 1992). This is the process of *vertical linking* within the spectrum of addiction services (NRV 1994). The local/regional level of drug policy-making is an opportunity to better gear the offered services to specific needs of substance-using populations in that area. The disproportionate policy attention to drug use is at least recognized, and the need to balance this with education on smoking, alcohol use, and legally prescribed substances is also expressed by the government.

The *horizontal linking* (NRV 1994) of the whole sector of addiction care with other relevant sectors in society (vocational training/job market, primary health care, mental health care, police/prison system, educational system, youth care) shows that the time of isolation of addiction care is over, not just because the professional addiction care wants to cooperate with these sectors to make their work far more effective, but because these other sectors increasingly realize they are better off with some knowledge of drug use in the current sociopolitical context. Normalization of drug use also means that knowledge and skills need to be normalized: every medical doctor, nurse, social worker, and psychologist should have some basic education and training in drug use and addictive behavior patterns (NIAD 1991).

Stepped care is the concept used today in the Netherlands to organize an effective care system (Vermeulen 1995). When a client comes for help, the least intensive services are provided first. When this less intensive strategy of service provision clearly fails to help the client, a more intensive next step is considered. The matching of client needs on the one hand and the possibility of choice between differentiated services on the other hand always directs this process. Client centeredness and a comprehensive continuum of care services are crucial in this effective approach. The less intrusive an intervention is, the better for continuity in the life of a client and the less the chances for chronic dependence on service provision (residential or ambulatory hospitalization). "Optimal autonomy" of a client is always the general objective of any care intervention (Majoor 1996). Stepped care also makes it possible to manage the costs of treatment in an effective way because the very expensive clinical treatment of drug clients will be used only when clearly indicated by failure of less intensive interventions.

Integration of the fields of care and cure for drug users has now been realized. There is concern about whether the small, community-based organizations that are now almost entirely integrated in large-scale regional organizations for addiction care and prevention will lose their own cultural "flavor" and with that their effectiveness. There is also some criticism of the bureaucracy of these big regional addiction centers, and especially of the resulting lack of flexibility to react to the rapid developments in the illegal consumer market. History shows, though, that when the lowest threshold program for this target group starts making its threshold higher, another individual or agency will create a new program. That is the law of experience in this field. In time the new service provider will also be integrated or institutionalized, but the grass roots will always produce new grass when the season is there.

THE PREVALENCE OF HARD DRUG USE

Although it is hard to make valid estimates of illegal drug use, precisely *because* of its illegality, all existing estimates show that the number of hard drug users in the Netherlands (25,000, or 0.16 percent of the total population) is relatively low compared to Europe's average (0.27 percent), according to the Dutch Inter-Governmental Drug Policy Report "Continuity and Change" (Ministry of Foreign Affairs et al. 1995). The number of heroin users under the age of 21 in the Netherlands is relatively low, even among vulnerable groups, and has continued to fall in recent years (Kuipers et al. 1993).

It is unclear how widespread the use of cocaine is in the Netherlands (Spruit 1997). Lately there has been more crack use in the big cities. An interesting line of research introduced by Cohen (1989) focused on the study of cocaine users in *nondeviant* subcultures. His findings provide detailed insight into the self-control mechanisms around cocaine use by a group of socially integrated persons. Of the experimental group, 6 percent experienced cocaine-related problems in such a way that they thought about asking for professional assistance. In the end, 1 percent really went for help (Cohen 1989, Cohen and Sas 1993).

Methadone has been an important part of the Dutch harm reduction approach. By the beginning of the 1980s, it was already clear that a methadone policy aimed only at abstinence from opiates was not tenable. In general, the more liberal policy on methadone provision that immediately followed had different objectives. Crime prevention, prevention of social deterioration, research, access to high-risk groups for prevention and care interventions, and prevention of public nuisance are pragmatic Dutch policy objectives. Since then, an extensive network for methadone provision consisting of municipal health services, drug care agencies, and general practitioners has developed in the Netherlands. More than 80 percent of methadone clients are on a maintenance schedule. The average dosage is 46.0 milligrams (De Zwart and Mensink 1996, Driessen 1992). Methadone provides an example of the development from cure to care. It can also be seen as another example of social experimentation with approaches to drug care. Again, we see a process of gradually stretching the inner political consensus until reachable objectives are obtained.

In the latest policy document of the Dutch government (Ministry of Foreign Affairs et al. 1995), the issue of heroin prescription is raised again with serious resolutions for an extensive research project in several Dutch cities. The project will provide injectable and noninjectable heroin to a small number of very ill or otherwise seriously problematic heroin users (Ehlers 1995, Inspectie Volksgezondheid 1995, 1996, Nadelmann 1995). Only by conducting social experiments will we keep on finding better answers to the social drug problem.

THE TAMING OF DRUG RELATED CRIMINALITY

Other important criteria to consider when judging a drug policy are the issues of drug-related crime, the public nuisance caused by the drug trade, and the status quo of the field of law enforcement regarding illegal drugs. For the Dutch government it is absolutely clear that some of the public images around the subject of crime and drugs are myths. Consider the latest national policy document:

> The impression is sometimes given that responsibility for most nuisance and the vast majority of thefts and burglaries lies with addicts, and that all addicts provide for themselves by committing criminal offenses. This impression is far from accurate. . . . [Ministry of Foreign Affairs et al. 1995]

These myths are to be tackled by an extensive effort to provide the general (national and international) public with a more realistic picture of the situation of drug users in the Netherlands. This will ultimately serve the drug policy objective of normalization that is nowadays less overtly mentioned by the Dutch government. Normalization is institutionalized, and this in itself creates a protective effect from the international community.

Ten to 20 percent of the total crime committed in the Netherlands—including the unresolved cases—is estimated to be accounted for by drug users. Research shows that 25 percent of the criminal drug users are responsible for most of the drug-related crime. Almost half of this "criminal anyway" group was already involved in criminal activities before they became dependent on illegal drugs (Bieleman et al. 1995). One third of property offenses in larger cities in the Netherlands is attributable to drug users. Across the country as a whole, the figures are somewhat lower (Korf and Leuw 1992, Spruit 1997).

In 1996 around 50 percent of the prison population consisted of drug-dependent persons (Spruit 1996). This was caused mainly by the relatively long prison sentences for violations of the Opium Law (Swierstra 1994). The juggling between law enforcement and public health objectives is difficult. Still, they work together, although sometimes grudgingly, to serve both ends. Recently, many new programs and innovative approaches—including coercive treatment—have been put in place to use the prison time to deliver care and cure services. For the cure programs, drugfree wings of prisons are created, where prisoners are in voluntary treatment for their addiction on the condition of urine analyses. Methadone provision, counseling, social rehabilitation, probation work, and other interventions are provided.

Strangely, there is one omission in the policy regarding drug users and the general prison population: there is virtually no effective AIDS prevention policy in Dutch prisons. The Justice Department still does not want to admit publicly that there is drug consumption (and sex) in prisons. Nonetheless, they create drugfree prison wings for the motivated user who wants to stop. With that action you acknowledge there is drug trade and use in prisons. Considering the Dutch pragmatic tradition, certain simple measures like the availability of safe use and safe sex materials in prisons should then be organized in a low-key way. It is truly shameful that this is scarcely the case. Increasing the prevalence of high-risk behaviors for HIV and hepatitis infections, such as sharing injection equipment and unprotected (anal) sex, are the results of this ostrich-policy (Majoor 1994a).

A second issue in the context of taming drug criminality is the public nuisance caused by drug users in the communities where they live, hang out, and/or purchase drugs. Again, there is the tendency to attribute public nuisance to drug users in a too generalized and undifferentiated manner. Other marginalized groups are equally responsible for nuisance and threatening the experience of public safety. Moreover, it should be noticed that a lot of nuisance is caused by drug tourism, especially along the borders and in the bigger cities (Braam 1995, Leuw and Aron 1995).

Still, it is important to take these social cues seriously. In 1990 a National Workgroup was established to come up with recommendations that would solve the issue. In 1993 the workgroup published a report titled "Drugs and Nuisance" in which an integrative approach was presented. The report emphasized a policy that employed a combination of criminal law, civil law, alien law, and administrative law (Blom and Van Mastrigt 1996).

Using the rising international pressure on the Netherlands to change its drug policy, in combination with the internal nuisance problems in certain communities, the Justice Department tried to take on more leadership in formulating and implementing Dutch drug policy. Consequently, the report of this workgroup recommended, almost exclusively, repressive measures to combat the problems around drug-related nuisance.

In the latest drug policy report from the government (Ministry of Foreign Affairs et al. 1995), combating the public nuisance problem remains a major policy objective. According to the wishes of the House of Parliament, an Inter-Administrative Task Force on Public Safety and Care for Addicts has been formed. The task force combines—according to the traditional Dutch problem-solving approach—the different parties involved to find a (new) effective compromise on the issues of public nuisance and law enforcement on the one hand and drug care and prevention on the other. The task force is also responsible for implementing the policy that is agreed upon. It represents more of a balance between public health and justice objectives in the context of leadership in determining Dutch drug policy. Still, the growing influence of the Justice Department—and its more repressive solutions—is palpable. We now can say that the inner consensus seems to have reached its boundaries. The stretch space is fully occupied, yet the inner and outer pressure keeps on rising.

Another factor in the diminishing hold of the Health Department on drug policy is the decentralization of care and prevention funding to local and regional authorities. Moreover, many more voices at the governmental level come into the discussion around the national drug policy nowadays. A new consensus had to be found: greater priority to drug trafficking and organized crime, a stricter policy regarding coffee shops with the objective of bringing down their number, and a way to combat the drug-related public nuisance problems. The further developed national consensus speaks clearly in the new constellation of drug policy objectives.

Besides these important new gestures to the troubled communities in the Netherlands—and to the European partners—the strong emphasis on quality of care and prevention remained. Experiments with preventive strategies and heroin maintenance are also main objectives in the 1995 drug policy report "Continuity and Change," prepared by the Ministry of Foreign Affairs and other Dutch ministries. In this combined report from the Departments of Foreign Affairs, Health, Justice, and Internal Affairs, the "self" and the "other" are one again.

The third area to discuss in the context of evaluating Dutch drug policy is the costs of enforcing drug laws in comparison with those of other countries, each with its own drug policy. Tax money is social money to be used to serve the collective good in a humane way. The more cost-effective a government is in its policies, the more satisfied the constituency will be. If it is important to the individual taxpayer to get his or her money's worth, then cost-effectiveness of policy measures is a major criterion for evaluating (drug) policies.

A comparison between the drug policy costs of law enforcement and health care in the United States and the Netherlands provides insight into the level of cost-effectiveness of two opposing drug policies: the repressive U.S. model and the more liberal Dutch model. The number of convictions and prison sentences for drug felonies per 1,000 persons is more than five times higher in the U.S. than in the Netherlands. The U.S. per capita prison population incarcerated for drug felonies is sixteen times higher than that of the Dutch population (CBS 1991, Kraan 1996, Reuter 1992). In the United States, between 1980 and 1994, the number of inmates incarcerated in federal prisons for drug law violations increased by 850 percent. In the same period the number of inmates in state prisons incarcerated for drug law violations increased 1,055 percent (Lindesmith Center 1996).

The costs per capita of drug law enforcement are more than four times higher in the U.S. than in the Netherlands. The costs per capita of health care for drug users are more or less the same in the U.S. and the Netherlands (Bureau of Justice Statistics 1992, CBS 1991, Kraan 1996). According to a recent RAND report (Caulkins et al. 1997), the general conclusion is that the U.S. "mandatory minimum drug sentences are not justifiable on the basis of cost-effectiveness at reducing cocaine consumption, cocaine expenditures, or drug-related crime" (p. xvi). Another conclusion is that treatment is by far the most cost-effective of the alternative cocaine control strategies (Caulkins et al. 1997).

Shenk (1996) stated in an article on U.S. drug policy: "Putting a murderer in jail means one less murderer on the street. Putting a drug dealer in jail means a job opening" (p. 10). Here we are speaking to the pragmatic and cost-effective side of a drug policy. What are the results, and how much is the collective cost? The numbers speak for themselves. What cannot be estimated in numbers, though, is the vast amount of human suffering caused by the repressive approach.

PUBLIC HEALTH OBJECTIVES

In describing Dutch drug policy as "harm reducing," "normalizing," and "pragmatic," the main policy objectives are linked to public order and, especially, to public health. An important dimension of the social drug problem is the somatic symptoms presented by drug users. Examples are complications due to extended use of contaminated street drugs, bad nutrition, overdosing, bad vein care, treatment of abscesses and cotton infections, women's health issues, and several infectious diseases, including HIV, TB, hepatitis A, B, and C, and sexually transmitted diseases (STDs).

Illegality causes a lack of regulation in the drug market. In a destructive spiral of violence and crime, the prices of street drugs will be relatively high. Without quality control, the health of drug consumers is endangered. Still, the results show that the differentiated circuit of care and prevention services in the Netherlands is working quite effectively.

The first criterion to look at when measuring the results of a drug policy in the context of public health is the number of fatalities from drug overdoses. The number of deaths from drugs per 100,000 of the population is at least twice as high in other countries than it is in the Netherlands. Moreover, unlike in other parts of the world, it is not rising (De Zwart and Mensink 1996). Rossi (1995) compared the data from the UN report, "Substance Abuse Related Mortality: A World Wide View" (UN 1994), and concluded that the number of drug-related deaths per capita in the Netherlands is seven times lower than that of the United States.

Another criterion to consider when evaluating the results of the public health objectives in Dutch drug policy is the number of AIDS cases in the injecting drug user population. In the early 1980s the government made the clear political choice that the fight against AIDS had more priority than the fight against drugs. The prohibitive policy of artificial scarcity (as occurs in the United States with paraphernalia laws) creates a situation in which sterile syringes for intravenous drug users are still not easily available. HIV infection and other infectious diseases (like hepatitis B and C) are therefore a frequent side effect of being an intravenous drug user in the current sociopolitical context because syringes must be shared among drug users (Gezondheidsraad 1996). Public health is well served by a comprehensive circuit of care and prevention services targeted at intravenous drug users. General costs for medical care will benefit from such a public health policy for intravenous drug users.

Approximately 10 percent of the total number of reported AIDS cases in the Netherlands are injecting drug users (De Zwart and Mensink 1996). The average percentage for Europe is 39 percent, while the U.S. estimates the percentage at around 50 percent of the total number of reported cases.

This percentage includes the following statistical categories: gay men who inject drugs, heterosexual contact with an injecting drug user, and the many pediatric AIDS cases that are drug related (HIV/AIDS Surveillance Report 1997). In the Netherlands it is especially salient that the incidence of new AIDS cases has been dropping since 1993 (De Zwart and Mensink 1996). The Dutch health authorities feel the epidemic is more or less under control.

Regarding the effects of prevention strategies on safer practices, there are indications that 60 percent of the heroin-addicted sex workers now use condoms, as against 20 percent in 1986 (Van Ameijden 1994). Another result of prevention messages, and of responsible practices by drug users, is the observed trend of long-term heroin users in the Netherlands switching from injecting to "smoking" heroin from heated aluminum foil. Between 1992 and 1995 the number of needles exchanged in Amsterdam went down by 29 percent. One of the biggest needle exchange programs in Amsterdam reported an exchange rate of 99 percent over 1996, that is, that 99 percent of the syringes distributed were returned. This demonstrates that Amsterdam drug users have been taking responsibility for safe disposal of used syringes (Viergever 1997).

A big part of the success of HIV prevention programs in the Netherlands is the result of easy access to the high-risk group of injecting drug users, mainly through methadone maintenance programs. Realistic estimates show that the comprehensive Dutch drug care system reaches 60 to 80 percent of all hard drug users (De Zwart and Mensink 1996, Ministry of Health, Welfare, and Sport 1993). There is broad and low-threshold access to sterile syringes and other paraphernalia for injecting drug users. Originally, before AIDS became known as a drug-related disease in the early 1980s, needle exchange programs in the Netherlands were established to prevent the further spread of hepatitis among injecting drug users. When the Dutch became aware of the AIDS epidemic, the government decided to flood the market of drug consumers with safe injection equipment in the context of public health. Fifteen years later the statistics on AIDS among injecting drug users show the wisdom of this policy decision.

The results of Dutch drug policy seem promising when the main criteria are compared internationally. Most of the still problematic areas of the drug problem in Dutch society—public nuisance, criminality of drug purchases, drug tourism, organized crime involved in (inter)national trade, the enormous amount of "black" money that threatens our economy and the general democratic order—are heavily related to the decision by the *world* community to prohibit these drugs. Under these international circumstances, the Netherlands is harvesting positive results with its drug policy of enlightened pragmatism (Moisi 1997). The positive results are replicated only in countries or states where the same policy choices are made. The international prohibitive context creates limits to this ongoing process of experimenting with the social drug problem within the national context. These limits have more or less been reached, nationally and internationally: nationally, because after twenty-five years the process of adaptation to "alien" drugs has reached a point where the conflict between "condoning" and "repressing" has to be resolved; internationally, because the European community demands harmonization of drug policies.

CONCLUSIONS

THE LIMITATIONS OF DRUG POLICY

The landscape of drug policy is varied in the Western world. It ranges from repressive and prohibitive policies to rather liberal and humane ones. In the past decade the drug situation has worsened in many countries, judged either by the number of drug-associated deaths or the amount of drugs seized by the authorities. Moreover, the social consequences of illicit drug use—such as drug-related crime, drug selling in public, or drug users loitering in formerly "safe" neighborhoods—have become visible and are defined as popular problems. The trend has caused an increasing number of people to plead for a change in drug policy (Reuband 1995).

With regard to the correlation between drug policy and the use of drugs, one can conclude that it is shortsighted and illusory to hope that *any* drug policy will have much effect on the supply or demand for drugs. Comparative studies of epidemiological findings in European countries indicate that rates of drug use in countries with liberal drug policies are neither higher nor lower than they are in countries with a more repressive policy (Reuband 1995). The *costs* of a prohibitive drug policy, however, as in the United States, are many times higher for the taxpayer than they are in countries with a more pragmatic, yet still humane, approach, as in the Netherlands.

It is obvious that the current repressive drug policies affect entirely different areas from those usually assumed (Baum 1996, Drucker 1995, Gordon 1994, Reuband 1995). The effects might be sought less in the prevalence rates, as evidenced by the example of the increase in cannabis use over recent years in countries with cannabis policies that vary from very prohibitive (in the United States, France, and Sweden) to more liberal (Netherlands). The prevalence of drug use is no less in countries with a prohibitive approach. In 1993, 12 percent of the U.S. population—or 15.5 million people—reported any illegal drug use during that year (USDHHS 1994).

The effects of drug policy are more apparent in patterns of use, physical complications, public health issues (especially HIV/AIDS and hepatitis), racism, crime rates, and even erosion of human rights. What has been proved by now is that repressive drug policies create a mix of serious biopsychosocial harms. Within a multifactor approach to drug use, the factor "prohibitive drug policy" has become singularly important in *causing* and *maintaining* a lot of drug-related harm (Majoor 1996). In contrast, informal social control mechanisms and sociocultural attitudes seem to be more important in creating and maintaining the use of drugs in a society than formal control mechanisms and drug availability (Fromberg 1993, Reuband 1995).

It seems reasonable to conclude that a drug policy reflecting an understanding of these informal social control mechanisms and sociocultural attitudes creates the protected (or regulated) space for acculturation of a substance over a longer period of years. The statistics and the qualitative data suggest that such a drug policy serves the public interest best on the most important of criteria: public health, public order, and cost-effectiveness.

AIDS AS A CHALLENGE

AIDS has been a major factor to challenge the prohibitionist ideology, as we have seen. For countries like the Netherlands and Australia, the integration of harm reduction services at the moment the high-risk relationship between injecting drug use and AIDS became apparent has worked very well. In terms of public health objectives the harm reduction policies have been a major success. Other countries have waited, and most are still waiting. Blinded by the illusion of control, countries like the United States keep on ignoring the major disaster of the war on drugs and the failing AIDS policy for (injecting) drug users.

The only way to account for this is willful ignorance: there is something more important than the fact that so many drug users are infected with HIV, criminalized, and marginalized. Since 1987, injecting drug users represent the biggest percentage of new HIV infections in New York City and State (NYSDOH 1997). Ten years later, needle exchange, the empirically proven, most effective preventive strategy, is still banned by city and federal politics (Des Jarlais et al. 1996, National Academy of Sciences 1996, *Lancet* 1995). Needle exchange is available to only 18 percent of the injecting drug-using population of New York city, and possession of syringes remains illegal. In 1998 it is only the funding of New York State that keeps the existing needle exchange programs in New York alive. In a recent article in *The Lancet*, Lurie and Drucker (1997) presented—after analyzing many data sources—some conservative estimates, of sad proportions, however: HIV infections associated with the lack of a national needle exchange program in the United States are estimated at around 10,000 so far (on the basis of a 33 percent incidence reduction because of the implementation of needle exchange programs). The

cost to the U.S. health care system of treating these preventable HIV infections is $538 million. If current policies are not changed, they estimate an
additional 11,329 preventable HIV infections by the year 2000 (Holmberg
1996, Lurie and Drucker 1997).

What can be more important than these facts? What creates this stun-
ning lack of pragmatism and cost-effectiveness regarding important public
health issues like AIDS, hepatitis, and STDs? What can be more important
than saving or relieving the lives of so many citizens with minor fiscal investments compared to the costs of the war on drugs? In 1997 the yearly
budget of the National Drug Control Strategy in the United States is almost
$15 billion (White House 1996). Prohibitive world drug policies have created
an illicit drug industry that accounts for 8 percent of the world trade. In
1997 drug trafficking is a $400 billion-a-year worldwide trade (UN1997). Ille-
gal drugs are bigger business than all exports of automobiles.

Only with users of illicit drugs is there the confounding problem of the
effects of morality in politics. Moralistic judgments take over, and zero tolerance through punishment and treatment becomes the only possible answer.
The Netherlands took a different road with the same illicit drug users by
formulating a policy characterized by acceptance and integration; it is client-
centered and focuses on meeting people's needs and listening to why they
use and how they manage their drug use.

The coping mechanism that addictive behavior often represents is an
important cue to where the group or a community is. Freedom of expression
as a postmaterialist purpose for policy development means that the main
culture has to listen to and look at expressions of subcultures that might be
different, or even threatening. The use of drugs like cannabis, heroin, cocaine, amphetamines, and MDMA has become part of our culture within
three decades, whether we want it or not. These drugs have become part of
who we are as a society, which we have failed to learn at increasing social
and economic cost.

Nowadays there are two approaches taken in drug policy. In the first
the authorities take over the responsibility for citizens' behavior and tell them:
"Just don't do it, because if you do take drugs I will punish you severely."
The other approach is for a government to strive to make users responsible
for self-managing their drug use by creating safe boundaries to protect the
individual *and* the public. Within these safe boundaries the process of acculturation can take place until the individual citizen, and the social control of
families and communities, can take over.

The United States and other countries with repressive drug policies are
saturated with a rigid morality that blocks out any evidence of a failing policy.
Collective emotions prevail where the rational comparison of concrete policy
results should reign. The incredible inefficiency of repressive drug policies

on all important criteria is fascinating to experience because it forces one to probe the causalities of destructive collective tendencies in a society. An interesting hypothesis in this context is that repression and prohibition as a policy stem from a fear ridden (materialist) attitude toward new social phenomena that feed the need to be "in power," the illusion of control. The main purpose for policies in a materialist society is to maintain public order. The "unknown" for the collective—in this case represented by illicit drugs—creates a threat to public order that has to be eliminated to stay in control, or better, to sustain the safety of the "known." As Wever (1995) concludes: "Maybe the abolition of the 'Federal Monopoly on Drug Policy' will create a lot of space for other, more effective ways of regulating individual and social drug problems" (p. 29).

There seem to be two major factors in American society that fuel a severe, prohibitive drug policy. They may explain the collective fear that is translated into a concrete war on drugs with many casualties and extremely high costs, while none of the policy objectives is even faintly reached. These two factors are *ethics* and *racism*.

ETHICS

Ethics builds a practical philosophy dealing with moral concepts and behavior. In past centuries, and until recently, people handed over their moral responsibility to higher authorities like the church, political powers, or philosophical systems. The dangers in handing over moral responsibility remain social control and repression. In postmaterialist society the schism is that no authority is capable of prescribing universal ethical rules. The danger herein is egocentrism and indifference in some of the members of society: individuals are thrown back on their own authority and moral responsibility. Morality must entail taking responsibility for "the other," your fellow beings, with whom you exist in a group.

The double-sidedness of moral behavior is always present. How do we exert moral responsibility? The answer profoundly defines the relationship between the state and the individual in a society, in that the setting of moral boundaries moves between two extremes. Either you say you know what is good or bad for the individual, which turns moral responsibility into repression (as we have learned well from the histories of materialistic societies), or you say I leave the individual totally free, which could lead to indifference for fellow citizens. The moral society and the individual have to find their balance between these extremes. That is the challenge for the government and the citizen in a postmaterialist society. Intense dialogues between people, displaying controversial opinions, are welcome and necessary. It seems that more noise diminishes the chance for repression.

In the example of drug policy in the Netherlands, we saw how international pressure imposes a materialist context for the social drug problem there, while the national drug policy reflects a postmaterialist approach. The many advisory committees reflecting different interests and goals were forged into a compromise that shows a consistent liberal drug policy over the past three decades that designs the relationship between individual and state on the issue of illicit drug use. The collective agrees not to punish those who use drugs, but to punish those who make big profits out of the illegal drug trade. Individuals who turn to criminal behavior to purchase their drugs will be punished, but we provide them with care and cure services during their incarceration. Within this policy framework the authorities keep on experimenting with new approaches and try to react to new trends in an innovative way. They will always be limited, though, by international obligations. These limitations are "the water in the wine" of the compromise between the Netherlands and the international community. The Netherlands belongs in the international community. Our national policy ("the self") will therefore always be defined by the "other."

There is no clear definition of moral concepts and behavior in a postmaterialist society. The dialogue between the mentioned extremes of "control" or "letting go" is exactly the challenge of this stage of civilization. The danger lies in trying to overcome the insecurity of the double-sidedness of morality by a longing for rigid and predictable rules that will take away the tension of difficult moral choices, and in fact takes away the personal responsibility for our fellow beings, and our communities (Bauman 1995, Majoor 1995). The fear of losing control seems a prominent driving force behind the war on drugs in the United States. The war sustains the illusion of control. Fear-based thinking and its resulting draconian measures create a "safe and known" image for many citizens, and so builds a constituency. No statistics or empirical findings can overrule this illusion of arriving at the total "cure": a drugfree society. Even all the contradictions presented by empirical knowledge about the use of alcohol, nicotine, and prescription drugs do not have any impact in this context. Illicit drugs are demonized by the USA authorities, and now they represent a public image that it is heroic to fight against as a citizen, a police officer, and especially as a politician (Baum 1996, Gordon 1994).

Regarding the situation in the United States, it seems crucial to move to a more postmaterialist approach in which the authority dares to get out of the way and give the individual more responsibility. The locus of control has to be guided from mass toward individual control. That is very hard in the U.S. because of the other important factor that is causal in maintaining a repressive drug policy. That major factor is racism.

RACISM

If the perception of individual fellow citizens in a society is blinded by a historically defined pigmentocracy, a class society is constructed with first-, second-, and third-class citizens. The legacy of many decades of racism is found in the statistics on poverty, public education, teenage pregnancy, unemployment, crime/violence, incarceration, AIDS and other health issues, and substance use (Gordon 1994).

The fastest-growing underclass in the United States consists in large part of African-Americans, but special attention should be given to the Latino population, which is growing rapidly and facing a comparable disaster as a result of the collective treatment by the main culture. Day (1995) reports that in 1993 there were almost two and a half times as many white injecting drug users in the United States as there were black injecting drug users. Still, one in three young African-American men is now under criminal justice control. In 1991 the population of drug law violators in state prisons consisted of 3.5 percent white nonhispanics, 60 percent African-Americans, and 37 percent hispanics (Lindesmith Center 1996). Black and Latino injectors are respectively five and three times more likely to get AIDS than are white injectors (Day 1995).

The war on drugs in the U.S. is the bureaucratization of prohibition politics. Prohibition really means excluding certain things, persons, and groups because they threaten some status quo. The result is marginalization, becoming outcast. In the urban ghettos of U.S. society we find the overwhelming truth of this reality. Refined through decades of social marginalization, the color of skin has become a source of anger and fear that perpetuates itself (Gordon 1994). Millions of fellow citizens are doomed to a life of mere survival. The answers to very basic security needs that lay the foundation for moving toward a more civilized collective are absent in these communities. This reality is the responsibility of a collective. It is something to consider as a group. The only way out of this self-maintaining destructiveness is to give the responsibility back to the individual, whatever the skin color.

If we are to learn from the lessons of Dutch drug policy, it is of utmost importance to realize that no conclusions can be drawn without taking the context of social security into consideration. Dutch drug policy is rooted in the realization that *any* social problem (poverty, racism, illegal drugs, homosexuality) is a problem because society marginalizes certain groups by its written and unwritten rules. It is based on the notion that drug use as a social problem is just one of the symptoms of social marginalization of certain groups.

The Dutch collective morality says it is inhumane to have collective systems that marginalize people, and we also know that it creates an enormous collective cost. In this context illegal drug use becomes a social phenomenon that should be "normalized"–in the sense of *integrated*—in our collective endeavors, and "shrunk" to individual proportions. Then harm reduction, in terms of public health *and* crime *and* ethics—and even in terms of costs—is truly possible.

CONTINUUM OF DRUG CARE SERVICES

To reduce the harm of prohibitive drug policies, we have to maneuver between extremes, and look for a middle course. The cannabis experiment in the Netherlands teaches us that a drug policy that creates space for a slow adaptation to a certain drug works best in terms of normalization and harm reduction.

Meanwhile, some drug users get into trouble and need help. The Dutch approach has proved that taking good care of the relatively few drug users who are in trouble helps to reduce the negative collective image of illicit drug use to more normal proportions. An effective drug care provision reflects the complex nature of addiction. Heterogeneity of the client population, high risk status for AIDS and other infectious diseases, and high relapse rates after treatment are the most important reasons in the field of addiction for building a differentiated spectrum of services. Stepped care is a concept used to describe the professional approach to differentiated drug care provision. The least intensive services are provided first. When this less intensive strategy of service provision clearly fails to help the client, a more intensive next step is considered. The matching of client needs on the one hand and the choice between differentiated services on the other always directs this process. Client-centeredness and a comprehensive continuum of care are crucial in this effective approach. The less intrusive an intervention is, the better for continuity in the life of a client and the less the chances for chronic dependence on service provision. "Optimal autonomy" of a client is always the general objective of any care intervention. Stepped care also makes it possible to manage the costs of care in an effective way because the very expensive clinical treatment of drug clients will be used only when clearly indicated by failure of less intensive interventions.

There is a big call in the United States for more drug treatment slots. I wonder about that client "need." If a comprehensive care continuum for drug users who need help (including care/harm reduction *and* cure/treatment services) were created, the present call for *treatment* slots would probably disappear. Moreover, the present treatment capacity would be used in a much more effective way in terms of helping a client stay abstinent after treatment and in terms of dropout rates.

THE FUTURE OF DUTCH DRUG POLICY

It seems that the Dutch have come full circle. The first legislation on drugs in the Netherlands during the 1920s was induced by international pressure and passed in a deafening collective silence because there was no perceived social drug problem. In the 1970s Dutch society was confronted with a clear drug problem, and approached it in the old tradition of social problem solving: compromise between humane and pragmatic interests. The result was a drug policy that was stretched to the boundaries of the international fear-based repressive approach. Enough national experimental space was found to develop a normalizing and effective drug (and AIDS) policy compared to international statistics. In "splendid isolation," a different approach to the social drug problem was developed.

The serious jump toward a bigger international community in the 1990s started building international pressure on Dutch drug policy again. Creation of the European Union focused international attention on the Netherlands vis-à-vis its drug policy. Holland now is literally identified with the demonized image of illicit drugs that become the threat to a harmonized European drug policy.

The Netherlands have come full circle in the development of their drug policy. The pioneer stage is over. The history of contemporary Dutch drug policy started with international pressure dictating national decisions. The country then went its own way and started experimenting with harm reduction and normalizing of drug use. Now international politics seem to be back as a main force that drives our national drug policy. The next ten years will be of crucial importance to the question of whether the Netherlands can continue their normalizing approach to drug use. The proceedings will not happen in silence this time because the drug issue is front page news nowadays. "The more noise . . . the less chance for repression" (Bauman 1995, p. 5). Whether all this noise will save the benefits of Dutch drug policy is hard to predict. In Europe no fellow countries fully support the Dutch approach to illicit drug use in the political arena. The issue in general is not of enough importance as an internationally shared subject of interest. Economic interests are the driving force behind the European Union and most international relationships, certainly now that our massive ideological enemy—called communism—has dissolved.

Can a minor political issue like drugs stand the storm of (inter)national economic interests? Dutch history teaches us the most probable answer: if the scapegoat of illicit drug use keeps enhancing the unification of Europe, as the shared enemy does to otherwise rival tribes in a war, then the Netherlands' drug policy will be sacrificed by the European community on the altar of international economic interests. As a small country in a strategic spot in Europe, the Netherlands needs the international relationships and cannot afford isolation, or even dissonance.

Policies represent our self-image and our image of the other, and in the end they represent emotions. In its ability to deal with social phenomena such as "the drug problem" in an effective and humane way, a society shows its maturity in terms of civilization. Let us hope that the bad results of repressive drug policies will convince the world community that a more liberal model is needed. But that is a rational assumption, and we are trying to solve a problem that is defined by emotions. Emotions do not care about rationalities.

The Netherlands may have a wise story to tell about its experiences in drug policy, but it is the international community that will make the decision concerning a more humane and effective solution. For that the fear of the unknown must be overcome. That will be a hard and long process, because *"the mildest suggestion for change is a death-threat to some status quo"* (Bach 1988).

REFERENCES

Baan Committee Report; Werkgroep Verdovende Middelen (1972). *Achtergronden en risico's van druggebruik*. Den Haag: Staatsuitgeverij.

Bach, R. (1988). *One*. New York: Dell.

Baum, D. (1996). *Smoke and Mirrors: The War on Drugs and the Politics of Failure*. New York: Little, Brown.

Bauman, Z. (1995). Ode aan de dubbelzinnigheid. Interview with the English sociologist Zygmunt Bauman about his book *Life in Fragments*. Peter Giesen, *De Volkskrant*, Het Vervolg, 20 mei.

Bieleman, B., Snippe, J., and De Bie, E. (1995). *Drugs binnen de grenzen, harddrugs en criminaliteit in Nederland; schattingen van de omvang*. Groningen/Rotterdam: Stichting Intraval.

Blom, T., and Van Mastrigt, H. (1996). The future of the Dutch model in the context of the war on drugs. In *Between Prohibition and Legalization: The Dutch Experiment in Drug Policy*, ed. E. Leuw and I. Haen Marshall, pp. 255–281. Amsterdam/New York: Kugler.

Braam, R. (1995). *Cannabis in Utrecht, deel 4: Buurten bij de koffieshop*. Utrecht: Centrum voor Verslavingsonderzoek, Universiteit van Utrecht.

Bureau of Justice Statistics (1992). *Drugs, Crime and the Justice System*. Washington, DC: U.S. Department of Justice.

Caulkins, J. P., Rydell, C. P., Schwabe, W. L., and Chiesa, J. (1997). *Mandatory Minimum Drug Sentences: Throwing Away the Key or the Taxpayers' Money?* Santa Monica, CA/Washington, DC: RAND, Drug Policy Research Center.

Central Bureau of Statistics (CBS) (1991). *Criminaliteit en Strafrechtspleging 1989*. Den Haag: SDU Uitgeverij.

Cohen, P. (1989). *Cocaine Use in Amsterdam in Nondeviant Subcultures*. Amsterdam: Instituut voor Sociale Geografie, Universiteit van Amsterdam.

Cohen, P., and Sas, A. (1993). *Ten Years of Cocaine. A Follow-up Study of 64 Cocaine Users in Amsterdam*. Amsterdam: Instituut voor Sociale Geografie, Universiteit van Amsterdam.

————, eds. (1996). *Cannabisbeleid in Duitsland, Frankrijk en de Verenigde Staten*. Amsterdam: CEDRO, Institute for Social Geography, University of Amsterdam.

Day, D. (1995). *Health Emergency—The Spread of Drug-Related AIDS among African-Americans and Latinos*. Washington, DC: Drug Policy Foundation.

De Kort, M. (1995). *Tussen patient en delinquent. Geschiedenis van het Nederlandse drugsbeleid*. Hilversum: Verloren.

De Loor, A. (1989). *XTC bestaat niet*. Amsterdam: Adviesburo Drugs.

———— (1990). *AIDS Preventie begint niet bij de buren*. Amsterdam: Adviesburo Drugs.

———— (1992). *The Safe House Campaign*. Amsterdam: Adviesburo Drugs.

———— (1993). *Hash Coffeeshops and their Patrons*. Amsterdam: Adviesburo Drugs.

Des Jarlais, D. C., Marmor, M., Paone, D., et al. (1996). HIV incidence among injecting drug users in New York City syringe exchange programmes. *The Lancet* 348:987–991.

De Swaan, A. (1988). *In Care of the State: Health Care, Education and Welfare in Europe and the USA in the Modern Era*. Cambridge: Polity Press.

De Zwart, W. M., and Mensink, C. (1996). *Jaarboek Verslaving 1995—over gebruik en zorg in cijfers*. Houten/Diegem: Bohn Stafleu Van Loghum/NIAD.

De Zwart, W. M., Mensink, C., and Kuipers, S. B. M. (1993). *Kerngegevens over roken, drinken, druggebruik en gokken onder scholieren ouder dan 10 j*. Utrecht: Nederlands Instituut voor Alcohol en Drugs (NIAD).

Driessen, F. M. H. M. (1992). *Methadonclienten in Nederland*. Rijswijk/Utrecht: Ministerie van WVC/Bureau Driessen.

Drucker, E. (1995). Harm reduction: a public health strategy. *Current Issues in Public Health* 1:64–70.

Ehlers, S. (1995). Maintenance tests readied in Australia, Netherlands. *The Drug Policy Letter* 27:13.

Engelsman, E. L. (1986). *Drug policy: Is the cure worse than the disease? To a process of normalization of drug problems*. Paper presented at the 15th ICAA International Institute on Prevention and Treatment of Drug Dependence, Amsterdam/Noordwijkerhout, April.

———— (1989). Dutch policy on the management of drug related problems. *British Journal of Addiction* 84:211–218.

Fromberg, E. (1990). *XTC, Hard Drug of genotsmiddel*. Amsterdam/Lisse: Swets & Zeitlinger.

———— (1993). Prohibition as a necessary stage in the acculturation of foreign drugs. In *Psychoactive Drugs and Harm Reduction: From Faith to Science*, ed. N. Heather, A. Wodak, E. Nadelmann, and P. A. O'Hare, pp. 127–136. London: Whurr Publishers Ltd.

Fromberg, E., and Jansen, F. (1993). *The Drugs Information Monitoring System*. Utrecht: Nederlands Instituut voor Alcohol en Drugs.

Fromberg, E., and Majoor, B. (1993). *Dutch drug policy: past, present and future*. Paper presented at the Drug Policy Foundation Conference, Washington, DC, November.

Gezondheidsraad (National Health Council) (1996). *Commissie Hepatitis B: Bescherming tegen Hepatitis B*. Rijswijk: Gezondheidsraad, Publication No. 1996/15.

Gordon, D. R. (1994). *The Return of the Dangerous Classes - Drug Prohibition and Policy Politics*. New York/London: W.W. Norton & Company.

HIV/AIDS Surveillance Report (1997). *U.S. HIV and AIDS cases reported through December 1996*. Washington, DC: U.S. Department of Health and Human Services; CDC National AIDS Clearinghouse, vol. 8, No. 2.

Holmberg, S. D. (1996). The estimated prevalence and incidence of HIV in 96 large US metropolitan areas. *American Journal of Public Health* 86:642–654.

Hulsman Committee Report (1971). *Ruimte in het Drugbeleid*. Meppel: Boom/Stichting Algemeen Central Bureau voor de Geestelijke Volksgezondheid.

Inglehart, R. (1971). The silent revolution in Europe: intergenerational change in post-industrial societies. *American Political Science Review* 65:991–1017.

―――― (1981). Post-materialism in an environment of insecurity. *American Political Science Review* 75:880–900.

Inspectie Volksgezondheid (1995, 1996). *Jaarverslagen 1994 en 1995.* Rijswijk: VWS.

(ISAD) Interdepartementale Stuurgroep Alcohol—en Drugbeleid (ISAD) (1985). *Drugbeleid in beweging; naar een normalisering van de drugproblematiek.* Den Haag: Staatsuitgeverij.

Janssen, O. J. A., and Swierstra, K. (1982). *Heroinegebruikers in Nederland; een typologie van levensstijlen.* Groningen: Instituut voor Criminologie, Universiteit van Groningen.

Kaplan, C. D., Haanraadts, D. J., Van Vliet, H. J., and Grund, J. P. (1996). Is Dutch drug policy an example to the world? In *Between Prohibition and Legalization: The Dutch Experiment in Drug Policy,* ed. E. Leuw and I. Haen Marshall, pp. 311–335. Amsterdam/New York: Kugler.

Korf, D. J., and Leuw, E. (1992). *Druggebruik, drugverslaving en criminaliteit.* In *Drugspreventie, achtergronden, praktijk en toekomst,* ed. W. R. Buisman and J. C. Van der Stel, pp. 88–105. Houten/Zaventem: Bohn Stafleu Van Loghum.

Korf, D. J., Muller, G., Freeman, M., and Lettink, D. (1993). *Drugstoerisme in de grensstreek.* Amsterdam: Amsterdams Bureau voor Onderzoek en Statistiek O+S.

Kraan, D. J. (1996). An economic view on Dutch drugs policy. In *Between Prohibition and Legalization: The Dutch Experiment in Drug Policy,* ed. E. Leuw and I. Haen Marshall, pp. 283–309. Amsterdam/New York: Kugler.

Kuipers, S. B. M., Mensink, C., and De Zwart, W. M. (1993). *Jeugd en riskant gedrag.* Utrecht: Nederlands Instituut voor Alcohol en Drugs.

The Lancet (1995). Editorial: Coming clean about needle exchange. 346, No. 8967, p. 1377.

Leuw, E., and Aron, U. (1995). *Een orienterend veldonderzoek naar het functioneren van 'coffeeshops'.* Den Haag: Interimverslag van het vooronderzoek 'Coffeeshops', Ministerie van Justitie, WODC.

Lindesmith Center (1996). *Factsheet: Drug Prohibition & The U.S. Prison System.* New York: The Lindesmith Center.

Lurie, P., and Drucker, E. (1997). An opportunity lost: HIV infections associated with lack of a national needle-exchange programme in the USA. *The Lancet* 349:604–608.

Maalste, N. (1995). *Cannabis in Utrecht, deel 3: Stamgasten van de koffieshops.* Utrecht: Centrum voor Verslavingsonderzoek, Universiteit van Utrecht.

Majoor, B. (1990). *Community-based reinsertion of drug users in the Netherlands.* Paper presented at the 2nd Technical Euro-Arab Seminar on Drug Misuse Problems, Council of Europe, Strasbourg, September.

―――― (1992). *Samengaan in zorg? - actuele ontwikkelingen in beleid en werkveld.* Paper presented at the NIAD-conference 'Who cares?', Utrecht, April.

―――― (1994a). *An Ostrich in AIDS-land.* Summary of the Mini-Conference on AIDS & Detention - the policy, Rotterdam, December.

―――― (1994b). *Helping the helpers—a plea for structural support of heart workers.* Paper presented at the Vth International Conference on the Reduction of Drug related Harm, Toronto, March.

―――― (1995). *Ethics and Harm Reduction.* Paper presented at the Ist North American Harm Reduction Conference, New York, June.

―――― (1996). *New Approaches in Drug Care.* Course Curriculum, European Addiction Training Institute, Jellinek Consultancy, Amsterdam.

Maslow, A. H. (1954). *Motivation and Personality.* New York: Harper.

Ministry of Foreign Affairs, Ministry of Health, Welfare and Sport, Ministry of Justice, Ministry of the Interior (1995). *Drugs Policy in the Netherlands: Continuity and Change.* Rijswijk: Staatsuitgeverij.

Ministry of Health, Welfare and Sport (1993). *Drugs en Overlast.* [*Drugs and Nuisance.*] Rijswijk: WVC.

—————— (1995). *Stadhuis en House; handreikingen voor gemeentelijk beleid inzake grootschalige manifestaties en uitgaansdrugs.* Rijswijk: VWS.

Moisi, D. (1997). Frankrijk kan arrogantie jegens Nederland beter laten vallen. *NRC-weekeditie.* 14 januari, 11.

Nadelmann, E. (1995). Beyond Needle Park: the Swiss maintenance trial. *The Drug Policy Letter* 27:12–14.

National Academy of Sciences (1996). *Preventing HIV Transmission: The Role of Sterile Needles and Bleach.* Washington, DC: National Academy Press.

National Council on Public Health (NRV) (1994). *Kwaliteitsbeleid Verslavingszorg.* Zoetermeer: NRV.

Netherlands Institute for Alcohol and Drugs (NIAD) (1991). *Jaarverslag Afdeling Opleiding & Methodiekontwikkeling 1990.* Utrecht: NIAD.

New York State Department of Health (NYSDOH) (1997). *AIDS in New York State, 1996 Edition.* Albany: NYSDOH Bureau of HIV/AIDS Epidemiology.

Noorlander, E. A. (1985). *Gedrag van heroinegebruikers, het zogenaamde Junkie-syndroom.* Paper presented at the Spring Conference of the Dutch Association of Psychiatrists, May.

Penning, G., Fromberg, E., and Majoor, B. (1988). De KGOD. Intern Memo, Project Deskundigheidsbevordering Drughulpverleningsinstellingen, FZA; also in: *Jojo Info Bulletin. 2.*

Reuband, K.-H. (1995). Drug use and drug policy in western Europe—epidemiological findings in a comparative perspective. *European Addiction Research* 1:32–41.

Reuter, P. (1992). Hawks ascent: the punitive trend of American drug policy. *Daedalus* 121(3): 15–22.

Rossi, C. (1995). Evaluating world drug policies - towards a cost-effectiveness analysis of initiatives undertaken. *The International Journal of Drug Policy* 6(4):238–242.

Shenk, J. W. (1996). Reconcilable differences. *The Drug Policy Letter* 31:9–10.

Silvis, J. (1982). Narcotica-verdragen lossen geen problemen op. *NJB. 33.* 913–918.

Spruit, I. P., ed. (1997). *Jaarboek Verslaving 1996, over gebruik en zorg.* Houten/Diegem: Bohn Stafleu Van Loghum/Trimbos Instituut.

Swierstra, K. E. (1994). Drugscenario's; Paars regeerakkoord, roze toekomstbeelden. *Justitiele Verkenningen* 20(8):116–124.

Swierstra, K. E., Janssen, O. J. A., and Jansen, J. H. (1986). *De Reproductie van het Heroinegebruik onder nieuwe lichtingen. Heroinegebruikers in Nederland—part II.* Groningen: Instituut voor Criminologie, Universiteit van Groningen.

UN Report (1994). *Substance Abuse Related Mortality: A Worldwide Review.* Vienna: United Nations International Drug Control Program, Vienna International Center.

—————— (1997). *The World Trade in Illicit Drugs.* Vienna: United Nations International Drug Control Program, Vienna International Center.

U.S. Department of Health and Human Services (USDHHS) (1994). *National Household Survey on Drug Abuse: Population Estimates 1993.* Washington, DC: Substance Abuse and Mental Health Services Administration, DHHS Publication No. (SMA) 94-3017.

Van Ameijden, E. (1994). *Evaluation of AIDS Prevention Measures among Drug Users; The Amsterdam Experience.* Wageningen: Ponsen en Looijen.

Van Epen, J. H. (1984). *De algebra van de behoefte.* Paper presented at Sophia Hospital for Children, Rotterdam, November.

Vermeulen, E. (1995). Structuring treatment and counselling processes at the Jellinek—problem-oriented evaluation and registration method (PER). *Jellinek Quarterly* 5.

Viergever, B. (1997). Spuitenruil in Amsterdam and Rotterdam. *Mainline* 1:21.

Visser, R. (1994). *Het uitgaanscircuit in 1994: uitdagingen en mogelijkheden voor drugpreventie.* Verslag van het Nationale Drugpreventie Debat, Amsterdam.

Wever, L. J. S. (1995). *Vijfentwintig jaar drugsbeleid van de Nederlandse overheid: terugblik en evaluatie.* In *Handboek Verslaving*, pp. A4000-1–A4000-31. Houten: Bohn Stafleu Van Loghum.

——— (1996). Drugs as a public health problem: assistance and treatment. In *Between Prohibition and Legalization: The Dutch Experiment in Drug Policy*, ed. E. Leuw and I. Haen Marshall, pp. 59–74. Amsterdam/New York: Kugler.

White House (1996). *National Drug Control Strategy Budget Summary 1997.* Washington, DC: The White House.

Wodak, A. (1992). HIV infection and injecting drug use in Australia. *Journal of Drug Issues* 22:549.

Zinberg, N. E. (1984). *Drug, Set, and Setting - The Basis for Controlled Intoxicant Use.* New Haven, CT/London: Yale University Press.

8

A Call for an Anti-War Movement

Kevin Alexander Gray

> The racists, that are usually very influential in the society, don't make their move without first going to get public opinion on their side. So they use the press to get public opinion on their side. When they want to suppress and oppress the Black community, what do they do? They take the statistics, and through the press, they feed them to the public. They make it appear that the role of crime in the Black community is higher than it is anywhere else.
>
> What does this do? This message—this is a skillful message used by racists to make the whites who aren't racist think that the rate of crime in the Black community is so high. This keeps the Black community in the image of a criminal. It makes it appear that anyone in the Black community is a criminal. And as soon as this impression is given, then it makes it possible, or paves the way to set up a police-type state in the Black community, getting the full approval of the white public when the police use all kinds of brutal measures to suppress Black people, crush their skulls, sic dogs on them, and things of that type. And the whites go along with it. Because they think that everybody over there's a criminal anyway . . . .
>
> —MALCOLM X[1]

My sincere thanks to Efia Nwangaza, Dr. Eva Elisabet Rutström of the University of South Carolina, David Kennison, Frances Close, Dr. Dawn Days of the Dogwood Center, Eric Sterling of the Criminal Justice Policy Foundation, Drs. James Lynch and Ruth Lane of American University, and Glenn Gray for their comments, contributions, and support in the preparation of this chapter. Also, thanks to all the people who shared their stories in hopes for an end to the war. And to my son Brian.

INTRODUCTION

On the street, war has dehumanizing slang. The "slingers" are "shaking out" or selling to the crackheads, lunchboxes, and fiends—the users. The "skeezers" sell their bodies for a crack rock. In years past crack-addicted prostitutes were called "rock stars." To build a "rep," short for reputation, a slinger has to be willing to protect his "spot" or territory. His employers then elevate him to "banger," one "who works in blood and bullets." If a slinger is good in "putting in work" in the "game," whatever that "game" may be, he then becomes a "baller" or "high-rolling hustler."[2] Despite the language or who provides the description, the most common perception of the drug problem is that "it's a black thing!" or a "G [gangsta]-thang!" For white America, the drug problem has a black face. Consequently, this provides the validation for the law enforcement targeting of blacks. Many believe that the dealers are all black because that is what they see on television. The language of the streets and office suites, politics, culture, and media is that of dehumanized dark faces. Dehumanization strips away an individual's humanity and attempts to insert stereotypical, collective properties. It fosters the tyrannical and regressive policy known as the "war on drugs" to the exclusion of policies that focus on the public health implications of substance abuse. It also encourages the undermining of civil liberties and violations of human rights protections. Both the war on drugs and conventional wars practice dehumanization of victims in the mind of the aggressors. In addition, the drug war effects dehumanization of victims in the victims' own minds. Often the combatants (as opposed to communities of innocent bystanders) share a lack of respect for human rights—life, liberty, and property. Furthermore, the aggressors and the victims are united in their hostility to human rights just as drug dealers and users are united in their commitment to the eventual destruction of human life.

Television reflects, monitors, and records where they are waging the government's war. Programs such as COPS seldom, if ever, show police engaged in "dynamic entries" (kicking in doors) out in suburbia. They do not show some soccer mom lying facedown on her living room floor wearing only her underwear. Usually the scene is of the police versus the "violent" drug lawbreakers, who are often portrayed as black. The television war is a real war that America wages against its own citizens. The faces on the floor, the hoods of cars, the pavement, in the dirt, or up against the wall are generally black, Latino, or poor. This may account for the incredulousness that white America feels toward reports that illicit drug usage is prevalent among their children.

Other forms of media, popular culture, and even artistic expression also serve to reinforce the dehumanization needed to wage war. Popular culture images have advanced the notion of the violent and sexually promiscuous underclass; an example being the "gangsta" rappers' portrayal of young black men as angry urban guerrillas locked in a genocidal/suicidal/fratricidal lifestyle. The rappers are often surrounded by black women called "hoochies," a contemporary twist on the myth of Jezebel, the promiscuous black woman. Douglas Kellner of the University of Texas posits that ideology (popular culture) can "seduce individuals into identifying with the dominant system of values, beliefs, and behavior. Ideology replicates their actual conditions of existence, but in a mystical form in which people fail to recognize the negative, historically constructed and thus modifiable nature of society."[3]

The drug war has spread from the urban ghettoes and rural communities of color "across the tracks" to all neighborhoods of color. It is common to witness detained minority motorists with their car trunks open and their personal belongings spread on the side of the road. Police roadblocks are a way of life in neighborhoods of color. Often, when a police stop is made, a questionable search is conducted and if no contraband is found, a black motorist receives what is commonly called a "nigger ticket"—issued to head off any possible legal action or formal complaint. Moreover, stories abound about routine traffic stops that become life-threatening events. Additionally, many black motorists have experienced being surrounded by three or more patrol cars for the issuance of a traffic citation or warning.

The "war on drugs" particularly affects how children are viewed, valued, and treated by society. First, the perception created by the war is that youth are abnormally violent. The dehumanizing portrayal of the current youth subculture as more violent than past generations has resulted in a corresponding erosion of the rights of minors. Warrantless search of lockers, drug-sniffing dogs, and urine testing for athletes have become commonplace in the public schools. Many state and federal laws now allow minors as young as 13 to be tried as adults. This is one of the few areas that society grants minors equal value to adults. Ordinarily, minors do not receive the same rights, protections, or value as adults. It might be assumed that since many in the black community have a child, relative, or friend under some type of penal supervision, they would eschew any attempts at dehumanization. However, it seems that tacit acceptance of the portrayal of youth as abnormally violent has taken place. Since the fear of youth is promoted, solving the drug abuse problem takes a backseat to control and containment. This promotion of fear gives irresponsible adults an escape from facing their responsibility for the problem of so-called incorrigible youth. Instead of dealing with the problems of youth, one often hears stereotyping comments such as, "If you look at them [youth] hard they will cuss you out or shoot you." Fear also creates irresponsible parents. Fear lowers resistance to dehumanization and they surrender parental responsibility to the state. The surrender takes the form of more police with an overabundance of power, boot camps, regressive "youth-oriented" legislation, curfew laws, and schools that are more reminiscent of penal facilities than educational institutions. Consequently, lack of parental responsibility coupled with the increased reliance on control and containment has caused children to resent and lose respect for adults and institutions, especially in the face of the erosion of and disrespect for their equal protection and due process rights. Worse, society witnesses a diminution in value that the child places on all life. These are the dynamics that make for a more violent society.

Hereafter, the war on drugs will be called simply the "war." Let us call it what it is. For many policy experts the information, assumptions, and conclusions of this essay are not new. This chapter is written for those living in an already hostile environment further exacerbated by the so-called "war on drugs." It offers ammunition in the struggle for justice and peace. The ammunition includes exposing the connection of history, politics, policy, and personalities, and how each has fostered the war. A primary theme of this essay, as expressed in the foregoing quotation made by Malcolm X in 1965, is that those who harbor and advance the racist notion that the black community is a community of criminal deviants promote war. Consequently, racism is a primary ingredient in the drug war.

Throughout United States history, racial stereotypes have determined individual actions and interactions, public policy, and group and state conduct. In this context the war is a continuation of attitudes that fostered U.S. participation in the Maafa (slave trade),[4] slave and Black Codes, Jim Crow laws, and state-sponsored segregation. Stated more strongly, the war reflects white supremacy, militarism, or fascism and a total disregard for fundamental civil liberties and human rights. Drug warriors aim these assaults primarily at people of color but the war affects all citizens.

The racial disparity in sentencing overall, and drug sentencing in particular, is reminiscent of the Black Codes and Jim Crow laws—ethnic discrimination against blacks by legal enforcement to contain and control. The sentencing disparity is an obvious disregard for equal protection under the law. In California, for example, records show that between 1988 and 1994 not one white defendant was convicted of a crack offense in the federal courts serving Los Angeles and six other southern counties since the federal government enacted mandatory sentencing in 1986. As reported in *The Los Angeles Times*, nearly all white crack offenders were convicted in state court, where sentences were less severe.[5] Blacks and Latinos were routinely referred to federal courts where jail sentences are commonly much longer than those meted out by the state. Further, the racial and ethnic composition of U.S. jails and prisons and the categorizations within the prisons harken back to the days of segregation. Inmate discipline and rewards (for example, percentages of inmates, by race, in solitary confinement or lockdown, prison work assignments, parole, pardons, probation, work release, and job placement) can all be shown to have racially disparate applications.

American racism is economic in origin and effect. Slavery emerged for economic reasons and racism made inhumane violations of human rights palatable to a majority. The drug war is simply a continuation of the legacy of American economic racism. As for the war being indicative of slavery, the argument is simple. A steady depletion of inner-city business capital and jobs has occurred over the past two decades. Manufacturing jobs have moved from the United States to cheaper labor markets abroad, and immigrant migrant laborers do much of the field or unskilled work.[6] This has made the lack of proper education and skill training among blacks obvious, and created large scale unemployment and underemployment. The poor, unskilled, underemployed, and unemployed black has become the raw material for the unprecedented expansion of the prison-industrial complex. The poor and dispossessed are a recognizable, bountiful, and easily harvested raw material. They are the chattel. Many states and localities use inmate labor for a variety of tasks. This state of affairs is also tantamount to chattel slavery. Chances are, if one is a black, Latino, or poor, one might end up in jail. In the past decade the building of jails has outpaced the building of public housing and schools in many areas. Moreover, the government has demolished and not replaced many older public housing projects. This is not to imply that building more public housing or expanding the welfare state is a solution to the economic problems of the poor. It is merely an example of public policy priorities that make jail one of the few places left for the poor to go.

The war provides a place for both semiskilled and skilled workers. Many of those who once held professional positions and semiskilled jobs in manufacturing now find themselves building and operating the infrastructure of the prison-industrial complex. They are the bail bondsmen, lawyers, judges, police, those who build and supply the prisons, prison guards, social workers, educators, instructors at the various criminal justice academies and criminal justice courses at community and technical colleges, private security officers, home security technicians and salespersons, and many others. Many states and localities depend on prison construction and operation as an integral part of their economies. According to the Census Bureau, federal, state, and local governments increased their prison construction spending from $4 billion in 1975 to $30 billion in 1994. This represents a 612 percent increase between 1970 and 1990. Furthermore, in 1994, spending on construction and operations of prisons increased twice as fast as the growth in overall state spending, according to the National Conference of State Legislatures.[7] In many rural areas the prison has replaced the mill or the factory as the primary employer. In the coalfield region of southwest Virginia the unemployment rate hovers around 20 percent and it is difficult recruiting manufacturers. Building four prisons resulted in the creation of 800 to 1000 jobs.[8] As with any industry, there must be a product that satisfies real or imagined need. The product offered by the prison-industrial complex is the illusory and euphemistic promise of a "safe and secure quality of life"—threat reduction. For war supporters successful threat reduction is measured by an increase in the black jail population (see Figure 8-1, arrest rates for blacks and whites age 18 and older), longer sentences for those convicted of a crime, and more punitive treatment while incarcerated. These increases have come as a direct result of drug arrest and prosecutions.[9]

The charge of conspiracy is raised in the drug debate. The conspiracy charge is not a new one. It is usually linked to the genocide of blacks and covers a variety of concerns. Whatever the concern may be, some blacks maintain the belief that there are small, secret groups of white racists tucked away somewhere plotting policies deleterious to blacks. Awareness of the Tuskeegee syphilis experiment evoked allegations of conspiracy. Long before it was publicly revealed that political operatives in the Richard Nixon White House used crime as an issue to attack blacks or the *San Jose Mercury News* articles exposed possible Drug Enforcement Administration (DEA) and Central Intelligence Agency (CIA) involvement in the drug trade,[10] the cry of conspiracy percolated within the black community. Many blacks now see conspiracy in the disproportionate spread of AIDS and the disproportionate drug arrests in the black community. Business practices of corporate America have long been suspect. The once secret, now public, actions of executives at Texaco oil and Avis car rentals only validated the cries of conspiracy theorists. They see conspiracy in the educational system and in a popular culture that promotes what some feel is a sanitized, majoritarian portrayal of slavery and history. It is felt that the portrayal reinforces the denial that many whites have regarding the economic disparity unjustly created by slavery and racial discrimination. However, historical interpretations, institutions, and popular culture images are functions or outgrowths of supremacy. Fundamentally, with institutional white supremacy and white male hegemony firmly in place, conspiracy is unnecessary. All that a white, majoritarian society needs to endure is maintenance of the status quo. Most people, of whatever race or ethnic origin, unless they are totally disengaged from institutional society, knowingly or unknowingly participate in the maintenance of white supremacy. White supremacy is not only the Ku Klux Klan with its white men in robes. White supremacy is the unjust institutional and structural control by whites. In the American context it is generally controlled by those of Anglo-European descent, although the definition of *white* has expanded throughout the years to include almost everyone except those of African origin. To some extent society and culture often views *white* more as an economic term than a racial classification. White supremacy is the conspiracy. The war helps to maintain and advance it as status quo. Thus, ending white supremacy and curing dispossession are the primary issues to be addressed for genuine reform to take place.

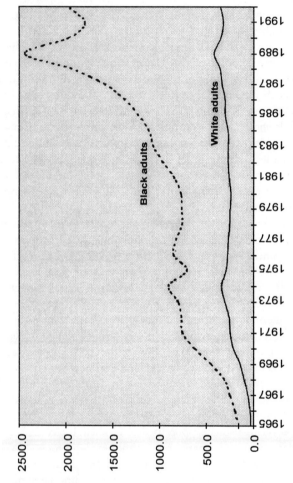

Figure 8–1. Among persons age 18 and older, the arrest rate for drug violations for blacks has grown much more rapidly than the arrest rate for drug violations for whites, 1965–1992

Source: U.S. Department of Justice

At the birth of this nation, the Founding Fathers dispossessed enslaved blacks. Racism was used to rationalize dispossession for the sake of white privilege. Dispossession is denial of capital and access to capital. The Founding Fathers legally defined enslaved Africans as property with no rights whites were bound to respect. They denied them equal opportunity, due process, equal protection, and economic rights. The goal of abolitionism was to secure those rights for all and to repair the damage caused by denial of those rights. This goal has also long been the framework for the human rights struggle. At the signing of the Declaration of Independence the Founding Fathers betrayed the abolitionist cause with the codification of slavery. While the Thirteenth Amendment ended the legal condition of chattel slavery, it failed to eliminate the *effect* that was dispossession. It is dispossession that *causes* and *maintains* racial economic disparity. Abolitionism was about ending dispossession, not just ending the treatment of individuals as property or ending the legal condition of slavery. Once one pulls a knife from a person's chest, one must stop the hemorrhaging or eventually the victim will die. Ending slavery removed the knife. The United States government has yet to treat the hemorrhaging.

When addressing dispossession in America, inevitably one must also address denial. Denial is ignoring the obvious. It is in the expectation placed on African-Americans that they accept thirty years of affirmative action policy as restitution for 300-plus years of slavery and state-supported discrimination— the hemorrhaging. In a legal sense restitution is making amends for an injustice. Affirmative action policy is a conservative remedy to address past and ongoing economic inequities and injustices. Many believe that affirmative action policy is restitution-avoidance policy that has failed to redress the dispossession that epitomizes the phrase "justice denied." The outward expression of white denial is in such wide-ranging comments as, "My ancestors never owned slaves," or "They have had enough time to catch up." While these comments seem to express very different sentiments, both share a denial of both history and economics—current and past. As for the first comment, in most wars the rich and powerful use the poor to defend their interest. Such was the case with nonslave-owning farmers and commoners who fought to defend the economic interest of the wealthy that included the institution of slavery. Many also fought for the possibility of themselves becoming slave holders. Then and now, many whites also participate in supporting and creating institutions and policies that maintain the status quo of dispossession. The second comment is usually either a manifestation of ignorance or a racist view that assumes that blacks cannot catch up due to some genetic predisposition. Both sentiments deny that a horrific injustice occurred and that United States society and government incurred a debt because of that injustice. Government is the obvious focus of debt collection because the injustices were sanctioned and promulgated by government. Sentiments of denial also seem grounded in the belief that blacks have or are somehow benefiting at the expense of white entitlement to privilege. Entitlement to privilege simply means that one group believes that it is uniquely qualified or entitled to rule. The privileged group sees economic, social, and political control as a birthright. Alternatively, its members view participation and power sharing with other groups as at the controlling group's disadvantage, pleasure, or "tolerance." Nonetheless, the reality is that the original injustice to blacks has enriched and continues to enrich many whites unjustly. The interplay of these issues is called the "cultural conspiracy." It applies to a laundry list of issues—from affirmative action, attacks on multiculturalism and racial diversity, and welfare program cutbacks to curfews in neighborhoods of color. The perception is that these issues, along with the politics and the popular culture environment that surrounds them, are somehow the result of conspiracy, inspired by denial and linked to genocide. Some theorists credit this conspiratorial environment with spawning so-called "hate radio" and the notion of the "angry white male."

While many acknowledge the war's failure and others cry conspiracy, there has been an unwillingness to challenge the failure of the current drug policy beyond rhetorical attacks. The violence of the war will end when those most adversely affected decide that enough is enough. The war must stop at the front. Blacks, Latinos, and the poor, all those ground up in the onslaught, must resist the genocidal impact and implications of the war. Activists, reformers, and community intellectuals must support the resistance by providing a connected and cogent argument identifying and explaining the impact and implications. Current drug policy leads to further expansion of the prison-industrial complex, specifically to the detriment of people of color and to society overall. Moreover, current policy has not eliminated or decreased drug usage. Therefore, the subject of legalizing drugs must no longer be taboo. Reformers need not feel embarrassment, shame, or fear when engaging in advocacy for the complete legalization of all drugs. Debating which drugs should or should not be banned encourages confusion and obfuscation. Legalization is a tactic available to counter the mass criminalization and militarization of civil society that has been another by-product of the war. Legalization is the abolition of all illegal possession laws, criminal statutes, and regulations concerning the production, distribution, possession, or consumption of drugs—leaving only those laws that protect consumers from deception and fraud. Some support a policy of decriminalization because it may be more palatable and social acceptance is easier to obtain. In defining the difference, decriminalization is the abolition of laws that make it a crime to use substances deemed illicit. Under decriminalization the government maintains control of how they dispense a particular drug. Legalization infers that protecting one from oneself is not a legitimate function of government.

Launching a rhetorical attack on the diversion of funds from education improvement to prison construction takes little effort. The difficult part comes with offering a strategy to end what is now common. There has been a noticeable silence on the issue of legalization for fear of advocacy being labeled as soft on crime. Supporting legalization attracts the new pejorative label of "liberal." When former Surgeon General Joycelyn Elders supported holding discussions on the issue of legalization, she had very little support from any quarter, including the black community. The drug abuse problem is a health problem as opposed to a crime problem. Legalization is not promoting or condoning drug use. Drug use is sometimes very harmful to people. The problem is that the drug war is not stopping the harm from drug use but it is adding the harm from drug prohibition. In this respect, legalization, or ending drug prohibition, is a means of achieving a more constructive and humane drug policy. Citizens must ask the question, "Are we winning the war on drugs?"

Direct and political action is essential in the antiwar effort. Opposition to current drug laws must take place at local, state, and federal levels. Opposition has to express itself at city and county councils, in the courthouse, at the statehouse, and at the White House. In addition, war opponents must consider direct action tactics such as jury nullification in drug cases. Jury nullification gives the individual juror the power to judge the law. Some declare that the criminal justice system is utterly racist and beyond reform. As a result, they advocate that black jurors set black defendants free no matter the crime. Jury nullification is not simply setting criminals free or setting a person free because of their color. Jury nullification signals public disapproval of the current policy and empowers individuals to act on the unfairness of current laws. Moreover, political action must take place. Policy reformers must educate the electorate on the cost and consequences of current drug policy. Political candidates who support policies that maintain the war must then face opposition from those seeking change. Opposition to candidates who advocate social policy that results in dehumanization must be vocal, organized, and expressed at the ballot box.

This essay does not intend to provide justification or comfort for those who would assign blame for their drug condition based solely on their status as a victim. Drug users who happen to be black know that American society is racist; the scar of slavery and discrimination remains and they do not get a reasonable chance in the criminal justice system. Nevertheless, choices and consequences for individuals remain. Surrendering one's rights should never be a choice. One should make legal choices only after obtaining clear information. Those who do not have clear information and enter a plea out of ignorance have surrendered to the war. Volunteer recruits in the war are those who know the war is violating their rights but surrender their rights out of fear or convenience. While challenging a racist legal system is both difficult and dangerous, acquiescence grants approval to the conduct of the war.

Participation in the war by a specific group of volunteer recruits must stop. Their participation is perhaps more dangerous and irrational than that of those previously mentioned. They are the black elected officials and leaders who condemn the consequences of the war but continue to support the conduct of war. The war is a means of social control and containment and has led to an expansion of the criminal underclass. Support of the war in any respect allows society to escape its responsibility for the dispossession created by the initial absence of justice.

Reformers should reject regressive policy measures wrapped in the language of justice and equality. Many "liberal" leaders call for the equalization of drug sentencing (which is nothing more than equalized suffering). Equalization means more whites in jail, not fewer blacks. This is another diversion from the goal of ending the war, and in many ways continues to erode support for the human rights struggle. The goals of that struggle remain the advocacy and protection of due process and equal protection rights and equal opportunity and economic justice for the dispossessed. These provided the framework for Dr. Martin Luther King's "Poor Peoples' Campaign" and they can do the same for a new antiwar or antidispossession movement. This essay seeks to explain why and how the war is waged and offers a defense and offense against it. This strategy involves attacking stereotypes and the process of dehumanization and confronting and ending dispossession. War opponents must recognize allies, drug warriors, and profiteers. Most important, reformers must engage in the advocacy of rational drug policies and humane legal alternatives. Government forfeits its moral authority to tell its citizens to stop killing when it has a policy of killing. It cannot command citizens to "stop the violence" and respect human life when it engages in a violent war that does not respect human life. The "war on drugs" is a failure for many reasons. Reformers must focus their efforts and energies on encouraging a new generation of antiwar activists armed with a compelling argument for ending the war. In turn, these activists must educate and mobilize those outside and inside mainstream structures (church, civil rights groups, etc.) on the ravages of war. This is not to suggest that the church community intervene in a way that would result in constitutional violations. Such violations include church-supervised punishment or religious indoctrination as a substitute for or a companion to punishment. Religion is not a substitute for curing dispossession. Nevertheless, reformers ought to encourage involvement from the religious community. When mainstream groups become supportive of the antiwar effort, it becomes easier for elected officials to support policies that some may view as "liberal," "radical," or whatever pejorative label the drug warriors attempt to place on opposition to the war. No effort for social change starts in the main. It starts with a few people who attempt to draw a crowd. The crowd gives the politician the will to act.

WAGING WAR

> One in three young black men in the United States is under criminal justice control at a cost of $6 billion every year. One in 15 black men is incarcerated. 683,200 black men are behind bars, compared with 674,400 white men. Blacks make up 12% of the U.S. population, 13% of drug users, but 55% of convictions for drug possession. It takes five grams of crack to get five years in federal prison versus 500 grams of cocaine. In 1992, 89.7% of all those in state prison on drug possession charges were black or Hispanic. 94% of crack defendants in federal courts in 1994 were black. Because addicts often share dirty needles, AIDS is now the leading cause of death for black men ages 25 to 44. For black injecting drug users, the risk of getting AIDS is seven times the risk of dying from an overdose.[11]

Whenever government wages war on something, more often than not that something turns out to be people. The government's drug war targets black people. Countless anecdotal examples exist on the insidiousness of the war. A case encountered while researching this essay describes the pervasiveness of the war. The story involves a black man in his early forties named Delane from a rural county in South Carolina. Delane is a carpenter by trade. He repairs mobile homes, puts up sheet rock, paints, and does other building-related jobs. He does not make much money, but would be considered in the lower middle-income level. Society commonly labels him working class. Before accepting an invitation to his friend's cookout (which turned out to be a "stakeout"), he had avoided the label of a convicted drug felon. Delane tells the story of being invited to a weekend cookout by a co-worker named Melvin. He went to the cookout and, upon arriving, asked for Melvin, the friend who invited him. A man who was later revealed to be an undercover police officer told Delane, "Melvin is gone to get beer." Delane told the person to tell Melvin he came by. As he turned to leave, three undercover agents grabbed him and threw him to the ground. His friends in the car, thinking that they were robbing him, got out of the car to help him. They arrested them too. Delane and his friends were taken inside the host's house and ordered to sit on the floor in handcuffs. When Delane went into the house, he found himself with several other people, many of whom he knew, sitting on the floor in handcuffs. One person, Al, resisted and "got some knots upside his head." Police promptly arrested all who stopped by and asked for the cookout's host. They arrested and formally charged about thirty persons with intent to buy crack-cocaine, including Melvin, the cookout's host. We should note that no physical evidence—crack-cocaine—was found or presented in court. Asking for the host qualified as grounds for arrest. Upon being taken to the county jail, defendants were not allowed to call family or legal counsel for at least twenty-four hours. Delane had just gotten his paycheck cashed and the police "confiscated every dime in [my] pocket." After spending the weekend in jail, they released him on a $2,500 bond. A year passed and they called up Delane's case on the docket. Unlike the other defendants, he at first chose to plead not guilty. Yet nervous because his court-appointed attorney was absent, Delane changed his plea to guilty. The judge, skeptical of Delane's decision, raised his bond and ordered him back to jail "to give him some time to think" about accepting the "deal" the police gave the other defendants. The deal was a felony drug charge—intent to buy—although no physical evidence was presented; 240 hours of community service—which consisted of washing police cars, doing repairs around the jail, and picking up trash on the highways; one year probation—suspended upon completion of community service; twelve months' suspension of driver's license; and loss of voting rights. The latter can be returned only on completion of state supervision. Although it seems that Delane accepted the deal out of expedience, he claims that he felt powerless and isolated and had to take it. Delane's final comment reflects the growing concern of black voter disenfranchisement due to the war. He stated, "The bad thing about what happened was that it was right before elections. And they had van loads of us going to jail that weekend."

One cannot have war without an enemy. The first act of the drug warriors was to claim that they were protecting citizens from an evil enemy—illicit drugs. One cannot wage war against a substance, however, so the drug warriors' attention predictably shifted to identifying a living, breathing enemy. An enemy that society deems to have less value than whites—blacks. After identifying the enemy, war supporters peppered the air with cries of national unity and war metaphors. Metaphors helped create a militaristic environment. Criminologists Peter B. Kraska and Victor E. Kappeler write:

> Metaphors play a central role in the construction of and reaction to social problems: they act to organize our thoughts, shape our discourse, and clarify our values (Ibarra and Kitsuse 1993; Spector and Kitsuse 1987). Sociologists have documented the spread of the medical metaphor—defining social problems as "illnesses" to be treated by medical professionals—as an important trend in twentieth-century social control (Conrad and Schneider 1992; Conrad 1992) . . . . The ideological filter encased within the war metaphor is "militarism," defined as a set of beliefs and values that stress the use of force and domination as appropriate means to solve problems and gain political power, while glorifying the tools to accomplish this—military power, hardware, and technology (Berghahn 1982, Eide and Thee 1980, Kraska 1993).[12]

When the enemy is a targeted group of people, they face immediate dehumanization. Martin Luther King, Jr. often called dehumanization *thingification.* Public acceptance of the growing incarceration rate is due in large part to the continuing *thingification* of blacks. Rather than picturing the black and Latino fathers, mothers, brothers, and sisters that they are jailing, politicians and demagogues dismiss them as criminals—the "enemy." The obvious consequence of dehumanization is an erosion of respect for human rights and the constitutional protection of those rights.

Additionally, because of where they are conducting the war, historical racism, and so on, the war and crime link to race politics. Race politics is a form of "wedge politics." Wedge politics is designed to separate—to drive a wedge through a group's connection to the whole of society and to drive a wedge through group cohesiveness. It intends to dismiss the political significance of a group. Nixon's use of crime to attack blacks is the most often cited example of wedge politics. Wedge politics in a racial context is analogous to race-baiting. There is an abundance of examples of contemporary race-baiting. The image of the black man behind bars remains a staple of crime and race politics. Race politics is evident in George Bush's 1988 Willie Horton "political ad" and in Bill Clinton's Stone Mountain "photo-op" (posing in front of a phalanx of black Georgia prison inmates during the 1992 Presidential election). It is a cornerstone of United States politics to exploit people's legitimate fear of crime. Political posturing on crime cultivates illegitimate racial animosity and prejudice that have neutralized citizen opposition to the war.

Dehumanization has a variety of elements; nonetheless, in the drug war racism is the most obvious. The war's propaganda reinforces the notion that the enemy possesses an inherent or genetic predisposition to violence. This validates disproportionate state action and control. Since the objects of scorn have no humanity, they are not worthy of justice or even of life. During World War II, the Japanese were labeled "Japs" and assigned a variety of stereotypes. This made the decision to drop atomic bombs on them seem somewhat less barbaric. During the Vietnam War, the North Vietnamese became "Charlie" or "gooks," which partly explains why the United States could not envision losing a war to a group of "pajama-clad commies." When whites enslaved Africans for their labor and they exterminated North American aborigines for land, they respectively called them "dumb savages" and "noble savages." In the war, black men are labeled "predatory" in an attempt to reinforce dehumanization. Labeling black youth as "predatory" arose from attacks against foreign tourists in Florida in the early '90s. It was also used (along with the term "wilding") to describe incorrigible youth in New York City. In 1993, during the heat of the crime debate, news programs such as NBC's Meet the Press revived and popularized the D. W. Griffith Birth of a Nation stereotype of the black male "predator."[13] Naturally, all crimes are predatory in nature. Milwaukee serial killer and cannibal Jeffrey Dahmer was surely predatory; however, he was not a black or a teen when he committed his crimes. Further-

more, neither Dahmer nor Colin Ferguson—the Long Island Rail Road killer—
had any arrests before their murderous acts. To apply the term *predatory* based
on age reinforces the perception of the youthful offender as more violent than
the adult offenders. To apply race simply implies that black youth offenders
are more violent than all others.

Society and culture also seduce the targets of the war into believing the
negative things said or written about them. This makes their surrender to the
war against them easier. Slogans such as "black-on-black crime," when used
by black leaders, insinuate that black intraracial crime is more insidious than
black interracial crime. It implies that black criminals should spare their brothers (that is, criminals should choose their victims based on race). In contrast,
pundits and politicians seldom refer to crimes committed by whites against other
whites as "white-on-white crimes." Criminologists commonly know that whites
commit crimes against other whites and blacks commit crimes against other
blacks at roughly the same rate of occurrence. Most crimes are neighborhood
crimes. Moreover, victims and perpetrators are generally known to one another. To categorize neighborhood crime as differing racially is an attempt to
portray black crime as more insidious and violent. Moreover, the notion of
the black perpetrator preying on whites is not only unfounded, but it is deliberately used to stir the fears and passions of whites. Political scientists James
Lynch and William Sabol assert that the black underclass poses less of a threat
to whites than the white underclass because it (the black underclass) is segregated residentially and therefore is less proximate to the working and middle
classes than is the white underclass.[14]

Many black politicians and community leaders have been manipulated
into adopting racist arguments and stereotypes that support the lie that blacks
are more violent than whites. The seduction has taken place partly because
many white liberals have changed their positions and beliefs about social justice. Liberalism was in vogue during the '60s and '70s. White officials then
exhibited a greater willingness to look at the causes of crime. Liberalism involved believing that doing something about the human condition was part
of the solution. Today it seems that liberals have apparently abandoned this
mode of thinking for a mind set supporting inherent racial pathologies. Taking their cues from the white liberals, along with a lack of a consistent focus
on cause, often puts black leadership at odds with itself. Case in point: calling
drug laws racist but telling kids "to turn those suspected of dealing in to the
authorities." Such a request is fraught with obvious contradictions. It says that
although the system is unjust, some are unworthy of justice. Black leadership
has been unable to find a cogent vision, language, and message to strike at
dispossession created by white supremacy. So they have followed the liberal
lead and capitulated to the dominant (conservative) ideology of the time.
Consequently, they often promote the vision, language, and message of the

forces that society has historically arrayed against them. In 1994 civil rights activist Jesse Jackson made an "off the record" comment that media widely reported during the crime debates. The comment suggested dehumanization, promotion of the dominant ideology, and lack of focus on the central problem of dispossession. Jackson stated: "There is nothing more painful to me at this stage in my life than to walk down the street and hear footsteps and start thinking about robbery and then see somebody white and feel relieved."[15]

Jackson traditionally criticizes stereotypical characterizations. Nonetheless, that comment provided succor to those harboring racist attitudes and beliefs. Perhaps it was "painful" to Jackson because he realized that the stereotypes of war had seduced him too. No matter the reason, the message in effect tells whites that he can understand and does not blame them for being racist because he too is relieved that the person walking behind him is not black! This suggests that any white person is justified in fearing black people. Some insist that we cannot fault Jackson for his fear of the stranger behind because making a risk assessment for the likelihood of being victimized by crime is reasonable for people. Still, Jackson made his comments in the crime debate. Several things come to mind when one considers Jackson's public pronouncement of fear. Jackson often mentions the 319 death threats he received during his bids for the presidency.[16] It would be revealing to know the number of blacks issuing threats. The answer would no doubt prove his fear misplaced. Jackson is a public figure. The civil rights leader made his comments in the middle of a policy debate and observers can assume that he was addressing public policy. His comments were supportive of policies that result in discriminatory treatment for those other than "somebody white." Such statements often justify curfews, random searches, and similar policies. There appeared to be no risk assessment of personal danger, only a political assessment. Jackson, it seemed, wished to remain politically visible by not appearing soft on crime. The effect of the comment was that it gave Jackson "credibility" in the prevailing conservative political order. (In fairness to Jackson, as the consequences and pressures on the black community due to the drug war increased, he sought to mobilize the black church community around the increased incarceration rate. Jackson encouraged ministers to set up bail funds for nonviolent drug offenders as well as church-based mentoring programs. He also criticized the government's focus on the building of prisons at a rate twice that of public housing or school construction. Jackson also condemned the sentencing disparity and was openly critical of black ministers' support of the 1994 Crime Bill with its Sixty-two death penalty provisions.)

Before war supporters fully insert troops into a war zone, the enemy's resistance must be broken down to a manageable level. Many tools and techniques to crush resistance are reminiscent of both slavery and Reconstruction. Enslaved Africans needed a traveling pass or a specific reason to be anywhere, and their masters imposed curfews from dusk to dawn. It was during

Reconstruction that loitering and vagrancy laws were first imposed to maintain order and control of blacks. The Black Codes made it unlawful for more than two blacks to congregate simultaneously in the same area. Columbia, South Carolina offers an example of a modern-day black code. In the 1980s the city council passed an ordinance that allows police to decide if a bystander is "aimlessly" loitering.

In addition, the "victims' rights" movement produced a concomitant erosion of human rights protection. This erosion of rights involved not only criminal defendants and prisoners but all those suspected of being involved in illegal activities. The Founding Fathers established the criminal justice system to settle disputes between parties, not direct arbitration and restitution. Instead of duels, private tribunals, vigilantism, and such, an "impartial" criminal justice system was set up. Both the alleged perpetrator and the victim surrendered the right of private settlement to the courts. The premise of justice was that defendants were innocent until proven guilty, and protection of the innocent was paramount. The first was a protection against false or fraudulent charges; the latter led to the establishment of the writ of habeas corpus to ensure the protection of the innocent. Battle cries by victims' rights advocates that "criminals have too many rights" undermined the foundational premise of the criminal justice system. Now many blacks view the justice system with suspicion and mistrust. In the cities, 80 to 90 percent of the criminal defendants are black men.[17] In the current environment criminal defendants are guilty until proven not guilty. Passing regressive laws that aim to punish and exclude rather than rehabilitate and include is easier when the perception exists that criminals have too many rights. "Truth in sentencing"—the crack-cocaine racial sentencing disparity[18] aside—became a euphemism for sending the convicted to jail in record numbers for longer periods. As the war progressed, state and federal "three-strikes" legislation passed with little opposition from elected officials or the public in spite of objections from judges, criminologists, and civil libertarians. Reagan-era[19] drug policy inspired the resurgence of boot camps and chain gangs, the removal of exercise equipment from prisons, and the end of conjugal visits. Along with press restrictions on contacts with inmates and limits on other types of visits (friends, for example), inmates face an increased disconnection from family and community. Many friends and family members would rather avoid the dehumanizing experience of strip searches or having their children, even babies in diapers, patted down for contraband. One would assume that the more contact with the outside world, the easier the transition would be for the inmate returning to his or her community. Still, it seems that prison officials are more concerned with making sure the outside world remains ignorant of conditions inside jails than what type of individual emerges from their facilities. This ensures that a human face is not placed on the "enemy" and they get just what they deserve—punishment or elimination.

Once society identifies, dehumanizes, and strips the enemy of his or her rights, it sends the troops into the war zone. Supporters give the troops overwhelming resources and power to accomplish their mission. In the war the police are the troops and undercover agents are the spies. Often the task of the spy, like that of most covert operatives, is deception. Ascribing a single description to the drug informant is difficult. They can range from the sheer opportunist to those concerned about solving a crime problem. Resources include money and equipment. The number of troops deployed or the caliber and newness of their weapons do not measure power. The lack of personal liberties measures police power. The more liberties restricted, the more power granted to the soldier/police. At best, the hope is that the police will act responsibly and in "good faith." At worst, society does not care about police conduct because it believes that the police are ridding society of criminals. In any case, when police deploy into a neighborhood and the balance of power tilts toward them, abuses may occur. This is particularly true in an environment described using war metaphors. In a militaristic environment the widely popular community-based policing becomes a means of gathering covert information for the war effort. Community policing is also used as a public relations device to gain acquiescence to the war. The coercive nature of militarism encourages tyranny and abuse that citizens are often powerless to combat. Any charges of abuse meet with disbelief, scorn, or a "they deserve it" attitude by the public-at-large. Police frequently respond to abuse with claims of ignorance, negligence, or the often used "acting in good faith" excuse.*

The rise in the number of SWAT teams is also a dangerous trend in the militaristic environment. SWAT stands for Special Weapons and Tac-

---

*The classic example of policy tyranny can be gleaned from the actions and attitudes of the Los Angeles Police Department before the Rodney King beating was captured on videotape. Before the nation witnessed the brutality of the police on film, complaints by affected citizens were ignored or dismissed by most whites. Gangsta rap was emerging as a means of alternative reporting. Artists, such as Los Angeles-based Ice-T (Tracy Marrow) and Tupac Shakur, told tales of urban combat between the police and the black community. The theme of police abuse was common in the music of young people. Marrow's reporting on police violence and urban warfare/retaliation on his album "Cop Killer," met with attack, denial, and reprisal by mainstream institutions. His record contract was canceled as police organizations and politicians (including then President George Bush) across the country condemned Marrow and his work. Then the King video became public. After the King incident, it was revealed that there were over 45,000 unresolved complaints of police abuse languishing at the U.S. Department of Justice. Still, as evidenced by the first trial of the officers involved, an all-white jury freed the officers based on the stereotyping of King as an "animal" who somehow got what he deserved. Talk of the "thin blue line" separating "them from us" enabled jurors to suspend their knowledge that the officers' actions were inappropriately violent. Police practices in Los Angeles and other cities did not change after the King incident nor did practices change after the rebellion following the first trial verdict. Moreover, recent cases of police abuse have been uncovered in Washington, New Orleans, Philadelphia, New York, Miami, Detroit, Pittsburgh, and other police departments across the country.

tics. Police researcher Peter Kraska conducted a survey of 600 law enforcement agencies serving cities with populations of 50,000 or more and found that 90 percent have active SWAT teams. In SWAT units formed since 1980, their use has increased by 538 percent. He also found that two out of three rural departments have active paramilitary units. Kraska calls this "militarizing Mayberry," and states that the mission of the SWAT unit has expanded from highly specialized actions to drug-related "dynamic entries" and gang suppression. Seventy-five percent of their mission is devoted to serving high-risk warrants, mostly through drug raids. The teams often move through neighborhoods in armored or special vehicles with an assortment of weapons and equipment such as battering rams, chemical agents (tear gas and pepper spray), assault rifles, and 9mm, fully automatic machine guns.[20]

The drug warriors target the "enemy" by use of a "profile." The profile allows police to make cursory assumptions about who they suspect is apt to engage in criminal activities. How one "fits the profile" can depend on many things. It can be something as obvious as gender, race, and age. Profiling can encompass the area one drives through or lives in. It can be the time of day that one drives down a highway or the fact that one drives on a certain road at all. Profiling takes into account one's car and its "gold" accessories. Those driving with tinted car windows, any type of neon light, and chopped or hydraulic suspensions are always suspect. It can be a haircut: dreadlocks (hairstyle associated with Rastafarians) mean reefer smokers. One style of dress—baggy pants and oversized jacket—means gangbanger. In addition, "colors" are some dead giveaways. It can be "eyeballing" a police officer or looking away. To travel with a crowd or to travel alone can be reasons for detention by police. Profiling can entail anything, everything, and nothing. The most often used profile is that of being a young black man. Consequently, the number of these "profiled" individuals from targeted areas going to jail is on the rise. To this extent the drug warriors' battle plan is a success. The data presented in Figure 8-2 show the rapid and disparate increases in drug arrest of blacks and black youth under 17 from 1965 to 1992. Figure 8-3 shows the likelihood of arrest of black and white drug users for possession, in 1993: blacks over 18 were seven times more likely to be arrested for drugs than whites.[21]

While young black men are the most targeted group in the war, Reagan-era drug policy has also snared a disproportionate number of black women in its web. The group with the greatest increase in correctional supervision during the past decade has been black women. Between 1989 and 1991 the rate of correctional supervision for black women rose 78 percent due to drug-related arrests[22] and criminal prosecution of pregnant drug users.[23]

Some raise the question, "What about those in the black community who are begging for police protection?" In the war zone everyone of color "fits the profile," including those begging for police to "protect" them. Every resident of the area becomes subject to arrest and search. If one is always sub-

Figure 8–2. Among youth age 17 and under, the arrest rate for drug violations for blacks has been growing while the arrest rate for whites rose in the 1970s and then fell, 1965–1992

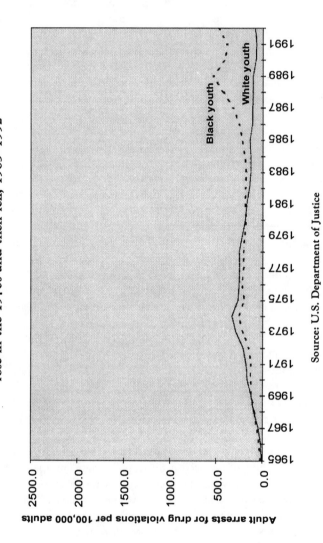

Source: U.S. Department of Justice

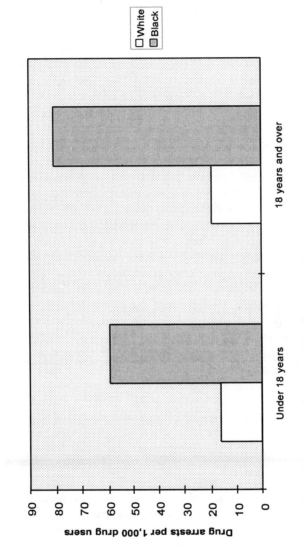

Figure 8–3. Black drug users were much more likely than white drug users to be arrested for drug possession, 1983

Source: U.S. Department of Justice

ject to arrest, one is no longer secure. Anyone who happens to be black faces an increased threat of being dehumanized, detained, escorted, arrested, and imprisoned, despite class or status. The threat of "dynamic entry" increases because police can create probable cause or assert "reasonable suspicion" (a standard lower than probable cause) to go into any house or apartment. The claim is that their deployment into neighborhoods of color represents a "crisis," "emergency," or "war." "DWB" (driving while black)[24] and even the act of walking down the street has become grounds for reasonable suspicion. Uncovering the economic impact created by the disparate issuance of traffic tickets would be interesting since violations have an impact on insurance rates. Disproportionate ticketing can lead to insurance company redlining. The police stop a black motorist under the pretense of a traffic violation and then ask the motorist, "Are there any drugs or weapons in the car?" They ask to search and most motorists acquiesce. If they find drugs, in come the troops en masse. If they do not find contraband, issuance of the "nigger ticket" justifies the stop. Police view as uncooperative any attempt by the motorist to assert his rights. A rights-conscious motorist often arouses police suspicion, perhaps even contempt. If a motorist chooses not to agree to an officer's request, more than likely the car will be searched anyway. In November 1996 the American Civil Liberties Union filed a motion in Federal Court in Baltimore asking for a contempt of court fine against the Maryland State Police for violating a 1994 settlement agreement to make highway drug stops without regard to race. The ACLU cited the police agency's reports showing that 73 percent (600 of 823) of the motorists stopped on Interstate 95 between suburban Baltimore and Delaware from January 1995 to November 1996 were black. An ACLU survey the summer of 1996 found that only 17 percent of the drivers on that 44-mile segment of Interstate 95 were black. In addition, police found nothing in 70 percent of those searches.[25]

Profiling and targeting of individuals using race and color as a determinant ultimately reaches all economic classes within a racial group because class is not as readily apparent a social marker as is skin tone. The war expands the black underclass and extends into the black middle class. Lynch and Sabol found that, for blacks who were not in the underclass—that is, for blacks with connections to labor markets and mainstream institutions—the increase in drug incarceration rates between 1986 and 1991 was the largest increase of any group. They argue that, since blacks are segregated residentially and underclass blacks are proximate to non-underclass blacks, or are more so than with whites, the law enforcement targeting strategies may be unable to distinguish class differences as simply as for whites. Consequently, strategies targeted at the underclass may have large spillover effects into the non-underclass.[26] This is a polite way of saying that all blacks and Hispanics generally look the same to police. Law enforcement officials also employ the widespread use of "John Doe" warrants for mass roundups of suspects. The John Doe warrant contains a vague description of a suspect, an age range, and the estimated weight of the unnamed, unknown, alleged suspect. Thus police can make anyone they wish (provided they are of the same race) fit the warrant. Where the John Doe warrant leaves off, some localities have passed "loitering with intent to distribute" laws. These ordinances target individuals who hang out or pass through areas designated by police to be high drug areas. Moreover, local ordinances make anyone and everyone within "reasonable proximity" of an unclaimed stash of drugs culpable for possession of the stash. The war also uses the tactic of punishing people who might not have committed a crime, but who lived in the same home as a "suspect" or knew of the suspect's activities.[27] This breeds abuse, not only by the police, but by neighbors hoping to protect themselves, their family members, or their friends from prosecution or investigation. Often, mere groundless accusations from anonymous informants, often paid, create "reasonable suspicion" that becomes probable cause for arrest.

Opponents of the war in Southeast Asia rallied and sang songs to protest its failure, and argued that it had accomplished nothing. If whether or not this war has curbed illicit drug usage is a measurement of success, then our country's current domestic war is also a failure. It too has accomplished absolutely nothing for scores of blacks. The total quantity of cocaine consumption remains at historically high levels. In addition, hard-core crack users are just as addicted as ever. Revealing true intent without possessing the power to read minds is impossible. The hidden intent may be ideology, racism, profit, or political gain. War has had the effect of increased incarceration of scores of young black women and men. (The increase in incarceration rates is even more sinister if there is validity to the charge that the crack-cocaine epidemic was promoted in the black community by agencies and agents of the United States government to provide financing for the Contra war.) If increased incarceration of these people is the goal, then the war is a success. The Sentencing Project reported that from 1980 to 1984 crime fell steadily, by a total of 15 percent. Then, from 1984 to 1989, crime rates rose by a total of 14 percent. Thus, in a decade, prison population increased and crime went down. Prison population then continued to increase and crime increased; therefore, the cause-and-effect relationship is far from certain.[28] Increased incarceration rates beget an increase in the criminal underclass. Data exist to confirm the growth of the underclass along with the growing income gap between the rich and poor. The average offender is a high school dropout who goes to jail poor and returns to the street poorer. With cutbacks in educational programs, the education received by most inmates is a real crime. After inmates serve their time, they return to where the drug warriors harvested them. Inmates who feel that society unjustly imprisoned them are not "well adjusted" or rehabilitated citizens. Because of conditions in many jails and prisons, a more violent person may emerge after incarceration. Most people emerge from jail disconnected from society and stigmatized. This can make finding "legitimate" employment difficult. Also, many ex-offenders lose their right to vote. According to the Sentencing Project, approximately 1.4 million African-American men are currently or permanently disenfranchised from voting because of a drug-related conviction.[29] Thus they have no economic or political power and no economic or political future.

Many in society have adopted the arguments and stereotypes that support the lie that blacks are more violent than whites. The stereotype of the "violent" and "predatory" black male is central to the justification of the war. "They sell drugs because they are lazy and don't want to work!" "They shoot and kill each another because they are more violent than everyone else!" These sentiments are common among those supportive of tyrannical and oppressive social policies. The reality is that one *is* working when one sells drugs. One reason those drug sales proliferated in minority communities is the lack of entry-level employment for the young. Communities of color have also experienced a general lack of capital development. For many of those engaged in drug sales, pushing is the most dependable source of employment in their neighborhoods. Drug dealers are capitalists, entrepreneurs who sell drugs to satisfy their material needs, real and imaged. For black men in the 18–24 age group, their reported unemployment rates in the mainstream economy have remained consistently high over the past decade. In 1991 the official government unemployment rate was 36.5 percent. Reported unemployment among black women in the same age group for the same period was 36.1 percent. The National Urban League estimated the unofficial or "hidden" unemployment rate for black men *and* black women in this age group at 56.9 percent.[30] Thus employment in drug trading fills the void created by surplus labor and a lack of economic opportunity. Next is the issue of whether drug dealing is more violent than other occupations. Illicit drugs, a valued commodity more costly than gold, require the same type of physical protection as does gold. Valued commodities usually require armed protection. Those protecting gold and those protecting illicit drugs use force appropriate to protect their products. Both will, and do, use violence when thought necessary. Because certain drugs are illegal, violence is the only method the drug dealer has to protect his investment. Moreover, the use of violence is the only measure a drug dealer has to select and appraise his employees. Consequently, the young dealer engages in violence to build a "rep" or to protect his "spot." This is the same kind of protectionism that the United States engaged in during the battle for oil in the Persian Gulf War.

The war seems to rest on the notion that leaders, whatever their political affiliation, ideology, or race, always seeks to act in the best interest of society. Citizens hope that their leaders will place their own interest second, and that they are fair-minded and just. However, neither the legacy of Ronald Reagan and George Bush nor the promise of Bill Clinton and Al Gore constitutes a successful campaign against drug abuse in the United States. Instead, they have promoted and maintained a war that erodes the rights of all citizens, but selectively targets those who lack the financial ability to defend their way through the justice system. Ninety-five percent of all African-Americans detained by this system have to rely on an overstressed, underfunded public defender system.[31] Moreover, cutbacks in treatment programs and educational and training opportunities for inmates make it apparent that the war is not concerned with enabling ex-addicts to become productive members of society. If protection of rights and humane treatment of addicts had been goals, then Reagan-era policy would be considered a failure. Instead, drug warriors fill the prisons beyond capacity and prison building is a growth industry. For those who seek rehabilitation as a goal, the policy has offered tyranny, violence, dehumanization, further dispossession, and hopeless entrapment of those in the ever-expanding underclass. These are some factors that contribute to the personal need to self-medicate.

The war paints with a broad brush, coloring everyone in the black community as potential lawbreakers in one stroke. Reform lies in confronting the myths, scapegoating, and stereotyping that are inherent in the war, drawing a line between fact and fiction. Exposing myths entails critical analysis of the popular culture and the environment in which stereotyping and war supporters perpetuate racial myths. Stereotypes perpetuate ignorance that breeds fear and hostility. Thus reformers should expose and reject those who use stereotypes. Speaking "truth to power" involves recognizing and challenging war hawks, no matter what their political party affiliation or race.

Those cultivated to be the criminal underclass must be the spearhead of an antiwar struggle. The war ensures their continued subjugation. Wars create prisoners of war, and drug war POWs serve as convenient props for ambitious politicians. The politicization of the victims of war is a significant step in organizing opposition to the war. (There appears to be growing awareness by inmates of their POW status as evidenced by the 1996 uprisings by black inmates in federal and state prisons over the crack and cocaine sentencing disparity.) Organizing and mobilizing the families, friends, and relatives of those incarcerated is crucial to resistance. In addition, opponents of the war must make it clear to society-at-large that oppressive social policies have dire consequences: destabilization of communities and the eventual destabilization of civil society. Communities with an ever-expanding, stigmatized criminal underclass face a violent future and an ever-growing war. Reform must seek an end to a violent present and a more violent future.

Few leaders and organizations are standing up for the rights of the poor. Inmates and criminal defendants have even less support. Fewer still are the leaders who have the long-term vision to recognize the ultimate impact on everyone's rights should the war continue. The notion exists that a conflict exists between "prisoners' rights" and "victims' rights." Obviously, the victims' rights movement has more public support. Often, when the public imagines "prisoners' rights," they think about inmates having access to cable television and weight-lifting equipment, not habeas corpus or fair treatment while incarcerated. Traditional institutions and groups, church and fraternal organizations, and civic and civil rights groups must take steps to provide political support for the incarcerated and their families.

The task of reformers is to learn, understand, and expose the strategies and tactics employed to maintain the many false assumptions of the war. To reverse the "success" achieved by the drug warriors, reformers must debunk their assumptions. Those assumptions are that increased incarceration rates suggest success in obtaining safety and security, that is, threat reduction; citizens should be willing to surrender certain rights for threat reduction; an increase in the criminal class is good for society; as certain groups and people are sufficiently more dangerous than others, they require control and containment; police are fair and always follow the rules; those claiming concerns about solving the problem of crime place society's interest before their own. A variety of contradictions are evident when these assumptions are examined. Ultimately, the public-at-large must understand clearly that ending the war—changing drug policy—is a progressive step toward more secure communities. Therefore, success is obtaining safe communities through humane policies. Reform must advance economic solutions over militarism. It must maintain a harm reduction and health focus over dehumanization and criminalization. Reformers must also confront the racism, stereotyping, and scapegoating, by all who employ it.

The tough job for policy reformers is overcoming the taboo associated with advocating drug legalization as a rational alternative to the war. Legalization is a means of ending the violence associated with the drug war. Drug sales employment will continue until government and business fills the economic void in the affected communities. Many argue that legalization will increase access, thus increasing usage and the number of those addicted to drugs. Right now, the drug addict has unimpeded access to illicit drugs, inside and outside jail. Why a person has a particular addiction is best left for another essay. However, the war puts drugs on the *black* market instead of the open market. This encourages high prices and high profits for the suppliers. Because profits are so high, suppliers are encouraged to expand their territory and use whatever means necessary to protect that territory. This is what has created the phenomenon of the pusher or "slinger." Legalization drives down the price of illicit drugs. Not many addicts will pay a corner pusher an inflated price for medication of questionable quality if they can purchase it cheaper at the corner drugstore. Also, reformers must address the health questions. Poverty is miserable and depressing. Not to validate or condone crack use, crack is the poor person's antidepressant medication—of questionable quality. The poor do not go to the public mental health clinic or a psychiatrist's office to get a prescription to ease the pain of poverty. The poor rarely have the income to afford professional psychiatric treatment. They most often seek out the corner pusher. The rich simply get a doctor to write a prescription for their problems of depression. Use of drugs by the middle class and rich to cope is not only legal but considered a rational response to their particular malady. Another health concern is AIDS. The main reason there is an AIDS crisis among addicts is that they share needles. Allowing addicts to purchase clean needles reduces short- and long-term health care cost because it reduces the spread of the HIV virus. As for the violence of the war, although competition between corner drugstores is often fierce, there have yet to be any reports of gunfire between local pharmacists. Moreover, the police are not kicking in doors at corner drugstores. Just as the shooting stopped when alcohol prohibition ended, the same will occur when drug prohibition is no longer policy. The problem of addiction is a legitimate concern. Still, an increase in police power and the building of more jails and prisons has not provided a solution. In the black community a root cause of the substance abuse problem lies in dispossession. Thus, to solve systemic and structural problems, any vision of change involves a focus on dispossession.

DISPOSSESSION

Dispossession is denial of justice, past and present. In economic terms it is the injustice caused by denial of capital and access to capital that belies the racial disparity in poverty, accumulated wealth, and business capital. The term *dispossession* more accurately describes the economic problems facing blacks than more common descriptions such as *poverty* or *disenfranchisement*. Economists define poverty as *substandard consumption* and disenfranchisement as *substandard political power*. Both are due to the lingering effects of dispossession that is substandard ownership of capital. In this regard, slavery and racial discrimination are viewed as devalued or stolen labor, and institutional denial of access to capital. The result is economic marginality.[32] Persistent racial disparity in educational and employment opportunities is symptomatic of dispossession. In human rights and civil liberties' terms it is the injustice caused by the denial of due process, equal protection, and equal opportunity rights. As an instrument of white supremacy and white male hegemony, dispossession maintains social order and control. Dispossession and racism are interwoven. Both are about political and economic power used to maintain a privileged position seen as an entitlement by many whites. The war, as a tool of dispossession, is a manifestation of oppressive social order and control measures over an economically marginal group. Consequently, the war has been enormously successful for maintaining social order and control over a population that has historically faced economic marginality and has lacked the sociopolitical means to fight deleterious policy.[33] Legalization of drugs is merely a tactical response that aims at an effect of dispossession. It provides a respite from the violence of the drug war, but it does not solve the fundamental problem of dispossession. Members of the marginalized group may opt for other illicit occupations if drug sales employment ends and legitimate opportunities are limited or nonexistent.

Dispossession is difficult to cure for many obvious reasons. First, the cure involves dispelling the notion of white entitlement to privilege and changing the nature of institutions that protect such privilege. This would change the social order. Change brings a natural fear of uncertainty. A change in what is considered common is painful because it challenges history and a majority culture's sense of itself. Some whites fear that they would have to give up material wealth and status with a change in social order. Accordingly, they feel that they have a personal stake in maintaining the current social, political, and economic structure. The backlash against multiculturalism in education and diversity in the workplace and in electoral representation exposes the fight to preserve supremacy and hegemony. The notion of the "angry white male" or a constant media and pundit focus on the relative strength, attitudes, and importance of white male voters is also a reflection of a backlash against attacks on white male hegemony. Curing dispossession exacts recognition of an economic injustice, the incurring of debt, and payment of restitution. While some charge that affirmative action attempts to right a wrong with a wrong, others see affirmative action policy as a recognition of injustice and an attempt to redress it. Yet affirmative action, as race-based preference in hiring, government contracting, and school admissions, deals only with the symptoms of dispossession: it could never provide a cure. This is why many economists, activists, and scholars often call it conservative, restitution-avoidance policy. Nonetheless, even if society or government acknowledges a debt, the ongoing difficulty in addressing dispossession from a policy perspective is the size of the debt and/or the form of restitution.

Both "conservative" and "liberal" social policy maintain the condition of dispossession. The "conservatism" of the Reagan era attacked poor people on three fronts. First, "conservative" policies cut and restricted access to benefit programs. This intensified the vulnerability of those poor citizens whose economic dependence on the government had been seeded by "liberal" welfare-state policies of the '60s. The vulnerability was further exacerbated by an increase in the number of people struggling at the bottom for unskilled jobs while the labor demand was for high-end technological jobs. "Liberal" welfare-state policies cultivated a permanent underclass by promoting social programs whose economic gains for the poor were limited to consumption rather than production. Little emphasis was placed on the capital accumulation necessary for full participation in a capitalist economy. This channeled many poor into illicit drug employment. Second, "conservative" budget cuts limited the ability of poor people to challenge the erosion of substantive constitutional rights by cutting back on legal services funds and, in essence, denying them attorneys. (Legal services for the poor evolved out of the Kerner Commission.) Third, "conservative" courts curtailed the constitutional protection against unlawful search and seizure in acquiescence to a Republican administration's execution of its domestic wars, the "war on drugs" and the "war on crime," both of which were financed by a Democratic Congress.

An antiwar movement must be an antidispossession movement. The movement must resist what passes as ideology in the current social, political, economic, and cultural context. White supremacy, as an ideology, is the belief and practice that all that is good, human, valuable, worthwhile, civilized, and right is European-based or white. Defenders of the status quo see it as establishing a universal standard. When countering the status quo ideology of white supremacy, reformers must present rational alternatives to fill the resulting voids. For activists and reformers from communities of color, structural alternatives are not diversions such as the promotion of pseudonationalism, separatism, and racial chauvinism. One cannot right a wrong with a wrong. One must right the wrong. Diversions usually benefit those who support dispossession. The goal of reform is economic, social, and political inclusion and expansion. Reform should also seek a reverse in the trend of the growing permanent underclass. Ultimately, solving the problem of dispossession requires justice. In economic terms, abolitionists, activists, and many economists see justice as restitution. Many across the United States, from religious groups to political leaders, are now calling for racial "reconciliation," "repentance," and "redemption." However, achieving any of the three without restitution will be difficult. In a religious sense, acts of faith or contrition grant redemption. In a political or legal sense, if one is aggrieved, injured, or harmed by another, the person committing the injustice is liable for damages. Justice means restitution—paying the debt. No justice, no peace!

THE PROFITEERS

The profiteers generally fit into one of these categories: (1.) those who have an inherent interest in maintaining the status quo—including ideologues and politicians seeking power within the prevailing social order; (2.) those claiming an entitlement to privilege—for them the war represents "threat reduction" and the protection of material wealth (the notion of threat reduction may be viewed as false by opponents of the war, but those seeking to maintain the status quo see the threat as real); (3.) those seduced, co-opted, and manipulated by ideologues, politicians, and private interest, including those who are considered members of the war's targeted group; (4.) those with private interests (this group claims a "legitimate" profit motive), including (but not limited to) those involved in correctional privatization efforts and those other participants in the security industry; (5.) the drug elite—the kingpins who control the manufacturing, supply, and distribution of illicit drugs; and (6.) those who earn a living from the war's delivery system, including the police (to include the various state and federal law enforcement agencies), military organizations, courts, lawyers, and all other prison-industrial complex employees.

Politicians have historically used the issue of crime for political profit. It has become a ritual for politicians to take photos with police and swear their support of war. They swear their allegiance to the "war on crime" or the "war on drugs." In 1992 Bill Clinton promised a national police force and 100,000 additional police on the street to fight the war. During the 1996 presidential campaign, Republican candidate Bob Dole of Kansas accused Clinton of being responsible for increased drug use among teens. Predictably, he used a gathering of law enforcement personnel to make his charge. Dole then promised, if elected, to escalate the war. He concluded by proclaiming, "Just don't do it," a parroting of Nancy Reagan's "Just say no" sloganeering. However, Clinton provides the best example of maintaining the racial status quo using co-optation and manipulation with his use of the image of Martin Luther King, Jr. If one wished to co-opt an influential black leader, King is the person one would choose for several reasons. King is the most revered of black leaders. Moreover, he cannot respond to a misappropriation of his message and philosophy. Therefore, Clinton's attempt to co-opt the message of King is somewhat successful. The co-optation influences black public opinion on the issue of crime and expands the war with the support of those most negatively affected by that expansion. Building on his "new Democrat" "law and order" image, Clinton linked crime to blacks when he went into Memphis to speak before the predominantly black Eighty-eighth Annual Holy Convocation of the Church of God in Christ in November 1993. In the pulpit where King last preached, Clinton cast off the Cold War, revised King's philosophy, and supplanted the domestic war focus in a patronizing tone. He presumed to speak for King, stating:

> How would we explain it to Martin Luther King if he showed up here today and said, "Yes we won the Cold War. Yes without regard to race, if you play by the rules, you can get into a service academy or a good

college. How would we justify the things we permit that no other country in the world would, explain that we gave people the freedom to succeed and we created conditions in which millions abuse that freedom to
destroy the things that make life worth living, and life itself? We cannot."
Clinton continued, "If King were to reappear by my side today . . . he
would say, 'I did not live and die to see young people destroy their own
lives with drugs and then build fortunes destroying the lives of others . . .
This is not what I died for.' "[34]

Clinton, by misappropriating and revising King's message in a black venue,
painted crime black and played to race politics. Mainstream media affirm the
revisionism by not challenging what Clinton says against King's actual philosophy on crime, poverty, and dispossession and government's role in curing the problems.

Political leaders, professional athletes, celebrities, and other well-known
figures from within dispossessed communities are often seduced, co-opted, and
then manipulated into giving "credibility" to the war. This allows the leadership of the majority to advance whatever punitive, regressive, or oppressive
measures, or distraction, they wish to use. Some members of the dispossessed
community profit because the status quo rewards them with privileges not
extended to other members of their group. They "tolerate" them for being an
anomaly or "not like the rest of them." Society and its functionaries often seduce
and manipulate many dispossessed without their knowing it has been done.
At times seduction and co-optation occur out of ignorance or naiveté. At other
times the manipulated person seeks seduction or co-optation, believing them
to be a way of gaining recognition by the status quo. Jesse Jackson cited an
example of seduction at an April 1997 gathering of ministers in Memphis,
Tennessee, to mark the assassination of Martin Luther King, Jr. Jackson scolded
a group of "influential" black ministers who had accepted an invitation to meet
with Clinton before enactment of the 1994 Crime Bill. Apparently Clinton
persuaded the Christian clergymen to accept the sixty-two additional death
penalty provisions in the bill in return for such "crime reduction" programs as
"Midnight Basketball." Jackson referred to the nonfunded recreation program
as "fluff." Later, Congresspersons Charles Rangel of New York and Maxine
Waters of California met with Clinton to discuss the additional death penalty
statutes and the draconian nature of the crime bill. In response to the lawmakers' concerns, they said that Clinton praised the black ministers for endorsing the bill. According to Jackson, Rangel was crestfallen. Jackson charged
that the Congressional Black Caucus opposed the 1994 Crime Bill; however,
the ministers undercut their elected representatives by endorsing the bill without first meeting with them. The ministers got a photo-op with the President. In exchange, the chief executive gained support for an expansion in
the use of the death penalty.[35]

Seduction and co-optation lie on both the left and right sides of the political spectrum. We can also see it in the liaisons between sides. C. Delores Tucker of the National Political Congress of Black Women entered an "antirap" liaison with conservative William Bennett, former secretary of education. The relationship suggests seduction. Tucker became an agent of both conservatives and liberals. She not only supports the war, but also advocates the restriction of rights within the dispossessed community. Tucker proposed the restrictions as a solution to cultural misogyny and urban "violence." She frequently blasts the culture of the underclass as immoral and abnormal. This generalization reinforces dehumanization and ignores the degrading environment and consequences of dispossession. Tucker's liaison gives conservatives a cover to continue their suppression of the underclass and liberals a cover to continue their control of it. The control takes the form of calls for suspension of free speech, support for government-mandated school prayer, the suggestion of martial law using federal and state troops, and a proposed network of police informants. Such tyranny falls under the guise of addressing crime and "immorality" in minority communities. The conservative political agenda shifts the public focus to guns, drugs, music, movies, television, video games, crime, and violence—everything but the real cause of the problem, the institutional, government-sanctioned, economic violence waged against the black community, and the dispossession created by that violence.

Blacks, Latinos, and the poor are the targeted raw material in the prison-industrial complex. Private and public entrepreneurs not only profit financially from housing incarcerated citizens, but they are also able to select laborers for a variety of profit-producing tasks. Prisoners are now doing jobs from road and infrastructure repair to manufacturing furniture. Prison labor is now used for "marking up" or converting the Library of Congress's archive holdings for use on the Internet. Inmates manufacture blue jeans and package computers. High prison occupancy means high profits. The delivery system of the drug war, the criminal justice industry, like most exploitative capitalist ventures, produces wealth for a few. Many companies with familiar names profit from the $30 billion dollar a year[36] prison-industrial complex. Goldman, Sachs and Company, Prudential Insurance of America, Smith Barney, Shearson, Inc., Merrill Lynch and Company, Westinghouse Electric Corporation, and Corrections Corporation of America[37]—all have an interest in maintaining the war. Corporate support of the war effort is grounded in profit, not rehabilitation or solving the abuse problem. They have little concern about group dispossession—unless solving the problem will lead to greater profits. Next in line are the media conglomerates such as BMG/Arista, Sony, and Time Warner. These companies make huge profits exploiting the high unemployment, consumer-obsessive behavior, sexual and racial stereotypes, and the need for recognition of those trapped in the "'hood." Often they try to shield themselves from public criticism by subcontracting their rap music interest to "independent" labels and using arm's-length distribution entities. For instance, Interscope Records and Universal Music Group, which owns half of Interscope (Universal was formally known as MCA Music Entertainment Group), serves as the distribution company for "independent" label Death Row Records, which was the home to murdered rapper Tupac Shakur. Interscope's parent company is Seagram's (the liquor company). Death Row is the west coast gangsta rap rival to the east coast's Bad Boy Entertainment. Bad Boy was home to murdered rapper Christopher Wallace, also known as The Notorious B.I.G. Other "independents," such as Lynch Mob Records, have company names that exploit stereotypes and artists who are encouraged to "keep it real." In the cases of Shakur and Wallace, both were victims of the so-called "East Coast/West Coast Rivalry." Their last albums suggest the dehumanizing and hopeless focus of their industry. Shakur's last recording was If I Die Tonite, and Wallace's contributions to the rap world include his first album, Ready to Die, and his last album, Life After Death. Both artists' final work made millions for their record companies.[38] While many artists come from middle-class suburbia, those "ballers," "bangers," and "slingers" from the 'hood who do "make it" generally have their pain and anger exploited for short-term perks. Those perks include living in a rented home and the ability to drive a luxury, leased car.[39] Many fail to receive fair compensation for their work and are discarded after record company promoters harvest new and hungrier voices. Raising the issue of gangsta rap music with its purveyors and exploiters is not to stifle the pain, misery, or debauchery emanating from the music. Nor is it a challenge to their free speech rights. The music will change when society changes the way it views and treats the poor.

Television programs, such as Real Stories of the Highway Patrol, America's Most Wanted (and its local spawns), and COPS, are now staples of the entertainment industry. Not surprisingly, this manifestation of "trash TV" appeals to the very people who end up in the back of police cars. Network television offers up NYPD Blue, New York Undercover, Law and Order, and a host of prime-time cop shows. These programs reinforce the war mentality and provide a numbing effect on citizens to the abuses of law enforcement. The illusion cast by these programs is that the police will conduct themselves as if a television camera is always following them around. The Rodney King video, of course, shows us what racist police will do when they think no one is looking. The connection between the cop show and the officer on the street is apparent. Cop shows support the drug warriors. Producers of the "real life" shows want excitement. Challenging unregulated police power is irrelevant to shows buoyed by the exercise of power. The result is a steady broadcast of shoot-outs, chases, dynamic entries, stings, and the like. Plus, when all is said and done, the officer on the screen gives the pitch for needing more men, money, and equipment. They prod citizens with the oft-used refrain, "There are more criminals than police and the bad guys have better arms."

The war produces an ever-increasing profit margin for members of the privileged drug elite. The elites are those who manufacture illicit drugs and control the lucrative drug distribution networks. Most illegal drugs are produced and initially distributed by an elite group of unscrupulous "businessmen" who rely on the government's war to protect their cartel from price competition in the marketplace by eliminating their competitors, at taxpayer expense, thereby guaranteeing outrageously high profit margins. The government's war also immunizes the drug elite from product liability. The police hunt down the victims of debilitating and dangerously misrepresented drugs as criminals. The drug warriors in that way deny victims the right to sue producers or distributors in the courtroom. Despite printed warning labels, smokers and government—both state and federal—now go to civil courtrooms and sue companies that manufacture cigarettes from government-subsidized tobacco crops. States are also suing the tobacco companies for their share of health care cost. However, they permit users of crack-cocaine to see the inside of courtrooms only as criminal defendants on their way to government-operated prisons where the illegal drug traffic rivals that on the streets. Escape from product liability allows the drug elite to invest more money in protecting their product. When governments buy bigger and better weapons, the cartels purchase bigger and better weapons. Also, when drug warriors threaten profits, the drug elite purchases governments and government officials, such as in Mexico and Panama, just to name a few.

"Kingpins," "Czars," and CEOs come and go with the flow of business. Although the drug elite make lots of money, no one group or identifiable figure is making or controlling it all. To attack the elite on their own soil takes the cooperation of governments and their citizens. Any attack on them, especially in their own countries, could expand the war in the classic military sense. A military expansion of the war would pit poor people from one country against poor people in another country. Also, in the drug-producing countries where the cartels rule, leadership changes. When governments jail or kill a publicly identified kingpin, another person steps in to take the risk and reap the profits. Still, there are no identifiable United States or foreign drug kingpins or Mafia bosses that society can focus its anger on, although the drug elite has a highly organized and efficiently operated the drug distribution structure. Additionally, the use of the term *kingpin* evokes a bit of skepticism. Law enforcement frequently applies the term from the street-level slinger all the way up to the head of a cartel.

For law enforcement agencies, local and national, the war is a boon. War supporters divert government funds not only from social programs but also from the economic growth and development normally stimulated by peacetime investment. The diverted funds purchase equipment, weapons, and SWAT teams, and build and maintain prisons and other institutions characteristic of a society at war. In the war, the suspension of civil liberties increases police powers. This suspension of rights is the most significant profit for law enforcement. In a material sense, property and money seized by police agencies provide secondary financing for many of those same agencies. However, property foreiture by law enforcement has led to abuse. In Jefferson Davis and Cameron parishes in southwestern Louisiana along Interstate 10, out-of-state travelers, particularly minorities, were stopped without cause, arrested, and had their property seized without evidence of drugs in their cars. Under state law, to sue for a return of their seized assets, uncharged citizens must pay the highest bond in the nation—10 percent of the property's value or $2,500, whichever is greater. The burden of proving their innocence is on the citizen. In Louisiana, 60 percent of seizure proceeds goes to the law enforcement agency that seized the property, 20 percent goes to the district attorney, and 20 percent goes to the state judges' judicial expense fund.[40] Obviously, seizure laws represent a conflict of interest that encourages law enforcement officials to abuse their power.

A specific group that has gained employment in the prison-industrial complex prompts particular attention—those blacks who join police agencies. In the past, civil rights organizations had to sue municipalities to increase the number of blacks on police forces across the country. Having a proportional number of minority officers and a minority police chief is commonplace for a city with a significant minority population. Who better to preside over a system that incarcerates an ever-increasing number of minorities? In the past, when police agencies were headed by a preponderance of white men, at the first word of police abuse a minority community would investigate and mobilize if warranted. Many blacks are now supportive of their black police chiefs, whatever the abuses that take place under their watch. Blacks worry that if they are critical of their black chief, his replacement might be a white person. Some black chiefs and officers, however, act similarly to the "stereotypical" white racist cop. Moreover, when they abuse a black or minority citizen, black and white citizens grant them immunity from charges of racism because of their color. They grant this immunity although they are often carrying out the mandate of a racist system.

The military has also profited from the war. In 1993 South Carolina deployed National Guard units to so-called high-crime areas. In the summer of 1996 National Guard troops conducted weekend training in targeted neighborhoods in Washington, D.C. Trying to curb drug crime, guard units would post troops in military vehicles on street corners where suspected drug trafficking was taking place. These areas were exclusively black. However, many residents did not see military deployment as an effective method of dealing with the drug problem. Use of the military is solely a police-state response that ignores the causes of poverty and crime. Military occupation did not affect suppliers and manufacturers, only increased the jail time for young black pushers and users. National Association for the Advancement of Colored People (NAACP) officials in South Carolina noted that military personnel arrested several citizens. Still, no change occurred in economic conditions or the drug abuse problem in the targeted communities. The drug dealers simply shifted their activities to another location. Meanwhile, war supporters still compelled residents to surrender their privacy rights as troops shone lights in windows at night and everyone became a suspect. For state military organizations, looking for a new role in a post-Cold War society, the domestic war provided the opportunity to find relevance, a new role, and new enemies to conquer.

When a politician uses the war to gain office and power, the profit is in winning the office he or she seeks. For those who support that politician, the profit is in maintaining an ideology and social order that keeps them on top or on the job. Legitimate corporations profit from the war because citizens have perceived their actions as providing a needed service. Most citizens have no idea or do not care about corporate expansion and involvement in the prison-industrial complex—unless that expansion directly affects them. The "legitimate" profiteers receive a handsome return on their investment, yet this is apt to change as the cost of war escalates. The antiwar goal is to persuade the executives and corporations to take an "enlightened self-interest" view toward investing in poor and dispossessed communities.

Plenty of everyday people profit from the war as it gives them employment and the means to care for their families. In addition, the jobs give them a sense of identity and self-worth. The insidiousness of the war lies in the fact that so many individuals and organizations gain identity and function in maintaining the war effort. Without the war many unemployed people would fight for jobs—including many middle-class black people who believe that they have made some small foothold through affirmative action. The fear may be that if attention shifts from crime and prisons, a huge economic void would result. Because so many people profit in so many ways, attention must be directed to the system itself. The "war on drugs" is a by-product of the system and ideology of white supremacy. It is the perpetuation of this system that has caused so much pain in the black community.

The United States spends $44 billion a year on police, prisons, judges, probation officers, and parole officers. Yet, with the increase in spending, drug usage remains unabated in this country. With only 5 percent of the world's population, the United States still consumes more than 50 percent of the world's drugs. Furthermore, this nation incarcerates black males at a rate nearly five times greater than for black males in South Africa. The United States imprisons more people per capita than any other country in the world. Also, this country spends an estimated annual expenditure of $35,000 (per prisoner) to feed, house, and care for inmates locked in our prisons.[41] Reversing such trends is not a goal of trash television. In addition, more police with better guns have not abated illicit drug use. As for those behind bars, in some states inmates are charged room and board. This creates the possibility that, after years of incarceration, ex-offenders may return to the streets in financial debt to the state. This type of scheme only perpetuates and increases the intergenerational nature of dispossession.

The war has its profiteers. However, contrary to popular opinion, they are not those bejeweled and bedecked, Tommy Hilfiger-wearing, gold-accented Lexus cruisers. Nor are they the poor, young blacks and Latinos occupying the jails and prisons. The cruisers are engaged in pure, dead-end consumption. They are not investing in anything because everything they have is at risk of confiscation. The war is successful in promoting drug traffic, thereby assuring its longevity. It has also enlisted the support of its victims, thereby ensuring almost no opposition.

Finally, Clinton was correct regarding King's disappointment over the economic status of blacks and the violence dispossession produces. Nonetheless, King would have denounced the racist innuendo that the black community was inherently more criminal than the white community. King believed that poverty and ignorance breed crime, whatever the racial group. He was explicit about the government's culpability and responsibility for the ongoing economic violence against the poor and blacks.[42] King challenged the lack of economic justice, citing urban decay as a symptom of dispossession. Whenever asked who he thought was responsible for inner-city crime and blight, King often quoted Victor Hugo: "If a soul is left in the darkness, sins will be committed. The guilty one is not he who commits the sins, but he who causes the darkness."[43] King's last speech was a call for economic boycotts against banks that redlined and industries that refused to hire blacks. King was killed in Memphis while leading garbage workers fighting for labor rights and calling for an end to the Vietnam War. He said that the war took away resources from the dispossessed. King died trying to change the status quo and fighting against economic dispossession. Therefore, the idea of King supporting the war, totalitarian-style crime bills, and the racist hysteria that replaced meaningful public discourse is hard to conceive. Casting crime in a race context reinforces group dispossession; it provides the illusion of safety and security to those claiming an entitlement to privilege. The solution rests with a focus on ending dispossession. Minority business ownership and self-determination, rather than food stamps and economic dependency, erode dispossession. The economic power of the marketplace, not the police power of government, reverses those factors that perpetuate conditions of poverty. The conditions of poverty breed the contempt for human life and the disregard for property rights that are the roots of drug abuse and crime in the United States.

PEACE AND JUSTICE

It is not enough for the Negro to declare that color-prejudice is the sole cause for their social conditions, or for the white South to reply that their social condition is the main cause of prejudice. They but act as reciprocal cause and effect, and a change in neither alone will bring the desired effect. Both must change, or neither can improve to any great extent. The Negro cannot stand the present reactionary tendencies and unreasoning drawing of the color-line indefinitely without discouragement and retrogression. And the condition of the Negro is ever the excuse for further discrimination. Only by a union of intelligence and sympathy across the color-line in the critical period of the Republic shall justice and right triumph.

—W. E. B. Dubois[44]

The way to peace is through justice. In advancing the antiwar effort, the dispossessed, facing the most oppressive conditions, must take to the offense through direct and political action. They must show a renewed understanding and assertion of their human rights. The role of the reformer is to offer humane solutions for dealing with symptoms of dispossession. Ending drug prohibition, or making drugs legal, would at the least make drug producers more accountable for the health care cost associated with addiction. At best, it would relieve the violence associated with the industry and end the state of house arrest and the resulting dehumanization that exists in many communities of color. A social movement with drug legalization as a tactic, along with the reinstitution of individual human rights, strikes a blow at the elite within the drug distribution structure. Should the erosion of rights continue to occur, individual and organizational efforts will predictably become more demonstrative. Society will witness an increase in emphasis on the delegitimization of institutions associated with the drug war. It is just as predictable that the initial focus of delegitimization will be law enforcement agencies and the criminal justice system. If the politicization of the poor, blacks, and other minorities intensifies, more violent social disorder will spark more extreme police-state measures. Thus an end to drug prohibition, or legalization, while intended to lessen inhuman treatment of addicts and violations of human rights, is a preventive measure to avoid an increase in social disorder and greater restrictions on rights.

In war, tactical diversions—for instance, the "bait and switch" or "divide and conquer"—keeps those opposed to the war fighting skirmishes instead of the main battle. A diversion is easy to recognize because those who practice it can rarely provide a rational explanation of where certain policies lead. Often their responses are full of hyperbole and emotionalism, or are merely a parroting of existing policies and policy statements. Society manipulates many dispossessed defectors into leading the diversionary charge, not just conservative talk radio hosts or the black conservative Republican legislators. A defector can be anyone who feels that he or she profits from diversion for maintenance of the status quo. Diversions can come from the paternalistic liberal or from religious leaders. Consequently, minority communities should reject diversions from all quarters, and demand a positive and productive strategy to end the economic dispossession and violence in their community. Drug warriors and those seduced by them should be identified and their message confronted by the war's opponents. However, this is not a primary focus of the antiwar effort. The antiwar effort is proactive in its attack on tyrannical politics. Achieving reform is about challenging irrational policies, not merely attacking personalities. Reformists should encourage defections on the other side. Accordingly, reformists must leave the back door open for proponents of war to change their minds. This does not mean that one drags the half-dead along, or engages as a primary mission in a fight with defectors trying to change their minds. Further, reformists ought not merely hold the line until traditional, recognized, and institutional leadership comes to the front of the battle. Antiwar activists must charge ahead and show the way by example. Fresh young recruits will join a noble cause. Strategically, education, mobilization, and resistance are key ingredients in countering regressive social policies. Therefore, reformers must build grassroots participation in organizations that promote drug policy reform and those that attempt to address dispossession. Linkage between new and traditional structures, such as Families Against Mandatory Minimums (FAMM) and the NAACP, is vital. Reformists must also create new grass-roots structures dedicated solely to the structural problems of, and a structural remedy for, dispossession. All must engage in mobilization and direct action to coerce politicians into changing the tone and substance of the drug debate or to support politicians seeking progressive reform. Group cohesiveness and the ability to mobilize a politically focused constituency is critical to policy reform. The communities punitively affected by Reagan-era drug policy do not have resources equal to those seeking to maintain the status quo; thus their human capital is their greatest resource. Thomas "Tip" O'Neil of Massachusetts once said, "All politics are local." Local structures influence national politics and shift the tone of the debate from one centered on criminal justice remedies to debate that regards drug abuse as a health care concern. The substantive effect of a change in tone would also strike at the rapid growth of the prison-industrial complex. The antiwar effort must act at least as rapidly as that growth. Instead of waiting for media or politicians to decide the saliency of the issue, reformers should go to the churches to meet with ministers, and speak to groups within the community and to local elected officials. The most obvious and compelling ammunition for ending the war is the disproportionate spending on the construction of jails and prisons as opposed to the construction of schools and even public housing. In the '90s jail has become the new form of public housing and moreover, has the potential to further resegregate American society. Only by attacking dispossession can reformists reverse this trend.

Proponents of war always ask the citizenry to give up some of their liberties during the conduct of war. Proponents of the "war on drugs" ask the citizenry to "give up some rights" to fight crime and drug abuse. However, their request erodes the foundation of "innocent until proven guilty," the cornerstone of jurisprudence for any free society. From the very beginning, the Founding Fathers defined rights as limits on democratic power. The American Revolution occurred in the wake of the experience of living under a police state. British soldiers conducted house-to-house searches to enforce harsh tax laws and seize literature hostile to the Crown. Those searches were feared then as drug dealers and burglars are feared today. The architects of the Constitution sought to prevent the much-feared recurrence of injustices suffered at the hands of the standing army in colonial America—injustices such as the imprisonment and detention of citizens without a judicial officer's determination of the existence of "probable cause" to believe that the individual had committed a crime. The Second, Third and Fourth Amendments along with the writ of habeas corpus protects those rights. They ensure that military and police power remains subservient to private citizens with the means to defend their liberty. Those inside and outside the war zone must ask themselves how many additional rights they should surrender to agencies such as the Bureau of Alcohol, Tobacco and Firearms, Drug Enforcement Administration, Federal Bureau of Investigation, and the Central Intelligence Agency. Do citizens want these organizations operating with impunity in their neighborhoods? Do they want their children to grow up in an environment where the acronyms for these agencies are everyday expressions? A right is a limitation on the power and authority of government. The purpose of the Bill of Rights is to protect against the tyranny of the majority and excessive government power. Thus antiwar activists must be steadfast in their support of these protections and must teach the meaning of rights.

Citizens must not allow the war mentality to prevail. They must challenge and reject war metaphors, which breed other war metaphors, as illustrated in this text. If reformers fail, the current environment of racism, dehumanization, and dispossession will worsen. As the number of blacks, Latinos, and poor locked away in prisons continues to grow, then, to quote Malcolm X, "the chickens will come home to roost." To put an end to the genocidal implications of the war, those who proclaim their commitment to law and order founded on the Constitution and the Bill of Rights must join a new, domestic, antiwar movement. That movement must restore and safeguard the protection of life, liberty, and property here at home. If reformers are successful in ending the "war on drugs," and attacking dispossession, the nation will be well on its way to a more secure future. It is hoped that those on the front line are willing to join in this effort.

Here is one last story that is a sign of encouragement. In the country, rural America, a pickup truck is often a person's most prized possession. One morning, as I was riding down the road (in my truck), I noticed a big red Ford "dually," a 4 x 4 pickup with a sticker on its chrome-plated bumper. This four-door truck had all the extras—tinted windows, custom striping, CB and mobile phone antennas, the works. Pulling up beside it I noticed a bumper sticker that read, "This Vehicle *Not* Purchased with Drug Money!" I followed the truck until its driver turned into a fast-food restaurant so that I could interview him. The driver was a black man in his mid to late fifties named Jesse. I asked him why he had the bumper sticker and his reply was an obvious one: "When I first bought this truck, the police would see a black man in a nice vehicle and pull me over and want to search. I got tired of it. A friend of mine knew what I had been repeatedly going through and he gave me this sticker. Now when the police stop me, it is often to ask where I got the sticker. Many of them think that it's funny and some have even called other officers to the scene to see it."

Policy reformers have many allies and supporters out there who need only to be encouraged to speak out against the war. They are people such as Jesse, who are tired of being stereotyped. They are working people like Delane, who realize that a decision made for convenience can have long-lasting effects. They are motorists like Tim, who is surrounded by six patrol cars and a paddy wagon, detained, searched, and given a ticket for a bad headlight. They are Cornelia Whitner, who is branded a bad mother and jailed because she has an addiction. The support base is the inmates and their families. For the antiwar activists, organizing will always start with a few. As Jesse Jackson puts it, "Rosa Parks did not start with a committee, she sat on the bus alone." An effort to change policy starts with a few. The drug war has had such a profound and devastating effect on blacks that a change in policy and direction can no longer be avoided by the community. Societal abuses have piled up to the point of change. Drug policy and its effects have produced the dynamic to create discontinuous change. The dispossessed must reject the basic assumptive paradigms of the drug war and replace them with new ones.[45] At the very least, legalization will create a more humane and less violent society. Ultimately, the human rights community has a responsibility to fight dispossession. It is a painful fight; still, pain is a part of the process of growth. The consequences of the current drug war have been painful. It is time that we learn from the pain and move on to a policy that will decrease incarceration and focus on treatment for those addicts who need help. Perhaps it is an overused cliché—nonetheless, when dealing with dispossession and its diversions, such as the "war on drugs," activists and reformers must "keep their eyes on the prize." Ending dispossession is the prize. The human rights community must end its retreat from dealing with the tyrannical and counterproductive laws now in place in society. It must move to reverse bad public policy. Policy can change with effort. Slavery was public policy. Jim Crowism was public policy. Separate but equal was public policy. It will take a new antiwar effort to end the bad policy known as the "war on drugs." Finally, one of the first rules of organizing is that you don't have to announce that you're going to fight, just fight. Those opposed to the war need not wait for someone to save them or fight for them. There is no need to wait for media or a crowd of people to hear the call. Those seeking changes just need to fight!

ENDNOTES

1. Bruce Perry, *Malcolm X: The Last Speeches* (New York: Pathfinder) 1989: p. 160.

2. Rob Marriott, "All That Glitters," *Vibe*, Vol. 5, No. 4, May 1997: pp. 54–56.

3. Douglas Kellner, *Media Culture: cultural studies, identity and politics between the modern and the postmodern* (London: Routledge) 1995: pp. 111–112. Kellner's revision of deconstruction is useful as a simple Marxian take on "false consciousness."

4. Marimba Ani, *Yurugu: An African-centered Critique of European Cultural Thought and Behavior* (Trenton: African World Press) 1994: p. xxi. *Maafa* is a Swahili term that means disaster, calamity, damage, injustice, misfortune, or catastrophe. Ani refers to it as " 'The Great Suffering' of our people at the hands of Europeans in the Western hemisphere." Africentrics use the word to depict what is considered the "African Holocaust"—"the great crime"—which was the enslavement of Africans, the slave trade, and the violence and death both produced.

5. Dan Weikel, "War on Drugs Targets Minorities Over Whites," *The Los Angeles Times*, May 21, 1995: p. 1. "Records show that federal officials prosecute nonwhites. . . . Virtually all white crack offenders have been prosecuted in state courts where sentences are far less. The difference can be up to eight years for the same offense."

6. Robert E. Scott, "Trade: A Strategy for the 21st Century," in *Reclaiming Prosperity*. Economic Policy Institute (Armonk: M. E. Sharpe) 1996: pp. 245–246. "Between 1980 and 1994, the U.S. current account balance, the broadest measure of income from trade in goods and services (including investment income) went from a surplus of $2.3 billion to a deficit of $151.2 billion. . . . When the U.S. imports more than it exports. . ., there is downward pressure on wages and an undermining of bargaining power of U.S. workers. . ."

7. Steven A. Holmes, "The Boom in Jails is Locking Up Lots of Loot," *The New York Times*, November 6, 1994: p. E3.

8. Paulette Thomas, "Rural Regions Look to Prisons for Prosperity," *The Wall Street Journal*, July 11, 1994: p. B1.

9. U.S. Department of Justice, FBI Uniform Crime Report, "Age-Specific Arrest Rates and Race-Specific Arrest Rates for Selected Offenses, 1965–1992": pp. 206–207 and U.S. Department of Health and Human Services, "National Household Survey on Drug Abuse: Population Estimates 1993": p. 18f, cited in Dawn Day, "Drug Arrest: Are Blacks Being Targeted?" *NewsBriefs*,

April 1995: pp. 22–27. Reproductions of the article are available through The Sentencing Project, Washington, D.C.

Although arrests per 100,000 for persons of all races for drug violations grew from a low of 26.7 in 1965 to 452.4 in 1993, the patterns for blacks and whites are distinctly different. In 1993 about 12 percent of both blacks and whites reported using illicit drugs. Yet in 1993 there were 136 arrests of blacks for drug violations per every 1,000 users versus thirty-one arrests of whites per 1,000 users. This suggests that blacks are arrested at a ratio of 4 to 1 when compared to white drug users.

10. Gary Webb, "Dark Alliance; America's 'crack' plague has roots in Nicaraguan war," *San Jose Mercury News*, August 18, 1996: p. A1. A three-part series on how Nicaraguan Contras in the '80s—aided by the CIA—provided a direct pipeline to a Los Angeles cocaine dealer who spread crack throughout Los Angeles, supplied rival gangs (the Crips and the Bloods), and shipped crack across the country.

11. Marc Mauer and Tracy Huling, *Young Black Americans and the Criminal Justice System: Five Years Later* (Washington: The Sentencing Project), October 1995.

12. Peter B. Kraska and Victor E. Kappeler, "Militarizing American Police: The Rise and Normalization of Paramilitary Units," *Social Problems*, Vol. 44, No. 1, February 1997: p. 1.

13. NBC News, Meet the Press, October 3, 1993. Host Tim Russert interviews columnist William Raspberry. Russert asks Raspberry to "speak to America," and to the "predatory youth." On October 17, 1993, Russert posits the same characterization of youth to Jesse Jackson. However, it is noted that the term *predatory* was commonly used during the 1993-94 public crime debates by columnists such as Raspberry of *The Washington Post*, Richard Cohen of *The New York Times*, and others.

14. James P. Lynch and William J. Sabol, "The Use of Coercive Social Control and Changes in the Race and Class Composition of U.S. Prison Population," paper presented at the meeting of the American Society of Criminology, Miami, Florida, November 9, 1994: p. 23.

15. Howard Fineman, "An Older, Grimmer Jesse," *Newsweek*, Vol. 123, Issue 2, January 10, 1994: p. 24.

16. Roger D. Hatch, *Beyond Opportunity: Jesse Jackson's Vision for America* (Philadelphia: Fortress Press) 1988: p. 109.

17. Marc Mauer and Tracy Huling, *Young Black Americans and the Criminal Justice System: Five Years Later* (Washington: The Sentencing Project) October 1995, cited in "Prisons," National Drug Strategy Network, *NewsBriefs*, Vol. VI, No. 9, December 1995: p. 11.

18. The Anti-Drug Abuse Act of 1988. The sentences for possession and distribution of cocaine base (crack) are 100 times greater than for powdered cocaine. This is commonly referred to as a "100 to 1" quantity ratio. "Crack" is the street term for cocaine base. Crack is manufactured by heating cocaine hydrochloride (powdered cocaine) and baking soda or some other cutting (diluting) additive. Five grams of crack cocaine carries the same penalty as 500 grams of powder cocaine. Congress passed these laws in 1986 and 1988. Opponents on the sentencing disparity claim that the law is arbitrary and irrational because it assigns such disproportionate penalties to two forms of the same substance. They argue that the law discriminates against African-Americans since the majority of those charged with crimes involving crack are black (92.6 percent of those convicted in 1992 for violations involving crack were black; 4.7 percent were white), whereas powder cocaine users are predominantly white.

19. The (Ronald) Reagan era is defined as that period beginning in 1978 and continuing through the Clinton administration. Reagan-era policies are considered as those derived from a fundamentalist, nationalistic, and "conservative" political agenda. However, the contemporary roots of the "war on crime" extend back to the Richard Nixon administration where the "get tough" movement was initiated within the context of the Civil Rights Movement, the urban riots of the '60s, and the social division created by the Vietnam War. Nixon's campaigning focused on a "return to normalcy." This spawned the contemporary "law and order" movement.

Still, it was Ronald Reagan who forced Democratic politicians to adjust their positions on crime to gain electoral support from a white, suburban political base.

20. William Booth, "Exploding Number of SWAT Teams Sets Off Alarms," *The Washington Post*, June 17, 1997: pp. A1, A10.

21. Dawn Day, "Drug Arrest: Are Blacks Being Targeted?" *NewsBriefs*, April 1995: p. 22–27.

FBI Uniform Crime Report. "Age-specific Arrest Rates and Race-specific Arrests for Selected Offenses, 1965–1992," (Washington, DC: U.S. Department of Justice) 1993.

FBI Uniform Crime Report, "Crime in the United States, 1993." (Washington, DC: U.S. Department of Justice) 1994.

22. Mauer and Huling, *NewsBriefs*: p. 11.

23. *See Whitner* v. *South Carolina*, Opinion No. 24468. Filed July 15, 1996. In a 3-2 decision, the South Carolina Supreme Court ruled that a woman could be held criminally liable for actions taken during pregnancy that might affect her viable fetus. In February 1992 Cornelia Whitner gave birth to a healthy baby who tested positive for cocaine. Two months later Whitner pleaded guilty to and was convicted of criminal child neglect and was sentenced to eight years in prison. Whitner filed a motion for postconviction relief in May 1993 arguing that she was wrongly charged and convicted and that she was given ineffective assistance of counsel. The conviction was overturned in state appeals court; however, the appeals court ruling was overturned by the S.C. Supreme Court, thus upholding the original conviction.

24. Paul W. Valentine, "Maryland State Police Still Targeting Black Motorists, ACLU Says," *The Washington Post*, November 15, 1996: p. A1, cited in National Drug Strategy Network, *NewsBriefs*, Vol. VII, No. 12, December 1996.

25. Ibid.: p. A1.

26. Lynch and Sabol: pp. 29, 30.

27. National Drug Strategy Network, "HUD Announces 'One-Strike' Rule for Public Housing Tenants," *NewsBriefs*, Vol. VII, No. 5, May 1995: p. 9. On March 28, 1996, HUD introduced a "zero-tolerance" policy designed to screen and evict tenants involved in drug or other criminal activity (59 Crl 1047). Referred to as "One Strike and You're Out."

28. Mauer and Huling, *Young Black Americans.* . . . : p. 58.

29. Marc Mauer, "Intended and Unintended Consequences: State Racial Disparities in Imprisonment," The Sentencing Project, January 1997: p. 26.

30. Billy J. Tidwell, ed., *The State of Black America, 1993* (Washington: National Urban League, Inc.) 1993: p. 259.

31. Mauer and Huling, *NewsBriefs*: p. 11.

32. Lynch and Sabol: p. 3.

33. Ibid.: p. 7.

34. Doug Jehl, "Clinton declares emotional appeal on stopping crime," *The New York Times*, November 14, 1993: p. A1.

35. Author attended Jackson's regional Rainbow/PUSH Coalition meeting in Memphis, Tennessee, April 3–4, 1997, to commemorate the assassination of Martin Luther King, Jr.

36. Paulette Thomas, "Making Crime Pay: Triangle of Interest Creates Infrastructure to Fight Lawlessness," *The Wall Street Journal*, May 12, 1994: p. A8.

37. Ibid.: p. A1.

38. Eric Boehlert, " 'Suge' Knight is sentenced to nine years in prison," *Rolling Stone*, Issue 758, April 17, 1997: p. 30. Also, Matt Henderson, "Notorious B.I.G., 1973–1997: The hip-hop community mourns as another rap star is gunned down": p. 30.

39. Rob Marriott, "All That Glitters": p. 59.

40. Deann Smith, "Foster to review drug forfeiture laws," *Baton Rouge Advocate*, January 5, 1997: p. B1, and Greg Garland, "I-10 drug searches," *Baton Rouge Advocate*, February 9, 1997: p. A1, cited in *NewsBriefs*, Vol. VII, No. 5, May 1996.

41. Marc Mauer, "Lock 'Em Up and Throw Away the Key: African-American Males and the Criminal Justice System" in *The African-American Male: A Second Emancipation* (Washington: National Urban League) 1993: p. 57.

42. Martin Luther King, Jr., *Stride Toward Freedom* (San Francisco: HarperCollins Publishers) 1986: p. 194.

43. Martin Luther King, Jr., "Next Stop: The North," in *A Testament of Hope: The Essential Writings and Speeches of Martin Luther King, Jr.* edited by James M. Washington (San Francisco: HarperCollins Publishers) 1986: p. 192.

44. W .E .B. Dubois, *The Souls of Black Folk* (New York: Bantam Books) 1903: pp. 131–132.

45. Jefferson M. Fish, "Discontinuous Change and the War on Drugs," Chapter 4 this volume.

Section IC
Social Science Analyses

9

The Opening Shots of the War on Drugs

Jerry Mandel

DRUG WARS BEFORE DRUG USE PROBLEMS

The telltale signs of the war on drugs—big profits, smuggling, organized crime, agent heroics and violence and corruption, disruption of the drug practices of a weak minority—sprang into existence after a federal law in 1862 set an exorbitant import duty on opium prepared for smoking. Long before there were any laws restricting any other form of opium, or any other drug except alcohol, the newspapers were reporting informants, dealer threats, and asset forfeitures as part of the trade in smoking opium. This chapter is about how the war on drugs developed, with opium smoking its sole focus for forty years and its main focus for another decade, from 1862 until opium smoking in the U.S. was so damaged (from 1909–1914) it never recovered. The data are framed by opening and concluding sections seeking the "lessons" from the history that would contribute to current debate over United States drug policy.

As I read it, the war on drugs preceded any drug use problem except alcohol. An opium smoking den in the U.S. was first described in a newspaper or magazine eight years *after* the war was initiated. Opium was the major medicine of the country, and at the very moment a law restricting opium smoking was passed, opiates were in greater demand than ever due to the wounds and battlefield conditions during the Civil War. Harsh laws against any other drug, except alcohol, had hardly ever been even mentioned in the U.S. So when the opening shots were fired, and for many of the early years of the war on drugs, there was no publicly recognized drug problem.

Racism was the prime reason for the initial half-century of the war on drugs. The war on drugs provided a venue for gratuitously punishing selected types of people while providing a rationale that one was really doing good. It enabled sadism without guilt or embarrassment, without legal or public censure. The titillating melodrama of the war on drugs—agent versus smuggler, good versus evil—served as a cover for the cultural oppression of the War On Drugs.

The major rationales for assailing opium smoking in China—that it destroyed economic productivity and eventually the family—were irrelevant in the U.S. context. During the initial decades of the war on drugs, the Chinese in the U.S. economically outperformed their white competitors by a lot, and there weren't enough Chinese women permitted into the U.S. to allow much of a family structure that any drug might undermine. U.S. laws against opium smoking were not initiated to save the put-upon Chinese but to further hurt them. Apart from the typically racist negative descriptions of opium smoking in the dens of the Chinese, there was virtually no public recognition of a drug problem in the U.S. until the 1900s.

The war on drugs made matters worse. Essentially, drug law enforcers are paid to make trouble among strangers they do not know or identify with. This was true in the first half-century of the war on drugs when the use and sale of smoking opium was not a crime, and hardly anyone in the U.S. outside the small Chinese communities knew anything about it.

The opening shots of the war on drugs raised the street price of opium prepared for smoking, changed the relationship of user and seller, and created a new set of experiences around the drug (such as investigation, search and seizure, and fine). The price alone influenced who smoked, how frequently and how much, and the status and other meanings attached to opium smoking. All the above problems were entirely imposed by the agents and their superiors, starting with Congress.

During the initial fifty years of contacts between agents enforcing drug laws and drug users, U.S. newspapers and magazines described those agents as rude, insensitive, frenzied, money-hungry, lying, corrupt, and racist as well as occasionally heroic. White opium smokers who had never previously used such concentrated manufactured drugs recreationally suddenly took up such drugs when smoking opium was so suppressed it became far more expensive, and riskier, than morphine or heroin. Even—or is that especially?—when the war on drugs succeeded, it made matters worse.

The goal of the war on drugs was not to end drug use but to wage the war itself. Smugglers and enforcers profited, often beyond what could previously be imagined, and the media and the public got a charge out of the new high stakes. Drug prohibition's emergence a half-century into the war on drugs escalated the melodrama.

The war on drugs created the drug problem.[1] Free of laws, opium smoking seems a reflective, subtle, delicate, sensual, stimulating ritual that rightfully had numerous devotees.

DECLARATION OF WAR

In 1862 the Customs Service discovered a new type of opium. It looked, felt, and smelled different from any other opium for which an import duty was imposed. This opium, prepared for smoking, was not recommended by doctors or sold in apothecaries or processed in factories for the medical profession or reported on in the U.S. mass media.[2] In the U.S., only the Chinese immigrants used prepared opium, bringing it with them from overseas.[3] Somehow, lawmakers who learned of this difference set an initial special duty on prepared opium at 80 percent ad valorem (80 percent of value) while all other opiates were taxed $2 a pound (when crude opium was reported selling at $6 a pound). Soon thereafter, prepared opium was taxed at 100 percent ad valorem, and other forms of opium at $1 a pound.

Why the special tax on smoking opium? Raising government revenues from the very poorest is mean, but meanness against Chinese immigrants began very soon after the first boatloads of them arrived in California soon after the gold rush. In 1861, according to the *San Francisco Bulletin* of May 6, the California Legislature Committee investigating crimes against Chinese was furnished "a list of 88 Chinamen . . . known to have been murdered by White people . . . probably a very small proportion of those who have been robbed and murdered." The Chinese opium smokers were not about to directly protest a special tax on their traditional drug use. Smuggling would be their response to the new law.

The ad valorem tax did not make opium possession a crime—just importing it without paying the duty. Seizures did *not* reduce the supply because they were resold at auction (possibly to the original importer). News of the huge tax must have spread instantly to mainland China because large-scale smuggling of smoking opium, using such contraptions as false-bottomed trunks and hollowed-out heels, emerged quickly. In 1864 a newspaper reported a conviction (and an acquittal) for smuggling and the red-handed capture of a smuggler.[4] The war was on.

RULES OF ENGAGEMENT

The war on drugs was ushered in with a bidding war. Given the enormous ad valorem duty, smugglers tried to bribe customs inspectors to overlook opium tins, and the Customs Service had to beat that offer for inspectors to enforce the law. Initially, a customs agent's reward for a drug seizure was 50 percent of net resale. Minutes after the special tax on smoking opium was known about, the ambiance of the San Francisco docks changed. Two populations imagined their fortunes rising—would-be smugglers and customs agents. If smoking opium sold for $6 a pound (plus tax) on the legal wholesale market, and almost that in auction, each pound seized by or slipped by an inspector was worth a day's salary to him.

VICIOUS AND AVARICIOUS: THE FIRST AND PROTOTYPIC NARCOTICS AGENTS

THE FIRST KNOWN CASE: U.S. VS. ONE CASE OPIUM

In January 1864 the courts—in *US vs. One Case Opium*—denied a customs inspector's claim that opium ready to be off-loaded was subject to seizure. The ship's captain had the suitcase of a Chinese passenger put in plain view, and notified customs officials the bag contained prepared opium and the owner would pay the duty.[5] The court fretted about these customs agents "lest their zeal in executing the revenue laws—stimulated, it may be, by the large personal interest they have in every seizure—betray them into unjustifiable violations of private rights."[6]

    In other words, the court prevented a frame-up by the agent. Drugs were only an alibi. It wasn't even the Chinese, though many agents were delighted to inflict whatever pain, whatever cost, they could. It was the money! With legal opium the U.S. Treasury got 80 percent ad valorem; with seized opium agents got half the net profit of resale. To agents it meant the difference between being poor and being a notch or two wealthier. Since the Chinese were easy prey, many agents felt there were no limits to their pursuit of rewards. No more than eighteen months after the special duty on smoking opium, the courts recognized this special nature of drug law enforcement.

FEEDING FRENZY: AGENTS GREET THE CHINESE IMMIGRANTS

The customs crew on the San Francisco docks probably aggressively searched each post-law steamer from China. A white minister sympathetic to the Chinese immigrants gave this account in 1877 of East-meets-West on the San Francisco docks.

Relays of Custom-house officials ... examine the men and their baggage. The Custom-house men go through (the baggage) without much ceremony. ... Custom-house officials [are] quite expert ... not only ... in detecting smuggled goods, they are also singularly careless in handling the personal effects of these poor fellows; and often wantonly destroy or (according to Chinese authority) unlawfully appropriate to their own benefit many little articles of personal baggage not subject to duty.[7]

How much opium was captured? How motivated were the customs inspectors? Though the reward for seizing opium dropped as low as 10 percent by the mid-1880s, a seizure of 250 pounds valued at $2,000 through the 1870s still meant a reward of a year's salary to the lower levels of dock watchmen and inspectors. The following list is incomplete, but gives an idea of the big seizures (most in San Francisco) during the twenty-five years after smoking opium was assigned a special tariff. The earliest "big seizure" I've read of was of $3,000 worth of opium in 1864. (The headline, "Another Large Seizure," suggests earlier ones.) In 1869 one ship from Asia yielded 1,000 pounds of opium, most found "in trunks having false bottoms," and another $12,000–$15,000 of it in "earthen pots, in cleats on the bottoms of boxes, in false covers, sides and bottoms ... in fact, every nook or corner where the owner thought there was a chance of smuggling it through." In 1875 untaxed opium (1,700 pounds valued at $25,000) was seized from a steamer from the orient. In 1880 a half-ton was seized from a steamer coming from south of the border. In 1882 a customshouse inspector seized 1,200 pounds of opium near the docks, and San Francisco police captured a boat containing 2,000 pounds of smoking opium rowing away from an anchored steamer. Seizures of 900 and 5,000 pounds were reported in 1886, and of 1,500 and 3,000 pounds in 1887, the last seized en route from a factory in Victoria, BC, to Chicago.[8] All the above captures occurred *before* the smuggling of prepared opium peaked as a result of the 1890 increase of the duty to $12 a pound.

AN AGENT'S DREAM KILLING: FOGARTY'S PROBE AND SLEEPLESS NIGHTS

Agents were motivated by money from even small seizures, but dreamed of the big score. Assistant surveyor John Fogarty had a special weapon to help realize his dream—"the biggest opium seizure ever made in this (San Francisco) port."

"Ever see Fogarty's probe? No? Well, it's a great tool. It'll go through the side of a house with a gentle push. It's made of Damascus steel and is tempered and pointed like a needle. Fogarty made several pokes with this probe and finally drew it out with 'dope' signs on it. He seemed terribly excited all of a sudden and called Inspector Holmes and put him on guard over the 'W.C.Y.' freight. Telling him not to let an ounce of it get out of his sight."[9]

A huge seizure of opium illustrated the greed of the agents. When a reporter caught up with Fogarty the day after his probe had hit the O-spot, he was:

> . . . looking sleepy about the eyes, not overclean as regards collar and cuffs. . . . [A dock worker said] "He [Fogarty] slept with it last night . . . [or] slept or not, but he was stowed away in the middle of it, right close to where the 'W.C.Y.' boxes were. He crawled out early this morning." [The day before] "Special Agent Tingle and Special [sic] McSweeney . . . borrowed Fogarty's probe, and commenced prospecting among the other freight. In about a minute there was a yell from Tingle, and he came to the front with more dope on the probe. Fogarty was paralyzed. He thought he had the whole business, but the freight Tingle and McSweeney made the find in was a totally different lot. It was a hundred cases of oil." [At this point Fogarty ordered all shipments of oil be confiscated.] "Mr. Fogarty was on the deck again all night last night, with a force of inspectors . . . guarding and probing the freight."[9]

The final tally showed $38,976 worth seized by Fogarty; $5,712 by Tingle and McSweeney.[10] Assuming a 10 percent reward for opium seizures, and salaries of $3 per day, Tingle and McSweeney earned four months' salary; assistant surveyor Fogarty, whose pay was higher, about three years' salary.

SURVEYOR BEECHER: BIG-TIME 1800s' CUSTOMS ENFORCEMENT

Fogarty's take illustrates the perquisites of high rank. They could mobilize more resources, order others around (e.g., to guard property), and seize entire shipments on suspicion. Line inspectors with skill, perseverance, and normal luck garnered rewards. Port surveyor Beecher, guarding more northern ports, made his record seizure in a daring venture as only a top administrator could.

Beecher acted on the tip of an informant who had missed his ship's departure from Portland on New Year's day. When, on the ship's return, he was told he had been replaced permanently, the sailor

> felt lonesome and again met his friend of Uncle Sam's custom house. . . . [I]t was not long before he remembered a number of barrels that had

been landed at the fishery in Kaasan Bay [Alaska]. Captain Beecher immediately telegraphed to the treasury department for permission to leave ... to Alaska and capture the opium. ... The collector and [informer] ... steamed away for Victoria [and met a pilot to guide them to Kaasan Bay, where a search by Beecher and ten men yielded fourteen barrels of prepared opium. The loaded cutter] had to force her way through ice to get out, the men at times having to get on floes and tow her. ... The ... opium seized [weighed] 3,012 pounds ... $45,000.[11]

The editorial comment on "The Kaasan Bay 'Find' in the (Portland) *Oregonian* was unconcerned about opium smoking, and thought smugglers were maligned:

Of all serious crimes ... smuggling ... least violates the consciences of men. It is a crime against law and against government, but not against morality. The smuggler robs no man. He buys his goods honestly in one market and sells them honestly in another. His offense is against an arbitrary regulation of government ... he simply fails to pay its demands. Many men otherwise honest are unable to see any moral turpitude in smuggling .... government, in exacting toll, plays the part of the highwayman.[12]

No mainstream paper in our lifetimes would so view drug smugglers.

AGENT CORRUPTION

The duty on prepared opium was an ideal law for corrupt agents. No one was hurt, no one paid extra except the "Celestials," whose testimony against whites was not accepted by the courts from 1853 to 1873.[13] The most corrupt agents were the most active and successful—without tough enforcement there was little incentive for smugglers to bribe agents and, besides, there was the possible big seizure and reward when no bribes had been paid.

Despite constant rumors of customs agent corruption, few agents were tried or convicted, or were fired or "quit" under pressure. Reverend Gibson wrote:

[I]t is strongly hinted, by those who ought to know something about it, that some of those Custom-house collectors are open to an arrangement with John Chinaman for a division of the profits, in which case, the officer although apparently practicing unusual diligence, is ... unable to detect any contraband.

The San Francisco press has more than once intimated the existence of an organized system of opium smuggling . . . 3 or 4 years ago an honest and efficient officer came near losing his life, because of his efforts to expose this ring. He has since been superseded in his office, without doubt through the political influence of this ring of smugglers.[14]

In 1882 two San Francisco city police officers captured a boat with 2,000 pounds of prepared opium on board as it was being rowed from a recently arrived steamer to San Francisco's shore. How the opium could be off-loaded from a steamer with eleven inspectors assigned to see this did not happen was cause for investigation.[15]

> After the news of the capture . . . a large delegation of Custom house officials set out for the office of the Chief of Police . . . to get possession of the seized goods. But [San Francisco Police] Chief Crowley stated that he would see . . . the seizure was properly conducted and . . . police officers got their just reward for the most important seizure of smuggled opium that has ever been made at the port.[16]

Though the collector of customs denied this story two days later, a reporter believed customs would struggle with police over who truly possessed the captured opium. Professional pride or personal greed, whoever had the seizure got the 10 percent reward.

In 1883 a Treasury department official estimated that in San Francisco

> during the last 10 years, over $6 million worth of opium has been smuggled in . . . systematically . . . by a ring of smugglers, assisted by prominent Government officials . . . receiving 30% of the spoils, the smugglers getting 70% . . . many men in this city who are reputed to be wealthy have made their money through smuggling opium.[17]

In 1888 the *San Francisco Examiner* (which William Randolph Hearst had published for a year) supported the allegation of a convicted smuggler that he had bribed officials in San Francisco. The reporter claimed "a new combination" of high-level smugglers had formed, including the ex-sheriff of San Francisco, the ex-assessor of San Francisco, and John T. Fogarty, deputy surveyor of the port. Fogarty threatened to sue for libel and the *Examiner* editorially welcomed the scrap.[18] What came of this is unknown, except a year later Fogarty was still at work, as evidenced by his seizure of 768 pounds of opium hidden on the steamer *Oceanic*.[19]

The greed of enforcers reached new levels in the case of Moy Jin Mun, "Chinese interpreter and opium expert for the Federal officials," who had informed customs that 1,200 tins of prepared opium were arriving aboard a steamer:

> He was very careful to stipulate that no mention should be made of him as having given the information on account of the feeling that he knew would be created against him in Chinatown . . . should it become known that he was the informer he would almost certainly be killed.[20]

The opium was found and seized, and to shield the interpreter's identity two freight clerks on the dock were put forward as informers to split the $5,000 reward, half of which was to be slipped under the table to the true informant. Somehow the money never got to Moy Jin Mun and he complained. The location of the reward money was a murky mess by the time the press reported it. In September 1892, fifteen months after the seizure, the informant's name was in print for all Chinatown to see, and he still hadn't received a dime.[20] Another paper the same day carried another version of the events. "In reality the seizure was not made, but opium was conveyed to the Custom House from the Pacific Mail dock as a blind." In fact, "this and other seizures were made systematically, . . . a plot to defraud the Government." One customs inspector was removed from office, and more action on the other "plotters," which included the deputy surveyor of San Francisco and a Colonel Evans, special Treasury agent, would be forthcoming.[21] This was high-level organized corruption, unprofessional conduct, ineptness, uncontrolled greed, and indifference to others' lives, even that of a professional employee and special ally. Whether Moy Jin Mun got the reward, or died shortly thereafter, is unknown.

In the late 1880s and early 1890s several high-level former and current customs officers were convicted, fired, or legally charged with corruption regarding opium smuggling. The former chief inspector of customs in Puget Sound (Edwin Gardner) was caught along the New York State/Canadian border with 1,500 pounds of prepared opium and later accused of selling 770 pounds of it, which had been stored in a customhouse, and paying customs employees to let him replace the seized-yet-sold opium with wooden blocks. One of his coconspirators was a deputy revenue inspector. Between his capture and his conviction, Gardner insisted that he was associated with a Herbert F. Beecher, U.S. Treasury special agent at Port Townsend, Washington, and that there had even been a $200 payment to him recorded on an expense list Gardner kept.[22]

In another case, the Treasury Department investigated

> the largest smuggling ring that ever engaged in the infamous traffic [in Chinese and opium]. . . .[C]orrupt Government officials in the North were as common as flies in summer. . . . Everybody connected with the ring had money to throw to the birds.[23]

A Portland grand jury in 1893 indicted for conspiracy the former collector at Portland, a former special agent there, six inspectors, and seven others. "The Secretary of the Treasury and the Attorney General are determined ... to put an end to the shameful practices which have for years given the district a scandalous notoriety in the country." "At the trials it was established that ... 30,000 pounds of opium had been smuggled into Portland ... from British Columbia in ... less than 12 months." The "huge conspiracy was proved" by convictions, though one of the 12 jurors voted to acquit the collector of Portland.[24]

□   □   □

Of the corrupt agents who were caught or brought to trial, certainly the research to date just scratches the surface. Up to now, data suggest that drug-related corruption among customs agents on the West Coast and Canadian border was endemic. It started near day one of the exorbitant special duty on prepared opium and got worse, involving more and higher ranked persons as time went on.[25]

Agent corruption did not reverse the impact of drug suppression policies but rather shaped the character of those policies. Matters would have been *worse* if customs officers had been honest, if assistant surveyor Fogarty had wielded his probe out of diligence and not greed. But an honest drug enforcement unit was a fantasy when a seizure could mean more money than a salary.

THE BILLION DOLLAR CONGRESS: THE TOP OF THE FEEDING FRENZY CHAIN

There was no better group to conduct an experiment on whether import laws affected the war on drugs than what the *New York Herald* at the time referred to as the Billion Dollar Congress of 1889–1890. It demonstrated that opium importation could be driven completely underground. Easily. Just tax prepared opium so much that the smugglers could beat the legal market's price. There was a point where loyal customers of legal suppliers either went underground or out of business. The Billion Dollar Congress found that point.

The duty on prepared opium was $10 a pound from 1884 to 1889, up from $6, which it had been since 1870 when "per pound" replaced ad valorem taxes. When the duty rose from $6 to $10 per pound, imports of opium for smoking skyrocketed in the months *before* the law took effect as merchants stocked up. They were three times higher in 1883 than in any previous year. The year *after* the law—1884—imports were near zero. After the stockpile was exhausted, imports picked up again, stabilizing at about 25 percent less than when the duty was $6. Everybody gained except opium smokers and the most honest merchants, "but they were only Chinese." Opium speculators made a killing, dishonest merchants could sell for under the legitimate price, smugglers thrived, and two types of inspectors did extremely well—honest and dishonest ones. The Treasury Department probably gained, as the duty per pound increased more than the loss from the decline in the weight. The Billion Dollar Congress ratcheted up the duty even more—to $12 a pound. At the start of 1889 the duty a Chinese immigrant would pay on a pound of opium was about two weeks' future earnings; by the end of that year he paid about two-and-a-half weeks' wages.

The *New York Herald's* special correspondent gave the most detailed coverage of the Billion Dollar Congress, smuggling just before and after the duty was raised to $12, import statistics, agents and corruption, the view of the populace at the centers of smuggling, and the interplay of all the above. Lengthy reports were datelined Winnipeg and British Columbia and several coastal cities in the northwestern U.S.[26] Smuggling, it was reported, had grown to vast proportions,[27] supported by the populace in places where opium was processed or the port from which it was shipped.[28] The smugglers knew the location and plans of agents and their boats, and besides this advantage had faster boats. Not every agent was corrupt, but corruption permeated the ranks.[29] If the increased tax had hindered drug use, that would be one thing, but the Chinese immigrants (whom the special correspondent and/or his *Herald* editor despised)[30] could smoke opium whenever they wanted for little more than before. The only loser was the U.S. Treasury because the increase in revenues per pound could not make up for the steep decline in imported opium for which a duty was paid.[31]

The *Herald* thought this decline in revenue was predictable, and therefore sinful. Congress must have known that smugglers would be the big gainers. An opium ring, to the special correspondent a huge, perfectly constructed and connected ring, controlled Congress. Ringleaders wrote the war on drugs' rules.

> The leaders of the opium ring ... induced the Billion Dollar Congress to impose a duty of $12 a pound upon opium, knowing that this would enhance the value of the drug, keep out legal importations and swell their profits on the smuggled opium. They persuaded the same Congress to enact legislation which places such a high license and heavy internal revenue tax upon manufacturers of opium in the United States as to effectually and absolutely keep out all manufacturers of the drug & leave the market entirely [to them].

> They control Senators and dictate the appointment of customs officers. When a customs officer proves too efficient, makes too many seizures

and keeps too bright a lookout they simply have him removed. This is especially the case with the Puget Sound customs district. This district has given the Treasury department more trouble than any other district in the United States.

A son of the late Henry Ward Beecher was appointed Collector of this district by President Cleveland. Almost the first thing the young man did was to trace and seize one lot of opium, valued at $40,000 .... Within a few months he had seized $130,000 worth of opium and was treading heavily upon the toes of the opium ring. The ring went to Washington and prevented the confirmation by the U.S. Senate of the nomination of Mr. Beecher....

There are two United States senators whose names are not far from taint in connection with this deal.[32]

☐   ☐   ☐

During the first three years of the $12 duty, from 1890–1893, the newspapers reported the greatest number of the highest level and most highly paid corrupt agents and the biggest, boldest, baddest smuggling operations in the thirty-year history of special taxation of prepared opium. Coincidentally, the percentage of resale that would be the reward to customs officers for drug seizures was *lower* than ever. As the legal reward declined, the temptation to be part of a smuggling operation must have been palpable for everyone working at a large port. Top-level customs officers at the two major Northwestern customs stations—Portland and Puget Sound—were convicted of "being on the other side." If the level of corruption got any higher, it would be in the Washington central office itself.

The *Herald's* special correspondent agreed with a port surveyor he'd interviewed that the only sane policy was to reduce the duty to about $2 a pound, which he thought Congress was going to do immediately. Policy suggestions, though, were secondary. The media (even the special correspondent) thrived on cops-and-robbers action—Fogarty's probe, Beecher's heroics, and what the guys in the seafront bars had to say about it all.

These tales of the Billion Dollar Congress show that the extent of the illicit traffic was a function of the structure, severity, and selective enforcement of the laws. Prohibition was not necessary to start the war on drugs. A 200 percent duty—the $12 tax on prepared opium—was sufficient to set off the trafficker versus narcs imagery that has been the staple war on drugs melodrama ever since. Smugglers versus agents was in place twenty years or more before the Harrison Act. The color and nationality of the victim changed; Mr. Big's probable country of origin changed; battering rams and outer space satellites replaced Fogarty's probe; big seizures now are valued in the scores of millions not the tens of thousands; and the drug seized is cocaine or marijuana, not prepared opium. But the melodrama was the same in the early 1890s as it is in the 1990s.

1894–1908: THE LOWER THE PENALTIES, THE LESS THE PROBLEM

(Reader beware! The next few paragraphs describe and document "no problem." Ending the war on drugs is far less exciting than initiating and escalating it. The action picks up soon.)

The Billion Dollar Congress proved that manipulating a simple customs duty could trigger off a war on drugs. After a few years during which smugglers thrived and corruption permeated top levels of customs inspectors, Congress in 1894 lowered the duty on prepared opium to $6 per pound. Almost immediately large-scale smuggling plummeted, and the newspapers suddenly (and for fifteen years) lost interest.

If the above is true, then the commonsense notion of how and why drug prohibition came to be is wrong. A "drug problem" did not emerge and spread like a cancer or epidemic, growing slowly but surely under the right conditions, until it caused such discomfort and pain that the situation cried out for remedy. Rather, a "drug problem" was turned on and off like a spigot. The Billion Dollar Congress turned it on; two congresses later it was turned off. *Drugs* were not a germ spreading among the most vulnerable, but a plaything of the most powerful. Commonsense cause and effect were reversed: drug policy *caused* drug problems.

I did not arrive at such radical conclusions lightly, nor was I confident that without special research they would weather the inevitable skepticism and criticism of the drug warriors and their captive audiences of the past few generations. When I began to write this chapter, my files had many drug stories before 1894 and after 1908, but next to nothing in between . . . even though access was provided to microfilm of thousands of pages of old newspapers from which *The Dope Chronicles: 1850–1950* were constructed.[33] So, I began a systematic study of key newspapers of the time.

THE MEDIA LOSES INTEREST WHEN PENALTIES DROP

Research Methods and Statistical Results

Eventually three increasingly detailed newspaper "samples" were drawn, partly because I was slow accepting the unconventional conclusions, partly because

I was hoping not to spend so much time reading papers via microfilm as I eventually did. Initially I tracked down the stories listed on the *New York Times'* indices for 1894–1905. The result—utter disinterest in drugs—was not sufficient because the opiate action (the Chinese smokers and their dens) was on the Pacific Coast. Further, the *Times* even then was rational and relatively staid and opiates were a hot issue, so maybe the *Times* was the wrong paper to read. Additionally, though the *Times'* indices were the best by far at the time, I still didn't trust their thoroughness and accuracy. So the first sample is off the mark, though close enough for a quick-and-dirty study.

Next I tried what I thought was the ultimate eye-straining big sample. Again the results seemed unconventional yet convincing. I was beginning to think I was on to something new, and then I met with Jim Baumohl—the most creative young researcher of the prelude to the Harrison Act of 1914—whose readings of the *Examiner*, in particular, had led him to believe that a real drug use problem had emerged in California in the late nineteenth century. So, I returned to The Stacks (it only felt like The Racks) for a third, larger, focused sample.

Sample 1. The New York Times' Index: 1894–1905. The *Times'* drug coverage tapered off to eight stories combined in 1894 and the next year (all but one on smuggling). From 1896 to 1905 it listed ten articles—one per year—on an opiate or cocaine, some not unfavorable to drugs. For 1906 to 1908, however, there were forty-one stories listed, twenty-six from overseas (twenty from China, none relating smoking opium among Chinese in the U.S. to those in Asia, and six from Europe); twelve on cocaine (six each in 1907 and 1908),[34] and three on opium. Some famous New York writers at the time mentioned opium smoking, for better or worse, but the *Times* didn't seem interested, at least in opiates, until 1909.[35]

Sample 2. The San Francisco Papers: 1894–1908. To determine news coverage in San Francisco, where the local newspapers have never been well indexed, three days per year each of the *Call*, *Chronicle*, and *Examiner* were read from 1894 through 1908. In all, 135 newspapers were read, nine different days per year for fifteen years.[36] *The 135 papers, combined, yielded less than a quarter of a newspaper page on a drug story.*

Sample 3. The San Francisco Examiner—William Randolph Hearst's Flagship Paper: 1894–1908. If any paper would feature exotic stories like drugs, it would be Hearst's first paper—the *San Francisco Examiner*—so it was oversampled. It was read five days per month, three months per year, between November 1894 and December 1908.[37] The total space allotted to non-alcoholic drugs in the *Examiner* in those 215 days, plus forty-two days read as part of Sample 2, plus all of February 1907 (looking for signs of recognition of California's first drug prohibition law), was under a page *for the combined 285 days.*

Content Analysis and Research Conclusions

The most parsimonious conclusion is that in the absence of something generating a war on drugs, without a reason for agents to actively disturb drug users, drugs—certainly opiates—are of little interest to the media. The $6 per pound tax on prepared opium was still a heavy penalty . . . and it still attracted the likes of ex-fireman Hansen who was the alleged smuggler of the drugs captured in by far the largest seizure reported in the sampled papers.

> Hansen used to shovel coal on the steamers plying between San Francisco and Honolulu and wore diamond rings while engaged in his occupation. When ashore he sported the finest clothes that could be bought . . . walking the streets with the freedom and elegance of a sugar planter.[38]

However, before the duty on prepared opium was dropped to $6 per pound, seizures of 471 pounds were not that rare, and the biggest cases were several times that. Likewise, to judge from the newspapers, almost all the agents who made their fortunes by selling their services to smugglers (or becoming smugglers) did so when that duty was $12, not $6, per pound. From 1900 to 1908 the only two stories on opium smuggling in the sampled newspapers were about agents who came up empty-handed: the discovery that between its seizure and public sale "someone extracted . . . [over 100 pounds of] opium from the boxes and refilled them with flour"[39], and an informant's tip that led to the seizure of a trunk full of ordinary clothes rather than of unstamped opium.[40]

A 1909 article—"Smuggled Opium"—showed how and why the substantial reduction in the tariff schedule substantially reduced the drug traffic.

> Now, the profit [in opium smuggling] is not sufficient to warrant many of the risks then taken and the expenses then incurred [in the 1880s] . . . [I]t comes in smaller quantities. . . . There are not the combinations that formerly existed and planned largely and systematically
>
> . . . [T]he hardest blow ever dealt that illegal industry was the act decreasing the duty upon opium. Successful smuggling depends upon three things: high duty, good demand, and small bulk. . . . Opium, when the duty was $12 a pound, combined the three points as almost no other article did.

[The main opium smuggler] must have a big profit to repay him for the risk. He had expenses, sometimes pretty heavy expenses, to cut down his apparent profit. Then he had to sell for less than the market price or there would be no advantage in buying from him. . . . Instead of being the $12 a pound represented by the duty, very likely his net profit was only $8 or $6 or even less. . . . Now deduct $6 from that net profit and see where he stands. . . . His expenses are as high as ever, and the buyer will insist upon approximately the same discount. An army of inspectors or revenue officers could not have hit as hard a blow as that. It . . . left the smuggling mainly to individuals and occasional small alliances where conditions were favorable and circumstances made the expenses light.[41]

The lack of media interest did *not* indicate that drug use was declining. At least two of the sampled San Francisco newspapers contained a short report on a legally imported (i.e., taxed) ten-ton shipment of opium.[42] When the import duty had dropped to $6 per pound,[43] legal imports more than doubled, from an annual average of 52,500 pounds of prepared opium in 1893–1894 to 118,500 over the next two years.[44] Given that we never know the amount of successfully smuggled drugs, at least it appeared that opium smoking was not declining much, if at all.

Of the "less than a page" the sampled San Francisco newspapers devoted to drugs, there were a few stories—typically a squib of two or three sentences—in which drugs were not part of a war on drugs (e.g., about duties paid on shipments of prepared opium, or of legal changes, or the endorsement by Chinese officials of morphia pills as a cure for opium smoking,[45] or of overdose/suicides).[46] A similar lack of interest in New York is suggested by the report of possibly the most money made from illegal "drugs" there at the time—$250,000—by a small manufacturer and a "regular organization" who sold *snuff* for twenty years without revenue stamps.[47] If opium had been a big issue, it certainly would have gotten headlines.

More revealing throughout the entire fifteen years was the absence of any mention of drugs when it would have been expected if drug use was widespread and "significant." There were violent struggles in both San Francisco and New York between rival local Chinese-American gangs, but never (in the sampled newspapers) is opium mentioned in this context. Likewise there were many stories of vice in Chinatown, concerning big profits and raids and trials, typically involving gambling but also prostitution and the enslavement of Chinese women, and sometimes prominently featuring agent corruption, but the one time in the sampled papers that stories mentioned opium smokers, the "dreamers" were peripheral to the hard-core vice as the police defined it (gambling).[48] When missionaries in China and the church's temperance work were the *Examiner's* "story of the week," there was no mention of opium.[49] Even when the Yellow Press pursued the removal of Chinese from the U.S., opium smoking did not rate a mention.[50] In sum, even if opium smoking had not decreased, the mass media's interest in it declined markedly. Opium use alone, without the huge profits and the war on drugs created by an exorbitant import duty, could not arouse even the Hearst editors, who were always on the prowl for a story that would sell.

DRUGS IN PRISON: AN ANOMALY AND PORTENT (1903)

Opiates in prison was the one new and relatively major story in the sampled papers. There were five stories in the *Examiner*, a total of two full columns, although several of them did not mention opium or drugs in the headline, and they involved a lot more than drugs. Two separate state prisons, over 100 miles apart, were described—San Quentin in 1898 and Folsom Prison in 1903. Did those stories indicate an emerging drug use problem that spilled beyond the prison walls that would (or should) generate interest in drug legislation, or were the stories and the phenomena described irrelevant to those laws?

The five stories are all about trafficking. No drug *use* problem is described, beyond claims that many prisoners were using. In Folsom, "at least 600 of the 800 convicts used opium when they could get it, and they seemed to get it pretty regularly," the prison directors were told.[51] It is unclear if the opium was taken in private or in groups. The form of opium used was, in San Quentin, opium pills, called a *ball* by prisoners:[52] In Folsom Prison a "morphine 'fiend' " claimed "at least 500 opium chewers in the institution."[53] Three stories do not mention any form in which an opiate was taken.[54]

The 1898 and 1903 reports of opium in prison had all the trappings of the war on drugs waged on San Francisco's docks in earlier decades: users paid exorbitant prices; smugglers' profits were extraordinary; law officers were easily corrupted and actively thwarted opium seizures; law enforcement barely dented the supply; the proportion of drugs intercepted was unknown; and there was violence related to the traffic.[55] Without public notice, lawmakers set the rules, which were responsible for all the *drug problems*.

Possibly the commotion over drug use in California prisons was a media exaggeration. Official prison studies after the 1903 report from Folsom did not deem opiate use widespread or important. A detailed front-page story of graft in San Francisco's jail did not hint of drugs there. And a biennial report of the State Board of Prison Directors (noted in 1910) reported that of San Quentin's population of 1,702, only thirty-nine (2 percent) were "addicted to liquor, tobacco, and opiates"; 487 had "no habits," "habits not stated" accounted for 348; and the remainder were addicted to liquor and/or tobacco only.[56]

What was the importance of prisoner drug use circa 1900 in the development of U.S. drug prohibition? How did it relate to opium smoking?

At the time, the forms of opium being used in San Quentin and Folsom were available legally and at a reasonable price in about every apothecary in the country, and there was no group scene, no illegal behavior, not even immorality associated with any nonsmoked opiate, except by prohibitionist exotics. Prisoner opiate use became a problem because it was taking place at all. Drugs were contraband. In earlier years it was combs, cookies, and the like. The problem was the context—the prison itself. This context created not only the problem, but the behavior itself. In the free world nobody took drugs, took opiates, as they did in prison. This was such unusual drug taking that one suspects that any behavior closely resembling it likewise bears the DNA markings of oppression.

In the free world, in the U.S., in California, if one wanted to socialize with an opiate, one typically smoked it. Even the whites. In 1878 there was even an "American opium-smoking society"—à la 1996's Cannabis Buyer's Club.[57] Typically, the Chinese in the U.S. smoked in the privacy of their enclaves, though white friends and paying customers could sometimes smoke with them. If some whites were curious, adventurous, or simply liked being around opium smoking, they could start a den or club of their own. Circa 1900 there were no opium eateries, no opium chewing clubs, not even laudanum drinking bars—they had opium smoking dens! Only in prisons were there ritually shared opium eats and chews.

Opium eating and chewing would become significant only if a crackdown on opium smoking succeeded, and eating and chewing (and sniffing and snorting) became the basis for both the dominant form of drug use and for the focus of government drug law enforcement. That would have to wait first for government to re-create and expand government agencies devoted to drug enforcement and for the narcs to grow and stamp out opium dens ... and even opium smoking was legal just about anywhere, de facto if not de jure, in 1908, the laws and their enforcers establishing rules only of etiquette (whom you might smoke with, where, with whose pipes, in whose place, who supplies the opium, etc.).

ONLY MISSIONARIES SEE AN OPIUM-SMOKING PROBLEM IN THE U.S.

Home-based U.S. missionaries persisted in seeing opium smoking as evil and they periodically called for action. In 1882 the former American Episcopal Missionary in China called for "the most severe repressive and prohibiting measures" and an end to the "duty on the abominable smoking opium, and its exclusion from the country must be absolute."[58] Two magazine articles on opium use in 1892 and 1896 by the superintendent of the Methodist Chinese Mission in San Francisco conveyed the old mood of a growing, menacing problem, spreading from the squalid Chinese quarters to the whites of the city. "It is no uncommon thing to see young men and even women of our race stealing into Chinatown at night for 'dope.' . . . Scores of dens are to be found outside of Chinatown . . . even . . . fashionable homes of the western suburbs." Many sentences in the two articles were identical, including statements on *changing* conditions, such as "the vice is spreading amongst depraved white people of both sexes."[59]

The U.S. missionaries were fighting against opium smoking as their brothers and sisters had done for over half a century in various outposts in Asia—China, India, Formosa, the Philippines—though in the amount of interest the print devoted to it, and even the emotional tone, the U.S. missionaries were much less devoted to this fight than their overseas-based compatriots. The missionaries' goal was always abstinence. Even from 1894 to 1908, tolerance toward drugs at least occasionally roused the missionaries; it put the press to sleep.

THE CALM BEFORE THE STORM (1894–1908)

Overall, the San Francisco newspapers from 1894 to 1908 conveyed an ambiance—drugs were irrelevant. There were lots of police raids on the Chinese: for fan-tan, lottery, and other gambling, and for smuggling people in on ships and across borders. In a report of eighty affidavits in 1908 claiming police harassment in Chinatown, there was no mention of opium.[60] The newspapers were "drugfree." The consequences of the $12 per pound tax had never been confronted by them, and the $6 per pound duty made drugs no longer newsworthy. The big opium story of 1899 was that the state assembly overrode the governor's veto 55—11, making the poppy the state flower.[61]

There wasn't a gambler in the Wild West in early 1908 who would have bet that a year later the U.S. would launch a full-scale war on drugs that would escalate time and again until the twenty-first century. Hadn't it been demonstrated that the lower the penalties, the smaller the drug problem? Wasn't the *drug problem* in nearly the only place where drugs were prohibited—in prisons?

1908: HAMILTON WRIGHT AND THE
GREAT LEAP FORWARD

Since 1862 opium—in particular, opium smoking—had been described as evil by many U.S. writers, but by the start of 1908 an onslaught against any opiate use had not happened. No person had led the charge, pushing the issue over the edge, into Prohibition.[62] Numerous laws regulating opiates were passed by Congress (such as the various tariff schedules for prepared opium) without debate and without being associated with a proponent or sponsor, but they never banned opiate use per se. Something held back the zealots (though the first drug prohibition laws were just emerging in a few western states). Almost every adult knew the effects of opiates—had taken it themselves for a range of illnesses and symptoms, or knew intimates who had, and understood that smoking opium was fundamentally the same class of drug as morphine or laudanum (minus the alcohol) or crude opium. Lots of people knew that the periodic diatribes about the evils of opium, particularly opium smoking, were hyperbole, but on the other hand hardly a soul took on the zealots, at least in public. In 1908 Dr. Hamilton Wright disrupted the national opium enforcement situation that, on the federal level, had been placid, for well over a decade.

Wright was in Washington, D.C. in mid-1908 when the State Department was looking for a scientist with experience in the Far East to be its third and last (and sole nonmissionary) delegate to a Shanghai Opium Commission scheduled for the start of 1909. Dr. Wright had been in Asia for years, and while there had discovered (incorrectly) that beriberi was an infectious disease. His wife was a senator's daughter and niece of three congressmen (and published at least two lengthy articles on drugs in 1909 and many more in the years to come). How he (or they) got the ban on the importation of smoking opium written and passed by February 9, 1909, is simple in outline, though amazing and amusing (and well documented by others).[63]

Shortly after joining the State Department, Wright publicized statistics showing that U.S. smoking opium imports went from 55,000 pounds per year from 1878 to 1882 to 177,000 pounds from 1903 to 1907 "while our Chinese population has actually decreased, [which] must mean that the evil is spreading among other races in this country." Wright notes an "estimate that there are probably over a hundred thousand Americans [i.e., non-Chinese] who smoke opium."[64] He also noted that "the greatest consumers of the drug are Chinese," and divided the Chinese smokers into four levels: "confirmed" (20 percent), "occasional" (30 percent), "on rare occasions" (25 percent), and "never" (25 percent).[65]

Neither Wright nor any contemporary brought up two factors that together would refute his notion of an alarming (and possibly any) spread of opium smoking in general, or among whites only. First, before opium for smoking was prohibited, the vagaries of import duties largely explained any rise or fall of legally imported opium. Second, in the U.S., since 1880, the combined white and black population had increased 83 percent while the Chinese population (as a response to the Exclusion Act of 1882 and anti-Chinese racism) declined 32 percent. Given that the *rate* of opium smoking was hundreds of times higher for Chinese than whites, it was quite possible that the *number* of white opium smokers soared, the *number* of Chinese opium smokers plummeted, and the per capita *rate* of such use remained the same as it had been for both whites and Chinese.[66]

Wright argued that the tripling of legal imports of prepared opium warranted restrictive laws in the U.S. to show good faith to the International Conference.

> [W]e had suggested the [1909 Opium Commission], primarily with the idea of guarding the weak morals of the Chinaman ... but it soon developed that we were importing into the United States, and legally importing, in our selfish greed to fill our own fat purses, undreamed of quantities of the same drug which we believed the Chinaman should cease to use. ... [W]e [are] now the greatest of the world's drug takers. ... The drug habit has spread throughout America until it threatens us with very serious disaster.[67]

Wright and Secretary of State Elihu Root

> tried to make the prohibition as simple as possible ... only the importation of opium for smoking was actually outlawed ... [so that the U.S. would, in the words of Root] "have legislation on this subject in time to save our face in the conference at Shanghai."[68]

Congressional opposition to the proposed law was quickly addressed and removed. "When the Act was approved [9 February 1909], the American delegation proudly and with dramatic flourish announced the victory to the commission, then in session."[69]

The connection of this first U.S. federal drug prohibition and China was ambiguous (beyond the U.S. acting "to save face"). The 1909 commission was suggested by Charles Brent, Episcopal bishop of the Philippines, in a 1906 letter to President Roosevelt, in response to a boycott of U.S. goods by merchants in China who were protesting the mistreatment of Chinese in the U.S. The act forbidding smoking opium imports supposedly showed China's delegates that the U.S. was acting in good faith, and the law's immediate effect was to punish tens of thousands of Chinese-Americans who smoked opium without causing any noticeable problem.

The mass media hardly noticed the passage of the Opium Smoking Import Act. There seemed to be a lack of principled *public* opposition to persons and policies that many privately might have found wrong and even detestable. According to the reports of modern historians, the opposition to Wright never fought over the consequences of the new drug prohibitions on the lowest social strata of users—those who would pay the most under the laws—or on crime and law enforcement.[70] Ergo, in the earliest years of federal prohibition the stance of Drug Crusader seemed unchallengeable in public, and the most obvious, harshest, community-disrupting consequences of the drug laws went unmentioned. With drugs, at least in late 1908 and early 1909, at the birth of government prohibition policies that utterly changed the character of drug use and sale, open, reasoned discussion on the relationship of policies to trafficking and the choice and conditions of drug use was stillborn.

IMPACT OF THE OPIUM IMPORT ACT OF 1909

Hamilton Wright, his State Department allies, and the 61st Congress paid little attention to the similarities between what would occur when the Opium Import Act took effect and what had followed the increased duties on opium imposed by the Billion Dollar Congress nineteen years previously. They never gave a clue that they understood that their proposed prohibition would revive the contest between agents and smugglers that follows these laws as day follows night, yet the fundamental conditions for a war on drugs were back in place, only at a new level and in a new context.

Each escalation in prohibition complicates the relationship between armed state agents and persons who want temporarily to be in "another world," though the exact consequences of any law are unpredictable. While not considered seriously by Congress, the Opium Import Act would lead, even before the Harrison Act was passed, to possibly the clearest victory of the war on drugs—the end of opium smoking—and had shown one of its greatest faults—in suppressing smoking opium it fostered the recreational use of more powerful synthetic drugs, morphine and heroin.

THE LAW PROVIDED A RETIREMENT BONUS FOR
LEGITIMATE DEALERS: STOCKPILED OPIUM
LASTED FOR YEARS

The 1909 Opium Import Act happened so quickly—less than nine months between the time the State Department interviewed Wright for a job and the President signed the bill—that even opium merchants were caught flat-footed. In the weeks just before the law took effect (April 1, 1909), "opium gamblers" ran "the price of [prepared] opium up to $40 and $45 a pound. It was worth from $9 to $12."[71] The merchants rushed to pay the duty on and import a stockpile of prepared opium—over 100,000 pounds of it, almost as much as the annual legal import in previous years. The merchants stood to make a killing . . . if opium for which a duty was paid before April 1 could be legally sold and used after then. By April 2 the collector of the port and the U.S. district attorney in San Francisco announced such sales were legal.[72] Merchants had been given a golden parachute.

How big a dent did the opium stockpile put in the illegal market, and how long did this depression last? The stockpiled opium probably was bought by the wealthier residents of Chinatown, who in 1909 could quickly raise several thousand dollars. Look Tin Eli, president of the Canton Bank, three years after the Opium Import Act went into effect and "it became unlawful for opium to be held even in a bonded warehouse," still had 300 five-tael tins (123 pounds) in his warehouse vault.

> The vault was built especially for the storage of opium, the agents say; and if their information is correct, has housed more than $1,000,000 worth of the drug. The vault of large dimensions was protected by a steel door of two layers of half inch steel."[73]

Ergo, a supply that could serve the entire market of opium smokers for most of 1908 actually lasted over three years.

USE PLUMMETED DUE TO THE LAW, ESPECIALLY, AT FIRST, AMONG WHITES

The steep rise in the street price (along with the massive stockpiling) immediately and substantially reduced the market for illegal smoking opium. This delayed the emergence of organized smuggling operations and large-scale corruption among agents, and sharply reduced the illegal profits and thus the size and power of the smuggling rings that did emerge. To comprehend this course of the war on drugs, it is necessary to group users the way Wright did—by race. The Chinese, then, were less than 1/1,000th of the U.S. population, though to judge from arrest stories and statistics over half the opium smokers were Chinese, and they smoked well over half the opium.

For the Chinese in the United States, opium smoking was a widely practiced, centuries-old tradition. The dens with their bunks, the pipes, and the lay-out, the "stoker" unobtrusively refilling and lighting the bowls, were part of a widely practiced ritual. For whites, particularly those who gravitated to dens run by and for whites or who smoked in their own rooms, the habit was more boisterous, less ceremonious. Whites were tourists; the Chinese were residents and at times guides.

When the 1909 Opium Import Act took effect, and the price and hassle of getting smoking opium skyrocketed, and the likelihood and consequences of getting caught with it soared, white and Chinese opium smokers responded differently. Most whites found comparable highs and scenes at a fraction of the cost by sniffing morphine, heroin, or even cocaine. The Chinese might cut back considerably (who but the rich could afford the new prices?),[74] but it wasn't a drug alone they were giving up so much as a long-standing tradition central to their community and a basic pleasure. The above interpretation would be consistent with several facts: at previous times, local crackdowns on opium dens resulted in whites, in particular, quitting smoking;[75] after 1909, whites were seldom arrested on opium smoking charges whereas Chinese were seldom arrested for other forms of opium;[76] many white morphine and heroin (and at times cocaine) users in several 1912–1915 studies reported first taking opium by pipe and switching right after the Opium Smoking Import Act took effect;[77] and even the most vociferous crusaders against opiates in the 1920s recognized that a switch in opiate use, primarily to heroin, took place starting in 1910.[78]

THE NEW FEDERAL WAR ON DRUGS
SLOWLY EMERGED: 1909–1910

As soon as the 1909 law took effect, San Francisco reporters covered the docks every time a steamer came in from the Orient, anticipating smuggler versus agent action, and tales of heroism, derring-do, and greed. Arrivals the first few months, however, yielded nothing.

The first smuggling arrest under the 1909 Act—a saloon keeper with eight tins (3.3 pounds) of smoking opium—was caught on a streetcar near the docks eight weeks after the law took effect. A month later customs inspectors seized 149 tins in Chinatown from his buyers. The bartender-informer was acquitted "after a half-hearted prosecution."[79] The seizures were in Chinatown, not on the docks, indicating agents were impatient for a big score. That such a small operation was newsworthy indicated the press wanted a return to the smugglers versus agents action that had sold papers through the early 1890s (and for the media would be the core of the war on drugs ever after).

For much of 1910 the San Francisco newspaper stories on opium smoking were often not local. In early 1910 seizures along the Mexican–U.S. border were as large as any reported in San Francisco: $10,000 worth was caught coming from Nogales; a smuggler in El Paso was caught with 700 tins.[80] By 1911, though, the few reported seizures of smoking opium coming up from Mexico were small and eventually (by 1912) the San Francisco press lost interest in this route.

The pursuit of prepared opium took customs inspectors far from the docks into urban neighborhoods where it was received and smoked. Raids in San Francisco's Chinatown in 1910 were ordered by collector of port

Stratton and sanctioned by U.S. attorney Black.[81] In 1913 a "recent order of [Treasury] Secretary McAdoo . . . [held] special Treasury agents responsible for the suppression of the smoking opium traffic in their districts."[82] Several newspaper stories read as if this was post-1909 policy, but customs inspectors two decades previously acted as urban narcotics officers. Federal customs officers raided Chinatowns in San Francisco,[83] New York City,[84] and Chicago[85] circa 1890 and 1910; in Seattle in 1889; in Denver in 1907; and in St. Louis in 1910.[86] Regardless of their motivations, the Customs Service looked as though it was staking out a claim for an additional role in narcotics law enforcement.

NO REWARDS FOR AGENTS = AGENT APATHY = FEWER AND SMALLER SEIZURES

The 1909 Act permitted a "moiety" ("2. one of the portions into which something is divided" [Webster's Tenth New Collegiate Dictionary, 1994]) be granted for information at the discretion of authorities, which the collector at San Francisco quickly requested be given his inspectors. An assistant secretary of the Treasury sent individual letters of appreciation, but denied the rewards:[87] "[N]ow that the importation of the drug is prohibited and all opium seized must be destroyed, there is no fund out of which rewards may be paid."[88] Adding insult to injury, in mid-1912 the daily salary of San Francisco's customs inspectors was cut from $4 to $3,[89] and later to $2.50, which led to "a universal feeling of discontent among the men"[90] and a steep decline in the street price of smoking opium.[91] In 1913 a new collector of customs at San Francisco said:

> "The searching of steamers in the past has been a joke . . . . as [men] have worked in the daytime only. . . . The guards are subject to tremendous temptations . . . . a salary of little over $800 a year. . . . A smuggler . . . offers him $100 for looking the other way for only five minutes."[92]

It's difficult to determine the extent of corruption that followed directly upon the 1909 Opium Import Act. Though the demand for imported smoking opium was deflated, the profit per pound of successfully imported opium and the consequences of getting caught were so high that smugglers must have become more sophisticated than ever to avoid detection. New York's port surveyor, Colonel Henry, whose first brush with opium smugglers was probably after the Opium Import Act took effect, no doubt exaggerated when he said:

Never in the history of smuggling have keener, more ingenious brains been devoted to the task of circumventing Government officials than at present are fixed upon illicit methods of furnishing New York with the immense, the startling, quantities which it consumes of this most dangerous of drugs.[93]

AGENT CORRUPTION: THE WAR ON DRUGS' CAMPFOLLOWER

San Francisco papers of that era revealed substantial agent corruption. In 1910 night watchman Freund was fired, gave information "disclosing the heads of the smuggling ring," and then begged not be reinstated for fear his co-workers would kill him. (This case involved the smuggling of Chinese, not opium, but it gave a flavor of the docks . . . and suggests that opium smuggling was not yet a major money-maker there.)[94] At the start of 1911 a major seizure—1,098 five-tael tins (about 500 pounds) valued at $44,000—occurred right after (and was attributed to) collector Stratton's replacement of the entire crew of night inspectors.[95] From February 1911 through September 1913 my files show only three stories of San Francisco dock worker corruption, two involving small amounts of opium[96] and one massive missed opportunity:

> It is known to the customs inspectors that the Mongolia brought 10,000 tins of opium into the port on this trip. Of this amount 2,000 tins have been landed. . . . The price of the drug is going down rapidly on account of the supply.[97]

Five days after the Mongolia had tied up, a grand total of 304 tins (125 pounds) had been seized, including twenty tins found on the ship's quartermaster and fifty on a customs night watchman as he hurried away from the docks. The local papers implied they knew something the customs agents didn't or pretended not to know.

In early 1913 three customs guards confessed to corruption, and another seven current or recently retired guards or inspectors and a watchman were indicted. One guard (Joseph) said he made an extra $4,000 per year (five to six times his salary) from illegal actions; another (Ellison) was rumored to have retired independently wealthy.[98] Apparently the involved agents did not split the results of their labors; it was each man for himself. The press claimed the opium ring had landed $1,000,000 of opium in San Francisco the previous three years.[99] Valued at $75 per pound, however, that was less than 4,500 pounds a year—not an extraordinary amount by the standards of the early 1890s.

ROUTINE ENFORCEMENT OF A STEADILY
SHRINKING MARKET

The level of agent corruption—the sheer amounts involved and the bravado of the most money-hungry agents—in the years immediately following the Opium Smoking Import Act did not approach that in the years just after the Billion Dollar Congress increased the duty on prepared opium imports to $12 per pound. The opium seizures in San Francisco from 1911 to 1913 likewise were much smaller than during that earlier era (though my newspaper records may be incomplete).

During the first half of 1911 the press sometimes reported "record seizures," but they were only so if the dollar value, not the quantity of drug, was considered. After mid-1911 the seizures fell considerably. Four in early 1911 involved a total of 1,750 pounds of smoking opium; the seven largest reported seizures that I can document from that time to late 1913 involved a total of about 800 pounds (see table below).

Seizures of 50 + Lbs. of Smoking Opium in San Francisco: 1911–1913							
S.F. Paper	Date	Lbs.*	$ Value	S.F. Paper	Date	Lbs.*	$ Value
Chronicle	1/26/11	450	$43,920	Chronicle	6/22/12	85	$8,000
Call	4/19/11	700	–	Call	6/26/12	165	–
Chronicle	6/2/11	370	$27,000	Call	7/21/12	75	$5,000
Chronicle	7/8/11	230	$14,000	Call	12/27/12	75	$5,000
Call	8/3/11	125	$12,000	Call	1/8/13	130	–
Call	12/15/11	130	$10,000				

* Usually reported as 5-tael tins, or sometimes "tins," which are 0.41 pound.

Why were the immediate post-opium smoking prohibition seizures *lower* than they were twenty years earlier? Any of the following reasons helps explain this drop: San Francisco's customs agents quit trying; more and higher placed agents were working for the smugglers "in the old days"; the smugglers were technically better than ever; smuggling routes shifted from the U.S.'s Pacific ports to alternative less guarded routes; the market was drying up.

THE END OF OPIUM SMOKING ... BEFORE
THE HARRISON ACT

Consider the war on drugs a mighty river, and my self-assigned task to discover and describe its earliest tributaries. Until now the focus has been on a single stream—the first I found that generated the war on drugs' trademark roar of smugglers and dealers and agents, of ill-gotten profits and corruption—the Customs Service's restrictions on the importation of prepared opium. The more restrictive the policy, (1) the higher the duty, (2) the larger and more organized and more creative the smugglers, (3) the more aggressive and corrupt the agents, and (4) the more interested the mass media. Reduce the tariff and the cacophony ebbed to the point where a *drug problem* was not discernible.

Until 1908 it was possible to pursue this stream without stirring up others that, from a broader perspective, contributed significantly to what became a roaring torrent. Then, to explain the sudden buildup in pressure, one has to bring in human megalomania (Wright, or the Wrights, mainly), international conferences, the State Department, even the appeasement of the prevailing Chinese emperor. Still, it was possible to focus on one, admittedly spreading, main stream . . . so long as one focused on drug policies in the east, south, or midwest regions, or the federal level.

However, there were two other streams that, in the years just before the Harrison Act, suddenly swelled, merged, and swamped the recreational users of opium, all but drowning the opium smokers in particular. These streams had meandered harmlessly, virtually unnoticed, for generations. Then the drug world's equivalent of the Bureau of Reclamation and the U.S. Army's Corps of Engineers stepped in and forever changed the natural, harmless flow of these streams.

One stream that in retrospect contributed to the demise of opium smoking was local laws against opium dens. The first such ordinance was passed in San Francisco in 1875, though similar laws were passed by state legislatures in Nevada in 1877 and many other states over the next few years. These laws banned the purchase and smoking of opium in "dens," though not the possession or use of smoking opium. It was like banning saloons but not alcohol. The intent of the lawmakers and the law enforcers, as reported in the press, was to prevent whites from smoking with Chinese. It was all right if Chinese smoked with other Chinese and whites smoked with their friends— just not together. Here and there, now and then, a local police force would interpret the law literally and arrest Chinese smoking in all Chinese dens, or the law would be broadened to include more than just smoking in dens, but these were exceptions. Into the early twentieth century, almost everywhere in the United States, if you paid the tax and did not smoke in an interracial setting, opium smoking was legal. If anything, given the Exclusion Act's impact on reducing the Chinese population in the U.S. while the white population was mushrooming, the fear of Chinese competition and the fears that Chinese men with their mysterious opium rituals somehow posed a threat to white male control of white women must have been less at the start of the twentieth century than it had been ten or twenty or thirty years previously.

The other stream that fed into the drowning of opium smoking seems at first glance to have nothing whatever to do with smoking. Early in the twentieth century the burgeoning pharmaceutical industry took major steps to professionalize, and one major way this was accomplished was to make the apothecary a special place for medicines. Medicines would be labeled (that was guaranteed by the Pure Food and Drug Act of 1906), but even more to the point certain medicines would be available only through apothecaries, and government would play the role of guaranteeing this. The prescription system was developed, along with the governmental agencies, to prevent noncompliance. To begin with, the drug chosen for circumscribed prescription-only distribution was the number one drug in the medical armamentarium of the day—opium.[100] In one sense, this had nothing to do with opium smoking because, though the apothecaries up to the time of the new prescription laws sold a wide variety of opiates, opium prepared for smoking was not one of them. Terminology had arisen noting this distinction, and opiate users were often classified as *smokers* or *eaters*, the latter meaning those who took opium in any manner except smoking.

The Harrison Act was the federal law that instituted the prescription system and provided for a federal drug enforcement apparatus. Many states had previously enacted similar legislation in the years just preceding it, however, though it was almost exclusively in the west that such laws preceded the 1909 federal ban on importing opium for smoking. In only one or two states were these laws enforced and enforced significantly enough to have an impact on opium smoking—most notably in California.[101] Coming on the heels of the Opium Smoking Import Act, a handful of agents, in just five years or so, essentially wiped out opium smoking within the U.S.

□   □   □

CALIFORNIA'S BOARD OF PHARMACY ATTACKS OPIUM SMOKING: 1907–1914

In 1905 the California legislature took "the sale of . . . drugs, medicines and poisons out of the hands of grocers, general dealers and department stores . . . placing it in the hands of those to whom it belongs"—pharmacists.[102] In 1909 the legislature "permitted the control of the distribution of narcotic drugs," in 1909 this act was amended to prohibit "*possession* of restricted narcotic drugs unless specifically authorized" by physicians, and in 1911 Assembly Bill 751 "provided that the possession of an opium pipe is a misdemeanor and a proof of use of the drug . . . [and] also provided that narcotic drugs and opium pipes can be destroyed after seizure."[103] To judge from the local newspapers, neither the 1907 nor the 1909 laws aroused any mass public interest, nor were they responses to obvious public social problems. As noted previously, systematic samples of 135 days of San Francisco newspapers, and 215 *San Francisco Examiners*, from 1894 to 1908, yielded minuscule concern over opium smoking and even less interest in any other illegal or subsequently illegal drug. The law itself never surfaced in the papers I read (though the sampling did not take account of the dates the various laws and amendments were approved). A special reading of the major paper of the state capital—the *Sacramento Bee*—seventeen of thirty-four days prior to the approval of SB 431 in 1907 revealed not a word about a drug law, and only one story on drugs.[104] If there was to be a publicly recognized problem, the agency charged with enforcing it would have to find a way to bring it to notice. The bills of 1907, 1909, and 1911 increased their ability to do just that.

The California Board of Pharmacy, the bureaucracy charged with enforcing those state laws, had a two-track enforcement policy, even before 1909. One focus was on pharmacists who sold opiates (or cocaine) to persons without a licensed physician's prescription or who otherwise violated the new state regulations. The other focus was on opium smokers: initially, especially, white women in Chinese dens. In a raid in 1908 two board of pharmacy inspectors assisted by eight San Francisco policemen raided four Chinatown dens, making twenty-three arrests.[105] Later that year the pharmacy board's secretary, Chas. Whilden, who seemed to have an instinct for publicity, claimed he had been "engaged in a night and day war on the local [San Francisco] Chinese opium dealers" because "white women, once they had acquired the habit, found it easy to gain access to the more luxurious dens of Chinatown."[106] It is unclear, however, if those 1908 raids were under the old law banning opium dens or a new law banning use of the drug entirely. Certainly, at the very start of 1909, as noted previously, San Francisco opium merchants placed orders for vast quantities of prepared opium to beat the federal ban on importing prepared opium, oblivious to any state law.

The 1909 California law, based on the recommendations of a joint meeting of the Board of Pharmacy and key members of the California Pharmaceutical Association,[107] clearly outlawed opium smoking. The first year the 1909 law was in effect, there were 222 cases "under the Pharmacy and Poison Laws," resulting in 161 convictions. Either eighty-one were "Chinese cases for violation of narcotic law"[108] or "[h]undreds of these Chinamen have been prosecuted by the Board."[109] By the end of that first year of the 1909 law, the pharmacy board's president was apologizing to pharmacists in a professional journal, claiming that "the Board is not in sympathy with technical prosecutions. . . . We warn 19 out of every 20 druggists that they are violating [sic], but sometimes a zealous inspector will make a prosecution on his own authority."[110] The following year, nearly the full weight of the board's agents and especially its prosecutors were used against Chinese. Reportedly 92 percent of the "335 persons who have been arrested and convicted for violating either the pharmacy or the poison laws . . . are members of [one of] the following societies: Bing Tongs, Hop Sings, Hip Sings, San Yips, and Suey Sings."[111] The years after that, 1912-1914, would be worse yet for the Chinese opium smokers, and 1914 would be the worst ever.

The pharmacy board had few agents—ten paid inspectors in 1910[112] and possibly fewer over the next few years, yet their impact was enormous. Their technique developed quickly, almost intuitively, and from 1908 to 1914 they seemed to perfect it. The Board of Pharmacy agents focused on one area at a time. A field agent or two went undercover for a few months to gather information. Then they made a sudden massive swoop, enlisting local police and deputizing volunteers for support in order to simultaneously raid ten or twenty times the number of dens they could on their own. The police and volunteers were notified of their missions only at the eleventh hour to guarantee that the "other side" was not tipped off in advance. In the 1908 raid previously noted, eight policemen were recruited to assist board agents. In 1910 forty deputies were mustered for raids in Bakersfield.[113] In October 1911 "58 deputy constables, especially sworn in for the occasion [most strikers from local Southern Pacific railroad shops] . . . raided 29 alleged opium dens in the local [Sacramento] Chinatown, taking about 150 prisoners and about $2,000 worth of contraband opium as well as hundreds of pipes and layouts. . . . About 15 white men were among the prisoners."[114]

The major focus, however, was on San Francisco, the biggest, most cosmopolitan and rambunctious city in California at the time. Its Chinese heritage community of about 12,000 contained about a third of California's Chinese, and three or four times more Chinese than New York City.[115] The pharmacy board's chief inspector, Fred Sutherland[116]—the first agent whose undercover work was described in detail, to my knowledge—had been in San Francisco "sleeping and eating among the drug users and dealers for 3 months in search of evidence."[117]

> Saturday evening, November 25th [1911], a posse organized under the direction of the California State Board of Pharmacy, descended upon the opium joints of Chinatown, San Francisco in what proved the largest and most successful raid ever conducted in California—or in any State for that matter. The posse . . . composed of 125 men in all—85 police officers, 15 deputies and inspectors of the State Board, and 25 drug clerks . . . .[118]

Before the night's work was over, sixty-two dens had been broken into in Chinatown.

Of the 210 persons captured, 85 percent were Chinese, though practically every report (in English) emphasized the white arrestees.

> Between those two types [a messenger boy and a "well-appearing young man"] and the degraded and withered Chinese . . . were found young white girls, negro men and women, a Chinese physician, soldiers, merchants, thugs, etc.[119]

A statement by Louis Zeh, secretary of the Board of Pharmacy, singled out the seven locations of dens where whites were arrested. Two young white women arrested at Bobby Bean's interracial den were mentioned in practically every story, and in the absence of any mention of other specific female personae they may have been the only white women arrested in that sweep. Regarding women, Chinese, and opium, things hadn't changed a whit in San Francisco since that initial anti-den law thirty-seven years previously.

In addition to the arrests, authorities seized $600 worth of opium,[120] 235 layouts, 282 pipes and stems, fifty-seven papers morphine (sic), and other paraphernalia.[121]

This first major sweep in San Francisco was a slaughter of the innocents. "The dash with which the raids were conducted and the unexpected invasion of the raiding forces took the quarter altogether by surprise."[122] If all arrested were regular users, and if 25 percent of Chinatown's residents were regular users, then 6 percent of its regular smokers were arrested overnight. More than a month after the raid, "of the hundreds of cases, not one verdict of 'not guilty' has been returned. The Board . . . now bids fair to give the death blow to the shameful traffic in San Francisco."[123]

THE UNPRECEDENTED TERROR TACTICS OF CALIFORNIA'S NARCOTICS AGENTS

If the price of opium is dependent on the difficulty of obtaining it, the Board of Pharmacy's raids, by increasing the risks and costs of dealing and using it, guaranteed that in California the price of smoking opium did not fall below the fourfold increase that occurred in anticipation of the effects of the 1909 Opium Smoking Import Act. However, the size of smuggling operations and the degree of agent corruption shrank even more as the Board of Pharmacy incarcerated some and intimidated many times more users and sellers.

The violence of narcotics agents, then as now, tends to be underreported, though in 1915 a reputable source claimed "a deputy [of the California Board of Pharmacy] jumped on the face of an accused Chinaman and left him apparently dead . . . [and in another case agents] chopped in a roof with axes in the search for contraband." According to the *Pacific Phar-*

macist, "these acts might be excused on one pretext or another." To them, spying on and framing pharmacists were more contemptible and less excusable than jumping on Chinese opium smokers.[124]

To terrorize the opium smoker it was not necessary to jump on an arrestee's face or convict the accused. The threat of arrest was often sufficient. During the initial year in which it had the power to arrest opiate users, according to the board's president, ". . . while convictions [of Chinamen] have not always resulted it had its good effects and we are informed that many fiends have left the larger cities and the State since our vigorous work."[125]

Similarly, after a Dr. Beechler, who ran a sanatorium, had been acquitted by a jury, the Board of Pharmacy agent in charge of the prosecution said:

> "We are in this fight to stay, even if we never get a verdict from a jury. As long as we know we are fighting in the right, we are going to keep on. Mr. Beechler will find out that it will cost him more for attorney's fees than it will for fines, and we will attain our aims in the end."[126]

In sum, narcotics agents, from virtually their moment of creation, took the law into their own hands to terrify, intimidate, and hound whichever users (and nonusers) they saw fit. The Chinese-Americans, unlike physicians who ran sanatoriums, could not make an issue of agent lawlessness.

HOLOCAUST: THE DESTRUCTION OF OPIUM SMOKING IN THE U.S.

In May 1912 the Board of Pharmacy gathered its seizures made in the last half of 1911 in the largest northern and central California counties (in cases that resulted in 1,500 arrests and 1,100 convictions). They made a bonfire of these seizures in the middle of Chinatown . . .

> ". . . of enormous dimensions, the heat of it cracking the windows and blistering the frontages of stores . . . so that the hose had to be turned on . . . flames . . . shooting 30 feet into the air . . . . The choking smoke spread its heavy mantle over Chinatown like a pall upon the dead."[127]

Board of Pharmacy inspector Sutherland and secretary Louis Zeh stacked the pyre, which was lit by the board's president and witnessed by 2,000 spectators, the entire Board of Pharmacy, and representatives of the local press. (This was not the world's first such occasion. In Foochow, China, "the oldest seat of missionary influence," shortly before 1911 "upward of 25,000 . . . pipes, bowls, plates, lamps and opium boxes" had been seized "or given up by reformed smokers" and destroyed in 10 public burnings.)[128] In San Francisco in 1912 (in addition to $20,000 worth of opium), 1,000 pipes, 2,000 smoker's lamps, 1,000 trays, 3,000 pipe bowls, and 100 "delicately adjusted oriental scales" went up in smoke.[129] "Some of the pipes that were destroyed were valued at $500 each," eight months' salary for a customs inspector. "They were 200 years old."[130] There were "pipes mounted in precious metal, chased and ornamented in designs of finest art." Some bowls had "a pedigree reaching back into the centuries and a price that could not be estimated by any rule of value."[131] Living works of art. "Chinese scholars would often get so attached to [opium pipe bowls] that they say 'I can't sleep without Fragrant Lady' . . . [and] there were bowls with tones [when smoked]."[132] "Ole Sam Sing," a distracted Chinatown denizen watching the fire of the opium smoking paraphernalia, provided the local color of the San Francisco *Chronicle's* coverage:

[Sam Sing] was conscious only of a dread in his heart. . . . It was to be a holocaust, a funeral pyre in which a million iridescent dreams were to be offered at the altar of that great god of the white man's called "hygiene." . . . [Sam Sing was left] pondering on the extravagance and strange vagaries of the white men.[133]

A similarly worded article in the *Drug Clerk's Journal* described the "funeral pyre" as "a sacrificial offering . . . to the newest God, 'The Uplift,' " and even picked up the word "holocaust" from the *Chronicle* story's headline.[134]

Several experts, though, were ecstatic, including Harvey Wiley, the former chief of the U.S. Department of Agriculture's Bureau of Chemistry who had inspired the Pure Food and Drug Act of 1906. "The burning of this opium," he said, "is a happy omen of the beginning of the end of drug addiction in this country."[135] Someone must have switched fortune cookies on him.

Fortunately, "before the match was applied, a moving picture machine made films of the scene . . . part of a moving picture drama which will portray the devilish evils of the narcotic shame, and will be sent around the world, crusading the extinction of the poppy."[136]

Less than two years later (ten months before the Harrison Act was passed), a similar pyre was erected in front of the old City Hall.[137] "Just before the torch was applied, [San Francisco's Mayor Rolph] suggested that it would be well to save the oldest and most elaborately decorated pipes and present them to the Golden Gate Museum . . . . [Thus] several pipes . . . more than 200 years old, were rescued."[138]

In both bonfires combined, almost 2,000 pipes, over 4,000 pipe bowls, well over 2,000 smoker's lamps and 1,000 trays, and about 500 scales were destroyed. (This was in addition to what was destroyed or stolen in raids.) If 10 percent of California's Chinese population possessed one opium smoking layout, close to their entire traditional opium smoking paraphernalia (which remained after the great earthquake and fire in 1904 razed San Francisco's Chinatown) was destroyed on those two pyres.

The only protest of the burnings of drugs and paraphernalia I have read, apart from the sarcasm of some reporters, was by "one of Los Angeles' leading clubwomen, Mrs. M. E. Johnson," yet she saw the "crime against humanity" to be the destruction of the drugs which, in 1915, were needed for the "wounded on the battlefields of Europe." To my knowledge, she too shed not a tear for the end of opium smoking.[139]

Translating percentages into behavior and emotions, the "holocausts" perpetrated by the California Board of Pharmacy, on top of their drug seizures and added to the work of the customs authority, probably inflicted blows on the traditional ritual of opium smoking from which the Chinese-American communities in California (51 percent of the U.S.'s Chinese in 1910) never recovered.

Opium smoking was successfully repressed because of the special nature of opium smoking as practiced by the Chinese. It was hard to conceal. It was a social ritual that required space—the "den" with bunks. Smoking opium's peculiar odor apparently stuck to walls and clothes, leaving telltale signs for those who knew what it was. Opium smoking required time—it wasn't just shoot up or snuff and be done with it. Opium was prepared in a special way, was bulkier than other forms of opium, and sticky. The layout was elaborate and bulky compared to powder wrapped in paper or even a syringe. An opium smoking layout couldn't be tucked in one's sock or flushed down the toilet when the front door was battered down. There must have been reluctance to throw away venerated art works such as opium pipes, bowls, scales, and so on. Opium smoking done right, as it had been done for hundreds of years in China (and in Chinatowns in the United States), was a narc's dream and thus a smoker's nightmare.

So, Chinese en masse stopped smoking opium, or cut back substantially. They did so for reasons different from the non-Chinese who went from one high, one social scene, to another, possibly thrilling in the greater charge of the more concentrated drug and, if of the demimonde, rejoicing in opportunities for vast profits in a new illegal enterprise. The Chinese quit smoking opium because they couldn't afford it, or dreaded taking the risk, or didn't have easy access to the paraphernalia required to smoke opium in the usual fulfilling manner, or didn't like the new ambiance of distrust bred by the pharmacy board or the federal inspectors . . . or any combination of the above (and probably more). Alternatives had little allure. The Chinese weren't interested in "taking drugs" per se, even in taking any kind of opiate. They weren't interested in being deviant—the combination of skin color and the local police attitudes guaranteed them that honor.

In sum, just before the Harrison Act was passed, smoking opium in the U.S. was on a steady, swift, downward course. A handful of Chinese smokers would continue, aging, dwindling in number, until becoming so few they just faded out of the picture. To return to the analogy that opened this section, the stream of customs duties on smoking opium was joined by other streams—the mini-Harrison acts of several states banning all nonmedicinal use of opiates and a federal import ban—and became a torrent that swept away opium smoking. All the energy that had built up against opium smoking, and a lot of the cumulated sediment, was released and found other streams—narcs and smugglers and images of evil users easily transferring to the non-Chinese users who were snuffing (and occasionally injecting) morphine and heroin. The non-Chinese replaced the opium dens, which had been the haunts of ne'er-do-well Tenderloin types for several decades, with their own drug-using and -dealing milieus. From 1914 on, white and black drug users and dealers would increasingly occupy drug agents who forever after would be unable to contain the leaks and undo the effects of periodic floods, which have seemed the course of recreational opiate use since the natural drain-off of opium smoking was destroyed.

AN ODE TO OPIUM SMOKING

SMOKING OPIUM IS TO HEROIN AS CHEWING COCA IS TO CRACK AS SMOKING MARIJUANA IS TO MARINOL

In recent generations heroin has been the only opiate considered by the public and even experts. Now, even those who try to visualize a post war-on-drugs drug policy assume future experimenters with opiates would try heroin. What else?

In 1909, however, smoking was the clear and in most places the only criminal form of an opiate; heroin was just a medicine. After heroin gained popularity as a recreational drug, it attracted a very different type of user from opium smokers, and very different types of scenes emerged about the two drugs, even though now we tend to imagine *all* opiates in the image of heroin—injected, under extreme repressive conditions.

THE SUBJECTIVE EXPERIENCE OF THE OPIUM SMOKER

What did it feel like to smoke opium in the manner of the Chinese? The many descriptions of opium dens in the U.S. before 1910 emphasized the "cold facts"—the architecture of a den, or the parts of the layout—but rarely captured any of the user's experience.

In 1952 the *New Yorker* published possibly the first lengthy description of that experience from the other side. The author, Christopher Rand, accompanied a Chinese opium-smoking friend to an opium den (or *divan* in that part of the world) just off the Chinese mainland. The friend, Mr. J. L. Fu, "was a graduate of an English university and a master of the English language." Fu was quoted as saying:

> "There are four things that are supposed to make [opium] smoking good, and in my opinion they are solid facts. . . .
>
> "The noise of soft rain on a windowpane. . . .
>
> "A lamp that is clear, or brilliant. . . .
>
> "The big noise of the pipe. Without the noise, there is no smoke. You wouldn't feel you were smoking. Indeed, you wouldn't be *smoking*.
>
> "Finally, and much the most important, is friendship."[140]

On its effects on the smoker, Fu said:

> "Your whole desire is to *do* things—with a friend or friends, not separately. Smoking makes you gregarious. . . .
>
> "Alcohol makes a swine out of a gentleman, some people say, but opium makes a gentleman out of a swine. . . .
>
> "It is like the works of God—not seen, not heard, but felt. Time is just suspended . . . [like] gears, opium makes the mind and the body change their gear ratio."[140]

Sounds great to me.

☐   ☐   ☐

In sum, add to the conclusions listed at the start of this article (the war on drugs precedes the drug use problem; the war is rooted in racism; the war shaped and worsened drug use; people enjoy the melodrama of fighting the war; the war on drugs created the drug problem) that *the war on drugs causes a collective memory loss of drugs in a free context,* which shackles the imaginations of those trying to ponder post war-on-drugs drug policy.

Thus the war on drugs stifles opposition. It destroys key databases about alternatives. We dread peace with opium because virtually all we can imagine is the current ragtag army of heroin junkies free of control. We can barely appreciate God's Own Medicine when used nonmedicinally, barely think of opium positively beyond lifting the heavy weight of oppression, let alone recall the noise of soft rain on a windowpane. The opening shots in the war on drugs also made a small noise, but they echoed long and louder and louder and louder.

ENDNOTES

1. After the Harrison Act of 1914, a small and ultimately unsuccessful group argued that government policies were a cause of drug use problems. One of its leaders, a doctor who later became a congressman (Dem. Brooklyn, N.Y.), wrote: "It is more than a coincidence that . . . sensational publicity . . . preceded this type of [drug] legislation . . . followed by . . . . underworld and spread of addiction of non-therapeutic origin among the youthful and curious": Lester Volk, "Certain Facts To Be Considered In Judging The Effects of Prohibition In Relation To The Use of Narcotics," *California State Journal of Medicine,* V. 21 (6), June 1923. (pp. 238–241).

2. In the late 1860s U.S. drug experts described opiate *eating* in the U.S. and opium *smoking* in China but seldom opium *smoking* in the U.S. Of those who did, Ludlow, returning home at 6 A.M., saw "an awful Chinese face" at "the door of an opium *hong.*" Since Ludlow failed to communicate in sign language, how he knew the "awful face" was an opium smoker is a mystery. (Fitzhugh Ludlow, "What Shall They Do To Be Saved?," *Harper's,* V. 35, 1887. [pp. 377–387]) Calkins warned of an opium *eating* menace, but his only comment on *smoking* opium was, "Cooly emigrants in California" imported "1½ pounds nearly for every soul of them." (Alonzo Calkins, "Opium and Its Victims," *Galaxy,* V. 4, May 1867. [pp. 25–36]). The only sentence in another article that suggests opium smoking contrasts "the miserable and groveling Chinese, who are fed on it [opium] almost from the cradle" and "educated and intellectual men in this country and in Europe" who *ate* opium, and were not to "be too much condemned." ("Opium Eating," *Lippincott's,* V. 1, April 1868. [pp. 404–409]). The first U.S. professional journal that focused on mind-altering drugs had several articles on opiates in 1869, but only one mentioned opium smoking in the U.S., and only in the last paragraph. The writer was alarmed that tobacco was mixed with opium and smoked. ("Opium Smoking," *The Probe,* V. 1, April 1869. [pp. 59–61]).

3. From 1850 until well into the twentieth century, the vast majority of Chinese immigrants in the U.S. were from Guangdong province's Pearl River Delta, at the southern tip of China, the same province where, in 1996, "one of the largest single hauls of heroin in history," 1,200 pounds, was captured. "Crime (and Punishment) Rages Anew in China," *NYT (International Edition),* July 11, 1996. (p. 1).

Abbreviations are: *New York Times* = NYT; *New York Herald* = NYH; *San Francisco Bulletin* = SF Bull; *San Francisco Chronicle* = SF Chron; *San Francisco Examiner* = SF Ex; *Rocky Mountain News* = RMN; *"Vertical File"* = VF)

4. "Verdict In The Opium Smuggling Case," *SF Bull*, January 16, 1864. (p. 3); "Another Large Seizure of Smuggled Opium," *SF Alta*, April 23, 1864. (p. 1).

5. Had the ship captain not testified, the seizure would have stood because Chinese testimony against a white was invalid in California courts between 1853 and 1873.

6. "Court Proceedings U.S. District Court," *SF Alta*, January 16, 1864. Similarly, in 1992 a detective killed a ranch owner in a raid searching for marijuana. The D.A. concluded "the L.A. Sheriff's Department was motivated, at least in part, by a desire to seize and forfeit the [$5 million] ranch for the government." Dan Baum, *Smoke and Mirrors: The War On Drugs and the Politics of Failure*, Little, Brown & Co., Boston, 1996.

7. Rev. O. Gibson, *The Chinese In America*, Cincinnati, Hitchcock & Walden, 1877.

8. "Another Large Seizure of Smuggled Opium," *SF Alta*, April 23, 1864 (p. 1); "Heavy Seizures of Opium," *SF Call*, May 21, 1869; "Seizure of Opium in San Francisco," *NYT*, July 30, 1869; "Seizure of Opium in San Francisco," *NYT*, April 17, 1875 (p. 8); "Smuggled Opium," *SF Daily Ex*, May 14, 1880; "Opium Smugglers," *SF Ex*, January 5, 1882 (p. 2); "The Opium Case," *SF Call*, March 10, 1882 (p. 1); "Smuggled Opium," *SF Ex*, May 14, 1886; "Heavy Opium Seizures," *NYT*, May 14, 1886 (p. 1); "An Opium Swindler Arrested," *NYT*, June 16, 1887; and "Large Smuggling In Opium," *NYT*, July 31, 1887.

9. "Oodles of Opium—Fogarty's Probe Driven Into $55,000 Worth of the Drug," *SF Ex*, May 14, 1887. (p. 4).

10. "The Big Opium Find," *SF Ex*, May 15, 1887. (p. 6).

11. "Pacific Coast: The Wolcott Seizes $45,000 Worth of Smuggled Opium," *Oregonian*, January 19, 1886. (p. 1); & "Recent Opium Seizure," *Oregonian*, January 22, 1886. (p. 3).

12. "The Kaasan Bay 'Find,'" *Oregonian*, January 21, 1886. (p. 2).

13. People vs. Hall, 4 Cal. 399 determined that Chinese could not testify against whites.

14. Gibson, op. cit.

15. "Opium Smugglers," *SF Ex*, January 6, 1882. (p. 2).

16. Ibid.

17. "The Profit of Opium Smuggling," *NYT*, Aug. 10, 1883. (p. 5).

18. *SF Ex*, Feb. 11–13, 1888, "Smugglers," and "The Latest Infamy," (Feb. 11, pp. 1 + 4); "The 'Fiends,'" " "Friend Finnegass," "Fogarty's Bean and Molasses," "The Work of Newsgathering," and "Consternation of the Ring" (Feb. 12, pp. 1, 2 + 4).

19. "More Opium Captured," *SF Chron*, April 23, 1889. The opium was "hidden in the hold of the ship, packed in behind a false wall made of sheet iron." Each of thirty-two packages "was encased in some waterproof material, lined with cork, in order to make it float if thrown overboard."

20. "China Informers' Fees," *SF Ex*, Sept. 24, 1892. (p. 3) In two gambling raids, NYC's police also revealed the names of local Chinese informers. "Avenging On Leongs Descend On Hop Sings" & "Chinese Puzzle Result of Wholesale Raids," *NYT*, May 31, 1909 (p. 9) and April 25, 1905 (p. 8), respectively. In an eerie parallel to Moy Jin Mun, there was a "murderous assault" on a Chinese interpreter in S.F. accused of "telling tales to the police about . . . an opium joint." *SF Chron*, Sept. 2, 1913. (p. 20).

21. "Customs Fraud at San Francisco," *NYT*, Sept. 24, 1892. (p. 1).

22. *NYT*, "The Opium Smuggling Case," Feb. 18, 1888; "After Opium Smuggler," Feb. 15, 1888 (p. 8); "Tracing An Opium Case," Feb. 28, 1888 (p. 8); "Gardner Found Guilty," November 29, 1888 (p. 3); and "The Opium Smugglers" (the same title on Feb. 12, 1888 (p. 2); August 22, 1888 (p. 2); and August 25, 1888 (p. 2). In the Feb. 15 story, "Gardner . . . insisted . . . that he was associated in the work with Capt. Beecher who was at one time Collector of Internal Revenue at Seattle . . . and whom he believed to be acting for the Government." The expense listing was reported on Feb. 28.

23. "The Trap Snaps," *SF Chron*, April 11, 1893. ("Herbert F. Beecher, the notorious smuggler who has been in trouble dozens of times for smuggling opium on Puget Sound, is at present employed as pilot on the revenue cutter that patrols the sound.")

24. "Smuggled Opium and Chinese," *NYT*, July 25, 1893 (p. 6); "The Chinese Conspiracy Case," *NYT*, December 26, 1893 (p. 1); and *Report of the Supervising Agent to the Secretary of the Treasury for FY ended 6/30/1894*, excerpt "Opium Smuggling On The Pacific Coast," in DEA Library, VF "Opium/History."

25. The only top federal narcotics officer ever dismissed because of corruption was Chief McNutt in 1929. Honesty and incorruptibility were important in choosing his replacement, Harry Anslinger. *See* Edward J. Epstein's *Agency of Fear* about the Nixon administration's venality in creating and appointing heads of drug agencies.

26. *NYH* articles on opium smuggling include: "Smuggled Opium and Opium Smokers," (Wash., D.C.), Oct. 13, 1890; "Opium Smuggling On Our Western Coasts," (Seattle), Dec. 28, 1890; "Opium Habit Now Fostered," (Winnipeg), Sept. 19, 1891; "Smuggling On Puget Sound," (Seattle), Sept. 19, 1891; "Smugglers Paths From Canada," (Winnipeg), late Sept., 1891; "A Paradise For Smugglers," (Victoria, B.C.), Oct. 12, 1891; "Opium Smuggling By Wholesale," (Port Townsend, Washington), Oct. 16, 1891; "Overland Paths For Smugglers," (New Westminster, B.C.), Oct. 19, 1891; and "Smuggling To be Checked," Nov. 13, 1891.

27. "Quite a number of officers of vessels plying between British Columbia ports and Seattle and Tacoma have grown comparatively rich within the past few months, although their salaries are not large." (*NYH*, op. cit. 12/28/1890) "Since the passage of the McKinley bill the (opium smuggling) business has assumed gigantic proportions . . . so lucrative that a number of new dealers have established themselves in [Victoria, B.C.] where prepared opium is manufactured in large quantities and is openly sold to all who wish to purchase, there being no law against its sale in the British province." A revenue cutter's captain said, "[T]he heavy duty on opium has led to an increase in smuggling. . . . The best thing the government could do would be to . . . put a lower duty on the prepared drug . . . and have the manufacturing done in this country [the US instead of Canada]." (*NYH*, op. cit., 12/28/1890).

28. "The sentiment of the people of [Victoria, B.C.] is favorable to the traffic and they will lend aid to a smuggler before they will give information to the officers." (*NYH*, op. cit., 10/12/1891).

29. "[T]wo Seattle police officers . . . used their official positions to secure 50 pounds of opium from a smuggler and then resold the captured booty. . . . [A] Canadian mounted police, seeing the big profit . . . derived from smuggling opium into the U.S., resigned from the force and embarked on that business." Further, "The impression prevails generally that many police officers . . . are secretly aiding and permitting the business to go on, for it is impossible that so much opium . . . should be carried in continually and the officers know nothing about it." (*NYH*, op. cit., 12/28/1890).

30. "Every Chinese laundry [is] a manufactory and every pigtailed and almond-eyed Celestial in the U.S. [is] a manufacturer of prepared opium for smoking purposes," (*NYH*, op. cit., Sept. 19, 1891).

31. Imports fell from 16,651 to 8,118 pounds from July to Sept. 1890 to the three months just preceding the McKinley Tariff Act. Even with the increased duty, customs collections fell from $166,500 to $97,400. (*NY Herald*, op. cit., 12/28/1890).

Conversely, when the duty fell from $12 to $6 per pound, revenues went up as legal imports of prepared opium rose from an annual average of 52,500 pounds in 1893-94 to 118,500 pounds in 1895-96. (Annual Report of the Supervising Special Agent to the Secretary of the Treasury for FY's 1895 and 1896, in DEA library, VF "Opium/History").

32. Op. cit. *NYH* Oct. 16, 1891.

33. Michael Aldrich provided me with three microfilm reels of drug stories in nineteenth

and early twentieth century newspapers—many of the original articles excerpted in *The Dope Chronicles: 1850-1950*, G. Silver, R. Ward, and M. Aldrich, eds., Harper & Row, NY, 1979.

34. Early in 1907 the *NY Evening Journal* launched a media blitz resulting in passage of the Smith-Frawley law restricting cocaine. No doubt publisher William Randolph Hearst exaggerated the problem as he was a candidate for NY's governor that year, so it's hard to say how much of the *Times'* coverage reflected a real drug problem or a response to a threat from a competitor.

35. In 1908, 97 percent of the U.S.'s smoking opium imports were registered in S.F. (145,345 + lbs.). *See* "Nations Uniting To Stamp Out The Use of Opium and Many Other Drugs," *NYT*, July 25, 1909. In 1890, a N.Y. writer sympathetic to immigrants disparaged the opium smoker who "puts mind and body to sleep to work out its deadly purpose in the corruption of the soul." (Jacob Riis, *How The Other Half Lives*, Dover Publications, NYC, 1971). A year later N.Y.'s police initiated a series of raids on opium dens. (Louis Beck, *New York City's Chinatown*, Appendix by Inspector Brooks, publisher unknown, 1898). Hostility toward opium smoking might have softened by 1896 when Crane wrote that police actions dispersed N.Y.'s opium smoking, which had been much practiced and flaunted by whites. (Stephen Crane, "Opium's Varied Dream," *Prose & Poetry*, "NYC 1896," Library of America, 1984).

36. For 1894-1908: *SF Call* = April 1-3 each year; *SF Chron* = February 1-3 & August 1-3, every other even year; and *SF Ex* = March 1-3 & September 1-3, every other odd year.

37. The *SF Ex* was read the 11th-15th of the month for: November 1894; January, March, and November 1895, 1898-1999, 1902-1903, and 1906-1907; and February, October, and December for 1896-1997, 1900-1901, 1904-1905, and 1908.

38. "Two Ships in From Honolulu," *SF Ex*, March 1, 1899. Hansen was not convicted.

39. "Administration Is Changed And So Has Opium," *SF Ex*, March 3, 1905. (p. 7).

40. "Loses Money, Gets Cold, but No Smuggler," *SF Ex*, November 11, 1906. (p. 23).

41. Elliott Flower, "Smuggled Opium," *Pearson's Magazine*, V. 21, March 1909, pp. 323-329.

42. "Heavy Shipment of Opium," *SF Chron*, August 1, 1896 (p. 7); "Big Shipment of Opium," *SF Ex*, March 1, 1899 (p. 10); & "The Opium-Seizure Scandal Increases," *SF Ex*, March 3, 1897 (p. 11). A dispute over $6 per pound of past duties ($200,000) fell outside the sampled dates. "Big Seizure of Contraband Opium," *SF Ex*, February 27, 1897. (p. 13).

43. Experts disagree on when the opium duty dropped. A contemporary historian cites a congressional report as proof it was July 1897 (David Courtwright, *Dark Paradise—Opiate Addiction In America Before 1940*, Harvard Univ. Press, Cambridge, 1982, Table 3); the *Report of the Supervising Agent to the Secretary of the Treasury for FY ended 6/30/1895*, excerpt "Opium Smuggling," in DEA Library, VF "Opium/History" dates the "tariff act of 1894 reducing the duty on smoking opium from $12 to $6 per pound."

44. Annual *Report of the Supervising Special Agent for the Secretary of the Treasury for FY 1895 and 1896*, in DEA Library, VF "Opium/History."

45. "Morphia Pill Endorsed As Opium Substitute," *SF Ex*, Oct. 11, 1898. (p. 32).

46. Most *SF Ex* stories on opiate ODs were squibs of suicides, sometimes involving alcohol or other drugs. Opiates, here, were in the category of strychnine, arsenic, wood alcohol, carbolic acid, and the exotic "knockout drops." Each was reported used in suicide attempts in the 1894-1908 *SF Ex* sample. The reported opium suicides tended to be early in the period sampled. Did the suicidal, too, lose interest when the media was quiet?

47. "Snuff Factories Raided," *NYT*, Sept. 11, 1902. (p. 2).

48. The most coverage given to vice in SF's Chinatown was from Feb. 11-14, 1901 when the Fisk Investigating Committee's hearings dominated the front pages of the *SF Ex*. In NY in 1905 the Parkhurst society actively attacked Chinatown's vice, but there gambling and gang violence were the issues. One raid on a tong's gambling den netted five Chinese, "dreaming over sizzling pipes of 'hop,'" whom the police did not arrest. See *NYT*, May 31, 1906, op. cit.

49. From October 11–15, 1901, the *SF Ex* covered the Episcopal Church's annual convention almost as if S.F. was hosting a national political convention.

50. The *SF Ex*'s banner headline on pages *1 & 2* of the story anticipating Congress would add restrictions the *SF Ex* was pushing to the Exclusion Act was "YELLOW JOURNALISM, 'The Journalism That Acts,' Wins a Fight To Keep Chinese Out Of The U.S.," *SF Ex*, March 15, 1902. (pp. 1 & 2).

51. "Opium Proof Wall May Solve The Problem," *SF Ex*, March 1, 1903. (p. 18).

52. "Hale Chastises His Officers," *SF Ex*, January 12, 1898. (p. 7).

53. *SF Ex*, March 1, 1903, op. cit.

54. "Hale's Corps of Tale-Bearers," *SF Ex*, January 11, 1898 (p. 12); "Warden Hale's Views On Prison Reforms," *SF Ex*, December 12, 1897 (p. 21); and "Pigeons Made To Smuggle Opium Into Prison," *SF Ex*, December 14, 1904. (p. 1).

55. "The prevalence of opium in San Quentin has caused many quarrels among the prisoners and has provoked at least one murder [and] the insurrection last June." *SF Ex*, January 12, 1898, op. cit.

56. "Jail Graft To Be Probed," *SF Ex*, Jan. 15, 1906; and R. E. Bering, "A Plea For a State Institution For The Treatment of Chronic Alcoholic and Drug Habitues," *California State Journal of Medicine*, 8 (7):237–241 (July 1910).

57. "The Opium Habit's Power," *NYT*, January 6, 1878. The only clue provided as to where the American opium-smoking society was located was "in a Western town."

58. John Liggins, *Opium: England's Coercive Policy and Its Disastrous Results in China and India*, Funk and Wagnalls, N.Y., 1882. (reprinted in G. Grob, ed., *American Perceptions of Drug Addiction, Five Studies, 1872–1912*, Arno Press, N.Y. [1981]).

59. Frederick J. Masters, "Opium and Its Votaries," *California Illustrated Magazine*, V. 1, May 1892, pp. 632–642; and "The Opium Traffic In California," *Chatauquan*, V. 24, October 1896, pp. 54–61.

60. *SF Chron*, August 21–23, 1908.

61. "Wins Against The Poppy," *SF Ex*, March 3, 1899. (p. 3).

62. Many states passed laws similar to the federal Harrison Act before 1914, some just before 1909, but hardly any enforced them except California. There the 1907 law resulted in thirty-five arrests of pharmacists before the year was out. "California Board Is Active," *Pacific Drug Review*, Portland, OR, Jan. 1908. (p. 8).

63. David Musto, Chapter 2, "Diplomats and Reformers," in *The American Disease*, Yale University Press, New Haven, 1973; and David Courtwright, *Dark Paradise*, Harvard University Press, Cambridge, 1982. Musto's analysis of Wright is terser and better captures his unique flamboyance and tactic. Musto also notes several enemies he acquired en route to getting the federal government's primary drug laws passed.

64. "The U.S. Opium Commission," editor, and Hamilton Wright, "Correspondence: U.S. Opium Commission," *JAMA* 51:678–679 and 688, August 22, 1908.

65. "Decries Immense Traffic in Opium," *SF Call*, December 27, 1908. (p. 5).

66. The following table is largely hypothetical, but shows Wright's data could be correct, and opium smoking was central to Chinese in U.S. but irrelevant to all but a wee fraction of whites. Population figures are from the US Census; total number of users is near Wright's estimates. Major assumptions regard: (1) the ratio of heavy : moderate : occasional users (assumed to be 2:3:4); (2) the relative amount consumed by each type of user (assumed to be 5:3:1 heavy:moderate:occasional users); and (3) the relative size of habits of Chinese versus non-Chinese (assumed to be twice as high for Chinese, for each type of user). Result: in the U.S. in the early 1900s the per capita rate of opium smokers among Chinese was 800 times that of non-Chinese, though three times more whites than Chinese "ever used."

Hypothetical: No. of U.S. Opium Smokers by Race: 1880 vs. 1909

	CHINESE (1910 Pop. = 72,000) 1880 Pop. = 105,800)				WHITE + BLACK (1910 Pop. = 91,600,000) 1880 Pop. = 50,000,000)			
	Heavy	Moderate	Occasional	TOTAL	Heavy	Moderate	Occasional	TOTAL
	% Who Smoke Opium				% Who Smoke Opium			
	10	15	20	45	0.025	0.0375	0.05	0.1125
	Number Who Smoke Opium				Number Who Smoke Opium			
1909	7,200	10,800	14,400	32,400	22,900	34,250	45,800	103,050
1880	10,580	15,870	21,160	47,610	12,500	18,750	25,000	56,250
	Amount of Opium Smoked				Amount of Opium Smoked			
	(5 lb. Avg.)	(3 lb. Avg.)	(1 lb. Avg.)	TOTAL	(2.5 lb. Avg.)	(1.5 lb. Avg.)	(.5 lb. Avg.)	TOTAL
1909	36,000	32,400	14,400	82,800	57,250	51,525	29,900	138,675
1880	52,900	47,600	21,200	121,700	31,250	28,125	12,500	71,875

67. Edward Marshall, " 'Uncle Sam Is The Worst Drug Fiend In The World', " *NYT*, May 12, 1911.

68. Musto, op. cit.

69. Ibid. Musto notes the 1909 ban on opium smoking imports was presented to U.S. audiences as important for foreign recognition of U.S. intentions, yet he could find no mention of the Act in any foreign publication.

70. Historian David Musto notes behind-the-scenes opposition to Wright and his ideas, mostly *after* 1909 when Wright maneuvered to eventually pass the Harrison Act. Within a year after the Commission, Wright was considered such a loose cannon that even his Shanghai partner, Bishop Brent, pleaded with him to quit, yet neither Brent nor any of his contemporaries I have read came out publicly against Wright. Musto, Ibid., and Courtwright, op. cit.

71. "Mystery In Big Lots of Opium Stored Here," *SF Ex*, March 31, 1909. (p. 3). Canada had recently passed drug prohibition acts, so Victoria, B.C., was no longer a manufacturing-distribution center for opium smoked in the U.S. Had it been, the street price of opium in the U.S. after 1909 would have risen less. However, a "false alarm" in December 1908—when Harvey Wiley of the U.S. Department of Agriculture claimed smoking opium was a dangerous drug and thus banned—triggered off stockpiling and a doubling in price, suggesting a "market" extremely sensitive to legal changes. (Since Wiley's order was not carried out, opium merchants and users might have underestimated future threats to their supply). See "What Will Chinatown Do When the Opium Gives Out?" *SF Chron*, December 2, 1908. (p. 5).

72. "Says Opium Here Is Safe" and "Opium Duty Is All Paid," both *SF Ex*, April 1 & 2, 1909. (p. 3 and 8, respectively).

73. "Canton Bank's Opium Seized As Contraband" and "Opium Seizure Case Is Continued To Today," *SF Call*, April 11 & 12, 1912. (p. 1 & 18, respectively). "Some Chinese . . . bank presidents" continued smoking opium for several decades, and were reportedly patients in the U.S. Public Health Service's narcotics hospitals in the late 1940s. See interview of Marie Nyswander in D. Courtwright, H. Joseph, and D. Des Jarlais, *Addicts That Survived—An Oral History of Narcotic Use In America*, University of Tennessee Press, Knoxville, 1989. (pp. 310–311).

74. "While the result of Uncle Sam's new order has not succeeded in altogether depriving the Chinese of his [sic] pipe, it had placed him on half rations. Economy is everywhere practiced

in Chinatown, and the smokers guard each little bit of opium as carefully as ship-wrecked sailors watch over the fresh water. Frequently a portion of opium, which used to be considered sufficient for just one smoke, is now divided among three or four smokers." In "Chinatown Has Opium Famine And Whites Are Sent To Asylum," SF paper and date unknown, attached to *Report of the California State Board of Pharmacy for FY Ending 6/30/1909*, Calif. State Archives, Sacramento.

75. "Deadly Drugs," RMN, December 12, 1880. (p. 2); and frequent reports from San Francisco in the late 1800s.

76. N.Y.C. data from Perry Lichtenstein, "Narcotic Addiction," *N.Y. Medical Journal* 100:962–966 (Nov. 14, 1914); Frank McGuire and Perry Lichtenstein, "The Drug Habit," *Medical Record* 90:185–190 (July 29, 1916); and Sylvester Leahy, "Some Observations On Heroin Habitués," *Psychiatric Bulletin of the N.Y. State Hospitals* N.S. V. 8: 251–263 (August 1915). A Californian was among the first to report a switch to injecting: "[I]t is only the vicious and criminal who . . . soon discards the filthy and nauseous surroundings [of the den] for the more seductive and less expensive needle." John Robertson, "The Morphin Habit: Its Treatment, and the Possibility of Its Cure," *Medical News* 73(9):257–260 (August 27, 1898).

77. Morphine and heroin were popular in the demimonde prior to the Harrison Act, as Courtwright, op. cit., noted. Often the shift from smoking opium resulted from the 1909 federal ban on imports. Even El Paso "had an army of smokers [but] two things happened in coincidence. The importation of opium was prohibited. The clumsy, expensive habit became almost impossible, unless one 'knew the ropes'. At the same time a new stepping-stone toward the hypodermic needle appeared. It was 'flake'—powdered cocaine. The victim inhales it like snuff." ("Hop + Dope Fiends Fast being Recruited From Better Families," *El Paso Herald*, June 15, 1913, pp. 10–11.) In places (i.e., California) earlier local bans had made opium smoking difficult and expensive. Whether this shift resulted from the pre-Harrison Act laws or was "spontaneous" is important for assessing whether drug laws were a cause or a response to a *drug problem*, but going deeply into this theme is beyond my scope here.

California sources noting the shift are: W.S. Whitwell, "The Opium Habit," *Pacific Medical and Surgical Journal* 30(6):321–338 (June 1887); Robertson, ibid.; R. Ellis Wales, "Held In Thrall by Morpheus," *SF Chron*, November 27, 1910 (Sunday Supp., p. 7); and Block, op. cit. N.Y.C. sources are: Lichtenstein, op. cit.; McGuire & Lichtenstein, op. cit.; Pearce Bailey, "The Heroin Habit," *New Republic*, April 22, 1916 (pp. 314–316); and (NYC) *Society for the Prevention of Crime Report 1916* (pp. 26 + 28). Also see Joseph McIver & George Price, "Drug Addiction," *JAMA* 66:476–480. (February 12, 1916).

78. According to the major proponent of drug prohibition in the 1920s, "the great expansion of narcotic addiction in America, given impetus by heroin, dates from about 1910." Rex Lampman, "Heroin Heroes: An Interview With Captain Richmond Pearson Hobson," *Saturday Evening Post*, September 20, 1924.

79. "Opium Smuggler Caught With Goods"; "Inspectors Seize Contraband 'Hop' "; and "Watch Liner For Opium Smugglers," all *SF Call*, May 25, 1909 (p. 1), June 22, 1909 (p. 5), and November 27, 1909 (p. 11), respectively.

80. "Opium Worth $10,000 Is Used As Evidence" and "Smuggler of Chinese and Opium Convicted," both *SF Call*, February 7, 1910 (p. 2) and April 18, 1910 (p. 3), respectively.

81. "Grand Jury To Delve Into The Bullion Theft," *SF Call*, December 20, 1910 (p. 3); and "Customs Inspectors Make Drug Seizure," *SF Chron*, Dec. 22, 1910 (p. 10).

82. "Arrest in Opium Raid," *NYT* September 16, 1913. (p. 7).

83. "Seizures of Opium" & "Hunt For Opium," *SF Chron*, Feb. 6, 1891 (p. 10) & Feb. 7, 1891, respectively; and "Inspectors Seize Contraband 'Hop,' " & "Drugs Seized In Raid Goes To State," *SF Call*, June 22, 1909 (p. 5) and Dec. 23, 1910 (p. 7), respectively. Also *SF Call*, Dec. 20, 1910, ibid.

84. *NYT* stories on customs agent NYC raids are: "They Smuggled Opium," January 31, 1891 (p. 9); "Opium Seizures," February 14, 1891 (p. 2); "Opium Arrests Continue," October 5, 1903 (p. 5); "Held As Opium Smuggler" (Hoboken), August 9, 1910 (p. 6); "Customs Men Raid Two Opium Shops," January 26, 1911 (p. 1); "Customs Men Raid Opium Supply Depot," October 7, 1911 (p. 3); "Arrest Physician After Opium Raid," January 31, 1913 (p. 7); & "Opium Raid Gives Tuner A Shock," November 22, 1913 (p. 1).

85. "The Opium Smuggler," *NYT*, August 22, 1888 (p. 2), and "U.S. Revenue Men Raid Opium Dens," *Chicago Daily Tribune*, January 1, 1912. (p. 3).

86. "Arrested for Drug Smuggling," *NYT*, Jan. 6, 1889 (p. 1), Edward Lehman II, "Death to Denver's Hop Alley," *RMN*, March 24, 1946; and "Raid On Chinese Yields Much Opium," *SF Call*, July 24, 1910. (p. 30).

87. "Appreciation, But No Jingling Coin," *SF Call*, March 15, 1910. (p. 5).

88. "Mongolia Yields More Contraband," *SF Chron*, June 26, 1912. (p. 12).

89. "Customs Men May Have Pay Restored," *SF Chron*, July 25, 1912. (p. 1).

90. "Inspectors Find Drug In Jacket," *SF Call*, June 22, 1912. (p. 13).

91. *SF Call*, June 22, 1912, ibid. Also see *SF Chron*, June 26, 1912, op. cit.

92. "Sailors To Guard Liner Chiyo Maru," *SF Chron*, September 4, 1913. (p. 22).

93. Davis Edwards, "Opium A Greater Menace to New York Than Liquor," *NYT*, October 20, 1910. (Pt. 5, p. 4).

94. "Suspicion Falls On Stratton's Department," *SF Chron*, December 11, 1910. (p. 27).

95. "May Impose Fine On Saunders For Opium," and "Customs Inspectors Deceive Smugglers," *SF Chron*, January 24 & 26, 1911 (last page & p. 4, respectively).

96. *SF Chron*, June 26, 1912, op. cit. and "Axle Grease Opium Brings Trouble to Customs Man," October 11, 1912. (p. 5).

97. *SF Call*, June 22, 1912, op. cit. A large dip in street prices "due to the great quantity of opium brought into this city [S.F.] the last few weeks" was noted eleven months previously in "Four Pickle Tubs Yield Opium Tins," *SF Call*, July 1, 1911. (p. 16).

98. "Smuggling Net Lands Ellison," *SF Ex*, September 1, 1913. (p. 13).

99. "Secrets of Opium Ring Laid Bare By Guards" and "Fourteen Out of Smuggling Ring Indicted," *SF Ex*, September 2 (p. 1) and 3, 1913.

100. Cocaine was also on the very short list of initially banned drugs, but by far the most widely used medicine—and thus the drug that had to be incorporated under a prescription system for it to substantially redefine professional practice—was opium.

101. The suppression of opium smoking occurred a few years earlier in Denver than in California; 1907 raids in Denver's Hop Alley "proved the death knell for the cobblestone alley [with] its innumerable 'hop joints' and opium dens. . . . Many . . . pipes seized in this raid were still [in 1946] in the possession of officers & agents. . . . Never again did it regain its reputation of being a street of solid dope dens." Lehman II, *RMN*, March 24, 1946, op. cit. These events in Denver had much less national impact than similar ones in Northern California because Denver's Chinese population was always considerably smaller, and shrunk in 1880 after "every Chinese abode in town may be said to have been destroyed" in an anti-Chinese riot ("Chinese Gone!" *Denver Weekly News*, November 3, 1880). Denver's Chinese population had once been 1,500 but was 270 in 1904 and 50 in 1921. ("Denver's Chinatown Worst In Country," *RMN*, Sect. II, p. 3, December 25, 1904; and Clyde Davis, "Denver's 'Hop Alley' Is Now A Quiet Place," *RMN*, Sunday Magazine, August 14, 1921.)

102. A. L. Leber, "California Laws Affecting The Pharmacist," *Pacific Pharmacist*, V. 1, Dec. 1907. (pp. 397–401).

103. "California Gets Little Drug Legislation," *Pacific Drug Review*, Portland Oregon, V. 23, April 1911 (p. 38).

104. The *Sacramento Bee* was read February 1–10 and 18–25, 1907, to pick up stories when a law was passed by the Senate (February 4) and the Assembly (February 21).

105. "Poison Sellers Face Heavy Fines" and "Net Woman In Opium Den Raid," SF Call, April 3, 1908 (p. 16) and April 6, 1908 (p. 14), respectively.

106. "Fighting To Save Women From Chinese Opium Traffic—'I Can Close Every Joint In The U.S.,' Says Man Who Has Barred White Patrons From The Dens of San Francisco," St Louis (Mo.) Star, August 7, 1908.

107. "Proposed Changes In The Pharmacy, Poison and Pure Drugs Law," Pacific Pharmacist, V. 2, Nov. 1908 (pp. 289–292).

108. E. T. Off, "A Summary of the Work Done By The State Board of Pharmacy," Pacific Pharmacist, V. 4, June 1910 (pp. 79–80).

109. E. T. Off, "The Work of the State Board of Pharmacy," Pacific Pharmacy, V. 4, June 1910 (pp. 75–77).

110. Ibid.

111. J. G. Munson, "Educational Requirements for the Betterment of Pharmacy In California and Bd. of Pharmacy Report," Pacific Drug Review, V. 24, July 1912 (p. 14).

112. E. T. Off, "The Work of the State Board of Pharmacy," op. cit. In reports of 1911–1912 drug raids in Central and Northern California, the same three names reappear. Possibly other inspectors were based elsewhere in the state or investigated only pharmacies.

113. "31 Opium Joints Raided and Druggists & Dr. Jailed," SF Call, October 11, 1910 (p. 1).

114. "Raid of Opium Dens In Sacramento," SF Chron, October 16, 1911 (p. 4).

115. The U.S. Census, Population 1910: General Report and Analysis, Vol. 1 listed 36, 248 Chinese in California, fewer than the Japanese in the state. San Francisco's "non-white or black" population was 15, 256, a large minority of whom I assume were Japanese, Indians, or other non-Chinese. New York City's non-white or black population was 4,430, again the majority of whom I assume were Chinese.

116. The Customs Service, and probably local antidrug forces, cultivated informers, such as for Beecher's strike at Kaasan Bay, or for sporadic Customs' forays in local Chinatowns, or the seizure following Moy Jin Mun's tip. Customs even sent an agent to China and back to get information on who smuggled opium and where they hid it on a transoceanic steamer. But a full-time field agent in the U.S., posing as a habitué was, to my knowledge, unreported until Sutherland.

117. "200 Seized In 62 Drug Dens," SF Call, November 26, 1911 (p. 17). Also see "Months Spent In Underworld to Trap Drug Sellers," SF Call, Nov. 27, 1911.

Arrestees in 1911 included Rose Mentor, proprietress of a drug store "believed by the inspectors to be the headquarters for the illicit selling of opiates in Chinatown . . . a young and attractive widow . . . of the Spanish type with dark eyes and hair and a flashing smile." (" 'Dope' Den Net Lands Woman In Prison," SF Ex, November 30, 1911 [p. 5]). "Inspector Sutherland obtained the conviction of the widow . . . and a few weeks afterward married her." ("Chief Inspector's Wife Is Named In Drug Graft," SF Ex, June 12, 1915 [p. 6]). Undercover, indeed.

That revelation may have been triggered by charges filed by Sutherland with the governor against a deputy San Francisco district attorney "who it was alleged divided protection money with [Pharmacy Board] Inspector White who is a brother of San Francisco's Chief of Police." ("Accused Members California Board Exonerated," Pacific Drug Review, Portland-San Francisco, V. 77 (4) July 1915 (pp. 18–19).) Sutherland also charged three other inspectors had accepted bribe money, and two of the seven men who comprised the Board of Pharmacy, and its secretary, had tried to block his investigation. Sutherland in turn was accused of insubordination and dishonesty by the board. In 1915 Sutherland was fired after hearings at which he was accused of corruption and of an attempt to double-cross the Board of Pharmacy. ("Sutherland Is Ousted As Drug Inquiry Climax," SF Ex, June 16, 1915. Also see Proceedings of the [CA] State Board of Pharmacy, June 11–August 3, 1915, California State Archives, Sacramento, CA).

118. "The Fight On The Narcotic Traffic," Drug Clerk's Journal, V. 1 (4) Jan. 1912 (pp. 42 + 44).

119. Ibid.

120. Six hundred dollars worth of opium seized in 62 raids—under $10 per raid—seems paltry, especially given that the police tended to exaggerate the value of seized drugs and the press uncritically reported that (in 1911 as ever after). Possibly not everything seized was turned in to higher authority. Unless the corruption was stupendous, however, the major cost of the raids was not the drugs seized. NY's police had earlier been more interested in destroying the opium layouts than making arrests. One time they ran across five Chinese smoking opium and "left the dreamers there, after taking away all of the . . . opium pipes." *NYT*, May 31, 1905, op. cit. Unconsciously, the police everywhere might have understood that only the drugs were replaceable. They were out to demolish a culture, not a habit.

121. The most details were in the *SF Call*, November 26, 1911, op. cit., "Two Hundred Are Arrested In Opium Dens," *SF Chron*, November 26, 1911 (p. 1), and *Drug Clerk's Journal*, V. 1 (4), op. cit. Also see "Raids On Opium Joints Net 200 'Dope' Victims," *SF Ex*, November 26, 1911 (p. 73).

122. *SF Ex*, ibid.

123. *Drug Clerk's Journal*, V. 1 (4), op. cit.

124. "The California Board of Pharmacy," *Pacific Pharmacy*, V. 8 (9), January 1915 (pp. 194–195).

125. Off, op. cit.

126. "State Board After Traffickers," *Pacific Drug Review*, V. 22, September 1910.

127. "Sad Chinatown Sees $20,000 Opium Bonfire," *SF Ex*, May 10, 1912 (p. 15). Also see "To Impress Fiends State Destroys Opium and Co-Narcotics In Chinatown," *SF Call*, May 10, 1912 (p. 5).

128. Edward Alsworth Ross, "China's Grapple With the Opium Evil," *Everybody's Magazine* 24 (4): 435–446 (April 1911).

129. "Old Sam Sing Beholds a Holocaust for His Good," *SF Chron*, May 10, 1912 (p. 18).

130. *SF Ex*, May 10, 1912, op. cit.

131. "State Board Presents A Spectacle," *Drug Clerk's Journal*, V. 1 (9), June 1912 (p. 41).

132. Christopher Rand, "Not Seen, Not Heard, But Felt," *New Yorker*, January 5, 1952.

133. *SF Chron*, May 10, 1912, op. cit.

134. *Drug Clerk's Journal*, V. 1 (9), op. cit.

135. Harvey Wiley, "An Opium Bonfire," *Good Housekeeping* 55:251–252. (August 1912).

136. *Drug Clerk's Journal*, V. 1 (9), op. cit.

137. "Opium Ashes Spirited Away," *SF Chron*, February 7, 1914 (p. 1).

138. Arthur Dahl, "A Twenty-Thousand-Dollar Pipeful," *Technical World* 27:392–393 (May 1914). This desire to save the unique artistry of the opium pipes while destroying the culture that created and used them is reminiscent of the Nazi Herman Goering's approach to the great paintings of Europe. Mayor Rolfe's view was echoed in an editorial in a California pharmaceutical journal: "It is a pity that the opium pipes are all destroyed. . . .It is only a question of a comparatively short time when these instruments will be passed out of existence." "Destruction of Contraband Opium," *Pacific Pharmacist* V. 7 (10), February 1914 (p. 245). Denver police, too, saved some opium pipes (for forty years at least), *RMN*, March 24, 1946, op. cit.

139. "Women Deplore Drug Destruction," *Pacific Drug Review—Portland, San Francisco*, V. 27 (12), Dec. 1915.

140. Rand, op. cit.

10

The Transition from Prohibition to Regulation: Lessons from Alcohol Policy for Drug Policy

Harry G. Levine, Craig Reinarman

Since the mid-1980s, growing numbers of Americans have noted the harshness, expense, and ineffectiveness of the war on drugs and of United States drug policy in general. As a result, policymakers, journalists, and the general public have increasingly sought alternatives to the current form of U.S. drug prohibition. These alternatives have included decriminalization, public health and harm reduction approaches, and even outright drug legalization. People have also looked for help to the history of America's experiences with alcohol prohibition and regulation.

In this chapter we review some major questions about the rise, effects, and fall of alcohol prohibition, and we examine the logic, rationale, and organization of the system of alcohol regulation instituted after repeal. We focus on lessons from alcohol prohibition that might be useful for understanding drug prohibition, and on various principles governing alcohol regulation that

An earlier version of this chapter was published in 1991 as "From Prohibition to Regulation" in a special issue of the *Milbank Quarterly* (Vol. 69, No. 3) and then in a book edited by Ronald Bayer and Gerald Oppenheimer, *Drug Policy: Illicit Drugs in a Free Society*, New York: Cambridge University Press, 1993. The ideas in the last section of this chapter are drawn from and developed in Craig Reinarman and Harry G. Levine, eds., *Crack in America: Demon Drugs and Social Justice.* Berkeley: University of California Press, 1997.

might apply to drug regulation. In the final section we assess the prospects for reducing the punitiveness and harshness of American drug prohibition and look at the forces in motion currently seeking to change U.S. drug policy.

Historical studies cannot provide simple and straightforward answers to the complex drug policy questions now confronting Americans. Closer attention to the story of alcohol prohibition and regulation, however, can help us better understand the inherent processes of drug prohibition while illuminating a wider array of policy options. To set the stage, we begin with a brief overview of the history of temperance, prohibition, repeal, and alcohol regulation.

TEMPERANCE, PROHIBITION, AND ALCOHOL CONTROL

The antialcohol, or temperance, movement was created in the early nineteenth century by physicians, ministers, and large employers concerned about the drunkenness of workers and servants. By the mid-1830s temperance had become a mass movement of the middle class. Temperance was not, as is sometimes thought, the campaign of rural backwaters; rather, temperance was on the cutting edge of social reform and was closely allied with the antislavery and women's rights movements. Always very popular, temperance remained the largest enduring middle-class movement of the nineteenth century (Blocker 1989, Gusfield 1986, Levine 1978, 1984, Rumbarger 1989, Tyrell 1979).

The temperance campaign was devoted to convincing people that alcoholic drink in any form was evil, dangerous, and destructive. Throughout the nineteenth century, temperance supporters insisted that alcohol slowly but inevitably destroyed the moral character and the physical and mental health of all who drank it. Temperance supporters regarded alcohol the way people today view heroin: as an inherently addicting substance. Moderate consumption of alcohol, they maintained, naturally led to compulsive use—to addiction.

From the beginning, temperance ideology contained a powerful strand of fantasy. It held that alcohol was the major cause of nearly all social problems: unemployment, poverty, business failure, slums, insanity, crime, and violence (especially against women and children). For the very real social and economic problems of industrializing America, the temperance movement offered universal abstinence as the panacea.

From roughly the 1850s on, many temperance supporters endorsed the idea of prohibition. After the Civil War the Prohibition party, modeled on the Republican party, championed the cause. Nineteenth-century prohibitionists believed that only when sufficient numbers of party members held office would prohibition be practical because only then would it be fully enforced.

In the twentieth century a new prohibitionist organization—the Anti-Saloon League—came to dominate the movement (Gusfield 1968, Kerr 1985,

Odegard 1928, Rumbarger 1989, Sinclair 1964, Timberlake 1963). The League patterned itself on the modern corporation, hiring lawyers to write model laws and organizers to raise funds and collect political debts. The League put its considerable resources behind candidates of any party who would vote as it directed on the single issue of liquor. By expanding the numbers of elected officials beholden to it, and by writing laws for those legislators to enact, the League pushed through many local prohibition laws and some state measures. In 1913 the League finally declared itself in favor of constitutional prohibition. Increasing numbers of large corporations joined the many Protestant churches that had long supported the League. Then, during the patriotic fervor of World War I, prohibitionists mobilized the final support for a constitutional amendment. Among other arguments, prohibitionists claimed that in the United States the heavily German beer industry was sapping American will to fight.

By December 1917 both houses of Congress had voted the required two-thirds majority to send to the states for ratification a constitutional amendment prohibiting the manufacture, sale, transportation, import, or export of intoxicating liquor. In November 1918 Congress passed the War Prohibition Act, which banned the manufacture and sale of all beverages that contained more than 2.75 percent alcohol. On January 16, 1919, Nebraska became the thirty-sixth state to ratify the Eighteenth Amendment, which was to go into effect in one year. In October 1919 Congress overrode President Wilson's veto to pass a strict enforcement act of Prohibition known by the name of its sponsor, Andrew Volstead, of Minnesota, chair of the House Judiciary Committee. The Volstead Act defined as "intoxicating liquor" any beverage containing more than 0.5 percent alcohol.

At midnight on January 16, 1920, the Eighteenth Amendment took effect. The famous minister Billy Sunday celebrated by preaching a sermon to 10,000 people in which he repeated the fantasy at the heart of the temperance and prohibition crusades:

> The reign of tears is over. The slums will soon be a memory. We will turn our prisons into factories and our jails into storehouses and corncribs. Men will walk upright now, women will smile, and the children will laugh. Hell will be forever for rent. [cited in Kohler 1973, p. 12]

Prohibitionism was not, as is sometimes implied, a public health campaign to reduce mortality from cirrhosis of the liver or alcoholic admissions to state hospitals. As Joseph Gusfield (1968) has pointed out, prohibitionists were utopian moralists; they believed that eliminating the legal manufacture and sale of alcoholic drink would solve the major social and economic problems of American society.

The many literary, photographic, and cinematic images of the Prohibition era capture some of the essential features of the period. Prohibition was massively and openly violated, and alcohol was readily available in most of the United States. New institutions and cultural practices appeared: bootleggers and speakeasies, hip flasks and bathtub gin, rumrunners smuggling in liquor, and Prohibition agents like Eliot Ness smashing down doors. Adulterated and even poisonous alcohol was sold and many people were locked up for violating prohibition laws. (For rich descriptions of the prohibition era, see Allen 1931, Allsop 1961, Cashman 1981, Everest 1978, Kohler 1973, Lyle 1960, Mertz 1970, and Sinclair 1964. Burnham [1968] offers perhaps the only serious scholarly case for the success of prohibition. For the most recent evidence and discussions of its failures see Miron and Zweibel 1991, Morgan 1991, and Thornton 1991.)

Public opposition to Prohibition began even before the Volstead Act passed, especially among labor unions, but organized opposition remained small and fragmented until 1926. Then one organization, the Association Against the Prohibition Amendment (AAPA), took over the campaign for repeal. Headed by Pierre DuPont and other powerful corporate leaders, the AAPA gathered increasing numbers of wealthy and prominent supporters, including many former prohibitionists. Although Prohibition would have been repealed eventually, the AAPA unquestionably accelerated the process (Kyvig 1979, Levine 1985, Rumbarger 1989).

Just as World War I had provided the necessary context for rallying popular support to pass prohibition, the Great Depression provided the necessary context for repeal. Prohibition's supporters had long argued that it would ensure prosperity and increase law and order. In the late 1920s and early 1930s, prohibition's opponents made exactly the same argument. Repeal, they promised, would provide jobs, stimulate the economy, increase tax revenue, and reduce the "lawlessness" stimulated by and characteristic of the illegal liquor industry.

The Depression also played a crucial role in undermining elite support for prohibition. To some extent, alcohol prohibition had originally gained the support of large employers because they believed it would increase worker discipline and productivity and reduce other social problems. The mass violations of national prohibition in the 1920s, followed by the depression of the 1930s, raised a new specter: prohibition, many came to believe, undermined respect for all law, including property law. This *lawlessness*, as people then termed it, frightened many of the rich and powerful—like Pierre DuPont and John D. Rockefeller, Jr.—far more than problems with worker efficiency (Kyvig 1979, Leuchtenburg 1958, Levine 1985). In addition, in the early 1930s the threat of revolt and revolution was in the air. There were food riots in many cities, unemployed people formed militant organizations, mobs stopped trains and took over warehouses of food. Socialists and communists held rallies of tens of thousands, angry armies of marchers camped in front of the White House, and some wealthy people had machine guns mounted on the roofs of their estates (Leuchtenburg 1958, Manchester 1974, Piven and Cloward 1971, 1977).

Those with wealth and power increasingly supported repeal, in part because they felt the need to do something to raise public morale and show that the government was in some way responsive to popular pressure in a terrible depression. In 1931 Matthew Woll, vice president of the American Federation of Labor and the sole labor member of the AAPA board, told President Hoover's National Commission on Law Observance and Enforcement (the Wickersham Commission) that workers were losing faith in the government's willingness to help them, and that Prohibition was causing them to further distrust and resent government. By 1932 a number of influential leaders and commentators also had concluded that legalizing beer would make workers feel better about government and take their minds off their troubles. Senators were told, "Beer would have a decidedly soothing tendency on the present mental attitude of the working men. . . . It would do a great deal to change their mental attitude on economic conditions" (Gordon 1943, p. 104). Walter Lippman argued, "Beer would be a great help in fighting off the mental depression which afflicts great multitudes" (Gordon 1943, p. 104). The Wickersham Commission explicitly pointed to the class resentment and lawlessness engendered by Prohibition in its report to Congress:

> Naturally . . . laboring men resent the insistence of employers who drink that their employees be kept from temptation. Thus the law may be made to appear aimed at and enforced against the insignificant while the wealthy enjoy immunity. This feeling is reinforced when it is seen that the wealthy are generally able to procure pure liquors, while those with less means may run the risk of poisoning. Moreover, searches of homes . . . have necessarily seemed to bear more upon people of moderate means than upon those of wealth or influence. [1931, pp. 54–55]

On November 16, 1932, the Senate voted to submit the Twenty-First Amendment—repealing the Eighteenth Amendment and returning to the states the power to regulate alcohol—to state conventions for ratification. On March 13, 1933, a few days after he was sworn in as president, Franklin Delano Roosevelt asked Congress to modify the Volstead Act to legalize 3.2 percent alcohol beer to provide needed tax revenue. By April 7, beer was legal in most of the country. On December 5, 1933, Utah became the thirty-sixth state to pass the Twenty-First Amendment. National alcohol prohibition was repealed, effective immediately.

In late 1933 and in 1934 bills creating state alcohol control agencies

sped through state legislatures. The model for most of the legislation had
been written by a group of policy-oriented researchers and attorneys associated with John D. Rockefeller, Jr., and with policy institutes he had created
or financially supported (Levine 1985). Within two years of repeal nearly every
state had an agency to supervise the sale and distribution of alcoholic beverages, and alcohol had ceased to be a controversial and politically charged
issue. The production, sale, and distribution of alcoholic beverages today is
still largely governed by the alcohol control structures designed and implemented at that time.

EFFECTS OF PROHIBITION ON CONSUMPTION, PRODUCTION, AND DISTRIBUTION

It has frequently been observed that drug prohibition tends to drive out the
weaker and milder forms of drugs, and to increase the availability and use of
stronger and more dangerous drugs (see, e.g., Brecher 1972). This has been
so often reported that many analysts speak of it as an "iron law" of drug
prohibition. This "law" holds because milder drugs are usually bulkier, harder
to hide and smuggle, and less remunerative. People involved in the illicit drug
business therefore frequently find it in their interest to do business in the
more compact and potent substances. For example, current interdiction efforts are most successful at capturing boats carrying many large bales of
marijuana; therefore, many drug smugglers have turned to smuggling cocaine
or heroin because it is easier and far more lucrative than smuggling marijuana (see Murphy et al. 1991).

This "law" of drug prohibition captures what happened during alcohol
prohibition. The major effect of the Eighteenth Amendment was to dramatically reduce beer drinking (and therefore total alcohol consumption). At the
same time, however, prohibition increased consumption of hard liquor (especially among the middle class). The fashionableness of the martini and other
mixed drinks among the middle class is in part a historical legacy of prohibition, when criminalization made hard liquor the most available form of
beverage alcohol.

Table 10-1 is drawn primarily from data gathered by the Rutgers University Center for Alcohol Studies and by historian William Rorabaugh (1979;
see also Miron and Zweibel 1991, and Williams et al. 1995). We added estimates of beer and wine consumption for 1925 and 1930 based on economist
Clark Warburton's classic study (1932) and adjusted the total consumption
figures accordingly. The table shows the per capita (15 years and older) consumption of absolute alcohol in spirits, wine, beer, and cider in the United
States over nearly three centuries.

Table 10-1. Absolute Alcohol Consumption in the United States by Beverage in Gallons of Absolute Alcohol Per Capita Drinking Age (15+) Population, from 1710 to 1993

Year	Spirits Absolute alcohol	Wine Absolute alcohol	Cider Absolute alcohol	Beer Absolute alcohol	Total Absolute alcohol
1710	1.7	< .05	3.4	–	5.1
1770	3.2	< .05	3.4	–	6.6
1790	2.3	.1	3.4	–	5.8
1800	3.3	.1	3.2	–	6.6
1810	3.9	.1	3.0	.1	7.1
1820	3.9	.1	2.8	–	6.8
1830	4.3	.1	2.7	–	7.1
1840	2.5	.1	.4	.1	3.1
1850	1.6	.1	–	.1	1.8
1860	1.7	.1	–	.3	2.1
1870	1.4	.1	–	.4	1.9
1880	1.1	.2	–	.6	1.9
1890	1.0	.1	–	1.0	2.1
1900	.8	.1	–	1.2	2.1
1905	.9	.1	–	1.3	2.3
1910	.9	.2	–	1.5	2.6
1915	.8	.1	–	1.5	2.4
1920	*	*	–	*	*
1925	.9	.2	–	.3	1.4
1930	.9	.2	–	.4	1.5
1935	.7	.1	–	.7	1.5
1940	.6	.2	–	.8	1.6
1945	.7	.2	–	1.1	2.0
1950	.7	.2	–	1.1	2.0
1955	.7	.2	–	1.0	1.9
1960	.8	.2	–	1.0	2.0
1965	1.0	.2	–	1.0	2.2
1970	1.1	.3	–	1.2	2.5
1975	1.1	.3	–	1.3	2.7
1980	1.0	.3	–	1.4	2.7
1985	.9	.4	–	1.3	2.6
1990	.8	.3	–	1.3	2.5
1993	.7	.3	–	1.3	2.3

Sources: Adapted from Rorabaugh (1979, p. 233) and Warburton (1932). Figures from 1980 and later are from Williams et al. (1995).
* Estimates for 1920 vary considerably and have been omitted.

Two factors stand out in these figures. First, although total alcohol consumption declined after 1915, the sharpest drop occurred between 1830 and 1840, nearly a century before Prohibition, when temperance first became a middle-class mass movement. Second, and more pertinent here, Prohibition led to a reduction in beer consumption, but to an increase in consumption of wine and spirits. From 1890 to 1915 beer accounted for more of the total alcohol consumed than did hard liquor. In 1915, for example, beer drinking accounted for nearly twice as much total alcohol consumed as spirits. Warburton compared alcohol consumption in the period 1911 to 1914 with that during the Prohibition years 1927–1930 and concluded that "the per capita consumption of beer has been reduced about 70 per cent . . . the per capita consumption of wine has increased about 65 per cent . . . [and] the per capita consumption of spirits has increased about 10 per cent" (1932, p. 260). This change was not permanent—after repeal, spirits consumption fell while beer consumption rose. By 1935 the alcohol consumed from beer equaled that from spirits, and by 1945 Americans were getting 50 percent more of their total alcohol from beer than from hard liquor.

CONSUMPTION AND PUBLIC HEALTH
UNDER PROHIBITION

The recent public debate about drug laws has increased interest in the effects of prohibition on public health, the economy, and social problems. These were very lively questions during Prohibition but have been largely ignored since. However, in the last two decades alcohol researchers in a number of countries have investigated at length the relationship between total per capita alcohol consumption and specific illnesses, especially cirrhosis of the liver. The data available for the Prohibition years in the United States will always be poor because it is impossible to get accurate consumption figures for an illegal substance. However, changes in the last fifty years in many countries that have kept accurate consumption and health statistics do allow some inferences about the relationship between overall alcohol consumption and cirrhosis. Although not all liver cirrhosis is caused by heavy drinking, much is. Furthermore, cirrhosis rates generally follow overall per capita consumption rates. These effects are mediated by dietary patterns, by type of alcoholic beverages consumed, and by when they are consumed. The level of health care people receive also affects cirrhosis death rates. In general, however, the positive relationship between alcohol consumption and cirrhosis holds: when consumption increases, cirrhosis increases (Bruun et al. 1975, Mäkelää et al. 1981, Moore and Gerstein 1981, Single et al. 1981).

One important way to evaluate the public health consequences of alcohol policies, then, is in terms of how they affect consumption. In 1932

Warburton pointed out that "except for the first three years, the per capita consumption of alcohol has been greater under prohibition than during the war period [1917–1919], with high taxation and restricted production and sale" (p. 260). As Table 10–1 suggests, both Prohibition and post-Prohibition alcohol regulation kept overall consumption down compared with the decades prior to Prohibition. Indeed, post-Prohibition regulatory policies kept alcohol use sufficiently low that it was not until the end of the 1960s, thirty-five years after repeal, that per capita alcohol consumption rose to the levels of 1915. Whatever public health benefits Prohibition achieved in terms of reducing consumption, alcohol regulation in the 1930s and early 1940s accomplished them as well. Further, this occurred despite the fact that (1) the post-Prohibition regulatory system had little or no public health focus, and (2) the liquor industry (like most other U.S. industries) gained increasing influence over the agencies that were supposed to regulate it. Our point here is *not* that U.S. alcohol control is a model of effective public-health-oriented regulatory policy (it certainly is not). Rather, until at least 1960, alcohol control worked almost as well as Prohibition in limiting alcohol consumption, and more effectively than pre-Prohibition policies.

It is also important to note that other nations achieved even greater reductions in per capita consumption than the United States—without the negative consequences of Prohibition. Robin Room (1988) has shown that in Australia a series of alcohol control measures instituted in the early twentieth century substantially reduced spirits consumption. More important, Australia's regulatory policies significantly reduced total alcohol consumption as well as the incidence of alcohol-related health problems, notably cirrhosis mortality. From a peak of 9.15 cirrhosis deaths per 100,000 in 1912, Australia's cirrhosis rate fell to 3.83 in 1933, and fluctuated between 3.15 and 5.12 for over twenty years. Room reports that mortality from alcoholic psychosis experienced a similar drop. All of this happened under regulated sale, not prohibition.

Great Britain's experience parallels that of Australia. England reduced overall consumption by instituting fairly stringent alcohol regulation at about the same time as the United States instituted Prohibition. Moreover, as Nadelmann notes (1989b), it reduced "the negative consequences of alcohol consumption more effectively than did the United States, but it did so in a manner that raised substantial government revenues" (p. 1105). By contrast, the U.S. government spent large sums attempting to enforce its prohibition laws, yet was unable to prevent the flow of money into criminal enterprises (1989b).

It is difficult to disagree with Nadelmann's conclusion that the "British experience [and, we would add, the Australian experience] strongly indicates that the national prohibition of alcohol in the United States was, on balance, not successful" (1989b p. 1105). Prohibition of course failed to fulfill the fantasies of prohibitionists about eliminating major social problems like poverty, unemployment, crime, and so on. Yet even in the less utopian terms of reducing total alcohol consumption, U.S. prohibition was no more effective than regulated sale in the 1930s and early 1940s. Prohibition, however, produced far more substantial negative side effects than did regulation.

Only a few other nations even tried prohibition laws, and only Finland instituted constitutional prohibition (repealing it before the United States and for many of the same reasons). Although there are today neotemperance movements in some Nordic and English-speaking (Canada, Australia, New Zealand, Great Britain) countries, which focus on the public health dangers of alcohol, these are not prohibitionist groups. Contrary to the claims and worries of the U.S. alcohol industry, there are no "neoprohibitionist" movements and no serious discussion anywhere about returning to prohibition. In the United States even many local prohibition laws have been replaced by regulation of some kind. More than fifty years after repeal of the Eighteenth Amendment, the consensus remains that alcohol prohibition was not sound public policy.

ALCOHOL PRODUCTION AND DISTRIBUTION
DURING PROHIBITION

During constitutional alcohol prohibition, consumption was influenced by the requirements of illicit production. It was much more profitable and cost effective to make and distribute distilled spirits (gin, vodka, whiskey, or rum) than beer. Beer is mostly water—only 3 to 6 percent alcohol. Production and storage of beer requires enormous tanks, many barrels, huge trucks, and a substantial investment in equipment. Hard liquor is 40 to 50 percent alcohol; it contains up to fifteen times more pure alcohol than beer. Because alcohol content was the main determinant of price, a gallon of spirits was much more valuable than a gallon of beer and also could be hidden and transported more easily. Furthermore, spirits could be preserved indefinitely, whereas beer spoiled very quickly. Large-scale beer bottling and refrigeration developed only in the 1930s, after repeal (Baron 1962, Kyvig 1979).

The rising supply of hard liquor came from many sources. Tens of thousands of people produced it in small, compact stills in sheds, basements, attics, and in the woods. It was also smuggled from Mexico, Europe, and Canada. Some of the largest names in distilling today entered the business or grew wealthy during the Prohibition era—notably the Bronfmans of Canada, who own Seagram's. A considerable amount of alcohol was also diverted from purported industrial or medical uses.

Wine consumption also increased during Prohibition, to about 65 per cent more than the pre-World War I period, according to Warburton (1932). Standard table wine contains 10 to 14 percent alcohol. Much of the wine was made for personal consumption and as a profitable side business by immigrants from wine countries, especially Italy. After the first few years of Prohibition, the California wine-grape industry experienced a boom and vineyard prices increased substantially. California grape growers planted hearty, thick-skinned grapes that could be shipped easily and used for small-scale and home wine making. Much of the California wine-grape crop was shipped to Chicago and New York in newly developed refrigerated boxcars. The grapes were bought right off the train by wholesalers, who resold them in immigrant neighborhoods. The homemade wine was then distributed to smaller cities and towns, where it was sometimes called "dago red" (Muscatine et al. 1984).

Although it is true that Prohibition provided a major boost for organized crime, it is not true (although widely believed today) that gangsters and large criminal organizations supplied most Prohibition-era alcohol. In Chicago and a few other large cities, large criminal gangs indeed dominated alcohol distribution, especially by the end of the 1920s. Most of the alcohol production and distribution, however, was on a smaller scale. In addition to homemade wines and family stills, people took station wagons and trucks to Canada and returned with a load of liquor. Lobster boats, other fishing boats, and pleasure boats did the same. Spirits and wine were also prescribed by physicians and available at pharmacies. Many people certified themselves as ministers and rabbis and distributed large quantities of "sacramental wine." Alcoholic beverages were made and sold to supplement other income during hard times. Prohibition thus shaped the structure of the alcohol industry in a distinctive way: it decentralized and democratized production and distribution (Allsop 1961, Cashman 1981, Everest 1978, Lyle 1960, Sinclair 1964).

Today as well, most people in the illicit drug business are small-scale entrepreneurs. Supporters of the drug war frequently suggest that elimination of the currently large-scale producers and distributors would have a lasting effect on drug production and distribution. There is no more evidence supporting this now than there was during alcohol prohibition. Much illicit drug production today is also decentralized and democratized. There is no criminal syndicate that, when eliminated, would stop the distribution of any currently illicit drug, or even reduce the supply for very long. Today some groups, families, and business organizations (like the so-called Medellín cocaine cartel) have grown very rich in the illicit drug business. However, just as Al Capone was quickly replaced, so have new producers taken the place of those cocaine "kingpins" who have been arrested. Indeed, after billions of dollars on interdiction have been spent by Customs, the Drug Enforcement Agency, and even the armed forces, there has been no lasting drop in the supply of cocaine. Even when interdiction does affect the supply of a criminalized substance, the effects are often ironic. The partial success of the Nixon administration's "Operation Intercept," for example, gave rise to what is now a huge domestic marijuana industry (Brecher 1972) that has become ever more decentralized and democratic as armed helicopter raids have increased.

In short, whereas prohibition regimes tend to be a boon to organized crime, they also increase the number and types of people involved in illicit production and distribution (Murphy et al. 1991, Williams 1989). Whether production occurs in a mob syndicate or a family marijuana patch, the result tends to be a shift toward production and sale of more concentrated forms of intoxicating substances. Recognition of such tendencies in the Prohibition era accelerated the process of repeal and informed the search for alternative regulatory systems.

ESTABLISHING AN ALCOHOL CONTROL SYSTEM

In 1933, at the very end of constitutional prohibition, the difficulties of creating an alcohol control system seemed formidable. In the years before constitutional prohibition in the United States, there had been little systematic control of the alcohol industry. The Eighteenth Amendment had not eliminated the business, but rather had profoundly altered its shape. In 1933 a sprawling illegal industry for producing and distributing alcoholic beverages was in place, composed of uncountable numbers of small independent distributors and producers, and some larger ones. For fourteen years this industry had kept the United States well supplied with alcohol. The mass patronage of this illicit industry—and the political and economic implications of such a popular display of disrespect for law—was a major factor in convincing Rockefeller and other prominent supporters of Prohibition to reverse field and press for repeal.

During Prohibition the liquor business was wide open. In most cities and many towns, speakeasies closed when they wished or not at all; they sold whatever they wanted, to whomever they cared to, at whatever price they chose. They decorated as they wished and had a free hand in providing food and entertainment. Producers had complete control over the strength of their alcohol and the means of its manufacture, including the products that went into it. Neither producers nor distributors paid any taxes (except for payoffs to police and politicians) and they were not regulated by any government agency. During Prohibition, the liquor industry was probably the freest large industry in America.

Alcohol control, on the other hand was premised on government intervention into every aspect of the liquor business. Controversial issues such as whether food must be served, women admitted, music and games banned, bars and bar stools allowed, all had to be settled. The number, types, and locations of on- and off-premise outlets and their hours of sale had to be determined. Producers had to be regulated to ensure that products were safe and of a uniform alcohol content. To eliminate untrustworthy or disreputable persons, both producers and distributors had to be screened, licensed, and made to pay taxes. Legal drinking had to be socially organized in a way that would not be an affront to the abstaining half of the population. Conversely, the control system could not make regulation so tight, or taxes so high, that drinkers would prefer to patronize illicit bootleggers or speakeasies. Americans, after all, were by then quite used to disobeying liquor laws.

Prohibitionists had always argued that the liquor business was inherently unregulatable. The onus was now on reformers to show that this was not true, and that they could create structures to make the industry obey laws and yield taxes. The task, as expressed in the catchall titles for alternatives to prohibition, was "liquor control" or "alcohol control" in the fullest sense of the terms. In short, repeal posed an enormous problem of social engineering. Constructing alcohol control, in fact, involved problems of government regulation so large and complex as to make some of the classic Progressive-era reforms—regulating meat packing, for example—seem paltry. Except for national Prohibition, postrepeal alcohol regulation is probably the most striking twentieth-century example of government power used directly to reshape both an entire industry and the way its products are consumed.

THE ROCKEFELLER REPORT

Prior to the passage of the Eighteenth Amendment, alcohol was regulated by cities, towns, and sometimes counties. State governments were rarely involved in regulating production or distribution. Prohibition then shifted control to the federal government. Postrepeal policy, however, made state governments chiefly responsible for devising and implementing a regulatory system. States could, and often did, then allow for considerable local option and variation.

By the end of the 1920s the Association Against the Prohibition Amendment had outlined some rough plans for alternatives to prohibition, but they had not been well worked out. The central principles of post-Prohibition alcohol control systems adopted by almost every state legislature were first fully laid out in a report sponsored by John D. Rockefeller, Jr., and issued in October 1933, shortly before repeal was ratified. Rockefeller's longtime adviser, Raymond Fosdick, was the senior author. Fosdick supervised the group of attorneys and policy analysts, most of whom worked with or for the Institute of Public Administration—a Progressive-era policy institute in New York that Rockefeller had funded for a number of years. The report was issued in press releases to newspapers and magazines over several weeks. Finally the Rockefeller Report (as it was called at the time) was released as a book, *Toward Liquor Control* by Raymond Fosdick and Albert Scott (1933).

Although few at the time recognized it, *Toward Liquor Control* had taken as its basic conclusions virtually all of the central recommendations made thirty years earlier by another elite-sponsored alcohol policy group called the Committee of Fifty. The Committee of Fifty, which was staunchly antiprohibitionist, had produced five books on various aspects of the "alcohol problem" around the turn of the century. Fosdick and the other study members had read the Committee of Fifty's reports and quoted them at length on the corruption and lawlessness resulting from earlier forms of local prohibition. The Rockefeller Report echoed the Committee of Fifty's conclusion that the legitimacy of the law must be of primary concern in liquor regulation. Both reports agreed that the specific content of the law mattered less than that the laws be obeyed. Both reports argued that alcohol regulation required a flexible system that could be continually monitored and adjusted. Further, both reports advised that, if at all possible, government should take over the selling of alcoholic beverages (Billings 1905, Levine 1983, Rumbarger 1989).

The specific plan for alcohol control suggested by *Toward Liquor Control*, and the Rockefeller Report's most controversial proposal, was that each state take over as a public monopoly the retail sale for off-premises consumption of spirits, wine, and beer above 3.2 percent alcohol. As Fosdick and Scott (1933) explained: "The primary task of the [State Alcohol] Authority would be the establishment of a chain of its own retail stores for the sale of the heavier alcoholic beverages by package only." This is the source of the term "package stores" still used today for liquor outlets in many states. The state-run outlets of Canadian provinces, and of Sweden, Norway, and Finland, were cited as working examples of such a plan. This quickly became known as the "monopoly plan" and at the time was usually called the "Rockefeller plan."

For those states not willing to establish government liquor stores, Fosdick and Scott proposed an alternative system: "regulation by license." They cited England as the best example of a working license system. A single, nonpartisan board appointed by the governor would have statewide authority to issue liquor licenses and regulate the industry. "Tied houses" would not be permitted—that is, no retail establishments could be owned directly by or under exclusive contract to a distiller or brewer.

Although it offered guidelines for a licensing system, *Toward Liquor Control* favored the monopoly plan. The possibility of increasing profits, said the authors, would encourage private businesses to sell more alcohol, to buy political influence and lax enforcement, and to violate laws. Rockefeller explained the chief advantage of government-owned liquor stores in his foreword to the book: "Only as the profit motive is eliminated is there any hope of controlling the liquor traffic in the interests of a decent society. To approach the problem from any other angle is only to tinker with it and to ensure failure" (Fosdick and Scott 1933). The irony of a Rockefeller warning about the dangers of the profit motive was not lost on observers in 1933. Rockefeller took such an anticapitalist position because, like others at the time, he had concluded, probably correctly, that government ownership brought greater powers to regulate and control behavior, and ensure obedience to the law.

For both plans, *Toward Liquor Control* outlined a detailed set of matters over which the state agency would have jurisdiction. These included the power to acquire real estate and other capital by purchase, lease, or condemnation; determine and change prices at will; establish a system of personal identification of purchasers; issue permits for and regulate the use of beer and wine for off-premises consumption and for on-premises consumption in hotels, restaurants, clubs, railway dining cars, and passenger boats; require alcohol manufacturers and importers to report on quantities produced and shipped; regulate or eliminate alcohol beverage advertising; determine the internal design, visibility from the street, hours and days of sale, number and locations of alcohol outlets.

In January 1934 a model law based on the guidelines of *Toward Liquor Control* and written by the staff of the Institute for Public Administration was published as a supplement to the *National Municipal Review*. The *Review* was the official journal of the National Municipal League, another Progressive-era policy organization supported by the Rockefellers. The model law and other supporting documents were widely circulated to legislators throughout the country in the months following repeal. State legislators, faced with difficult political choices and with little personal expertise in the complexities of liquor regulation, turned to the authoritative and virtually unchallenged plans of the Rockefeller commission—and the National Municipal League. In a letter in the Rockefeller Archives, one of the model law's authors estimated that the monopoly law was taken almost verbatim by fifteen states, and the licensing law served as the text or draft for many more (Gulick 1977, Levine 1985).

ALCOHOL CONTROL IN OPERATION

Postrepeal regulation transformed the alcohol beverage industry. Finland, the only other nation to have experimented with constitutional prohibition, had nationalized production of spirits. However, such proposals were not seriously discussed in the United States. Instead, production took the form of an oligopoly of relatively few corporations. By the end of the 1930s, four or five years after repeal, roughly four fifths of all distilled liquor made in the United States was manufactured by four corporations. The beer industry, although more diverse nationally because beer required quick and local distribution, was monopolized by region or area. Regulatory agencies preferred to deal with a few large corporations—they were easier to police and to make agreements with, and more likely to be concerned with keeping the image of the industry clean and respectable. This pattern of monopolization was not unique of course; most major American industries—steel, automobiles, soft drinks, chemicals, for example—were increasingly dominated by a few large corporations. (From at least the time of the National Recovery Act at the start of the New Deal, federal government policy often encouraged such concentration. The alcohol industry was exceptional only in how quickly many small producers were overtaken by a few dominant ones.)

Although production became oligopolistic, distribution was splintered and scattered. Perhaps the most important long-term innovation in post-Prohibition alcohol regulation was that it permitted the legal sale of alcohol at a wide variety of sites. Before Prohibition, the saloon had been a single, all-purpose institution—there one drank beer, wine, or spirits, and there one purchased for off-premises consumption a bottle of spirits or a bucket of beer. After repeal, alcohol control created several different types of establishments to sell alcoholic beverages. In most states special stores were designated for selling distilled liquor and wine—often they could not sell any food at all, or even cigarettes. Beer on the other hand was made relatively widely available in bottles and cans—with grocery stores and small markets licensed to sell it. In other words, after Prohibition, sale of bottled alcohol was increasingly separated from the public drinking place. This encouraged the privatization of drinking. Whether alone or with others, drinking became something more commonly done at home—where, it should be noted, drinking patterns were often moderated by family norms (see Zinberg 1984). By 1941 off-premises consumption accounted for the majority of alcohol sales (Harrison and Laine 1936, Kyvig 1979, p. 189).

The character of public drinking was significantly altered by these regulatory changes. A new class of licenses for on-premises consumption of beer only, or of beer and wine, was established and liberally issued to restaurants and cafeterias where eating moderated the character and effects of drinking. This separated the barroom selling distilled liquor and beer as a distinct institution. Many state alcohol control laws made provision for a local option whereby a county government could prohibit specific kinds of liquor selling within its borders. This option has been widely exercised. As late as 1973, of the 3,073 counties in the United States, 672 prohibited sales of distilled liquor by the drink for on-premises consumption, and 545 totally prohibited sales of distilled spirits (Alcohol Beverage Control Administration 1973).

Under alcohol control, all establishments licensed for on-premises consumption of spirits were specifically restricted in ways that shaped the cultural practice of drinking. In some areas control laws attempted to moderate the effects of drinking by encouraging food consumption. For example, spirit sales often were limited to bona fide restaurants with laws specifying how many feet of kitchen space and how many food preparation workers there must be. Most states established restrictions on the number of entrances and their locations (back entrances are usually prohibited); the times of day and days of the week when sales may occur; permissible decorations; degree of visibility of the interior from the street; numbers and uses of other rooms; distance of the establishment from churches, schools, and other alcohol outlets; whether customers may sit at a long bar—a counter in close proximity to the source of alcohol—or whether they must sit at tables and order drinks as one orders food; and the ratio of chair seating to bar seating.

The public character of drinkers' comportment was also regulated. Many states, for example, prohibit dancing or live music except under special license. Most gambling or betting is prohibited, and other games are restricted as well. For many years New York and other states did not allow barrooms to have pinball machines. Many states specifically ban the use of the word *saloon*, others the use of the word *bar*, and some forbid all words to indicate a drinking place. Until about 1980 most drinking establishments in California displayed only a name and a symbol: a tilted glass with a stirrer.

From a pre-Prohibition or Prohibition-era perspective, there are two surprising characteristics of postrepeal alcohol controls. First, most laws and regulations are *obeyed*. Almost all drinking places, for example, stop serving and collect glasses at the required hours; and they observe the regulations about tables, dancing, decorations, signs, entrances, and so on. By and large, this obedience has been relatively easily achieved through careful policing, coupled with the power to revoke or suspend licenses. Operating a liquor-selling business is usually quite profitable compared to other kinds of retail establishments, so owners tend to guard their licenses carefully. Minimum-age drinking laws constitute the one obvious exception to this regulatory success as well as one of the few remaining forms of prohibition. Second, postrepeal alcohol regulation is usually *not* perceived as especially restrictive by customers. The many layers of laws and regulations are rarely noticed; most drinkers take them completely for granted.

A third, less surprising characteristic of postrepeal alcohol control is that policy has not been aimed specifically at maximizing what earlier reformers had called *temperance*—meaning, above all, reducing habitual drunkenness or repeated heavy drinking. In his preface to *Toward Liquor Control* (Fosdick and Scott 1933), Rockefeller maintained that such problems could not be effectively addressed by liquor regulation and that they would have to be taken up by other agencies as part of broader educational and health efforts. Since repeal, these tasks have been adopted by a number of independent and government groups, notably Alcoholics Anonymous and the National Council on Alcoholism, various state and local alcoholism agencies, and, since the early 1970s, the National Institute on Alcohol Abuse and Alcoholism. In recent years some public health professionals have urged that the control system be used more self-consciously to reduce drinking and alcohol-related health problems. Such concerns have by and large been imposed on the system, however, and do not flow from its natural workings.

It is worth noting that whenever states propose adding public health concerns to the control system, the alcohol industry usually offers fierce opposition. This is why Rockefeller pushed to eliminate the profit motive from alcohol sales, even while advocating private production. This is also why Finland chose to organize both hard liquor production and sales as a state monopoly. As a result, the Finnish alcohol industry is relatively less powerful than the American industry, and the Finns have found it easier to make public health a part of their postrepeal control system.

On the other hand, despite all its flaws, postrepeal alcohol control did succeed in turning consumption away from hard liquor and back toward beer. Further, alcohol control (coupled with the Depression and World War II) did keep alcohol consumption below pre-Prohibition levels. In fact, as noted earlier, it was not until 1970 that the total alcohol consumption level of the drinking-age population reached the levels of 1915.

In 1936 a second volume of the Rockefeller-sponsored Liquor Study Commission Report was issued. *After Repeal: A Study of Liquor Control Administration* (Harrison and Lane 1936) analyzed the results of liquor control after "a two-year trial," and described the most important changes and innovations in liquor administration instituted since repeal. The overall thrust of the report was that, with some understandable exceptions, alcohol control worked extremely well. Other observers at the time drew similar conclusions (Sheppard 1938, Shipman 1940). Legalizing alcohol and then regulating it had accomplished what most temperance and prohibition supporters claimed was impossible: alcohol moved from being a scandal, crisis, and constant front-page news story to something routine and manageable, a little-noticed thread in the fabric of American life. For over fifty years alcohol regulation has quietly and effectively organized and managed the production, distribution, and sale of alcohol, as well as much of the social life associated with drinking.

The alcohol control system was and is coercive, although its coercion was not organized like that of Prohibition. This coercion was designed with a certain pragmatic precision that continues to function effectively. Some prohibitionist critics observed at the time of repeal that this system was shaped around the preferences of drinkers and the alcohol industry (Garrison 1933). But as the Committee of Fifty had recommended at the turn of the century, alcohol regulation was not designed to stop all drinking and eliminate the industry, but rather to promote "order, quiet and outward decency." This more modest goal has been largely achieved.

Despite frequent claims to the contrary, alcohol control has of course sought to legislate morality. It has not, however, sought to impose the morality of the nineteenth-century Victorian middle class, who took up the cudgel of temperance. Rather the alcohol control system legislates the more modern morality of the new business and professional middle class, of the corporate elite, and to some extent of the twentieth-century working class. Accordingly, unlike the use of marijuana, heroin, or cocaine, drinking has not been criminalized and pushed beyond the pale of normative and regulatory influence. Moreover, once it ceased to be outlawed, the alcohol industry was no longer dominated by unregulated, illicit entrepreneurs who shot at each other, developed organized crime syndicates, and paid off police and government officials. The leaders of the major alcohol industries are members of the economic establishment with an investment in maintaining order and obedience to law.

Now, over a half-century since Prohibition, it is easy to forget that all this was the outcome of self-conscious public policy and not the "natural" result of market forces or national Zeitgeist. The alcohol control system has worked sufficiently well that it usually goes unnoticed, even by students of Prohibition or American history. For purposes of devising new drug policy options, however, it is important to remember that this particular system was the self-conscious creation of a political and economic elite with the power to institute what it regarded as good and necessary. The alcohol control system they devised is not especially democratic; it does not really address public health or social welfare concerns; and it has produced enormous profits for a handful of large corporations that continue to fight public health measures. However, it has achieved what its designers sought to do: regulate and administer the orderly and lawful distribution of alcoholic beverages in a way that creates little controversy (Beauchamp 1981, Bruun et al. 1975, Levine 1984).

LESSONS FROM ALCOHOL CONTROL

Many different (even contradictory) lessons may be drawn from the story of legalization of alcohol production and sales and the establishment of alcohol control in the United States. Two seem particularly relevant for the drug policy. First, the legalization of drug production and sales and the establishment of drug control along the lines of alcohol control *is* a reasonable and practical policy option. Supporters of alcohol prohibition always claimed that alcohol was a special substance that could never be regulated and sold like other commodities because it was so addicting and dangerous. However, as the last fifty-five years of alcohol control and the experiences of many other societies have shown, the prohibitionists were wrong. The experiences of drug policy in other nations, and the experiences of U.S. pharmaceutical and drugstore regulation, suggest that most if not all psychoactive substances *could* be similarly produced, regulated, sold, and used in a generally lawful and orderly fashion. Therefore, it would mark a significant advance if the current U.S. debate on drug policy could be moved beyond the question of *whether* such a system of legalized drug control is possible; it is. Instead, we think debate should focus on whether a nonmoralistic assessment of the advantages and disadvantages of such a system make it desirable, and what different regulatory options might look like.

A workable system of at least partially legalized drug production and sales—of drug control—would have to be a flexible one, geared to local conditions, as Edward Brecher recommended more than 25 years ago in his landmark study *Licit and Illicit Drugs* (1972). The logic of such a flexible system was also outlined ninety-five years ago by the Committee of Fifty. As with alcohol control, drug control could be implemented so as to reduce substantially, if not eliminate, the illegal drug business and most of the crime, violence, and corruption it produces. Drug control with a public health orientation would also seek to encourage milder and weaker drugs and to make them available in safer forms accompanied by comprehensive education about risks, proper use, and less dangerous modes of ingestion. In other words, a public-health-oriented drug control regime would seek to reverse the tendencies that appear inherent under criminalization, in which production, distribution, and consumption are pushed into deviant subcultures; in which purity is not controlled, dosage is imprecise, and extreme modes of ingestion are the norm.

If a legalized drug control system were designed according to rigorous public health criteria, then the experience of alcohol regulation suggests that, in the long run, drug problems would probably not rise significantly above the levels now present under drug prohibition, and overall consumption might not rise either (see also Nadelmann 1989a). Similarly, if such a public health model of drug control were coupled with increased social services and employment for impoverished inner-city populations, then the abuse of drugs like heroin and cocaine might well be expected to decrease (Brecher 1972, Jonas 1990, Reinarman and Levine 1997).

Having said this, it is incumbent upon us to point to a second lesson that may be inferred from the history of alcohol control: it will be no simple matter to design such a system for drug control. It took a full-time, multi-year effort for the researchers and planners at the Institute of Public Administration to come up with a workable blueprint for post-Prohibition alcohol control. Furthermore, this system has been constantly adjusted ever since. A postdrug-prohibition control system will require far more research, planning, and experimentation, which in turn will require a Rockefeller-like willingness to invest the necessary resources. Useful lessons aside, all this begs a rather big question: Does the political will exist to try or even seriously consider alternative drug policies?

THAT WAS THEN, THIS IS NOW: THE POLITICAL
CONTEXT OF DRUG REFORM

The many differences between the situation of constitutional alcohol prohibition in the early 1930s and drug prohibition at the end of the twentieth
century make radical transformation of U.S. drug law seem unlikely in the
short run. In the 1920s only one substance was at issue. Now there are entire classes of them. Alcohol prohibition was repealed after only fourteen years.
But federal drug prohibition began nearly eighty years ago, when opiates and
cocaine were criminalized, and has been supplemented regularly ever since.
Marijuana was criminalized over fifty years ago, lysergic acid diethylamide
(LSD) twenty years ago, and MDMA (better known as "Ecstasy") in 1984
(Brecher 1972, Goode 1989).

The political context of alcohol, had been in popular recreational use for several millennia before Prohibition. By the early 1930s half of the adults in the United States
drank, and the vast majority of adults in most big cities wished to drink occasionally; they continued to do so during the Prohibition era. Local police were
rarely supporters of alcohol prohibition, and they themselves drank.

Today, however, despite widespread experimentation, even the most
popular illicit drug, marijuana, was used by only about 20 percent of all adults
in the last year. This is a sizable minority, but alcohol prohibition affected the
majority. Further, unlike the 1930s, drug prohibition is supported by most
police and politicians, who believe that all illicit drugs (except, perhaps, marijuana) are extremely dangerous and that no one should use them. There are
no longer any "wet" legislators to criticize prohibitionist policies and introduce
alternatives, only "drys" debating other "drys." To imagine a political context
for all currently illegal drugs comparable to that of alcohol repeal, we would
have to assume that most police and at least half of the elected officials in the
United States were moderate marijuana users, and that a sizable minority had
snorted powder cocaine and eaten psychoactive mushrooms.

In the "Roaring Twenties" a new, urban middle-class generation came to
maturity. They were the first post-Victorian generation and they tended to
oppose what they saw as the repressive, puritanical restrictions of temperance.
Further, by 1930 the political power of the Anglo-American middle class had
been diluted by a large number of immigrants from southern and eastern
Europe, who brought with them cultural traditions that regarded drinking as
a normal part of life. To them, alcohol prohibition seemed a bizarre custom
imposed by moralistic fanatics. By the early 1930s alcohol did not seem as
threatening to as many as it once had. Antidrinking sentiment was weaker
than it had been for 100 years, and it was becoming even weaker. Together
with the widely perceived failures of prohibition, these demographic and cultural shifts helped render national alcohol prohibition politically bankrupt.

There are today few comparable demographic or cultural changes. Most Americans are now as fearful of drugs as middle-class Americans were about alcohol at the start of the century. Current immigrants do not come from drug-using cultures. The baby boomers who popularized the recreational use of marijuana and other drugs in the 1960s are in middle age. While their own experiences with marijuana have made them more knowledgeable about that drug, they are also watching their health, limiting their consumption of illicit and licit drugs, and (as their own parents were) worrying about the drug use of their children.

Over and above natural citizen concern about very real drug problems, antidrug sentiment and support for punitive drug prohibition has been culti-vated by politicians' drug war speeches, mass media scare stories, and multimil-lion-dollar advertising campaigns to a degree that turn-of-the-century temper-ance crusaders would envy (Reinarman and Levine 1997). Indeed, the use of drinking as a scapegoat explanation for social problems, which was so promi-nent in nineteenth- and early twentieth-century temperance and prohibition-ist rhetoric, is reproduced in antidrug campaign rhetoric. Long-standing prob-lems like urban poverty, crime, and school failures are frequently blamed on drugs like crack and heroin. In another parallel with the nineteenth century, abstinence ("Just say no") and the utopian wish for truly effective prohibition are held up as the solutions to urban problems. Billy Sunday's panacea, quoted earlier, of solving America's economic and social problems through alcohol pro-hibition remains alive in the dream that effective drug prohibition and a rig-orous war on drugs can now solve the problems of America's poverty-stricken urban neighborhoods (Reinarman and Levine 1997).

Another difference, as we discussed earlier, was the crucial role of the Great Depression in turning the political and economic elite against prohibi-tion. With food riots and protest marches making headlines, popular discon-tent clearly helped shape the political context in which decisions about repeal and alcohol policy were debated. Despite all our contemporary crises, we are not yet facing the equivalent of the Great Depression. However, even an eco-nomic catastrophe would not necessarily soften attitudes about drug prohibi-tion as it did attitudes about alcohol prohibition.

During the 1920s, and especially the early 1930s, repeal advocates argued that ending prohibition would result in a windfall of revenues from taxes on alcohol sales and from money saved on enforcement. This generally did not come to pass, for the economic needs of a growing government in a deep de-pression were so great that the new revenue was quickly expended. Thus it cannot be automatically assumed that if drug prohibition were lifted, excise taxes on legal drugs and reduced enforcement costs would provide a fiscal boon for governments. With worsening federal and state deficits, much of this money also would be absorbed. Given the shamefully inadequate level of support now provided for drug treatment, however, it is still conceivable that revenues from taxation and licensing could finance the expansion of treatment, counseling, and education that any sound drug control system would require (see Schmoke 1990 and *Hofstra Law Review* 1990 for detailed proposals). In terms of the politics of reform, however, it remains unlikely that the potential fiscal advantages of repeal will by themselves move us toward significant change in U.S. drug law.

The political and intellectual energy that fueled the repeal of alcohol prohibition came from outside the Democratic and Republican parties, and the situation is little different today. In 1928 Al Smith campaigned against prohibition, but the Democratic party provided no leadership, organizational skills, or intellectual support for repeal. A few current political leaders have criticized the ill effects of drug prohibition, but almost all elected officials of both parties have appealed to the electorate by trying to prove only that they are more committed drug warriors than their opponents. Some politicians may join in opposing the war on drugs and working for decriminalization, but it remains unlikely that many candidates for national office will soon take leadership roles in a campaign for drug law reform.

To sum up: the current sociological, economic, and political conditions do not seem especially conducive for radical transformations in U.S. drug policy. At first glance the current context of drug prohibition does not compare favorably with the context in which alcohol prohibition was repealed. However, there are also many signs of shifts in attitudes about drug policies in the U.S and elsewhere, and many signs as well of a growing opposition to harsh drug war policies.

"THE TIMES THEY ARE A-CHANGING": FROM PUNITIVE DRUG PROHIBITION TO REGULATORY DRUG PROHIBITION

In the late 1980s and the 1990s a growing minority of the political and intellectual elite, and of the broader American public, came to support drug policy reform. As with alcohol prohibition in the 1920s, this support for drug policy reform had been generated in part by the cost, harshness, and ineffectiveness of drug prohibition itself. For example, there has been a major shift in media coverage and public opinion from 1986 (when the media and political hysteria about crack cocaine began) to 1996 (when California and Arizona passed medical marijuana initiatives and the media reacted favorably). We think these shifts are just the beginning, and that changes in attitudes and policy are likely to accelerate in the last years of the twentieth century and in the first two decades of the twenty-first century.

While some form of drug prohibition will likely persist in the U.S. for

many years, a considerable range and variety of policies are possible under the
umbrella of a broadly defined system of "prohibition." Among Western societies—all of which have drug prohibition—the U.S. is still at the most repressive end of the continuum.

We use the term *punitive drug prohibition* to name the system of drug law
and policy that came into existence in the U.S. in the 1920s and that has been
the dominant U.S. drug policy since that time. Punitive drug prohibition is
distinguishable from more humane and tolerant forms of drug prohibition by
its heavy reliance on criminal law and imprisonment for use and personal possession of illicit drugs. For nearly eighty years the centerpiece of U.S. drug
policy has been punishment of drug users by criminal law for possessing small
quantities of drugs for personal consumption or for small-scale dealing. And
U.S. drug prohibition has become more punitive over the years—dramatically
so in the 1980s. The committed punitiveness toward drug users sets the U.S.
apart from most other Western societies, each of which has some form of drug
prohibition. These other advanced industrial societies have instituted a broader
range of policy options while still retaining the formal prohibition on commercial production and sales that is required by international treaties.

Punitive drug prohibition can therefore be distinguished from more
tolerant and humane forms of drug prohibition—from what we call *regulatory
drug prohibition*. Though still prohibitionist, regulatory prohibition does not
rely so heavily on arresting and imprisoning men and women for possessing
and using illicit drugs or for small-scale dealing. Punitive drug prohibition and
regulatory drug prohibition can be pictured on a continuum. American policies fall toward the extreme punitive and criminalizing end. The policies of
the Netherlands, for example, especially its marijuana policies, fall toward the
noncriminalizing and regulatory end. Similarly, all forms of alcohol prohibition in the U.S. (throughout the nineteenth century and up to the present)
were varieties of regulatory prohibition because they never criminalized the
use of alcohol or the possession of it for personal consumption. Today many
towns and counties in the U.S. still retain forms of alcohol prohibition. But
no matter what the form of alcohol prohibition, personal possession and use,
even for minors, are not criminalized. The idea of "regulatory prohibition" may
seem peculiar to those used to U.S.-style punitive drug prohibition, but regulatory prohibition has been much more prevalent than punitive prohibition.

In the 1980s the war on drugs made U.S. drug policy even more punitive, expensive, and ineffective in reducing drug abuse. As a direct result, growing numbers of physicians, lawyers, scientists, professors, activists, journalists,
and even a few politicians began to openly question and criticize U.S. drug
policy and punitive drug prohibition itself. In the 1990s they have grown to
be increasingly formidable opponents of American drug policy. They have
pointed out the true costs of punitive drug prohibition, articulated alternative

policies, and made drug policy a contested terrain for the first time in decades. These opponents of punitive prohibition have introduced previously heretical ideas ranging from moderate drug policy reforms and harm reduction and needle exchange programs all the way to decriminalization and full legalization. They have made drug prohibition itself a topic of debate and research and called attention to the fact that U.S.-style drug prohibition is by far the most expensive and repressive of any industrial democracy. The drug policy reformers have been so successful that they prompted the Drug Enforcement Administration to hire a panel of experts to prepare a pamphlet for DEA agents and other prohibitionists explaining how to argue against them. The DEA pamphlet is entitled "How to Hold Your Own in a Drug Legalization Debate" (DEA 1994).

Critics of punitive drug prohibition cut across the political spectrum. They include the wealthy and powerful as well as the poor and powerless. They come from the political right and the left. There are elite professionals and grassroots activists. These opposition voices include such unusual suspects as former prosecutor and now mayor of Baltimore Kurt Schmoke; conservative publisher William F. Buckley, Jr.; Nobel Prize-winning free-market economist Milton Friedman of Stanford University; former Reagan administration Secretary of State George Shultz; longtime TV news anchors Walter Cronkite and Hugh Downs; international financier and philanthropist George Soros; former U.S. Surgeon General Dr. Joycelyn Elders; Nobel Prize-winning novelist Gabriel Garcia Marquez; and members of Congress such as George Crockett and Barney Frank. They have been joined by numerous judges across the court system, those appointed by Republicans as well as Democrats, and by a much larger array of scientists and university professors in medicine, law, and the social and physical sciences. In recent years a number of prominent individuals have come to see the harmful consequences of harsh drug prohibition and lent their support to drug law reform organizations such as the Drug Policy Foundation in Washington, D.C., The Lindesmith Centers in New York City and San Francisco, the National Organization for the Reform of Marijuana Laws in Washington, D.C., and the Harm Reduction Coalition in Washington, San Francisco, and New York.

By the mid-1990s, so many knowledgeable and influential people, from all professions and all points on the political spectrum, had raised so many critical questions about this country's harsh drug prohibition policies that they had become not only a recognizable but a "respectable" opposition. Between 1989 and 1995, trenchant critiques of punitive drug prohibition appeared in a broad range of highly regarded scholarly journals and popular periodicals, including *Science, The Lancet, Harper's, The New York Times, The Wall Street Journal, American Heritage, Harvard Law Review, The American Journal of Public Health, Atlantic Monthly, Daedalus, The Public Interest, Mother Jones, Wash-*

ington Monthly, Milbank Quarterly, Scientific American, Stanford Magazine, The British Medical Journal, The Nation, The Economist, The Journal of the American Medical Association, The Washington Post, Notre Dame Journal of Law, Ethics and Public Policy, Foreign Policy, The New Republic, National Review, The Humanist, and the *New England Journal of Medicine.* These writings dissected the flaws in and laid out workable, effective alternatives to the war on drugs and to American drug prohibition for a large and influential readership. At the level of ideas, floodgates have been opened that moral fundamentalists and other prohibitionists will probably not be able to close again.

In the professions closest to drug problems, for example, there appears to be majority support for alternatives to U.S.-style drug prohibition. The American Bar Association, the American Public Health Association, and the American Medical Association are not known for taking radical stands on public policy issues. Yet each has passed an official resolution criticizing existing drug policies and advocating reforms.

Many of the criminal justice professionals who confront drug offenders every day are opposing current drug policies. In 1993 more than fifty senior federal judges started a boycott of drug cases because they felt the drug control system was not working and that long mandatory sentences were often unjust. Many other local judges have also refused to hand out mandatory minimum sentences for minor drug offenses or are refusing to take drug cases altogether (Treaster 1993; see also Myers 1989). Dozens of police chiefs across the country have quietly made illicit drug use a low priority. The police chief of New Haven openly helped establish needle exchange programs and procedures to divert drug offenders to treatment and social service agencies. Former police chiefs such as Anthony Bouza, Joseph McNamara, Wes Pomeroy, and Frank Jordan (who later became the mayor of San Francisco) have publicly criticized punitive prohibition and called for decriminalization or public health approaches. A recent (nonrandom) survey (McNamara 1995) of some 365 police chiefs, police officers, district attorneys, and judges found that about 90 percent in all groups felt "the U.S. was losing the war on drugs." Many of them supported alternative approaches to drug policy. Even Raymond Kendall, head of the leading international police force, Interpol, admitted in 1993 that the war on drugs was "lost," and that "making drug use a crime is useless and even dangerous" (cited in Fratello 1993, p. 9).

Much of the media is likely to continue to support drug wars and harsh prohibition policies, but there have been a number of notable exceptions and there are signs that more will join them. Further, the media's penchant for new story lines has led at least some journalists to begin reporting the failures, costs, and consequences of the drug war, and to give space to its critics. By the mid-1990s dissenting voices and alternative visions had moved beyond the confines of scholarly journals and public affairs magazines to the more popular and mainstream media. For example, Walter Cronkite, who had once narrated a "Partnership for a Drug Free America" TV spot, produced for his own TV series an hour-long critique of the failures of the drug war and a positive review of alternative policies. An increasing number of nationally syndicated political columnists have written critically of drug wars and punitive prohibition. Many political cartoonists have satirized punitive drug prohibition for yielding a prison building boom when funding to schools and job training had been cut. We believe that these critics in journalism are signs of the significant undercurrents of opposition to U.S. drug policies at major institutions of influence and power.

Until recently, most African-Americans have been correctly perceived as staunch supporters of the drug war and often of punitive prohibition. Since at least the 1940s, heroin and other hard drugs have been more visibly available in urban black neighborhoods than in white neighborhoods. There have always been disproportionately more poor people in black neighborhoods; therefore, black communities have also had disproportionately more people with intractable life problems and disproportionately more people vulnerable to hard drug abuse. The black middle class and wealthy, including professionals, celebrities, and stars have usually avoided questions of drug policy or have taken relatively conventional and conservative stands. Black politicians, whatever their personal views, have typically represented the more culturally conservative sectors of the black community. For many years the single most visible and vocal drug warrior in the United States Congress was Representative Charles Rangel, a black Congressman from Harlem and part of the Upper West Side of Manhattan.

But there have always been opponents of drug wars and prohibition among African-Americans. In 1986 the mayor of Baltimore, Kurt Schmoke, electrified a meeting of the U.S. Conference of Mayors with his keynote address urging them to consider alternatives to drug prohibition, including decriminalization. Schmoke, a graduate of Harvard University and Yale Law School, served five years as an assistant district attorney prosecuting drug cases. His experiences convinced him that drug prohibition was bad for Americans in general and African-Americans in particular. Drug prohibition, he reasoned, created much needed employment for poor young men, especially blacks and Latinos, but only in criminal enterprises; and the "gangster" lifestyle of the young drug dealers distorted values and priorities in black neighborhoods. As a result, prohibition probably increased the spread of hard drugs in poor communities, and those young men in the drug business who were not killed frequently wound up in prison for a long time. Schmoke has not softened his views: he has continued to speak out for drug policy reform and helped convince the governor to allow needle exchange in Maryland. He has introduced other harm reduction measures in Baltimore, and he has been continually reelected.

Over time, growing numbers of black politicians and professionals have withdrawn their support for repressive drug policies or have openly endorsed alternatives. In recent years black politicians have outspokenly criticized the huge disparity in mandatory sentencing laws between those convicted of selling powder cocaine and those convicted of selling smokeable cocaine (crack). The former are disproportionately white, the latter almost entirely black; typically, crack sellers possess much less cocaine but receive mandatory sentences several times to ten times as long as the powder cocaine dealers. African-Americans in Congress along with civil rights, civil liberties, and legal reform organizations have been actively working together to reduce or eliminate this disparity. In 1996 the U.S. Sentencing Commission studied this issue and recommended ending these disparities. The U.S. Congress, however, overwhelmingly voted to retain them. That vote then sparked several riots in prisons overcrowded with young black men serving long mandatory sentences for selling small amounts of crack.

These injustices, along with rising AIDS deaths due to needle sharing, are leading more and more African-Americans to abandon their traditional support for punitive drug prohibition. Growing numbers of black journalists, lawyers, doctors, educators, and ministers are talking about alternatives to prison for drug offenders and questioning the use of prisons and criminal law to deal with drug problems. In part, the black middle class and professionals have been taught and moved by young African-American men and women who have become needle exchange and harm reduction activists in their own communities. Many of these activists are themselves former drug abusers; some are HIV positive or already have AIDS. They are insisting to their neighbors and families that the devastating effects of the drug war in their communities are more damaging and permanent than the effects of drug abuse. These activists have been passionate and articulate exponents of humane approaches to drug problems and advocates of more just social and economic policies. We believe it is likely that more and more African-Americans will come to join them in building humane and effective alternatives. (All of what we have written about the disproportionate effects of the drug war on African-Americans holds true for Hispanic Americans as well. Latino harm reduction and needle exchange activists have bravely brought the alternative perspectives on drug use and policy to their communities as well. And Hispanic professionals in all professions—medicine, law, education, social work, policing—and from all national groups are also increasingly rejecting punitive prohibition and looking for less harmful alternatives.)

Drug policy reform sentiments also have been making substantial headway in other Western industrial democracies. The U.S. has pushed punitive drug prohibition on other nations since the first international treaties outlawing opium at the start of the twentieth century (Bruun et al. 1975, Musto 1973).

But the cumulative consequences of such laws have recently reduced U.S. powers of persuasion. In 1994 Germany and Colombia joined Spain, Italy, the Netherlands, and Poland in moving away from harsh drug policies. In 1996 a Commission of the European Parliament voted to support decriminalization of cannabis. Canada and Australia have also taken steps to shift the axis of their drug policies away from criminal law toward public health. A growing number of local elected officials in Europe have embraced alternative drug policies, sometimes in defiance of their own federal laws. Their reasons are practical: public-health-based drug policies offer more promising results at the local level.

In recounting all these prominent opponents of punitive drug prohibition, we do not want to appear to be subscribing to the "great man" theory of history. Long before most of the people cited above went public with their criticisms, grass-roots activists were directly defying drug laws, often at great risk, to do what they found necessary to meet the human and health needs of drug users. Their work helped open the space in public discourse for the critics and laid the foundation for the alternatives to drug prohibition that are taking shape.

For example, beginning in the early 1980s AIDS activists and addicts spread the word in the hard-to-reach social worlds of injection drug users that sharing needles and syringes can lead to AIDS. They trained each other as volunteer "community health outreach workers" (CHOWs). They walked through the worst neighborhoods and flophouses of America's cities distributing information on AIDS risks and safe injecting procedures. They invented pocket-sized bottles of bleach for cleaning syringes and distributed them to injection drug users. They made referrals to drug treatment, health, and social service agencies. They passed out condoms and safe sex information so that needle-sharers who might be infected with HIV would be less likely to spread the virus to their sexual partners and children. When their shoe-leather ethnographic research found that this was not enough to halt the deadly epidemic, they organized, staffed, and scraped together funds for free needle exchange programs. They found ways to get supplies of technically illegal syringes. They formed associations like the North American Syringe Exchange Network and organized national and international conferences to share their epidemiological and practical knowledge. They got social scientists to help them collect the data necessary to evaluate the effectiveness of their efforts when the government refused to fund such research. And they did all this at their own expense, for no pay.

After years of working underground and risking arrest and jail, these activists had convinced enough police chiefs and city officials that needle exchange should be allowed to operate. By the mid-1990s numerous scientific studies supported their claims and over sixty major U.S. cities had needle exchange programs that reduce needle sharing, help addicts get the help they need, and remove tens of thousands of potentially HIV-contaminated needles each week from streets and parks. The drug war and harsh drug prohibition hindered needle exchange. But by making syringes illegal, scarce, and expensive, U.S. drug policy also made needle sharing inevitable and needle exchange necessary.

On another front, medical marijuana "buyers' clubs" have sprung up. Thousands of people suffering from serious diseases have found marijuana the most effective medicine, sometimes even a lifesaving one, and very often their own physicians have quietly recommended it. The ban on the medical use of marijuana is probably one of the most politically vulnerable parts of U.S. drug policy. Until 1997 the federal government repeatedly refused to allow even the research needed to test the medical efficacy of marijuana despite the fact that the medical use of marijuana has considerable public support. From March 31 through April 5, 1995, an independent polling firm (Belden and Russonello Research and Communications of Washington, DC) surveyed a random representative sample (for the American Civil Liberties Union) of over 1,000 American voters on their attitudes about medical marijuana. More than nine in ten were aware of marijuana's medical uses for glaucoma and nausea from chemotherapy. A surprising majority of 55 per cent favored its legalization for medical purposes, even when the survey question specified that evidence of its efficacy was not yet "conclusive." When the question included the phrase, "when proven effective," support rose to nearly nine in ten. These survey data suggest why a number of state legislatures have passed laws allowing physicians to prescribe marijuana to patients who need it, despite the federal government's refusal to allow such prescriptions. The California legislature passed medical marijuana bills in 1993, 1994, and 1995, each of which was vetoed by the Republican governor. In 1996 voters in California and Arizona passed medical marijuana initiatives by substantial margins, neither subject to veto. A national medical marijuana bill (HR 2618) that would allow physician prescription has attracted sixteen cosponsors in Congress, including several Republicans.

On this issue, as with needle exchange, a few courageous individuals have invoked the tradition of civil disobedience of Ghandi and Martin Luther King, Jr., to make an enormous difference in the lives of thousands of desperately ill Americans. Their defiance of punitive drug prohibition in the interest of humane medical treatment is a moral example that has inspired many others to take up this cause. Given the growth in public support for medical marijuana, it seems likely that continued suppression of it will only help raise public awareness of this additional cost of harsh drug prohibition: seriously ill and often dying patients suffer needless pain because they are denied a relatively safe and effective medicine for the sake of the war on drugs and its defense of a punitive form of drug prohibition.

The policy that we have called *punitive drug prohibition* is rooted in the assumption that illicit drugs are so dangerous that most illicit drug users will likely become abusers or addicts. Ironically, much of the behavior cited to support this assumption stems from the mind sets and social settings of use that are shaped by punitive prohibition itself. By making drug users deviants, our laws marginalize them in deviant subcultures. In a kind of self-fulfilling prophecy, their contact with criminal worlds is maximized while the potentially moderating influences of "normal" society are minimized. Informal social controls, on the other hand, approach users as people who are full citizens of society and who have a self-interest in getting and using information about the risks of the drugs they use. Of course, self-regulated drug use and informal social controls are more likely among those who have balanced lives, who can look forward to a decent life in the future, and who therefore have some stake in conventional life and society (Waldorf et al. 1991). Just as marginalizing drug use into deviant subcultures increases the likelihood of abuse, so does socioeconomic marginalization increase the likelihood of mind sets and the social settings that increase the likelihood of drug problems.

We believe this link between social justice and public health will hold whether the U.S. moves toward more drug wars or toward alternative policies based on harm reduction principles. If social inequality continues to increase, a larger portion of the population will be unable to build balanced lives or look forward to a decent life in the future. Under these conditions it is a virtual certainty that some minority of these dispossessed citizens will develop the distressed mind set and will find themselves in the distressed social settings that make hard drug abuse likely.

However, if more Americans join those who have already recognized that drug problems are embedded in and grow out of larger social problems, then the United States can start shedding the worst aspects of punitive drug prohibition and move in the direction of a more humane and effective drug policy—toward decriminalization and a regulatory prohibition of the sort that the Netherlands has pioneered and that other Western societies have increasingly adopted. This would constitute important steps in reorganizing American society so that more people have the sorts of lives and life chances, and the sorts of mind sets and social settings, in which the risks of drug-related harm are markedly reduced.

We are convinced that someday, as Edward Brecher predicted, most Americans will look back on drug prohibition and judge it to have been repressive, unjust, expensive, and ineffective—a failure. In the twentieth century a dozen major scientific commissions in Britain, Canada, and the United States have recommended alternatives to punitive drug policies. The United States is the only nation where these recommendations have been so consistently ignored (Levine 1994, Trebach 1989, Trebach and Zeese 1990). For starters,

these recommendations should be more widely discussed and better understood in the United States. The experiences of other nations and cities—
notably the Netherlands and Liverpool—also provide living examples of drug
policies that are more humane and, because they are linked to better social
policies, more *effective*. The full range of such alternatives to current drug
policy should be studied and debated—from futuristic visions to pragmatic
reforms that could be implemented immediately (Hofstra Law Review 1990,
Nadelmann 1989a, Trebach and Zeese 1990). For drug policy, such discussion is an essential part of the transition from punitive prohibition to regulation.

REFERENCES

Alcohol Beverage Control Administration (1973). *Licensing and Enforcement*, revised and updated
    by B. W. Corrado. Washington, DC: Joint Committee of the States to Study Alcoholic
    Beverages Laws.
Allen, F. L. (1931). *Only Yesterday: An Informal History of the 1920s*. New York: Harper.
Allsop, K. (1961). *The Bootleggers and Their Era*. London: Hutchinson.
Baron, S. (1962). *Brewed in America: A History of Beer and Ale in the United States*. Boston:
    Little, Brown.
Beauchamp, D. (1981). *Beyond Alcoholism: Alcohol and Public Health Policy*. Philadelphia: Temple
    University Press.
Billings, J. S. (1905). *The Liquor Problem: A Summary of Investigations Conducted by The Commit-
    tee of Fifty and the Origins of Alcohol Control*. Boston: Houghton Mifflin.
Blocker, J. (1989). *American Temperance Movements: Cycles of Reform*. New York: Twane.
Brecher, E. M. (1972). *Licit and Illicit Drugs*. Boston: Little, Brown.
Bruun, K., Edwards, G., Lumio, M., et al. (1975). *Alcohol Control in Public Health Perspective*.
    Helsinki: Finnish Foundation for Alcohol Studies.
Burnham, J. C. (1968). New perspectives on the prohibition "experiment" of the 1920s. *Journal
    of Social History* 2(51):1–67.
Cashman, S. D. (1981). *Prohibition, the Lie of the Land*. New York: Free Press.
Drug Enforcement Administration (1994). *How to Hold Your Own in a Drug Legalization De-
    bate*. Washington, DC: U.S. Department of Justice, Drug Enforcement Administration.
Everest, A. S. (1978). *Rum Across the Border*. Syracuse, NY: Syracuse University Press.
Fosdick, R. B., and Scott, A. L. (1933). *Toward Liquor Control*. New York: Harper.
Fratello, D. H. (1993). Parallel universes. *The Drug Policy Letter*, Spring, 9.
Garrison, W. E. (1933). Fitting the law to the lawless. *Christian Century* 50:1505–1506.
Goode, E. (1989). *Drugs in American Society*. New York: McGraw-Hill.
Gordon, E. (1943). *The Wrecking of the 18th Amendment*. Francestown, NH: Alcohol Information
    Press.
Gulick, L. (1977). Letter to Richard S. Childs, copy to Laurence S. Rockefeller, in Rockefeller
    Archives, May 2.
Gusfield, J. R. (1968). Prohibition: the impact of political utopianism. In *Change and Continuity
    in Twentieth Century America*, ed. J. Braeman et al. Columbus: Ohio State University Press.
——— (1986). *Symbolic Crusade: Status Politics and the American Temperance Movement*, 2nd ed.
    Urbana: University of Illinois Press.
Harrison, L. V., and Laine, E. (1936). *After Repeal: A Study of Liquor Control Administration*. New
    York: Harper.

Hofstra Law Review (1990). *A symposium on drug decriminalization* 18(3).

Jonas, S. (1990). Solving the drug problem: a public health approach to the reduction of the use and abuse of both legal and illegal recreational drugs. *Hofstra Law Review* 18:751–793.

Kerr, J. A. (1985). *Organized for Prohibition: A New History of the Anti-Saloon League.* New Haven, CT: Yale University Press.

Kohler, J. (1973). *Ardent Spirits: The Rise and Fall of Prohibition.* New York: Putnam.

Kyvig, D. E. (1979). *Repealing National Prohibition.* Chicago: University of Chicago Press.

Leuchtenburg, W. E. (1958). *The Perils of Prosperity: 1914–1932.* Chicago: University of Chicago Press.

Levine, H. G. (1978). The discovery of addiction: changing conceptions of habitual drunkenness in America. *Journal of Studies on Alcohol* 39:143–174.

—— (1983). The committee of fifty and the origins of alcohol control. *Journal of Drug Issues* 13:95–116.

—— (1984). The alcohol problem in America: from temperance to prohibition. *British Journal of Addiction* 79:109–119.

—— (1985). The birth of American alcohol control: prohibition, the power elite, and the problem of lawlessness. *Contemporary Drug Problems* 12:63–115.

—— (1994). Drug commissions, the next generation: 'to boldly go. . .' *International Journal of Drug Policy* 5(4):209–215.

Lyle, J. H. (1960). *The Dry and Lawless Years.* Englewood Cliffs, NJ.: Prentice-Hall.

Mäkelaä, K., Room, R. Single, E., et al. (1981). *Alcohol, Society, and the State. 1: A Comparative Study of Alcohol Control.* Toronto: Addiction Research Foundation.

Manchester, W. (1974). *The Glory and the Dream: A Narrative History of America: 1932–1972.* Boston: Little, Brown.

McNamara, J. D. (1995). Changing police attitudes support reform of national drug control policies. Paper presented at the 37th Annual International Conference on Alcohol and Drug Dependence, San Diego, CA, August.

Mertz, C. (1970). *The Dry Decade.* Seattle: University of Washington Press.

Miron, J. A., and Zweibel, J. (1991). Alcohol consumption during prohibition. *American Economic Association Papers and Proceedings* 81:242–247.

Moore, M., and Gerstein, D. R., eds. (1981). *Alcohol and Public Policy: Beyond the Shadow of Prohibition.* Washington: National Academy Press.

Morgan, J. (1991). Was alcohol prohibition good for the nation's health? Working paper. School of Medicine, City University of New York.

Murphy, S., Waldorf, D., and Reinarman, C. (1991). Drifting into dealing: becoming a cocaine seller. *Qualitative Sociology* 13(4):321–343.

Muscatine, D., Amerine, M., and Thompson, B. (1984). *The University of California Book of California Wine.* Berkeley: University of California Press.

Musto, D. (1973). *The American Disease: Origins of Narcotic Control.* New Haven, CT: Yale University Press.

Myers, M. A. (1989). Symbolic policy and the sentencing of drug offenders. *Law and Society Review* 23:295–315.

Nadelmann, E. (1989a). Drug Prohibition in the U.S.: costs, consequences, and alternatives. *Science* 245:939–947.

—— (1989b). Response to letters. *Science* 246:1104–1105.

Odegard, P. (1928). *Pressure Politics: The Story of the Anti-Saloon League.* New York: Columbia University Press.

Piven, F. F., and Cloward, R. (1971). *Regulating the Poor: The Functions of Public Welfare.* New York: Pantheon.

—— (1977). *Poor People's Movements.* New York: Pantheon.

Reinarman, C., and Levine, H. G. (1997). *Crack in America: Demon Drugs and Social Justice.* Berkeley: University of California Press.

Room, R. G. W. (1988). The dialectic of drinking in Australian life: from the rum corps to the wine column. *Australian Drug and Alcohol Review* 7:413–437.

Rorabaugh, W. J. (1979). *The Alcoholic Republic: An American Tradition.* New York: Oxford University Press.

Rumbarger, J. J. (1989). *Profits, Power, and Prohibition: Alcohol Reform and the Industrializing of America, 1800–1930.* Albany: State University of New York Press.

Schmoke, K. L. (1990). An argument in favor of decriminalization. *Hofstra Law Review* 18:501–525.

Sheppard, J. S. (1938). After five years, what has repeal achieved? *New York Times Magazine,* December 4.

Shipman, G. (1940). State administrative machinery for liquor control. *Law and Contemporary Problems* 7:600–620.

Sinclair, A. (1964). *Era of Excess: A Social History of the Prohibition Movement.* New York: Harper.

Single, E., Morgan, P., and Delint, J., eds. (1981). *Alcohol, Society, and the State. 2: The Social History of Control Policy in Seven Countries.* Toronto: Addiction Research Foundation.

Thornton, M. (1991). Alcohol prohibition was a failure. Policy Analysis Report No. 157. Washington, DC: Cato Institute.

Timberlake, J. H. (1963). *Prohibition and the Progressive Movement, 1900–1920.* Cambridge, MA: Harvard University Press.

Treaster, J. B. (1993). U.S. judges, protecting policies, are declining to take drug cases. *New York Times,* April 17, A7.

Trebach, A. S. (1989). Ignoring the great commission reports. *The Drug Policy Letter* (Sept.-Oct.):5.

Trebach, A. S., and Zeese, K. B., eds. (1990). *Drug Prohibition and the Conscience of Nations.* Washington, DC: Drug Policy Foundation.

Tyrell, I. (1979). *Sobering Up: From Temperance to Prohibition in Antebellum America, 1800–1860.* Westport, CT: Greenwood.

Waldorf, D., Reinarman, C., and Murphy, S. (1991). *Cocaine Changes: The Experience of Using and Quitting.* Philadelphia: Temple University Press.

Warburton, C. (1932). *The Economic Results of Prohibition.* New York: Columbia University Press.

Wickersham Commission (National Commission on Law Observance and Enforcement) (1931). *Report on Enforcement of the Prohibition Laws of the United States.* HR 722, 71st Congress, 1st Session. Washington, DC.

Williams, C. D., Stinson, F. S., Steward, S. L., and Dufor, M. C. (1995). Apparent per capita alcohol consumption: national, state, and regional trends, 1977–93. NIAAA Surveillance Report #35, December. Washington, DC: U.S. Department of Health and Human Services, Public Health Service, Institute of Health.

Williams, T. (1989). *Cocaine Kids: The Inside Story of a Teenage Drug Ring.* Reading, MA: Addison-Wesley.

Zinberg, N. E. (1984). *Drug, Set, and Setting: The Basis for Controlled Intoxicant Use.* New Haven, CT: Yale University Press.

11

Ending the International Drug War [1]

Ted Galen Carpenter

United State officials have waged a vigorous campaign against illegal drugs internationally as well as domestically. Washington has taken four approaches to eradicating the supply of such drugs: global agreements, regional and subregional agreements, bilateral agreements with drug-producing or drug-transiting countries, and unilateral coercive measures.

The U.S. government has long been involved in global efforts to stem the trafficking in illegal drugs. Indeed, the first of those measures, the 1912 Hague Opium Convention, predated the passage of the Harrison Act, America's domestic venture in drug prohibition. In the decades since the Hague Convention, the United States has been a signatory to other agreements, including the 1925 Geneva Conventions, the 1961 United Nations Single Convention on Narcotic Drugs, the 1972 Convention on Psychotropic Substances, and the 1988 United Nations Convention Against Illicit Traffic in Narcotic Drugs and Psychotropic Substances. Washington also gave tangible expression to its commitment to the terms of such agreements by supporting the programs of the UN Fund for Drug Abuse, the UN Commission on Narcotic Drugs, and other agencies.[2]

America's multilateral efforts include not only global conventions and agreements but a number of regional and subregional arrangements (especially with Latin-American countries). There is also a network of bilateral agreements with countries to facilitate drug eradication and interdiction and to prosecute related crimes, such as money laundering. Most of those agreements are with nations in the Western hemisphere, but they have been concluded with drug-producing countries in other parts of the world (e.g., Turkey and Thailand) as well. In addition to its involvement in multilateral and bilateral agreements, the United States has sought to shape the behavior of other nations on the drug issue through the threat of economic sanctions outlined in the International Narcotics Control Act of 1986 and its successor, the International Narcotics Control Act of 1988.

Washington has, in short, helped to erect a complex structure of international arrangements designed to enforce a drug prohibitionist strategy. Indeed, the United States has been, especially in recent decades, the principal architect of that structure. Any decision by U.S. leaders to change policy and opt for the legalization of drugs would therefore cause an array of international complications. The prospect of such complications is not a sufficient reason for rejecting the option of legalization, however. The horrendous domestic consequences of drug prohibition would be sufficient reason to choose a different course, regardless of the international reaction. Moreover, the possibility of an adverse reaction from some countries must be weighed against the frictions in relations already caused by Washington's attempts to coerce other societies into enlisting in the war on drugs. On balance, the United States would be better off internationally as well as domestically if it opted for drug legalization.

GLOBAL ANTIDRUG ARCHITECTURE

The modern era in international antidrug policy can be dated from the 1961 United Nations Single Convention on Narcotic Drugs.[3] That convention brought together, updated, and strengthened the various global accords that had been signed since the 1912 Hague Convention. The 1961 agreement put drugs that are often abused onto four schedules—schedules one and four included the drugs most likely to be abused—and then restricted their cultivation, production, transfer, and use. The convention limited the drugs on schedule one to medical and scientific uses and outlawed their possession, trade, or production for all other purposes. In addition to that broad prohibition, the convention contained several specific articles restricting coca, cannabis, and opium. Article 22 stated that the parties should prohibit cultivation of opium poppies, coca bushes, and cannabis plants if that was the best way to prevent illegal trafficking. Article 23 required any government allowing opium cultivation to set up an agency to license growers and to buy the entire crop produced. Such an agency would also have the sole right to export or to import opium. Article 24 limited the opium exports of producing countries and Articles 26 and 28 placed similar limits on the exports of cannabis and coca leaves. Article 27 did, however, allow for the cultivation of coca leaves for flavoring, provided the narcotic alkaloids in the leaves were removed. In a concession to countries where there were traditional uses of some drug plants (e.g., Andean populations' chewing of coca leaves), some restrictions were waived for a grace period of fifteen to twenty-five years, depending on the specific practice. Thus, although the convention made it illegal to cultivate coca to create cocaine, up until 1986 it was legal for local growers to cultivate coca to be chewed.

Other sections of the convention provided for various enforcement measures. A narcotics board was created to receive reports from participating countries stating the quantity of restricted drugs they expected to legitimately use in the coming year as well as reports detailing the consumption, import, export, seizure, and disposal of illegally produced drugs for the previous year. Article 39 mandated criminal penalties for people engaged in trafficking and other drug-related activities, subject to the laws and constitutions of the countries involved.

The 1972 Protocol Amending the Single Convention strengthened the 1961 convention in several ways.[4] It broadened the mission of the narcotics board, requiring the board to attempt to limit the cultivation and production of drug crops. The protocol also asked parties prohibiting cultivation to seize and destroy illicitly cultivated plants. Finally, it made drug offenses extraditable offenses.

Later in 1972 the international community adopted the Convention on Psychotropic Substances, which substantially extended and broadened the scope of the 1961 convention.[5] Whereas the 1961 convention had restricted only certain substances, and in fact dealt with a relatively small number of specific drugs, the Convention on Psychotropic Substances limited not only a new list of drugs (again on four schedules) and the products that contain them, but also any substance capable of producing dependence, hallucinations, depression, or elation due to stimulation of the central nervous system and any substance with the same potential for abuse as drugs on any of the schedules. In addition, whereas many enforcement provisions of the 1961 convention had been relatively vague, the 1972 convention mandated a number of specific enforcement procedures.

Although the latter convention allowed drugs on schedules two, three, and four to be used for medical and scientific purposes, it severely limited their use in various ways. In particular, it required licenses for the manufacture, trade, and distribution of such drugs. It also required prescriptions for the medical supply of drugs on those three schedules and required virtually everyone involved with a restricted drug—including manufacturers, importers, exporters, medical and scientific users, and distributors—to keep detailed records. To guarantee that the provisions of the convention would be met, it required periodic inspections of those records by the governments of signatory states. Restrictions on the drugs on schedule one (including marijuana) were even more severe. All uses of those drugs were prohibited—except for very limited medical use and scientific experiments, which then required all of the previously mentioned safeguards for schedules two, three, and four.

The 1972 convention also included enforcement provisions that strengthened those of its 1961 predecessor. Provisions included more extensive reports to the drug board, a request that countries increase cooperation to stop illegal drug traffic, and the criminalization of activity that violated any laws passed pursuant to the treaty.

The most recent and important global agreement is the 1988 United Nations Convention Against Illicit Traffic in Narcotic Drugs and Psychotropic Substances.[6] It reinforces many provisions of the 1961 and 1972 conventions and expands their enforcement by attacking money laundering and tightening controls over trade in drug precursors and other chemicals used to make drugs and equipment used to manufacture or process drugs. The convention also encourages greater cooperation among UN member-states through more liberal extradition proceedings, mutual legal assistance, and the establishment of multinational law enforcement and paramilitary teams to fight the drug war.

In Article 3 the convention lists various drug offenses and sanctions. It first restates the standard list of crimes from the 1961 and 1972 agreements and then requires countries to eradicate illicitly cultivated narcotic plants and eliminate the demand for narcotic drugs and psychotropic substances. It goes on to list a variety of new crimes. It is now an offense to manufacture, transfer, distribute, or possess equipment intended for drug plant cultivation or drug production. Financing of drug-related activities (cultivation, import, etc.) is barred, as is the knowing transfer or conversion of property derived from any drug offense or the concealment of the true nature of such property.

Signatories are obligated to pass legislation authorizing the confiscation of illicit drugs and their proceeds, and each country is requested to seize drug assets when asked to do so by another country. That obligation includes the collateral requirement that governments have legal access to domestic bank records—with all the implications for privacy rights of such a power. Signatories are also requested to expedite extradition proceedings for drug offenders. The parties are required to render several forms of mutual legal aid including taking evidence; effecting searches and seizures; and identifying or tracing proceeds, property, and instrumentalities for evidentiary purposes in drug-trafficking cases.

The final provisions of the 1988 convention require parties to take certain measures to prevent the transport of illicit drugs. Article 15 deals with commercial carriers and suggests that parties follow certain guidelines in handling baggage and that carriers train their personnel to identify suspicious consignments. Article 17 allows a party to request the assistance of other parties to prevent illicit traffic on a ship flying its flag. When a party believes that a ship flying another party's flag is trafficking in drugs, the first party can ask the flag state for authorization to board and search the vessel.

PROLIFERATION OF REGIONAL AND
BILATERAL AGREEMENTS

Washington has had a significant role in drafting all of the global agreements, and it has played a preeminent role in sculpting the provisions of the agreements and conventions enacted since the 1960s. That increasing prominence corresponds to a surge in the intensity of the U.S. commitment to the fight against both domestic drug use and international drug trafficking. The increased intensity has also been expressed in a variety of bilateral and regional (western hemispheric) initiatives.

One noticeable upsurge of attention and resources occurred in the 1960s and early 1970s as drug use became more prevalent in America. The United States and Turkey established bilateral arrangements for the suppression of opium poppy cultivation in the mid-1960s, and the administrations of Richard Nixon and Gerald Ford adopted even more aggressive programs with respect to marijuana cultivation in Mexico during the following decade.[7] The network of bilateral ties has steadily expanded since then. By 1996 the United States had major bilateral agreements with fourteen nations and more limited arrangements with dozens more. As just one measure of the extent of Washington's emphasis on that aspect of the international drug war, the Drug Enforcement Administration now maintains seventy offices in forty-nine countries.[8]

A second surge of U.S. pressure took place during the administrations of Ronald Reagan and George Bush—especially after 1986 when the United States officially declared drug trafficking a threat to national security.[9] The escalating U.S. emphasis on stemming the supply of illegal drugs was symbolized by the drug policy summit attended by Bush and the presidents of Colombia, Peru, and Bolivia in Cartagena, Colombia, in February 1990. The Declaration of Cartagena that emerged from that meeting proclaimed the formation of an "antidrug cartel." It committed the four governments to a comprehensive multilateral strategy to fight all facets of the drug trade. The Andean regimes pledged to increase their efforts to disrupt trafficking patterns, prevent the diversion of essential chemicals to drug production, and discourage illicit coca cultivation. The United States pledged to reduce the domestic demand for drugs and to increase assistance to the Andean countries to reduce the supply of illegal drugs, develop alternative sources of income for coca growers, and enhance interdiction capabilities.[10]

The Cartagena summit led to a noticeable increase in U.S. aid dollars to drug-source countries in Latin America. Counternarcotics assistance for Colombia during the first year included $21 million to support the national police as the lead antinarcotics force; nearly $72 million in foreign military assistance programs to provide equipment, services, and training for the counternarcotics efforts of the armed forces; and $3.7 million in economic and developmental aid. Antinarcotics aid to Bolivia included $15.7 million for programs to strengthen law enforcement and interdiction capabilities; $39.1 million in foreign military assistance funds to support the antidrug role of the armed forces (plus $7.8 million in Department of Defense equipment, services, and training); and $40.5 million in economic assistance. Peru received $20 million in law enforcement support and $4.3 million in economic support.[11] Antidrug aid has continued to flow to the Andean countries in the years since the Cartagena summit, although never the amounts originally hoped for by those countries. There is also little evidence that the aid given has had a significant impact on the quantity of illegal drugs coming out of those countries.

The Cartagena summit was followed two years later by a larger gathering of hemispheric leaders in San Antonio, Texas. In contrast to the Cartagena Declaration, the San Antonio Declaration was adopted by all members of the Organization of American States.[12] It calls on member states to appropriate funds to create new law enforcement training centers, share information about the activities of traffickers, provide one another with technical assistance to monitor drug trafficking, prevent the use of private aircraft and airfields for drug trafficking, establish means to verify the registry of vehicles suspected of trafficking, control chemicals used to manufacture drugs, and better monitor commercial carriers to prevent their use for drug smuggling. The document also reaffirms the 1988 UN convention provisions relating to money laundering, mutual legal assistance, and strengthening the administration of justice. The countries agree to seek agreements to share any assets seized from or forfeited by drug traffickers, to control the export of firearms, and to take other cooperative measures.

UNILATERAL MEASURES

Washington's growing enthusiasm for the international drug war in recent decades has led to increased pressure on regimes and societies that did not fully share that enthusiasm. Before the Reagan administration's escalation of the antidrug crusade, several countries, principally in the Third World, imposed no legal penalties for the possession and/or cultivation of various drugs, despite the governments' supposed obligations under the UN conventions. For example, marijuana cultivation was legal in Afghanistan, Bangladesh, India, Pakistan, and other nations. Bolivia, Peru, Uruguay, and Paraguay permitted the possession of coca leaf and its derivatives, and Bolivia and seven other countries tolerated coca cultivation as well. Opium poppy cultivation was legal in several countries, most notably Morocco and Pakistan.[13]

The absence of legal sanctions was not generally an oversight; it reflected significant differences in cultural norms between the United States and those countries. Some Third World societies exhibited a more permissive attitude toward moderate drug use. Opium had long enjoyed at least a quasi-legitimate status in Southeast Asia. Similarly, the populations of Ecuador, Bolivia, and Peru used raw coca and the coca plant itself for a variety of accepted purposes. Bolivian and Peruvian peasants in the Andes, for example, routinely chewed the coca leaf to dull hunger pains and to alleviate the physical stresses of work at high altitudes; coca tea was a mild stimulant routinely used and enjoyed throughout the society. Rural Jamaicans often drank tea brewed from marijuana for both social and medicinal purposes.[14] (Indeed, such traditional practices continue largely unabated to the present day.)

Given those cultural differences, many of the drug-source countries reacted with a mixture of apathy and hostility when U.S. leaders sought to enlist them in Washington's escalating campaign against drugs. Moreover, until recently, those societies did not have serious internal drug abuse problems; consequently Third World populations felt that they were being asked to radically alter their own traditions and assume onerous law enforcement burdens merely to alleviate a domestic American problem.[15]

Washington showed little tolerance for "slackers" in the drug war. One response was to pressure foreign governments to pass laws banning previously legal drug cultivation or possession. (More recently, similar U.S. coercion was evident in campaigns to "persuade" various countries to pass stringent statutes against money laundering—modeled after American laws.)

The centerpiece of Washington's coercive strategy has been the International Narcotics Control Act of 1988.[16] This statute requires "source" countries (drug-producing or drug-transiting nations) to participate in eradication and interdiction programs to be eligible for U.S. foreign aid and various trade preferences. The number of nations that must fulfill that requirement has been growing in recent years and now includes countries that are relatively minor players in the drug trade.

The "certification" process mandated by Congress requires the President to determine annually whether the government of a drug-source country has cooperated sufficiently in eradication and interdiction efforts. In certifying cooperation, the President is obliged to consider a variety of factors, but the principal question is whether a foreign government has achieved the maximum possible reduction in illicit drug production or trafficking. Although the standards give the President considerable latitude—and he can even waive the requirements if he states explicitly that doing so is in the national interest—congressional pressure to decertify recalcitrant regimes is omnipresent. Moreover, Congress has the power to reject the President's determination of compliance.

If the President does not certify that a drug-source country is in compliance—or if Congress overrules his certification—some sanctions are imposed automatically; others are at the discretion of the President.[17] The mere threat of decertification gives the United States a potent diplomatic and political weapon against reluctant governments, particularly in Latin America. Although the dismal record of U.S. bilateral and multilateral assistance programs throughout the world suggests that recipient countries would be better off without the crutch of foreign aid, the sudden withdrawal of U.S. subsidies could create major economic disruptions. The imposition of trade sanctions would have an even more devastating impact on nations whose economies are heavily dependent on access to the U.S. market.

Washington has frequently used the threat of sanctions to pressure the governments of drug-source countries. Actual decertification is relatively rare, and typically only countries in which the United States has little influence are decertified.[18] (The decertification of Colombia in 1996, however, suggests that U.S. policy may be getting bolder.)

The explicit or implicit threat of decertification is used against a wider range of regimes and with greater effect. A national interest waiver, for example, is an unsubtle warning that Washington is displeased and that decertification may be forthcoming the next year. That was clearly the message sent to Colombia in 1995 when President Clinton granted that country a national interest waiver. Bogotá's conduct did not change sufficiently in the Clinton administration's judgment, and Colombia was indeed decertified in 1996.

Sometimes messages of U.S. displeasure are sent even when the cooperation of other countries is officially certified. In its 1988 drug strategy report to Congress, for example, the State Department stated that although the law required justifications only for countries given a national interest certification, the department had "taken an unusual step and provided justifications for two countries that are certified as fully cooperating. We are sending a signal to Colombia and Mexico."[19] Only the most obtuse Colombian or Mexican official would have failed to discern the underlying threat: unless greater cooperation was forthcoming, the next report might recommend decertification and its attendant penalties.

An even more informal, but still potent, form of coercion was also evident when Washington announced that it was postponing $94 million in military and economic aid to Peru for fiscal year 1991 because it could not obtain an agreement from the government of Alberto Fujimori on a coordinated antidrug strategy.[20] The U.S. action was notable because Peru had been officially certified as cooperating with U.S. efforts. The timing of the announcement was also revealing; it occurred in the midst of intensive negotiations with Lima about the composition and orientation of antidrug programs. Postponing the delivery of aid moneys, therefore, was probably a tactical maneuver by Washington to gain a decisive advantage in those negotiations.

A similar informal threat was made to Mexico in 1996. In the weeks leading up to the annual certification announcement, Clinton administration officials repeatedly leaked reports to the news media that Colombia would be decertified and Mexico would probably be given a national interest waiver. The resulting press reports also suggested that administration officials were valiantly resisting pressure from influential members of Congress who wanted to see both countries decertified.[21] The official announcement came as a surprise, because although Colombia was decertified, Mexico received full certification without the national interest waiver. Nevertheless, the underlying message of the administration's preannouncement war of nerves was that Mexico was heading down the same path as Colombia and would ultimately end up at the same destination if major policy changes did not take place immediately.

PROBABLE INTERNATIONAL RAMIFICATIONS
OF LEGALIZATION

The United States has given great impetus to the international drug war and is the principal architect of an elaborate structure of unilateral, bilateral, and multilateral measures designed to wage that war. A decision by U.S. leaders to abandon the prohibitionist strategy would therefore have enormous repercussions. Foreign governments might well be bewildered by such a dramatic reversal of policy, and their reactions cannot be predicted with precision.

From a legal standpoint the international agreements and conventions to which the United States is a party would continue in force, even if Washington no longer adhered to their provisions. The United States could, of course, call for a global conference to formally repeal the various agreements. That step would at least afford U.S. officials the opportunity to present a detailed explanation of the reasons for the country's decision to withdraw from the prohibitionist system. (The United States could adopt a similar course on the regional level at a meeting of the Organization of American States.)

If the United States could convince the other members of the international community to terminate the legal framework of global drug prohibition, it would minimize the trauma and disruption caused by such a dramatic policy shift. It is just as likely, though, that many of the other UN member-states would use the occasion of a new conference to attempt to pressure the United States not to embrace legalization. The United States spent decades persuading, cajoling, and bribing other nations to wage a coordinated war against drugs; it is a bit much to expect those same countries to reverse course at Washington's call. A more practical strategy might be for the United States to renounce its international commitments and simply tolerate the probable recriminations, bruised feelings, and policy turbulence.

Ultimately, the issue is not whether the international system of drug prohibition would legally remain in effect after a U.S. withdrawal. The more pertinent question is whether such agreements would have any viability without U.S. support and participation. American proponents of the drug war point to the harassment sometimes meted out to the Netherlands by its partners in the European Union because of that country's de facto legalization of marijuana possession, and they warn that the United States might encounter similar problems.[22] Such concerns are misplaced; the U.S. is not the Netherlands. On the drug issue as on so many others, the United States is the 800-pound gorilla in the international system. It seems highly improbable that a collection of small and mid-sized states would attempt to continue waging a vigorous campaign against drug trafficking without U.S. leadership and contrary to Washington's policy preferences.

An American withdrawal from the international drug war would probably sound the death knell for that strategy. It is difficult to imagine, for example, the Latin-American countries being able to fulfill the pledges they made in the Cartagena and San Antonio declarations if U.S. antidrug aid moneys stopped flowing. That would be true even if those governments wanted to persist in the costly and often violent struggle against entrenched domestic political and economic constituencies that benefit from the drug trade. And there is considerable doubt that the Andean governments or the government of Mexico would have the inclination to do so.

Even if U.S. abandonment of drug prohibition did cause strained relations with some countries, the resulting friction could scarcely match the animosity that Washington's crusading policies have created. Indeed, the reaction in many nations, particularly the drug-producing and drug-transiting countries of Latin America, might well be relief. During the past quarter century or so, the United States has frequently played the bully, demanding that other governments and societies bend to Washington's views of how to deal with the problem of drug abuse. U.S. officials have shown little sensitivity to indigenous laws or customs that run counter to Washington's policy agenda. Those officials exhibit almost no understanding of, much less sympathy with, the difficulties encountered by foreign governments that are asked to confront powerful political and economic groups in the name of the war on drugs. Worst of all, foreign officials who dare to question the wisdom of America's drug policies have been subjected to campaigns of character assassination and demands for their removal from office.[23] That approach has created a sizeable reservoir of resentment.

In recent years serious frictions have even developed between the United States and the governments or populations of such distant drug-source countries as Myanmar (Burma) and Thailand.[24] But it is in the western hemisphere that Washington's "Ugly American" tactics have created the most problems.

In addition to the threat of decertification and the resulting economic sanctions, those tactics have assumed a variety of forms. U.S. ambassadors in source countries repeatedly demand that officials they suspect are involved in drug trafficking—or merely oppose the war on drugs—be dismissed. An interview by ABC News anchor Peter Jennings with then Bolivian president Jaime Paz Zamora in December 1992 suggested the extent of U.S. "influence" on political appointments in that country.

JENNINGS: Does the American ambassador in Bolivia have the power to make or break police officers, military officers, even politicians?
ZAMORA: (through interpreter) Without a doubt.
JENNINGS: Does this mean that if the U.S. ambassador doesn't like a man you've appointed to government, he can ask you to get rid of him?
ZAMORA: (through interpreter) Yes, in practice it works that way.[25]

Indeed, less than two years earlier, three high-level officials in Paz Zamora's government had been forced to resign because of U.S. pressure.

Washington's appetite for dictating political outcomes in Latin America has grown since the interview with Paz Zamora. U.S. officials have openly opposed Colombian president Ernesto Samper, who they charge knowingly received money from the drug cartels during his successful bid for the presidency. When Colombia's Chamber of Representatives examined the charges and exonerated Samper, the Clinton administration denounced the outcome and warned that the decision would make the imposition of economic sanctions more likely.[26] Whatever the merits of the allegations against Samper—and there is credible evidence of financial links between the cartels and his campaign, although it is not certain that Samper was aware of the contributions—the lack of U.S. respect for the political process in a sister democracy is palpable and infuriates many Colombians. The tensions between Washington and Bogotá have produced name-calling and an assortment of other nasty incidents that suggest a rapidly deteriorating relationship. Most recently, a close associate of Samper's publicly called Assistant Secretary of State Robert Gelbard a "liar," and the United States accused Colombia's secret police of tapping the U.S. ambassador's phone and following the ambassador whenever he left the embassy.[27]

The most odious example of Washington's Ugly American tactics was the U.S.-sponsored kidnapping of Mexican physician Humberto Alvarez Machain, whom the Drug Enforcement Administration accused of participating in the 1985 torture and murder of DEA agent Enrique Camarena. Frustrated by problems in getting the Mexican government to extradite Alvarez to the United States for trial under provisions of the treaty between the two countries, the DEA offered a bounty for his kidnapping, a lure that ultimately produced the desired result in 1990. The U.S. Supreme Court considered the sordid affair in June 1992 and ruled that the extradition treaty did not bar U.S. authorities from using other means to bring an accused party to trial.

From the standpoint of constitutional law, the Court's decision was relatively narrow. The majority certainly did not pass judgment on whether kidnapping was wise policy in terms of U.S. relations with hemispheric neighbors.[28] Throughout Latin America, however, the Court's ruling was widely interpreted as giving a green light to the executive branch to apprehend accused drug traffickers in another country without the consent of that country's government. Ill-considered comments by Bush administration officials exacerbated that fear, and the *Alvarez* case became a new symbol of Yankee arrogance.

The aftermath of the Court's decision (Alvarez's criminal trial) made matters even worse. To the chagrin of the DEA, a federal judge acquitted the accused with caustic comments about the weakness of the government's case. Instead of quietly accepting defeat, Washington then demanded that Mexico put Alvarez on trial to honor the spirit of the extradition treaty— the same treaty U.S. officials had circumvented up to that point. Not only did the demand deserve a prize for chutzpah, it again inflamed anti-U.S. sentiment in Mexico and elsewhere in the hemisphere.

But even if U.S. leaders were to become more subtle in their tactics, they would still be asking the governments of drug-source countries to do the impossible. The reality is that the drug trade has become an important— in some case vital—component of the economies of numerous nations. One expert estimates the total value of the global drug trade at $500 billion per year.[29] That estimate may be high; other studies cite figures of $180 billion to $300 billion.[30] Nevertheless, there is little doubt that the trade generates

billions of dollars each year for the economies of major drug-source countries, especially those in Latin America and Southeast Asia's golden triangle.
U.S. and Colombian officials, for example, believe that the narcotraffickers
invest $5 billion to $7 billion annually in that country—and that figure represents only about half of their total proceeds.[31] The commerce in illegal drugs
has become so lucrative in northern Mexico that traffickers reportedly pay
as much as $500 million a year just in protection money to corrupt officials.
Although that might seem an enormous outlay, it is a small portion of the
$10 billion to $30 billion the drug kingpins take in.[32] From the standpoint
of economics, demanding that the authorities in such countries as Colombia, Mexico, and Thailand wage a serious war on drugs is akin to demanding that Japan eradicate its electronics or automobile industry.

Predictably, such intense economic activity has given rise to powerful
political constituencies. Washington's prohibitionist strategy places incumbent regimes in a no-win situation. If they defy the United States (or even if
they appear evasive), they risk decertification and the resulting economic sanctions. Yet those governments run a serious political risk—as well as a risk to
the personal safety of public officials—if they respond to U.S. pressure and
try to put drug-trafficking organizations out of business. The violence that
has periodically convulsed Colombia during the past decade as successive
governments have attacked the Medellín and Cali cartels is merely an extreme example of that problem.

Given the economic realities, the U.S.-led international campaign against
illegal drugs has failed to make a significant impact on the supply. The figures in the U.S. State Department's 1996 *International Narcotics Control Strategy Report* confirm that point. Worldwide potential illicit production of opium
gum in 1995 was 4,157 metric tons; in 1994 it had been 3,409 and in 1987,
2,242. The pattern for coca leaf was only marginally more encouraging. The
1995 figure was 309,400 metric tons compared to 290,900 in 1994 and 291,100
in 1987. For cannabis it was 11,489 metric tons in 1995, 13,386 in 1994, and
13,693 in 1987.[33] The data merely confirm what many policy experts—even
those who do not favor legalization—have concluded for years: the international supply-side campaign against drugs has produced meager results.[34]

Legalization would hardly be a panacea internationally any more than
it would be domestically. Not all nations would follow the U.S. lead and
abandon their domestic prohibitionist strategies. Consequently, a black market
in drugs would continue to exist, although it would certainly be smaller and
have to operate in competition with a legal market. The existence of a legal
market would enable legitimate business people to enter the trade, and that
would assuredly have a beneficial effect on crime rates. One dare not be
excessively optimistic on that score, however. The most violence-prone criminal elements have had the trade to themselves for decades and have become

thoroughly entrenched. It would not be easy for honest businesses to displace them even in the legal market; the continuing presence of a parallel illegal market (albeit on a smaller scale) would make the task of displacement especially difficult.

The emergence of a legal market in drugs might also have disruptive effects on the economies of drug-producing and drug-transiting nations. One predictable outcome of the end of the U.S.-led prohibition regime would be a decline in the price of drugs at all points in the trade pipeline, as the "risk premium" would largely disappear. The decline in prices could be an unpleasant surprise to countries (or portions of countries) that have become economically dependent on the commerce in drugs. In essence, they would confront the consequences of a major recession in what had been a lucrative industry.

The political impact of such economic dislocations, especially on countries with already fragile economies (such as Mexico and the Andean nations) is not easy to predict. It is possible that a severe recession would fatally undermine regimes that in some cases have a shaky reputation for legitimacy with restless populations. But it is also possible that the recessionary effects of drug legalization would be relatively brief and that the decline of the drug trade would be a net positive for the economies of drug-source nations over the long term. That trade, although lucrative, has created numerous economic distortions. Talented entrepreneurs who might have made major contributions in other, more useful, fields were diverted into the black market. Capital that might have been invested in more constructive enterprises went instead to fund the commerce in illicit narcotics. Legitimate forms of agriculture frequently languished as growers concentrated on producing vastly more profitable drug crops.

The end of the black market premium would also mean an end to such systemic distortions. If the governments of drug-source countries pursue wise economic policies—minimizing the legal barriers to the formation of new businesses, allowing unfettered labor markets, and establishing low-tax environments—the end of the illegal drug trade will not necessarily usher in a prolonged period of economic decline. Much will depend, however, on whether the governments have the wisdom to adopt enlightened, pro-growth policies.

Despite the problems that may accompany the transition to a regime of drug legalization, the United States would be wise to end its commitment to international prohibition. It is a fatally flawed strategy that has poisoned America's relations with other countries, especially in the western hemisphere, and created needless difficulties for their populations. The global drug war, for all its elaborate legal and institutional mechanisms, has failed to have a significant impact on the supply of illegal drugs. It has been more than eight decades since the Hague Convention, and eight decades of failure ought to be enough evidence of the need for a new approach.

ENDNOTES

1. The author wishes to thank Cabell Westbrook for his valuable research assistance.

2. Useful discussions of the early phases of multilateral efforts to control illegal drugs and the U.S. role in those efforts include several chapters in *Drugs, Politics and Diplomacy: The International Connection*, ed. Luiz R. S. Simmons and Abdul A Said (London: Sage Publications, 1974).

3. Text of the 1961 convention in Congressional Research Service, *International Narcotics Control and United States Foreign Policy: A Compilation of Laws, Treaties, Executive Documents, and Related Materials*, Report prepared for the Committee on Foreign Affairs, U.S. House of Representatives, 103rd Congress, 2nd Session, December 1994, pp. 632–666.

4. Text in ibid., pp. 667–680.

5. Text in ibid., pp. 608–631.

6. Text in ibid., pp. 581–607.

7. *See* Carpenter, "The U.S. Campaign against International Narcotics Trafficking: A Cure Worse Than the Disease," Cato Institute Policy Analysis no. 63, December 9, 1985, pp. 13–15.

8. U.S. Department of State, Bureau for International Narcotics and Law Enforcement Affairs, *International Narcotics Control Strategy Report*, March 1996, p. 40.

9. For discussions of that decision and the subsequent escalation of the drug war in Latin America, *see* Ethan Nadelmann, "U.S. Drug Policy: A Bad Export," *Foreign Policy* 70 (Spring 1988) 142–159; Rensselaer W. Lee III, "Why the U.S. Can't Stop South American Cocaine," *Orbis* 32 (Fall 1988): 499–519; Ted Galen Carpenter and R. Channing Rouse, "Perilous Panacea: The Military in the Drug War," Cato Institute Policy Analysis no. 128, February 15, 1990; and Peter R. Andreas, Eva C. Bertram, Morris J. Blachman, and Kenneth E. Sharpe, "Dead End Drug Wars," *Foreign Policy* 85 (Winter 1991-92): 106–128.

10. The Declaration of Cartagena, White House press release, February 15, 1990.

11. Figures for all three Andean countries are included in "One Year Later: Update on Andean Drug Strategy," Department of State *Dispatch*, October 29, 1990, pp. 220–221.

12. Text in *International Narcotics Control and United States Foreign Policy*, pp. 689–702.

13. U.S. Department of State, *The Global Legal Framework for Narcotics and Prohibitive Substances*, June 29, 1979, pp. 7–13.

14. Ibid.

15. That attitude, although weaker than in the 1970s and 1980s, persists in some countries. For example, *see* Calvin Sims, "Defying U.S. Threat, Bolivians Plant More Coca," *New York Times*, July 7, 1995, p. A3; and Gabriel Escobar, "Keeping Coca a Cash Crop," *Washington Post*, September 29, 1995, p. A18.

16. International Narcotics Control Act of 1988, Public Law 100-690, November 18, 1988, 102 Stat. 4261–4295.

17. For a discussion of the certification process and the range of sanctions, see Raphael Francis Perl, "Congress, International Narcotics, and the Anti-Drug Abuse Act of 1988," *Journal of Inter-American Studies and World Affairs* 30 (Summer/Fall 1988): 19–52.

18. For example, in both 1990 and 1991 President Bush recommended the decertification of only four nations: Afghanistan, Iran, Syria, and Myanmar (Burma). With the possible exception of Syria in 1991, U.S. relations with those states were exceedingly strained or nonexistent, and there was utterly no prospect of aid programs, with or without certification. Similarly, in 1995 President Clinton declined to certify Afghanistan, Burma, Iran, and Syria. Such countries as Colombia, Bolivia, Lebanon, Pakistan, and Peru were given national interest certifications. U.S.

Department of State, Bureau for International Narcotics and Law Enforcement Affairs, *International Narcotics Control Strategy Report*, March 1995, p. vii.

19. "Presidential Certification of Narcotics Source Countries," *Department of State Bulletin*, June 1988, p. 48.

20. Michael Isikoff, "U.S. Postponing Some Aid to Peru," *Washington Post*, March 2, 1991, p. A8. The United States employed a similar tactic—"freezing" $84 million in aid funds—to coerce Panama to amend its banking statutes. As part of Washington's ongoing campaign against money laundering and drug crimes, U.S. officials specifically sought the elimination of various laws protecting the secrecy of accounts. See Clifford Lewis, "Panama–U.S. Accord Set on Bank Records," *New York Times*, April 4, 1991, p. D1.

21. For examples of such leaked stories, *see* David Johnston, "Clinton Urged to Cite Mexico for Drug Flow," *New York Times*, February 18, 1996, p. A1; William Branigin, "Mexican Commitment to Anti-Drug Efforts Questioned by U.S.," *Washington Post*, February 19, 1996, p. A10; and William Branigin and Molly Moore, "Political Overtones in Anti-Drug Dispute," *Washington Post*, February 22, 1996, p. A4. The reports of congressional pressure for decertification were not without foundation, as the adverse reaction to the administration's decision to certify Mexico as cooperative confirmed. David Johnston, "U.S. Decision on Mexico Drugs Draws Opposition in Congress," *New York Times*, March 8, 1996, p. A2.

22. William Drozdiak, "Dutch Drugs Irk Neighbors," *Washington Post*, November 11, 1995, p. A1; "Dialogue With France," *Rotterdam Algemeen Dagblad*, April 19, 1996, in *Foreign Broadcast Information Service Daily Report—Western Europe*, April 22, 1996, p. 5; and Barry Newman, "Holland and Morocco Have Hash in Common, as World's View Differs," *Wall Street Journal*, April 23, 1996, p. A1.

23. Perhaps the most egregious example occurred in 1994 when Colombia's prosecutor general, Gustavo de Greiff, had the temerity to suggest that drug legalization be discussed as a policy option. U.S. officials responded with a concerted campaign to discredit de Greiff and circulated ugly rumors that he was in league with the drug cartels, despite a dearth of evidence to support such allegations. For examples of the U.S. media offensive, *see* Jose De Cordoba, "Washington, Irked by Colombia Official, Ends Evidence-Sharing on Drug Cartels," *Wall Street Journal*, March 8, 1994; Pierre Thomas, "U.S. Criticizes Top Colombian Prosecutor over Behavior in War on Drugs," *Washington Post*, April 21, 1994, p. A20; and Douglas Farah, "U.S. Teamwork with Colombia against Drugs Coming Unstuck," *Washington Post*, June 12, 1994, p. A29.

24. For accounts of the recent tensions between the United States and Thailand, *see* Rajan Moses, "Top Thai Party Spurns U.S. Concern over Drug Ties," *Washington Times*, July 5, 1995, p. A11; Philip Shenon, "U.S. Warns Thais on Naming Cabinet Members Linked to Drugs," *New York Times*, July 6, 1995, p. A5; and Willis Witter, "Thais Angered by U.S. Attitude," *Washington Times*, July 6, 1995, p. A13.

Washington's negotiations to provide aid funds to the Burmese government to wage the war on drugs pleased Burma's military dictatorship but infuriated human rights groups and prodemocratic factions of the country's population. Jim Mann and Ronald S. Ostrow, "U.S. to Help Myanmar Fight Drug Production," *Los Angeles Times*, June 21, 1995, p. A4; and Ted Bardacke, "Burmese Drugs Offensive May Clear Way for Cash Injection," *Financial Times*, August 28, 1995, p. 4.

25. "Peter Jennings Reporting: The Cocaine War, Lost in Bolivia," ABC News, December 28, 1992, transcript, p. 10.

26. Douglas Farah, "U.S. Weighs Response to Clearing of Colombian Leader," *Washington Post*, June 14, 1996, p. 17; and Ben Barber, "U.S. May Respond with Sanctions to Clearing of Colombian President," *Washington Times*, June 14, 1996, p. A17.

27. "Colombian Secret Police Chief Quits after U.S. Accusations," *Washington Post*, June 19, 1996, p. A22.

28. Carlos Manuel Vasquez, "Misreading High Court's *Alvarez* Ruling," *Legal Times*, October 5, 1992, pp. 29–30.

29. Richard Clutterbuck, *Drugs, Crime and Corruption: Thinking the Unthinkable* (London: Macmillan, 1995).

30. *See*, for example, Paul B. Stares, *Global Habit: The Drug Problem in a Borderless World* (Washington: Brookings Institution, 1996).

31. Georgie Anne Geyer, "Narco Future in Colombia," *Washington Times*, May 29, 1994, p. B1. Important recent studies on the economic impact of the drug trade on the economies of individual countries include James Painter, *Bolivia and Coca: A Study in Dependency* (Boulder, Colo.: Lynne Rienner, 1994); Maria Celia Toro, *Mexico's "War" on Drugs: Causes and Consequences* (Boulder, Colo.: Lynne Rienner, 1995); and Francisco E. Thoumi, *Political Economy and Illegal Drugs in Colombia* (Boulder, Colo.: Lynne Rienner, 1995). A crucial earlier account dealing with the Andean countries is Rensselaer W. Lee III, *The White Labyrinth: Cocaine and Political Power* (New Brunswick, N.J.: Transaction, 1989).

32. Molly Moore and John Ward Anderson, "The Drug Fiefdom of Northern Mexico," *Washington Post*, April 28, 1996, p. A1.

33. U.S. Department of State, Bureau for International Narcotics and Law Enforcement Affairs, *International Narcotics Control Strategy Report*, March 1996, p. 25.

34. Recent examples include Clutterbuck; Stares; Mathea Falco, "U.S. Drug Policy: Addicted to Failure," *Foreign Policy* 102 (Spring 1996): 120–133; and Kevin Jack Riley, *Snow Job? The War Against International Cocaine Trafficking* (New Brunswick, N.J.: Transaction, 1996). *See* also Lee, *White Labyrinth*; and Nadelmann.

12

On the Reconstruction of Drug Education in the United States[1]

Rodney Skager, Joel H. Brown

Drug education[2] must change regardless of whether the war on drugs endures or policies emphasizing harm reduction, decriminalization, and legalization take its place. According to California high school students, alcohol and illicit drugs are still easy to obtain (Skager and Austin 1997). Moreover, research reviewed below reveals that conventional approaches to drug education have been ineffective in reducing use. The double failure to reduce supply and persuade youth to remain abstinent suggests that use of alcohol and other drugs among young people will remain common. Instead of chasing the fantasy of drug-free schools and communities, those responsible for drug education need to roll up their sleeves and tackle the world as it is.

Since the 1970s, parents and the public at large have been deeply concerned about the threat that drugs are perceived to have on children and society in general (Baum 1996). We share this concern in recognizing that abuse of both legal and illegal drugs is associated with serious harms to significant numbers of youth and adults. But we are also aware, as are most youth, that the majority of people who use alcohol or other drugs manage to do so without negative consequences to themselves or others. We believe that failure to acknowledge this and other uncomfortable realities has been counterproductive to the whole enterprise of prevention.

To comprehend the desperate need for change in this field, it is first necessary to show how ostensibly relevant social science theories have been applied to the formulation of drug prevention policies and programs, how competing interest groups work together to continue programs with questionable efficacy, how youth interpret and share information about drugs, and how they feel about these programs. This analysis will lead directly to proposals for alternatives. These themes divide the chapter as follows:

- A critical look at current principles and practices in drug prevention education for youth
- An examination of the cultural underpinnings of adolescent substance use
- A description of the relationships between interest group politics, policies, and prevention education practices
- What youth tell us about drug education
- An alternative model for prevention education

CURRENT MYTHS ABOUT WHY YOUTH USE DRUGS AND RELATED APPROACHES TO PREVENTION

From 1981 to 1996 the federal government spent approximately 13 billion on youth drug education (White House Office of Drug Control Policy 1996). This does not include state, local, and charitable expenditures, which would at least double and probably triple the federal contribution (Romero et al. 1994). Suffice it to say that many billions of dollars are spent annually on educating our youth about drugs. Yet analysis of the principles underlying current approaches to drug education reveals simplistic overgeneralizations about why young people try drugs and inappropriate interpretations of research findings.

ADOLESCENTS USE DRUGS BECAUSE THEY ARE IGNORANT OF THE CONSEQUENCES

The most widely accepted idea driving prevention is that teenagers use drugs because they lack accurate information about negative consequences associated with use. The commonsense notion underlying this assumption is that youth will choose abstinence if only given the "right" information. Yet information-oriented prevention programs, including widely used packaged curricula, have repeatedly proved ineffective in reducing alcohol and other drug use. Tobler's (1986, 1997) comprehensive assessments of prevention programs confirmed that informational strategies increased knowledge without affecting either attitudes or drug use. Nevertheless, faith in informational approaches remains particularly hard to shake. In part this may be because solutions to problems are defined in terms of the services institutions normally provide. Most prevention education goes on in schools, and the mission of schooling is development of knowledge and competencies rather than character or personality.

The flaw in the information approach is that early in adolescence, or even before, young people begin to acquire knowledge about drugs from their own sources. For example, they perceive that not all people who use drugs have problems, that there are differences between "hard" and "soft" drugs, that people who use marijuana usually do not "progress" to cocaine or heroin, and that alcohol is also a drug, but one widely used by both older adolescents and adults. In other words, much of the "right" information they are getting in school is actually wrong. Once this happens, drug education begins to be perceived as indoctrination rather than truth, and the seeds are planted for tuning out on the message as a whole.

ADOLESCENTS WHO USE DRUGS ARE DEVIANTS

The deviance hypothesis that formed the basis of problem behavior theory emerged first in studies by Jessor and Jessor (1977), who reported relationships between drug use and socially deviant behaviors such as lying, stealing, and delinquent behavior. At about the same time similar relationships for nonconformity and rebelliousness were associated with teenage drug use (Wingard et al. 1979), as were tendencies toward sensation seeking and sociability by other researchers (Kandel 1978). But how do these findings hold up on closer analysis?

At the beginning of an upswing in socially proscribed behavior it is not surprising that various notions of deviance would be enlisted as "explanations" of that behavior. In the mid-1960s illicit drug use among adolescents and even adults *was* deviant in a normative sense. Likewise, any use at all, rather than just heavy use, was more likely at that early stage to be associated with measures of psychological and social dysfunction. Today, with use of alcohol and marijuana common among young people, such across-the-board explanations seem both silly and suspiciously judgmental. Today it makes no sense to characterize all youth who experiment with drugs, or even the majority, as deviant and rebellious, when such labels are more likely to apply to the smaller subgroup whose use is clearly damaging to self and others. Unfortunately, this is still done, even among prevention experts, as witnessed by the following recent observations:

> The relationship between non-conformity and drug use takes on added significance for prevention programming because rebellious youth are

likely to be particularly susceptible to peer values and models. . . . This argument applies to adolescent extroverts as well. Sensation-seeking and sociability have been linked to marijuana and other drug use. . . . [Ellickson 1995, p. 98]

One reads these statements with amazement. High sensitivity to peer influence is normal in adolescence. A genuinely rebellious adolescent would *ignore* peer influence. Furthermore, the idea that extroverted and sociable adolescents are in "special danger" merely recognizes that healthy kids try drugs too, hardly justifying a theory that characterizes an entire group (about half of the age cohort by age 16) as deviant. There is ample reason to believe that drug use is engaged in by substantial numbers of young people with positive personal characteristics. For example, Evans and Skager (1992) found that 70 percent of academically successful high school students in two large-scale California surveys (one statewide and the other representative of a large county population) reported using alcohol, other drugs, or both.

An uncritical buying into war on drugs ideology is a large part of the reason that researchers have routinely lumped together all substance users, rather than distinguishing between heavy and occasional users. In doing so they go along with the assumption that all drug use is equivalent and that success in the war on drugs is properly measured by reducing total use rather than the number of users who experience problems associated with their use. By doing so, significant statistical relationships with other negative behavioral indicators are bound to emerge, even though such relationships may be based entirely on the small group of heavy users included in the larger group of users. In support of this point, Shedler and Block (1990) reported that heavy or abusive adolescent users as a group were characterized by psychological or social dysfunctions, while moderate or occasional users were not.

The deviance idea was later elaborated by the addition of so-called "risk" characteristics associated with family and environment. Educational services arising from this perspective were fielded as programs for "at-risk" youth who have increased risk of accidents, delinquency, or substance abuse (Bell and Bell 1993, Coie et al. 1993, Gillmore et al. 1991, Hawkins et al. 1987, 1992, Rossi 1994). The goal was to identify and intervene early with at-risk youth in the hope of averting problems later on. The failures of this model once it was applied in school-based programs have been chronicled. For example, "[M]any programs designed for "at-risk" students are based on a theoretical framework that functions to maintain the status quo by labeling certain students as deficient on the basis of characteristics over which students have no control" (Baizerman and Compton 1992, p. 73). In addition:

In many schools, this process results in the majority of students being identified as at-risk. This is hardly surprising, since the educational use

of the term "at-risk" does not meet the test of the public health definition—that is, it is not known whether the characteristics used for identification actually predict which students are most likely to drop out of
school . . . the whole field of education used the concept of risk as part
of an ideology, thereby joining science, mathematics, and morality. The
major use of this ideology is to construct a socioeducational population
of at-risk students and suggests that they are both the problem and its
cause. The school is absolved and can be expected only to "do the best
with limited resources." Whole schools and even districts are not thought
of as being at-risk; the problem and its sources are the students.
[Richardson 1990, p. 73]

One large-scale study examined how substance use prevention policies
based on risk factors translated into programs and concluded that the application of risk-oriented programs in California ". . . create policies that exclude those whom students themselves recognize as most in need of help;
they drive those, who already might be on the margins of the school system,
further out" (Brown and D'Emidio-Caston 1995, p. 482).

Drug education programs associated with deviance and risk theories have
shown little evidence of success (Brown and Horowitz 1993). Due to negative characterization and isolation of at-risk youth, such theories and the programs with which they are associated may have caused significant harm.

ADOLESCENT USE OF "SOFT DRUGS" LEADS TO USE OF
HARD DRUGS: THE GATEWAY THEORY

Proponents of an epidemiological perspective hold strongly to the *gateway
theory* of drug use. Derived from methodologically sophisticated but widely
misinterpreted studies such as that by Yamaguchi and Kandel (1984), the
gateway theory proposes that use of tobacco leads to use of alcohol and then
to marijuana followed by more dangerous drugs like cocaine and heroin. This
is the concept of *progression*.

The gateway theory is based on correlational, rather than causal, relationships. The fact that most heroin addicts tried cigarettes first, then alcohol, then marijuana, and then "harder" drugs does not mean that most young
people who try alcohol or marijuana will do the same thing. Youth soon
realize that relatively few people who experiment with these substances become addicted or progress to cocaine or heroin. Such impressions are supported by the relatively stable rates in heroin use throughout the last thirty
years and in the declines in cocaine use since the mid-1980s reported by
Everingham and Rydell (1994). Brown and D'Emidio-Caston (1995) have
shown that older teenagers are aware that the majority of their peers drink

alcohol occasionally and that substantial numbers have tried marijuana, but they do not see evidence of corresponding mass progression to harder drugs. These researchers also concluded that discrepancies between what young people are told in school about drugs and what they learn on their own leads to rejection of the message and doubts about the sincerity and expertise of those who deliver it.

The gateway theory as it has been applied to drug education thus overgeneralizes from the drug progression shown by some users to the much larger total population of occasional drinkers or users. Spokespersons for war on drugs policies obviously consider this theory to be an essential supporting argument for the abstinence message to youth. Of course, it is not really intended for adults, since it associates use of alcohol and tobacco with more or less inevitable progression to addiction. More than fifteen years ago Chng (1981) concluded that "drug education in the schools has failed . . . the goal of abstinence [is] one of the contributory factors for this 'failure'" (p. 13). We would counter that the goal of abstinence by youth may be appropriate, but not for the reason advanced in the gateway theory. More convincing and honest reasons are needed if we are going to continue to preach abstinence to intelligent young people.

Together, the deviance and the gateway theories have provided the conceptual basis for most school-based prevention education. Certainly the familiar "Just say no" campaign of the Reagan years implicitly or explicitly proclaimed that all substance use was dangerous or criminal. This message remains with us, having been extolled not so long ago by one of the 1996 presidential candidates.

ADOLESCENTS USE DRUGS BECAUSE THEY LACK SELF-ESTEEM

Another pervasive theory is that young people use alcohol and drugs because they lack self-esteem. Programs designed to address such presumed defficiencies were initially referred to as *affective* education. Like information approaches, affective education has also failed to reduce substance use (Schaps et al. 1986). A more comprehensive approach called *life skills* education has emerged more recently, though it has not yet penetrated the ordinary practice of prevention. In this approach *self-efficacy* (Bandura 1977), defined as the belief that one can perform important kinds of social behaviors competently, replaces the fuzzy, global concept of self-esteem. However, this merely reflects another kind of deficit theory. It assumes that young people use drugs because they do not feel good about themselves due to a lack of important social skills.

Why does low self-esteem as a cause of drug use remain a popular idea despite the failure of prevention strategies associated with it? Obsession with self and self-esteem may be inevitable in a highly individualistic society where individuals are often isolated and lack a sense of membership in a support-ive community (extended family, clan, etc.) (Cushman 1990). However, re-search (Skager and Kerst 1989) does not support the widespread conviction that the great majority of young people use substances because they feel bad about themselves (especially not those sociable adolescent extroverts), although lower self-esteem has been identified among heavy drug users (Ellickson 1995). Longitudinal research has established that children with low self-esteem and other personal problems were likely to abuse substances later on during ado-lescence (Shedler and Block 1990, Werner 1993). This same research found that adolescents who used drugs only occasionally showed no signs of these kinds of problems in childhood.

We suggest that the role of self-esteem as an explanation of substance use by all adolescents is an overgeneralization reflecting yet another patron-izing adult perspective. Lack of self-esteem cannot account for the widespread use of substances among adolescents throughout the last quarter century unless adolescence itself is conceived as a stage of sickness or vulnerability. Like the deviance theory, it implies that all young people who drink and use do so for the same reasons, and that all are equally vulnerable.

PEER PRESSURE IS RESPONSIBLE FOR INITIATION AND USE

Growing awareness that drug initiation and use is rooted in social interac-tions has stimulated alternative approaches to prevention. Influence of peers, the media, and even the family have been recognized. One significant prod-uct of this approach has been the development of curriculum strategies that teach resistance skills to counteract pressure from peers to try drugs and, in the case of alcohol and cigarettes, to evaluate and dismiss advertising mes-sages. Training in resistance skills has been incorporated into common pre-vention practice.

Accounting for initiation of substance use as the result of direct pres-sure from peers ignores the influence of curiosity, in itself obviously related to social messages. Skager and Austin (1997) report that, when asked why students used alcohol and other drugs, older adolescents ranked "to have fun" and "to see what it's like" well above "because their friends use." Blaming drug initiation on pressure from peers stigmatizes children and young people as both victims and perpetrators. Not only is such a view patently circular, it puts all of the blame on youth, conveniently absolving adults and the so-ciety they have created or at least inherited.

Direct pressure from peers is certainly not the only way, or even the primary way, in which social influence may work among teenagers. Implicit *assumptions* about what most kids are doing may be a more common motivation for trying alcohol and other drugs. Normative education, one version of the social influence model, differs from the peer pressure idea in proposing that young people form impressions about the behavior of their peers that are highly inaccurate, especially in the direction of overestimation. Believing that "everybody is doing it" or that important role models "are doing it" is a powerful motivating agent for adolescents as well as adults (Hansen and Graham 1991).

Early in the teen years normative education assesses (anonymously) actual levels of use among students. The results are likely to reveal that fewer peers have experimented with drugs than the students expected and that use itself, or various behaviors of peers while under the influence, are strongly disapproved of by most of the students. This information is used to focus on the social *acceptability* rather than the *personal consequences* of use. That adolescents might be more influenced by social disapproval than by warnings about health and legal consequences is a significant insight.

Evidence of the long-term effectiveness of social influence approaches is not promising, however. Programs combining resistance to both external and internal pressures have delayed initiation of illicit drug use, though they have been less effective with alcohol, due probably to the greater social acceptability of drinking (Ellickson 1995). Social influence methods have been incorporated in DARE (Drug Abuse Resistance Education), the most widely used prevention program. While the DARE curriculum was based on early social influence approaches, and also incorporates attention to media promotion of drug use, enhancing self-esteem, and resisting peer pressure, evaluations have shown it to be ineffective in reducing drug use (Ennett et al. 1994). These researchers also noted that the DARE curriculum is delivered by uniformed police officers using a traditional teaching style rather than the give-and-take, interactive-delivery approach that Tobler (1997) found to be associated with positive outcomes. They concluded that teaching style may be the critical factor accounting for the ineffectiveness of DARE. The recognition by Ennett and colleagues (1994) of the importance of interactive teaching style is significant in the light of what teenagers tell us they need from prevention education (the topic of a later section).

Life skills education (Botvin 1995) combines social influence and affective approaches by promoting the development of a variety of personal (self-appraisal, goal-setting, decision-making, anxiety management, etc.) and social (communication, overcoming shyness, making conversation, etc.) skills. The goal of this approach is to reduce motivation to use drugs by fostering competencies that contribute to a sense of personal self-efficacy in self-management and relationship with others.

The kinds of skills addressed in life skills education are important and probably in need of development in many young people. They are skills associated with successful living, not simply competencies that may reduce use of drugs. But there is resistance to the introduction of life skills curricula because they require significant time and money to implement. Haaga and Reuter (1995) point out that pressure to improve basic, work-related skills of graduates, presumably reading and mathematics, makes educators reluctant to allocate the necessary time to life skills courses.

Life skills approaches are also based on youth deficit theories of substance use. We have already cited research (Newcomb and Bentler 1988, Shedler and Block 1990, Werner 1993) demonstrating that deficit notions do not apply to the majority of youth who try alcohol and illicit drugs. Existing social influence curricula are also accommodated to the zero tolerance message, and thus must be evaluated on their success in reducing substance use for all youth rather than those who are most vulnerable to problems resulting from use. This seems to us to be a prescription for failure.

On the other hand, the incidence of substance use harmful to self or others might be reduced by focusing on offensive or otherwise undesirable behaviors of peers under the influence of alcohol or other drugs. Such a suggestion is of course anathema under current ideology on the grounds that it would be interpreted as giving permission to use. Yet when these techniques have been applied to alcohol *misuse* (defined as overindulgence or trouble with friends or adults), positive results have been reported for reducing rates of increase in problems associated with drinking among children who had already started drinking in upper elementary school, despite the fact that frequency or amount drunk did not change. Dielman et al. (1989) found that eighth-graders who had experienced the training in grade six showed lower rates of increase in instances of alcohol misuse. This result was later found to persist into grade ten (Shope et al. 1992).

In sum, the social influence approaches might be more effective if applied to socially unacceptable patterns of use. However, we believe that stress should be placed on enhancement of youth well-being in programs that are not grounded on false premises that all youth who use substances are deviant or afflicted by psychosocial deficits, especially since those young people are merely engaging in behaviors that adults either reserve for themselves (use of alcohol and tobacco) or openly violate (use of other drugs).

ADOLESCENT SUBSTANCE USE AND THE CONCEPT OF "NORMAL" PSYCHOSOCIAL DEVELOPMENT

Despite the fact that the overwhelming majority of adolescents experiment with alcohol and approximately half experiment with illicit drugs, theories based on adolescent deviance (nonconformity, rebelliousness, sensation seeking, and delinquency) or deficits (ignorance, low self-esteem or self-efficacy, susceptibility to peer pressure) are used to explain their behavior and serve as the basis for developing prevention programs. Recent highly significant research, though, suggests that a very different picture underlies adolescent substance use. This picture emerges when all adolescents who use substances are not lumped together, as is the case in most research relating to prevention.

In 1990 Shedler and Block reported longitudinal evidence collected from preschool to age 18 on the relationship between preexisting psychological characteristics and later substance use. This research compared adolescent abstainers, occasional users, and heavy users on measures of psychological health, school performance, and family dynamics as far back as the early years of childhood. Because of the quality of the research and the rarity and hence great significance of a data set with these kinds of long-term measures, these findings deserve special note.

- Adolescents who were classified as heavy substance users were found to be ". . . maladjusted, with signs of a distinct personality marked by interpersonal alienation, poor impulse control, and manifest emotional distress. . ."
- Adolescents who abstained from marijuana use were found to be ". . . anxious, emotionally constricted, and lacking in social skills."
- Those adolescents who experimented with substances were found to be the "psychologically healthiest."

The current functioning of the occasional users were the highest of any of the three groups. It is significant that the psychological difficulties of frequent users and abstainers were identified *before* any of the participants had initiated substance use. Consequently, heavy substance use was associated with long-standing psychological problems. Likewise, abstainers manifested their particular set of psychological characteristics well before the period of initiation of use by other participants. Abstainers were the only group who showed deficits in social skills, raising questions about the theoretical basis of the life skills education approach discussed above.

Similar results were found by Newcomb and Bentler (1988) in shorter duration (but technically state-of-the-art) research. Like Shedler and Block, these investigators found that the heavy users had psychological and social problems that predated drug use and that affected current functioning. Authors of both studies made it abundantly clear that they did not attribute the higher functioning of the occasional users to substance use itself, but rather to preexisting positive social (especially family) and psychological factors. This clear disclaimer did not forestall an avalanche of criticism of their findings by establishment figures, including the then-governor of California.

This evidence stands with a great deal of other evidence in suggesting that adolescent interest in, and willingness to experiment with, alcohol and drugs is now culturally transmitted. The situation is precisely analogous to the period of alcohol prohibition when drinkers refused to relinquish their right to drink alcohol. This is the reason substances are used on a moderate basis by a large number of psychologically healthy adolescents. The mechanism of cultural transmission does not depend on deficit or deviance models and takes into account two salient research findings for which none of the popular theories account. First, among older adolescents, experimenting with substance use is a norm, rather than aberrant behavior. Second, the majority of adolescents who use alcohol and other drugs manage to do so without serious consequences to themselves or others. Neither of these assertions, nor the research on which they are based, denies the proviso made at the beginning of this chapter that significant numbers of other adolescents and adults abuse substances in ways that harm themselves and others. Our main point is that current approaches to drug education and prevention in general result in punishment or exclusion of the abusers while at the same time failing to convince the majority of youth that they should choose abstinence.

CULTURAL UNDERPINNINGS OF ADOLESCENT SUBSTANCE USE

In confronting cultural norms and expectations, education is up against a very powerful adversary. Cultural trends are infinitely more difficult to address than mere ignorance or misinformation, conditions that are the ordinary focus of education. This is because *culture* as the term is used here transmits ideas about what is normal and expected, about how one is supposed to live, even how one has the right to live.

It has been argued elsewhere (Cushman 1990) that American culture actively supports substance use. Zinberg (1983) noted, for example, that interest in consciousness-changing illicit drugs was preceded by the emergence of consciousness-changing pharmaceutical drugs. The advent in the 1950s of drugs for the treatment of chronic anxiety, depression, and psychosis was widely discussed and appreciated then and now. The inappropriate distribution and use of medical psychotropic drugs is a frequently ignored aspect of problematic drug use today.

The deliberate targeting of youth in alcohol advertising and marketing does not require elaboration. Neither does the fact that films, television, and music have incorporated illicit drug use into popular art forms, just as they have incorporated a much more open (though often distasteful) view of sexuality. While entertainment and entertainers are criticized for promoting drug use, it may be more objective to suggest that popular art forms reflect rather than invent popular culture, or at least that there is an interaction between the two rather than a simple one-way causal relationship.

Findings from the latest California high school student survey (Skager and Austin 1997) reflect signs of cultural underpinnings that account for high levels of substance use among youth.

- Slightly over half of 16-year-olds in California high schools knew at least one adult who used marijuana once a week or more often.
- Most 12-year-olds said that a lot of what they knew about alcohol and other drugs was learned in school classes. In contrast, two thirds of 16-year-olds said they learned from their friends and four out of ten from their own experience.
- More than eight out of ten 16-year-olds reported that marijuana was easy or fairly easy for students to obtain, about as easy as it was to get alcohol.
- The majority of 16-year-olds believed that students got marijuana from their friends both in and outside of school and at teen social events.
- Only about a third said that students got their drugs from people they thought of as dealers.
- Six out of ten 16-year-olds believed that their peers used alcohol and other drugs to have fun or to see what it was like. More than half thought that having friends who used was another reason. Only about a third said it was because kids were bored.
- A majority of 16-year-olds had tried an illicit drug at least once in their lifetime. Over four in ten used marijuana in the preceding six months and one in four in the last month. Eight out of ten used alcohol, three quarters of those in the last six months, about half within the last month.
- Only about one in five 16-year-olds abstained from both alcohol and illicit drug use on a lifetime basis.
- Six out of ten 16-year-olds who reported that they used alcohol currently had done so without experiencing any problems. Over half of current drug users reported the same thing.

These findings suggest that the majority of high school students by mid-adolescence are very likely to have acquired culturally transmitted sources of information about alcohol and other drugs contradicting what they have been told in drug education classes. The majority of students may have liked or even admired the adult regular marijuana user they reported knowing (whether their perception about frequency of use is accurate is beside the point). Their own experience with alcohol and other drugs was likely to have been fun or interesting, also true of much of the second-hand experience gleaned from friends. They did not obtain drugs from the shady drug dealer in the official scenario, but rather from their peers. They usually obtained drugs at school or while socializing with their friends, and in doing so exercised what they believed to be a legitimate personal choice. The great majority undoubtedly consider drinking to be their natural right. For at least half the students in their late teens the same may be true for marijuana. Children entering the society of the teenager are likely to encounter and absorb these kinds of attitudes and norms. The immense significance to the adolescent of what other teens think and do is well established (Hansen and Graham 1991).

In such a cultural context, popular prevention theories about why young people try drugs appear silly or irrelevant. Rather than deviance, drug use is common. Rather than peer pressure, we have a developmentally normal tendency to imitate peers. Rather than low self-esteem, we have self-assertion in going against the rules laid down by the official culture. Rather than boredom, we have curiosity. Instead of poor decision-making skills, there is normal interest in having fun. All of this is supported by a developmentally sophisticated underground information transmission network that contradicts what students learn in prevention education. Most young people live in what to them must be a schizoid society in which alcohol and illicit drug use is condemned and forbidden to them by the official world of laws and authority, but is widely practiced in the culture they join as teenagers, in other words, their cultural world.

INTEREST GROUP POLITICS AND THE PRINCIPLES DRIVING DRUG EDUCATION

The research reviewed above reveals at best only very weak evidence for effectiveness of drug education programs based on the deviance and deficit theories, and that only for approaches used mainly on an experimental basis. Yet federal expenditures on traditional drug education approaches continue to grow. Long-term, methodologically sound research that should lead to different conceptions of the nature of the problem and to effective prevention strategies is ignored. This immensely frustrating rigidity in the system obliges us to ask what it is that protects the bankrupt status quo in prevention.

The answer to this question leads to the potent role of interest-group politics in drug education. The field is characterized by a relentless commitment to keeping things just as they are, except of course for continual increases in program funding. This situation is exactly parallel to that of law enforcement, which regularly requests and receives more funding for activities that for decades have failed to reduce illicit drug supplies.

In effect, we are confronted with a modern enactment of the folk tale about the king who paraded among his subjects while wearing no clothes. The courtiers and townspeople reacted by praising the elegant garments the king's tailors had persuaded him that he was wearing. Once committed to maintaining the illusion, they were fearful of the consequences to themselves if someone told the king that he was actually naked.

Two interest groups maintain the status quo in prevention. They are readily distinguished by their members' stance on a pair of deceptively simple, yet polar opposite, principles. These principles are:

- All illicit drugs are evil.
- All people who use drugs are evil.

The principles obviously distinguish people who want to protect youth from drugs from those who want to punish youth who use them. To buy into the education side of the drug war, one need accept only one of these principles. People who believe in both are of course the *echt* drug warriors. The seeming incongruity in the principles is that they allow for the assignment of blame to potentially independent agents, consciousness-changing chemicals versus people who use them. However, in America's social landscape, interest groups who might normally oppose one another often work together. This is accomplished by adopting common goals (in this case universal abstinence by youth) while pursuing different means to achieve those goals.

In a society in which competition for limited social welfare resources is keen, interest groups often have a stake in the creation of ambiguity that promotes psychological tension among the public. The perceived threat of drugs in American society has been escalated to such a level that humanitarians and moral hard-liners can join together, because each offers a strategy to replace "tension and uncertainty with a measure of clarity, meaning, confidence, and security" (Edelman 1964, p. 61). Given a broadly defined problem (adolescent drug use or abuse), which has an equally broad range of solutions (from saving innocent youth from the ravages of drugs to punishing other youths to save the rest), competing interest groups discover that they can share the resource pie while pursuing their own strategies.

INTEREST GROUP 1: HUMANITARIANS SAVING ADOLESCENTS FROM DRUGS

The first principle, that all illicit drugs are inherently evil, appeals to social and/or humanitarian interest groups composed of those who feel sympathetic toward people who use substances. For them, drugs are the enemy and users deserving of help.

The humanitarian perspective is readily expressed in the language of public health. In this language substance use becomes a disease, drugs are agents of that disease, and anyone who uses a drug, even if only occasionally, becomes a host, like the typhoid or tuberculosis carriers who are themselves not sick. The language of the humanitarian/public health model contributes significantly to public tension. An increase in occasional use is routinely characterized as an "epidemic," with consequent hysteria in the body politic. This interest group then promotes educational solutions ostensibly based on scientific principles. In this way it is possible to simultaneously foment hysteria while at the same time reassuring the public that something is being done about the problem. But given highly symbolic (and impossible) efficacy standards such as no youth substance use, combined with false reassurances about program effectiveness, one must wonder where the "human" in humanitarian really is?

The manner by which failure of current approaches is used to justify increased resources is illustrated by the following editorial published under the headline "An Ounce of Prevention Is Not Enough." The opening paragraph stated:

> Drug, alcohol, and tobacco use prevention programs reach less than half of the nation's school-children, and only a handful of the programs that exist contain all of the elements that are key to effective prevention according to Drug Strategies, a nonprofit group that is trying to promote more effective approaches to the nation's drug problem. [*Washington Post* 1996]

The *Post* editorial went on to quote the spokesperson for Drug Strategies to the effect that current fashion models look "the way heroin addicts look: strung out, undernourished and very, very, sick. Those images resonate for young girls who are susceptible to fashion. That's the way drugs work: It's this kind of pervasive collective notion of what is acceptable behavior."

Here we have a classic instance of humanitarian hyperbole. Use of heroin is associated with failure to provide drug education. This despite the fact that there is no evidence that significant numbers of American adolescents actually use heroin. A highly respected newspaper helps a humanitarian organization arouse ambiguity and tension about youth and drugs by establishing an ostensible linkage between the most evil drug of all and a pitiful state of naiveté among adolescents who have not been immunized by the right drug education.

To assuage public fears aroused by such a vision of victimized youth, the spokesperson for this humanitarian organization went on to assert that prevention programs that "work" had been identified. The organization was in fact helping fill the void through the nationwide distribution of a consumer guide for parents and school districts in which existing programs were given letter grades on various aspects of quality.

Examination of the apparently new programs rated in the booklet reveals that all were based on the familiar drugs-are-evil perspective that Beck (1998) has shown to be over 100 years old. A careful analysis of how this humanitarian interest group sought to reassure the public suggests that the at best equivocal findings of research on the effectiveness of current prevention programs must have looked rather different to those who assigned the ratings of quality. One can only wonder if form might have counted more than substance in determining which programs merited an overall "A" rating. It may even be that normal standards of effectiveness were sacrificed for symbolic reasons. For example, of the five programs in middle and high school grades that received overall A ratings, four did not receive all A ratings on individual components. How did three B-rated components result in an overall A grade for one program? How is it that one program receiving all A ratings was reported in the research literature (Ellickson et al. 1993) to have "negative [program] effects" for the most vulnerable students presumably in greatest need of help? The need to show that those in the know can offer a solution is a hallmark of interest-group politics. In other words, there have to be programs with A ratings lest the impression be given that drug prevention does not work.

INTEREST GROUP 2: MORAL HARD LINERS AND THE ADOLESCENT AS CRIMINAL DRUG USER

The moral hard-liners also view drugs—with the exception of alcohol, of course—as inherently evil. However, instead of providing public reassurance primarily through "effective" education, members of this interest group advocate punishment of substance-using adolescents as a way of setting an example for others.

The following pronouncement from the Bush White House in 1989 defined this position in a way that also acknowledged that part of the turf belonged to the humanitarians. After supporting resistance training as a prevention strategy, the White House called for a "firm moral stand that using drugs [all drugs] is wrong and should be resisted" (p. 50). In addition:

> School-based prevention programs should be reinforced by tough, but fair, policies on use, possession, and distribution of drugs. . . We can-

not teach them that drugs are wrong and harmful if we fail to follow up our teaching with real consequences for those who use them. Policies like these have been criticized for adding to the dropout problem. But experience shows that firm policies fairly enforced actually reduce the numbers of students who must be expelled for drug violations; most students choose to alter their behavior rather than risk expulsion. [1989, pp. 50–51]

In the world view of moral hard-liners, public confidence is reestablished by a confrontational approach in which zero-tolerance drug education is enforced by "real consequences for those who use them [substances]" (The White House 1989, p. 49)

So, while the humanitarians reassure the public by providing "effective educational programs," the hard-liners do the same thing with confrontational education and punitive consequences. Ideological differences between humanitarians and hard-liners are primarily symbolic as far as the youth drug problem is concerned. Each works in the same political environment to facilitate agendas of their own interest groups because they agree on the principle that drugs are evil. The two groups also fully accept the war on drugs goal of total abstinence (read as "zero tolerance" among the hard-liners) as the core goal for adolescent drug education. This shared understanding is wide enough to allow both interest groups to have an influence in the schools. Unfortunately, both the humanitarian "effective program" approach and the moral hard-liner "confrontational" approach promote retention of ineffective and virtually indistinguishable adolescent substance use and abuse programs. Not only have these programs failed to reduce substance use, but, as shown in the next section, they have alienated youth from the educational process. Two illustrations support these contentions.

First, despite reassurance that the problem will be solved by the best of the current approaches to prevention, high levels of drug education programs have often been implemented without signs of corresponding success (Tobler 1986, 1997). Brown and colleagues (1997) observed:

Recently, adolescent substance use has increased more quickly to higher levels than at any time in the past 15 years (Johnston, O'Malley, & Bachman, 1995). Usage increases occur among those youth who have received more drug education than any group since school-based drug education began. [p. 65]

The fact that substance use recently increased even where intensive programs were in place is consistent with our earlier summary of evaluation research on specific programs. Current approaches to prevention vary from the generally ineffective to the (at best) marginally effective.

Second, there is evidence of awareness in government that the confrontational approach has had highly undesirable side effects. Six years after the aforementioned policy was issued by the Bush White House, a new problem had emerged. Policies of detention, suspension, and expulsion were indeed dumping too many youth onto the streets. Researchers began to receive requests to submit proposals for dealing with the following kinds of problems:

> With the growing numbers of "at-risk" youth and the increased efforts of schools to reduce violence and maintain order, we anticipate that the number of children removed from regular classroom settings may increase significantly. This competition will serve to meet our responsibility to continue to provide a meaningful education for those troubled youngsters.

> Under the authority of the Safe and Drug-Free Schools and Communities Act, a competition will be conducted to create effective model projects to provide alternatives to expulsion, i.e. meaningful alternative forms of schooling outside the classrooms for children expelled or suspended from school. . . . The Department has established a "fast-track" schedule to conduct this competition. . . . [U.S. Department of Education 1995, pp. 1–2]

Federal dollars have been tied to implementation of moral hard-liner policies like the ones issued by the White House in 1989. One large-scale study (Brown and D' Emidio-Caston 1995) examining the transmission of these policies from government to schools found that "[t]hough the program was directed to assist 'at-risk' students, identification often preceded detention, suspension, or expulsion (p. 451) [and that] . . . many students wondered why drug, alcohol, and tobacco education services were not helping those most in need of such assistance, often purging them from the educational system" (p. 480).

These researchers concluded that such programs, "Help create policies that exclude those whom students themselves recognize as most in need of help; they drive those who already might be on the margins of the school system further out" (p. 482). When forty student focus groups in that same study were asked about the drug policy in their school, thirty-nine of them used the following descriptors: "detention, suspension, and expulsion" (p. 451).

For moral hard-liners, the get-tough policy responded to tensions about what do about the drug problem by establishing a clear and forceful strategy: remove those students from school who "just [failed to] say no." This strategy, while reassuring to the public and moral-hard liners, does not appear to have affected overall substance use among adolescents. Eventually, even government recognized such approaches created a problem: what to do about the new group of dropouts.

In conclusion, the two underlying moral principles have on one side spawned prevention education programs stressing the immorality and harm associated with drug use and on the other isolation and exclusion for those young people who are discovered to be involved with drugs. Humanitarians enlist the medical, mental health, public health, and education establishments as partners in efforts to stop youth from using alcohol and drugs. Depending on the magnitude of the infraction, moral hard-liners exclude the youthful violator from the school community, and in the process may also may enlist law enforcement, the judiciary, and corrections institutions.

Thus liberal humanitarians and moral conservatives have been able to climb into the same bed, each group pursuing its own agenda in the drug war, and between them managing to align with a remarkable array of government agencies and departments. Each side maintains public tension over adolescent substance use, assuaging that tension with promises about more education programs on the one hand and punitive measures that turn out to be counterproductive on the other. This partnership between opposites has been achieved at the cost of harm to many young people. It has also hooked a staggering array of institutions onto government funding in a seemingly permanent stalemate in the war on drugs.

Despite these tainted relationships, there are glimmers of hope. There is a small but strong research base for alternative models, and despite the symbolic politics of interest groups, program failures are beginning to trouble many parents. And, for the first time in years, our youth have weighed in on this topic. For the remainder of this chapter, we will examine the possibilities, propose an alternative drug education paradigm, and describe how this model fits with what youth want in their drug education.

WHAT YOUTH TELL US ABOUT DRUG EDUCATION

In the recent past, few if any researchers have examined how students feel about drug education and described what they wanted in such programs. The evaluation by Brown and colleagues (1997) provided this information. The overall findings were that students wanted more complete drug information, more panels and talks, and they wanted them delivered through a different educational process, one that included those who have used, and/or abused substances. No program will be successful unless we are willing to hear the voices, not only of thriving youth, but also at-risk youth. In this section we present some snapshots of what students wanted in their drug education.

A few elementary school students ("R" below for "respondent") described their drug educational process ("#" below for "interview identification members") and then told researchers ("I" below for "interviewer") what they wanted.[3]*

> R: Well like I said, he'll be talking about something and then when you like ask for more information he like really doesn't want to come out like and tell us the whole thing.
> I: Can you give me like—can you make up an example? (long pause, lead respondent heard making long "ah" sound) What do you mean he doesn't want to give you more information?
> R: Like he doesn't want to.
> R: He doesn't want to tell you everything about it.
> R: Everything like details.
> I: Why not?
> R: I guess that's just the way he is. I don't know.
> I: How do you guys feel about that?
> R: Depressed. Because if he's about talking to us about drugs and alcohol and all these kind of things he should come out with those, you know, he should talk to us the right—you know, with the whole thing, not just say a little bit and then just leave the rest behind. [#568, pp. 73–74]

Even at this age level, some students recognize that they want more complete substance use information. This elementary student feels "depressed" because he/she feels that the drug educator does not share with him "the whole thing."

Middle school student groups also wanted more information, although their messages were more sophisticated than those of elementary school students. The middle school students also wanted more information, but wanted it delivered to them by substance users or abusers. While often sarcastic, these students were aware that substances were "abused." They wanted more information through a different and more experiential process:

> I: What do you think that teachers or schools could do to really help kids with this stuff? If it could be really helpful, what?
> R: Um, try it and see if they like it! (being facetious?)
> I: Let them try it? I don't think that's gonna happen!
> R: And I doubt that they would like it.
> I: Yeah? Okay. What else can schools really do?

---

* The following dialogues are reprinted from Brown et al. 1997, copyright © by the American Educational Research Association and used by permission.

R: They should like, they should have a lot of things like that.

I: A lot of things like?

R: Like drugs and stuff. Like regular users and stuff like that. Someone that's had what it can do to your body and stuff like that.

I: Uh huh?

R: Keep you out of class, too!

R: They should bring like people that have done tobacco and like got messed up with their job or something! Stuff to show 'em that how you handle it. [#606, p. 76]

The following is from a second interview:

I: Um, do you think that any of the information that you got at school, at this school has influenced you either way in your own decision? As you get older and have to make those choices?

R: Not really.

I: You don't think that the class really had much impact?

R: No.

I: No? How about you? Do you think?

R: Yes. It had an impact.

I: It what?

R: They said it was like bad for you!

R: You just tell 'em that it's bad for you!

I: Oh, bad for you! I'm sorry! I didn't understand. Um, who do you think ought to be teaching you about alcohol and tobacco and other drugs?

R: Somebody who has had a real problem with it.

I: Okay, and does still have a problem?

R: No! They got over it.

I: Somebody got over it?

R: Probably someone who still has a drug problem. [#551, p. 76]

In addition to expressing sarcasm, these middle school students are telling us that they want more information delivered by substance users ("regular users") and abusers (people who have a "real drug problem") from outside the school. Rather than receiving "just the facts," students wanted to understand the experience of substance use and abuse. In isolation sarcasm might merely indicate common adolescent skepticism. However, given the specific linkages these students made to educational processes they actually experienced, the skepticism seems to reflect their reactions to prevention education.

Not surprisingly, it is among high school students that we find the best articulated statements about what students want in their drug education. Statements like these represent well articulated but typical high school student discussion:

R: Yeah, but the Health teacher doesn't really know, you know.

R: Oh yeah, the Health teacher doesn't know. He's reading from the book.

R: Yeah, he's just reading from the book and if they had brought someone in that knew and that like went through it I think it would be a lot better.

R: It's kind of like everybody knows that drugs and smoking are bad for you so it's not like a teacher can sit there and can pound it into you so you're not going to do it. I remember like in sixth grade our PE teacher would sit there (inaudible) and (inaudible) smoking, they all went along with it or whatever but it's like you are going to do it if you want, you're not going to listen to a teacher or a parent. If my parents sit there and say all the time, stop smoking, stop doing this, don't do anything, don't do any drugs, don't do anything bad when you go out. So they can say as much as they want, your best friend (inaudible), but you're only going to listen to yourself, it's not what they teach you, if you know it's bad.

I: Using or not using has something to do with your own decision?

R: [Loud responses from many voices] Yes. [#531, pp. 76–77]

By saying "the Health teacher doesn't really know" and "if they had brought someone in that knew and that like went through it, I think it would be a lot better," nearly all high school focus groups connected program inefficacy and lack of educator credibility with the kinds of changes they desired: (1) moving away from "no-use" educational processes and (2) being able to identify in some way with an educator whom they perceive as able to provide credible information.

At first, the next passage seems to indicate that students want more of what already exists in drug education: addicts sharing their harmful-consequences experiences with students. However, when interviewers probed, we found that they wanted more than that:

I: Who do you think should be teaching you about alcohol, tobacco, and drugs?

R: Someone outside the school.

I: For example?

R: I don't know, yourself.

R: No, I think someone who has been through it. (several voices speak at once, sounds as if they are in agreement with this statement)

R: Someone outside the school.

I: Recovering addicts?

R: They know the most because they have been through it. They know how it feels.

R: They only tell you—like their stories are interesting and you want to hear about it. You know when you're sitting in the class and you're reading out of a book, you know, cigarettes cause emphysema, it's like "that's great."

R: It's boring.

R: Yeah, so it's so boring, just like the other school classes, I mean, but we already know about it and that's not going to help us. We already know about it and it's not going to do anything.

I: So you agree with him that it needs to be an experiential thing.

R: (several voices at once) Yes.

R: If somebody does drugs and if a teacher says it does this to you, you're not going to stop unless something happens to you or you see something happen to someone else, you know, one of your close friends or something and then you think about it, because when you're doing drugs or drinking or whatever, you don't think anything is going to happen to you, you just think, you know. [#531, p. 77]

These students tell us that their programs are ineffective ("but we already know about it and that's not going to help us . . . it's not going to do anything"), and then go on to describe what they want: (1) "Someone outside the school"; (2) "Someone like yourself" (the interviewer, not a substance abuser); (3) "Someone who has been through it," delivering drug education. In sum, the students do not ask that there be no prevention education. Rather, they want prevention education delivered by guides who are both credible and authentic.

The final statement best summarizes the student view of the desired educational process:

R: I just want to say that I guess the best education would be the education that would allow you to evaluate yourself and allow you to evaluate your own personal beliefs and your morals and your values and take a strong look at what you're feeling and how you might have the possibility to be a substance abuser. [#530, p. 77]

ALTERNATIVE MODELS OF SUBSTANCE USE EDUCATION: HARM REDUCTION AND CONFLUENT EDUCATION

The deficit and deviance explanations for adolescent substance use underlie decades of failure by drug education. Knee-jerk acceptance of these explanations and their associated programs has closed the system to alternatives. But the price for maintaining this closed system has been severe. As youth perceive that drug education is little more than indoctrination, they respond by tuning out the message.

People use alcohol and other drugs to alter how they experience themselves and the world. The real-life consequences of use vary from harmless recreation and interesting perceptions and thoughts to self-destruction and serious social harm. Yet in the ostensibly humanitarian, public health model, no distinction is made between casual and abusive use. One of the authors of this chapter asked an epidemiologist how it was decided that an increase in overall use signified an epidemic. "An epidemic is any level of use higher than that we [our models] predict," he replied with a shrug.[4]

Our point has been that characterizing every rise in the number of teenagers who try a drug even once as an epidemic assures that policies will be adopted in a state of permanent hysteria, as indeed they have been. Understanding use as a phenomenon with origins in cultural trends that is heavily influenced by group norms and rituals, and that is likely to result in real harm to a relatively circumscribed minority of youth who can be identified and assisted, ought to bring a very different perspective to prevention. It might even be possible to present honest information, answer the questions that young people have, and enlist them in helping in prevention instead of sitting in sullen boredom and defiance as is so often the case under current prevention programs.

Human beings, whether teenagers or adults, *decide* to drink or use. Even alcoholics or addicts, before every drink or fix, can opt to put down the glass or the needle and pursue sobriety. The life stories of recovering alcoholics and addicts are replete with such moments of truth. Yet the public health perspective has been interpreted in a way that removes responsibility from the user, as if the drug were all-powerful and the user a mindless automaton. But the harms associated with current policies should inform us that placing responsibility where it belongs does not mean punishing young people when they do not make the choices we would like them to make. Rather, the focus needs to be on encouraging them to take responsibility for their decisions and actions, while making assistance available for those whose choices lead them into trouble.

To provide a sound basis for drug prevention education, a model for practice must facilitate understanding of the multiple reasons why people use drugs as well as for what kinds of people, conditions, and situations use is inappropriate. No doubt some proponents of current approaches would reply that this is too complex for youth prevention because there are many reasons why individuals use drugs in various situations. This response reveals an implicit recognition that many factors, personal and social, are indeed related to drug use and its consequences. It is hardly an excuse for doing more of the same in drug education.

But the most predictable response from currently dominant interest groups is that approaches that focus on harm reduction while abandoning the core principles of zero tolerance ideology—especially that all drugs are the same, equating any use with abuse, and an overblown theory of progression—will be perceived by youth as giving them permission to use. The flaw in this argument is that the great majority of older teenagers *already* feel that they have the right to drink, and at least half that they have a similar right to use marijuana. Use of other drugs has actually declined in recent years, and has never accounted for more than a small percentage of overall teenage use. Teenagers, despite what they hear over and over again in drug education, form their own conclusions about hard versus soft drugs. Like it or not, this is the way things are.

Zinberg (1983) did seminal work on how users control their alcohol and other drug use, work conveniently ignored since the drug war began. He explained that effects of specific psychoactive drugs are not constant (like medicines), but fluctuate widely depending on the psychological *set* (state) of the user, the social *setting* in which use occurs, and the properties of the particular *drug*. How Zimberg's principles of drug, set, and setting apply to the effects of alcohol surely requires no elaboration. For one of the authors it also recalls a first interview of a marijuana user in the late 1960s. The latter indicated that "marijuana takes you where you are going at a particular time" and went on to say that in his experience one should not use that drug when feeling angry or anxious or in an uncomfortable social situation. Later, as use of drugs continued to develop, there were similar observations about LSD, including the importance of a trustworthy guide and a secure situation on the occasion of first use.

Depending on the interaction between the possible effects of a drug, the personality of the user, and the nature of the social situation, the experience and its consequences can vary widely. Also depending on this interaction, abusive and addictive use may develop quite independently of the phenomenon of physical dependency and withdrawal symptoms associated with regular use of some drugs. The drug itself is only one of many factors determining the consequences of use.

Zinberg and colleagues (1977) studied controlled marijuana, psychedelic, and heroin users whose long-term moderate use was confined to specific social settings characterized by group sanctions against outside use and regulated by in-group rituals. They concluded that drug use could be controlled by social as well as psychological factors. Most people who drink or use manage to maintain sensible limits on their use. In fact, it would be more accurate to say that most drinkers and users are really not consciously concerned with "control" over their use. For example, moderate drinkers do not need to make pledges to themselves and others that they will never again have more than two drinks at a party. It is the abuser, the addict in the making, who, after repeated negative experiences, becomes preoccupied with limiting use.

Let us be clear on the issue of giving approval to teenage use. We advise young people to stay clean and sober and to obey the law. We do not advocate programs promoting substance use. Nevertheless, students tell us, and we believe them, that they need accurate information focused on reducing the potential harm arising from substance use and providing help for those who need it. This is what is usually referred to as a *harm reduction model*.[5] According to O'Hare and colleagues (1988), a harm reduction model applied to drug education includes the following suggestions:

> Provide young people with honest, factual information about drugs.
> Help them examine in a nonpunitive atmosphere their own attitudes about drugs and drug users.
> Help them understand people who experience drug problems, and foster a caring attitude.
> Help them avoid the harmful consequences of drug use by explaining secondary prevention (after initiation of use) strategies.
> Raise awareness of the legal, health, and social implications of their own drug use.
> Help them understand the role of drug use in past and present societies and cultures.

To this we would add:

> Acquaint them with the signs of drug dependency in self and others and the nature of intervention and treatment.

Adopting a harm reduction approach in prevention is only the first step in fully acknowledging the sophistication of today's youth. It does not address how such programs could be delivered. Teenagers tell us they want a change in the *process* of drug education, that is, how it is delivered to them. Students want to be more aware about issues they think important and to take responsibility for their actions. For them, awareness and responsibility are defined by an educational process that incorporates two goals: (1) a learning process characterized by trust, caring, and a sense of full participation that (2) (and in our words) promotes in youth the integration of thinking, feelings, and actions, both about and within themselves, as well as relative to their role as a member of groups and in other social contexts (Brown 1996, DeMeulle and D'Emidio-Caston 1996).

As revealed in the focus interview transcripts, students want drug educators to be facilitators. They want an honest, give-and-take process, rather than authorities presiding over a top-down process in which canned information is fed to a passive audience. When poorly trained educators, using confrontational and deficit model approaches, tell teenagers what to think about substances and how to think about them, responsibility is taken away. When adults merely tell teenagers that they should take responsibility for themselves ("Just say no!"), they are actually preventing them from going through a necessary developmental process engendering maturity and acceptance of responsibility. A harm reduction model, if properly implemented, can allow educators to be facilitators without taking responsibility away from youth.

Currently, the American educational system is undergoing its first major restructuring since John Dewey at the turn of this century. Much more attention is being paid to how we educate teachers. Teacher educators, it is hoped, are training student teachers to teach *with* students rather than *at* them. The role the teacher establishes relative to the student may be one of the most important factors in drug education. Given youth's informed and sophisticated (but not necessarily accurate) drug information network, the educator cannot get away with simply reading facts from a curriculum guide warning about the dangers of drugs. D'Emidio-Caston and Brown (1998) found that students at all educational levels want to voice and examine their questions about drugs with understanding teachers, and, conversely, that they are highly sensitive to the inadequacies of teachers who do not or cannot facilitate such a process. It is possible to be a caring, knowledgeable, facilitating teacher without advocating substance use. We suspect that this is part of any successful education for today's youth, and it is most certainly necessary for effective drug education.

How might educators in a restructured learning environment work with students who may be vulnerable to abusive use of substances? A great deal of evidence suggests that youth in even the most challenging life circumstances can be successful, if only their well-being is promoted through enhancing resilience rather than through stigmatization and isolation (Werner 1989, 1990, 1993). One of the most effective ways to do this is to provide time to talk and someone to listen. This can be any adult who bonds with a child and gives him or her support and understanding through the most difficult life circumstances. In the educational system this can be achieved through two processes. With most youth, facilitators should work with small groups that confidentially, openly, and honestly discuss youth experience and values. For those students with an actual or potential substance use difficulty, various kinds of student assistance programs should be available as alternatives to banishment and expulsion.

One of the most destructive tactics associated with current drug policy results in young people seeing peers known to have substance abuse difficulties being banished from school. Witnessing such a process demonstrates to them that the educational system does not care about them. We submit that an effective, humane, and even efficient educational process would focus on promoting the well-being of all students and assisting those who need help. Making appropriate programmatic distinctions between students who need help and those who require honest information and the opportunity to process it in an accepting learning atmosphere would benefit schools as institutions as well as their students.

Finally, students tell us that they want contact with people who have had problems with substances as well as with people who have had some experience, but without associated problems. Unfortunately, programs in which ex-drug addicts told students about their disastrous addictions are generally perceived by young people as just another kind of scare tactic. Most youth simply do not see how they themselves could ever get into the desperate situations related by recovered addicts in their personal stories. We choose to interpret the underlying message to be a request for adult guides who are *credible*. If such teachers are properly educated themselves and allowed to be candid and truthful, the issue of prior personal experience with substances is no longer relevant.

CONCLUSIONS

Today we are mired in a drug education corrupted by drug war ideology. Inappropriate theories and the programs they generate, when combined with highly symbolic interest-group politics, have resulted in policies and programs that are ineffective and worse. Current programs are underpinned by a deficit view of youth and programmatically marred by inaccurate or incomplete information and educational processes that alienate intelligent teenage students. Prevention today is also marred by highly punitive responses against those who "do not hear the message." Many youth respond to this situation through an alternative cultural information network that usually, but not always, gives them the information they seek through processes they are more likely to trust. As a new wave of research reveals continued failures in drug education, the opportunity for making positive changes is now emerging.

Based on realistic developmental models of adolescence, harm reduction programs can combine with confluent education processes for more effective drug education.

We believe that a cost-benefit analysis of the outcomes of harm reduction approaches in drug education would reveal significant benefits to our society, including improved educational outcomes, more participation from youth as citizens, decline in youth criminal activity, and significant reductions in life-endangering behaviors associated with substance use. Programs representing these paradigm shifts should be implemented and evaluated. But they cannot be evaluated using traditional methods, as Horowitz and Brown (1996) have explained. They propose an evaluation approach that more realistically reflects the social world of youth, is more dynamic than traditional evaluations, and would reveal more accurate explanations of the findings than are currently provided through evaluation strategies based solely on simplistic experimental designs inherited from laboratory science.

It is time to begin applying the knowledge base about effective educational practices to drug education. In doing so, we must have the courage to take chances inherent in a democratic society. This means allowing young people to become aware and informed, while at the same time expecting them to balance opportunity with personal responsibility. Drug education can be seen as a forum for acquainting youth with what education really is: a process in which learners are given the opportunity to engage themselves with all of the information that is relevant to a complex issue and then decide how to apply it in their own lives. But most of all, a transformed drug education will allow us to stop punishing youth who are merely learning how to set their own life's boundaries, and start helping those who really need it.

ENDNOTES

1. *Drug education* as used in this chapter refers to education that seeks to prevent or reduce the use of any psychoactive substance, especially alcohol and illicit drugs, but also psychoactive pharmaceutical drugs used without a valid prescription. While we are aware that tobacco has the most damaging effects on health of any substance used illicitly by youth, we do not consider tobacco and its active ingredient, nicotine, to have psychoactive properties in the same sense that alcohol and marijuana or cocaine do. However, virtually all of what we propose in this chapter applies to tobacco education as well.

2. The accuracy of reports by adolescents on anonymous, paper-and-pencil questionnaire surveys assessing use of illicit substances is often questioned. While researchers generally assume that underreporting use is more common than exaggerating use, Marquis (1981), in a review of several studies of reports on sensitive topics that could be corroborated against independent, objective checks on validity, found little evidence of systematic misrepresentation. However, reports based solely on students currently in school *do* underestimate use for an overall age cohort by not including data from peers who have dropped out of school. Horowitz and Austin (1997) found that school dropouts had significantly higher rates of use of all substances than youth attending school.

3. Each student quotation represents the most articulate exemplar of a given category of statements in the large-scale study of school drug education conducted by Brown and his colleagues (1997). The categories were established by means of the constant comparative method used in the grounded theory approach described by Glaser and Strauss (1967) and Strauss and Corbin (1990).

4. From an interchange at a meeting of the Substance Abuse Research Consortium, Sacramento, CA, September 24-25, 1996.

5. The particular prevention strategies proposed here under the broader concept referred to as *harm reduction* are limited to drug education. Pragmatism is the principle underlying all specific approaches to harm reduction. The latter thus begins with the recognition that some significant level of alcohol and other drug use by youth (and adults) will continue regardless of efforts at suppression. Whatever the particular area of application, harm reduction attempts to identify and mitigate (1.) the harmful consequences of substance use itself as well as (2.) the many additional harms that result from implementation of the laws and practices fostered under war on drugs policies. As such, harm reduction involves reform in many social institutions, especially education, public health, law enforcement, and the courts.

REFERENCES

Baizerman, M., and Compton, D. (1992). From respondent and informant to consultant and participant: the evolution of a state agency policy evaluation. In *Minority Issues in Program Evaluation*, New Directions in Program Evaluation, no. 53, ed. A. M. Madison, pp. 5-15. San Francisco: Jossey-Bass.

Bandura, A. (1977). *Social Learning Theory*. Englewood Cliffs, NJ: Prentice-Hall.

Baum, D. (1996). *Smoke and Mirrors: The War on Drugs and the Politics of Failure*. Boston: Little, Brown.

Beck, J. E. (1998). 100 years of "just say no" versus "just say know": reevaluating drug education goals for the coming century. *Evaluation Review* 22(1):15-45.

Bell, N. J., and Bell, R. W. (1993). *Adolescent Risk Taking*. Thousand Oaks, CA: Sage.

Botvin, G. J. (1995). Principles of prevention. In *Handbook on Drug Abuse Prevention*, ed. R. H. Coombs and D. Ziedonis, pp. 19-44. Boston: Allyn and Bacon.

Brown, J. H., ed. (1996). *Advances in Confluent Education, Vol. 1: Integrating Consciousness for Human Change*. Greenwich, CT: JAI Press.

Brown, J. H., and D'Emidio-Caston, M. (1995). On becoming at risk through drug education: how symbolic policies and their practices affect students. *Evaluation Review* 19(4):451-492.

Brown, J. H., D'Emidio-Caston, M., and Pollard, J. (1997). Students and substances: social power in drug education. *Educational Evaluation and Policy Analysis* 19(1):65-82.

Brown, J. H., and Horowitz, J. E. (1993). Deviance and deviants: why adolescent substance use prevention programs do not work. *Evaluation Review* 17(5):529-555.

Chng, C. L. (1981). The goal of abstinence: implications for drug education. *The Journal of Drug Education* 11(1):13-18.

Coie, J. D., Watt, N. F., and West, S. G., et al. (1993). The science of prevention: a conceptual framework and some directions for a national research program. *American Psychologist* 48(10):1013-1022.

Cushman, P. (1990). Why the self is empty. *American Psychologist* 45(5):599-611.

DeMeulle, L., and D'Emidio-Caston, M. (1996). Confluent education: a coherent vision of teacher education. In *Advances in Confluent Education, Vol 1: Integrating Consciousness for Human Change*, ed. J. H. Brown. Greenwich, CT: JAI Press.

D'Emidio-Caston, M., and Brown, J. H. (1998). The other side of the story: student narratives on the California drug, alcohol, and tobacco education programs. *Evaluation Review* 22(1):95-117.

Dielman, R. E., Shope, J. T., Leech, S. L., and Butchart, A. T. (1989). Differential effectiveness of an elementary school-based alcohol misuse prevention program. *Journal of School Health* 59:255-263.

Edelman, M. (1964). *The Symbolic Uses of Politics*. Chicago: University of Illinois Press.

Ellickson, P. L. (1995). Schools. In *Handbook on Drug Abuse Prevention*, ed. R. H. Coombs and D. M. Ziedonis, pp. 93-120. Boston: Allyn and Bacon.

Ellickson, P. L., Bell, R. M., and McGuigan, K. (1993). Preventing adolescent drug use: long-term results of a junior high program. *Journal of Public Health* 83(6):856-861.

Ennett, S. T., Tobler, N. S., Ringwalt, C. L., and Flewelling, R. L. (1994). How effective is drug abuse resistance education? A meta-analysis of project DARE outcome evaluations. *American Journal of Public Health* 44(9):1394-1401.

Evans, W. P., and Skager, R. W. (1992). Academically successful drug users: an oxymoron? *Journal of Drug Education* 22(4):353-365.

Everingham, S. S., and Rydell, C. P. (1994). *Modeling the Demand for Cocaine*. Drug Policy Research Center, Santa Monica, CA: Rand Corporation.

Gillmore, M. R. Hawkins, D. J., Catalano, R. F., et al. (1991). Structure of problem behaviors in preadolescence. *Journal of Consulting and Clinical Psychology* 5(4):499-506.

Glaser, B. B., and Strauss, A. L. (1967). *The Discovery of Grounded Theory: Strategies for Qualitative Research*. New York: Aldine.

Haaga, J. G., and Reuter, P. H. (1995). Prevention: the (lauded) orphan of drug policy. In *Handbook on Drug Abuse Prevention: A Comprehensive Strategy to Prevent the Abuse of Alcohol and Other Drugs*, ed. R. H. Coombs and D. Ziedonis, pp. 3-17. Boston: Allyn and Bacon.

Hansen, W. B., and Graham, J. W. (1991). Preventing alcohol, marijuana, and cigarette use among adolescents: peer pressure resistance training versus establishing conservative norms. *Preventive Medicine* 20:414-430.

Hawkins, J. D., Catalano, R. F., and Miller, J. Y. (1992). Risk and protective factors for alcohol and other drug problems in adolescence and early adulthood: implications for substance abuse prevention. *Psychological Bulletin* 112(1):63-105.

Hawkins, J. D., Lishner, D. M., Jenson, J. M., and Catalano, R. F. (1987). Delinquents and drugs: what the evidence suggests about prevention and treatment programming. In *Youth at High Risk for Substance Abuse*, ed. B. S. Brown and A. R. Mills, pp. 81-131. DHHS Publication No. ADM 87-1537; reprinted 1990 as ADM 90-1537. Washington, DC: U.S. Government Printing Office.

Horowitz, J. E., and Austin, G. (1997). *Findings from an exploratory survey of substance use and other risky behaviors among California school dropouts*. Paper presented at the annual meeting of the American Educational Research Association, Chicago, March 27.

Horowitz, J. E., and Brown, J. H. (1996). Confluent education and evaluation research. In *Advances in Confluent Education, Vol 1: Integrating Consciousness for Human Change*, ed. J. H. Brown. Greenwich, CT: JAI Press.

Jessor, R., and Jessor, S. L. (1997). *Problem Behavior and Psychosocial Development: A Longitudinal Study of Youth*. New York: Academic Press.

Johnston, L. D., O'Malley, P. M., and Bachman, J. G. (1995). *National Survey Results on Drug Use from the Monitoring the Future Study, 1975-1994*. Rockville, MD: U.S. Department of Health and Human Services, National Institute on Drug Abuse.

Kandel, D. B., ed. (1978). *Longitudinal Research on Drug Use: Empirical Findings and Methodological Issues*. Washington, DC: Hemisphere-Wilen.

Marquis, K. H. (1981). Response errors in sensitive topic surveys: estimates, effects, and correction options. R-2710/12-HHS, RAND, April.

Newcomb, M. D., and Bentler, P. M. (1988). *Consequences of Adolescent Drug use: Impact on Psychosocial Development and Young Adult Role Responsibility*. Beverly Hills, CA: Sage.

O'Hare, P. A., Clements, I., and Cohen, J. (1988). *Drug education: a basis for reform.* Paper presented at the International Conference on Drug Policy Reform. Bethesda, MD, November.

Richardson, V. (1990). At-risk programs: evaluation and critical inquiry. *New Directions for Program Evaluation* 45:61-75.

Romero, F., Bailey, J., and Carr, C. (1994) *California Programs to Prevent and Reduce Drug, Alcohol, and Tobacco Use Among In-School Youth: Annual Evaluation Report.* Prepared by the Southwest Regional Laboratory for the California Department of Education. Los Alamitos, CA: Southwest Regional Laboratory.

Rossi, R. J. (1994). *Schools and Students at Risk: Context and Framework for Positive Change.* Thousand Oaks, CA: Sage.

Schaps, E., Moskowitz, J., Malvin, J., and Schaeffer, G. (1986). Evaluation of seven school-based prevention programs: A final report on the Napa project. *International Journal of the Addictions* 21:1081-1112.

Shedler, J., and Block, J. (1990). Adolescent drug use and psychological health: a longitudinal inquiry. *American Psychologist* 45(5):612-630.

Shope, J. T, Dielman, T. E., and Butchart, A. T. (1992). An elementary school-based alcohol misuse prevention program: a follow-up evaluation. *Journal of Studies on Alcohol* 53(2):106-121.

Skager, R. W., and Austin, G. (1997). Sixth Biennial Statewide Survey of Drug and Alcohol Use among California Students in Grades 7, 9, and 11. Sacramento, CA: Crime Prevention Center, Office of the Attorney General, California Department of Justice.

Skager, R. W., and Kerst, E. (1989). Alcohol and drug use and self-esteem: a psychological perspective. In *The Social Importance of Self-Esteem*, ed. A. M. Mecca, N. J. Smelser, and J. Vasconcellos, pp. 248-293. Berkeley: University of California Press.

Strauss, A., and Corbin, J. (1990). *Basics of Qualitative Research.* Newbury Park, CA: Sage.

Tobler, N. S. (1986). Meta-analysis of 143 adolescent drug prevention programs. *Journal of Drug Issues* 16:537-567.

—— (1997). Effectiveness of school-based drug prevention programs: a meta-analysis of the research. *Journal of Primary Prevention* 17(3).

Washington Post (1996). An ounce of prevention is not enough. Editorial, June 7.

Werner, E. E. (1989). High risk children in young adulthood: a longitudinal study from birth to 32 years. *American Journal of Orthopsychiatry* 59(1):72-81.

—— (1990). Protective factors and individual resilience. In *Handbook of Early Childhood Intervention*, ed. S. Mesiels and J. Shonkoff, New York: Cambridge University Press.

—— (1993). Risk, resilience and recovery: perspectives from the Kauai longitudinal study. *Development and Psychopathology* 5:503-515.

White House (1989). *National Drug Control Strategy.* Washington, DC: Office of National Drug Control Policy.

White House Office of Drug Control Policy (1996). *National Drug Control Strategy Budget, 1981-1996.* Washington, DC: Office of National Drug Control Policy.

Wingard, J., Huba, G., and Bentler, P. (1979). The relationship of personality structure to patterns of adolescent substance use. *Multivariate Behavioral Research* 14:131-143.

U.S. Department of Education (1995). *Request for Funding Announcement,* June 14.

Yamaguchi, K., and Kandel, D. (1984). Patterns of drug use from adolescence to young adulthood: II. Sequences of progression. *American Journal of Public Health* 74:668-672.

Zinberg, N. (1983). *Drug, Set, and Setting.* New Haven: Yale University Press.

Zinberg, N. E., Harding, W. M., and Winkeller, M. (1977). A study of social regulatory mechanisms in controlled illicit drug uses. *Journal of Drug Issues* 7(2):117-133.

PART II

APPROACHES TO LEGALIZATION

Introduction

Given the substantive background provided by the first half of this book, the second half, "Approaches to Legalization," discusses a variety of proposals, with a variety of rationales, for a variety of forms of legalization.

Section IIA, "General Considerations," contains three chapters that offer three different kinds of overviews of issues related to legalization.

In Chapter 13 James Ostrowski looks at developments since his 1989 comprehensive cost-benefit analysis of drug prohibition. He shows that the social problems caused by prohibition continue as a result of the continuation of the same failed policies, and then explains why prohibitionist arguments against legalization continue to remain unpersuasive. Among the prohibition-related social problems that remain, the author discusses the permanent crime wave, the disproportionate imprisonment of minority men (thereby creating fatherless single-parent families), the swamping of the courts with drug cases, falling prices for cocaine and heroin despite increased law enforcement, an increase in drug-related medical emergencies and AIDS, and a loss of civil liberties.

From there he goes on to ask why the cost-benefit argument has failed thus far to persuade a majority of Americans, and discusses six reasons: (1) people's skepticism about statistics, (2) the subjective component involved in evaluating costs and benefits, (3) people's ignorance of the consequences of

current policy, (4) the bureaucratic self-interest of those involved in drug prohibition, (5) the war on drugs as a religious war that is not open to evidence
or logic, and (6) the willingness of white suburbanites to pay for the destruction of inner-city minority neighborhoods so that they can feel safe.

While I am more optimistic about the future than the chapter's author,
his presentation does convey a vivid picture of the intellectual climate that
reformers confront.

In Chapter 14 Richard M. Evans analyzes the words in the phrase *drug
legalization*. He discusses a variety of approaches to changing current policy,
from de jure and de facto decriminalization, limitation of access (through prescriptions, licensing, and/or restrictions on places where substances can be
used), and regulation and taxation to complete legalization—in which currently
illicit substances would be no different from any other commodity.

At this point I would like to digress to react to an interesting point that
the author makes along the way. It is that alcohol prohibition—even though
it was codified in a constitutional amendment—was actually much weaker than
drug prohibition, since possession of small amounts of alcohol for personal use
was never a crime. In other words, Prohibition was an example of what we
would now call *decriminalization*.

One might ask why it is then that—even though there was a constitutional amendment—Prohibition fell so rapidly once its counterproductive, black-
market-creating aspect became evident. Clearly it wasn't because alcohol is not
dangerous. From what was known at the time, it appeared to be the most
dangerous psychoactive substance. Only when we became aware of tobacco's
initially less obvious but ultimately more devastating health effects did we realize that a more dangerous substance existed.

The answer seems to be, rather, that too many people used alcohol. Thus,
even under a regime of decriminalization, it was not politically sustainable to
direct governmental power against so large a proportion of the population. In
order for prohibition to "work," the target needs to be a smaller minority, so
that a significant majority of the population can cloak its scapegoating in the
garments of moral outrage. In other words, cocaine and heroin are useful substances to demonize because relatively few people want to use them. (This is
because their negative effects are easy to see. For example, people can smoke
while working, or drink during a lunch break, but cocaine and heroin are not
"worker friendly" substances—using them has not been found to be career
enhancing.) Because relatively few people want to use them, however, the
government cannot build up a "prison industrial complex" with a war against
only "hard drugs."

Marijuana is a more problematic substance because well over a quarter
of the population has used it—enough to mobilize a huge criminal justice bureaucracy, but beginning to approach the numbers that made alcohol prohi-

bition untenable. If only marijuana—and no other substances—were legalized, then the war on drugs would shrink dramatically, prisons would close, and many drug warriors and criminal justice bureaucrats would be looking for jobs.

We now know that tobacco is the most dangerous substance, even more dangerous than alcohol, because it is responsible for many more deaths—both direct (e.g., more lung cancer than cirrhosis of the liver) and indirect (e.g., more people killed by secondhand smoke than by drunk drivers). Since a much greater proportion of smokers than of drinkers are heavy users and have difficulty stopping, the more devastating effects of smoking are harder to avoid. Thus, if any substance should be prohibited because of its disastrous effects on society, it is tobacco.

Unfortunately, as we have seen from the case of alcohol, it would be a dreadful idea to make tobacco illegal. The magnitude and viciousness of the black market that would develop, and the "breathtaking" speed of its appearance, would make the current drug war disaster pale by comparison. The only argument in favor of making tobacco illegal is that to do so would create so colossal a calamity so quickly that the entire regime of drug prohibition might collapse along with it. No matter how strongly one is opposed to drug prohibition, however, nothing could justify putting the country through so pointless a social catastrophe. (This ends the digression.)

In Chapter 15 Stanley Neustadter reviews a range of legislative options based on actual bills that have been presented to state legislatures. These legislative models roughly correspond to the range of public health policy options discussed in Chapter 14, but do not yet include bills for complete legalization. The chapter discusses bills legalizing marijuana alone, as well as omnibus/all drugs bills; and it also refers to two other approaches not yet submitted as bills.

International treaties and federal laws would supersede new state laws, even if enacted, but the repeal of drug prohibition in a number of states would increase the enforcement burden on the federal government—a tactic that was used successfully by the movement to repeal alcohol prohibition. In addition, passing state laws for one or another form of legalization would be a dramatic sign to politicians around the country of a significant shift in voter opinion. (Perhaps the 1996 success of medical marijuana referenda in California and Arizona is a harbinger of such a change.)

After reviewing the range of current bills, the chapter goes on to present fifteen policy issues that must be considered in drafting legalization legislation. These issues, which include taxation, liability waivers, home growers, drug testing, prescription drugs, and the fate of large numbers of people imprisoned for activities that will cease to be criminal, require careful thought. Many of them are discussed elsewhere in this book.

Section IIB, "A Range of Options," contains nine chapters, each of which presents a different approach to legalization. The chapters are arranged in an approximate sequence from the most limited (change the government's classification of licit and illicit substances—and, by implication, any penalties associated with them—to reflect scientific evidence of dangerousness) to the most sweeping (legalize all substances at all dosage levels). These differing proposals cover a vast intellectual territory, and include public health, rights-based, and mixed stated and/or implied rationales for many different and often overlapping policies. Furthermore, the disciplinary backgrounds of the authors and the kinds of evidence and modes of argument they use to support their various suggestions come from constitutional law, economics, philosophy, political science, psychiatry, and psychology. Thus many of these chapters invite readers to consider and reflect on their proposals as self-contained entities before comparing them to others or choosing elements from among several different ones.

In Chapter 16, Robert S. Gable condenses findings from a wide range of experimental studies to classify twenty psychoactive substances—legal, prescription, and illegal—on the two key dimensions of acute toxicity and dependence potential. His presentation makes it easy to see that the penalties for using the various substances bear little relationship to their dangerousness.

I would like to react briefly to the clear implication of this chapter that any prohibitionist penalties that do exist should be roughly proportional to the dangerousness of the substances involved. The fact that this is not the case, and that repeated efforts to achieve this kind of appropriateness have been consistently rebuffed over the years, makes one wonder about the motivation of governmental policymakers. As I see it, the demonstration in Part I of the book, that prohibitionism has been used as a way of legitimizing the mistreatment of minority groups, points to the dark side of our irrational classification of substances.

In Chapter 17 Lester Grinspoon makes the case for medical marijuana, a subject he has explored in great detail in his other writings. He discusses a wide range of therapeutic uses for this substance, which if legal would have the dual advantages of low cost and low toxicity.

In Chapter 18 Robert W. Sweet and Edward A. Harris present a philosophical and constitutional argument for the decriminalization of all substances. In addition, they call for continuing discussion of policy alternatives—especially public health options—that would go even further.

Sweet and Harris describe, analyze, and respond to the views of the libertarian psychiatrist Thomas Szasz, who argues that all psychoactive substances (including prescription drugs) should be treated like other goods and should be available for adults to purchase in the free market. Like Szasz, the authors begin by attacking the emotionally charged symbolism, metaphors, and myths that pervade and distort the drug policy "debate." Those not familiar with Szasz's writings will be repaid by reading the well-chosen quotations that appear in both the text and notes.

The authors base their decriminalization alternative on the right of adults to self-determination, and explain why they understand that right as one of the unenumerated rights protected by the Ninth Amendment to the Constitution. The "right to self-determination" refers to individuals' ability to make and implement informed choices about their own conduct—which is practically a definition of the value of "individualism" that social scientists have found to be central to our culture.

In Chapter 19 Eric E. Sterling argues not only that drug prohibition has failed, but that the drug problem can never be solved—it can only be managed. As a result, he advocates a pragmatic course of trying out a variety of public health and criminal justice policies in an evolving attempt to see what works best, instead of a comprehensive regulatory scheme.

The chapter begins with a discussion of twelve principles for managing the drug problem, and then goes on to identify a series of key issues and offer a variety of approaches to them. Here are a few examples: licenses for adults to use various substances (including alcohol), which could be lifted if rules governing responsible use are broken—along with insurance for substance users to pay for damage done while under the influence; lockable beer sections of refrigerators (as a counterpart to liquor cabinets) to keep alcohol away from children; suggestions for the development of a medical marijuana industry; and a proposal that driving under the influence of drugs and alcohol be controlled by tests of impaired performance rather than chemical tests.

As these examples indicate, the author would replace the global "Just say no/don't even think about drugs" approach by a more molecular one of specifying a series of issues and trying out different solutions for each one. Some of these prevent abuse through information, education, and humane treatment; others confront users with a swarm of bureaucratic gnats (making abuse awkward, inconvenient, expensive, and less fun) instead of hitting them over the head with a sledge hammer (throwing them in jail for years).

In Chapter 20 I discuss a series of initial steps, short of legalizing cocaine and heroin, that can be taken to significantly reverse the damage caused by drug prohibition. In addition, I make three general proposals concerning the context of legalization, which are aimed at fostering a more rational and humane drug policy.

In Chapter 21 Mary M. Cleveland provides an economic perspective on drug legalization, illustrated by a series of informative tables and figures. She presents federal drug use statistics—which confirm what readers can recognize in patterns of alcohol use—that there are a small proportion of abusers, a larger proportion of regular users, and a substantial majority of occasional users. Combining this information with knowledge about patterns of use of different substances, she argues for downsizing the drug war and proposes three very different policies for marijuana, cocaine, and heroin. Implicit throughout her chapter is the idea of using economic tools to construct a public health policy that offers the best chance of minimizing drug abuse among troubled youth.

In Chapter 22 Ethan A. Nadelmann reviews the logic and implications of a range of approaches to drug policy whose advocates he characterizes as "hardcore libertarians," "progressive legalizers," "progressive prohibitionists," and "reactionary prohibitionists" (or "pharmacological Calvinists"). In response to the libertarian "supermarket model" of legalization, he offers a complex "right of access" or "mail-order" proposal. This would allow adults to buy small amounts of all substances by mail, for personal use, from a single (most likely governmental) supplier, in a somewhat inconvenient manner that includes a deliberately built-in time delay. He presents a variety of reasons for believing that the effects of legalization on increasing abuse would be quite limited. (For example, polls show that few would use currently illegal substances if they became legal.) Instead, he discusses changes in patterns of use and abuse of differing substances that would be likely to follow changes in policy.

In the course of explaining and discussing the rationale for this proposal, the chapter calls attention to many of the key issues that need to be considered in designing a new drug policy, and examines a range of opinions in a search for common ground.

In Chapter 23 Steven B. Duke and Albert C. Gross advocate legalizing virtually all widely used substances so as to avoid the greater costs of prohibition, but propose a variety of forms of regulation to minimize the dangers of drug abuse. These include restricting the places where drugs can be used; preventing juvenile access; encouraging employee assistance programs; licensing the refining, production, and distribution of psychoactive substances; and banning their advertising.

Finally, in Chapter 24, Mark Thornton provides a libertarian economic rationale for legalizing all substances at all dosage levels. He argues that market forces, taxes, liability laws, and social pressures will be sufficient to control drug consumption, as they were in the nineteenth century.

We should remember that in the nineteenth century, when everything was legal in the United States, alcohol—not opiates or cocaine—was the substance singled out as most dangerous and most requiring governmental control. Many members of the temperance movement used opiates, which were freely available in hundreds of patent medicines, and physicians treated pain more successfully than they do today. If opiates—which are more difficult to stop using than any substance except nicotine—were not viewed as a serious danger in the nineteenth century, then it is likely that the dangers of relegalizing everything have been greatly exaggerated. While only a minority of voices in the legalization movement advocate the libertarian free market solution, it is an important position with a distinctive and well-thought-out rationale; it deserves a serious hearing as part of the general debate over what to do.

The chapters in Part II do not exhaust all current proposals for legalization, but they do provide a clear sense of the issues involved. They include both public health and rights-based rationales, and cover the range of options from the most limited to the most sweeping. They should provide an adequate basis for readers to think through for themselves how best to go about legalization. By helping to shift the debate from whether to legalize to how to legalize, it is hoped that this book will contribute to reforming our current drug policy.

Section IIA
General Considerations

13

Drug Prohibition Muddles Along: How a Failure of Persuasion Has Left Us with a Failed Policy

James Ostrowski

INTRODUCTION

In 1989 the Cato Institute published my comprehensive cost-benefit analysis of the so-called "war on drugs," or as I prefer to call it, drug prohibition.[1] In that article I attempted to provide, for the first time since national drug prohibition was begun in 1914, a statistical evaluation of the actual consequences of drug law enforcement. I concluded that drug prohibition was a spectacular failure, nowhere near the break-even point of efficacy. Specifically, I concluded that drug prohibition had created a permanent crime wave, fostered a criminal subculture in inner-city neighborhoods, increased the dangers of using drugs, caused widespread official corruption, overburdened courts and prisons, and destroyed civil liberties, and had done all this without stopping the massive flow of drugs to those who had a strong desire to use them.

Reviewing the long history of official efforts to stamp out the use of various mind-altering drugs throughout the centuries, I concluded that these wars were doomed to failure because:

> drugs motivate some people—those who most need protection from them—more than any set of penalties a civilized society can impose, and

even more than what some less than civilized societies have imposed. The undeniable seductiveness of drugs, usually considered a justification for prohibition, thus actually argues for legalization. The law simply cannot deter millions of people deeply attracted to drugs. [Id., pp. 33–34]

That being the case, the failure of the war on drugs "is guaranteed because the black market thrives on the war on drugs and benefits from any intensification of it. At best, increased enforcement simply boosts the black market price of drugs, encouraging more drug suppliers to supply more drugs" (Id., p. 6).

In short, those who would make drug prohibition work are confronted by "the sheer impossibility of preventing consenting adults in a free society from engaging in extremely profitable transactions involving tiny amounts of illegal drugs"[2] (Id., p. 6).

The report concluded that drug prohibition annually causes about 8,250 deaths and costs the economy about $80 billion, without having markedly reduced drug consumption from what it had been prior to national prohibition in 1914.

The American people, however, rejected the seemingly radical prescription of drug legalization urged upon it by numerous critics of drug prohibition in the late 1980s. Thus we have experienced eight more years of drug prohibition, spanning the presidencies of George Bush and Bill Clinton. Though the idea of ending the war on drugs and instituting some form of drug legalization continues to be discussed in the media and in academia, in 1998 the nation as a whole does not appear to be significantly closer to ending drug prohibition than it was in 1989. As will be demonstrated below, the basic problems caused by drug prohibition remain with us in greater or lesser degrees. Further, the arguments made against legalization by prohibitionists are unpersuasive. Why then has the cost-benefit argument failed to persuade a majority of Americans that it is time to change drug policy? This chapter will attempt to answer that question in the final section.

THE STATE OF THE DRUG "WAR"

CRIME

The United States remains in the midst of a permanent crime wave. There were 42 million crimes in the United States in 1994, including 11 million crimes of violence.[3] Politicians and supporters of drug prohibition boast that crime has decreased in recent years. That is like saying your temperature has gone down from 105 to 104. The FBI reported that the murder rate in 1995, down 7 percent from 1994, was eight per 100,000.[4] That is almost twice as high as the murder rate in the 1950s.[5] Ever since the 1970s, when Richard Nixon called drugs America's public enemy No. 1 and initiated the current "drug war," we have lived—and died—with intolerably high levels of crime and violence. We now live with levels of crime and murder and assault that were common during the gangster era of Al Capone. Of course, that crime wave was caused by the prohibition of alcohol.[6]

This current and seemingly permanent crime wave is also the result of drug prohibition. It began in the early '70s with President Nixon's war on drugs and continues today even after our million man march to jail. As The New York Times reported in January 1996, "The country continues to suffer through the most prolonged crime wave since the days of the wild West."[7] ... "Despite recent reports that crime is decreasing, violent crime in the United States is a ticking time bomb that will explode in the next few years as the number of teenagers soars." [8]

IMPACT OF DRUG PROHIBITION ON MINORITIES

There are 1,584,000 Americans behind bars.[9] About 388,000 are in prison on drug charges,[10] but several hundred thousand more are there because drug prohibition stimulates violent crime and property crime. Over 60 percent of these prisoners are black or Hispanic.[11] We sometimes wonder why we have so many single-parent minority households. Just do the math. We have locked up the men. One third of the young black men in America are in prison, on probation, or on parole,[12] and the single biggest reason is criminal drug prohibition. It has now become clear that those who support drug prohibition are in favor of putting a lot of young black men in prison, a fate from which most will never fully recover: "Those who spend time in correctional facilities are compelled to adopt the values and violent tactics necessary to survive in these facilities. They then bring these antisocial survival tactics out to the streets." [13]

The arrest rate for drug offenses among blacks is significantly higher than for whites, even though the vast majority of drug users are white.[14] Walk into any criminal court in a large American city and you get the feel of what Jim Crow must have been like in the 1950s: whites in charge up front; blacks in the back waiting to be arraigned on drug-related charges.

Prohibition-related violence is also a major reason why blacks have a lower life expectancy than whites[15] and why blacks continue to lag behind whites in economic progress. It is difficult to resist the temptation to call the war on drugs a war on blacks.

OUT-OF-POCKET COST OF DRUG PROHIBITION

In 1989 I estimated that drug prohibition costs about $10 billion per year out of pocket, a relatively small figure compared with other governmental expenditures. Total national expenditures on drug law enforcement are now perhaps $25 billion. That figure may still seem small given total national governmental expenditures of well over $1 trillion. However, the money spent on drug prohibition does have a significant deleterious impact on society. First, the courts are forced to deal with criminal drug cases at the expense of dealing with civil cases. These civil cases drag on for years, imposing enormous suffering on civil litigants, and causing a perception of the impotence of the civil justice system. It is precisely the huge expenditures earmarked for Social Security and other programs that prevent additional funding for civil justice. Second, the devotion of scare resources to drug enforcement takes investigative, prosecutorial, judicial, and correctional resources away from the fight against violent crime.

ENFORCEMENT EFFORTS

Despite some claims to the contrary, drug enforcement has remained vigorous in recent years. The drug offense arrest rate rose from 256 per 100,000 in 1980 to 437 per 100,000 in 1993.[16] Those incarcerated on drug charges have risen from about 52,000 in 1980 to 388,000 in 1995.[17] Drug seizures have remained steady in recent years.[18]

DRUG PRICES

One of the main goals of drug prohibition is to raise the retail price of illegal drugs so as to decrease their economic availability and therefore their use. Thus a prime test of the effectiveness of prohibition is its impact on the street price of illegal drugs. The United States Sentencing Commission, in its 1995 report "Cocaine and Federal Sentencing Policy," stated that:

> Prices for crack cocaine and powder cocaine dropped dramatically during the 1980s. Since 1990, however, prices generally have remained constant or increased . . . crack cocaine generally is sold for $5, $10, or $20 in single-dosage quantities ranging from 0.1 to 0.5 a gram . . . although quantities in some areas have gradually decreased as dealers seek greater profits per sale. . . .The relatively low price for a dose of crack cocaine makes it more affordable to lower-income persons. * * * In some saturated urban markets, the DEA reports even lower 1992 prices (Detroit: $3 per vial; Philadelphia: $2.50 per vial; New York City: $2 per vial). [http://www.acsp.vic.edu/lib/vssc/chapter4.htm]

As for heroin, its price has been *decreasing* while its purity has been *increasing*.[19] Thus, in spite of substantially increasing enforcement efforts, the street prices of drugs have not been significantly reduced in recent years.

DRUG-RELATED MEDICAL EMERGENCIES

Among the more reliable drug-related statistics are those kept by the Drug Abuse Warning Network (DAWN). DAWN keeps records of drug-related medical emergencies in major hospitals throughout the country. According to a recent DAWN report, drug-related visits to emergency rooms have generally been increasing in recent years:

> The rate of drug-related episodes per 100,000 population increased 32 percent from 167 in 1990 to 221 in 1994 and the rate per 100,000 emergency department visits rose 31 percent during the same period from 451 to 591. . . . Cocaine-related episodes in 1994 were at their highest level since the DAWN survey began. The proportion of drug-related episodes that are heroin-related has increased steadily from 4 percent in 1978 (11,700 out of 323,100) to 13 percent in 1994 (64,200 out of 508,900). After a drop in 1990 (33,900), increases continued in 1991, 1992, and 1993 (35,900, 48,000, and 63,200, respectively); however, there was no change in 1994. Heroin-related episodes were at their highest level in 1994, since the DAWN survey began. [http://www.health.org/pubs/94dawn/annualtot.htm]

These numbers suggest that claims of sharp reductions in drug use may be exaggerated.

AIDS AND OTHER DISEASES

Drug prohibition-related AIDS continues to spread as a result of needle sharing by drug users. Further, the jailing of large numbers of prisoners with AIDS in overcrowded facilities with AIDS has caused a resurgence of tuberculosis in jails. According to Andrew A. Skolnick:

> Inmates infected with HIV and TB are at high risk for developing active TB and spreading it in prison and when they are released, in the community. Overtaxed medical staffs at correctional facilities are not able to detect and treat many of the infectious cases. . . . The rates of TB in some jails have skyrocketed. In 1988, the case rate in the general population was 13.7 per 100,000. Case rates in correctional facilities have been as high as 400 to 500 per 100,000.[20]

SUMMARY AND ANALYSIS OF THE NUMBERS

In recent years more money has been spent on drug enforcement, more people have been arrested, and more people have been incarcerated than ever before. These efforts have not been successful in reducing the retail price of cocaine or heroin on the street. There is some reason to believe that fewer people are using drugs. At the same time, however, drug-related medical emergencies have increased. Crime rates have declined slightly in recent years. The reasons for this decline are not clear. However, the United States remains mired in historically high and socially intolerable levels of crime.

What does all this mean? The United States spends a significant amount of money on drug law enforcement and incarcerates a huge number of persons convicted of drug crimes. Most of the inmates are black or Hispanic. Drug prohibition is also causally related to the violent and property crimes that plague our society. Though rates of these crimes have declined slightly, that is little comfort to most people, whose quality of life suffers from the perception and reality of a crime-ridden society. As a result of high levels of crime, the United States now incarcerates a truly incredible number of persons—nearly 1.6 million.

Whether recent and modest declines in drug use are because of changing attitudes or the threat of imprisonment is not clear. However, drugs continue to be used by millions of Americans at relatively stable prices and those users visit emergency rooms in steadily increasing numbers. Whether those visits are caused by the inherent danger of drugs, the lack of quality control over their ingredients, or the lack of less potent legal alternatives is open to question.

CIVIL LIBERTIES

The courts now routinely justify arrests and searches of suspects if they occur in a "drug-prone neighborhood." [21] Further, courts have explicitly stated that police officers no longer need specific evidence of a violation of drug laws in order to arrest suspects: "No longer do courts require as prerequisite to a finding of probable cause the observation of a 'hallmark' of a drug transaction, such as plastic vials, tinfoil packets or glassine envelopes." [22]

The same New York court, in another case, explicitly signed on to the war on drugs at the expense of the right to privacy guaranteed by the Fourth Amendment: "In a probable cause analysis, the emphasis should not be narrowly focused on a recognizable drug package or any other single factor, but on an evaluation of the totality of circumstances. . . [I]n order for society to keep pace with the war on illegal drugs, law enforcement must be as flexible and creative as the drug traffickers." [23]

A fair translation of the last sentence is: "In order for society to keep pace with the war on drugs, the courts must be flexible and creative with the Fourth Amendment." Such ideas have consequences. According to the supposedly liberal courts of New York State, police officers no longer need to see specific evidence of a drug transaction before making an arrest. All they need is to observe money changing hands on the street in a "drug-prone" (read: black) neighborhood. In Buffalo, New York, for example, a white man, Mark Virginia, was seen speaking to a black man late at night in a "drug-prone neighborhood." Money changed hands. For this "crime" the police arrested this innocent man and killed him in an ensuing struggle. No drugs were ever found. It turned out that the white man was the employer of the black man.[24] The *Buffalo News* explained: "The interaction between a white man and a black teenager in the wee hours of the morning could have raised the suspicion of police." [25] Ideas have consequences. Sometimes, ideas can kill.

In the now-famous case in New York City in which Judge Harold Baer was attacked by President Clinton and by Senator Dole for suppressing evidence obtained in an illegal search, it is quite likely that if the suspects had been *white* and had loaded a few duffel bags into a car in a *white* neighborhood, there would have been no arrest and no calls for impeaching a federal judge. In that case the police officer defined the drug-prone neighborhood as "everything north of 155th" street in Manhattan![26]

The actual facts of the case are far less lurid than we are led to believe. A woman is double-parked at 5:00 A.M. on a street in Manhattan. Four men carrying duffel bags approach her car. They open the trunk and put the duffel bags in the trunk. They give her the keys and she pulls away. There was conflicting testimony as to whether the men fled when the police pulled up; the judge concluded that they had not fled. Stripped of its association with a "drug-prone neighborhood," there is simply nothing in these facts probative of illegality. Thus it is that race has become the prime factor in determining which Americans are suspected and investigated for drug crimes.

There is no escaping the fact that, because the drug market tends to attract young, poor, minority males, minorities in general will be subjected to increased suspicion and harassment from law enforcement officials. This is true on the streets of our cities, where a new "crime" has been identified in recent years—"DWB"—driving while black. It is true on the highways, and in bus stations and airports where drug profiles used by drug enforcers inevitably point to ethnic minorities. Blacks and Hispanics are therefore permanent victims of drug prohibition, even though only a tiny percentage of these groups have anything to do with selling illegal drugs. The most appropriate symbol of drug prohibition is a white cop pushing the head of a young black man into the sidewalk while making a drug arrest.

THE PROHIBITIONISTS FIGHT BACK

The first reaction of prohibitionists to calls for drug legalization in the late '80s was the classic strategy of ignoring the issue so as not to dignify their opponents. Eventually, however, the prohibitionists perceived an increase of support for legalization, if not among the public in general, certainly among "intelligent laypersons." Anecdotal evidence suggested that a surprising percentage of the highly educated supported drug legalization. Fearful that this cadre, through osmosis, would gradually shift public opinion against prohibition, prohibitionists left the "Rose Garden" and explicitly campaigned against legalization.

Typical of the antilegalization literature are the 1996 book *Hep-Cats, Narcs, and Pipe Dreams*[27] by Jill Jonnes; a pamphlet entitled "Speaking Out against Drug Legalization," published by the Drug Enforcement Administration in 1994; and a 1995 report by the Center on Addiction and Substance Abuse entitled "Legalization: Panacea or Pandora's Box." Interestingly, all three works were published at a time when legalization was no longer the front page news it had been from 1988 through 1990. These works were selected for analysis here because of the prominence of the authors and the degree of attention bestowed on their publications, as well as the representative nature of the antilegalization arguments they set forth.

Hep-Cats, Narcs, and Pipe Dreams, written by a journalist with a doctorate in American history, describes itself as a "history of America's romance with illegal drugs." It is that, until the last chapter when its apparent ultimate purpose is unveiled: to polemicize against drug legalization. Curiously, however, the book's bibliography and footnotes evidence no familiarity with major legalization literature. Perhaps that is why the author follows standard and fallacious prohibitionist methodology: anecdotally describe the harmful drug use prohibition has *failed* to prevent, then imply that this failure is an argument against legalization. When, in contrast, she attempts to adduce evidence of the harm that prohibition has *succeeded* in preventing, she fails.

She alleges that, prior to the advent of national prohibition, there were about 450,000 drug "addicts" or about 0.6 percent of the population.[28] How many do we have now? "We have five hundred thousand heroin addicts and 2 million cocaine addicts," she writes, or about one percent of the population.[29] That means that prohibition has apparently "succeeded" in increasing the number of drug users five and half times, while the population has increased only three and a half times. According to the author's own figures, the *rate* of drug use has *increased* by one third under prohibition. The failure of prohibition to reduce drug use below preprohibition levels in not addressed in the book.

The book does feature unsupported predictions of massive increases in drug use under legalization. Such predictions, however, are mere thought experiments by a biased advocate, the results of which are never in doubt. The great *historical* experiment of legalization proved otherwise. At a time of wide drug availability, when life was much tougher than it is now; when medicine was primitive, illness commonplace, and knowledge about the dangers of drugs primitive, only a tiny segment of the population used cocaine or heroin.

It is also puzzling why the author deems prohibition a success that had been forgotten by the 1970s. She notes that as early as the 1920s, "not only were the nation's slums awash in illegal cocaine, heroin and morphine, so too was the glamorous, never-never land, Hollywood." [30] She further notes that in Chicago in the 1930s, there were enough drug users around so that 2,500 "addicts" were "studied" by a researcher.[31]

All three prohibitionist tracts attempt to turn the legalization analogy to alcohol and tobacco against legalization by the following argument: so many people use these drugs because they are legal. One could just as well argue that they are legal because so many people want to use them. Conversely, the drive to legalize drugs is handicapped by the public's lack of interest in consuming extremely potent drugs. Alcohol and tobacco, however, because of their more moderate impact, are easily integrated into everyday life. In addition, both are extremely pleasant to the user and so pleasant in some cases that the users could be considered "addicted." These drugs have won out over other drugs over the years because of these characteristics.

If, as prohibitionists argue, the more potent drugs such as the opiates and cocaine turn regular users into subhuman, useless parasites, that fact in itself is a strong deterrent to using them. Even when these drugs were legal, they were not nearly as popular as alcohol and tobacco are today. Also, there is an *illegal* drug that can serve as the basis for comparison in this context. Most reasonable people consider the effects of marijuana to be less dramatic than those of heroin and cocaine. Why is marijuana always more popular than cocaine and heroin in the illegal drug market? Simply because it is, and is perceived to be, less harmful and less disruptive to life than the other drugs. If cocaine were as popular as marijuana, the black market would supply it as readily. It might be argued that marijuana is more available and more popular because it more socially acceptable. However, the reason it is more acceptable than cocaine is that it is perceived to be less harmful. Thus the marketplace itself, that dreaded realm where people make up their own minds, has shown an ability to distinguish between more dangerous drugs and less dangerous drugs (there being no such thing as a safe drug).

All three antilegalization tracts have little to say about substitution effects. A substitution effect occurs when a person deterred from illegal drug use turns instead to a legal harmful drug. The main reason why legalizers believe it important to point out the harmful effects of alcohol, nicotine, and other legal drugs is that those drugs are likely to be used by those deterred from illegal drug use. For example, a person who wishes to be artificially depressed, if deprived of heroin, will get drunk. Being chronically drunk is as socially destructive as being under the influence of heroin, and is almost certainly more physically harmful. Thus it is not clear that forcing a troubled person to switch from heroin to cheap wine is beneficial.

What about forcing a person to switch from cocaine to tobacco? Tobacco can be quite harmful to health both in the short term and the long term. Heavy cocaine use seems to render one incompetent to function. However, is smoking benign in its behavioral effects? Anecdotal evidence suggests a strong correlation between smoking and criminality, as a visit to any jail will confirm. (Bring a gas mask.) Smoking in fact would appear to be the perfect "criminogenic" drug: it both stimulates and depresses. It must be an efficient depressant indeed if it gives comfort to a man about to be torn apart by bullets from a firing squad. How much child sexual abuse has been stimulated by cigarettes? How much guilt over the same has been short-circuited in the brain by nicotine? What, ultimately, is the good in forcing one to switch from cocaine to nicotine? As economist Jeffrey A. Miron argues, the "prohibition of drugs may not significantly reduce externalities [harm to third parties] because it simply results in a substitution toward consumption of other goods that also create externalities." [32] Prohibitionists have never been able to prove that those deterred from drug use by prohibition will not seek equally or more destructive mind-altering alternatives.

The author of *Hep-Cats* also appears to have overdrawn the image of drugs inevitably leading people who use them to become wastrels: " 'Practically all of the addicts under our observation who had been engaged in occupations requiring any real effort, either mental or physical, had been forced to abandon them.' " [33] That same author, however, tells us that cocaine "could help [workers] tolerate the 'extraordinarily severe work of loading and unloading steamboats, at which, perhaps, for seventy hours at a stretch, they would have to work without sleep or rest, in rain, in cold, and in heat. . . .' " [34]

The lead author of *Legalization: Panacea or Pandora's Box* is Joseph Califano, who appears to have succeeded William Bennett as the leading spokesperson against legalization. Califano led the Great Society's "War on Poverty," its domestic version of the war in Viet Nam. Now he has thrown his prestige behind the war on drugs. This is clearly a man committed to the use of massive centralized coercion to improve society; a man at home in the twentieth century.

The premise for the use of government coercion is the perception that large numbers of persons would not choose to engage in certain behavior desired by the coercers. It is precisely the function of coercion to negate the ability of people to make choices. It can be fairly said that Califano, like all prohibitionists, holds to an elitist view that large numbers of Americans would make the wrong choices if drugs were legalized. He says as much: "There are more than 50 million nicotine addicts, some 18 million alcoholics and alcohol abusers, and 6 million illegal drugs addicts. Making illegal drugs legal would drive the number of marihuana, heroin, and cocaine users closer to the number of alcohol and tobacco users." [35]

Califano's paper argues that lowering the price of potent, mind-altering drugs guarantees a huge increase in consumers. Surely, however, one who believes that drug use is dangerous will not change that view simply because the price of the dangerous drugs declines. Consider other potentially dangerous activities such as skydiving, bungee jumping, and mountain climbing. Most people have no desire to engage in these activities because they perceive them to be dangerous. How many non-sky divers would suddenly consent to being pushed out of a plane—for free?

Economist Miron writes:

> [M]any people may have no desire to consume any quantity of such goods no matter how low the price. . . . If, at least in part, the world consists of individuals who may have some demand for these goods at positive prices and others who do not, then it is likely that those who have the greatest desire to consume such goods are the ones already doing so. The important implication of this view is that extrapolation from elasticities [of demand] estimated on the basis of existing consumers is likely to overstate the increases in consumption that would occur as the result of lower prices under legalization. [36]

Califano's paper tries to argue that alcohol prohibition "did not generate a crime wave." [37] The sole evidence for this remarkable assertion is that "homicide experienced a higher rate of increase between 1900 and 1910 than during Prohibition, and organized crime was well established in cities before 1920." [38] In fact, crime did increase during the years of alcohol prohibition— 1920–1933—when compared with the years before and after. The repeal of Prohibition led to a decline in the murder rate for eleven consecutive years and a decline in the rate of assaults with a firearm for ten consecutive years. [39]

The main problem with "Speaking Out against Drug Legalization" is its publisher. The Drug Enforcement Administration is probably the most biased source for information about drug policy. Under legalization, the DEA's power and size would be greatly diminished, if not eliminated entirely. [40] Also, legalization would be a tremendous blow to the DEA's prestige and image, an admission that their core purpose has been a failure. When money, power, and ego are all at stake, an institution is likely to issue a self-serving and stilted report. (See also below.)

Further, the concept of a law enforcement agency injecting itself into a political debate is troublesome, to say the least. The mandate of the DEA is to enforce drug laws. It has no business whatever spending public money to influence public opinion on a political issue. To allow government agencies to use public money and resources to enter a political debate that threatens their very existence is a distortion of the democratic process. The First Amendment gives citizens the right "to petition the government for a redress of grievances" without ending up on what is in effect an enemies list entitled "Who's Who in the Legalization Debate" on the last page of this odd publication.

THE IMPORTANCE OF COST-BENEFIT ANALYSIS

Cost-benefit analysis attempts to reduce complex and highly emotional political and moral issues to numbers—supposedly neutrally derived—that purport to offer a more or less scientific solution to a social problem. For a variety of reasons, cost-benefit analysis has proved ineffective in causing large swings in public opinion on the issue of drug legalization. Though this fact is most noticeable in the failure of legalizers to convince a majority of Americans to support their proposal, it is equally true that numbers-crunching prohibitionists have failed to eliminate the large core of legalization supporters who have kept the issue alive since the late '80s.

STATISTICAL SKEPTICISM

One obvious problem with cost-benefit analysis is suspicion of statistics and numbers. It is sad that statistics have been sufficiently abused for propaganda that the average person is rightly skeptical of them. As Benjamin Disraeli said, "There are three kinds of lies: lies, damn lies, and statistics." After an opponent quoted the above passage in a debate on legalization, I responded, "I am glad you are attacking statistics in general, but not *my* statistics."

The truth is, however, that people, particularly people opposed to your position, are indeed skeptical of *all* statistics, not merely those whose fallacies are apparent. During a televised debate I once pointed out that the murder rate had increased during alcohol prohibition, and had declined for eleven straight years after repeal. The philosophy professor who opposed me in the debate said I was wrong. During a commercial break I showed him a chart from my Cato Institute report based on U.S. Census data, which proved that I was correct. He remained unconvinced, pointing out that it was not actually a U.S. Census chart, but a chart I had created from U.S. Census data.

I suppose that if I had showed the actual Census data, he would have alleged a typographical error. This type of statistical skepticism allows people who oppose legalization to somewhat lazily reject prolegalization cost-benefit analyses.

THE SUBJECTIVITY OF VALUE

A more fundamental problem with cost-benefit analysis is that it purports to "measure" costs and benefits, which phenomena are inherently incapable of being measured. Harm, value, cost, and happiness are subjective concepts pertaining to purely mental phenomena. As economist Murray Rothbard frequently observed, these phenomena are not subject to any objective interpersonal measurement or mathematical calculation. For example, drug prohibition may increase my risk of being mugged by a drug user trying to raise funds for drugs. Another person might think that the high price of drugs makes it less likely that he will be tempted to use them. There is no way to conclude scientifically that my increased risk of mugging is more or less important than another person's decreased risk of giving in to the temptation to use drugs. Thus cost-benefit analysis founders in this epistemological quagmire.

IGNORANCE OF CONSEQUENCES

Randy Barnett argues against cost-benefit analysis on the ground that "policy makers suffer from a pervasive ignorance of consequences." [41] A good example of the ignorance of policymakers is a 1987 survey done by the National Institute on Drug Abuse of state drugs officials concerning the rate of HIV infection among intravenous drug users in each state. The study indicated that states in which the sale of clean needles was banned had rates of HIV infection *six times higher* than in comparable neighboring states. The only problem was that the study was entirely unknown to the policy community since the study was unpublished.

Even if such a study had been widely published, lawmakers could claim that circumstances had changed and a new study is needed. Alternatively, they could claim that such studies do not eliminate all risks of changes in policy. Ultimately, no cost-benefit study will answer all the questions policymakers posit. In fact, a bizarre game has been played out in the legalization debate: the prohibitionists spend most of their time thinking up questions that cannot be answered because no human being, including proponents of drug legalization, could answer such questions without being able to predict the future, which is impossible. Prohibitionists continually boast that legalizers do not know what will happen tomorrow if we legalize drugs. They are blithely unconcerned that they do not know what will happen tomorrow if we do *not* legalize drugs.

BUREAUCRATIC SELF-INTEREST

Another critical reason why mere cost-benefit arguments fail to carry the day is the influence of special interest group politics. When a policy inflicts a moderate amount of harm on millions, but confers tremendous benefits to thousands, the policy is likely to continue. The thousands of beneficiaries will expend large amounts of resources to preserve the policy (see, e.g., the DEA pamphlet discussed above), while the millions of moderate victims will *not* spend equal amounts to obtain only a small benefit. The laws governing special interest group politics operate on drug policy just as they operate on farm policy. Those who monetarily benefit from drug prohibition are legion: drug enforcement agents, the police, prison guards, drug treatment centers, sellers of legal drugs such as alcohol and tobacco, organized crime, and drug dealers. While law enforcement officials' essentially unified front against legalization may be the product of sincere deliberation, it may also be reflective of another kind of deliberation described by Ambrose Bierce: "the act of examining one's bread to determine which side it is buttered on."

WAR ON DRUGS AS RELIGIOUS WAR

The issue of drug legalization stirs up deep-seated feelings that, for want of a better word, can best be described as religious in nature. The drug issue is religious in the sense that it involves a conflict over ultimate moral values, values that cannot be proved true or false by generally accepted methods. On the one side are those who believe it morally imperative that human beings pass through life with their "natural" consciousness more or less intact. On the other are those who believe that the pharmacological manipulation of consciousness, while potentially dangerous, is morally unobjectionable.

Just as cost-benefit analysis would not have stopped the inquisitors from tracking down and punishing heretics in the Middle Ages, crime and AIDS "body counts" do not stop modern drug warriors from crusading against drugs. They are not deterred by the sight of prohibition-caused street violence because they believe that such costs, to the extent they even acknowledge their existence, are trivial in comparison with the ultimate value of achieving a "drug-free" America. These crusaders, who count among their ranks millions of Americans, simply do not want to live in a world where recreational drug use exists, and they are willing to pay virtually any price, *and have others pay virtually any price*, to achieve that goal. Cost-benefit arguments simply do not register with millions of Americans who view the war on drugs as akin to a religious war.

The only civilized way to deal with irreconcilable conflicts in ultimate values is to declare freedom of religion and let each go his or her own way. That is the last thing the prohibitionists have in mind. Rather, their solution to the problem of the irreconcilable conflict of values over drugs is to inflict on those who disagree with them all the force and violence they can muster.

SOCIOECONOMIC DISTORTION

Hep-Cats does have a virtue lacking in other prohibitionist literature. The author frankly admits that prohibition imposes enormous costs on inner-city neighborhoods so that suburbanites can feel protected from drugs:

> The reality is that the great mass of Americans rightly fear illegal drugs and want them kept as far away as possible. If that means violent drug markets are confined to (and ruining) inner-city neighborhoods and prisons are filled to bursting, middle-class Americas accept that price. All they know is heroin and cocaine are not available at the local mall.[42]

Though the notion that drugs are not available "at the local mall" is a bit fanciful, the passage inadvertently provides yet another explanation for the failure of antiprohibitionist cost-benefit analyses to persuade the American people to end drug prohibition: a perceived threat to the welfare of white suburban teenagers—legalization—is given greater weight than the actual harm prohibition causes to urban minority teenagers.

We must therefore leave the realm of cost-benefit number crunching to resolve the issue of legalization versus prohibition. First, *is it right* to deliberately impose huge costs on readily identifiable and mostly minority communities so that mostly white suburbanites can feel safer? Second, *is it dangerous* to social peace to do so? Actions have consequences. One consequence of investigating, arresting, and jailing huge numbers of young black males is the creation of a festering and lingering resentment in the black community. In this regard it is worth noting that America had race riots in its two largest cities in recent years. As this chapter was being written, a third race riot broke out in St. Petersburg, Florida, sparked by the police killing of a young black male. According to a city councilman, when the police come into black neighborhoods, they have "their guns cocked and their attitudes cocked." [43] Tensions are inevitable when largely white police are regularly forced to arrest and jail large numbers of young black males on drug charges. As the author of *Hep-Cats* notes in the title of her chapter attacking drug legalization: "You have to pay up somewhere along the line" (p. 413).

CONCLUSION

The events of the last eight years indicate that the persuasive case made for legalization in the late 1980s remains intact. Prohibition is enormously costly and destructive and its benefits are largely unknowable, unprovable, and probably modest. Legalizers believe the costs outweigh the benefits. Prohibitionists believe the benefits outweigh the costs. Most Americans currently side with the prohibitionists. Because of the inherent limitations of the cost-benefit form of policy argument, they have not been persuaded by the cost-benefit studies of the legalizers. That being the case, unless Americans begin to grasp the linkage between drug prohibition, social unrest, and the erosion of civil liberties, it is likely that drug prohibition will continue for the foreseeable future. In a perfect world, all of the costs of drug prohibition would be born by those who support it. But this is not a perfect world, as the war on drugs has taught us.

ENDNOTES

1. "Thinking About Drug Legalization," Policy Analysis 121, May 25, 1989 (also available on the Internet).
2. *Id.*
3. Bureau of Justice Statistics: National Crime Victimization Survey (1994).
4. FBI Press Release, Oct. 13, 1996.
5. U.S. Bureau of the Census, *Historical Statistics of the United States, Colonial Time to 1970, part 1*, Washington, D.C. (1975, p. 414).
6. Cato report, pp. 1–2.
7. Jan. 28, 1996, Sect. 4, p. 5.
8. Jan. 6, 1996, p. 6.
9. Bureau of Justice Statistics.
10. Source: Lindesmith Center, 1996.
11. Statistical Abstract of the United States (SAUS), p. 217.
12. Marc Mauer, "The Drug War's Unequal Justice," in *The Drug Policy Letter* (Winter 1996), p. 11.
13. Jerome Miller, quoted in A. Skolnick, " 'Collateral Casualties' Climb in Drug War," JAMA, June 1, 1994, pp. 1636, 1639.
14. *Id.*
15. N. McBride, "Violence cited in lagging life expectancy among US blacks," in *The Christian Science Monitor* (Dec. 27, 1988), p. 3.
16. SAUS 208.
17. Source: Lindesmith Center, 1996.
18. SAUS 208.
19. Source: DAWN.

20. Skolnick, *supra* at 1638–1639.

21. E.g., *People* v. *Jones*, New York Appellate Division, New York Law Journal, June 13, 1996.

22. *Id.*

23. *People* v. *Schlaich*, New York Appellate Division, New York Law Journal, April 18, 1996.

24. Buffalo News, April 14, 1996, p. C1.

25. *Id.*

26. *United States* v. *Bayless*, United States District Court, S. D. N. Y. , New York Law Journal, Feb. 6, 1996.

27. Scribners: New York.

28. *Id.* at 25; the population in 1900 was about 76 million. Statistical Abstract of the United States (1995), p. 8.

29. *Id.* at 425. The population of the United States in 1994 was about 260 million. Statistical Abstract at page 8.

30. *Id.* at 60.

31. *Id.* at 57.

32. "Drug Legalization and the Consumption of Drugs: An Economist's Perspective," in *Searching for Alternatives: Drug Control Policy in the United States*, p. 71 (M. Krauss & E. Lazear, eds; Hoover Institution Press: Stanford, CA).

33. *Id.* at 48.

34. *Id.* at 32.

35. p. 35.

36. Miron, *supra* at 72–73.

37. p. 32.

38. *Id.*

39. U.S. Bureau of the Census, *Historical Statistics of the United States, Colonial Time to 1970, part 1*, Washington, D.C. (1975, p. 414).

40. As a criminal defense lawyer, the author of this chapter would likely lose income if drug prohibition is repealed.

41. "Curing the Drug Law Addiction: The Harmful Side Effects of Legal Prohibition," in *Dealing with Drugs, The Consequences of Government Control* (R. Hamowy, ed., 1987).

42. *Id.* at 426.

43. *New York Times*, Oct. 26, 1996, p. 8.

14

What Is "Legalization"?
What Are "Drugs"?

Richard M. Evans

A premise of this book is that drug prohibition and the war that has been waged for a quarter century for its sake are recognized by a majority of the voting public as not only having failed to protect the nation from the problems associated with illegal drugs, but as having done a lot more harm than good in the process. A further premise is that majority support exists for coming to terms with drugs in ways other than with police, prisons, and propaganda. Many call it *legalization*.

What, exactly, *is* legalization?

It isn't exactly anything. The term has been employed to describe a chaotically wide range of proposals. Some plans turn control over nonmedical drugs to doctors; some allow sales in liquor and drugstores; some contemplate merely not arresting people for small quantities and keeping the business of production and distribution illegal. Some would create a free and open market in drugs and treat them like any other commodity. Some forbid advertising. Some permit drugs to become constituents in other products. The varieties and variables of legalization are endless.

A portion of this chapter previously appeared in the papers of the 1990 International Conference on Drug Policy Reform, *The Great Issues of Drug Policy*, Arnold S. Trebach and Kevin B. Zeese, editors, Drug Policy Foundation, Washington, DC, 1990.

The legalization plans that have been put forward have very little in common, except, perhaps, for one feature: acquisition, possession, and use of the now-legal drug by responsible adults stops being the business of the state, stops putting at risk one's liberty or property. Within that broad standard lies a menagerie of "legal" schemes. Although the criminal and civil justice apparatuses retain a prominent role in protecting public health and public safety, under "legalization" plans the government does not intrude on personal autonomy with regard to drug acquisition or consumption by adults that is not visibly harmful.

At issue is not how drugs *ought* to be legalized, but how they *might* be. Responses draw upon the imaginations of legislators and writers who have proffered a variety of nonprohibitionist options. "Nonprohibitionist" because they reject total prohibition, a system in which, if we are talking about illicit drug X, all use of or commerce in drug X by all persons in all circumstances is a crime, and hence the business of the criminal justice system.

In the broadest sense legalization means something other than prohibition and war. But as one cannot fairly describe modern alcohol policy as the absence of speakeasies and bathtub gin, one cannot describe drug legalization as the absence of street dealers and turf wars. As the public debate over legalization develops, it becomes the duty of both proponents and detractors to be clear about just what they mean by the word *legalization*. The aim of this chapter is to survey a range of possible meanings, and to propose a framework upon which they and others can be compared and examined.

As the sine qua non of legalization is legal access to drugs for responsible adults, this chapter excludes consideration of "medical marijuana" or "hemp" reforms. These measures and initiatives, worthy though they may be for medical or industrial purposes, bear no connection to legalization. Exempting small categories of people from the prohibition laws (chemotherapy patients, licensed hemp farmers) has little to do with repealing prohibition entirely and allowing access to most adults.

FORMS OF LEGALIZATION

Over the past two decades a wide variety of plans have been put forward in the name of legalization. Most seem to fall into one of three general categories: *decriminalization* plans, *limitation* plans, and *regulation and taxation* plans.

Falling outside this grouping are calls for outright legalization, in which drugs would be produced, bought, and sold like any ordinary commodity. The most eminent advocate of treating drugs like ordinary goods is Thomas Szasz, M.D., whose prolific and eloquent writings make a strong case for a free market in drugs, free of government involvement.[1] Antiprohibitionists speak affectionately of the tomato model, in which commerce in and use of drugs would carry a level of government regulation comparable to tomatoes, that is, merely the usual agricultural regulations and pure food rules, and perhaps an ordinary sales tax.

If drugs are to be treated under the law like tomatoes, magazines, medicines, or toothpaste, it is hardly necessary to conjure a new set of rules about where and to whom they can be sold, or to what extent they may become ingredients in other products, or how they are to be taxed, and if their potency is to be regulated, and in what forms they may be sold. All that is needed is to latch on to the existing commodity that best illustrates the favored approach. Free market proponents can bring clarity and spirit to the debate over how to legalize drugs by simply filling in the blank: drugs should be as legal as————.

Recent pressure on the tobacco industry appears to be giving rise to a new form of legalization that may come to be called the "new cigarette model." The "landmark settlement" reached in June 1997 between the tobacco industry, state attorneys general, and plaintiffs provides for the elimination of advertising and marketing designed for underage smokers; stronger warning labels on cigarettes packs; full disclosure of ingredients; prohibition of tobacco use in public places, workplaces, and fast-food restaurants; and regulation of nicotine as a drug by the Food and Drug Administration.[2] Notably, there is no talk of prohibition. If these restrictions are codified, and the new cigarette scheme is successful in curbing smoking by the young, reducing threats to the public health, and reimbursing government its costs, it is entirely possible that the new cigarette model could provide a legalization protocol at least for marijuana, if not for other drugs as well.

DECRIMINALIZATION

In the context of drugs, the word *decriminalization* entered the popular lexicon during the '70s, and was used to describe changes to the marijuana laws in eleven states.[3] The changes were modest. Under them, marijuana remained illegal under both state and federal law, and one could still be prosecuted and punished for simple possession of marijuana. The difference was that such possession of a small quantity was no longer an offense under state law for which one could lose one's liberty (be arrested) upon being caught. And, typically, such charges did not carry the risk of creating a permanent criminal record. As a result, prosecutions for marijuana were said to resemble prosecutions for speeding or other traffic offenses: a ticket and fine, and possibly a court appearance, but offenders were not arrested on the spot and taken in.

Because these reforms involved changes to the written law applicable to possessing a small amount of marijuana, they can be described as de jure decriminalization. This can occur in one of two ways: by an act of a legislative body (state legislature, city council),[4] or by a court.

The best example of court-made decriminalization is the 1975 case of
Ravin v. State of Alaska, in which the Supreme Court of Alaska, having considered the right to privacy amendment in the Alaska constitution, found
"no adequate justification for the state's intrusion into the citizen's right to
privacy by its prohibition of possession of marijuana by an adult for personal consumption in the home," a decision that had the result of removing
criminal penalties for the violation of the statutory prohibition laws to the
extent declared constitutionally infirm.[5]

In 1990 an initiative election strongly backed by then President Bush's
"drug czar," William Bennett, "recriminalized" marijuana, restoring criminal penalties for the possession of small amounts. Since then, however, in cases that
have not been reported or appealed, trial courts have dismissed prosecutions
on the grounds that a voter initiative making new statutory law cannot change
the constitution or the way it is interpreted, thus neutralizing the effect of
the initiative.

It is important to observe that, notwithstanding the *Ravin* decision, marijuana has remained illegal in Alaska, as in all states, under federal law; hence
Ravin cannot be said to have "legalized" anything. What *Ravin* did, rather, was
to cede to federal authorities the responsibility for enforcing the marijuana laws
as to persons using or growing it in the privacy in their home. There are no
reports, however, of any such federal prosecutions in Alaska.

In New York City, however, federal authorities in June 1997 demonstrated their prowess and willingness for street-level prohibition enforcement.
In cooperation with New York City police, they conducted a sweep of Washington Square Park in Greenwich Village, arresting, in the words of *The New
York Times*, "dozens of marijuana dealers who the authorities say return again
and again after serving short sentences."[6]

In a further example of court-made de jure decriminalization, the Constitutional Court of Colombia in 1994, citing Article 16 of the Constitution,
which provides that "All people have the right to the free development of their
personalities with no more limitation than those imposed by the rights of others and by the legal order," declared unconstitutional a law mandating intern-
ment for "the user or consumer who, according to a legal medical report, is in
a state of drug addiction, even if it is the first offense."[7] The decision did not
affect commerce in drugs, which remains prohibited.

A colorful precedent to such de jure decriminalization can be said to have
occurred three generations ago. The experience deserves to be recalled in some
detail, not only because it is an interesting story, but because it answers objections frequently raised today about alleged "conflicts" between static federal
law and changing state laws.[8]

The year was 1923, the state was New York, the governor was Al Smith,
and the drug was alcohol. Three years had passed since the 18th Amendment

to the United States Constitution, prohibiting "the manufacture, sale, or transportation of intoxicating liquors,"[9] was adopted. Every state but Maryland had enacted its own version of the Volstead Act, the federal law implementing the new prohibitions. Neither the Prohibition Amendment nor the Volstead Act prohibited the possession of beverage alcohol, so what is now called "decriminalization" was then called "prohibition."

In only a few years, state courts became jammed with liquor cases. Illicit commerce in alcohol caused rampant violence; organized crime moved in. In response to the crisis, State Senator Louis Curvillier introduced a measure he claimed would give badly needed relief to the criminal justice system. It was ingeniously simple, and cost nothing. The measure merely repealed the state prohibition laws, and replaced them with nothing.

Since alcohol remained prohibited on the federal level, Senator Curvillier's bill would hardly be said to "legalize" it; rather, it merely shifted the burden of enforcing the prohibition laws from state to federal authorities. With surprisingly scant opposition—consisting largely of tired old jeremiads about the evil of drink—the bill passed the legislature and landed on Governor Smith's desk.

Smith, a popular Democrat, was a rising star in national politics. He anguished over whether to sign the bill, fearful that approval would forever cost him the presidential nomination he wanted so badly. After listening exhaustively to all sides, he waited until the last possible moment to declare his approval of the Curvillier bill.

His long and tortuous statement explaining his decision was classic Al Smith. He was a New Yorker and New Yorkers did not like Prohibition, and it should not be necessary to explain why. But since he could not put it that way, he indulged his fertile wit to make a case that repeal of the state prohibition laws would actually *strengthen* the national prohibition effort. Here, for example, he challenges the argument that repeal of state prohibition laws "sends the wrong message," as it would be put today:

> The repeal of the [state prohibition law] will mean that violations of the Volstead Act will hereinafter be prosecuted by the federal courts. This, to my mind, seems to be desirable, as it will fix in the minds of offenders the thought that they have violated a federal statute intended to effectuate an amendment to the Constitution of the United States, rather than have them harbor the thought that they are simply standing against what a great many of them may be led to believe is merely a local regulation.[10]

With the enactment of the Curvillier bill, the burden of enforcement in New York shifted to federal authorities for the ten remaining years of Prohibition. Because federal enforcement was limp, New York escaped much, if not most, of the Prohibition-related violence that plagued other large cities like Chicago and Detroit. And that is why, in old movies set in New York during the period, Prohibition police are called the "feds." They *were* the feds, and *only* the feds.

Smith received the nomination of his party for President in 1928, but lost the election to Herbert Hoover. His opposition to Prohibition, and his Catholicism, are said to have contributed to his defeat. (Four years later, FDR's embrace of repeal contributed significantly to his election.)

The forms of reform described are examples of de jure decriminalization, because all involve some tinkering with the statutory law. None involved major policy changes. In the '20s, alcohol commerce remained illegal under federal law, and in the '70s, marijuana remained illegal under federal law, despite repeal or lessening of state laws.

As war between nations can be defined as the failure of diplomacy, domestic war can be seen as the failure of policy. Nations may reduce hostilities without signing formal peace treaties and without declaration of victory or surrender by either side. Weapons are put down, but not away. Rhetoric softens. The belligerents cool down. That, in short, is decriminalization: a détente in the war on drugs.

The cooling-off can occur de facto as well, where there are no changes in the laws appearing on the books, but they are enforced less stringently than before. In his book *Marijuana: Costs of Abuse, Costs of Control*, Mark A. R. Kleiman calls this approach "enforcement reduction," and recommends it as the "best alternative for dealing with the nation's marijuana problem."[11]

The clearest picture of de facto decriminalization of drugs by enforcement reduction can be seen in Amsterdam. There, "soft drugs" (marijuana and hashish) remain illegal, but are widely tolerated by law enforcement authorities. Cannabis is openly available for purchase in coffee shops. The drug prohibition laws remain on the books, but are not enforced against soft drugs.

Veterans of the '60s and '70s recall a time when marijuana was used widely with minimal concealment, even in states that did not decriminalize. A modicum of discretion was sufficient to retain one's liberty. Police and the public were tolerant, if not approving, of personal marijuana use.[12]

Among avenues of drug law reform, de facto decriminalization has the distinct advantage of not requiring the complicity of the legislature. Police officers, one recalls from elementary civics, work for the executive branch of government, whose job it is to *execute* and carry out the laws. All it takes to institute such a policy of reduced enforcement is the will of a single executive— a mayor, governor, or president—and the political moxie to carry it off.

Although decriminalization, whether de jure or de facto, is frequently mentioned as a preferable alternative to prohibition, two principal problems haunt it as a permanent policy option. The first is that under decriminalization, as the term is used here, the drug market remains illegal, and underground networks of illegal suppliers and distributors continue to supply the public demand for drugs. With no legal commerce there are no taxes paid or collected, no FDA-like controls over purity and dosage, and no legal and peaceful remedies for settling industry disputes that inevitably occur. Criminal organizations remain in control of drug production and distribution (except, one speculates, in the case of cannabis, where backyard gardens may well supply most consumers). If the goals of "legalization" are to protect the public safety and public health, prevent abuse, and halt the crime associated with prohibition, decriminalization, whether de jure or de facto, is not an attractive candidate for significant and long-term reform, as the war continues against production and supply networks.

The other serious drawback to decriminalization as a policy option is that although it goes far in abating the harms created by drug prohibition, it does nothing to address the problem of drug abuse, that is, problems arising out of excessive or otherwise inappropriate *consumption* of drugs. Hence a number of legalization advocates have urged schemes to protect people from drugs by drawing lines in new and different ways.

LIMITATION

The basic idea is that if people's access to drugs is limited, their problems with drugs are thus limited. Limits can be imposed on the categories of people who are permitted access, on the quantity of drugs, and the circumstances under which they are available. In a sense, total prohibition might be called the ultimate limitation scheme, in that it attempts to limit availability of drugs to everybody, but that option is not among those under review here.

A familiar example of the limitation approach is today's prescription drug model, where only those holding permits (prescriptions) from physicians are given access, and then only in limited quantities. This appears to be what Mayor Kurt Schmoke of Baltimore, an early and unflagging critic of the drug war, has in mind when he urges that the drug problem should be treated as a public health problem, not a law enforcement problem.[13] His commissioner of public health has spoken of "medicalization," calling for "machinery within our society to allow the medical profession to deal with the problem of addiction."[14]

Medicalization makes the medical profession the arbiter of who shall have legal access to nonmedical drugs and who shall not, as it now is in the case of pharmaceuticals. Thus marijuana use would require a physician's okay[15] whether for medical or nonmedical purposes.

It's dubious that the "medical profession" would gladly become gatekeepers for nonmedical drug users. When doctors hold the key to the nonmedical drug cabinet, they may find themselves deciding who should and who should not

be permitted to get high on a Saturday night, a function that is not likely to
enhance public health, the medical profession, or Saturday nights.

Should drug users be licensed, like drivers? The suggestion has been
made that in order to use drugs legally, people should take a class and pass
an examination, proving to the satisfaction of authorities that they can handle
drugs. Then, under one plan, the user would receive a plastic card and a
PIN number, with which drugs would be obtainable from an ATM-like
machine. Before dispensing the drugs, however, the machine would check
to see that the consumer's state-approved quota had not been exceeded.[16]

Another approach is to limit the places were drugs can be used. Ronald
Dworkin, M.D., urges "institutionalization."[17] He would set up addiction-main-
tenance programs operating out of deliberately drab government clinics. "Addicts" would go "to obtain their fix," and stay until the drugs wore off.[18] An
intricate system of locks and gates would attempt to prevent drugs and individuals under the influence of drugs from getting out, although it is not clear
how such efforts would be any more successful keeping drugs out of prisons
today.

By granting to qualifying individuals a right of legal access to drugs, limitation schemes do not replace the prohibition laws, but instead carve out
exceptions to them. For those who do not qualify under the exceptions, the
prohibition laws remain in place, with a law enforcement apparatus equipped
to come down on drug use and commerce that remains off limits. Thus limitation plans could not be expected to change significantly the prohibition
landscape in terms of illegal drug markets. Unlimited supplies of drugs will
remain available illegally for those who do not qualify for legal access, raising serious questions about the efficacy of imposing limits in the first place.

REGULATION AND TAXATION

It is the absence of such limits that characterizes regulation and taxation models, of which the familiar alcohol and soon-to-change tobacco systems stand
as examples.

The principal function of regulation and taxation is to drive out the illegal market by recognizing a legal market with which the illegal market cannot
compete. Its essence is that just about any adult can obtain drugs legally—
and, if using them responsibly, avoid scrutiny of the police. In other words, if
the taxes are paid and the other rules observed, production and distribution
of drugs carry no criminal penalties.

Current alcohol and tobacco schemes are fairly characterized as regulation and taxation, though neither provides a compelling "model" for other
drugs. Given the nearly half-million deaths caused annually by alcohol and
tobacco, and the close association between violent crimes and alcohol, one

cannot argue persuasively that American alcohol and tobacco policies are a total success—although prohibition is not seen as a preferable alternative. Since a regulation and taxation scheme for drugs would build on that experience and take a different form, it is not correct to say that where drugs are regulated and taxed, they are treated "just like wine," or "just like cigarettes."

A variety of bills have been introduced in state legislatures, and several initiatives proposed, having as their aim some sort of regulation and taxation plan for drugs. Typically, they received a polite, if not serious, reception. None has been vigorously examined or debated, or enacted into law. Like castles in the sky, they are visions sculpted in exquisite detail, but visions nonetheless.

The first drug legalization and taxation schemes applied only to marijuana. In 1971 a bill was introduced in the New York Senate by Senator Franz Leichter,[19] which would set up a Marijuana Control Authority to license and control commerce in cannabis the way commerce in alcohol is currently licensed and regulated, except that advertising would be forbidden. The Leichter bill was introduced regularly during the '70s, and by 1979 had attracted a number of cosponsors, including Senator Joseph L. Galiber, who in 1989 expanded the scope of the Leichter bill to include all illegal drugs, and proffered a bill he unambiguously called "A Bill to Make All Illegal Drugs as Legal as Alcohol."[20] Under the Galiber bill, all "controlled substances" could be sold by licensed doctors or pharmacists under a license issued by the State Controlled Substances Authority, which is granted authority to make all necessary rules for drug production, distribution, and sales.

A comprehensive cannabis regulation and taxation bill was introduced in Massachusetts in 1981.[21] The Cannabis Revenue and Education Act regulated commercial production and distribution of cannabis, and imposed a tax based on THC content. Half of the net tax proceeds collected went to a Cannabis Education Trust, set up to conduct a public education campaign against marijuana abuse.

The only comprehensive bill for the regulation and taxation of cannabis at the federal level was called the Cannabis Revenue Act,[22] drafted in 1982 by a group of lawyers and economists called the National Task Force on Cannabis Regulation. Rather than simply laying out a single legalization scheme, the proposal left the door open for variations from state to state as to how cannabis might be legalized.

If the CRA were enacted into federal law, states would have three options:

- Option A permits any state to retain its prohibition laws, opting out of legalization altogether, as some states remained "dry" following the repeal of federal prohibition in 1933. The local picture would not visibly change. State prohibition laws continue to govern. Illicit com-

merce and use may decline, as consumers are more likely to prefer
"clean" drugs, that is, those that carry enforceable assurances of freedom from contamination or adulteration, even it means traveling or
enlisting the aid of a friend in another state. States not changing their
laws would not share in the new federal revenue.

- Under Option B, states would repeal local prohibition laws and pass
  laws dealing only with distribution of cannabis to minors and driving under the influence. Without further regulation the state could
  plug into, and thus qualify for revenue from, the new federal scheme,
  which imposes the usual regulation on all levels of commerce in cannabis, from production to consumption: it licenses people to engage
  in the business, it collects the tax, it protects consumers from fraud
  and adulterated cannabis, it prohibits advertising, and it imposes penalties on people who violate the new laws. And it sends revenue to
  state capitols.

  Under Option B this picture of legal cannabis emerges: licensed retailers would sell it in one-ounce packages packed loose like pipe tobacco or herbal tea. The package would bear a tax stamp, and the
  label would reveal the origin of the cannabis, the identity of the
  contents by species and variety, the net quantity, potency, and a cautionary label. Licensees would be strictly liable for security lapses and
  sales to minors.

- Option C for the states, under the Cannabis Revenue Act, was for
  the state to impose its own regulatory or taxation scheme, or both,
  in addition to the federal regulation imposed by the CRA. For example,
  states could impose license quotas, prohibit public use, or earmark
  revenue for a particular use. However, states would not be eligible
  for revenue sharing if they legislated in conflict with certain elements
  of the federal law.

  The picture under option C: a patchwork of laws, like alcohol and
  tobacco regulation today. In some states drugs might be sold in state-
  owned and -operated stores, and in others by state-licensed retailers.
  They could be open around the clock, or closed by law after 11 P.M.
  and on Sundays and holidays. Home delivery, like for pizzas, may be
  legal in some states and banned in others. Packaging requirements,
  taxation levels, even content regulation would differ from state to
  state, but in all states that legalize, access to cannabis is legal for adults.

In the year following publication of the Cannabis Revenue Act, regulation and taxation bills drawing on the CRA were introduced in the state
legislatures of Oregon and Pennsylvania. The Oregon bill[23] restricted retail
sales to state-operated stores and earmarked all the revenue to local school
districts and local law enforcement. The Pennsylvania bill removed all sanctions from personal cultivation and possession (up to 2.2 pounds) and subjected the commercial cannabis industry to regulation by the Department of
Agriculture, restricting retail sales to state-owned liquor outlets.[24]

In the 1990 session of the Missouri legislature, a bill that would license the production, distribution, and sale of all drugs was introduced by Rep. Elbert Walton.[25] The sales tax is set at a flat rate of 25 percent of retail. Unlike the other regulation and taxation models, the Missouri bill imposes strict limits on where drugs may be used, prohibiting the use of "controlled substances" "in the presence of a minor under the age of eighteen years or outside the confines of a private residence or in a place of public accommodation or private residence or in a place of public accommodation or conveyance" . . . in other words, prohibiting drug use in bars, restaurants, offices, or cars, and even at home if the kids are around.

A novel feature of the Missouri plan is that it expands the conventional definition of cannabis, giving statutory recognition to the species *cannabis Americana*, with a nod to botanists who developed this new domestic species of cannabis as law enforcement focused on border interdiction.

Also in 1990 a creative initiative measure was proposed in Oregon, called the Oregon Marijuana Initiative (OMI). Had OMI reached the voters and obtained their approval, an exception would have been carved out of current cannabis prohibition laws, allowing personal use and cultivation, with a certificate from the county health department, available for $50 each with the revenue going to county drug and health programs.

In a significant article in the Summer 1992 issue of *Daedalus* [reprinted in this volume as Chapter 22], Ethan Nadelmann suggests what he calls a "right of access" or "mail-order" model. Adults would be able to obtain through the mail "a modest amount of any drug at a reasonable price reflecting production costs and taxes,"[26] while other sales of drugs would remain prohibited under local, state, or federal law.

In 1993 a Washington (state) grass-roots organization called the Washington Citizens for Drug Policy Reform sponsored an initiative for a new marijuana policy, to be known as "regulated tolerance." Under the WCDPR's plan, private adults would be legally able to grow and possess up to a "personal use quantity" without sanction by the criminal law, and without having to obtain any license. Cultivating, transporting, and selling more than a personal use quantity would require a license from a cannabis control authority. Determining that quantity is left to the courts. The proposed law prescribed a tax of $15 per ounce of cannabis "at standard cured moisture content," to be collected and paid by sellers.[27]

The measure permits the retail sale of "cannabis products made from flowering female tops other than seeds," which suggests the prospect of a wide variety of cannabis-containing products being marketed, from soft drinks to pastries to chewing gum. This contrasts with the 1982 Cannabis Revenue Act, which legalized the sale of cannabis in its natural form only, specifically prohibiting sales in derivative or constituent forms.

Although not with the level of eloquence with which Governor Al Smith of New York, in 1923, told the feds to take a hike, the WCDPR initiative throws an unambiguous barb at the other Washington, to wit,

> Sec. 21. State agencies shall refrain from enforcing any provision of United States criminal law not consistent with the purposes of this act, to avoid a waste of resources.[28]

In 1997 two "legalization" initiatives were independently promoted in Oregon. The Oregon Drugs Control Amendment would amend the state constitution to require that laws "regulating" controlled substances be passed, and to forbid that such laws "prohibit adult possession of any controlled substance."[29] The legislature is directed to work out the regulatory details for dealing with a list of issues, which is duplicated here as it provides a useful checklist for any new regulatory scheme.

    a. A minimum legal age of not greater than 21 years;
    b. Reasonable limits on adult personal possession;
    c. Adequate public health and consumer safeguards;
    d. Adequate manufacturing, price, import, and export controls;
    e. Penalties for violations, provisions for enforcement;
    f. Exceptions for controlled scientific research;
    g. Exceptions under medical and/or parental supervision;
    h. Exceptions for traditional, spiritual practices;
    i. A defined legal level of impairment;
    j. Promotion of temperance, moderation, and safety;
    k. On-demand substance abuse and harm reduction programs.[30]

Curiously, the amendment provides that "[i]n no case shall the State of Oregon ever make a net profit from the manufacture or sale of controlled substances."[31]

Making a profit, on the other hand, is a chief objective of the other Oregon initiative. It is called the Oregon Cannabis Tax Act (OCTA), and has been proffered by an organization called the Campaign for the Restoration and Regulation of Hemp. In a lengthy preface, the Act traces the history and benefits of industrial, medical, and recreational cannabis, and the failings of its prohibition. The existing Oregon Liquor Control Commission is renamed the Oregon Intoxicant Control Commission and is assigned authority to regulate, by licensing, the cultivation and processing of cannabis. Licensed cultivators sell their crop only to the Commission. After processing, it is sold in OICC stores at such price as will "generate profits for revenue to be applied to the purposes [of the statute] and to minimize incentives to purchase cannabis elsewhere, to purchase cannabis for resale or for removal to other states."[32] Industrial hemp falls outside the definition of "cannabis," and its regulation is beyond the jurisdiction of the Commission.

The initiative goes on to specify the disposition of "profits" from the issuance of licenses and sale of cannabis. After administrative and enforcement costs, 90 percent goes to the general fund, 8 percent to the Department of Human Resources "to fund various drug abuse treatment programs on demand," 1 percent "to create and fund an agricultural state committee for the promotion of Oregon hemp fiber, protein and oil crops and associated industries," and 1 percent "to the state's school districts, appropriated by enrollment, to fund a drug education program."[33]

Uniquely among cannabis legalization proposals, the initiative goes on to lay out the essential elements of an acceptable curriculum for young people. Rejecting prohibitionist doctrine, which has traditionally dominated drug education, the proposal instead requires that the curriculum

1. Emphasize a citizen's rights and duties under our social compact and to explain to students how drug abusers might injure the rights of others by failing to fulfill such duties;
2. Persuade students to decline to consume intoxicants by providing them with accurate information about the threat intoxicants pose to their mental and physical development; and
3. Persuade students that if, as adults, they choose to consume intoxicants, they must nevertheless responsibly fulfill all duties they owe others.[34]

Finally, like the Oregon Drug Control Amendment, the OCTA turns a stern face to federal law. Section 474.315 provides:

As funded by [this law], the Attorney General shall vigorously defend any person prosecuted for acts licensed under this chapter, propose a federal act to remove impediments to this chapter, deliver the proposed federal act to each member of Congress and urge adoption of the proposed federal act through all legal and appropriate means.[35]

The varieties of legalization are infinite. What is intrinsic to the species, however, is that the sumptuary practices of adults are not the business of the state. This leaves ample room for experimentation by the states with controls—or not—over advertising, driving, content and form, taxation levels, and the other significa of tolerance.

WHAT ARE "DRUGS"?

At first glance the question seems simple, even simplistic. One need merely consult the federal Controlled Substances Act[36] or its counterpart in the states. In these prohibition laws, one will find listed, in exquisite detail, the chemical compounds for the "control" of which the war is being waged. Might it follow then that the answer to what do we mean by *drugs*, when we speak of legalizing them, is right there?

It sounds plausible at first. After all, illegal drugs are what we see on the 11:00 news; you don't hear about shootouts between beer distributors. But if the CSA definition is employed, and "illegal drugs are made legal," laws concerning a huge multitude of chemical compounds are thereby changed. The notion of prescription drugs will cease to exist. Lest advocates of legalization be wrongly accused of going too far, it is incumbent upon them to specify exactly *which* drugs are to be excised from the list of "controlled substances," and regulated, if at all, in ways not involving criminal or civil sanctions for adults using them responsibly.

Most of the regulation and taxation plans described in the previous part of this chapter relate only to marijuana. If marijuana alone is an issue, then the problem of defining *drugs* can be left for another day, as marijuana is easily severable from other illegal drugs, economically, culturally, and pharmaceutically. If the intent, however, is to legalize more drugs than marijuana, but not all those on the prohibited list, then it becomes necessary to draw and explain new lines between the legal and the illegal. Shall we legalize heroin but not cocaine? Amphetamines but not barbiturates?

When that problem is solved—that is, determining what drugs, *exactly*, are to be legalized—another emerges: What happens to those drugs remaining on the prohibited list? Will they fall into the wrong hands, cause harm to abusers, carry risks of contamination and adulteration, and threaten the public safety by perpetuating a violent and criminal production and distribution system? To protect the public from those harms, will we continue to wage domestic war, but with fewer drugs as targets?

Let us ask the question "What are drugs?" a different way: What drugs threaten public health and safety to the extent that the state is justified in imposing restraints and controls? The destructive ones, naturally, but they are already legal! Indeed, opponents of drug legalization often cite the failures of alcohol and tobacco legalization as examples of why drugs should not be legalized. They have a point. When drugs are legalized, the mistakes of alcohol and tobacco policy—widespread advertising, for example—must be scrutinized carefully.

In terms of morbidity, toxicity, and social disruption, alcohol and tobacco dwarf illegal drugs. If drug policy reform is about measures aimed at protecting us from such destruction, then a posteriori a broader definition of "drugs" is in order.

The broader definition of "drugs" is well established, though rarely invoked when talking of policy reform. When Congress created the U.S. Food and Drug Administration, it declared that drugs are articles "(other than food) intended to affect the structure or any function of the body."[37] The leading drug education program puts it more colloquially to fifth graders: "any substance other than a food that affects the body or the way it works."[38] Alcohol, nicotine, caffeine, laxatives, and headache remedies are all thus drugs.

If the point of the drug laws is to protect public health and safety and curb abuse, perhaps a more promising approach lies in urging public cognizance of the broader definition, fixing in the public psyche a new, larger category of substances deserving of serious national concern. Substances in this category will be treated differently: they will not be commercially available to young people; they will be taxed at a level at least to pay for the harm they cause;[39] people who use them irresponsibly will get in trouble; children will learn to avoid problems with them; laws will protect consumers from impurities.

What do we call this larger category? Several years ago, in a small town in Massachusetts, a school committee charged with reviewing the local drug education curriculum used the term *TAOS*, an acronym for tobacco, alcohol, and other substances. The committee wrote:

> "Drug-free" may be a clever slogan, but it is an unnatural condition. We look around us and see drugs everywhere: not illegal drugs, necessarily, but legal drugs like alcohol, nicotine, caffeine, sleeping pills, wakeup pills, cold pills, prescription medications, inhalants and all the myriad of preparations offered us at drug stores and supermarkets and hawked on the evening news.[40]

The committee called it "the ubiquity of drugs: they seem to be everywhere." Any drug education curriculum that pretended otherwise was defective: "Children will be exposed to TAOS as they grow older—as they will be exposed to automobiles and dangerous tools and sex and other hazards of adulthood— and what is important is that they act responsibly. It is unrealistic to expect any of our children not to encounter TAOS as they grow up."[41]

Legalizing drugs is about coming to terms with troublesome realities, and one of those realities is the insufficiency of our vocabulary. To legalize drugs effectively will be to redefine them; to redefine them will be to rename them; to rename them will be to unify them. As the legalization debate develops, one awaits the emergence of a new term to embrace the broader meaning, giving a broader swath to the benefits of reform.

CONCLUSION

Defining legalization and specifying the drugs so legalized is complex in the abstract, but in actuality, fairly simple: it's what emerges, bit by bit, piece by piece, state by state. As confidence in prohibition yields to the point of tolerating use by responsible adults, legalization can be said to have occurred.

The greatest impediment to legalization is hardly our inability to devise good legal schemes. This point was driven home years ago, when a congressional aide chuckled to a small group of legalization activists who had exhaustively devised a detailed plan. "A comprehensive bill? Heck, that's no problem," he grinned. "If we need to regulate something, we just call the legislative staff and ask 'em for a bill. It's usually on your desk in a week. The government is very good at figuring out how to regulate something. You name it, we can regulate it."

The greatest impediment to legalization is the mountain of opprobrium toward drugs and drug users, defended by a multitude of scorn, that block serious talk of reform. It is natural that the opprobrium should exist, as in the name of "prevention" the public has been bombarded with messages demonizing drugs and viciously attacking drug users, the most prominent example of which are produced and distributed by the Partnership for a Drug-Free America.

All the reforms mentioned in this chapter presume that the level of opprobrium will recede. If not, legalization will remain merely a vision, that castle in the sky, intriguing perhaps, but not to be considered seriously by political leaders.

Unless that level of opprobrium falls and stabilizes at a level commensurate with the dangers of drugs, attempts may be made in the name of "reform" to replace criminal penalties with draconian "civil" sanctions. Such sanctions could be far more oppressive and intrusive than criminal prohibition. Imagine a form of legalization where there is no risk of being arrested, surely, but the right to drive a car, have custody of your children, operate a retail business, get a passport, buy or sell real estate, or even take out library books will require proof of abstinence. Future generations may then look back on the last decades of the twentieth century as the golden years of prohibition.

Legalization is more than changing laws. In the long run, it means trying to accomplish the same goals as prohibition: protecting public health and safety; curbing abuse, especially among the young; and eliminating the crime and violence associated with illicit drug trafficking. In the short run, legalization means changing the way we think about drugs. When drugs are legal, there will be little confusing of drug use with drug abuse, or the harm done by drugs with the harm done by drug prohibition. Teachers and parents will recognize that educating young people to avoid problems with drugs is not merely a matter of infusing them temporarily with fear and scorn. Consumers will understand that the legal status of a drug has little to do with the drug's safety. Drug-related crime will be distinguished from prohibition-related crime.

Legalization confers upon citizens both the benefits and the burdens of personal autonomy. Drug users will face less risk to their health and their liberty, but will be held accountable for their conduct affecting others. A major challenge to the architects of legalization will be to devise a system that imposes on consumers a profound sense of responsibility for the consequences of their drug use.

When talk is of legalizing drugs, identifying what is meant by "legalizing" and what is meant by "drugs" is a modest but necessary first step before attention is turned to how best to do it. Unlike the "bogus ideal" deprecated by Justice Oliver Wendell Holmes, what it means to legalize drugs must not "dwell in generalities and shirk the details."[42]

ENDNOTES

1. Szasz, T. (1992). *Our Right to Drugs, The Case for a Free Market*. New York/Westport/London: Praeger.

2. Cigarette makers in a $368 billion accord to curb lawsuits and curtail marketing, *The New York Times*, June 21, 1997, p. 1.

3. The eleven states that decriminalized marijuana statutorily are Alaska, Oregon, California, Minnesota, Colorado, Nebraska, Mississippi, Ohio, North Carolina, New York, and Maine.

4. Milwaukee aldermen cite fairness in easing marijuana punishment, *Milwaukee Journal Sentinel*, May 14, 1997, p. 1.

5. *Ravin v. State*, 537 P. 2d 494 (1975).

6. Police, U.S. agents seize marijuana dealers in Greenwich Village, *The New York Times*, June 21, 1997, p. 21.

7. Republic of Colombia, Constitutional Court Sentence No. C-221/94 C-221/94, Record No. D-429, Alexandre Sochandamandou, Demandant, May 5, 1994.

8. *The New York Times*, December 31, 1996.

9. The entire text of the 18th Amendment reads as follows:

> Section 1. After one year from the ratification of this article the manufacture, sale, or transportation of intoxicating liquors within, the importation thereof into, or the exportation thereof from the United States and all territory subject to the jurisdiction thereof for beverage purposes is hereby prohibited.

> Section 2. The Congress and the several States shall have concurrent power to enforce this article by appropriate legislation.

> Section 3. This article shall be inoperative unless it shall have been ratified as an amendment to the Constitution by the legislatures of the several States, as pro-

vided in the Constitution, within seven years from the date of the submission hereof
to the State by the Congress.

10. *The New York Times*, June 2, 1923, p. 1.

11. Kleiman, M. A. R. (1989). *Marijuana: Costs of Abuse, Costs of Control*, p. 182. New York: Greenwood.

12. According to FBI Uniform Crime Statistics, arrests for marijuana have risen from ten per 100,000 population in 1965 to 224 per 100,000 population in 1995.

13. Schmoke, K. It's worth a try, *The New York Daily News*, March 11, 1990, p. 2.

14. Speech before the 1989 Biennial Conference of the American Civil Liberties Union, Madison, Wisconsin.

15. E.g., Mikuriya, T., M.D. (1989). A comprehensive proposal to legalize drugs. *California Physician*, December, p. 19. *See* also Medicalization of drug abuse control. *Drug Policy 1989–90, A Reformer's Catalogue*, The Drug Policy Foundation, Washington, DC, p. 239.

16. Wilmot, R. S., and Ryan, T. M., The drug license. *Drug Policy 1989–90, A Reformer's Catalogue*, The Drug Policy Foundation, Washington, DC, p. 146.

17. Dworkin, R. (1990). Drugs and the principle of utility. *Baltimore Evening Sun*, May 30, p. 9.

18. Legalization schemes that grant or withhold legal rights or benefits based on whether one is an "addict" run up against the reality that the preponderance of drug users are not drug addicts. Limiting those eligible for legal drugs to "addicts" may well encourage nonaddicted users to join that category by increasing their drug use so as to meet the "addict" standard.

19. Senate Bill No. 4944, February 16, 1971, 1971–1972 session; Senate No. 3980, Assembly No. 6025, March 15, 1979, 1979–1980 session.

20. S. 1918, 1989–1990, regular session of the New York Senate.

21. House No. 1737, 1981 session.

22. The regulation and taxation of cannabis commerce. Report of the National Task Force on Cannabis Regulation, December 1982. The author was chairman of the Task Force.

23. Senate No. 497, 1983 regular session.

24. Commonwealth of Pennsylvania, The Pennsylvania Marijuana Cultivation Control Act of 1983, introduced by Sen. T. Milton Street.

25. State of Missouri, House Bill No. 1820, 85th General Assembly.

26. Nadelmann, E. A. (1992). Thinking seriously about alternatives to drug prohibition. *Daedalus*, 121:3 (Summer), p. 113.

27. Initiative Measure 595 (1993, Section 10(1)).

28. Initiative Measure 595 (1993, Section 21), State of Washington.

29. The Oregon Drugs Control Amendment, Section 1 (1997).

30. Op. cit., Section 3.

31. Op. cit., Section 6.

32. Oregon Cannabis Tax Act, Section 474.055.

33. Op. cit., Section 474.075(3).

34. Op. cit., Section 474.055(d).

35. Op. cit., Section 474.315.

36. 21 U.S.C. 801 et seq.

37. 21 U.S.C 321 (g) (1).

38. DARE Officer Training Manual, 1984, p. 93, revised 1994.

39. Grinspoon, L. M.D. (1990). The harmfulness tax: a proposal for the regulation and taxation of drugs. *North Carolina Journal of International Law and Commercial Regulation*, vol. 15, No. 3, June.

40. Report of the Committee to Review the Tobacco, Alcohol and Other Substance (TAOS) Curriculum, Ashfield–Plainfield (Massachusetts) Regional School District, Sanderson Academy School Council, June 6, 1994, p. 6, *www.lindesmith.org/tletaol.html*.

41. Op. cit., p. 7.

42. Letter to Harry Drinker, quoted in *Family Portrait*, by Catherine Drinker Bowen, Little, Brown & Company, Boston, 1970.

15

Legalization Legislation: Confronting the Details of Policy Choices

Stanley Neustadter[1]

INTRODUCTION

The messiah of drug legalization has not yet arrived, but the prohibitionists can hear the heavens rumbling with skepticism and with concomitant expectations of a different future. Increasingly large cohorts of the public and even of law enforcement personnel are sensing the futile and Sisyphian nature of using the penal law and prisons as a response to drug use and sale. The citizenry is coming to realize how costly the penal drug war is in terms of dollar expenditures and the sacrifice of civil liberties, and that the drug war, rather than the drugs themselves, is the gratuitous and avoidable cause of many societal distortions. Drug prohibition is wearily shuffling in tattered robe and floppy slippers toward its deathbed, and the only truly undecided questions are how expensive the funeral is going to be, and what the postprohibitionist generation of drug policy will look like.

While many reformers have spoken and written about legalizing drugs, remarkably little thought or energy has been devoted to detailing the legislative nuts and bolts of the legalization scheme that will replace current prohibitionism.

The scarcity of legislatively oriented thinking makes legalizers too often seem like utopians, architectural dreamers able to talk wistfully about a new edifice they plan to erect, but unprepared to tell skeptics how much concrete will be needed for the foundation, what kind of framing will be erected, whether the siding will be brick or wood, the angle of the roof, or the size and number of the rooms inside. No one is seriously going to consider risking an investment in such a structure until specifications are drawn and revealed.

Though reformers tend to speak only in general policy terms, there are in fact several legislative models available.[2] Several bills have been drafted, sponsored, and filed in state legislatures; a few others have been proposed by reformers but either have not been reduced to legislative language or have not been sponsored as bills by any legislators. All, however, give the reader, despite the unavoidable legalese that burdens any legislation, a fairly clear idea of how currently proscribed substances might be made available in the postprohibitionist universe.

These bills have one essential feature in common: they foresee a government-regulated market modeled more or less on today's alcohol market instead of the current across-the-board prohibition. None of the bills is a pure libertarian model, which calls for a complete withdrawal of government involvement in the drug market, and none would allow drugs to be bought and sold free of any government controls, as though they were, say, radishes or umbrellas.

The devil, of course, is in the details, and the proposals vary markedly in precisely how they design the regulated drug future. But each in its own way reflects policy judgments on some of the key issues that any serious reformer must candidly recognize, confront, and resolve, and offers reformers a broad menu of alternatives. Needless to say, many of these issues overlap and cannot be resolved independently of the resolution of other issues, and all of them present not only policy dilemmas but political ones as well.

It would be useful, then, first to outline the salient and distinctive features of these bills, describe some of the proposals that have been discussed but not yet written up in legislative form, and finally, identify the key policy issues and how these bills and proposals set about to resolve them.[3]

An initial caveat is in order. As most of the bills have been proposed as *state* legislation, it is important to note that, for all practical purposes, even if enacted, state legalization bills will remain purely hortatory in nature and effect until the federal government exercises its prerogatives to withdraw from international treaties obliging it to take steps to repress drug trafficking within its borders. Until drug law policy is fundamentally changed at the national level, a state whose legislature implemented a regulated marketplace for currently proscribed substances would likely be greeted by a U.S. Justice Department lawsuit, premised on solemn treaty obligations,[4] to enjoin deployment of the state legalization scheme.

Pending an equivalent shift in federal policy, then, the most a single state could accomplish on its own would be to repeal its own criminal drug statutes, thus leaving it entirely to federal law enforcement operatives to enforce federal drug laws within the state, without any help from state law enforcement.[5] Since the states now carry the overwhelming portion of the onshore drug law enforcement burden, state enactment of simple repealers (i.e., legislation that simply erases criminal drug laws from its books, but that does not also legislatively create a state-regulated drug market) might be a plausible first step toward forcing the federal hand.

Accordingly, the legislation proposed to date as state enactment is useful to reformers as much for its prospects of becoming the eventual legislation for any single state as for providing models of the kind of legislation that will be eventually enacted on a national level.

There are two major categories of bills: marijuana-only bills, and the omnibus legalization bills that would legalize the sale and possession of virtually all nonmedical substances.

MARIJUANA BILLS

The 1981 Massachusetts Cannabis Revenue & Education Bill:[6] This bill would create the Cannabis Control Authority to regulate the commercial production and distribution of marijuana, with different licenses required for importation, cultivation, processing, and retailing activities. The number of marijuana retail outlets could not exceed the number of alcohol retail outlets, and the minimum age for purchase and use would be 18. Marijuana would be retailed in three different THC potencies: less than 2 percent, 2-5 percent, and 5 percent and more, and would be taxed accordingly. Half of the net revenues would be earmarked toward drug education. The bill prohibits all marijuana advertising.

1979 Florida Local Option Marijuana Bill:[7] This bill would give each of Florida's counties the individual option to permit the cultivation and sale of marijuana. The bill prescribes little in the way of detail, except to limit marijuana sales to already licensed alcohol retailers, and to provide for a state sales tax of 4 percent plus a 10 percent tax dedicated to the reduction of county and local taxes. All regulatory details are to be delegated to the counties.

1983 Oregon Marijuana Control Bill:[8] This bill places the entire regulatory and administrative responsibility in the hands of the state treasurer. It allows home growing and processing for personal use, up to five plants annually or one kilogram of smokable product. All commercial (defined as nongratuitous) cultivation, processing, or retailing must be licensed. Licensed cultivators may grow up to 1,000 plants per year. The treasurer is to purchase the plants from the cultivators at a fixed price per plant. The treasurer is to contract with licensed processors, who clean, test, package, and label the product. Retailers sell the processed marijuana at fixed prices, depending upon THC content, as adjusted biannually according to the consumer price index. All retail proceeds go to the treasurer, who pays the cultivators and the processors, and then covers the administrative expenses. The balance of the retail proceeds are evenly divided by law enforcement and local school districts. The minimum age of a purchaser is set at 21.

1983 Pennsylvania Marijuana Cultivation Bill:[9] This bill is almost identical to the 1983 Oregon bill, except that the state department of agriculture, rather than the state treasurer, oversees the operation, and the profits go into the general state fund and are not earmarked for any specific purpose.

1982 Cannabis Revenue Act:[10] This bill was designed as a federal prototype for the regulation and taxation of commercial activity in marijuana, and was the progenitor of the Oregon, Massachusetts, and Pennsylvania bills described above. It designates the U.S. Secretary of the Treasury as the chief regulator, and requires licenses for the commercial cultivation, processing, and retailing of marijuana. The cultivation and possession of personal-use amounts are allowed, no more than twenty-five plants or five pounds of crude cannabis. Noncommercial transfers of marijuana are allowed. The minimum age for purchase or use is 18. The processors are obliged to accurately label the product to reveal THC content, species and variety, origin, and the identity of the processor, and the label would also display a detailed warning on the side effects and possible consequences of use.

Taxes are based upon the per-ounce THC content: $20 for less than 2 percent; $25 for 2-4 percent; $35 for 4-6 percent, and $45 for more than 6 percent. The licensed processor, who cleans, tests, packages, and labels the product, is responsible for collecting the tax; the processor is obliged to remit 90 percent of his gross receipts (sales receipts plus tax receipts) to the Secretary of the Treasury. A portion of the remitted revenues goes to the general fund of the U.S. Treasury. The other portion is distributed, under a prescribed formula, to those states that have elected to permit, in a manner consistent with the federal enactment, commerce in marijuana within their borders. Those states that opt to continue with their marijuana prohibitionist policies would receive no marijuana-generated funds from the U.S. Treasury.

OMNIBUS/ALL DRUGS BILLS

1989 Drug Crime Prevention Bill:[11] This is a federal bill that legalizes the licensed cultivation, manufacture, and sale of all drugs except PCP ("angel dust"), for which severe penalties would remain. Patterned rather closely after New York's Alcohol & Beverage Law, the bill prohibits manufacturers and wholesalers from having any financial interest in retail operations and forbids quantity discounts and sales promotions. Sales to minors (minimum age: 21) are harshly punished. The bill requires all drugs to be packaged in blister packs containing no more than the single dosage unit specified for each drug.[12] The states retain the prerogative to impose nonpunitive taxes on drug sales, and also retain the right to prescribe nonpenal sanctions to discourage drug use (e.g., loss of various welfare, housing, or unemployment benefits; grounds for divorce or child custody). But states that attempt to prohibit the commerce in drugs forfeit their eligibility for federal funds for law enforcement, correction, and drug and alcohol treatment.

1990 Missouri Bill:[13] This bill allows the licensed manufacture and sale of all currently illegal substances, but also allows unlicensed cultivation and manufacture for personal use, and unlicensed gratuitous transfers as well. It imposes a flat state sales tax of 25 percent. It also sets forth a strict prohibition on use of drugs (1) in the presence of anyone less than 18 years of age, (2) outside the confines of a private residence, or (3) in a place of public accommodation or conveyance.

1995 Galiber (NY.) Bill:[14] This bill, like the 1989 federal bill, draws heavily on New York's alcohol legislation, and would legalize the manufacture, wholesaling, and retailing of all drugs through a licensing and regulatory body, the Controlled Substances Authority. All drugs except marijuana would be sold through licensed private retail outlets. Marijuana would be sold through liquor stores, and the marijuana commerce would be jointly regulated by the Alcohol Beverage Commission and the Controlled Substances Authority. No single retail purchase could exceed ten "usual doses," a quantity to be determined by the Authority. The Authority is empowered to add or remove substances requiring licenses from the list, and to promulgate the rules and regulations designed to further the bill's general legalization goals. The bill imposes a flat 5 percent sales tax on all sales, and the tax revenues are dedicated entirely to the treatment of addiction to controlled substances. Addiction to a controlled substance is not to be considered a "disability."

OTHER APPROACHES NOT YET REDUCED
TO LEGISLATIVE DRAFT

The "medical" models: Baltimore mayor Kurt Schmoke has been the most publicized advocate of medicalizing the distribution of drugs, but has spoken only generally, and has provided few details of how this would work.[15] Dr.

Tod Mikuriya has proposed that hard drugs be made available only to adults, and only to those adults who have passed written and physical examinations to demonstrate both their need for drugs and their ability to understand proper usage and the consequences of abuse. A variation on this theme proposed that drugs would be available to adults who take classes and pass an examination designed to test their ability to cope with drugs. Passage of the exam would entitle the user to an ATM-like card to be used in drug-dispensing machines.[16]

Ethan Nadelmann has proposed a legalization scheme that would have the government distribute drugs through a vast mail-order system; he has not reduced this proposal to legislative draft, but has described it in some depth in Chapter 22.[17]

BASIC POLICY ISSUES TO BE CONTEMPLATED BY LEGALIZATION DRAFTERS

The following paragraphs identify fifteen areas of concern to any legislator seriously contemplating introducing a bill to legalize drugs. As will become obvious, any number of these areas, while theoretically distinct, overlap to one degree or another with one or more other issue areas. Though posed here purely as matters of policy, in the realm of legislation, there is no gainsaying the role of political palatability in the ultimate resolution of these questions.

ALLOCATION OF FEDERAL/STATE PREROGATIVES

Both levels of government have been legislating in the drug control field for decades, and both levels will certainly want to have a voice in whatever scheme replaces current prohibition. It would seem that there are two polar possibilities. The federal government could enact simple repealers of all federal penal drug statutes, and declare the states free to do as they pleased with the issue.[18] The key practical drawback here is that this will inevitably result in at least some, possibly many, "dry" states.

This can have consequences that some consider undesirable: citizens of bordering states flocking to buy in the "wet" states. Both Amsterdam and Zurich have experienced this phenomenon. Closer to home, so did New York State when its minimum drinking age remained 18 long after all neighboring states had raised the minimum age to 21; Louisiana has a similar problem today. State-by-state disparities tend to create pressure on wet states to become dry or on low-minimum-age states to become high-minimum-age states. A parallel problem could emerge intrastate: certain counties might want to remain dry or might choose to set disparate minimum age limits.

The other extreme would be to grant the federal government exclusive authority to define and administer the new drug control regime, completely preempting state prerogatives. While this has the virtue of ensuring clarity and nationwide uniformity, it eliminates the value of having different states devise creative or experimental local methods of deploying and operating a drug control system.

The more sensible approach would seem to reside with a workable middle ground: federal legislation would repeal federal penal drug statutes and would erect a federal regulatory scheme that would allow the states reasonable flexibility in administrative and regulatory details, but with strong monetary incentives to toe the federal line. In other words, the country's core drug policy would be determined at the national level, and states that adopted policies that were designed or that tended to undermine or frustrate overall federal regulatory policy would suffer fiscal penalties.[19]

EQUAL ACCESS TO ALL DRUGS?

This problem has several facets. Is it wise to allow heroin, for example, to be as easily available as marijuana? If not, by what legislative or regulatory mechanism should the distinctions in accessibility be determined? Some reformers would argue that certain drugs should not be legalized at all, and that, for those drugs, the current prohibitionist approach should remain intact. Or, instead of a pure prohibitionist model for those substances (say, heroin and cocaine), perhaps there should be a medical model, analogous to methadone clinics dispensing maintenance doses to certified addicts. But under a medical model, what happens to nonaddicted casual users? Will there be enough doctors willing to make addict certification and drug dispensing their professional undertaking? What will be the responses of medical schools and medical associations to such a proposal? In any event, will changing the drug barrier from a cop to a medic do anything to eliminate black market trafficking and the enormous law enforcement machinery currently operating to eliminate it?

If the medical model seems a problematic substitute for prohibition of the most "dangerous" drugs, what other mechanisms might be available to deal with the fact that some drugs are more perilous to users than others? Stringent licensing requirements? Fewer retail outlets? Different drugs available at different outlets? In alcohol regulation many states allow beer, wine, and spirits to be sold only at separate outlets. Shorter retailing hours? Smaller amounts available for individual sales? Higher tax rates on the more "dangerous" substances? By what criteria is dangerousness to be ascertained and measured, and by whom? To what extent does *any* differential accessibility scheme encourage the continuation of black markets? To what extent should fears of reemerging black markets drive new drug policy?

APPROPRIATE LEVEL OF RETAIL PRICE
AND TAXATION RATE

Should different substances be taxed differently? What level of taxation can be maintained without driving the final sales price so high that black markets would be encouraged? This latter question has received scant econometric attention,[20] but sorely needs it. The various bills seem to just pluck numbers from the air, but tax rates must be determined only after serious analysis. An equally thorny problem is reckoning the base cost of cultivating or manufacturing the substances. Because the "crime tariff" (the premium over base cost that the criminal charges for the risk of producing and trafficking in illegal substances) is responsible for most of the retail street price of drugs under the current prohibitionist system, it is difficult to project the true base cost in a free market solely from current price patterns. Moreover, manufacture/cultivation, wholesaling, and retailing would involve significant personnel and regulatory compliance costs whose dimensions must be also be estimated. Without those projections it is difficult to project a sensible retail sales price, without which no tax rate can be rationally calculated.

Figuring retail prices and tax rates is further complicated by another factor: with cultivation/manufacture open and legal, small-plot farming and garage lab production will disappear and be replaced by economies of technology and scale. In the longer run this will have the inevitable effect of dramatically reducing the base unit product cost, which will in turn impact taxation policy. For example, an ounce of marijuana whose wholesale cost is $20 in the first year of legalization may well cost only $1 in year five. To the extent the tax rate is based on wholesale product *cost*, revenues would diminish as production efficiencies increase.

Some, but by no means all, of these problems can be simplified or eliminated if the new drug commerce is operated as a government monopoly. There would be no taxes as such, just "profits" represented by the balance remaining after the state has paid all expenses of cultivation, manufacture, processing, and retailing.

Even after these calculations are made, other questions remain. Who decides what the tax rates should be, the legislature or the regulatory agency? In most jurisdictions, if not all, tax policy may be set only by elected officials, yet regulators are more likely to have a keener grasp of commerce itself, and could make wiser, speedier taxation decisions out of public view. If the new drug scheme is a concurrent state/federal one, how should tax revenues be divided? How should the likely competition between state and federal governments for the lion's share of the tax dollar be managed? In any event, should revenues, whether at the federal or local level, be specifically earmarked for, say, drug treatment and education? For reduction in local income or property or sales taxes? For local law enforcement? For government's expenses in administering the new drug scheme? For the general treasury? In any event, should legalization proponents announce an estimate of how much revenue might reasonably be generated by the new regime?[21]

LEGISLATING THE DETAILS

How much of the regulatory scheme (e.g., label warning language, sale unit for each drug, time/place sale and use restrictions) should be detailed in the legislation? Is it wiser to leave that to the regulatory body that these bills envisage and create? Does that dampen criticism or invite it? To what extent will the politicians, other public figures, the drug warriors, and the public insist that the details be spelled out in advance? Politicians might well prefer to pass the buck on those details to the regulatory agency, while others might want to know all the details in advance. To what extent should any new drug legislation expressly answer questions such as, "Will an airline pilot be able to go down to the local store and buy crack?"?

LIABILITY WAIVERS

Holding manufacturers and sellers harmless from any product liability claims to users is a feature of some of these bills. But what about manufacturer/retailer liability to third parties harmed by users under the influence of legally purchased substances? Is the alcohol/gun model appropriate for liability to the nonusing third party?

DEGREE OF GOVERNMENT INVOLVEMENT
IN LEGALIZED MARKET

Although the analogies are gross and imperfect, the other legalized "sin" markets—alcohol and gambling—provide convenient comparisons. In terms of government involvement, should the new drug scheme resemble, for example, state lotteries or rather licensed casinos?[22] Lotteries are run virtually entirely by state agencies staffed by state employees; though some peripheral functions are contracted out (e.g., manufacturing the machines that print out the tickets; paying retailers a tiny commission on each ticket sold), the whole system is operated by government functionaries as a monopoly. There is no tax on each sale of a lottery ticket: the government simply keeps the balance of revenues after administrative costs are paid.

Casinos, however, are typically overseen by a state regulatory agency. The actual casino operations themselves, though tightly monitored by the regulators, are entirely managed by licensed private hands, staffed wholly by private enterprise. The state realizes revenues by taxing casino proceeds.

With respect to the drug market, should the government cultivate, process, and sell the product, and keep what is left after covering those costs? Should it leave the cultivation and processing to licensed private operators who will then sell it (at what price? free market or fixed?) to the government, which will then operate as the wholesaler/retailer? Many states operate the liquor market in this fashion. Or should the government leave the whole enterprise in private hands, with its involvement limited to licensing/regulatory matters? Should the government/private mix be different for different substances? Should these decisions be made at the national or local level?

Intense government involvement, particularly in the preretail phases of the drug market, would be politically attractive to civil service unions but they might also end up to be more costly enterprises, requiring ever-increasing higher total retail prices to support, creating the risk that underpricing and unregulated black markets would eventually emerge.[23] Even if pervasive government involvement translated into greater government revenues, many might find it unseemly for the government to be in the actual business of importing, cultivating, processing, and retailing substances that once were completely illegal and thought by many to be immoral as well.

PRESCRIPTION DRUGS

Some prescription drugs—for example, valium, barbiturates, opiate-based pain-killers—are commonly abused through both overprescription and black market availability: Should these drugs be available without prescription under the new scheme? What is the nature of the intersection between the new recreational drug scheme and federal regulation of prescription medications, substances originally designed for the treatment of medical conditions but that have been put to recreational use as well?

DESIGNER DRUGS

New substances work their way into use from time to time. How does the new regime deal with this phenomenon?

HOME GROWERS

Of particular importance to the doper-legalizers, but theoretically a more general, if less widespread, phenomenon with other drugs as well, are the consumers who grow their own. It is worth noting that current alcohol regulations allow individuals to brew limited quantities of their own beer and wine. How about cooking up your own personal-use pile of Quaaludes or speed? What about growing your own coca leaves to chew yourself? To make into cocaine for your own use? What about buying cocaine through legal retail outlets and rendering it down to crack for your own use? This in turn suggests other questions: Does it make sense to legalize/regulate coca leaves but not cocaine, cocaine but not crack, opium leaves but not heroin or morphine?

LICENSING USERS

Inevitably there will be calls from skeptics and die-hard warriors who say no legalization scheme should even be contemplated unless it requires that users be licensed, the argument being that if we require licenses for the recreational use of cars and guns, why not for drugs? Along the same lines, there may be calls to have retailers keep records of purchasers (perhaps through the issuance of drug ID cards) and amounts sold to each one. Are these wise ideas? If not, how are they best countered? May the same goals be achieved by measures less onerous to privacy and civil liberties concerns?

PARENT–CHILD DRUG TRANSFERS

Current law has an expansive definition of "sale" of drugs, and forbids not only typical cash-and-carry transactions, but gratuitous transfers—gifts—as well.[24] All legalization bills would lift penal sanctions on adults for licensed sales, and for gratuitous transfers between adults, but would retain penal sanctions, often harsh ones, against transfers to those under 21 years of age (except for the 1982 Cannabis Revenue & Education Act, which set the age at 18).

Yet parents might well want to introduce their teenage offspring to some drugs both to remove the "forbidden fruit" attraction of drug use (if Mom and Dad do this, how cool could it be?) and to teach safe-use methods. This, of course, is what many families do today with respect to introducing their children to alcohol, even though, under current alcohol regulations, it is illegal. Should the new legislation deal with this explicitly? Should this particular dog be left to sleep, like parent–child alcohol transfers?

CURRENTLY INCARCERATED DRUG OFFENDERS

How will the new scheme affect them? Not at all, unless the legislation says otherwise. This was a problem when alcohol prohibition was repealed by constitutional amendment (as opposed to ordinary legislative enactment), and where the number of inmates affected was, compared to current drug inmate populations, insignificant.[25]

A number of options suggest themselves: (1.) a direct and immediate legislative commutation of all drug sentences; (2.) a complete legislative commutation combined with some sort of limited parole supervision depending upon the severity of the sentence; (3.) a staggered legislative commutation depending upon the severity of the sentence either with or without parole supervision; (4.) a case-by-case approach, requiring each defendant to petition the sentencing judge, with legislation providing guidelines to judges, with right of appeal. A parallel issue involves remissions of forfeitures obtained under the former laws.

DRUG TESTING

Does a legalization scheme call for a different approach to drug testing? Does it warrant testing a broader—or narrower—segment of society on a routine basis? Only on a probable-cause basis? Should the criteria change from mere presence of drugs in the system to impairment of function?

NONPENAL SANCTIONS FOR DRUG USERS

This issue is analytically distinct, but closely related to the drug-testing issue noted above. Both issues are likely to be resolved on the basis of whether, and in what manner, the public perceives that drug use will significantly increase after legalization. Many proponents of legalization argue that even if overall usage increases, the drugs available will be safer and, more important, less potent. The theory is that the "iron law" of drug prohibition—that criminal laws virtually guarantee that smugglers will market only the most compact shipments of the most potent substances—will no longer operate in a regulated market, and that most drug users, given the choice, would normally opt for milder forms of drugs, preferring a cocktail-like buzz to a blottoed binge.

Even if the future ultimately bears out the truth of these plausible theories, the public's perception of legalization's likely harvest might well be quite different. Citizens might well seek comfort in knowing that the law contains other measures—nonpenal in nature—that would act to deter drug use.

The possibilities are endless. Eligibility for all sorts of public benefits (welfare, housing, veterans, Social Security, Medicare, unemployment insurance, driving and occupational licenses) might be denied on the basis of a failed mandatory drug test or on other proof of drug use. Assuming that the Constitution would impose some limits on the denial of public benefits solely on the basis of using a legal substance, it is not at all clear what would prevent, for example, a legislature from making drug use a ground for divorce or a factor in awarding child custody.

Moreover, the Constitution is unlikely to provide protection from purely private sanctions: legislation allowing a landlord to evict a tenant for drug use. If measures such as these become part of the legalized drug landscape, reformers whose anti-prohibitionism is driven largely by libertarian sentiments might find the drug peace scarcely more attractive than the drug war; the brawny arm of the penal law would be replaced by the slithery tentacles of insidiously intrusive nonpenal sanctions.

DECRIMINALIZATION OF DRUGS AND THE ANTITOBACCO-SMOKING MOVEMENT

There is a certain *Godzilla vs. Rodan* quality to the irony that as drug prohibitionism draws more and more skepticism, tobacco prohibitionism gains ever more favor. The two movements seem, at least on the surface, to be dissonant and at cross-purposes. The arguments in favor of one seem to undermine the arguments in favor of the other, even though, at least to date, the antismoking forces are not calling for criminal sanctions against sale and possession of cigarettes. How are these cross-currents to be navigated? On the other hand, insofar as both movements share at least one goal in common—to control rather than outlaw perilous recreational substances—there may be some productive common grounds available for both movements to strengthen one another, particularly if, as currently seems plausible, the Federal Drug Administration acquires regulatory prerogatives over tobacco products.

CONCLUSION

These are thorny issues whose resolution requires not only sage and informed policymaking, but astute political judgment as well. Formulating wise and effective policy will require the contributions of more than just earnest drug policy reformers. It will draw upon the expertise of several disciplines, including economics, pharmacology, taxation, medicine, and public administration; it will also seek to learn from the accumulated experience of those who have dealt with alcohol and gambling regulation.

Alcohol prohibition has been a favorite fount of lesson-learning and moralizing for drug warriors and drug reformers alike, and perhaps it would be worthwhile to look to the aftermath of alcohol prohibition's repeal to learn how best to fashion the legislation that will establish the postdrug prohibitionist universe.

As the 21st Amendment repealing alcohol prohibition was being considered for ratification, John D. Rockefeller Jr. sponsored a study to recommend legislation to be implemented following repeal. Eventually published as a book, *Toward Liquor Control*,[26] the study provided the blueprint for virtually all the state legislation that was thereafter enacted. The Rockefeller study was undertaken by a handful of attorneys and policy wonks, but compared to the legalization of alcohol, legalization of currently controlled substances is far more complicated and will require the active participation of a broader array of thinking from far more people, and far greater time to complete. The extant legislative proposals do not reflect the kind of probing and far-reaching analyses required for the task.

ENDNOTES

1. The author is indebted to Richard Evans, Esq., whose encyclopedic knowledge and shrewd observations were invaluable to the preparation of this chapter.

2. I use the word *available* advisedly. Bills that are proposed and filed, but never enacted, are exceedingly difficult to find as they are seldom housed in any bibliographically accessible manner and are thus virtually impossible to 'research' or locate in any systematic way. Nor has a complete collection of these bills been privately published. A couple of them were reprinted by the Drug Policy Foundation [DRUG POLICY 1989–1990: A Reformer's Catalogue]. See endnote 11. Most of the others were brought to my attention by Richard Evans, Esq., to whom I am deeply indebted.

3. I have *not* covered the more narrowly targeted legislation often characterized as "harm reduction" measures: (a) eliminating mandatory minimum sentences for various types of drug crimes and drug offenders; (b) providing easier access to clean hypodermic needles, either through the authorization of needle exchange programs or over-the-counter sales of needles; (c) "medical marijuana" bills to ease or eliminate restrictions on both the use of marijuana in the course of medical treatment and research into its possible medical benefits; (d) limiting the government's prerogative to pursue forfeitures in drug prosecutions, imposing broader due process protection upon the government when it seeks forfeiture, broadening "innocent owner" defenses to forfeiture actions, and prescribing proportionality limitations on the amount or value of property the government may claim in forfeiture proceedings. Nor shall I discuss legislation, much of it enacted by several states in the 1970s, which, though it drastically reduced the penalties for sale and possession of marijuana, did not purport to legalize such conduct [*e.g.*, NY Penal Law Article 221,"Marijuana Reform Act," L.1977, Ch 360]. The harms that these measures are designed to reduce would largely disappear under virtually any legalization scheme.

4. For example, the Convention on Psychotropic Substances signed in Vienna on February 21, 1971; the Single Convention on Narcotic Drugs signed in New York on March 30, 1961. These treaties, and others, typically allow any signatory to unilaterally withdraw from its treaty obligations upon prescribed notice to the other signatories.

5. There is precedent for this approach. In 1923 Governor Al Smith signed the Cuvillier Bill, which repealed New York's alcohol prohibition laws, which shifted the entire burden of enforcing prohibition to the federal authorities. In 1990 Governor Mario Cuomo, though he did not call for repeal of the state's drug laws, suggested that local prosecutors dump their drug arrests on federal prosecutors' offices as a way to encourage Washington to assume a greater share of the drug law enforcement burden. In 1993 Massachusetts reformers drafted a one-page bill that would remove the word *marijuana* from the state's drug laws, thus ceding marijuana enforcement entirely to the federal government; the bill awaits a legislative sponsor.

6. Massachusetts House Bill #1737/1981, introduced by Representative Card, and drafted by Richard Evans, Esq.

7. Florida Senate Bill (unnumbered) introduced by Senators Gordon and Barron in April 1979.

8. Senate Bill #497/1983, sponsored by the Oregon Senate Committee on the Judiciary.

9. Unnumbered Senate Bill sponsored by Senator Street.

10. The earlier version of this bill was drafted in 1982 by the National Task Force on Cannabis Regulation, led by a pioneer in legalization legislation, Richard M. Evans, Esq., of Northhampton, Massachusetts. Its most current version has been reprinted in DRUG POLICY 1989–1990: A Reformer's Catalogue (Trebach & Zeese, eds.) [Drug Policy Foundation, Washington, DC: 1989], at pp. 429–451.

11. Nancy Lord, M.D., LL.B., drafted this bill while a law student at Georgetown University Law School. It has been published in DRUG POLICY 1989–1990: A Reformer's Catalogue (Trebach & Zeese, Eds.)[Drug Policy Foundation, Washington, DC: 1989], at pp. 371–399.

12. The dosage units are derived in part from FDA dosage regulations and in part from Goodman & Gilman, *The Pharmacologic Basis of Therapeutics* (7th Ed. 1985) [letter from Nancy Lord to author dated 18 November 1989].

13. Missouri House Bill #1820, introduced by Representative Walton in February 1990 [85th General Assembly, Second Session].

14. New York State Senate Bill #4771, introduced May 3, 1995, by the late Senator Joseph L. Galiber. Senator Galiber had long been active in trying to lessen the role of the penal law in drug policy, and had led the fight in the 1970s to decriminalize personal-use amounts of marijuana in New York. An earlier, and rather different, version of this bill was published in DRUG POLICY 1989–1990: A Reformer's Catalogue (Trebach & Zeese, eds.)[Drug Policy Foundation, Washington, DC: 1989], at pp. 400–428.

15. Schmoke, *An Argument in Favor of Decriminalization*, 18 Hofstra L.Rev. 501, 523–525 (1990).

16. For more complete descriptions of these proposals, see *Medicalization of Drug Abuse Control and The Drug License*, articles in DRUG POLICY 1989–1990, A Reformer's Catalogue [Drug Policy Foundation: Washington, DC: 1989], at p. 239.

17. There are some key problems with this proposal: huge administrative costs of packaging and labeling the products for mail; verifying the age eligibility of buyers; the delay between the buyer's desire for a drug and its delivery; the uncertain security of mails; and resolving claims of nondelivery or receipt.

18. For an interesting analysis sponsoring a 10th Amendment states-rights approach, see Benjamin & Miller, *Undoing Drugs: Beyond Legalization* [Basic Books, NY: 1991].

19. In fact, the federal government has already used this carrot-and-stick approach in the drug policy arena with considerable effect. The Federal Drug Offenders Driving Privileges Act provided that states that decline to enact legislation stripping drivers' licenses from people convicted of drug offenses will have their matching federal highway funds cut off [See 23 U.S.C. {104(a)(2)}]. Virtually all states got the message and enacted the requisite legislation.

20. The only recent scholarly economic analysis I have been able to locate is Caputo & Ostrom, *Potential Tax Revenue from a Regulated Marijuana Market: A Meaningful Revenue Source*, 54 Am.J. Econ. & Sociol. 475 (1994). *But see* Garber, *Potential Tax Revenues from a Regulatory Marketing Scheme for Marijuana* 10 J. Psyched. Drugs 217 (1978). Extrapolating from alcohol and tobacco tax experience and from available statistics on marijuana usage patterns, the authors derive a broad estimate of the range of tax revenues that might be generated through a legalized marijuana market. However, the authors have no particular legalization model in mind, and do not propose any particular tax structure or tax rate. They tacitly assume that the government will be operating (not just licensing others to do so) the entire marijuana industry,

from cultivation to processing to retailing, and seem to equate "taxes" with "profits." Yet the tax issues do not exist in a vacuum, and can be confronted or resolved only within the framework of specific legalization models.

21. Cost-benefit and cost-effectiveness analyses have been marshaled by drug policy debaters, but not always sagely because there are so many variables. For a trenchant examination of the problem, see Warner, *Legalizing Drugs: Lessons From (and About) Economics*, 69 Milbank Quarterly 641–662 (1991).

22. Another apt contrast would be between race tracks (entirely in licensed private hands) and off-track betting parlors and lotteries (operated wholly by government employees).

23. New York's experience with its Off Track Betting Corporation [OTB] is soberingly instructive. Established more than twenty years ago, OTB operates a statewide chain of betting parlors where customers can bet on horse races through OTB's own pari-mutual wagering. OTB earns its revenues by taking an off-the-top percentage of the total OTB wagering pool. In its earlier years the percentage was fairly low, but still made the state a tidy profit. For reasons not entirely apparent, though, OTB's administrative costs ballooned over the years, forcing it to take ever larger shares from the wagering pool, which meant, of course, that fewer pari-mutual dollars were available to the winning bettors, who made less on a winning OTB bet than they would have made had they placed the same bet at the racetrack. Bookies, whose business was seriously dented in the early OTB years, have slowly reemerged to former levels as they operate leaner nonunion enterprises and can offer better payoffs on winning bets than OTB. As a result, OTB barely breaks even.

24. A recent New York case fairly reflects the law in almost all jurisdictions. *People v. Starling*, 85 N.Y.2d 509, 650 N.E.2d 387 (1985).

25. *See generally, United States v. Chambers*, 291 U.S. 217, 233 (1934); Note, *The Status of Liquor Crimes and Forfeitures Following Repeal*, 2 Geo.Wash.L.Rev. 395 (1934); Annotation at 89 A.L.R. 1514 (1935).

26. By Raymond Fosdick and Albert Scott [Harper: New York, 1933]. For a more complete discussion of the Rockefeller group, see Levine & Rainerman, *From Prohibitionism to Regulation*, in CONFRONTING DRUG POLICY, R. Bayer & G. Oppenheimer (Eds.) [Cambridge U. Press: 1993], at pp. 160–193.

Section IIB
A Range of Options

16

Not All Drugs Are Created Equal

Robert S. Gable

If we are concerned about the external pollutants that threaten our environment we should be equally concerned about internal pollutants—like marijuana products. For sheer survival, we must defend ourselves against both kinds of pollution.

—JACQUES IVES COUSTEAU,
cited in Schuchard (1993)

Consider this: The risks of caffeine are greater than THC in every way. . . . Caffeine is physically addicting (with headache as the most often cited withdrawal symptom) and can cause unnecessary stress, lightheadedness, breathlessness and an irregular heartbeat or much worse in larger-than-average doses. Marijuana isn't even remotely as dangerous—no deaths by overdose, no physical addiction and minimal health risks . . . .

—D. LARSEN (1996)

Opinions about the nonmedical use of psychoactive substances are plentiful and contradictory. The disputes tend to focus on the dangers of "drugs" in general, without thoughtful consideration of the different physical and psychological risks among substances. The public is not to blame. Relevant data are difficult to obtain, and in some cases remain highly speculative. Nonetheless, under political pressure to "do something" about drug abuse, legislators tend to pass awkwardly structured statutes with heavy penalties. In the Narcotics Penalties and Enforcement Act of 1986 (U.S. Code, vol. 18, sec. 3553), for example, cocaine is mislabeled as a "narcotic drug."

This chapter briefly reviews empirical criteria for making comparisons of drug risks, tentatively summarizes a substantial portion of available information, and recommends several basic drug control guidelines.

CRITERIA FOR DRUG COMPARISONS

The manner in which a question is asked often determines the answer. This situation certainly applies to the task of comparing the dangers of recreationally used psychoactive substances. My approach to the task of drug comparison was admittedly a personal and pragmatic one. As the parent of a college-age son who was experimenting with a variety of drugs, I became personally interested in drug abuse issues about six years ago. I imagined two nightmare scenarios regarding my son's drug use: first, that I would get a call from a hospital emergency room saying that he was dying; second, that he would become addicted to a substance in a way that would lead to a downward spiral of arrests and health problems. Therefore I decided to compare recreational drugs on two variables—acute toxicity and dependence potential.

ACUTE TOXICITY

The traditional laboratory measure of toxicity has been the *therapeutic index* (Nies 1990). The therapeutic index is calculated by first determining the amount of the drug that is necessary to produce the desired effect in one half of an animal population (typically, mice). This dosage level is referred to as the *effective dose* for 50 percent of the animals, or "ED_{50}." Similarly, the *lethal dose* is determined by observing the amount of the drug that causes death in 50 percent of the animal population, the "LD_{50}." The ratio of the LD_{50} to the ED_{50} provides a one-point estimate of how selective, or nontoxic, a substance is in producing a desired effect.

Figure 16–1 (modified from Julien 1995) illustrates the effective dose (ED) and the lethal dose (LD) curves of a hypothetical drug. Fifty percent of the

Figure 16–1. Dose Response Curves

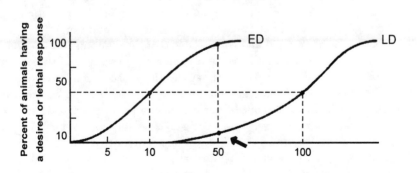

Drug dose (milligrams)

animals have the desired reaction at the 10-mg dosage level, while 50 percent die at the 100-mg dosage level. Figure 16-1 shows that at the 50-mg dose (indicated by the arrow and vertical dotted line), 90 percent of the animals will show the desired response (ED), and 10 percent of the animals will die (LD). Thus the therapeutic index of the hypothetical drug is 10 (100:10).

Now consider our most common recreational substance, alcohol. The LD_{50} of alcohol is estimated to be 270 grams taken orally within five minutes on an empty stomach by a 70-kg human who is a nondrinker. Assuming 13,500 mg of alcohol per 12 fluid ounces (a typical beer having 5 percent alcohol by volume), 270 g of alcohol would be equivalent to twenty beers. The effective dose, ED_{50}, of alcohol is assumed to be 27 g, the amount in two beers. Therefore the "therapeutic index" is $LD_{50}:ED_{50} = 270:27 = 10$ (the same as our hypothetical drug).

Obviously, the likelihood of drinking twenty beers within five minutes is a near impossibility because the large fluid volume may trigger regurgitation. Thus, in this example, the route of administration acts as a protective mechanism. Conversely, if alcohol were taken intravenously—as was recommended at one time as a postsurgical analgesia (Dunham 1951)—it would be much more dangerous.

The six most common routes of drug administration are oral, smoked, intranasal, intravenous, intramuscular, and by inhalation. Oral administration is the most common route, and generally the least susceptible to acute toxic insult because the substance is metabolized in the liver prior to absorption into the bloodstream. However, the slower and variable absorption rate of ingested substances means that regulating the drug's effects is more difficult. Injection of the drug into the vein or muscle produces a more prompt reaction, but leaves less margin for error and runs the risk of infection from nonsterile needles. Inhalation also provides rapid absorption, and avoids the unpredictability of ingestion; however, nonvolatile materials (such as in cigarette smoke and cocaine vapor) have been linked to serious chronic illnesses. Intranasal administration has a slower initial onset of action than inhalation or intravenous injection, but is more rapid and controllable than ingestion or intramuscular injection. The route of administration is related to the severity of subsequent addiction (Gossop et al. 1992) as well as the risk of acute lethality.

The therapeutic index will change as the purpose for use of the drug changes (i.e., the ED is modified). For example, a sedative-hypnotic such as phenobarbital will be relatively safe if the goal is sedation; it will be less safe if the goal is general anesthesia. A dose still higher than that needed for anesthesia may dangerously depress respiratory and vasomotor functions, and therefore lead to coma and death. Most sedative-hypnotics, with the exception of diazepines (e.g., diazepam), again fall into the therapeutic index range of 10 if the goal is intense relaxation or a hypnotic effect (Trevor and Way 1992).

It may seem that a substance with a therapeutic index or safety margin of 10 means that it can be used with little risk. Not necessarily so. Note again Figure 16-1 where a 50-mg dose of the hypothetical drug caused a 10 percent death rate in order to obtain the desired effect in 90 percent of the animals. It must be emphasized that different substances have different "dose–response curves." That is, the amount of the drug needed to go from the minimum to the maximum of a desired or of a lethal effect (i.e., slope of the curve) is unique for each substance. The therapeutic index reflects the relationship of the desired effect and the lethal effect at only *one* point on the curve.

The fact that the therapeutic index is based on the percentage of a population that responds in a particular manner is in itself recognition of the variability of drug responses among individuals. Age, gender, genetic background, and general health status are factors known to impact drug reactions because these factors influence drug distribution, absorption, metabolism, and excretion. Furthermore, an individual's responsiveness to a drug may progressively decrease as a consequence of prior use. This process of "drug tolerance" results in a larger dose of the drug being required to elicit the same effect as a previous smaller dose. Both neuroreceptors in the brain and drug metabolizing enzymes in the liver are involved in such adaptation.

Environmental and motivational factors also play a role in drug response. For example, the LD_{50} point for amphetamine sulfate in mice was reduced by approximately one half when the animals were confined to small (rather than large) floor-area jars. But even more dramatically, the LD_{50} was almost ten times lower when the mice were housed with other mice rather than in isolation (Falk and Feingold 1987, Lasagna and McCann 1957). Similarly, Essman (1983) reported that amphetamine reduced aggressive behavior in isolated mice, but increased it in grouped mice.

A classic laboratory study that used morphine, pentobarbital, and a placebo with humans demonstrated that—depending upon incentives—pentobarbital and morphine varied from being a stimulant to a depressant to having no effect at all (Hill et al. 1957). Mello and Mendelson (1970) reported that more signs of intoxication occurred when alcohol was served by researchers than when identical doses of alcohol were self-administered by the participants. A similar tolerance to drug effects, as a function of established drug-use ritual, was noted by Siegel (1989).

DEPENDENCE POTENTIAL

Dependence potential is a multidimensional construct and can be defined in various ways. The definition is a critical determinant of how various substances get ranked with respect to their addictive risk. One measure of risk could be the "capture ratio" of a substance. That is, of the people who try a drug, what proportion of them will encounter some period of time during which their use of the drug is not fully under their voluntary control? By this measure, tobacco is probably at, or near, the top (Kozlowski et al. 1989). Heroin and cocaine also show a high relapse rate despite the user's acknowledgment that the substance is harmful.

A different criterion for dependence potential can be the onset of withdrawal symptoms when the drug is not available after prolonged use. This measure is the traditional *negative reinforcement* paradigm of addiction. Alcohol, heroin, and short-acting barbiturates get top billing by this standard (Jaffe and Martin 1990).

Another way to assess dependence potential is to measure the strength of the drug as a *positive reinforcer*. Users often self-administer a substance in order to induce euphoria, confidence, sensuality, or novel sensory experiences. This form of dependence is motivated primarily by a desire to repeat a rewarding experience rather than to avoid withdrawal symptoms. Cocaine, opiates, and amphetamines are probably the most addicting drugs by this standard (Hilts 1994).

Finally, another measure of dependency is the drug's severity per unit of time. In other words, how detrimental is the drug to the physical and psychological welfare of a person who is dependent on the substance for a month or a year? By this measure, smoked cocaine competes with intravenous heroin as the most dangerous. Alcohol would probably be ranked second among common psychoactive substances.

PROCEDURE AND RESULTS

An inquisitive person can easily find consumer reports comparing the merits and cost of different brands of aspirin, cigarettes, and wine. In the midst of a fading "drug war," one would not expect to find any popular articles comparing the benefits and dangers of alcohol, amphetamines, and marijuana. Nonetheless, it seems not unreasonable that laboratory reports comparing acute toxicity and dependence potential among substances would exist in the psychopharmacological literature. In fact, such reports are relatively rare across different *classes* of drugs (e.g., stimulants, depressants, and hallucinogens). A few notable studies making broad comparisons include Gossop and colleagues (1992), Heishman and colleagues (1989), Haertzen and colleagues (1983), Henningfield and colleagues (1991), and Iwamoto and Martin (1988).

The present study began by interrogating seven on-line databases (Biosis Previews, Current Contents, Embase, Health Periodicals Database, Medline, PsychInfo, Toxline) using the descriptors "therapeutic index," "toxicity," "dependency," "dose," "dosage," and "reinforcement," accompanied by the names of various drugs. This procedure yielded approximately 12,800 English language citations. Many were redundant; others appeared, on the basis of their titles, to be irrelevant because they dealt primarily with pharmacokinetics, drug design, therapy, or legal matters. Eventually, a total of approximately 350 articles or book chapters was located, photocopied, and catalogued for twenty different psychoactive substances.

Ethyl alcohol far exceeded all other substances as a topic of investigation; caffeine came in second and nicotine third. These are not the most consciousness-altering nor the most addictive substances, but their legal status circumvents the cumbersome and politically sensitive approval procedure that is necessary for research with illicit substances (cf. Strassman 1991). Opium and mescaline had the fewest reports on toxicity and dependence potential.

Estimates of the therapeutic index and the dependence potential of the twenty psychoactive substances are presented in Table 16-1. The effective dose is the estimated amount of the substance that will produce the desired psychological effect in a 70-kg adult who has not developed a tolerance to the substance by sustained prior use. The dosage amounts refer to the quantity of active substance administered; it does not include the amount of inactive material used as a filler or medium. Substances are presumed to be administered within approximately five minutes. The route of administration (e.g., oral, intranasal, smoked) is listed for each substance in Table 16-1. The lethal dose is an estimate generated from nonhuman laboratory animal studies and from emergency room or coroner office reports. One difficulty in making an estimate of the median lethal dose is that animal species may vary greatly in their reaction to a drug. For example, the LD_{50} of injected MDMA for rats is apparently half of what it is for mice (Logan et al. 1988). And, as previously noted, the external test conditions may also have a profound effect on the LD_{50}.

Determining the lethal dose of a drug in emergency room situations is even more difficult. One cannot be sure of the purity of substance that patients claim they have used, and a large majority of patients have ingested alcohol in addition to the putative substance. Details regarding the published sources used to arrive at the LD_{50} estimates can be found in Gable (1993).

The term *safety margin* is used in Table 16-1, rather than *therapeutic index*, because the intended uses of the substances are nonmedical in nature. The numbers are presented solely for the purpose of comparing substances, not as a precise quantification of safety. Even though absolute magnitudes of risk remain uncertain, this quantification can give policymakers a basis for systematically ranking risks and for establishing priorities for intervention programs.

The "Dependence Potential" column in Table 16-1 is an attempt to combine the positive and the negative reinforcement definitions of dependence po-

Table 16–1. Safety Margin and Dependence Potential of Psychoactive Substances[1]

Substance	Effective Dose	Lethal Dose	Safety Margin	Dependence Potential
Narcotics				
Heroin (IV)[2]	4 mg	30 mg	7	Very high
Morphine (IM)	10 mg	90 mg	9	High
Opium (SM)	100 mg	800 mg	8	High
Depressants (sedative-hypnotics)				
Barbiturates				
Secobarbital (OR)	100 mg	2500 mg	25	Moderate
Benzodiazepines				
Diazepam (OR)	2 mg	2000+ mg	1000+	Moderate
Ethanol	27 g	270 g	10	
Alcohol (OR)	(2 beers)[3]			Moderate
Methaqualone (OR)	75 mg	10,000 mg	130	High/moderate
Stimulants				
Amphetamines (OR)	10 mg	200 mg	20	Moderate
Caffeine	100 mg	10,000 mg	100	
Coffee (OR)	(1.5 cup)[4]			Low/moderate
Cocaine	100 mg	2500 mg	25	
powder (IN)	(5 lines or ¼ g)[5]			High/moderate[6]
Cocaine	15 mg	375 mg	25	
("crack") (SM)	(1 rock)[7]			Very high
Nicotine	1 mg	60 mg	60	
Tobacco (SM)	(1 cigarette)			High
Anesthetics				
Ketamine (IM)	50 mg	1300 mg	26	Low
Nitrous oxide (INH)	1 liter[8]	24 liters	24	Low/moderate

[1] After Gable (1993). The information presented here should not be used as a dosage guide. Significant differences exist with respect to a person's physiological and psychological reactions. The dosage indicated is the estimated median amount for an average 70-kg adult human who has not developed tolerance to the substance.

[2] IV = intravenous, IM = intramuscular, INH = inhaled, SM = smoked, OR = oral (swallowed), IN = intranasal (insufflation/snorting). Substances are presumably administered within approximately 5 minutes.

[3] Assumes 52,500-ml body fluid (adjusted for 75% absorption on an empty stomach by 70-kg male human) and 13,500 g of 5% alcohol by volume per 12-oz beer container, resulting in 25.7 mg/100 ml blood alcohol per beer within 15 minutes.

[4] Assumes ground coffee at 65–120 mg caffeine, instant coffee at 50–100 mg, per 148-ml (5 oz) cup.

[5] Based on a "line" of approximately 50 mg, or "¼ gram" total, containing 40% cocaine, 60% adulterants.

[6] Intranasal cocaine powder usually shows mild to moderate physical withdrawal symptoms, but compulsive drug-seeking (i.e., psychological dependence) is sometimes vigorous and sustained.

[7] 100-mg street "rock" of free-base cocaine with 15% inactive residues (e.g., baking soda), smoked in pipe with approximately 20% cocaine intake.

[8] The effective dose is roughly equivalent to street use of two balloons, one half of a 3.5-L "whippet" cartridge, or one 1.5-L whipped cream can of approximately 100% N_2O with 70% of the contents inhaled. The lethal dose estimate would approximate six normal breaths of 100% N_2O,

Substance	Effective Dose	Lethal Dose	Safety Margin	Dependence Potential
Phencyclidine (PCP) (SM)	5 mg (1 "Sherman")[9]	200 mg	40	Moderate/high
Hallucinogens				
LSD-25 (OR)	50 mcg	14,000 mcg[10]	280	Very low
MDMA (OR)	125 mg	1875 mg	15	Moderate/low
Mescaline (OR)	350 mg	6000 mg	17	Very low
Psilocybin (OR)	4 mg (4 'shrooms)[11]	14,000 mg	3500	Very low
Cannabis				
Marijuana (SM)	1.5 mg (½ joint)[12]	4000 mg	2600	Low/moderate

Table 16–1. (continued)

based on average respiratory gas exchange capacity of an adult human of 4 L. Commercial N_2O cartridges and whipped cream dispenser cans have been found to contain numerous contaminants.
[9] One PCP cigarette ("Sherman") sprinkled with, or soaked in, 15-mg phencyclidine with 33% absorption by pulmonary route.
[10] Assumes 0.2 mg/kg for a 70-kg human, based on interpolated LD of 0.3 mg/kg in rabbits and 0.1 mg/kg in an elephant.
[11] Assumes 1 mg of indole alkaloids per mushroom. (One gram of dry weight mushrooms contains approximately 2 mg of psilocybin; however, the potency varies greatly between specimens, and "street 'shrooms" may be contaminated with LSD or PCP.)
[12] There are great variations in the efficiency of the smoking process. This calculation is based on a medium street-grade 700-mg cigarette containing 1.5% delta-9-THC with approximately 30% intake.

tential outlined earlier in this chapter. A graphic representation of dependence and toxicity is presented in Figure 16–2. The most dangerous substances (i.e., opiates) are clustered in the lower right corner because they have the highest dependence potential and the greatest toxicity. In contrast, psilocybin ("magic mushrooms"), which is in the upper left corner, has the lowest addiction potential and the least toxicity. Orally ingested psilocybin, with a safety margin of 3500, is 350 times "safer" than alcohol with a safety margin of 10. Again, these are only estimates, but there seems to be little doubt about the relative position of most (not all) of the substances with respect to one another.

An obvious and important limitation of the two-dimensional comparison in Figure 16–2 is best illustrated by the location of psilocybin. Although it is "safe" with respect to potential lethality and addiction, its potency in altering consciousness makes it much less socially benign than, say, caffeine. Driving a car after ingesting psilocybin is obviously less acceptable than after drinking a cup of coffee. *The consciousness-altering potency of a substance, and the conditions under which it is used, must be factored into any comprehensive assessment of safety.*

Figure 16–2. Safety Margin and Dependence Potential
of Psychoactive Drugs

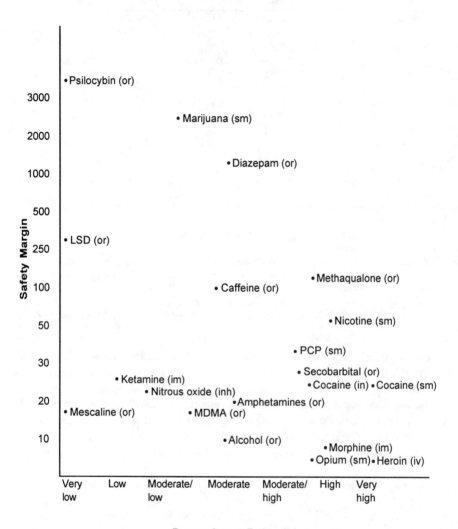

im = intramuscular, in = intranasal, inh = inhaled, iv = intravenous, or = oral,
sm = smoked

POLICY GUIDELINES

Drug regulation in some form is generally agreed to be necessary. Unfortunately, many of our present drug laws are ill-informed and anachronistic. Consider, for example, the Anti-Drug Abuse Amendments Act of 1988 (21 U.S. Code, vol. 21, sec. 1504), which stated: "It is the declared policy of the U.S. Government to create a Drug Free America by 1995." The target date has come and gone, but the increased penalties that Congress imposed for a wide range of drug offenses are still on the books. This is not an isolated case of legislative error. There are at least three other well-known failed attempts to eliminate or prohibit activities involving public health risks: the Delaney Amendment forbidding any carcinogens in food additives (U.S. Code, vol. 21, sec. 348), denial of economic considerations in certain provisions of the Clean Air Act (U.S. Code, vol. 42, sec 7409), and the zero tolerance drug policy of the U.S. Customs Service (Thomas 1989). Eventually, all these regulations were circumvented or rescinded. Realistic and enforceable policies do not come easy in a climate of public fear.

Here are four principles that might guide the development of a pragmatic drug control strategy:

1. Harm will occur.

Archaeological studies indicate that psychoactive substances have been used since prehistoric times (Westermeyer 1988). It seems reasonable to proceed on the premise that the use of psychoactive substances, of some type and to some degree, is inevitable. Laws to control drug use may reduce risks, shift risks, or increase risks, but they cannot *eliminate* them (MacCoun 1993). Taxation, regulation, and prohibition are the most common strategies to reduce the consumption of a commodity. All three create their own reaction in terms of substitution, evasion, or black markets. For example, given a free choice, both laboratory (Mello and Mendelson 1978) and sociological (Burglass 1985) studies suggest that people prefer marijuana to alcohol. When laws against marijuana are stringently enforced, the use of cocaine and alcohol appears to increase (DiNardo 1991, Harrell and Peterson 1992), thus increasing health risks. In short, there are no riskfree options in drug policy.

2. Harm reduction is a necessary, but not sufficient, drug control strategy.

Thoughtful scholars such as MacCoun and colleagues (1996) note that harm reduction, like most interventions, has pitfalls and uncertainties, but they recommend its integration into our national drug control policy. A reasonable first step would involve state-level experiments, accompanied by a rigorous evaluation of various economic and social effects on both users and nonusers.

Unfortunately, harm reduction is only a partial answer because it focuses exclusively on potential negative consequences. It ignores the personal positive value of the drug experience itself. By analogy, consider the situation in which you had $100 that you wanted to protect from loss. The most direct and cautious action would be to put the money in a safe deposit box. This would be a strict harm reduction strategy. The money would not, however, earn interest. At a modest 3 percent annual inflation rate, the $100 would be almost worthless in thirty years, and you would have been burdened with the safe deposit box rental fee. In the absence of certain knowledge about the future, the only way to prevent this loss of equity would be to take a risk and invest the money in some enterprise. Risk reduction is not a free good.

The lesson is this: the only way to achieve long-term harm reduction is to assume short-term risk in order to gain compensatory benefits. Assuming a risk matrix for drugs as illustrated in Figure 16–2, we should begin a rational exploration of trade-offs. Perhaps the concept of "risk investment," rather than "risk reduction," would better describe realistic policy alternatives to drug prohibition.

3. Benefits should be acknowledged.

If drugs had adverse effects only, there would no use or abuse. Just as drug users tend to overlook possible costs (e.g., impurity of illicit substances, neurotoxicity), nonusers tend to ignore potential benefits. The assertion, for example, that "increased use of marijuana regardless of potency offers a multitude of negative consequences and no benefits" (Vocci 1995) does not explain why marijuana is used in the first place. It also precludes reasonable discussion of how regulatory agencies might go about assessing benefits and costs.

Numerous first-person reports have been published describing the perceived experiential benefits of psychoactive substances (e.g., Brookhiser 1993, Hindmarch and Stonier 1995, Johnson 1988, Shulgin and Shulgin 1992, Stolaroff 1994). Two early self-studies include those of Victor Robinson (1925), a physician using marijuana, and philosopher William James (1902), using nitrous oxide. Another noteworthy self-study was that of Bennett (1960), who subjected himself to a series of standardized tests after having eight recreational drugs administered blindly to him.

In a sociological study comparing the psychological effects of amphetamines, hallucinogens, and MDMA, persons who used all three drugs distinguished MDMA by the terms *closeness to others*, *accepting*, *sensual*, and *euphoria* (Solowij et al. 1992). The negative side effects (e.g., insomnia, loss of appetite, and irritability) were generally similar for the three substances, with MDMA being less severe. Given the perceived benefits and rather minimal side effects of a substance such as MDMA, why is its addiction potential moderately low (see Figure 16–2)? With repeated use of MDMA, there is a rapid development of tolerance to the desired effects, and at the same time the short-term aversive effects become more pronounced (Peroutka 1990). A simple hedonistic calculus on the part of the users seems to control its use. It should be noted, however, that vulnerable populations such as juvenile delinquents seem more heavily influenced by rewards than by deterrents (Piliavin et al. 1986). Why not consider a partial "technological fix" to the drug problem? Permit the development of patentable, nonprescription designer drugs (with self-limiting, short-term benefits) that will be voluntarily substituted by users for more harmful illicit drugs. This recommendation is not intended to negate the importance of the social context of drug use, which may contribute as much, or more, toward drug abuse than the pharmacology of the substances (cf. Hartnoll 1990).

4. Amend the federal regulatory framework.

The legal definition of a *drug* is, in part, "articles (other than food) intended to affect the structure or any function of the body of man or other animals. . ." (*U.S. Code*, vol. 21, sec. 321g). In one sense this definition is too broad. It could be interpreted to regulate even distilled water if a distributor attached a label claiming (accurately) that the water could improve digestion and prevent renal failure. On the other hand, the primary federal regulatory statute (*Controlled Substance Act, U.S. Code*, vol. 21, sec. 811) is too restrictive. All substances that lack accepted medical use are placed in Schedule I under the regulatory taxonomy established by that statute. Schedule I substances cannot be distributed legally. Apparently, the logic of Congress was that a substance without medical use has no other legitimate benefit and therefore should be totally prohibited.

Schedule I has become a "taxonomic wastebasket" for any nonmedical substance even if there is evidence of significant educational, religious, palliative, or recreational benefits (Gable 1992). Tobacco and alcohol were specifically excluded from this statute, for political reasons at the time. It is hoped that the current debate about tobacco will be leveraged into a full-scale examination of the current illogical regulatory framework.

If we care about our progeny, we want to leave them "better off" than we were at their age. Because we cannot predict the exact nature of the threats to their well-being, the "better off" must be something in the way of a generalized attitude toward life—an attitude characterized by resourcefulness, honesty, resilience, and compassion. These virtues are appropriate not only for the next generation, but would serve us well now as we work toward a more enlightened relationship with psychoactive substances that have the power to entertain, inspire, and kill.

REFERENCES

Bennett, C. C. (1960). The drugs and I. In Drugs and Behavior, ed. L. Uhr and J. G. Miller, pp. 596–609. New York: Wiley.

Brookhiser, R. (1993). The DEA's prescription for reefer madness. The Leaflet. National Organization for Reform of Marijuana Laws 22: 4.

Burglass, M. E. (1985). The use of marijuana and alcohol by regular users of cocaine: patterns of use and style of control. In The Addictions: Multidisciplinary Perspectives and Treatments, ed. H. B. Milkman and H. J. Shaffer, pp. 111–129. Lexington, MA: Heath.

DiNardo, J. (1991). Are marijuana and alcohol substitutes? The effect of state drinking age laws on the marijuana consumption of high school seniors. Santa Monica, CA: RAND Corp.

Dunham, J. S. (1951). Intravenous alcohol in surgery. What's New, pp. 26–28, No. 163. Abbott Laboratories, North Chicago, IL.

Essman, E. J. (1983). Amphetamine alters aggressive behavior in differentially housed mice: changes in regional brain serotonin receptors. Psychological Reports 53, 662.

Falk, J. L., and Feingold, D. A. (1987). Environmental and cultural factors in the behavioral action of drugs. In Psychopharmacology: The Third Generation of Progress, ed. H. Y. Melzer, pp. 1503–1510. New York: Raven.

Gable, R. S. (1992). Regulatory risk management of psychoactive substances. Law and Policy 14:257–276.

——— (1993). Toward a comparative overview of dependence potential and acute toxicity of psychoactive substances used nonmedically. American Journal of Drug and Alcohol Abuse 19:263–281.

Gossop, M., Griffiths, P., Powis, B., and Strang, J. (1992). Severity of dependence and route of administration of heroin, cocaine and amphetamines. British Journal of Addiction 87:1527–1536.

Haertzen, C. A., Kocher, T. R., and Miyasato, K. (1983). Reinforcements from the first drug experience can predict later drug habit and/or addiction: results with coffee, cigarettes, alcohol, barbiturates, minor and major tranquilizers, stimulants, marijuana, hallucinogens, heroin, opiates, and cocaine. Drug and Alcohol Dependence 11:147–165.

Harrell, A. V., and Peterson, G. E. (1992). Drugs, Crime, and Social Isolation: Barriers to Urban Opportunity. Washington, DC: Urban Institute Press.

Hartnoll, R. (1990). Non-pharmacological factors in drug abuse. Behavioural Pharmacology 1:375–384.

Heishman, S., Stitzer, M. L., and Bigelow, G. E. (1989). Alcohol and marijuana: comparative dose effect profiles in humans. Pharmacology Biochemistry & Behavior 31:649–655.

Henningfield, J. E., Cohen, C., and Slade, J. D. (1991). Is nicotine more addictive than cocaine? British Journal of Addiction 86:565–569.

Hill, H. E., Belleville, R. E., and Wikler, A. (1957). Motivational determinants in modification of behavior by morphine and pentobarbital. Archives of Neurology and Psychiatry 77:28–35.

Hilts, P. J. (1994). Is nicotine addictive? Depends on whose criteria you use. New York Times, August 2, p. C3.

Hindmarch, I., and Stonier, P. D., Eds. (1995). Human Psychopharmacology: Measures and Methods, vol 5. Chichester, England: Wiley.

Iwamoto, E., and Martin, W. (1988). Critique of drug self-administration as a method of predicting abuse potential of drugs. In Problems of Drug Dependence, ed. L. S. Harris, pp. 457–465. Rockville, MD: National Institute of Drug Abuse.

Jaffe, J. H., and Martin, W. R. (1990). Opioid analgesics and antagonists. In Goodman and Gilman's The Pharmacological Basis of Therapeutics, ed. A. G. Gilman, T. W. Rall, A. S.

Nies, and P. Taylor, 8th ed., pp. 485–501. New York: Pergamon.

James, W. (1902). *The Varieties of Religious Experience*. New York: Mentor, 1958.

Johnson, C. (1988). Psychedelics: A woman's rite of passage. *Psychedelic Monographs & Essays* 3:17–23.

Julien, R. M. (1995). *A Primer of Drug Action: A Concise, Nontechnical Guide to the Actions, Uses, and Side Effects of Psychoactive Drugs*, 7th ed. New York: Freeman.

Kozlowski, L. T., Wilkinson, D. A., Skinner, W., et al. (1989). Comparing tobacco cigarette dependence with other drug dependencies. *Journal of the American Medical Association* 261:898–901.

Larsen, D. (1996). The Vancouver Harm Reduction Club. *Cannabis Canada: Canada's Magazine of Marijuana & Hemp*. Dec. 20, http://www.hempbc.com.

Lasagna, L., and McCann, W. P. (1957). Effect of "tranquilizing" drugs on amphetamine toxicity in aggregated mice. *Science* 125:1241–1242.

Logan, B. J., Laverty, R., Sanderson, W. D., et al. (1988). Differences between rats and mice in MDMA (methylenedioxymethylamphetamine) neurotoxicity. *European Journal of Pharmacology* 152:227–234.

MacCoun, R. J. (1993). Drugs and the law: a psychological analysis of drug prohibition. *Psychological Bulletin* 65:613–628.

MacCoun, R. J., Reuter, P., and Schelling, T. (1996). Assessing alternative drug control regimes. *Journal of Policy Analysis and Management* 15:330–352.

Mello, N. K., and Mendelson, J. H. (1970). Experimentally induced intoxication in alcoholics: a comparison between programmed and spontaneous drinking. *Journal of Pharmacology and Experimental Therapeutics* 173:101–116.

———— (1978). Marijuana, alcohol, and polydrug use: human self-administration studies. In monograph 20: *Self-Administration of Abused Substances*, ed. N. A. Krasnegor, pp. 115–124. Washington, DC: National Institute on Drug Abuse.

Nies, A. S. (1990). Principles of therapeutics. In *Goodman and Gilman's The Pharmacological Basis of Therapeutics*, ed. A. G. Gilman, T. W. Rall, A. S. Nies, and P. Taylor, 8th ed. pp. 618–630. New York: Pergamon.

Peroutka, S. J. (1990). The recreational use of MDMA. In *Ecstasy: The Clinical, Pharmacological, and Neurotoxicological Effects of the Drug MDMA*, ed. S. J. Peroutka, pp. 100–120. Norwell, MA: Kluwer Academic Publishers.

Piliavin, I., Thornton, C., Gartner, R., and Matsueda, R. L. (1986). Crime, deterrence, and rational choice. *American Sociological Review* 51:101–119.

Robinson, V. (1925). *An Essay on Hasheesh*. New York: Dingwall-Rock.

Schuchard, M. K. (1993). Marijuana: an environmental pollutant. *International Drug Report* 34:3–6. Published by PRIDE, National Parent's Resource Institute for Drug Education, Inc., Atlanta, GA. (Original source of quotation not cited.)

Shulgin, A., and Shulgin, A. (1992). *Pihkal: A Chemical Love Story*. Berkeley, CA: Transform Press.

Siegel, S. (1989). Drug anticipation and the treatment of dependence. In Research monograph 84: *Learning Factors in Substance Abuse*, ed. B. A. Ray, pp. 1–24. Bethesda, MD: NIDA.

Solowij, N., Hall, W., and Lee, N. (1992). Recreational MDMA use in Sydney: a profile of "ecstasy" users and their experiences with the drug. *British Journal of Addiction* 87:1161–1172.

Stolaroff, M. J. (1994). Thanatos to Eros: Thirty-Five Years of Psychedelic Exploration. Berlin: VWB, Verlag für Wissenschaft und Bildung.

Strassman, R. J. (1991). Human hallucinogenic drug research in the United States: a present day case history and review of the process. *Journal of Psychoactive Drugs* 23:29–38.

Thomas, P. (1989). Prosecuting the U.S. drug war: hard policy versus politics. *Los Angeles Times*, August 20, sec. 5, p. 3.

Trevor, A. W., and Way, W. L. (1992). Sedative-hypnotics. In *Basic and Clinical Pharmacology*, ed. B. G. Ketzung, 5th ed. pp. 306–321. Norwalk, CT: Appleton & Lange.

Vocci, F. J. (1995). Letter to Richard Cowan from Deputy Director, Medication Development Division, National Institute on Drug Abuse. In *Ongoing Briefing* February 7, p. 4. Washington, DC: National Organization for Reform of Marijuana Laws.

Westermeyer, J. (1988). The pursuit of intoxication: our 100-century-old romance with psychoactive substances. *American Journal of Drug and Alcohol Abuse* 14:175–187.

17

Marihuana: An Old Medicine for a New Millennium

Lester Grinspoon

In September 1928 Alexander Fleming returned from vacation to his laboratory and discovered that one of the petri dishes he had inadvertently left
out over the summer was overgrown with staphylococci except for the area
surrounding a mold colony. That mold contained a substance he later named
penicillin. He published his finding in 1929, but the discovery was ignored
by the medical establishment and bacterial infections continued to be a leading
cause of death. Had it aroused the interest of a pharmaceutical firm, its development might not have been delayed. More than ten years later, under war-
time pressure to develop antibiotic substances to supplement sulfonamide,
Howard Florey and Ernst Chain initiated the first clinical trial of penicillin
(with six patients) and began the systematic investigations that might have
been conducted a decade earlier (Hayes et al. 1993).

After its debut in 1941, penicillin rapidly earned a reputation as "the
wonder drug of the '40s." There were three major reasons for that reputation: it was remarkably nontoxic, even at high doses; it was inexpensive to
produce on a large scale; and it was extremely versatile, acting against the
microorganisms that caused a great variety of diseases, from pneumonia to
syphilis. In all three respects cannabis suggests parallels.

Cannabis is remarkably safe. Although not harmless, it is surely less toxic than most of the conventional medicines it could replace if it were legally available. Despite its use by millions of people over thousands of years, cannabis has never caused an overdose death. The most serious concern is respiratory system damage from smoking, but that can easily be addressed by increasing the potency of cannabis and by developing the technology to separate the particulate matter in marihuana smoke from the cannabinoids (prohibition, incidentally, has prevented this technology from flourishing). Once cannabis regains the place in the U.S. pharmacopoeia that it lost in 1941 after the passage of the Marihuana Tax Act (1937), it will be among the least toxic substances in that compendium.

Medical cannabis would be extremely inexpensive. Street marihuana today costs $200 to $400 an ounce, but the prohibition tariff accounts for most of that. A reasonable estimate of the cost of cannabis as a medicine is $20 to $30 an ounce, or about 30 to 40 cents per marihuana cigarette. As an example of what this means in practice, consider the following. Both the marihuana cigarette and an 8-mg ondansetron pill—cost to the patient, $30 to $40—are effective in most cases for the nausea and vomiting of cancer chemotherapy (although many patients find less than one marihuana cigarette to be more useful, and they often require several ondansetron pills). Thus cannabis would be at least 100 times less expensive than the best present treatment for this symptom.

Cannabis is remarkably versatile. Let me review briefly some of the symptoms and syndromes for which it is useful. I will briefly consider only the most common present medical uses of marihuana.

CANCER TREATMENT

Cannabis has several uses in the treatment of cancer. As an appetite stimulant marihuana can help to slow weight loss in cancer patients. It may also act as a mood elevator. But the most common use of cannabis in cancer treatment is the prevention of nausea and vomiting in patients undergoing chemotherapy. About half of patients treated with anticancer drugs suffer from severe nausea and vomiting—not only unpleasant but a threat to the effectiveness of the therapy. Retching can cause tears of the esophagus and rib fractures, prevent adequate nutrition, and lead to fluid loss. Some patients find the nausea so intolerable they say they would rather die than go on. The antiemetics most commonly used in chemotherapy are phenothiazines like prochlorperazine (Compazine), the relatively new ondansetron (Zofran), and the newer granisitron (Kytril). Unfortunately, for many cancer patients these conventional antiemetics do not work at all or provide little relief.

to strain To vomit without bringing anything up.

The suggestion that cannabis might be useful arose in the early 1970s when some young patients receiving cancer chemotherapy found that marihuana smoking, which was of course illegal, reduced their nausea and vomiting. In one study of fifty-six patients who got no relief from standard antiemetic agents, 78 percent became symptom-free when they smoked marihuana (Vinciguerra et al. 1998). Oral tetrahydrocannabinol (THC) has proved effective where the standard drugs were not (Lucas and Laszlo 1980, Sallan et al. 1975). But smoking generates faster and more predictable results because it more easily raises THC concentration in the blood to the needed level (Chang et al. 1979). Also, it may be hard for a nauseated patient to take oral medicine. In fact, there is strong evidence that most patients suffering from nausea and vomiting prefer smoked marihuana to oral THC (Grinspoon and Bakalar 1993).

Oncologists may be ahead of other physicians in recognizing the therapeutic potential of cannabis. In the spring of 1990 two investigators randomly selected more than 2,000 members of the American Society of Clinical Oncology (one third of the membership) and mailed them an anonymous questionnaire to learn their views on the use of cannabis in cancer chemotherapy. Almost half of the recipients responded. Although the investigators acknowledge that this group was self-selected and that there might be a response bias, their results provide a rough estimate of the views of specialists on the use of Marinol (dronabinol, oral synthetic THC) and smoked marihuana.

Only 43 percent said the available legal antiemetic drugs (including Marinol) provided adequate relief to all or most of their patients, and only 46 percent said the side effects of these drugs were rarely a serious problem. Forty-four percent had recommended the illegal use of marihuana to at least one patient, and half would prescribe it to some patients if it were legal. On average, they considered smoked marihuana more effective than Marinol and roughly as safe (Doblin and Kleiman 1991).

GLAUCOMA

Cannabis may also be useful in the treatment of glaucoma, the second leading cause of blindness in the United States. In this disease, fluid pressure within the eyeball increases until it damages the optic nerve. About a million Americans suffer from the form of glaucoma (open-angle) treatable with cannabis. Marihuana causes a dose-related, clinically significant drop in intraocular pressure that lasts several hours in both normal subjects and those with the abnormally high ocular tension produced by glaucoma. Oral or intravenous THC has the same effect, which seems to be specific to can-

Something derived   to dose with a sedative

nabis derivatives rather than simply a result of sedation. Cannabis does not cure the disease, but it can retard the progressive loss of sight when conventional medication fails and surgery is too dangerous (Helper et al. 1976).

It remains to be seen whether topical use of THC or a synthetic cannabinoid in the form of eyedrops will be preferable to smoking marihuana for this purpose. So far, THC eyedrops have not proved effective, and in 1981 the National Eye Institute announced that it would no longer approve human research using these eyedrops (Roffman 1982). Other natural cannabinoids and certain synthetic cannabis derivatives are still being studied. But smoking marihuana (six to ten times a day) seems to be a better way of titrating the dose than taking an oral cannabinoid, and most patients apparently prefer it.

SEIZURES

About 20 percent of epileptic patients do not get much relief from conventional anticonvulsant medications. Cannabis has been explored as an alternative at least since 1975, when a case was reported in which marihuana smoking, together with the standard anticonvulsants phenobarbital and diphenylhydantoin, was apparently necessary to control seizures in a young epileptic man (Consroe et al. 1975). The cannabis derivative that is most promising as an anticonvulsant is cannabidiol. In one controlled study, cannabidiol in addition to prescribed anticonvulsants produced improvement in seven patients with grand mal convulsions; three showed great improvement. Of eight patients who received a placebo instead, only one improved (Cunha et al. 1980). While again the evidence is anecdotal, there are patients suffering from both grand mal and partial seizure disorders who find that smoked marihuana allows them to lower the doses of conventional anticonvulsant medications or dispense with them altogether (Grinspoon and Bakalar 1993).

PAIN

There are many anecdotal reports of marihuana smokers using the drug to reduce pain: postsurgery pain, headache, migraine, menstrual cramps, arthritic pain, and so on. In particular, marihuana is becoming increasingly recognized as a drug of choice for pain that accompanies muscle spasm. This kind of pain is often chronic and debilitating, especially in paraplegics, quadriplegics, other victims of traumatic nerve injury, and people suffering from multiple sclerosis or cerebral palsy. Many of these sufferers have discovered that cannabis not only allows them to avoid the risks of opioids for pain relief, but also reduces muscle spasms and tremors, sometimes allowing them to leave their wheelchairs (Petro 1980). Cannabis may act by mechanisms different from those of other analgesics. Some new synthetic cannabinoids might prove to be especially effective as analgesics—a possibility implied by the recent discovery of cannabinoid nerve receptor sites in the brain and other organs (Matsuda et al. 1990, Munro et al. 1993).

AIDS

[handwritten annotation: a fully conscious state in which pain is not felt]

The American AIDS epidemic first came to notice in 1981, and by now more than 311,000 Americans have died of the disease. Nearly one million are infected with the HIV virus, and perhaps as many as half a million are ill. Although the spread of AIDS has slowed among homosexuals, the reservoir is so huge that the number of cases is sure to grow. Women and children as well as both heterosexual and homosexual men are now being affected; the disease is spreading most rapidly among inner-city black and Hispanic intravenous drug abusers and their sexual partners. The period of incubation is variable, but averages eight to ten years. It appears that almost all infected persons will eventually become ill. Opportunistic infections and neoplasms can be treated in standard ways, and the virus itself can be attacked with antiviral drugs, of which the best known is zidovudine (AZT). Unfortunately, AZT, along with some of the newer drugs used in the treatment of AIDS such as the protease inhibitors, sometimes causes severe nausea that heightens the danger of semistarvation for patients who are already suffering from nausea and losing weight because of the illness.

Marihuana is particularly useful for patients who suffer from AIDS because it not only relieves the nausea but retards weight loss by enhancing appetite. When it helps patients regain lost weight, it can prolong life. The synthetic cannabinoid dronabinol (Marinol) has been shown to relieve nausea and retard or reverse weight loss in patients with HIV infection, but most patients prefer smoked cannabis for the same reasons that cancer chemotherapy patients prefer it: it is more effective and has fewer unpleasant side effects, and the dosage is easier to adjust.

AFFECTIVE DISORDERS

Cannabis was first proposed as a treatment for depression by Jacques-Joseph Moreau de Tours in 1845 (Moreau de Tours 1857). During the next 100 years his proposal was supported and disputed in a number of medical papers. The most recent study on cannabis and depression was undertaken in 1973. Eight hospitalized patients were given either THC or a placebo for up to a week. The THC did not help them, and in four it produced discomfort and anxiety so serious it had to be withdrawn (Kotin et al. 1973). But the patients were not prepared for the experience of an altered state of consciousness, and the brief duration of the trial must also be considered. Standard antidepressants often require three weeks or even longer to work. Today, among the minority of depressed and bipolar patients who do not respond to any of the standard antidepressants or find the side effects unbearable, some have discovered that whole smoked marihuana is more useful than any legal drug (Grinspoon and Bakalar 1997). This evidence is anecdotal, and large-scale clinical studies will eventually be required.

□   □   □

The above comprise the symptoms and syndromes for which cannabis is most commonly used today. But there are others for which there is compelling anecdotal evidence. They include migraine, severe pruritis, premenstrual syndrome, labor pain, hyperemesis gravidarum, asthma, osteoarthritis and other rheumatoid disorders, pseudotumor cerebri, Crohn's disease, and tinnitus, to name a few (Grinspoon and Bakalar 1997).

Marihuana has more in common with penicillin than safety, low cost, and medical versatility. There are also historical parallels. Just as World War II provided the impetus for research on penicillin as an antibiotic, the AIDS epidemic is now exerting some pressure on researchers to explore cannabis as a medicine. But it took more than ten years to recognize the medical potential of penicillin, and its systematic exploration was long delayed by lack of interest and resources. For similar reasons the urgently needed large double-blind clinical studies on cannabis have not yet begun. In this case progress has been delayed largely because the medical establishment and government authorities are stubbornly committed to wild exaggeration of marihuana's dangers when it is used for nonmedical purposes. In fact, the potential dangers of marihuana when taken for pleasure and its usefulness as a medicine are historically and practically interrelated issues: historically, because the arguments used to justify public and official disapproval of recreational use have had a strong influence on opinions about its medical potential; practically, because the more evidence accumulates that marihuana is relatively safe even when used as an intoxicant, the clearer it becomes that the medical requirement of safety is satisfied.

If any other drug had shown similar promise, public and professional interest would be intense. But the U.S. government, in its zeal to prosecute the war on drugs, has been doing everything it can to reduce that interest and prevent the fulfillment of marihuana's medical promise (Grinspoon et al. 1995). Cocaine and morphine (Schedule II drugs) are legally available as medicines; marihuana is not. In 1972 an effort began to put marihuana in

Schedule II, a classification that would allow doctors to prescribe it. Finally, in 1988, after years of hearings in which scores of witnesses presented impressive evidence of marihuana's medical usefulness, an administrative law judge recommended that it should be transferred to Schedule II. The Drug Enforcement Administration rejected the recommendation and was upheld on appeal. (For a comprehensive discussion of the various social and legal arrangements that would make marihuana available as a medicine, the reader is referred to the chapter titled "The Once and Future Medicine" in Marihuana, the Forbidden Medicine [L. Grinspoon and J. B. Bakalar, 1997].)

Given that cannabis is such a remarkably safe, versatile, and effective medicine, and could be a remarkably inexpensive one if the prohibition tariff were eliminated, why is the United States government so adamantly opposed to any arrangement that would legalize it? We can only speculate about the answer, but at least three possible reasons come to mind:

1. The government has been exaggerating the dangers of recreational marihuana for almost seventy years. It has spent many millions of dollars in efforts to demonstrate some harm that would justify prohibition. Since 1967 more than 10 million Americans have been arrested on marihuana charges, and many of them have had to serve long prison sentences. Careers have been ruined and families bankrupted or destroyed. The damage is beyond estimation. It is difficult for the government to turn around now and say, "Sorry, we made a mistake." Governments don't readily acknowledge mistakes.

2. There are now considerable vested interests in maintaining prohibition. The drug war has created a vast enforcement and "educational" bureaucracy, a drug-abuse industrial complex that parallels the military-industrial complex produced by the Cold War and is just as difficult to unseat. Forfeitures of drug dealers' property fill the coffers of the drug control system, supplemented by the illegal seizures of corrupt drug agents. The drug war juggernaut also sustains a growing industry devoted to examining the hair and urine of citizens for traces of marihuana and other drugs. The pharmaceutical companies and drug-testing laboratories that profit from this practice do not want to see it ended. A mirror-image industry on a smaller scale develops techniques for defeating the drug tests and markets them in such magazines as High Times. Illicit marihuana dealers, of course, also profit from the present system, and so do the people who provide hydroponic lighting and control equipment to growers who seek safety from the law by moving indoors. All in all, a large and growing investment of capital and human resources is involved.

3. Finally, marihuana has become a symbol charged with cultural tensions. Along with psychedelic drugs, it was seen as a catalyst of the antiestablishment movement of the 1960s and 1970s. Many regarded the free speech,

no normal

civil rights, and anti-Vietnam War movements as socially healthy and exciting expressions of a vibrant democracy. But others saw these movements as
symptoms of a society out of control—just look how those marihuana-smok-
ing young people dressed and wore their hair. Even today, culturally conservative people are fearful of marihuana. The establishment plays to this fear
by exaggerating the harmful potential of the drug and especially by presenting its users as deviant. Successful middle-class marihuana users passively cooperate with this campaign when they keep their use secret and allow the
television camera's lens to focus on latter-day hippies.

It is distressing to consider how many lives might have been saved if
penicillin had been developed as a medicine immediately after Fleming's discovery. It is equally frustrating to consider how much suffering might have
been avoided if cannabis had been available as a medicine for the last sixty
years. Initial enthusiasm for drugs is often disappointed after further investigation. As Sir William Osler put it, "We must use new drugs quickly while
they are still efficacious." But it is not as though cannabis were an entirely
new agent with unknown properties. Studies conducted in the past ten years
have confirmed a centuries-old promise. I believe that as restrictions on research are relaxed, and this promise is realized, cannabis, one of the oldest
medicines, will come to be recognized as a wonder drug of the new millen-
nium.

REFERENCES

Chang, A. E., Shiling, D. J., Stillman, R. C., et al. (1979). Delta-9-tetrahydrocannabinol as an
    antiemetic in cancer patients receiving high-dose methotrexate: a prospective, randomized
    evaluation. *Annals of Internal Medicine* 91:819–824.
Consroe, P. F., Wood, G. C., and Buchsbaum, H. (1975). Anticonvulsant nature of marihuana
    smoking. *Journal of the American Medical Association* 234:306–307.
Cunha, J. M., Carlini, E. A., Pereira, D. L., et al. (1980). Chronic administration of cannabidiol
    to healthy volunteers and epileptic patients. *Pharmacology* 21:175–185.
Doblin, R., and Kleiman, M. (1991). Marihuana as antiemetic medicine: a survey of oncologists'
    attitudes and experiences. *Journal of Clinical Oncology* 9:1275–1280.
Grinspoon, L., and Bakalar, J. B. (1993). *Marihuana, the Forbidden Medicine.* New Haven, CT:
    Yale University Press.
——— (1997). *Marihuana, the Forbidden Medicine,* rev. ed. New Haven, CT: Yale University Press.
Grinspoon, L., Bakalar, J. B., and Doblin, R. (1995). Marijuana, the AIDS wasting syndrome,
    and the U.S. government. *New England Journal of Medicine,* Letters to the Editor,
    333(10):670–671.
Hayes, G. W., Keating, C. L., and Newman, J. S. (1993). The golden anniversary of the silver
    bullet. *Journal of the American Medical Association* 270(13):1610–1611.
Hepler, R. S., Frank, I. M., and Petros, R. (1976). Ocular effects of marihuana smoking. In *Phar-
    macology of Marihuana,* vol. 2, ed. M. C. Braude and S. Szara, pp. 815–824. New York:
    Raven.

Kotin, J., Post R. M., and Goodwin, F. K. (1973). Delta-9-tetrahydrocannabinol in depressed patients. *Archives of General Psychiatry* 23:345–348.

Lucas, V. S., and Laszlo, J. (1980). Delta-tetrahydrocannabinol for refractory vomiting induced by cancer chemotherapy. *Journal of the American Medical Association* 243:1241–1243.

Matsuda, L. A., Lolait, S. J., Brownstein, A. C., et al. (1990). Structure of a cannabinoid receptor and functional expression of the cloned cDNA. *Nature* 346:561–564.

Moreau de Tours, J.-J. (1857). Lypemanie avec stupeur; tendance à la démence—traitement par l'extrait (principe resineux) de cannabis indica—Guerison. *Lancette Gazette Hôpital* 30:391.

Munro, S., Thomas, K. L., and Abu-Shaar, M. (1993). Molecular characterization of a peripheral receptor for cannabinoids. *Nature* 365:61–65.

Petro, D. J. (1980). Marihuana as a therapeutic agent for muscle spasm or spasticity. *Psychosomatics* 21:81–85.

Roffman, R. A. (1982). *Marihuana as Medicine*. Seattle: Madrona.

Sallan, S. E., Zinberg, N. E., and Frei III, E. (1975). Antiemetic effect of delta-9-tetrahydrocannabinol in patients receiving cancer chemotherapy. *New England Journal of Medicine* 293:795–797.

Vinciguerra, V., Moore, T., and Brennan, E. (1988). Inhalation marihuana as an antiemetic for cancer chemotherapy. *New York State Journal of Medicine* 88:525–527.

18

Moral and Constitutional Considerations in Support of the Decriminalization of Drugs[1]

Robert W. Sweet, Edward A. Harris

A more appropriate conceptual framework for the drug problem is the metaphor of cancer. Dealing with cancer is a long-term proposition. It requires the mobilization of support mechanisms—human, medical, educational, and societal, among others. To confront cancer, we must check its spread, deal with its consequences, and improve the prognosis. Resistance to the spread of cancer is necessary, but so is patience, compassion, and the will to carry on. Pain must be managed while the root cause is attacked. The road to recovery is long and complex.[2]

GEN. BARRY R. MCCAFFREY, Director
Office on National Drug Control Policy

[Rep. Bob Barr, R–Ga.] took direct aim at McCaffrey when he said it was disparaging to those dying in foreign anti-drug battles for the Clinton administration to shun the "war on drugs" metaphor and replace that with "cancer." "Where in God's name did that notion come from?" Barr scoffed.[3]

INTRODUCTION

For more than three decades we have been fighting the war on drugs. From the initial identification of this country's "drug problem," this policy issue stands out as unique because it has always been conceptualized and addressed by our government, at all levels, in metaphorical terms. Every facet of the discussion of drugs has been filtered through the metaphor of war, and it has become such a habit that it is virtually impossible for us to think about the issue without doing so from within this rhetorical framework.

Even on the constitutional level of the debate concerning drugs, the rhetoric of the war on drugs is most evident. The policies of the United States government toward the use of illegal drugs by its citizenry is not a "war"; there is no genuine foreign "enemy" against whom this "war" is or even can be waged. Rhetorical skills notwithstanding, no foreign nation can be identified as responsible at the point of production on the coca farms in the mountains of Colombia or in the poppy fields of the Middle East and Asia. And at home, the government and the courts distinguish between "us"—we who are morally upright and voluntarily comply with the drug laws—and "them"—those who are morally defective.[4] It is through the rhetoric, however, that our leaders seek to establish that, when it comes to drug use, it is in our best interests for our government to intervene on our behalf to protect us against ourselves. And it is we who are directly affected when metaphor is confused with reality, and the conceptual apparatus of war is taken literally to justify abridging our constitutional rights.[5]

While the "war on drugs" metaphor continues to permeate public and private conceptualization of the drug issue, 1997 marked a radical shift in this country's official drug policy. The Clinton administration rejected the "war on drugs" metaphor as the official metaphor for its drug policy and replaced it with the extended metaphor or analogy of "drugs as cancer."[6] This paradigm shift began the previous year with the emergence of retired Army General Barry McCaffrey as President Bill Clinton's drug "czar." At his confirmation hearing in 1996, McCaffrey articulated for the first time the notion that the "war on drugs" metaphor was "inadequate" and advanced the alternative analogy of drugs as cancer.[7] At public appearances throughout 1996 he repeatedly insisted that the old metaphor be rejected in favor of the "drugs as cancer" analogy.[8] This became the official position when McCaffrey presented the Clinton administration's 1997 National Drug Control Strategy to the House Subcommittee on National Security, International Affairs, and Criminal Justice.[9]

The significance of this paradigm shift cannot be overstated. By rejecting the earlier metaphor, the administration rejected the proposition that there was a war that could be "won": "The metaphor of a 'war on drugs' is misleading. Wars are expected to end. Addressing drug abuse is a continuous challenge; the moment we believe ourselves to be victorious and free to relax our resolve, drug abuse will rise again."[10] The critical response to the administration's position was immediate. Representative Bob Barr attacked McCaffrey at the House Subcommittee hearing and accusatorially demanded to know who within the administration came up with the idea of changing the way we talk about the drug problem.[11] To those, like Barr, who have confused metaphor with reality—and they are many—it *is* a war out there that is being fought, and to give up the metaphor is to surrender in a real war, to a real demonic force that will subjugate and destroy us.[12]

Despite the attacks on the new analogy, the fact remains that the administration is still defining its policy from within the conceptual framework of a rhetorical device. The enemy has moved from being "out there" to being "inside" us. Unfortunately, but more realistically, the administration has not given us much hope by selecting an insidious disease for which there is no known cure and which too often results in an excruciatingly painful death— ironically, a death whose pain can be tempered only by the use of drugs, some of which are currently outlawed by prohibition.

The fact that the drug issue can be discussed at the highest levels of government only in metaphorical terms with mythological demonic imagery constitutes an unmistakable warning to us that something is seriously wrong. Although billions of dollars have been spent and hundreds of thousands of people have been jailed, the most recent statistics show that drug use continues to increase in this country.[13] While Rome burns, our leaders fiddle. The discussion about this nation's drug policy and what ought to be done has been transformed into a heated debate over the *appropriateness* of metaphors, as if identifying the most appropriate metaphor would somehow illuminate substantive solutions to the myriad problems related to drugs and prohibition.

This chapter is a plea for rational, substantive dialogue concerning drugs and the alternatives to the prohibitionist policy that has failed so spectacularly for more than thirty years. Before such a dialogue can take place, it is necessary to cut away the layers of the rhetorical framework of myths and metaphors that have been carefully crafted to reflect back to the public the distorted image of drugs as a terrifying demon, a terrifying enemy, a terrifying disease—a horrific thing that threatens each and every one of us with death and destruction, while giving prohibition the appearance of invincibility. When the drug issue is viewed through this obscuring lens, the very possibility of rational dialogue is destroyed. Any policy other than prohibition is simply unthinkable.

Thus the preliminary task of clearing a conversational space in which rational dialogue can take place is daunting. However, it is a task that Thomas Szasz has been pursuing for more than two decades with a unique combination of a zealot's passion and a scientist's cold logic. We begin our examination of the drug issue by critically considering Szasz's formidable—and we think largely successful—efforts to demythologize the war on drugs through his critique of the language used to justify the policy of prohibition and the suspect assumptions underlying it. We then identify and examine certain moral and constitutional considerations raised by the drug issue. These considerations support the rejection of prohibition and the adoption of a policy of decriminalization. Ultimately, we favor a drug policy that would be comparable to the nation's current policy and legal framework regulating alcohol, and we suggest that support for such a policy—based on a right to self-determination—may be derived from the Ninth Amendment of the Constitution.

SZASZ'S ASSAULT ON THE WAR ON DRUGS

SZASZ AS CASSANDRA

Whenever the domains of the law and psychiatry intersect, as they increasingly do, Thomas Szasz stands at the crossroads, emphatically denouncing the traditional principles and claims of the practitioners of psychiatry and psychology as they attempt to influence the law and the legal process. Although his emphatic voice is often heard as a lone cry from the wilderness, he has time and again rallied to a cause weighty forces that have successfully challenged the conventional wisdom on a number of issues.[14] And while he remains a controversial figure at every turn, Szasz nonetheless commands the respect owed a serious thinker whose radical ideas are grounded in a wealth of knowledge and a healthy skepticism of tradition and are set forth with a rhetorical flair that is simultaneously compelling and provocative.[15] He first shocked the legal and medical professions with his 1960 article "The Myth of Mental Illness," in which he argued that the medical model was inappropriately applied to conditions of so-called "mental illness" and denied the reality of illnesses of the mind.[16] His words and works have been quoted and referred to in more than seventy-five court opinions, ranging from the United States Supreme Court[17] to the Family Court of New York[18]; and even when his position on an issue is not adopted, the force of his analysis does not go unacknowledged by legal or medical experts.[19]

During the past twenty years he has returned repeatedly to the theme of drugs and advanced the proposition that the individual has a moral right to possess and use drugs freely.[20] We view Szasz's work as particularly compelling and timely because, in rejecting the "war on drugs" metaphor, the Clinton administration and drug czar McCaffrey are offering arguments first formulated by Szasz twenty years ago. Moreover, during these same twenty years, Szasz has decried the war on drugs as a pressing and significant issue, not merely because of the poll results favoring the war on drugs and the billions of dollars spent on it, but also because so many Americans feel that the end of winning this so-called war justifies the use of many highly questionable means, including the suspension of many fundamental constitutional rights and liberties. Most recently, in his book *Our Right to Drugs*,[21] Szasz focuses on the moral principles surrounding the issue of drug use in support of the simple and astonishing proposition that every American has the right to possess and use drugs with the same freedom that attaches to any other specie of property.

The Hypocrisy of the "Drug War" Vocabulary

According to Szasz, drug education constitutes pharmacological disinformation that has reached the highest ranks of our political system, affecting the attitudes of presidents both past and present.[22] He concludes:

> In American society, hypocrisy pervades pharmaceutical life and relations. If the state (official medicine) certifies you as sick and gives you drugs—regardless of whether you need them or not, whether they help you or not, even whether you want them or not—then you are a patient receiving treatment; but if you buy your own drugs and take them on your own initiative—because you feel you need them or, worse, because you want to give yourself peace of mind or pleasure—then you are an addict engaged in drug abuse. This outlook on life and the policy it engenders rest on a medical imagery that idolizes the therapeutic state as benevolent doctor, and demonizes the autonomous individual as a person who is both a criminal and a patient and whose sole aim in life is to be high on drugs and low on economic productivity. The result is the medicalization of drug use—the political elite assured access to the drugs they want from their physician-suppliers, the rest of the people denied drugs cheaply and legally for sale in Third World countries.[23]

Thus we exist in a state of perpetual ambivalence, irrationally wavering under the twin delusions of "pharmacological phobia and pharmacological hubris": on the one hand, the phobia that " 'dangerous drugs' cause 'epidemics' and 'plagues' " is accepted to be a genuine threat, while on the other, hubris is mistakenly confused with scientific knowledge, resulting in the unwarranted belief that all maladies can be cured by some existing or yet-to-be-discovered drug.[24] The misleading effects of these delusional forces are then compounded by the very atmosphere of hypocrisy underlying every aspect of the individual's view of drugs, from legal use to illegal abuse.

Szasz debunks the phobia by placing the "danger" of "dangerous drugs" in its proper and almost universally ignored context, noting that "no drug is dangerous so long as it remains outside the body; and every drug—even the seemingly most innocuous, such as aspirin or vitamin A—is potentially dangerous for certain persons, in certain doses."[25] Moreover, while all drugs have the potential of being genuinely dangerous when they are ingested, the danger of addiction, which is the quintessential psychiatric concept used to justify the war on drugs, is illusory in Szasz's view.

According to Szasz, the medical model has been employed illegitimately to describe "mental illnesses" such as drug addiction and to prescribe the appropriate treatments to "cure" them. However, the danger simply is not there because the concept of addiction is itself only a metaphor without any literal physiological component. At most, the person who takes drugs can develop a bad habit, not an addiction, and he continues to have both the moral and legal capacity to be responsible for his drug use and its consequences. Therefore, the dangers posed by currently illegal drugs can be easily remedied in two steps: first, the role of state intervention is to be reduced to the bare minimum of preventing the mislabeling of drug products; and second, each individual assumes responsibility for himself and for his own actions.

The present ideological commitment supporting the war on drugs denies the concepts of free will, dignity, and personal responsibility in drug use. The individual is treated in a degrading manner by an illegitimately paternalistic state that intentionally disseminates false and misleading information for the personal gain of those whose livelihoods, positions, and power are critically linked to the war on drugs.[26] It follows that the repeal of the current drug prohibition is the only morally coherent alternative to the morally bankrupt war on drugs.

Szasz is consistent in his commitment to individual liberty and autonomy, and his call for the repeal of drug prohibition extends not only to those drugs that are currently considered "dangerous" and deemed illegal but also to all prescription drugs. Only by giving the individual the free choice to decide as he will about the kind and amount of drugs he consumes can the integrity and dignity of the individual qua responsible agent be respected. It follows from this view of the individual that the legitimate role of government regarding drugs is sharply limited to that of monitoring the quality of drugs, minimizing impediments to the free market, and ensuring that they are labeled accurately so that the individual can make rational and informed decisions about the drugs he chooses to use.

Of course, the prospect of all drugs being available to adults[27] raises a chorus of concerns, each of which Szasz addresses consistently within the libertarian framework he embraces. In response to the concern that a free market in drugs would have a negative impact on economic productivity, Szasz asserts that this is an issue of family stability, cultural values, education, and social policies, not an issue about the availability of drugs. In response to the concern that Szasz's policy would result in drug-crazed people committing criminal acts, he contends that this image is a fiction created by psychiatry; it is an inversion of the truth. Drugs are not an inducement to crime, rather, prohibiting drugs is. Finally, in response to the concern that if drugs were available to the extent sanctioned by Szasz the suicide rate would increase as it became

easier to kill oneself, he argues that this fear is based on an illegitimate paternalism. If a person wants to kill himself and wants to do so in a relatively
painless manner by overdosing on some kind of drug, that person has the right
to do so.

Drugs as Scapegoat

Szasz analyzes the tension between personal freedom and governmental restraint
as it relates to drugs, characterizing it as the "American ambivalence" that has
ended with the "holy utopia" becoming transcendent and obliterating the distinction between vice and crime.[28] As a society, we have capitulated in the
face of the ambiguities accompanying responsibility and choice "in a free pharmaceutical market" and have "colluded with physicians and politicians to have
the state put us under its medical tutelary protection."[29] The result is that we
have been driven by fear—fear of having to accept responsibility for ourselves
and our actions as free and rational agents—to locate the source of our problems in the inanimate matter of drugs. It is now drugs that play the role of
our social scapegoat, replacing the actual scapegoat that was driven from the
Jewish community each year.[30]

By scapegoating drugs, however, we have not only given up an important part of our inalienable right to drugs qua property, we have also embraced
the "therapeutic paternalism" of rampant government intervention in our lives.[31]
We now find ourselves tolerating and even championing further governmental encroachments on our constitutionally protected rights in order to fight
the perceived scourge of the scapegoated drugs.[32]

Drugs as Property

In *Our Right to Drugs* Szasz builds his analysis of rights—and specifically, *the*
right to drugs—on the axiom that a substance, commonly viewed as a drug, is
property. Szasz's property-based position has its roots in the tradition of classical liberalism or libertarianism, stretching from John Locke[33] and John Stuart
Mill[34] to Ludwig von Mises,[35] Milton Friedman,[36] Friedrich Hayek,[37] and Robert Nozick,[38] and states that the individual's rights to property and personal
liberty sharply constrain the power of the state to limit the personal use of
property.[39]

Szasz traces the evolutionary development of the concept of property from
Madison through the concept of the person as property and the government's
attack on personal choice via methods he terms "therapeutic slavery."[40] In
analyzing freedom, Szasz notes that its primary characteristic is choice, that it
is a personal right to be exercised by the individual, and that its exercise is
antithetical to government power, the very purpose of which is to limit choice,

presumably for the benefit of the society. The efforts of the government to eliminate choice with respect to drugs are outlined by Szasz, extending even to the forfeiture cases and noting Justice William O. Douglas's dissent in *Calero-Toledo v. Pearson Yacht Leasing Co.*, in which he ridiculed "the fiction that the inanimate object itself is guilty of wrongdoing."[41] It is that fiction that Szasz would replace with the personal responsibility to ingest whatever one pleases in order to avoid what he terms "chemical statism."[42] He correctly notes:

> Thus, all that the therapeutic demagogues need to do is declare a particular drug to be the embodiment of transcendent disease-producing evil and, presto, we have the perfect modern medicomythological scapegoat. This *pharmakos* (Greek for scapegoat) is not a person, so why should it have any rights? It is an ominous threat, causing deadly dangerous diseases, so what rational person would come to its defense?[43]

LOCATING SZASZ'S RADICALISM

Although Szasz's libertarian commitments to the minimal state and the conclusion that the state has no legitimate right to interfere with a free and rational individual's use of drugs appear to place him within the mainstream of the proponents of classical liberalism, his claims and the principles from which he derives them are even more radical in nature. The extreme character of Szasz's assault on the war on drugs is readily apparent when Szasz's work is considered against the background of that of Friedrich Nietzsche. Szasz's polemic against the current war that is raging in the United States against "dangerous drugs" and "drug abuse" parallels that of Nietzsche's lifelong project of effectuating a "revaluation of all values"[44]—of destroying and transcending the categories and concepts that served only to enslave the great and the noble, while giving power to the weak, the petty, and the envious.[45]

In Nietzsche's view of the history of the western world, generations of moralists, theologians, and do-gooders—namely, those who were physically, mentally, and spiritually weak, and who were terrified by free will, personal responsibility, and life itself—had gained devastating control over the strong and self-reliant lovers of life. They had achieved this control by reconceptualizing human behavior and experience in such a way that what was originally described by the lover of life as "good" was now defined by the moralist to be "evil," and what was formerly "bad," namely, that which is unpleasant and life-negating, was now labeled "good." With this conceptual framework firmly in place, the moralists and theologians could keep the lovers of life in a state of perpetual submission by waging a war on immorality, which permeated every aspect of human relations: social, political, legal, and spiritual. Those activities that the lover of life held to be "good" were now "evil sins," and he was threatened with prison in this life and eternal imprisonment and torture in an awful hell in the next if he gave in to his impulses to do that which he deemed to be natural and good.

The moralists and theologians asserted their legitimacy as the leaders in this war and justified their otherwise irrational assertions and hyperbolic rhetoric by willfully misleading their victims with fraudulent claims of paternalistic virtue. They claimed that they were selflessly leading the charge in the war on immorality out of a love of humanity, and that their authority to do so was based on their access to privileged knowledge regarding what is "in the best interest of all." Thus the weak could enslave the strong by duping the strong into believing that it was quite simply in the latter's best interest to acquiesce. Nietzsche's writings call the lovers of life—the "free spirits"—to arms to throw off the yoke of oppression by rejecting the war on immorality and everything that went with it.

When the works of Szasz and Nietzsche are placed side by side, one is immediately struck by the similarities in their unforgiving tone and focused urgency as they reject the status quo and call for radical change. Szasz is motivated by the same anger and disgust that led Nietzsche to characterize his day as the "Twilight of the Idols," and to urge the free spirits, who were simultaneously strong enough to act according to their own wills and able to assume responsibility for their own actions, to finish off, once and for all, the destructive and enslaving "idols" of contemporary morality, religion, philosophy, and politics. Most appropriately, Nietzsche characterized his methodology as "philosophiz[ing] with a hammer,"[46] and the fundamental principles underlying his view of the human being consisted of the complementary notions of will and responsibility.

Szasz, too, has taken up nothing less than a formidable hammer that he wields effectively against the hyperbolic rhetoric, mythologies, bad science, and the campaigns of misinformation now used by moralists, theologians, politicians, and do-gooders[47] to justify the war on drugs in the United States qua "therapeutic state," the home of "chemical statism" and "drug socialism," and all that goes with it. But he does more than merely bash the policies and programs of the status quo and the government's continuing commitment to a drug-free society. Ultimately, he undertakes his transformative project with such skill and analytical insight that even the most hardened drug warrior will be forced to reflect on alternatives to what is compellingly presented as a hopeless march forward in a misguided cause that is resulting in more misery, carnage, and waste than if no war were being waged at all.

The similarity between Szasz's attack on the war on drugs and Nietzsche's attack on the war on immorality, however, provides a useful literary comparison between the rhetorical styles of two otherwise disparate thinkers. Nietzsche's work serves as an illuminating background against which to read Szasz's work for a number of reasons: it locates Szasz within an important and provocative group of radical social commentators and philosophical thinkers; it provides important insights into the methodological approaches Szasz employs and the logical structure of his position; and finally, it helps to describe Szasz's substantive view of society and our place as individuals in it.[48]

Szasz as "Edifying" Thinker

One may be tempted to see Szasz as part of a radical *tradition* that stretches back from Nietzsche and continues to the present. However, the use of the term *tradition* is distinctly inappropriate and would serve to misdescribe the shared aspects of the methods and objectives of those with whom Szasz would identify. Goethe, Kierkegaard, Nietzsche, Santayana, William James, Dewey, the later Wittgenstein, the later Heidegger, and, more recently, Wilfrid Sellars,[49] Paul Feyerabend,[50] and Richard Rorty[51] are figures who "resemble each other in their distrust of the notion that man's essence is to be a knower of essences. . . . These writers have kept alive the suggestion that, even when we have justified true belief about everything we want to know, we may have no more than conformity to norms of the day."[52] Rorty explicitly rejects the idea that he and these other important thinkers are members of a shared and identifiable tradition. Rather, he describes this group of radicals as revolutionary thinkers who have moved on the periphery of the history of modern philosophy.

In Rorty's view, there are two kinds of revolutionary thinkers:

> On the one hand, there are revolutionary philosophers—those who found new schools within which normal, professionalized philosophy can be practiced—who see the incommensurability of their new vocabulary with the old as a temporary inconvenience, to be blamed on the shortcomings of their predecessors and to be overcome by the institutionalization of their own vocabulary. On the other hand, there are great philosophers who dread the thought that their vocabulary should ever be institutionalized, or that their writing might be seen as commensurable with the tradition.[53]

The former are "systematic" philosophers who are in the mainstream, building on the continuing tradition that reaches from the past to the present and, with them, on into eternity. In contrast, the latter are "edifying" philosophers who remain intentionally peripheral. They are reactive and "know their work loses its point when the period they were reacting against is over. . . . [They] destroy for the sake of their own generation."[54]

Rorty's classification can be readily generalized to account for the distinction between systematic and edifying thinkers in all fields, and when one considers and classifies those significant contemporary thinkers in the fields of psychiatry, psychoanalysis, and medicine, Szasz comes to mind as one who squarely falls within the group of the "edifying" rather than the "systematic."[55]

Szasz's Humanism

Traditional psychiatry and psychology posit the literal existence of the mind and its various states as a given. From this assumption the tradition then rationalizes the treatment of the human being, any human being, as a datum that can be examined in a detached and wholly objective manner.[56] Szasz shares the same objective pursued by the edifying philosophers identified above, namely, that of humanizing human beings and rejecting the attempt to see them only as objects about whom systematic thinkers have gained access to privileged truths regarding their ultimate essence—in this case, truths about the essence of their minds. He calls for the humanization of the sciences generally and the medical sciences in particular by reintegrating the human being as the *subject*, not merely the object, of the issue under consideration.[57]

The by-products of edifying discourse about the human condition include not only the reintroduction of the human being as subject into the issue under consideration, be it metaphysics or biology, but also the possibility of new truths coming to light about the human condition. Rather than attempting to answer the key questions regarding the human condition in a definitive manner by imparting wisdom derived from the privileged access to the objective truth, the edifying thinker simply aims to keep the conversation going by sending it off in new directions. And it may be the case that

> [s]uch new directions . . . engender new normal discourses, new sciences, new philosophical research programs, and thus new objective truths. But they are not the point of edifying philosophy, only accidental byproducts. The point is always the same—to perform the social function which Dewey called "breaking the crust of convention," preventing man from deluding himself with the notion that he knows himself, or anything else, except under optional descriptions.[58]

It is just such a conversation that Szasz has been engaged in and contributing to for four decades.[59]

The Method and Structure of Szasz's Edifying Discourse

Initially, one may be surprised and even disappointed by the lack of a rigorous and systematic argument in Szasz's approach to drugs. However, upon recognizing that Szasz is engaging in a project of edifying discourse at the periphery of the issues he addresses, the reader can appreciate the presentation Szasz offers. To say that Szasz's argument is neither systematic nor rigorous is not to say that Szasz presents no argument. Rather, this statement merely serves to highlight the fact that the argument he does present is of a particular kind—one that is less familiar and more challenging to the typical reader in this area precisely because the project in which Szasz is engaged falls outside mainstream traditions and undertakes an aggressive assault upon these traditions.

The Primacy and Power of Language. As an edifying thinker, Szasz's motivation is reactive rather than constructive in nature.[60] He is reacting against the "therapeutic state" and all of the institutional devices it employs to secure and support the status quo from the language it uses and the laws it enacts to the distorting and dehumanizing interpersonal relationships it forces on its citizenry. Rather than formulating a sustained and systematic argument, Szasz offers his readers, just as the edifying thinkers identified above offer theirs, arguments that are conveyed in the literary devices of metaphor, analogy, satire, parody, and aphorism,[61] each of which is loaded with stiff doses of irony.[62] Take, for example, Szasz's characterization of the success of the war on drugs:

> [T]he assertion that the War on Drugs is failing, or is not working, is—
> in a fundamental sense—false. It is terribly misleading. The War on Drugs
> *is* working just fine, thank you. [Its] primary purpose is to elect politi-
> cians. Hasn't it done wonders for [them]? When confronted with social
> policy, we must always ask: "*Cui bono?*" The War on Drugs is not sup-
> posed to help the addicts, or the people who get mugged by criminals
> on the street, or the patients who get AIDS from contaminated blood
> because selling clean syringes is illegal in America. It is supposed to help
> [politicians].[63]

The first line of attack undertaken by the edifying thinker is on the vocabulary of the tradition in an effort to demystify terms that have come to have a privileged descriptive status merely through their repetitive use by "professionals" and "experts."[64] Therefore, what initially distinguishes Szasz from other critics of the war on drugs and places him squarely within the ranks of the edifying thinkers is his attack on the vocabulary employed by both sides in the war.

For decades Szasz has played the role of edifying etymological debunker of the vocabulary now used in the war on drugs through his sustained challenge of the basic concepts and categories of psychiatry and psychology.[65] In *Insanity: The Idea and Its Consequences*, Szasz presents a classically edifying analysis of the concept of mental illness as metaphor, arguing that mental illness is a metaphorical, not literal, disease.[66] This conclusion follows from his analysis of the history of the concept of mental illness, during which time what began as a metaphor was literalized into "an illness *like any other illness* (that is, always and without a doubt a disease of the brain)."[67] In the end, purely metaphorical concepts are now held to describe physical realities because the vocabulary of the psychiatrist and psychologist have been chanted with a mantralike precision, with an unwavering faith in the privileged access these experts have to the truth about the mind and its health, by both professional and layman alike. A further conclusion following from this analysis is that the treatment of mental illness through psychiatric intervention is, at most, a metaphorical treatment using psychopharmacology, not a physiological treatment of a literal disease.[68]

In light of his preoccupation with the vocabulary of traditional psychiatry, it comes as no surprise that Szasz compels us to reflect upon the logical coherence and soundness of the assumptions, principles, and objectives of the traditional approach to that subject by using linguistic devices to present his analysis. In order to communicate through an edifying discourse, Szasz is forced to push conventional vocabulary beyond its limits and look for alternative ways to express himself. It is for this reason that he eschews systematic arguments that are constrained by the very assumptions and principles of the tradition he rejects, and formulates his argument by using the aforementioned literary devices.[69] Ultimately, Szasz rejects the traditional view of the mental disease of drug addiction as a metaphorical construct patterned after literal physiological diseases, and he argues for this claim by formulating and deconstructing a number of metaphors such as "drugs as scapegoats," "crack as genocide"[70] and "drugs as devils."[71] The substance of this metaphorical assault on the metaphor of drug addiction and its practical consequences for an alternative to the war on drugs are considered in greater detail below.

Perspectivalism and the Illusion of the Mental. As noted, Szasz's underlying theoretical commitment is to the individual as an autonomous and responsible agent, and his refutation of mental illness turns on his denial of its reality. More formally, this amounts to a refutation of the objectiveness of the mind and mental predicates. In other words, the mind is a metaphorical construct and, as such, it is entirely subjective and even illusory in nature. This explains the need for psychiatrist and patient to resort to a conversation in metaphors rather than in literally descriptive terms. This analysis of the mind and mental illness is "perspectival"[72] in nature and parallels Nietzsche's perspectivalist attack on traditional morality. Reflection on the nature of this attack as it is employed by both Szasz and Nietzsche is useful not only because it reveals the depth and sophistication of Szasz's argument, but more importantly because, for our present purposes, it provides insights into the strategies and content of an adequate response to Szasz's argument that can avoid a dismissive charge that any criticism is just another sorry manifestation of the dehumanizing and objectified tradition.

According to Nietzsche, such objectivity is not only self-deceiving, it is also impossible, and any attempt to live according to this objective morality results in further self-frustration and self-estrangement. The objectified person is reduced to an instrument, a mirror: "Whatever still remains in him of a 'person' strikes him as accidental, often arbitrary, still more often disturbing. . . . He recollects 'himself' only with an effort and often mistakenly; he easily confuses himself with others, he errs about his own needs and is in this respect alone unsubtle and slovenly."[73]

Nietzsche concludes that if this objectivity is the cause of alienation and degeneration of humanness, the true and natural essence of the human being must be contained in the subjective part of the person, namely, in his own perspective. Nietzsche advances this notion in his claim that "at the bottom of us, really 'deep down,' there is, of course, something unteachable, some granite of spiritual *fatum*, of predetermined decision and answer to predetermined selected questions."[74] It is a change from the traditional morality founded on the concept of objectivity—on the idea that certain people have figured out just how things really are. There is simply no single morality that can be derived objectively through the employment of one's faculty of pure reason a priori.

This is precisely the form that Szasz's argument takes regarding the objectification of the human mind by psychiatry and psychology. The abstract mind-in-itself, which is the object of psychiatric and psychological study, does not exist; it is merely a figurative extrapolation of the subjective perceptions of individuals who use medical metaphors to describe their experiences to the "experts." Szasz's attack on the mind and its health parallels exactly Nietzsche's perspectivalist attack on morality. One could simply replace the vocabulary of the tradition that Nietzsche finds so objectionable with the traditional vocabulary Szasz finds offensive to formulate the latter's refutation of the objective reality and givenness of mental illness.[75]

The Edifying Critique. Szasz's edifying discourse is an assault on the vocabulary of the war on drugs. It is inevitable, then, that Szasz has treated his critics and those advocating alternative proposals to end the war as illiterates who are unwittingly using a vocabulary that is nothing more than a language of a nonexistent mythological world as if it could be used to describe the realities of the human condition. He laments that, "having become used to living in a society that wages a relentless War on Drugs, we have also lost the vocabulary in which to properly articulate and analyze the disastrous social consequences of our own political-economic behavior vis-à-vis drugs."[76] Thus the traditional vocabulary fails to correspond to reality, and it necessarily prevents those using it from effectively grappling with the actual problems posed by drug use.

These considerations regarding Szasz qua edifying thinker also explain why he is so relentlessly critical of those who would appear to be natural allies, namely, those who, like the reviewers, are calling for the decriminalization of drugs. From his position on the periphery, Szasz is unable to distinguish drug war warriors from committed legalizers. What is of central importance to him is that they are speaking the same corrupt language and use the same vocabulary to articulate their morally vacuous positions. The fact that there may be a difference—even a sharp divergence—in the positions that are being advocated is ultimately irrelevant because the mere use of the language of the war on drugs is to concede the critical assumptions and principles to the warriors that Szasz so vehemently rejects.

Among Szasz's "intellectually bankrupt legalizers," one finds William F. Buckley, Jr., the editors of The Wall Street Journal and The New York Times, Ethan Nadelmann, Eric Sterling, Lester Grinspoon, and author Sweet.[77] In fact, Szasz formulates his general objection to the legalizers' shared project by characterizing author Sweet's 1989 position, calling for legalization, taxation, and government control, as "even more lawless than what the prohibitionists mean by criminalization,"[78] and Szasz finds the suggestion of the psychiatric treatment of addicts to be particularly offensive. Even Milton Friedman, whose free-market economic analysis and libertarian commitment to the liberty, autonomy, dignity, and responsibility of the individual are cited by Szasz as critical insights into the necessary failure of the war on drugs, does not escape Szasz's wrath on two fronts mentioned above for unwittingly attempting to attack the war on drugs on the terms set by the antidrug warriors.[79]

Szasz has also critically addressed one of the frequently cited aspects of the drug debate, the effect of drugs on the African-American and Hispanic communities in the United States. He unabashedly charges that the war on drugs is "a war on blacks."[80] He notes the views, and what he considers the hypocrisy of some African-American leaders, Reverend Jesse Jackson in particular, and is characteristically persistent in praising the position of the Black Muslims and the example of Malcolm X in simultaneously rejecting both the degrading meddling of the therapeutic state in their community and the use of drugs on moral and religious grounds as a matter of personal choice and self-discipline.[81]

THE LIMITATION OF SZASZ'S ANALYSIS

Just as an adequate response to Nietzsche's perspectivalism requires the critic to identify and analyze some human feature or desire that transcends the individual's perspective,[82] a truly effective response to Szasz must join his attack by demonstrating that there is something that transcends the individual's perspective that can be the object of psychiatric study without alienating and dehumanizing individuals. We attempt to offer such a response below, but do so only by addressing the narrow issue of drug addiction.

Policies toward the drug issue have been cyclical, from free choice to taxation, regulation, prohibition, and therapeutic treatment.[83] Despite the rhetoric of the war on drugs, its futility is quietly resulting in a shift from prohibition, prosecution, and interdiction to treatment, education, and prevention. Szasz seeks to overleap any intermediate steps and return to the libertarian practices of the nineteenth century: market access to all drugs, including illegal and ethical or prescription drugs.

Any challenge to Szasz's effort must rest on grounds that he would find unacceptable—the need to address perhaps in greater depth the demonology and the misperceptions abroad in the land. A further explication of the development of the demonology and scapegoating attached to drugs and the masking and transfer of other social concerns in the slogans of the drug war would have been particularly helpful from an author with his credentials.

The Genuine Dangers of Drugs and Drug Abuse

While Szasz makes crystal clear what he terms the moral issue, he does not address in sufficient depth the most commonly cited consequences of his libertarian position—a drugged-out population and an overwhelming increase in the number of addicts. Here a dispassionate collection and review of the literature in the field would have supplemented and reinforced Szasz's conclusions. Of course, Szasz denies the need for such analysis on two grounds that are now familiar: first, there is no such thing as addiction, there are only bad habits; and second, any negative social consequences of recognizing the individual's right to drugs are irrelevant in light of the positive affirmation of individual autonomy, dignity, liberty, and responsibility that such recognition would necessarily entail.

Szasz's appeal to these and other propositions is, nonetheless, limited. In fact, his analysis provocatively ends by having raised many questions but without Szasz explicitly admitting that they remain unanswered. To say that there is no such thing as addiction because mental illness is only metaphorical does not definitively resolve the genuine issue of the physiological impact of drugs on the individual.

The Physiological Reality of Addiction

One can agree with Szasz that what is needed is a demystified description of the functioning of the brain in place of the metaphorical vocabulary of "folk psychology."[84] This is a familiar project undertaken by contemporary philosophers in dealing with the "mind-body problem," the age-old conundrum regarding the relationship and interaction between the immaterial mind and the physical body and the epistemological implications of that relationship.[85]

However, the burden is upon Szasz to provide, at least, an argument in support of the conclusion that mental illness and addiction are irreducible to neurophysiological states or to offer a positive analysis of the physiology of addiction.[86] Szasz simply moves too fast through his syllogism from the premises that there are no such things as mental illness and addiction to the conclusion that drugs are not dangerous and cannot debilitate the moral agency or legal capacity of the user. While Szasz's linguistic analysis is illuminating and provocative, ultimately we are still left with physical brains and powerful chemicals that certainly affect those brains if not wreaking havoc on them.

The serious shortcoming of Szasz's work to this point is that he ends his analysis precisely where it would be the most fruitful, that is, with a new beginning in which the physiology of "addiction"—or to use a term more acceptable to Szasz, *excessive use*—was analyzed. Ultimately, it may be the case that the concept of addiction cannot survive the sort of descriptive reduction of mental states to physiological brain, but the burden is squarely on Szasz to demonstrate that the concept of addiction would in fact be eliminated or, at least, that it is of no practical, physiological, moral, or legal significance. In the end, the most significant questions arising from Szasz's polemic remain unaddressed: Does the mental phenomenon of addictive behavior survive the reductive move from the mental to the physical or can it simply be eliminated entirely? And what are the genuine (neuro)physiological effects of so-called "dangerous" drugs?

Addiction should be demystified as a demon and placed in an appropriate perspective as a disorder in many forms such as alcoholism, drug dependence including caffeine and tobacco, and eating disorders, among others, with causative factors including genetic predisposition, family and social environment, and emotional trauma. The state of knowledge, or the lack of it, regarding the ability to predict addictive rates, would have been a welcome addition to his presentation. A comparison between the operation of alcohol, tobacco, marijuana, and cocaine, for example, might well have reinforced his thesis that drug use can be controlled through responsibility and choice.[87] In any event, the identification and analysis of rights should be accompanied by an equally effective delineation of consequences.

Despite these limitations, there can be no doubt that Szasz forces us to address the consequences of his reasoning, and to struggle to defeat, accept, or distinguish his conclusions. What has been raised is one of the most challenging and vexing issues in society: the role of criminal law and the tension between the interests of the state and the individual. The rhetoric of the war on drugs has swept these issues away by a wave of flawed assumptions and hyperbolic fear, and Szasz has reclaimed these issues for us and demands that we subject them to critical scrutiny. In the following sections we undertake such a critical examination of these issues by identifying and analyzing, in turn, certain moral and constitutional implications of the war on drugs. We conclude that the moral and constitutional considerations speak strongly against the policy of prohibition and ultimately support the adoption and implementation of a policy of decriminalization.

THE MORAL IMPLICATIONS OF DRUG PROHIBITION

TWO KINDS OF MORAL ARGUMENTS

To qualify as a *moral* argument, the question the argument must address is what the actor *ought* to do in a particular situation, regardless of whether the actor is an individual or a state, rather than merely what the actor should or could do.[88] Here we are concerned with the state as actor in legislating and enforcing the laws of prohibition and the individual as actor in asserting moral claims against the state's action. However, it is imperative to note that a moral argument against prohibition neither entails nor implies a moral prescription in favor of drug use. The moral question of what laws a government ought to enact and enforce is logically independent of the question of what the individual ought to do. The denial of this fact of logic has led prohibitionists to assert as axiomatic that any move away from prohibition and the war on drugs by the government will necessarily constitute the government's tacit approval of drug use. On this confused view, merely discussing alternatives to prohibition in a public forum is thought to be sufficient to send "the wrong message" and encourage drug use.

In general, two kinds of arguments have been formulated to answer the question What ought the state to do with regard to drug use?—consequentialist or cost-benefit arguments[89] and rights-based arguments.[90] Versions of these types of arguments have been formulated by both advocates and opponents of prohibition laws.[91]

The most common consequentialist arguments involve appeals to either economics or health concerns. The economic arguments have the general form of either (1) drugs ought to be criminalized because their use inflicts substantial costs on society that outweigh the total benefits derived therefrom,[92] or (2) drugs ought not to be criminalized because such criminal laws exact substantial costs from society that outweigh the total benefits derived therefrom.[93] The health arguments have the general form of either (1) drugs ought to be criminalized because their use inflicts substantial damage on the health of the person using them that outweighs the total benefits the person gains through drug use, or (2) drugs ought not to be criminalized because in the act of criminalizing they are made more dangerous and inflict more damages on the person using them than they would if they were legal. Of course, these statements are only general *formulas* of arguments, and, as such, each can and has been fleshed out in an array of distinctly different and even incompatible ways.[94]

In contrast to the consequentialist arguments, the rights-based argument is at once the most difficult to formulate and has the potential for having the most radical outcome because it requires both an elucidation of its assumptions and principles and an unwavering commitment to those principles regardless of where they may lead.[95] Again, the variety of rights-based theories is profound, ranging from those grounded on natural law and natural rights[96] to those formulated by Immanuel Kant and more recently by John Rawls,[97] which employ a priori reasoning, or a thought experiment assessing the needs and desires of an individual under ideal or constrained circumstances, to determine the character and extent of an individual's rights.[98] But despite these differences among arguments, the proponents of the war on drugs draw support for their position from the shared claim that there is a fundamental moral principle proscribing drug use that overrides all consequentialist considerations and that the government has a right to enforce.[99]

CONSEQUENTIALIST JUSTIFICATIONS FOR DECRIMINALIZATION

While Szasz has made various references to the economic and social costs of the war on drugs in his writings, he has not discussed in detail what he terms the *practical argument* based on a cost-benefit or utilitarian analysis. As we have argued elsewhere,[100] we find the practical moral argument of consequentialism to provide compelling support for the conclusion that prohibition is wrong and must be given up in favor of decriminalization. Regardless of the factors one considers in the utilitarian calculus—whether they be economic, social, health, or safety—the devastating harms continue to outweigh the few benefits.[101]

There is no hard evidence to establish that ending the present prohibition on drugs would increase their use in the long run or that people are restrained from using drugs only by 21 U.S.C. § 846 and comparable statutes.[102] On the contrary, some experts maintain the addiction rate is roughly comparable for all mind-altering drugs, including alcohol, around 10 to 15 percent.[103]

We have noted previously the staggering price we are paying in dollars to finance the current war on drugs.[104] But that price does not include the equally staggering price we are paying if constitutional rights are ceded in the face of the fear of the present so-called drug *epidemic*.[105] A survey of the rights of the individual that have been curtailed in the name of the war on drugs is sobering:[106] the elimination of an accused's right to pretrial release for most charges under the Controlled Substance Act;[107] heightened restrictions on postconviction bail;[108] and invasions into the attorney–client relationship through the use of the criminal forfeiture provisions of the Comprehensive Crime Control Act.[109] Moreover, the federal judiciary approved every wiretap request in 1990, and the annual requests for wiretaps were up more than 400 percent from 1980.[110]

In recent years the Supreme Court has cut back Fourth Amendment rights. It has relaxed the criterion that must be satisfied to secure a search warrant.[111] In cases involving illegal drugs, the Court has permitted the issuance of search warrants based on anonymous tips and tips from informants, some of whom have proven corrupt and unreliable,[112] permitted warrantless searches of fields, barns, and private property near a residence,[113] permitted warrantless surveillances of a home,[114] lowered the permissible ceiling for aerial warrantless searches to 400 feet;[115] and upheld the use of evidence obtained under the color of defective search warrants on the ground that the officers executing the warrant acted "in good faith."[116] When taken together, these various holdings effectively have been characterized as "the drug exception to the fourth amendment."[117]

The protections of the Fourth Amendment are not the only ones that have been adversely affected. The rights supposedly secured by the Fifth, Sixth, and Eighth Amendments also have been diminished.[118] In addition to the Court's actual holdings, *dicta* in cases like *Arizona v. Fulminante*,[119] and dissents[120] can be viewed as an effort to enhance the war on drugs at the expense of individual rights.

The question raised by this altered view of constitutional rights is not whether the government deserves to win cases involving drug offenses; rather, the question is whether the social benefit supposedly resulting from and used to justify this intrusion is truly worth the cost.[121] However, within the context of the rhetoric of the war on drugs, this question is dismissed out of hand on the assumption that the government and the courts are warranted in taking these and even more drastic measures to fight this scourge. But before the government continues infringing upon enumerated and explicitly recognized unenumerated constitutional rights in the name of the good of both the individual and society, it must be asked whether such paternalistic intervention justified only by the rhetoric spawned by a "war zone" mentality is constitutionally permissible.[122] We suggest that it is not.

RIGHTS-BASED ARGUMENTS AND AN ABSOLUTE MORAL RIGHT TO DRUGS

Szasz's argument is rights-based rather than consequentialist in nature. It was noted above that Szasz's argument is grounded on the identification of drugs as property and takes positive shape through the project of reactively exposing the moral bankruptcy of the present policies and practices and their theoretical underpinnings.[123] It is also an argument that reverberates throughout Szasz's writings as it has shaped his discussion of the numerous legal issues he has addressed over the years, including the involuntary commitment and treatment of the so-called mentally ill, the insanity defense, and the fitness requirement to stand trial.[124]

The theoretical underpinnings of Szasz's rights-based position against the criminalization of drugs are not novel; as was discussed above, his accounts of natural rights and of individual liberty and responsibility fall squarely within the tradition of classical liberalism or libertarianism.[125] In an early article Szasz stated his central libertarian "prejudice" in the following terms: "[T]o be a fully human person one must be free and responsible, and must treat others as free and responsible persons. This prejudice is diametrically opposed to, and is therefore incompatible with, the prejudice that animates and informs involuntary psychiatry and those who defend or support its principles and practices."[126] It is precisely this priority of autonomy, individual commitment, and liberty over the unavoidable benefits of protected interests, or *forced* happiness, that is the quintessential principle of political liberalism in its various forms, including classical liberalism or libertarianism.

Szasz's rejection of mental illness complements his libertarian skepticism of governmental power and his libertarian commitment to the freedom and responsibility of the individual. This compatibility among the various principles he espouses is secured by a commitment to a radical libertarian metaphysic of morals.[127] Thus his rejection of mental illness and addiction has significant implications for his moral and political theories, especially as they relate to drugs. His entire discussion of the drug issue is premised on a view of free will and moral autonomy that goes beyond a political commitment to individual liberty to a categorical rejection of determinism at the metaphysical level. This "deep" point can be simply stated as follows: because there is no such thing as mental illness or addiction, there is no rational basis for ever invoking them as valid reasons to relieve the individual of the moral and legal responsibility for his actions. Therefore, regardless of the way in which the individual exercises his free will and regardless of the impact those choices and actions may have on his mind and character, that individual continues to be a morally responsible agent who is capable of acting freely.

This view is compatible with his denial of the physical reality of all mental illnesses, including insanity and drug addiction.[128] Implicit in this underlying thesis is a rejection of not only metaphysical determinism[129] but also a denial that drugs have the property of impinging on one's moral autonomy and capacity to will.[130] Szasz draws a basic distinction between bad habits and illness and places drug "addiction" in the category of the former.[131] It follows that "[t]he drug user's 'problem'—assuming *he* thinks he has a problem—is that he has a habit, say smoking, he wants to quit. To break his habit, he must want to stop smoking more than he wants to continue smoking."[132] Under this description the drug user is at all times a morally *and legally* responsible agent.[133]

Szasz summarizes his position in the following succinct language:

> I don't see how anyone can take seriously the idea of personal self-determination and responsibility and not insist on his right to take anything he wants to take. . . . That doesn't mean, obviously, that it's a good thing to take certain drugs.[134] It most assuredly can be a very bad thing. But a person must, if he is to be free, have the right to poison and kill himself. As, indeed, he now does with tobacco, but not with marijuana; with alcohol, but not with heroin.[135]

In light of Szasz's commitment to a strong version of individual autonomy, Lockean natural rights, and individual responsibility, it necessarily follows that the sphere in which the state can function legitimately is narrowly limited to that of securing the individual in the exercise of his rights, including his right to drugs qua property.

DERIVING A RIGHT TO DRUGS FROM THE CONSTITUTION

While Szasz has cast his thesis as a pure moral question, relying as he does on Locke and the early property rights held in the early days of our Republic, the issue has become substantially more sophisticated in today's world as our society has grown in size, complexity, and diversity and has extended its boundaries and concerns well beyond our national borders. Szasz correctly notes the overwhelming desire for order on the part of most members of the society, but perhaps underestimates the difficulty of applying the social contract to the problems of today. However, even Szasz concedes the desirability of law against the possession of dynamite.

Szasz has suggested that the individual has a constitutional right to grow and use drugs. He grounds this right in the protected property and privacy rights enunciated in the Declaration of Independence and by the Supreme Court in *Griswold* v. *Connecticut*[136] and *Roe* v. *Wade*.[137] Szasz's analysis suggests that the government's enforcement of its laws against drugs constitutes an unconstitutional taking of property in violation of the express provisions of the due process clauses of the Fifth and Fourteenth Amendments. If drugs are "property" and fall within the protective spheres of the Fifth and Fourteenth Amendments, then the right to drugs is an enumerated right that needs no Ninth Amendment protection and the constitutional analysis of the status of a right to drugs is over.

This avenue of constitutional analysis is not available, however, because of Supreme Court decisions arising out of the context of Prohibition which have held that there is no constitutionally protected fundamental property right in alcohol or drugs.[138] Thus the criminalization of those substances under the present state of constitutional authority does not infringe on the individual's protected property rights and does not constitute an unconstitutional taking.[139] While one may disagree with the logic of the Supreme Court's refusal to recognize alcohol and drugs as property for constitutional purposes, these decisions necessarily define the parameters within which the present constitutional debate on drugs can take place.[140]

All too frequently, what should have been the cornerstone of any prohibitive measure endowed with a criminal sanction, that is, harm to another, has been overlooked. Conduct that the society regards as offensive, although it is done exclusively in the privacy of one's home, has been criminalized.[141] Perhaps the enactment of motorcycle helmet laws is but a simplified projection of the concept that society can and should regulate the conduct of individuals when it deems such conduct harmful, not particularly to the society but to the individual. There is little, if any, empirical evidence that the use of criminal law for this purpose is effective.

This view, validating unenumerated rights held by the individual for his or her benefit, gained little expression in the law until the development of what has been defined as the right to privacy—the vehicle for the justification of a series of rights, including the right to make one's own choices about having children.[142] To date, these rights have been derived from the "penumbral rights" of "privacy and repose," which have been identified by reading simultaneously various amendments in the Bill of Rights.[143] However, despite the overwhelming public interest in the war on drugs and the amount of attention paid to the legal dimensions of that war, there has been no serious attempt to examine the constitutional dimension of the moral right to possess and use drugs within the framework of Ninth Amendment jurisprudence, for example.[144]

THE NINTH AMENDMENT

Of the various amendments[145] identified as contributing to the penumbra of the right of privacy, the Ninth Amendment consistently has received the least attention by the courts.[146] The watershed case for Ninth Amendment jurisprudence was *Griswold* v. *Connecticut*, in which Justice Arthur Goldberg noted that

> the Ninth Amendment shows a belief of the Constitution's authors that fundamental rights exist that are not expressly enumerated in the first eight amendments and an intent that the list of rights included there not be deemed exhaustive. . . . The Ninth Amendment simply shows the

intent of the Constitution's authors that other fundamental personal rights should not be denied such protection or disparaged in any other way simply because they are not specifically listed in the first eight constitutional amendments.[147]

Since *Griswold*, the Ninth Amendment has been raised and considered in hundreds of opinions. When the Supreme Court has turned its attention to the Ninth Amendment, however, it has interpreted the amendment "in a manner that denies it any role in the constitutional structure."[148] Nonetheless, the Ninth Amendment has become a cottage industry for legal scholars as the debate rages over its place and function in the constitutional scheme,[149] and it remains a "sleeping giant" within the framework of protecting the fundamental rights of the individual.[150]

The Ninth Amendment succinctly provides that: "The enumeration in the Constitution, of certain rights, shall not be construed to deny or disparage others retained by the people."[151] The fundamental question is whether this sparse statement was intended to function merely as a principle of construction, that is, a declaration that there are some rights existing independently of government that cannot be legitimately encroached upon by the federal government but also whose encroachment does not give rise to a cause of action in federal court,[152] or as a substantive principle that refers to specific unenumerated rights that nonetheless may be identified and protected by federal courts.[153] In determining which interpretation is the most accurate, much effort has gone into analyzing the intentions of James Madison regarding the Ninth Amendment's formulation and the antifederalist concerns that motivated its adoption.[154] And it is noteworthy that this project united proponents of "originalism" and "activist egalitarians"[155] in the common task of deciding what the Framers meant by "rights retained by the people" and whether they intended those rights to be justiciable.[156] Only those who live in dread of the possibility of what they characterize as undemocratic judicial activism have refused to join in this project by misleadingly asserting an alleged originalist claim that the amendment was flawed from its inception and simply can be ignored without any adverse consequence.[157]

Various writings of the Framers and discussions surrounding the ratification of both the Constitution and the Bill of Rights tend to establish that the Framers understood unenumerated rights referred to in the Ninth Amendment to be *fundamental substantive*, as opposed to procedural, rights.[158] A paramount concern of the Framers was that an imperfect enumeration in a bill of rights would endanger unenumerated substantive rights. Thus the Ninth and Tenth Amendments, the former reserving rights and the latter limiting powers, were specifically designed to protect fundamental substantive rights of the individual by explicitly limiting the government's powers. Furthermore, these fundamental substantive rights could be said to derive from at least two sources: natural law and positive law.[159]

Those interpretations that support the conclusion that the Ninth Amendment was intended by the Framers to be given substantive effect as a repository of unenumerated but identifiable rights that are justiciable in federal courts against both state and federal governments seems to us to be the most consistent with the historical evidence surrounding the adoption of the amendment and the most appropriate in securing the overall coherence of the constitutional scheme.

DETERMINING NINTH AMENDMENT RIGHTS

The methodology for identifying positive rights in the Ninth Amendment requires locating the asserted right in the state's constitution, statutes, or common law and sorting out any conflicts arising from claims made by Congress pursuant to the Supremacy Clause.[160] The methodology required to identify unenumerated natural rights obviously is more involved than that used to identify unenumerated positive rights, but ultimately this methodology is analogous to that of the common law: it is "a gradual process of judicial inclusion and exclusion."[161] This process is *gradual* precisely because of the textual and structural constraints limiting the kinds of rights that can be recognized at any given time,[162] and it begins with the determination of whether the alleged unconstitutional activity of the government in suppressing the asserted right violates any express constitutional provision.[163] If the asserted right is protected, there is no need to appeal to the Ninth Amendment. If the asserted right is not protected, then a further determination must be made about whether the activity infringes an unenumerated right.

This next step requires an assessment of the *fundamentality* of the asserted right. It is at this point that Justice Goldberg's formulaic rules come into play. In *Griswold*, Justice Goldberg required the court to "look to the traditions and collective conscience of our people" and to "the emanations of specific constitutional guarantees and . . . experience with the requirements of a free society."[164] Fundamentality is determined, therefore, by considering the "traditions and collective conscience of our people,"[165] and the court can look to various factors in assessing the traditions and collective conscience of the people.

These factors include the following: a textual foundation in the Constitution for the asserted right, albeit implied or attenuated;[166] a historical justification for the claim that the right is authentically fundamental in nature by locating it in "the organic law of the nation, the states, the colonies, or the common law";[167] a showing that it is a pervasive right, "generally recognized by a significant portion of contemporary society as one *inextricably connected with the inherent dignity of the individual*";[168] and finally, a showing that the exercise of the asserted right is theoretically and practically consistent with the exercise of the fundamental rights of others. The theoretical component requires that the party asserting the right be able to demonstrate that it is "plainly inferable" from the axioms of natural law theory,[169] while the practical component requires the asserted right to pass the familiar balancing test to which the enumerated rights are regularly subjected.[170] Thus, once it is established that the right is fundamental in nature, the burden is on the government to demonstrate that it has a "substantial" interest in taking any action that encroaches on that right, and subjecting the right and the governmental action to a balancing test effectively determines just how compelling the need for governmental action is.[171]

Like enumerated rights, unenumerated rights can best be understood to have a presumptive claim of validity insofar as they promote individual liberty.[172] This presumption holds that "individuals are constitutionally privileged to engage in rightful behavior—acts that are within their sphere of moral jurisdiction—and such behavior is presumptively immune from government interference."[173] Thus individuals are presumed free to act within boundaries of their common law rights, and this presumption places the burden on the government to justify its activities to a neutral third party, a judge, before it may legitimately encroach on an individual's asserted right.[174]

Finally, it is also important to note the qualitative difference between enumerated and unenumerated rights. Justice Goldberg's reliance on traditions and the collective conscience of society as the foundational touchstone of unenumerated rights necessarily implies that these rights can and will change as society changes. It is this malleability that gives the Ninth Amendment its open texture and allows for its ability to accommodate the needs and conditions of contemporary society.[175]

THE RIGHT TO SELF-DETERMINATION[176] AS A FUNDAMENTAL CONSTITUTIONAL RIGHT

Szasz's position merits serious consideration insofar as it suggests there are various possible rights regarding the manufacture, possession, and use of drugs that could be asserted under the Ninth Amendment either as part of a natural right to drugs grounded in natural law or as positive rights grounded in state law. In view of the authorities noted above, which have rejected Szasz's Fifth Amendment argument and property contentions, the question can be fairly put whether there is any issue left to consider, the Ninth Amendment notwithstanding. However, property rights are of a different quality than the more abstract rights to protected conduct, such as free speech, religion, and press. It is this vital distinction that warrants examining the further constitutional implications of Szasz's positions with regard to the right to self-determination.[177]

Textual Foundation

The initial challenge is that of phrasing the asserted right in the appropriate manner to facilitate an inquiry into the textual basis for such a right.[178] When the right has been narrowly defined as, for example, the right to possess and smoke marijuana[179] or the right to privately possess cocaine,[180] the courts have consistently refused to recognize it as one that is fundamental in nature.[181] However, when the right to ingest substances is considered in more general terms[182] as the right to self-determination,[183] a right logically and practically related to the right to privacy,[184] the right to self-ownership,[185] and the right to recreation,[186] a more coherent argument can be made for the proposition that the right to ingest consciousness-altering substances has a textual foundation in the Constitution. This textual foundation is found precisely in those penumbras and emanations identified by Justices Douglas and Goldberg in Griswold.[187]

Similarly, the reasoning in Griswold lends support for the claim that there is a fundamental right to self-determination. In arguing for the ban on contraceptives, the State of Connecticut asserted that the law was warranted by the genuine state interest in discouraging extramarital relations.[188] Justice Goldberg rejected this reasoning on the grounds that contraceptives were widely available and that they served purposes additional to preventing conception, such as preventing disease.[189] Thus the only state interest that might have justified this ban was the prohibition of nonprocreational sexual relations within or without the marital relationship,[190] but this was not a defensible interest. Another way of phrasing this conclusion is that Griswold stands for the proposition that there is a fundamental right to self-determination, that is, a right to determine with one's spouse how to use one's body and whether to engage in the intimate activity of nonprocreational sexual relations,[191] a right derived from the penumbras and emanations of the Bill of Rights and the fundamental rights to life, liberty, and happiness.[192] Therefore, to the extent that Griswold sets forth a textual foundation for the right to marital privacy and recreation, an analogous textual foundation for the right to personal privacy and self-determination can be formulated.[193]

Historical Justification

Szasz's historical review of the emergence of the therapeutic state and the subsequent war on drugs supports the conclusion that the right to administer to one's own body has historical justification.[194] The negative[195] right to be free from governmental interference with regard to the manufacture, possession, and use of drugs was respected from colonial times to 1907.[196] And it was only with the Harrison Narcotic Act of 1914[197] and the Food, Drug, and Cosmetic Act of 1938 that individuals were no longer able to possess narcotics freely or to determine what counted as therapeutic drugs and as legitimate medical treatment.[198] Therefore, it is not unreasonable to conclude that the asserted right to drugs was implicitly recognized in the organic law of the nation, the states, the colonies, and the common law for several hundred years up to 1938.

Pervasiveness

In *Griswold*, Justice Goldberg found that the state's argument regarding the antiextramarital relations rationale was suspect in light of the "admitted widespread availability to all persons in the State of Connecticut, unmarried as well as married, of birth-control devices for the prevention of disease. . . ."[199] The conclusion suggested by this finding is that the "widespread availability" and the implied demand that supported it counted strongly toward the Connecticut public's recognition of the right to nonprocreational sexual relations as a *pervasive* right, a right that a significant portion of contemporary society viewed as being inextricably connected with the inherent dignity of the individual.[200]

Two considerations suggest that the right to self-determination qua the right to use drugs may be considered to be a pervasive right. First, Szasz's analysis of the relationship between the exercise of the individual's free will regarding drugs and the concepts of autonomy, dignity, and moral responsibility provides support for the claim from within the framework of his libertarian moral theory. Of course, one need not accept all of the implications of Szasz's libertarianism to assert reasonably that the individual's informed decisions about what he will or will not ingest are related in a significant manner to these basic concepts. A commitment to the individualism espoused by either classical[201] or contemporary[202] liberal theory is sufficient so long as it acknowledges the logical and practical relationship between the concepts of self-ownership and self-determination on the one hand and the concepts of autonomy, dignity, and moral responsibility on the other; and it is not unreasonable to assert that the scope of the recognition of this relationship satisfies the criterion of pervasiveness.

Second, the empirical data regarding drug use in the United States provides additional support for the significance of the recognition of a right to drugs. In light of the compelling arguments that have been offered by Szasz, Husak, Duke, and others in support of the proposition that both casual drug users and addicts alike can be held to act autonomously in their choosing to take drugs,[203] both groups of users can be understood to be asserting a right to drugs in their acts of defying the present prohibitionist laws.[204] Thus the 21 million to 25 million Americans who have used cocaine and the 70 million who have used some kind of illegal drug[205] can be counted in the calculation to determine the pervasiveness of the recognition of self-determination qua the right to drugs. Furthermore, just as the widespread availability of contraceptives in Connecticut in 1964 was viewed as significant support for the claim that the right to nonprocreational sexual relations was held to be a pervasive right, so too can the widespread availability of controlled and illegal drugs be viewed as significant support for the claim that a significant portion of the public recognizes the right to drugs as a fundamental right.[206]

Theoretical Consistency

The right to self-determination is theoretically consistent with other fundamental rights and not only can be readily derived from the axioms of natural law but is itself an axiom. Self-determination, both in the narrow technical sense in which we are using the term and in its usual more general sense, is recognized as both a "basic good" in natural law theory and as a good that can be derived from the other basic goods.[207] Natural law and natural rights theory begins with a framework of basic values that are required for an individual's well-being. These include life—self-determination in the general sense, knowledge, play (recreation), aesthetic experience, sociability (friendship), practical reasonableness—ordering one's life so that actions and habits conform with one's own practical attitudes, and personal responsibility.[208]

Practical Consistency

It is the question of the practical consistency of the right to drugs with other fundamental rights that is the most complex of the issues raised by a rights-based argument in favor of decriminalization. In answering this question, it is necessary to balance the exercise of the right to self-determination against other competing rights; and at the outset of such a balancing analysis, *pace* Szasz, a general right to manufacture, possess, and use all drugs at all times and in all places by all people cannot survive even when governmental encroachment on this fundamental constitutional right is subjected to the requisite heightened level of scrutiny. Ultimately, the key factor in determining the scope of the right to self-determination is, as Szasz also recognizes, the threat that the exercise of that right poses to the safety of the public.[209]

The question of practical consistency requires an analysis of each drug[210] considered individually and the time, manner, and place[211] of its use asserted as part of the right held by the individual and the harm of that use on the individual and others. The harm principle[212] applied in this calculation focuses on the harm that the right to drugs would inflict on the relevant *compelling* interests of the government, which include the well-being of the individual and the exercise of constitutionally recognized rights by others. Thus it is a rights-

based rather than a utility-based calculation that employs the latest data supplied by sciences and that is expressed in a demythologized vocabulary—that
is, a vocabulary that reflects and incorporates the latest developments in the
relevant scientific disciplines—to facilitate the dispassionately rational analysis
of the competing rights claims.

While the government has a legitimate interest in the well-being of the
individual, that interest and its ability to act in a paternalistic manner to protect the individual from him- or herself are necessarily limited by the priority
the government must give to the individual's liberty, autonomy, and dignity.
Isaiah Berlin brings into sharp focus the dangers of paternalism:

> [I]f the essence of men is that they are autonomous beings—authors of
> values, of ends in themselves, the ultimate authority of which consists pre-
> cisely in the fact that they are willed freely—then nothing is worse than
> to treat them as if they were not autonomous, but natural objects, played
> on by causal influences, creatures at the mercy of external stimuli, whose
> choices can be manipulated by their rulers, whether by threats of force
> or offers of rewards. To treat men in this way is to treat them as if they
> were not self-determined. "Nobody may compel me to be happy in his
> own way," said Kant. "Paternalism is the greatest despotism imaginable."
> This is so because it is to treat men as if they were not free, but human
> material for me, the benevolent reformer to mold in accordance with my
> own, not their freely adopted purpose.[213]

Concerned about the excesses of Connecticut's paternalistic foray into
the marital bedroom, Justice Goldberg found in *Griswold* that the governmental interest in question could be served in a more discriminately tailored
manner than the present prohibition that "sweep[s] unnecessarily broadly,
reaching far beyond the evil sought to be dealt with and intruding upon the
privacy of the [individual]."[214] Therefore, in place of criminal sanctions against
drug use, the governmental interest in the well-being of the drug user can be
served best by controlling the quality and labeling of drugs[215] and by increasing
the availability of drug treatment to those seeking such assistance.

The most compelling governmental interests at issue turn on the prevention of harm to others as a result of recognizing and protecting the
individual's right to drugs. While the practical consequences of recognizing
the right to drugs is hotly contested across the spectrum by champions of
the war on drugs predicting calamities of biblical proportion, by proponents
of decriminalization predicting a return to the Garden, and moderates on
both sides betting on more realistic outcomes, the constitutional consequences
of recognizing this right are quite straightforward. The foremost constitutional
issue is that of balancing the drug user's rights against the rights of others,
and this is the kind of question that courts confront on a daily basis by using

the familiar analytical tools of the balancing test.[216] Therefore, defining the scope of the right to drugs as a fundamental constitutional right poses no greater difficulty than defining the scope of other unenumerated constitutional rights that have been recognized and protected previously by the Court.[217]

CONCLUSION

Szasz's unwaiveringly persistent and coldly logical voice from the wilderness— although extreme most of the time—should give us pause. Regardless of whether his theory of the mind, addiction, mental illness, and other mental predicates is ultimately right or wrong, his critique of our nation's drug policy strips away the obscuring layers of myths and metaphors and shatters the distorting mirrors that have transformed the reality of drugs into a collection of hideous demons. Our elected leaders and other concerned drug warriors have used these mythical demons to terrorize the public into unreflectively accepting the devastating policy of prohibition as the only solution to the drug issue. Any other alternative is simply *unthinkable*!

Once the myths, metaphors, and mirrors are swept away, it is possible to take a step back from the heated battle and reflect dispassionately on the war on drugs. By subjecting our nation's drug policy to the scrutiny of the consequentialist calculus discussed above ("Consequentialist Justifications for Decriminalization"), the staggering costs—measured not only in terms of money but also in terms of health, safety, civil rights, and human dignity and autonomy—and paltry benefits of the war on drugs come into clear focus. Moreover, the staggering cost of fighting the newly framed battle of drugs as cancer will continue endlessly into the future with no promise of finding a "cure" for the terminal disease. The consequentialist analysis compels the conclusion that alternatives to prohibition *must* be sought.

Our demystified consequentialist conclusion is as follows: if what we are doing is not working, if the driving force behind the use of drugs is money, or the lack of it, then it is time to consider alternatives to the status quo, including the alternative of abolishing the prohibition, that is, to cease treating indulgence in mind alteration as a crime. Simply put, we propose that drugs should be regulated as alcohol now is. The model is the repeal of Prohibition and the end of Al Capone and Dutch Schultz.

This conclusion is reinforced further by the rights-based moral analysis of prohibition discussed above ("Rights-Based Arguments and an Absolute Moral Right to Drugs"). We join with Szasz and others who call for reform that centers responsibility for conduct on the individual instead of the society. In place of laws criminalizing individual choice and self-determined actions of the autonomous individual, the emphasis should be on a policy that would maximize the responsibility and capacity of the individual to make an informed choice concerning his or her conduct. What should be criminalized is conduct that results in harm to others, and the policy we favor—like the current policy concerning alcohol misuse—would support, publicize, and enforce stiff criminal sanctions against persons whose conduct under the influence of drugs resulted in harm to another's person or property.

Given the present complicated state of the law, legislative reform is the preferred vehicle by which this change of direction can be achieved. Our analysis of the Ninth Amendment suggested that support for such reform may be found in the Constitution. Decriminalization could be accomplished by the legislative repeal of federal prohibition; the setting of federal standards for the dispensation of drugs and their taxation; and the availability of funding and revenue to state and local governments that would undertake to provide education and drug abuse prevention programs, identify chronic users, research drug-blocking alternatives for the addict, and increase the number of therapeutic treatment centers. Immediate consideration should be given to making methadone available to the 200,000 heroin users who now seek it instead of only to the 30,000 for whom slots are available in existing programs. Residential treatment should be made available for anyone who meets a defined threshold of addiction, and anyone beyond that threshold should be permitted to obtain drugs only after medical intervention. The manufacturing, resale, and distribution of drugs outside the enacted regulatory regime would of course remain a federal crime. With greater proportionate resources available for enforcement and adjudication, punishment for violation would be swifter, surer, and equally—or perhaps even more—punitive than at present.

We count no fewer than five benefits that would follow immediately from the decriminalization of drugs: first, the elimination of the profit motive from the sale of illegal drugs would reduce violence and corruption. Well-financed gangs, drug dealers, and drug-related random violence, which currently plague our streets and devastate our neighborhoods, and are as well a substantial cause of corruption of our public officials and law enforcement officers would disappear. Second, revenue generated by taxing drugs, plus the billions of dollars that would be spent fighting the war on drugs, would be available to finance research, education, prevention, and rehabilitation programs. Third, the elimination of drug prosecutions and harsh mandatory minimum sentences currently imposed on nonviolent drug offenders would keep otherwise law-abiding people with their families and productively working on the job—instead of languishing for years at the taxpayers' expense while truly dangerous criminals are returned to the streets because of the overcrowded conditions of our prisons. This would have the added benefit of freeing up substantial state and federal resources to prosecute those criminals and crimes that actually threaten the health and safety of our communities and nation. Fourth, a healthier nation would emerge as a result of a better educated citizenry making informed decisions concerning drug use, the elimination of the death and destruction caused by impure drugs currently sold on the streets, and more effective rehabilitation of those who are addicted to drugs and now avoid treatment because of the illegal status of drugs. An additional benefit of decriminalization from the consequentialist perspective and *the* definitive consideration from a rights-based perspective is that the government would respect the autonomy and dignity of the individual—and the individual's right to self-determination—by repealing prohibition and allowing the individual to make personal decisions concerning drug use.[218]

The shared lie of the war on drugs and drugs as cancer policies is that drug use is at the center of this universe of problems related to drugs. The truth is that drug use—and more important, drug *abuse*—are symptoms of more serious social ills that include an inadequate commitment to education, a lack of economic opportunity, a lack of commitment to our society, dishonesty in high places, and the end of altruism. These are the real problems of which drug use is merely an effect, and the drug warriors take the easy way out by ignoring the real problems and setting their sights on simply shooting the messenger of these disquieting tidings.

Addressing the underlying causes of drug use and abuse, providing safe narcotics, and treating users would ultimately result in a healthier America. If it is otherwise, it will be because our citizens have lost the capacity to act affirmatively and determine for themselves the kind and quality of lives they will lead, and to reach out with concern and compassion to those in need of assistance and direction in their lives.[219] If we are not willing to be responsible for ourselves and to be our brothers' keepers, then we will have to become our brothers' jailers, and this ought not to be an acceptable alternative to a nation that professes to prize personal liberty. The catalyst behind this proposed legislative reform comes not only from the consequentialist cost-benefit analysis of the war on drugs but also from considerations of the fundamental rights and principles that underlie the system of government and that are protected by the Constitution. While our foray into Ninth Amendment jurisprudence, like Szasz's denunciation of the present state of the fields of psychiatry and psychology, is far from being free of controversy or doubt, we suggest that the consideration of fundamental rights can and should illuminate and advance the discussion concerning drugs.

The greatest single problem in the current "debate" on the war on drugs is the lack of rational dialogue. The tendency is for each voice to assert the definitive position on the issue to which all others are to acquiesce in silence. Given the scope of what is at stake, however, it is precisely rational dialogue that is so desperately needed, and it is only through such dialogue that we can reconsider our own views about the autonomy, dignity, and moral responsibility of the individual, and the sphere in which the constitutionally empowered and constrained government of the United States may function legitimately.

ENDNOTES

1. Portions of this chapter were previously published in *Just and Unjust Wars: The War on the War on Drugs — Some Moral and Constitutional Dimensions of the War on Drugs*, by Robert W. Sweet and Edward A. Harris. 87 Nw. U. L. Rev. 1302-73 (1993) (book review).

2. Testimony of Barry R. McCaffrey before the House Committee on Government Reform and Oversight, Subcommittee on National Security, International Affairs, and Criminal Justice, February 27, 1997.

3. Carolyn Skorneck, *Drug Policy Chief Takes Offense at Criticism of His Strategy*, ASSOCI-ATED PRESS POL. SERV., Feb. 27, 1997 (reporting Barr's questioning of McCaffrey following McCaffrey's testimony before the House Committee on Government Reform and Oversight, Subcommittee on National Security, International Affairs, and Criminal Justice, February 27, 1997).

4. *See* Dan Baum, *The War on Drugs, 12 Years Later*, A.B.A.J., Mar. 1993, 72.

5. For example, "[t]he Court justified its decision to permit pretrial preventative detention, in *U.S. v. Salerno*, 481 U.S. 739 (1987), by explicitly comparing the war on drugs to a war against another nation, ruling that in times of 'war or insurrection . . . the government's regulatory interest in community safety can . . . outweigh an individual's liberty interest.'" Baum, *supra* note 4, at 73.

6. THE NATIONAL DRUG CONTROL STRATEGY, 1997 at 5-6.

7. Testimony of Barry R. McCaffrey before the Senate Judiciary Committee, Feb. 27, 1996 ("The metaphor 'war on drugs' is inadequate to describe this terrible menace facing the American people. Dealing with the problem of illegal drug abuse is more akin to dealing with cancer"). It is clear that McCaffrey understands the difference between metaphors and analogies. For McCaffrey, the "war on drug" metaphor was inadequate precisely because it could not be extended to an analogy to describe the drug problem. Once one attempts to identify the *enemy*, the *armies* involved, the *end objectives* and the *means* to achieve those ends, the "war on drugs" metaphor collapses. *Id.* ("the United States does not wage war on its citizens").

8. *See, e.g.*, *Q&A Barry R. McCaffrey, Director, National Drug Control Policy*, SAN DIEGO UNION-TRIBUNE, June 2, 1996; CBS This Morning (CBS television broadcast, Apr. 30, 1996); Mark Brown, *Drug "Czar" Puts New Label on Old Problem*, CHICAGO SUN-TIMES, Apr. 3, 1996.

9. *See supra* note 6.

10. *See supra* note 6, at 5.

11. *See supra* note 3.

12. *See* Bob Barr, *Commentary*, WASH. TIMES, June 19, 1997 ("what we now have is a drug strategy that is more apology than action, more excuse than explanation, and, in effect, is little more than a parenthetical entry in an administration's domestic platform"); Michael Hedges, *Can't Win Drug War, U.S. Draft Concedes*, PITTSBURGH POST-GAZETTE, Feb. 10, 1997; Michael Hedges, *War on Drugs May End, Clinton Seeks to Fight Use as a Disease*, CHICAGO SUN-TIMES, Feb. 9, 1997.

13. According to the annual government survey released on August 6, 1997, "drug use continued to increase among those 18 to 25 years old last year, to 15.6 percent from 14.2 percent in 1995, and those using cocaine monthly increased to 2 percent from 1.2 percent. Heroin and cocaine use among young adults rose sharply. There were 141,000 new heroin users reported in

1995, most of them under 26." Christopher S. Wren, *Fewer Youths Report Smoking Marijuana, But Overall Use of Illegal Drugs Is Unchanged*, N.Y. TIMES, Aug. 7, 1997, at A18.

14. The issues on which he has been the most vocal include the involuntary commitment and treatment of the mentally ill, the insanity defense, and the fitness requirement to stand trial. *See, e.g.,* THOMAS SZASZ, LAW, LIBERTY, AND PSYCHIATRY (1963); THOMAS SZASZ, THE MYTH OF MENTAL ILLNESS (rev. ed. 1974); THOMAS SZASZ, PSYCHIATRIC JUSTICE (1965); THOMAS SZASZ, PSYCHIATRIC SLAVERY (1977); THOMAS SZASZ, THE SECOND SIN (1972); George J. Alexander & Thomas Szasz, *From Contract to Status via Psychiatry*, 13 SANTA CLARA L. REV. 537 (1973); George J. Alexander & Thomas S. Szasz, *Mental Illness as an Excuse for Civil Wrongs*, 43 NOTRE DAME L. REV. 24 (1967); Thomas Szasz, *Involuntary Psychiatry*, 45 U. CIN. L. REV. 347 (1976); Thomas Szasz, *Psychiatry, Ethics, and the Criminal Law*, 58 COLUM. L. REV. 183 (1958); THOMAS SZASZ, *The Right to Health*, in THE THEOLOGY OF MEDICINE 100 (1977) [hereinafter THE THEOLOGY OF MEDICINE]. Additionally, Szasz's analysis of the false distinction between voluntary and involuntary hospitalization is now being applied to nursing home residents. See Cathrael Kazin, Comment, *"Nowhere to Go and Chose to Stay": Using the Tort of False Imprisonment to Redress Involuntary Confinement of the Elderly in Nursing Homes and Hospitals*, 137 U. PA. L. REV. 903, 907 n.18 (1989).

15. For discussions of Szasz's influence, see SUSAN M. CHANDLER, COMPETING REALITIES: THE CONTESTED TERRAIN OF MENTAL HEALTH ADVOCACY 41 (1990); Grant H. Morris, *The Supreme Court Examines Civil Commitment Issues: A Retrospective and Prospective Assessment*, 60 TUL. L. REV. 927, 928 (1986); Delila M. J. Ledwith, Note, *Jones v. Gerhardstein: The Involuntarily Committed Mental Patient's Right to Refuse Treatment with Psychotropic Drugs*, 1990 WIS. L. REV. 1367, 1372–74.

16. *See* Thomas S. Szasz, *The Myth of Mental Illness*, 15 AM. PSYCHOL. 113 *passim* (1960); Thomas Szasz, *Repudiation of the Medical Model*, in PSYCHOPATHOLOGY TODAY: EXPERIMENTATION, THEORY AND RESEARCH 47 *passim* (William S. Sahakian, ed., 1970); *see also*, Linda C. Fentiman, *Whose Right Is It Anyway?: Rethinking Competency to Stand Trial in Light of the Synthetically Sane Insanity Defendant*, 40 U. MIAMI L. REV. 1109, 1118 n.29 (1986) ("Just what constitutes 'mental illness' or indeed, whether it even exists as a medical entity, has been the source of intense debate ever since Thomas Szasz first wrote *The Myth of Mental Illness*").

17. *See Eddings v. Oklahoma*, 455 U.S. 104, 126 (1982); *O'Connor v. Donaldson*, 422 U.S. 563, 585 n.5 (1975).

18. *See In re Andrea B.*, 405 N.Y.S.2d 977, 983 (N.Y. Fam. Ct. 1978).

19. Referring to the American Psychiatric Association Statement on the Insanity Defense, the Fifth Circuit noted that "[t]he APA has not adopted the extreme views of Thomas Szasz, but it has definitely repudiated the ideology of Karl Menninger. The psychiatrists no longer want the criminal law to change to conform to deterministic psychiatric concepts . . . ." *United States v. Lyons*, 731 F.2d 243, 246 n.4 (5th Cir. 1984), quoting Phillip E. Johnson, *Book Review*, 50 U. CHI. L. REV. 1534, 1548 (1983) (reviewing NORVAL MORRIS, MADNESS AND THE CRIMINAL LAW (1982)).

Szasz is a controversial and formidable force even when he is not personally in the courtroom. In *Nowitzke v. State of Florida*, 572 So. 2d 1346, 1352 (Fla. 1990), the Florida Supreme Court held that the trial court committed a reversible error by allowing the jury to hear an exchange between the defense's psychiatric expert and the state attorney regarding Szasz's public repudiation of the expert as a "hired gun."

20. For Szasz's earlier related discussions regarding drugs and drug use, see THOMAS SZASZ, CEREMONIAL CHEMISTRY: THE RITUAL PERSECUTION OF DRUGS, ADDICTS, AND PUSHERS (1974) [hereinafter CEREMONIAL CHEMISTRY]; THOMAS SZASZ, *The Ethics of Addiction*, in THE THEOLOGY OF MEDICINE, *supra* note 14, at 29 *passim*.

21. THOMAS SZASZ, OUR RIGHT TO DRUGS: THE CASE FOR A FREE MARKET (1992).

22. One is reminded of the furor created in the media by President Bill Clinton's non-use of marijuana. *See* Gwen Ifill, *Clinton Admits Experiment with Marijuana in 1960s*, N.Y. TIMES,

Mar. 30, 1992, at A15.

23. SZASZ, *supra note* 21, at 94.

24. *Id.* at 69.

25. *Id.* at 61.

26. *Id.* at 90–94.

27. Szasz's analysis supports the conclusion that only adults, *not children*, have a right to drugs. This conclusion follows from his scathing critique of the content of the current "drug education" efforts and the "casualties of the children's drug crusade," *id.* at 77–84, and from his identification of the legitimate limits that should be imposed on the right to drugs, *id.* at 161–64.

28. *Id.* at 31, 58.

29. *Id.* at 43.

30. Szasz first addressed the concept of "the drug as scapegoat" in *Ceremonial Chemistry. See* CEREMONIAL CHEMISTRY, *supra* note 20, at 19–27. Szasz has examined the concept of scapegoating in a variety of contexts other than that of drugs, including the scapegoating of homosexuality, which Szasz identifies as "the model psychiatric scapegoat." *See* THOMAS SZASZ, THE MANUFAC-TURE OF MADNESS 242–59 (1970). *Cf.* FRIEDRICH NIETZSCHE, BEYOND GOOD AND EVIL 59–76 (Walter Kaufmann ed. & trans. & R. J. Hollingdale trans., 1966); (analyzing the phenomenon of scapegoating with regard to the enslavement of free spirits who were strong enough to act and accept responsibility for their actions by the weak and envious); FRIEDRICH NIETZSCHE, ON THE GENEALOGY OF MORALS 33–43, 120–28 (Walter Kaufmann trans., 1969) [hereinafter GENEALOGY OF MORALS] (same). *See also* RICHARD L. MILLER, THE CASE FOR LEGALIZING DRUGS 109–24 (1991) (discussing "the myth of drug abuse"); *infra* text accompanying notes 27–31 (discussing the similarities between Nietzsche's and Szasz's methodologies).

31. SZASZ, *supra* note 21, at 47; *see also id.* at 73.

32. Szasz notes the public support for governmental encroachment on constitutional rights in the name of the war on drugs. *Id.* at 43.

33. *See* JOHN LOCKE, *The Second Treatise of Government: An Essay Concerning the True Original, Extent, and End of Civil Government, in* TWO TREATISES OF GOVERNMENT 265, 285–302 (§§ 25–51) (Peter Laslett ed., student ed. 1988) (3d ed. 1698).

34. *See* JOHN STUART MILL, ON LIBERTY (Currin V. Shields ed., Bobbs-Merrill 1956) (1859).

35. According to Mises, "the task of the state consists solely and exclusively in guaranteeing the protection of life, health, liberty, and private property against violent attacks. Everything that goes beyond this is an evil." LUDWIG VON MISES, LIBERALISM IN THE CLASSICAL TRADITION 52 (Ralph Raico trans., 3d ed. 1985); *see also id.* at 18–23 (defining fundamental concepts of classical liberalism: property, freedom, and peace).

36. *See* MILTON FRIEDMAN, CAPITALISM AND FREEDOM (1962).

37. *See, e.g.,* FRIEDRICH A. HAYEK, THE CONSTITUTION OF LIBERTY 71–84 (1960) (discussing the fundamental concepts of individual liberty and responsibility); 1 FRIEDRICH A. HAYEK, LAW, LEGISLATION AND LIBERTY: RULES AND ORDERS 94–123 (1973) (discussing the "law of liberty"); 3 F. A. HAYEK, LAW, LEGISLATION AND LIBERTY: THE POLITICAL ORDER OF A FREE PEOPLE 153–76 (1979) (discussing the failure of modern philosophy, sociology, law, and psychology to give individual freedom its due).

38. *See* ROBERT NOZICK, ANARCHY, STATE, AND UTOPIA 171–82 (1974).

39. Isaiah Berlin distinguishes between "negative" liberty as "freedom from" and "positive" liberty as "freedom to," and he locates the libertarian view of property under the former rubric. ISAIAH BERLIN, *Two Concepts of Liberty, in* FOUR ESSAYS ON LIBERTY 118, 124, 126, 127 (1974); *see also* NOZICK, *supra* note 38, at 26 (the only legitimate state is one that functions analogously to the night watchman: it is "limited to the functions of protecting all its citizens against violence, theft, and fraud, and the enforcement of contracts").

40. SZASZ, *supra note* 21, at 9. For a discussion of Szasz's development and use of this con-

cept, see CEREMONIAL CHEMISTRY, *supra* note 20, at 137–39.

41. 416 U.S. 663, 693 (1974) (Douglas, J., dissenting).

42. SZASZ, *supra* note 21, at 26; *see also supra* note 31.

43. SZASZ, *supra* note 21, at 29.

44. FRIEDRICH NIETZSCHE, *The Antichrist, in* THE PORTABLE NIETZSCHE 565, 568 (Walter Kaufmann ed. & trans., Penguin Books 1976) (1954).

45. *See* NIETZSCHE, BEYOND GOOD AND EVIL, *supra* note 30, at 110–18; NIETZSCHE, GENEALOGY OF MORALS, *supra* note 30, at 120-28; FRIEDRICH NIETZSCHE, THUS SPOKE ZARATHUSTRA: A BOOK FOR ALL AND NONE 99–102 (Walter Kaufmann trans., Penguin Books 1978) (1954).

46. The phrase comes from the subtitle of Nietzsche's book, *Twilight of the Idols. See* FRIEDRICH NIETZSCHE, *Twilight of the Idols: Or, How One Philosophizes with a Hammer, in* THE PORTABLE NIETZSCHE, *supra* note 44, at 463.

47. Szasz's profiles of anti-drug crusaders include unsympathetic portraits of Nancy Reagan, Father Bruce Ritter, President John F. Kennedy, Betty Ford, and Kitty Dukakis. SZASZ, *supra* note 21, at 77–82, 85–86, 97.

48. Additionally, like Nietzsche, Szasz is a prolific writer and each book is simultaneously a kaleidoscope, which reflects and refines his previous work, and each is a freestanding statement to further some aspect of the charge taken up before. Not surprisingly, Szasz has turned his hammer against Nietzsche, denouncing him as exemplifying "the 'mad Übermensch,' the 'inhuman (superman) mental patient.' " SZASZ, THE UNTAMED TONGUE: A DISSENTING DICTIONARY 87 (1990).

49. *See, e.g.,* WILFRID SELLARS, SCIENCE AND METAPHYSICS: VARIATIONS ON KANTIAN THEMES (1968); WILFRID SELLARS, *Empiricism and the Philosophy of Mind, in* SCIENCE, PERCEPTION AND REALITY 127 *passim* (1963) (refutation of the "Myth of the Given," i.e., the claim that there is an objective "given" external to individuals that is the object of any single individual's sense perception of that object); WILFRID SELLARS, *Grammar and Existence: A Preface to Ontology, in* SCIENCE, PERCEPTION AND REALITY, *supra*, at 247 *passim* (rejecting "the move from empirical statements to statements asserting the existence of *entities* of a higher order than perceptible individuals").

50. *See, e.g.,* PAUL FEYERABEND, AGAINST METHOD (Verso ed. 1978) (1975); 1 PAUL K. FEYERABEND, PHILOSOPHICAL PAPERS: REALISM, RATIONALISM & SCIENTIFIC METHOD (1981); 2 PAUL K. FEYERABEND, PHILOSOPHICAL PAPERS: PROBLEMS OF EMPIRICISM (1981); PAUL FEYERABEND, SCIENCE IN A FREE SOCIETY (Verso ed. 1982) (1978).

51. *See, e.g.,* RICHARD RORTY, CONSEQUENCES OF PRAGMATISM (1982); RICHARD RORTY, CONTINGENCY, IRONY, AND SOLIDARITY (1989); RICHARD RORTY, PHILOSOPHY AND THE MIRROR OF NATURE (1979) [hereinafter RORTY, MIRROR OF NATURE]; 1 RICHARD RORTY, PHILOSOPHICAL PAPERS: OBJECTIVITY, RELATIVISM, AND TRUTH (1991); 2 RICHARD RORTY, PHILOSOPHICAL PAPERS: ESSAYS ON HEIDEGGER AND OTHERS (1991).

52. RORTY, MIRROR OF NATURE, *supra* note 51, at 367. *See also* W. V. QUINE, *Ontological Relativity, in* ONTOLOGICAL RELATIVITY AND OTHER ESSAYS 26, 54-55 (1969) ("Ontology is indeed doubly relative. Specifying the universe of a theory makes sense only relative to some background theory, and only relative to some choice of a manual of translation of the one theory into the other.").

53. RORTY, MIRROR OF NATURE, *supra* note 51, at 369.

54. *Id.*

55. A good indicator that one is an edifying as opposed to a systematic thinker is the sort of terms used to qualify the person as being on the periphery. Szasz has been described in the following terms: Dr. Tanay, the psychiatrist labeled by Szasz as a "hired gun," *see supra* note 19, described Szasz to the jury as "a person who has been generally recognized as holding views that are really bordering on the ridiculous," *Nowitzke v. Florida,* 572 So. 2d 1346, 1350 (Fla. 1990); "Dr. Szasz has been treated as somewhat of a pariah by the psychiatric establishment," Lois G. Forer, *The Prisoner and the Psychiatrist,* 31 EMORY L. J. 61, 62 n.2 (1982); "the renegade

psychiatrist, Thomas Szasz," Andre W. Scull, *The Theory and Practice of Civil Commitment*, 82 MICH. L. REV. 793, 800 (1984); "the controversial writings of Thomas Szasz," Stacy E. Seishnaydre, Comment, *Community Mental Health Treatment for the Mentally Ill—When Does Less Restrictive Treatment Become a Right?*, 66 TUL. L. REV. 1971, 1972 (1992).

56. The systematic thinker has as his goal the definition of objective truth about how things really are. However, "[t]o see the aim of philosophy as truth—namely, the truth about the terms which provide ultimate commensuration for all human inquiries and activities—is to see human beings as objects rather than subjects, as existing *en-soi* rather than as both *pour-soi* and *en-soi*, as both described objects and describing subjects." RORTY, MIRROR OF NATURE, *supra* note 51, at 378; *see also* FEYERABEND, AGAINST METHOD, *supra* note 50, at 17–22 (science is an essentially anarchistic enterprise: theoretical anarchism is more humanitarian and more likely to encourage progress than its law-and-order alternatives). The point is that, by holding oneself out as being in search of *the truth*, one is prone to claim access to privileged knowledge of objective truth and engage in the misguided task of passing judgment on the human condition from a detached and a historical perspective that fails to conform with the reality of the human condition—as did the moralists, theologians, and philosophers whom Nietzsche attacked, and as do the doctors, scientists, psychologists, psychiatrists, politicians, and even judges whom Szasz now attacks. At least, that is the shared claim of Szasz, Nietzsche, Sellars, Feyerabend, and Rorty.

57. *See* THOMAS SZASZ, *Illness and Indignity*, *in* THE THEOLOGY OF MEDICINE, *supra* note 14, at 18, 23 ("Do your utmost to exercise your skills in healing, but do not do so by sacrificing dignity, either your patient's or your own. . . . For . . . what does it profit a man if he gains his health but loses his dignity?"); THOMAS SZASZ, *The Moral Physician*, *in* THE THEOLOGY OF MEDICINE, *supra* note 14, at 1, 16–17 ("The biologist's or physician's claim that he represents disinterested abstract values—such as mankind, health, or treatment—should be disallowed; and his efforts to balance, and his claim to represent, multiple conflicting interests . . . should be exposed for what they conceal, perhaps his secret loyalty to one of the conflicting parties or his cynical rejection of the interests of both parties in favor of his own self-aggrandizement.").

58. RORTY, MIRROR OF NATURE, *supra* note 51, at 378–79.

59. In response to a question about the centrality of the freedom of the individual in his conception of humanism, Szasz offers a discussion of the interrelationship between humanism, individual autonomy, and edifying discourse:

> [H]umanism is not this or that way of living, but the diversity that results from the economic, political, and psychological circumstances that permit one person to live one way and another, another way. . . . [A]utonomy [of the individual to choose as he sees fit] has no meaning outside of a political and socioeconomic context that provides and protects the range of choices available. . . . Humanism is usually thought of primarily in ethical and psychological terms. I want to emphasize the political criteria and ideas. And among those, there is one notion I want to single out, and that is *dissent*. After all, authorities never object to people agreeing with them. . . . So it's disagreement that must be nurtured and protected. In short, instead of thinking of humanism as this or that kind of life-style or ideology, I think we should think of it more as the right to disagree and reject authority [i.e., the mainstream tradition]—religious authority, educational authority, medical authority—and of course the right to take one's chances with one's own judgment and decision. . . . The idea is this: the Fall was really not a fall but a rise—a rise from infantilism to humanism.

THOMAS SZASZ, *Medicine and the State: A Humanist Interview*, *in* THE THEOLOGY OF MEDICINE, *supra* note 14, at 145, 161–62.

     60. *See id.*

     61. Nietzsche extols the power of the aphorism in the following aphorism:

> Praise of aphorisms. —A good aphorism is too hard for the tooth of time and is not consumed by all millennia, although it serves every time for nourishment: thus it is the great paradox of literature, the intransitory amid the changing, the food that always remains esteemed, like salt, and never loses its savor, as even that does.

FRIEDRICH NIETZSCHE, *Mixed Opinions and Maxims* (1879), *in* GENEALOGY OF MORALS, *supra* note 30, at 174, 176. Szasz has recently written a book that is almost entirely aphoristic in form. *See* THOMAS SZASZ, THE UNTAMED TONGUE, *supra* note 48.

     62. A representative sampling of Szasz's aphoristic statements in *Our Right to Drugs* addresses the following subjects: the legality of guns, but not sterile syringes, SZASZ, *supra* note 21, at 43; the fact that abortion was illegal twenty years ago, but now a pregnant woman who uses pre-scription drugs may be prosecuted if she does not have an abortion, *id.* at 68; the Reagan and Bush administrations' commitment to family values included an attack on the very core of fam-ily relationships by encouraging and congratulating parents and children who turned in each other to the authorities for drug use, *id.* at 78; the fundamental characteristic of the therapeutic state, as matters of medical principle and social policy, is that "*it prevents sane adults from taking the drugs they want, and insane adults from rejecting the drugs they do not want*," *id.* at 132; medical madness: "First, doctors plead for the prohibition of opiates, to prevent people from using the drugs to kill themselves; then, doctors discover that people kill themselves because they have been deprived of opiates, and plead for letting the patient have more opiates," *id.* at 142; and the ironies of the availability and unavailability of drugs: "[N]arcotics are available, *ad libitum*, in the streets. Only in medical settings—in hospitals and doctors' offices—is the availability of narcotics so restricted that patients are harmed as a result," *id.* at 142.

     63. *Symposium Proceedings: Roundtable Discussion*, 11 NOVA L. REV. 939, 957–58 (1987) (Szasz's comments).

     64. *See infra* notes 77–80 and accompanying text.

     65. *See* THOMAS SZASZ, *Language and Lunacy*, *in* THE THEOLOGY OF MEDICINE, *supra* note 14, at 86, 95, 98–99 (calling on "linguistic humanists" to "battle against [psychiatry], one of the most vicious contemporary sociopolitical creeds that wages war against human freedom and dignity by corrupting language" and warning that the battle will only be won "not because we are reasonable or well-meaning, rational or liberal, religious or secular, but rather because we protect and perfect our souls by protecting and perfecting our language"). Compare Szasz's ef-forts to debunk the concept of mental illness with Nietzsche's analysis of the etymological sig-nificance of "good" and conceptual transformation of that term, and his analysis of the creation of such "moral-psychological terms" as "selflessness" and "sanctification" and of such "physiological terms" as "hypnotization." *See* NIETZSCHE, GENEALOGY OF MORALS, *supra* note 30, at 27, 131.

     66. *See* THOMAS SZASZ, INSANITY: THE IDEA AND ITS CONSEQUENCES 135–69 (1987) [hereinafter INSANITY]. *Accord* THOMAS SZASZ, INSANITY AND IDEOLOGY (reprint ed. 1991); SZASZ, THE MANU-FACTURE OF MADNESS, *supra* note 30; SZASZ, THE MYTH OF MENTAL ILLNESS, *supra* note 14; Szasz, *The Myth of Mental Illness*, *supra* note 16.

     67. SZASZ, INSANITY, *supra* note 66, at 141. Szasz argues that lumping together bodily dis-eases and mental diseases in the same class results in a basic Rylean "category mistake" whose logical error can be perceived readily in the following example: "Diabetes and depression are both diseases because they both cause suffering; eagles and bats are both birds because they both fly." *Id.* at 168; *see* GILBERT RYLE, THE CONCEPT OF MIND 15–16 (1949) (mind–body dualism or the "'dogma of the Ghost in the Machine' . . . is one big mistake and a mistake of a special kind. It is, namely, a category-mistake. It represents the facts of mental life as if they belonged to one

logical type or category . . . , when they actually belong to another. The dogma is therefore a philosopher's myth").

In his 1960 paper Szasz described this category mistake in greater detail and in the more formal terms of epistemology, arguing that the Ghost in the Machine is not just a philosopher's myth but also one wholeheartedly embraced and championed by psychiatrists and psychologists:

> [The] error in regarding complex psychosocial behavior, consisting of communications about ourselves and the world about us, as mere symptoms of neurological functioning is *epistemological*. In other words, it is an error pertaining not to any mistakes in observation or reasoning, as such, but rather to the way in which we organize and express our knowledge. In the present case, the error lies in making a symmetrical dualism between mental and physical (or bodily) symptoms, a dualism which is merely a habit of speech and to which no known observations can be found to correspond. . . . In medical practice, when we speak of physical disturbances, we mean either signs (for example, a fever) or symptoms (for example, pain). We speak of mental symptoms, on the other hand, when we refer to a patient's *communications about himself, others, and the world about him.* . . . [T]he statement that "X is a mental symptom" involves rendering a judgment. The judgment entails . . . a covert comparison or matching of the patient's ideas, concepts, or beliefs with those of the observer and the society in which they live. The notion of mental symptom is therefore inextricably tied to the social (including ethical) context in which it is made in much the same way as the notion of bodily symptom is tied to an *anatomical* and *genetic context.*

Szasz, *Myth of Mental Illness, supra* note 16, at 113-14. *Cf.* RORTY, MIRROR OF NATURE, *supra* note 51, at 70-127 (refutation of the reality of the mind and of mental predicates such as pain and pleasure on the basis that they are part of the vocabulary of an inaccurate and outmoded "folk psychology" that must be replaced with purely physiological concepts and categories to describe sense perception); SELLARS, *Empiricism and the Philosophy of Mind, in* SCIENCE, PERCEPTION AND REALITY, *supra* note 49, at 127 (refutation of the epistemological mistake that there is a "given" in perception).

68. See SZASZ, INSANITY, *supra* note 66, at 162-66.

69. See *supra* note 61 and accompanying text. To emphasize the distinction between bodily illness and mental illness, Szasz formulates an analogy using the distinction between a television set and a television program:

> In short, bodily illness stands in the same relation to mental illness as a defective television set stands to a bad television program. Moreover, when minds are called "sick," metaphor is strategically misinterpreted and systematically mistaken for fact— and the doctor is sent for to "cure" the "illness." It is as if a television viewer were to send for a television repairman because he disliked the program he sees on the screen. Television repairmen fix screens, while the television writers fix scripts. No one confuses their respective functions. But nearly everyone now confuses the functions of body healers or doctors with those of mental healers or psychiatrists.

Szasz, *Involuntary Psychiatry, supra* note 14, at 362-63.

70. Szasz, *supra* note 21, at 59-66, 111-24. The entire book *Ceremonial Chemistry,* is written in a metaphorical form about concepts that Szasz perceives to be metaphors, as is indicated

by the section headings: "Pharmakos: The Scapegoat" (with a chapter entitled, "The Scapegoat as Drug and the Drug as Scapegoat"), "Pharmacomythology: Medicine as Magic," and "Pharmacracy: Medicine as Social Control." See Szasz, Ceremonial Chemistry, supra note 20.

71. See id. at 89–103.

72. "Perspectivalism" or nonfoundationalism denies the existence of the given or of absolutes, and therefore necessarily entails the denial of a privileged position from which one can pass judgment on the truth or correctness of a person's actions, beliefs, and so on. In other words, there is no objective "view from nowhere." See generally Thomas Nagel, The View From Nowhere (1986); Rorty, Mirror of Nature, supra note 51, at 165–212; Joan C. Williams, Rorty, Radicalism, Romanticism: The Politics of the Gaze, 1992 Wis. L. Rev. 131, 131–34 & n.1.

73. Nietzsche, Beyond Good and Evil, supra note 30, at 127.

74. Id. at 162.

75. See supra note 67.

76. Szasz, supra note 21, at xiv.

77. Representative Charles Rangel is identified and criticized as the paradigm of the intellectually bankrupt antidrug warrior. Id. at 101–02.

78. Id. at 103.

79. Id. at 147.

80. Id. at 115.

81. See Szasz, supra note 21, at 121–24; Ceremonial Chemistry, supra note 20, at 89–103. The Black Muslim's approach is particularly attractive to Szasz because it is one that is logically coherent and based on the fundamental principles of individual autonomy, responsibility, and dignity. The approach is one of the few that reflects the logical coherence of being consistent in its commitment to the principle of abstaining from all self-indulgent pleasures. Nadelmann has cited both the Mormons and the Puritans for similar consistency in their respective positions toward alcohol, tobacco, and drugs of all kinds. See Ethan Nadelmann, The Case for Legalization, in The Crisis in Drug Prohibition 13, 33 (David Boaz ed., 1990). In these religious traditions, no distinction is made among tobacco, alcohol, and illegal drugs.

82. Such as the desire to justify one's actions to others—a desire that transcends the individual's perspective.

83. See David F. Musto, The American Disease: Origins of Narcotic Control (1973); David F. Musto, Opium, Cocaine and Marijuana in American History, Sci. Am., July 1991, at 40 passim.

84. See Stephen P. Stich, From Folk Psychology to Cognitive Science (1983) (critical analysis of treatments of the semantic content of mental states such as beliefs, thoughts, and desires); see also Rorty, Mirror of Nature, supra note 51, at 213–56 (raising "suspicions about psychology" and analyzing the problems arising out of the traditional theory of knowledge based on Descartes's model of the mind as the mirror of nature, which allows only for the individual to have privileged access to his purely subjective mental states. This privileged access allows that individual to explain his actions but necessarily precludes him from justifying his actions to others).

85. Rorty would welcome Szasz's rejection of mental illness and addiction as a purely mental phenomenon. "The more directly relevant reasons for suspicion [of psychology] are those which suggest that psychologists should be more mechanistic rather than less, that they should cut straight through the mental to the neurophysiological." Rorty, Mirror of Nature, supra note 51, at 217. Two of these reasons are "the urge toward unified science" and "the fear of ghosts." Id. at 217, 218. It is the latter fear that is debunked by Sellars's argument against the givenness of the mental, which leads to the conclusion that when we engage in introspection, there is no non-physical item present to a nonphysical observer. Id. at 243.

Two distinct approaches to the issue of redescribing immaterial mental states in terms of physical brain states have been formulated and refined: "reductive materialism" or the "identity thesis" and "eliminative materialism." For discussions of reductive materialism, see, e.g., James

W. Cornman, *The Identity of Mind and Body*, in MATERIALISM AND THE MIND–BODY PROBLEM 73 *passim* (David M. Rosenthal ed., 1971) [hereinafter MATERIALISM]; DAVID LEWIS, *An Argument for the Identity Theory*, in 1 PHILOSOPHICAL PAPERS 99 *passim* (1983); J. J. C. Smart, *Sensations and Brain Processes*, in MATERIALISM, *supra*, at 53 *passim*. For critical discussions of this strategy, see PAUL M. CHURCHLAND, MATTER AND CONSCIOUSNESS 26–34 (1984); Judith Jarvis Thomson, *The Identity Thesis*, in PHILOSOPHY, SCIENCE, AND METHOD: ESSAY IN HONOR OF ERNEST NAGEL 219 *passim* (Sidney Morgenbesser et al. eds., 1969). For discussions of eliminative materialism, see, *e.g.*, PAUL K. FEYERABEND, *Materialism and the Mind–Body Problem*, in 1 PHILOSOPHICAL PAPERS, *supra* note 50, at 161 *passim*; Richard Rorty, *Mind–Body Identity, Privacy, and Categories*, in MATERIALISM, *supra*, at 174; Richard Rorty, *In Defense of Eliminative Materialism*, in MATERIALISM, *supra*, at 223. *Cf.* STICH, *supra* note 84 (critical analysis of treatments of the semantic content of mental states such as beliefs, thoughts, and desires). For critical assessments of eliminative materialism, *see* CHURCHLAND, *supra*, at 43–49; DANIEL C. DENNETT, BRAINSTORMS 190–229 (1981); Richard J. Bernstein, *The Challenge of Scientific Materialism*, in MATERIALISM, *supra*, at 200.

86. Szasz has furthered his analysis on these issues in his most recent book, *The Meaning of Mind*. THOMAS SZASZ, THE MEANING OF MIND: LANGUAGE, MORALITY, AND NEUROSCIENCE (1996).

87. *See, e.g.*, MILLER, *supra* note 30, at 125–57; John P. Morgan, *Prohibition Is Perverse Policy: What Was True in 1933 Is True Now*, in SEARCHING FOR ALTERNATIVES: DRUG-CONTROL POLICY IN THE UNITED STATES, 405 *passim* (Melvyn B. Krauss & Edward P. Lazear eds., 1991) [hereinafter SEARCHING FOR ALTERNATIVES].

88. For a discussion of the logical and moral implications of the term *ought*, see Edward A. Harris, Note, *Fighting Philosophical Anarchism with Fairness: The Moral Claims of Law in the Liberal State*, 91 COLUM. L. REV. 919, 927 n.38 (1991).

89. From the time of Jeremy Bentham, this form of argument has been referred to as "utilitarian," to wit, one in which decisions to act are made by comparing the number of "utils"— units of happiness—alternative actions would produce and opting for the optimal util-producing activity. *See* HENRY SIDGWICK, THE METHODS OF ETHICS 411–17, 460–95 (Hackett 1981) (7th ed. 1907); Jeremy Bentham, *An Introduction to the Principles of Morals and Legislation* (2d ed. 1823), in 2 BRITISH MORALISTS 1650–1800, at 313, 313–46 (D. D. Raphael ed., 1969); JOHN STUART MILL, *Utilitarianism* (1863), in UTILITARIANISM AND OTHER WRITINGS 251, 256–78 (Mary Warnock ed., 1974).

90. *See* RONALD DWORKIN, TAKING RIGHTS SERIOUSLY 171–77 (1978) (discussing goals-based, rights-based, and duty-based moral theories). In the jargon of moral philosophy, rights-based arguments and theories are given the technical name *deontological*. Deontological reasons are "reasons for an agent to do or avoid certain actions. They do not spring from the consequences of those actions, but rather from the claims of those with whom we interact to be treated by us in certain ways. One who believes in deontological values believes that no matter how good our ends are, we are not supposed to hurt people, or tell lies, or break promises in their pursuit." Christine M. Korsgaard, *The Reasons We Can Share: An Attack on the Distinction between Agent-Relative and Agent-Neutral Values*, SOC. PHIL. & POL'Y, Winter 1993, at 24, 41.

91. This necessarily oversimplified statement is not intended to deny that various other significant kinds of moral theories could be and have been formulated to address these issues. For discussions of the varieties and complexity of moral theories, see generally C. D. BROAD, FIVE TYPES OF ETHICAL THEORY (1930); CHARLES E. LARMORE, PATTERNS OF MORAL COMPLEXITY (1987); ALASDAIR MACINTYRE, A SHORT HISTORY OF ETHICS (1966).

92. The consequentialist argument is rarely advanced independently as a justification for the criminalization of drugs. Rather, it is usually presented as a reactive argument warning of the anticipated effects of changes in the current law, and when it is advanced, the argument takes the form of "legalization would be an 'unqualified national disaster' and would create many more addicts." Stephen Labaton, *Federal Judge Urges Legalization of Crack, Heroin and*

Other Drugs, N.Y. Times, Dec. 13, 1989, at A1. This is not surprising in light of the acknowledged dearth of quantitative data and cost-benefit studies that support policies and laws of the war on drugs. *See* James Ostrowski, *The Moral and Practical Case for Drug Legalization*, 18 Hofstra L. Rev. 607, 642 n.162 (1990).

93. Kurt Schmoke, mayor of Baltimore, summarizes the consequentialist argument in favor of decriminalizing drugs as follows: "Advocates of drug decriminalization do not base their position on a belief that people have an inherent right to use drugs. . . . Advocates simply view decriminalization as preferable to present policies. This view reflects the notion that decriminalization is a means to a much desired end: controlling the problem of drug abuse through the public health system, not the criminal justice system." Kurt L. Schmoke, *An Argument in Favor of Decriminalization*, 18 Hofstra L. Rev. 501, 506 n.25 (1990).

94. One of the most compelling and prolific advocates of drug decriminalization working within the consequentialist framework is Ethan Nadelmann. A representative sampling of his works includes: Ethan A. Nadelmann, *Beyond Drug Prohibition: Evaluating the Alternatives*, in Searching for Alternatives, *supra* note 87, at 241; Ethan A. Nadelmann, *The Case for Legalization*, 92 Pub. Interest 3 (Summer 1988); Ethan A. Nadelmann, *Drug Prohibition in the United States: Costs, Consequences, and Alternatives*, 245 Science 939 (1989); Ethan A. Nadelmann, *Should We Legalize Drugs?: Yes*, Am. Heritage, Feb.–Mar. 1993, at 42; Ethan A. Nadelmann, *Thinking Seriously About Alternatives to Drug Prohibition*, 121 Daedalus 85 (1992). For additional consequentialist arguments in favor of drug decriminalization based on economic and health considerations, see, *e.g.*, Milton Friedman, *The War We Are Losing*, in Searching For Alternatives, *supra* note 87; Mark A. R. Kleiman & Aaron J. Saiger, *Drug Legalization: The Importance of Asking the Right Question*, 18 Hofstra L. Rev. 527 (1990); Ostrowski, *supra* note 93; Kurt L. Schmoke, *Drugs: A Problem of Health and Economics*, in The Crisis in Drug Prohibition, 9 (David Boaz ed., 1990); Steven Wisotsky, *Exposing the War on Cocaine: The Futility and Destructiveness of Prohibition*, 1983 Wis. L. Rev. 1305.

95. *See* Immanuel Kant, Groundwork of the Metaphysic of Morals 89–90, 100–04 (H. J. Paton trans., 1964) (1785); *see also* Immanuel Kant, Critique of Practical Reason 90, 136 (Lewis White Beck trans., 1956) (1788).

96. *See generally* John Finnis, Natural Law and Natural Rights (1980); Leo Strauss, Natural Right and History (1953); Richard Tuck, Natural Rights Theories: Their Origin and Development (1979).

97. *See generally* John Rawls, A Theory of Justice (1971); John Rawls, *The Basic Liberties and Their Priority*, in Liberty, Equality, and Law 1 *passim* (Sterling M. McMurrin ed., 1987); John Rawls, *Justice as Fairness: Political not Metaphysical*, 14 Phil. & Pub. Aff. 223 *passim* (1985); John Rawls, *Kantian Constructivism in Moral Theory: The Dewey Lectures 1980*, 77 J. Phil. 515, 535, 554 *passim* (1980).

98. *See* Bruce A. Ackerman, Social Justice in the Liberal State (1980); David Gauthier, Morals By Agreement (1986); *see also* Ostrowski, *supra* note 92, at 627–31 (discussing the natural rights theory of Douglas Rasmussen and the neo-Kantian theory of Hans-Hermann Hoppe).

99. Identifying the various forms of arguments used in the debate surrounding the war on drugs serves both a descriptive and an explanatory purpose. It describes the sort of arguments that are available to a proponent of a particular position, and it explains why the debate has made such little progress in most quarters. The language of the consequentialist is distinctly different from that of the rights-based theorist, and at some point a breakdown in communications between the consequentialist and the rights-based theorist is inevitable even when both are on the same side of the issue. Furthermore, a conflict over fundamental principles in competing rights-based arguments often stalls communications. Thus, while one consequentialist may be able to persuade another to give up a position by using new or better data in her cost-benefit analysis, the debate between antagonistic rights-based theorists often never gets started because the commitment each side has to its respective principles necessarily precludes the pos-

sibility of even countenancing the other side's position. Therefore, in considering the various arguments advanced on these issues, it is important to distinguish not only between kinds of arguments but also between types of arguments that may be inherently irreconcilable within a particular category of argument.

100. *See* Sweet & Harris, *supra* note 1, at 1329–38 (discussing the economic and social statistics of prohibition).

101. STEVEN B. DUKE & ALBERT C. GROSS, AMERICA'S LONGEST WAR: RETHINKING OUR TRAGIC CRUSADE AGAINST DRUGS AND RIGHTS 160–199 (1993), DOUGLAS HUSAK, DRUGS AND RIGHTS, 145–207 (1992).

102. Ostrowski has identified the mistaken axiom of prohibition as follows:

> The fatal flaw in the policy of prohibition is that those who need to be protected most from drug use—hard-core users—are those who will not be deterred by laws against drugs. These individuals consider drug use to be one of their highest values in life. They will take great risks, pay high prices, and violate the law to achieve this value. The remainder of the population consists of moderate drug users and non-drug users. These are people who have developed the individual or social resources which allow them to avoid harmful legal drug use.

Ostrowski, *supra* note 92, at 674.

103. *See The Federal Drugstore*, NAT'L REV., Feb. 5, 1990, at 34, 37–38 (interview with Michael S. Gazzaniga). *See also* Steven Jonas, *Solving the Drug Problem: A Public Health Approach to the Reduction of the Use and Abuse of Both Legal and Illegal Recreational Drugs*, 18 HOFSTRA L. REV. 751, 785–86 (1990) (no substantial increase in use of marijuana in states that decriminalized it in the 1970s); Ostrowski, *supra* note 92, at 675 (after decriminalizing marijuana in the Netherlands, use declined); *Holland's Drug Policy: War by Other Means*, ECONOMIST, Feb. 10, 1990, at 50 (Dutch have abolished most drug-related crime and are reducing drug use).

104. *See* Sweet & Harris, *supra* note 1, at 1329–38.

105. The effectiveness of this campaign of fear is evidenced in the results of a *Washington Post/ABC* News poll from September 1989: "62 percent of the respondents were willing to give up 'a few' freedoms in order to curb drug use; 67 percent would allow police to stop cars at random to search for drugs; 52 percent would allow the police to search without court order the homes of people suspected of selling drugs, even if some homes were searched by mistake; 71 percent would make it against the law to show the use of illegal drugs in the movies." SZASZ, *supra* note 21 at 43.

In the face of this popular support, the courts and the government have actively curbed various fundamental constitutional rights in the name of the war on drugs. *See* DUKE & GROSS, *supra* note 101, at 122–45; Michael Z. Letwin, *Report from the Front Line: The Bennett Plan, Street-Level Drug Enforcement in New York City and the Legalization Debate*, 18 HOFSTRA L. REV. 795, 816–27 (1990); Steven Wisotsky, *Crackdown: The Emerging "Drug Exception" to the Bill of Rights*, 38 HASTINGS L.J. 889, 909 (1987) [hereinafter Wisotsky, *Crackdown*]; Steven Wisotsky, *A Society of Suspects: The War on Drugs and Civil Liberties*, POL'Y ANALYSIS, Oct. 2, 1992, at 1, 1–29 [hereinafter Wisotsky, *Society of Suspects*].

106. *See* Wisotsky, *Crackdown*, *supra* note 105, at 900–03; *see also* Wisotsky, *supra* note 95, at 1418–23 (examining constitutional limitations in the name of the war on drugs); Wisotsky, *Society of Suspects*, *supra* note 105, at 12–29 (updating review of the encroachment on constitutional rights in the name of the war on drugs); Steven Wisotsky, *Not Thinking Like a Lawyer: The Case of Drugs in the Courts*, 5 NOTRE DAME J.L. ETHICS & PUB. POL'Y 651, 653, 659–82 (1991) (analyzing the distinctly nonlawyerlike rhetoric employed by courts in drug cases and corresponding failure of the courts to advance "the cause of intelligent debate about drug policy").

See generally Stephen A. Saltzburg, *Another Victim of Illegal Narcotics: The Fourth Amendment*, 48 U. Pɪᴛᴛ. L. Rᴇᴠ. 1 *passim* (1986); Richard Wasserstrom, *The Incredible Shrinking Fourth Amendment*, 21 Aм. Cʀɪм. L. Rᴇᴠ. 257 *passim* (1983).

107. This was brought about through the passage of the Comprehensive Crime Control Act of 1984, 18 U.S.C. § 3142(e) (1997).

108. *See* 18 U.S.C. § 3143 (1997).

109. 18 U.S.C. § 1963(a)(3) (1997); 21 U.S.C. § 853(a) (1997).

110. *See* Baum, *supra* note 4, at 73.

111. *See id.*; Duke and Gross, *supra* note 101, at 123–28.

112. *See Illinois v. Gates*, 462 U.S. 213 (1983); *McCray v. Illinois*, 386 U.S. 300 (1967); *see also 60 Minutes* (CBS television broadcast, Mar. 28, 1993).

113. *See Oliver v. United States*, 466 U.S. 170 (1984).

114. *See California v. Ciraolo*, 476 U.S. 207 (1986).

115. *See Florida v. Riley*, 488 U.S. 445 (1989).

116. *See Maryland v. Garrison*, 480 U.S. 79 (1987); *Massachusetts v. Sheppard*, 468 U.S. 981 (1984); *United States v. Leony*, 468 U.S. 897 (1984); *see also* Wisotsky, *Crackdown*, *supra* note 164, at 897, 908.

117. Wisotsky, *Crackdown*, *supra* note 105, at 910–21 (discussing the numerous encroachments on Fourth Amendment rights in the name of the war on drugs); *see also supra* note 106.

118. *See, e.g., California v. Acevedo*, 111 S. Ct. 1982 (1991) (abandoning the former *Chadwick-Sanders* rule to expand the "automobile exception"); *Florida v. Bostick*, 111 S. Ct. 2382 (1991) (legitimizing practice of "working the buses" in holding that no "seizure" occurs for Fourth Amendment purposes so long as "a reasonable person would feel free to decline the officer's requests or otherwise terminate the encounter"; implicitly overruling prior test in which determination was based on whether the individual felt "free to leave"); *Arizona v. Fulminante*, 111 S. Ct. 1246 (1991) (despite a vast body of precedent to the contrary, a majority of the Court concluded that the admittedly coerced confession of a defendant ultimately sentenced to death was subject to "harmless error" analysis. Adding insult to injury, the Court made this radical departure in *dictum*); *Harmelin v. Michigan*, 111 S. Ct. 2680 (1991) (outside of capital punishment, the Eighth Amendment contains little or no proportionality requirement); *Payne v. Tennessee*, 111 S. Ct. 2597 (1991) ("victim impact" evidence is admissible at capital sentencing hearing; overruling prior precedent holding that such evidence was per se inadmissible at a capital sentencing hearing because it serves no purpose but to appeal to the sympathies and emotions of jurors).

119. 111 S. Ct. 1246 (1991).

120. *See, e.g., Hudson v. McMillan*, 112 S. Ct. 995, 1004 (1992) (Thomas, J., dissenting).

121. *See* Wisotsky, *Crackdown*, *supra* note 105, at 909.

122. While times change, the "war zone" rhetoric does not, and the disgrace of the governmental action of interning Japanese-Americans during World War II stands as a sharp warning against both the soundness of this rhetoric and the kinds of reactive measures it justifies the government to pursue. *See Korematsu v. United States*, 323 U.S. 214 (1944); David G. Savage, *House OKs Extra $400 Million to Internees*, L.A. Tɪᴍᴇs, Sept. 17, 1992, at A13.

123. *See supra* text accompanying notes 34–44.

124. *See supra* notes 14, 31, 66.

125. *See supra* notes 33–43 and accompanying text. Szasz's political and moral theories center on a commitment to the liberty and responsibility of the individual. He shares this commitment with Locke, Mill, and the Founders of the United States. *See* Lᴏᴄᴋᴇ, *supra* note 33, at 315, 330–51 (§§ 73, 95–126); Mɪʟʟ, *supra* note 34, at 102 ("[T]he strongest of all arguments against the interference of the public with purely personal conduct is that, when it does interfere, the odds are that it interferes wrongly and in the wrong place"); Jᴏʜɴ Sᴛᴜᴀʀᴛ Mɪʟʟ, Tʜᴇ Lᴏɢɪᴄ ᴏꜰ ᴛʜᴇ Mᴏʀᴀʟ Sᴄɪᴇɴᴄᴇs 35–60 (Open Court 1988) (1872) (discussing the laws of the mind, the

science of psychology, and "ethology" or the science of the formation of character); JAMES WIL-
SON, *Of the Natural Rights of Individuals*, in 2 THE WORKS OF JAMES WILSON 585 (J. D. Andrews
ed., 1896); Randy E. Barnett, *Reconceiving the Ninth Amendment*, 74 CORNELL L. REV. 1, 17–18
(1988) (discussing James Madison's view regarding natural rights).

126. Szasz, *Involuntary Psychiatry*, *supra* note 14, at 347.

127. The metaphysical theory of libertarianism asserts the reality of the freedom of the will
and derives from that assertion the necessary falsity of determinism. *See* C. D. Broad, *Deter-
minism, Indeterminism, and Libertarianism*, in FREE WILL AND DETERMINISM 135 *passim* (Bernard
Berofsky ed., 1966); C. D. Campbell, *Is "Freewill" a Pseudo-Problem?*, in FREE WILL AND DETER-
MINISM, *supra*, at 112 *passim*; John Stuart Mill, *The Freedom of the Will*, in FREE WILL AND DETER-
MINISM, *supra*, at 159 *passim*; Jean Paul Sartre, *Being and Doing: Freedom*, in FREE WILL AND DE-
TERMINISM, *supra*, at 174 *passim*; David Wiggins, *Towards a Reasonable Libertarianism*, in ESSAYS
ON FREEDOM OF ACTION 31 *passim* (Ted Honderich ed., 1973).

For critical discussions of the problem raised by determinism for free will and moral re-
sponsibility, see generally BERNARD BEROFSKY, DETERMINISM (1971); PETER VAN INWAGON, AN ESSAY
ON FREE WILL (1983); A. J. Ayer, *Freedom and Necessity*, in FREE WILL, *supra* at 15 *passim*; Wilfrid
Sellars, *Fatalism and Determinism*, in FREEDOM AND DETERMINISM 141 *passim* (Keith Lehrer ed.,
reprint ed. 1976); Peter van Inwagon, *The Incompatibility of Responsibility and Determinism*, in
MORAL RESPONSIBILITY 241 *passim* (John Martin Fischer ed., 1986). *But see* Phillipa Foot, *Free
Will as Involving Determinism*, in FREE WILL AND DETERMINISM, *supra*, at 95 *passim* (statement of
"reconciliationist" position that free will entails determinism); R. E. Hobart, *Free Will as Involving Determination and Inconceivable without It*, in FREE WILL AND DETERMINISM, *supra*, at 63 *passim*
(same).

128. That is, all mental illnesses are diagnosed without there being any physiological component to the illness such as physical damage to the brain. *See* SZASZ, MYTH OF MENTAL ILL-
NESS, *supra* note 14, at 34–37, 45–47.

129. *See supra* note 127.

130. Therefore, although Szasz denies the thesis of metaphysical determinism he goes even
further in claiming that no matter what one does to oneself, one remains a morally responsible
agent.

131. Szasz's axiomatic proposition is that "bad habits are not diseases." SZASZ, *supra note* 21,
at 91. *Accord* Thomas S. Szasz, *Bad Habits Are Not Diseases*, LANCET, July 8, 1972, at 83–84.

132. SZASZ, *supra* note 21, at 162.

133. It has been noted that while Szasz has been popular among civil rights advocates on
some issues, "[n]ot all civil rights lawyers appreciated the conservative implications of Szasz's
libertarianism. For example, Szasz would virtually abolish the insanity defense on the ground
that individuals should be held absolutely responsible for their criminal acts, regardless of their
mental conditions." Ledwith, *supra* note 15, at 1372 n.38.

134. This is simply to acknowledge the distinctions between *rights* and *goods*: one has a right
to do many things whose consequences are not necessarily a good for that person. *See generally*
RICHARD B. BRANDT, A THEORY OF THE GOOD AND THE RIGHT (reprinted 1984).

135. SZASZ, *supra* note 59, at 154.

136. 381 U.S. 479 (1965).

137. 410 U.S. 113 (1973); Szasz follows Locke in holding that each individual's body is his
own property and that the right of self-ownership (the right to do with one's body whatever one
will) precedes all political rights. SZASZ, *supra* note 21, at 4–5, 8–9.

138. *See, e.g., Crane v. Campbell*, 245 U.S. 304 (1917) (no private property right in intoxicants such as alcohol).

139. *See supra* note 138; *infra* note 181.

140. This being the case, we ultimately focus on the Ninth Amendment as a legitimate and
open avenue within those parameters that merits serious consideration.

141. *See, e.g., Bowers v. Hardwick,* 478 U.S. 186 (1986) (the Constitution does not confer a fundamental right upon homosexuals to engage in sodomy); Jed Rubenfeld, *The Right of Privacy,* 102 Harv. L. Rev. 737, 747-52 (1989). For a comprehensive discussion of the "harm principle," see 1 Joel Feinberg, The Moral Limits of the Criminal Law: Harm to Others 45-51 (1984); 3 Joel Feinberg, The Moral Limits of the Criminal Law: Harm to Self 21-23 (1986).

142. One of the earliest and best known statements of the right to privacy is that of Justice Louis Brandeis, in *Olmstead v. United States,* 277 U.S. 438 (1928): it is "the right to be let alone—the most comprehensive of rights and the right most valued by civilized men." *Id.* at 478 (Brandeis, J., dissenting). For Brandeis's seminal explication of the right to privacy, *see* Samuel D. Warren & Louis Brandeis, *The Right to Privacy,* 4 Harv. L. Rev. 193 (1890). *See also* Laurence H. Tribe, Abortion: The Clash of Absolutes 92-99 (paper ed. 1992) (reviewing the history of the right to privacy).

While the right to privacy is most closely associated with the Ninth Amendment, a variety of unenumerated rights have been recognized by the courts over the years. These have included the following: the right to retain American citizenship, despite criminal activities, *Afroyim v. Rusk,* 387 U.S. 253 (1967); *Trop v. Dulles,* 356 U.S. 86 (1958); the right to receive equal protection from the states and the federal government, *Mapp v. Ohio,* 367 U.S. 643 (1961); *Bolling v. Sharpe,* 347 U.S. 497 (1954); the right to vote, subject only to reasonable restrictions to prevent fraud and unequal weighting of ballots, *Swann v. Adams,* 385 U.S. 440 (1967); *Harper v. Virginia Bd. of Elections,* 383 U.S. 663 (1966); *Reynolds v. Sims,* 377 U.S. 533 (1964); *Baker v. Carr,* 369 U.S. 186 (1962); the right to a presumption of innocence, *Jackson v. Virginia,* 443 U.S. 307 (1979); *In re Winship,* 397 U.S. 358 (1970); *Speiser v. Randall,* 357 U.S. 513 (1958); *Tot v. United States,* 319 U.S. 463 (1943); the right to use the federal courts and other governmental institutions and to encourage others to use these processes to protect their interests, *N.A.A.C.P. v. Button,* 371 U.S. 415 (1963); *In re Slaughter-House Cases,* 83 U.S. (16 Wall.) 36 (1873); the right to associate with others, *N.A.A.C.P. v. Alabama,* 357 U.S. 449 (1958); *De Jonge v. Oregon,* 299 U.S. 353 (1937); the right to travel within the United States, *Shapiro v. Thompson,* 394 U.S. 618 (1969); *Edwards v. California,* 314 U.S. 160 (1941); *Crandall v. Nevada,* 73 U.S. (6 Wall.) 35 (1867); the right to marry or not marry, *Zablocki v. Redhail,* 434 U.S. 374 (1978); *Loving v. Virginia,* 388 U.S. 1 (1967); the right to education, *Griffin v. County Sch. Bd.,* 377 U.S. 218 (1964); *Brown v. Board of Educ.,* 347 U.S. 483 (1954); *Bolling,* 347 U.S. at 497; the right to educate one's children so long as minimum state standards are met, *Pierce v. Society of Sisters,* 268 U.S. 510 (1925); *Meyer v. Nebraska,* 262 U.S. 390 (1923); the right to choose and pursue a profession, *Gibson v. Berryhill,* 411 U.S. 564 (1973); *Meyer,* 262 U.S. at 390; *Allgeyer v. Louisiana,* 165 U.S. 578 (1897); and the right to attend and report on criminal trials, *Richmond Newspapers, Inc. v. Virginia,* 448 U.S. 555 (1980). *See* Randy E. Barnett, *Forward: The Ninth Amendment and Constitutional Legitimacy,* 64 Chi.-Kent L. Rev. 37, 58 (1988) (citing W. Murphy et al., American Constitutional Interpretation 1083-84 (1986)); Barnett, *supra* note 125, at 32 n.106 (same); Raoul Berger, *The Ninth Amendment,* 66 Cornell L. Rev. 1, 1-2 (1980).

143. *Griswold,* 381 U.S. at 485 (1965).

144. "In sophisticated legal circles, mentioning the Ninth Amendment is a surefire way to get a laugh. ('What are you planning to rely on to support that argument, Lester, the Ninth Amendment?')." John Hart Ely, Democracy and Distrust 34 (1980).

145. In the opinion of the Court in *Griswold v. Connecticut,* 381 U.S. 479 (1965), Justice Douglas identifies penumbras emanating from the First, Third, Fourth, Fifth, and Ninth Amendments, which create specific zones of privacy and which, when taken together, create a zone of privacy surrounding a couple's decision to use contraceptives. *Id.* at 484-85.

146. Prior to *Griswold,* the Supreme Court addressed the Ninth Amendment in only seven cases, and in those, the Court's treatment was superficial at most. *See* Russell L. Caplan, *The History and Meaning of the Ninth Amendment,* 69 Va. L. Rev. 223, 224 n.5 (1983); Calvin R. Massey, *Federalism and Fundamental Rights: The Ninth Amendment,* 38 Hastings L.J. 305, 305 n.1

(1987); Eugene M. Van Loan, III, *Natural Rights and the Ninth Amendment*, 48 B.U. L. REV. 1, 1 n.3 (1968).

However, in the years since *Griswold*, when the Supreme court turned its attention to the Ninth Amendment, the Court has interpreted the amendment "in a manner that denies it any role in the constitutional structure." Barnett, *supra* note 125, at 2. Barnett notes that the "singular exception" to his conclusory assertion is *Richmond Newspapers, Inc. v. Virginia*, 448 U.S. 555, 579 n.15 (1980), in which the "plurality based its opinion, in part, on the Ninth Amendment." Barnett, *supra* note 125, at 2 n.6.

147. 381 U.S. 479, 492 (1965) (Goldberg, J., concurring). For a representative sampling of the literature generated by *Griswold*, see Caplan, *supra* note 146, at 225 n.12.

148. Barnett, *supra* note 125, at 2. Even in *Griswold*, after Justice Goldberg gives life to the Ninth Amendment as an amendment that must have "effect," 381 U.S. at 490-91 (quoting Chief Justice Marshall in *Marbury v. Madison*, 5 U.S. (1 Cranch) 137, 174 (1803)), he virtually snuffs out that life by denying that the amendment can be applied against the states or that it "constitutes an independent source of rights protected from infringement by either the States or the Federal Government," *id.* at 492.

The one exception to this proposition regarding the Court's treatment of the Ninth Amendment is *Richmond Newspapers, Inc. v. Virginia*, 448 U.S. 555 (1980), in which a plurality of the Court relied, in part, on the Ninth Amendment to justify the protection of the right to attend and report on criminal trials. *See supra* note 146.

149. For a representative sampling of the literature on the Ninth Amendment, *see* THE RIGHTS RETAINED BY THE PEOPLE: THE HISTORY AND MEANING OF THE NINTH AMENDMENT 399-403 (Randy E. Barnett ed., 1989); Van Loan, *supra* note 146, at 2 n.11 (citing articles, notes and comments published in the year following the Supreme Court's decision in *Griswold*).

150. We consider the Ninth Amendment to be a sleeping giant in contrast to Robert Bork's disdain for it as an "inkblot," *see infra* note 157, and to the view of it as "that old constitutional jester" whose meaning is "almost unfathomable" and eluded Justice Jackson as an impenetrable "mystery," *see* Caplan, *supra* note 146, at 223 (reviewing disparaging comments directed toward the amendment); *supra* note 144.

151. U.S. CONST. amend. IX.

152. This is the claim that the Ninth Amendment identifies an area of "no-power," an area in which the federal government and judiciary have no power to act. *See* Berger, *supra* note 142, at 9, 23-24; Leslie W. Dunbar, *James Madison and the Ninth Amendment*, 42 VA. L. REV. 627, 641 (1956); Geoffrey G. Slaughter, Note, *The Ninth Amendment's Role in the Evolution of Fundamental Rights Jurisprudence*, 64 IND. L.J. 97, 104 (1988); *see also* Norman Redlich, *Are There "Certain Rights . . . Retained by the People"?*, 37 N.Y.U. L. REV. 787, 807 (1962). In fact, the no-power argument is one of no fewer than four distinct arguments that reject the substantive value of the Ninth Amendment. *See* Jordon J. Paust, *Human Rights and the Ninth Amendment: A New Form of Guarantee*, 60 CORNELL L. REV. 231, 238 (1975) (distinguishing and analyzing what are critically characterized as misguided arguments that confuse the role of the Ninth Amendment for the constitutional protection of human values and liberties). Andrzej Rapaczynski and Michael McConnell have formulated more compelling arguments that the unenumerated retained rights implicated by the Ninth Amendment may not be justiciable. *See* Michael W. McConnell, *A Moral Realist Defense of Constitutional Democracy*, 64 CHI.-KENT L. REV. 89 *passim* (1988); Andrzej Rapaczynski, *The Ninth Amendment and the Unwritten Constitution: The Problems of Constitutional Interpretation*, 64 CHI.-KENT L. REV. 177 *passim* (1988). *But see* Lawrence G. Sager, *You Can Raise the First, Hide Behind the Fourth, and Plead the Fifth. But What on Earth Can You Do with the Ninth Amendment?*, 64 CHI.-KENT L. REV. 239 *passim* (1988) (critically assessing the strengths and weaknesses of McConnell and Rapaczynski's arguments).

153. *See generally* BENNETT B. PATTERSON, THE FORGOTTEN NINTH AMENDMENT 51-56 (1955); LAURENCE H. TRIBE, AMERICAN CONSTITUTIONAL LAW § 11-3, at 774-75 (2d ed. 1988); Sotirios

A. Barber, *The Ninth Amendment: Inkblot or Another Hard Nut to Crack?*, 64 Chi.-Kent L. Rev. 67 *passim* (1988); Barnett, *supra* note 125, at 1 *passim*; Massey, *supra* note 146, at 305 *passim*; Lawrence E. Mitchell, *The Ninth Amendment and the "Jurisprudence of Original Intention*," 74 Geo. L.J. 1719, 1729-30 (1986); Redlich, *supra* note 152, at 810-12; Van Loan, *supra* note 146, at 1 & *passim*.

154. For discussions of the historical aspects of the adoption of the Ninth Amendment, *see* Ely, *supra* note 144, at 34-38; Barnett, *supra* note 125, at 9-11; Berger, *supra* note 142, at 3-9; Caplan, *supra* note 146, at 223 *passim*; Dunbar, *supra* note 152, at 627 *passim*; Calvin R. Massey, *Antifederalism and the Ninth Amendment*, 64 Chi.-Kent L. Rev. 987 *passim* (1988); Massey, *supra* note 146, at 307-11; Mitchell, *supra* note 153, at 1736-41; Van Loan, *supra* note 146, at 3-23.

155. Calvin Massey uses this term to describe positions taken by Charles Black, John Ely, Laurence Tribe, and Louis Henkin, among others. *See* Massey, *supra* note 146, at 312 n.33.

156. For informative discussions of these two approaches to statutory interpretation and judicial review, *see* James L. Oakes, *The Proper Role of the Federal Courts in Enforcing the Bill of Rights*, 54 N.Y.U. L. Rev. 911 (1979); *see also* R. George Wright, *Two Models of Constitutional Adjudication*, 40 Am. U. L. Rev. 1357 *passim* (1991) (characterizing and analyzing the two competing kinds of approaches to judicial review as "foundationalism" and "coherentism"); David B. Anders, Note, *Justices Harlan and Black Revisited: The Emerging Dispute between Justice O'Connor and Justice Scalia over Unenumerated Fundamental Rights*, 61 Fordham L. Rev. 895 *passim* (1993) (analyzing the positions of Justices Scalia and O'Connor against the background of the approaches characterized as "originalism" and "fundamental rights theory").

157. This position is championed by Robert Bork. In his view, Madison and company were attempting to do something positive by alluding to unenumerated rights but botched the attempt by drafting the amendment so poorly that one can do nothing more with it than ignore it as if it were an unsightly "inkblot" on the parchment. *See The Bork Disinformers*, Wall St. J., Oct. 5, 1987, at 22; *see also* Robert H. Bork, The Tempting of America 183-85 (1990) (criticizing the view attributed to Ely that the Ninth Amendment is "a warrant to judges to create constitutional rights not mentioned in the Constitution"); Office of Legal Policy, Wrong Turns on the Road to Judicial Activism: The Ninth Amendment and Privileges or Immunities Clause 8-27 (1987) (report to then-Attorney General Edwin Meese III, concluding the Ninth Amendment to be a rule of construction and not the source of any rights that would trump granted federal or state powers); Antonin Scalia, *Originalism: The Lesser Evil*, 57 U. Cin. L. Rev. 849, 854-62 (assessing the defects of "nonoriginalism" and "originalism," while arguing for the latter).

For devastating critiques of Bork's position qua paradigm of the "New Right constitutionalism," the incoherence of this piecemeal approach to the Constitution, and the disingenuousness of the constitutional revisionism that masquerades as originalism, *see* Barber, *supra* note 191; Randy E. Barnett, *A Ninth Amendment for Today's Constitution*, 26 Val. U. L. Rev. 419 *passim* (1991); Ronald Dworkin, *The Concept of Unenumerated Rights*, 59 U. Chi. L. Rev. 381, 385-391 (1992); Sanford Levinson, *Constitutional Rhetoric and the Ninth Amendment*, 64 Chi.-Kent L. Rev. 131 *passim* (1988); Ronald Dworkin, Book Review, *Bork's Jurisprudence*, 57 U. Chi. L. Rev. 657, 663-74 (1990); Stephen Macedo, Book Review, *Originalism and the Inescapability of Politics*, 84 Nw. U. L. Rev. 1203 *passim* (1990).

158. *See* Van Loan, *supra* note 146, at 13-15; Mark A. Koral, Comment, *Ninth Amendment Vindication of Unenumerated Fundamental Rights*, 42 Temp. L.Q. 46, 50-53 (1968).

159. Natural law is "the longstanding position in moral and legal theory that human law is in some sense derived from moral norms that are universally valid and discoverable by reasoning about human nature or true human goods." Kent Greenawalt, Conflicts of Law and Morality 161 (1987); *see also* H. L. A. Hart, The Concept of Law 152 (1961) (fundamental claim of natural law theory is that "there are certain principles of true morality or justice, discoverable by human reason without the aid of revelation even though they have a divine ori-

gin"). The most sophisticated and compelling version of natural law theory that has been formulated in recent years is that of John Finnis. Finnis notes that "[t]he principal concern of a theory of natural law is to explore the requirements of practical reasonableness in relation to the good of human beings who, because they live in community with one another, are confronted with problems of justice and rights, of authority, law, and obligation." FINNIS, *supra* note 96, at 351. While Finnis counts "religion" as a universally discoverable "basic good," he explains that "religion" reduces to the recognition and acceptance, by believer and nonbeliever alike, of the responsibility to choose what one is to be and to do. *Id.* at 90. This gloss suggests that the concepts of moral self-determination and self-realization most accurately approach Finnis's intended meaning of the term *religion* and serves to minimize the theological baggage usually associated with the theory.

"Though the framers distinguished between natural law and positive law, they were anything but meticulous in maintaining that distinction when debating the necessity of a Bill of Rights." Massey, *supra* note 146, at 314 n.47.

For a more thorough discussion of these sources of unenumerated fundamental rights, *see* Sweet & Harris, *supra* note 1, at 1356-64.

160. *See* Sweet & Harris, *supra* note 1, at 1358-61.

161. Van Loan, *supra* note 146, at 39 (quoting *Davidson v. New Orleans*, 96 U.S. 97, 104 (1877)).

162. *See* Sweet & Harris, *supra* note 1, at 1357.

163. *See* Koral, *supra* note 158, at 54 (footnote omitted). Koral notes that the manner in which the right is characterized may be determinative of whether it is protected by an express constitutional right: "The more narrowly the right is characterized, the more difficult it will be to find an express constitutional provision that protects it. If the right is characterized broadly enough, there will be an express constitutional provision under which it falls." *Id.* at 54 n.53; *see also Thornhill v. Alabama*, 310 U.S. 88 (1940). This discussion of Ninth Amendment methodology follows the test to determine whether a right is protected by the Ninth Amendment proposed by Koral, *see* Koral, *supra* note 158, at 54-55, and employs the factors identified by Massey, which a court should consider in recognizing an unenumerated natural right, *see* Massey, *supra* note 146, at 330-31.

164. *Griswold v. Connecticut*, 381 U.S. 479, 493 (1965) (citations and internal quotations omitted).

165. *Id.* (quoting *Snyder v. Massachusetts*, 291 U.S. 97, 105 (1934)).

166. This requirement addresses Ely's concern about the open-textured nature of the Ninth Amendment and his rejection of a purely extra-textual appeal to notions of natural law. *See* ELY, *supra* note 144, at 12 (content of the Ninth Amendment and other open-ended clauses "should be derived from the general themes of the entire constitutional document and not from some source entirely beyond its four corners"); *see also* Douglas Laycock, *Taking Constitutions Seriously: A Theory of Judicial Review*, 59 TEX. L. REV. 343, 366-67 (1981) (reviewing ELY, *supra* note 144) (unenumerated rights are derived only from the penumbras and emanations of the text); Levinson, *supra* note 157, at 149-50 (discussing Ely's and Laycock's concerns).

167. Massey, *supra* note 146, at 331. Of course, the Court has the discretion to break with the past and do more than react to social changes. As Van Loan notes, in recognizing Ninth Amendment rights the Court can act "as a moral vanguard for the inculcation of new ideas and new values in certain segments of the populace." Van Loan, *supra* note 146, at 37. This simply highlights the fact that these factors are neither sufficient nor necessary in determining the fundamentality of an asserted right.

168. Massey, *supra* note 146, at 331 (emphasis added).

169. *Id.* at 331 n.136. For a thorough discussion of these axioms and basic right-defining values, *see, e.g.*, FINNIS, *supra* note 96, at 63-75, 81-97.

170. As Redlich has pointed out, "[t]he Ninth and Tenth Amendments, unlike other portions of the Bill of Rights, should be viewed as dealing not with absolute rights but generally with preferred rights, where the balancing of interests is appropriate." Redlich, *supra* note 152, at 812.

171. *See Simon & Schuster, Inc. v. Members of New York State Crime Victims Bd.*, 112 S. Ct. 501, 514 (1991) (Kennedy, J., concurring); *United States v. O'Brien*, 391 U.S. 367, 377 (1968); *Zemel v. Rusk*, 381 U.S. 1 (1965); *Loper v. New York City Police Dep't.* 802 F. Supp. 1029 (S.D.N.Y. 1992), *aff'd*, 999 F.2d 699 (2d Cir. 1993); *Young v. New York City Transit Auth.*, 903 F.2d 146, 157 (2d Cir.), *cert. denied*, 498 U.S. 984 (1990).

172. *See* Barnett, *supra* note 125, at 34–37.

173. *Id.* at 35.

174. *See id.* at 36–37.

175. We view this open texture as a continuing advantage built into the Ninth Amendment and not something that should be eliminated through an attempt to identify, once and for all, the various unenumerated rights it may imply, as Ely suggests. *See* ELY, *supra* note 144, at 38–41; *see also Adamson v. California*, 332 U.S. 46, 69 (1947) (Black, J., dissenting) (objecting to the power of the natural law to periodically expand and contract constitutional standards, enabling the Court to conform them to its conception of what constitutes "civilized decency" and "fundamental liberty and justice").

176. The term *right to self-determination* is used below in a technical sense to refer to a general right to determine for oneself what to put into and do with one's body. An aspect of this right is what Szasz refers to as the right to drugs, that is, the right to choose whether to take drugs internally, what drugs to take, and in what manner to take them (be it by ingestion, inhalation, or injection). *See* SZASZ, *Medicine and the State*, *supra* note 59, at 154 ("I don't see how anyone can take seriously the idea of personal self-determination and responsibility and not insist on his right to take anything he wants to take"). That is, it is a right to control one's own level and state of consciousness, as well as the physical condition of one's body. Less controversially, an aspect of this right to self-determination is the right to choose what kind and how much food to eat or whether to eat at all. *Cf.* TRIBE, *supra* note 142, at 87, 131 (discussing a woman's right to abortion in terms of the fundamental right to liberty, which entails the concepts of dignity and privacy, as an alternative to the right of privacy); Dworkin, *Unenumerated Rights*, *supra* note 157, at 415 ("A state may not curtail liberty, in order to protect an intrinsic value, . . . when the decision has very great and disparate impact on the person whose decision is displaced.").

177. As we have argued elsewhere, even in the absence of federal decriminalization by legislation, state court determinations finding a right to ingest mind-altering substances under their own state constitutions might well be appropriately protected by the Ninth Amendment despite the claims of the Supremacy Clause. *See* Sweet & Harris, *supra* note 1, at 1358–61.

178. For a discussion of the significance of the manner in which the right is phrased, *see supra* note 163.

179. While holding that the private possession of marijuana by adults at home for their personal use *is* constitutionally protected, the Supreme Court of Alaska acknowledged the Massachusetts Supreme Judicial Court's decision in *Commonwealth v. Leis*, 243 N.W.2d 898 (Mass. 1969), in holding that there is "no constitutional right to smoke marijuana, that smoking marijuana [is] not fundamental to the American scheme of justice or necessary to a regime of ordered liberty, and that marijuana [is] not locatable in any 'zone of privacy.'" *Ravin v. State*, 537 P.2d 494, 502 (Alaska 1975); *see also National Org. for Reform of Marijuana Laws v. Bell*, 488 F. Supp. 123, 133 (D.D.C. 1980) ("Private possession of marijuana, not being what Justice Stewart called an 'established constitutional right,' cannot be deemed 'fundamental.'").

180. *See Wolkind v. Selph*, 495 F. Supp. 507, 510 (E.D. Va. 1980), *aff'd mem.*, 649 F.2d 865 (4th Cir. 1981) (classification of cocaine as a Schedule II drug satisfies rational basis test because

private possession of cocaine is not a fundamental constitutional right); *see also United States* v. *Solow*, 574 F.2d 1318, 1319–20 (5th Cir. 1978); *United States* v. *Marshall*, 532 F.2d 1279, 1287–88 (9th Cir. 1976); *State* v. *Erickson*, 574 P.2d 1, 12 (Alaska 1978).

181. *See Crane* v. *Campbell*, 245 U.S. 304, 308 (1917) (Supreme Court has refused to find any right of private possession of intoxicants such as alcohol).

182. *See supra* note 163.

183. *See supra* note 176.

184. *See Ravin* v. *State*, 537 P.2d 494 (Alaska 1975) (recognizing state constitutional right to possess and smoke marijuana at home). *See also Griswold* v. *Connecticut*, 381 U.S. 479, 484–85 (1965) (reviewing the various cases addressing the penumbral rights of "privacy and repose" in support of claim that "the right of privacy . . . is a legitimate one"); *Boyd* v. *United States*, 116 U.S. 616, 630 (1886) (Fourth and Fifth Amendments described as protection against all governmental invasions "of the sanctity of a man's home and the privacies of life").

185. *See* THE DECLARATION OF INDEPENDENCE para. 1 (U.S. 1776) (penumbral value of the Bill of Rights implicated in the fundamental right to liberty enunciated in the Declaration of Independence).

186. The right of recreation is implied in the concepts of liberty and happiness set forth in the Declaration of Independence. In *Olff* v. *East Side Union High Sch. Dist.*, 404 U.S. 1042 (1972), Justice Douglas identifies recreation as a fundamental right implied in the concept of "liberty":

> The word "liberty" is not defined in the Constitution. But, as we held in *Griswold* v. *Connecticut*, it includes at least the fundamental rights "retained by the people" under the Ninth Amendment. One's hair style, like one's taste for food, or one's liking for certain kinds of music, art, reading, *recreation*, is certainly fundamental in our constitutional scheme—a scheme designed to keep government off the backs of people.

Olff, 404 U.S. at 1044 (Douglas, J., dissenting from denial of *certiorari*) (footnote and citations omitted, emphasis added). *See* HUSAK, *supra* note 101.

187. For a compelling discussion of the reasons for accepting Justice Goldberg's analysis of the right to marital privacy derived from the Ninth Amendment instead of either Justice Douglas's reliance only on the penumbras and emanations of the various amendments or Justice Harlan's reliance on the due process clause of the Fourteenth Amendment, see Sanford Levinson, *Constitutional Rhetoric and the Ninth Amendment*, 64 CHI.-KENT L. REV. 131, 135–43 (1988).

188. *See Griswold*, 381 U.S. at 498 (Goldberg, J., concurring).

189. *Id.*

190. *See Eisenstadt* v. *Baird*, 405 U.S. 438, 443 (1972) (affirming First Circuit's finding that the statutory goal of the anticontraception laws at issue was to limit contraception and nonprocreational sexual relations); David A. J. Richards, *Constitutional Legitimacy and Constitutional Privacy*, 61 N.Y.U. L. REV. 800, 847 (1986); *see also id.* at 836 & nn.217, 218 (discussing the views of Augustine and Thomas Aquinas in which they consider nonprocreational sexual relations as constituting murder, thereby justifying the Church's ban on contraceptives).

191. While this right is limited in *Griswold* to the marital relationship, it could be expanded to extramarital relationships under the penumbra of the First Amendment right of association.

192. This analysis also suggests an argument for the recognition of a right to recreation in *Griswold*, that is, the right to engage in the intimate *recreational* activity of nonprocreational sexual relations. Tribe makes a similar point when he suggests that "[w]hat is really protected as a fundamental right in the contraceptive cases is the right to engage in sexual intercourse without having a child." TRIBE, *supra* note 142, at 94.

193. *In National Org. for Reform of Marijuana Laws* v. *Bell*, 488 F. Supp. 123 (D.D.C. 1980),

the court refused to find a constitutional right of privacy to possess marijuana and distinguished *Griswold's* right to privacy from the asserted right of privacy to possess marijuana in one's home on the ground that "[t]he act of smoking does not involve the important values inherent in questions concerning marriage, procreation, or child rearing. Moreover, its use predominantly as a 'recreational drug' undercuts any argument that its use is as important as, e.g., use of contraceptives." *National Org. for Reform*, 488 F. Supp. at 133 (footnote and citation omitted). In its analysis the court not only dismisses the value of "recreational" activity but actually counts the recreational aspect of the activity against the significance of the activity. In doing so, however, the court necessarily fails to grasp both the recreational aspect of nonprocreational sexual relations implicitly recognized in *Griswold* and the significance of the fundamental right to recreation that individuals have in their pursuit of life, liberty, and happiness.

194. For a detailed account of the history of the war on drugs, *see* Musto, *supra* note 83; Musto, *supra* note 83.

195. For a discussion of negative and positive liberty and the difference between them, *see* Berlin, *supra* note 39.

196. Szasz quotes Thomas Jefferson's reference to the significance of bodily self-ownership as a political issue: "[I]n France the emetic was once forbidden as a medicine, the potato as an article of food. . . . Was the government to prescribe to us our medicine and diet, our bodies would be in such keeping as our souls are now." Szasz, *supra* note 21, at 5. The federal government made its first incursion into the drug market with the passage of the Food and Drugs Act of 1906. Food and Drugs Act, Pub. L. No. 59-384, 34 Stat. 768 (1906). The asserted purpose of this act was to control the quality and labeling of food and drugs.

197. Harrison Narcotic Act, Pub. L. No. 63-223, 38 Stat. 785 (1914).

198. Szasz, *supra* note 21, at 41, 52.

199. *Griswold v. Connecticut*, 381 U.S. 479, 498 (1965) (Goldberg, J., concurring).

200. *See* Massey, *supra* note 146, at 331.

201. *See supra* notes 34-39.

202. William Galston has described the liberal society as being characterized by two key features: "individualism and diversity. To individual corresponds the liberal virtue of independence—the disposition to care for, and take responsibility for, oneself and to avoid becoming needlessly dependent on others." William A. Galston, Liberal Purposes: Goods, Virtues and Diversity in the Liberal State 222 (1991). For discussions of contemporary liberalism and versions of liberal theory, *see, e.g.*, Ackerman *supra* note 98; Richard Flathman, Toward a Liberalism (1989); Gauthier, *supra* note 98; Larmore, *supra* note 91; Stephen Macedo, Liberal Virtues: Citizenship, Virtue, and Community in Liberal Constitutionalism (1990); Rawls, *supra* note 97; Joseph Raz, The Morality of Freedom (1986); Edward A. Harris, Note, *From Social Contract to Hypothetical Agreement: Consent and the Obligation to Obey the Law*, 92 Colum. L. Rev. 651 *passim* (1992); Harris, *supra* note 88, at 919 *passim*.

For criticisms of liberalism and the priority it places on individualism, *see, e.g.*, John Dunn, Rethinking Modern Political Theory: Essays 1979-83 (1985); Alasdair MacIntyre, After Virtue: A Study in Moral Theory (1981); Alasdair MacIntyre, Whose Justice? Which Rationality? (1988); C. B. Macpherson, The Political Theory of Possessive Individualism: Hobbes to Locke (1962); Carole Pateman, The Problem of Political Obligation: A Critique of Liberal Theory (1979); Michael J. Sandel, Liberalism and the Limits of Justice (1982); Roberto M. Unger, Knowledge and Politics (1975); Robert Paul Wolff, The Poverty of Liberalism (1968).

203. *See* Husak, *supra* note 101, at 100-30; Duke and Gross, *supra* note 101, at 146-59; *see also* 1 Feinberg, *supra* note 141, at 45-51 (discussing the harm principle); 3 Feinberg, *supra* note 141, at 21-23 (same).

204. Of course, this claim is tempered by the recognition of the physiological reality of addiction as it is defined by the current state of scientific knowledge, and it necessarily will change as our scientific knowledge advances.

205. *See* HUSAK, *supra* note 101, at 124.

206. *See supra* note 179.

207. *See* FINNIS, *supra* note 96, at 86–87 (discussing the basic values of self-determination and recreation). Again, the right to self-determination qua the right to drugs is intimately related to the right to recreation.

208. *See id.* at 86–90; *see also id.* at 139–44 (playing with others and friendship). Note that natural law theory does not prioritize one basic good over another; they are co-equal. *See id.* at 92 (each basic value is "equally self-evidently a form of good" and when focused on, each can be regarded as the most important). Furthermore, the identification of co-equal basic goods must be distinguished from the identification of the right, that is, the right qua what one ought to do. *See generally* BRANDT, *supra* note 134. A theory of the right tells the individual how to prioritize across and within kinds of goods. Simply to recognize recreation as a good is to leave open the question about the specific forms of recreation that an individual ought and ought not to undertake. Therefore, to say that recreational drug use is a basic good is not to condone that use as a preferred form of recreation. Rather, it is to acknowledge the right of the individual to choose it from among the various recreational activities with which he is presented. In fact, we strongly assert that using drugs recreationally is not a preferred form of recreation and suggest that "natural" alternatives to drug-induced highs are preferable. *See* ANDREW WEIL & WINIFRED ROSEN, FROM CHOCOLATE TO MORPHINE: EVERYTHING YOU NEED TO KNOW ABOUT MIND-ALTERING DRUGS 174–77 (rev. ed. 1993) (distinguishing between being drugged and being "high," and discussing alternative sources for highs).

209. In discussing the scope of the government's legitimate power to limit the right to drugs, Szasz considers the government's right to regulate the driving of cars because a driver's "behavior may be a threat to the safety of the public." SZASZ, *supra* note 21, at 162. Thus Szasz advocates the continued prohibition of drug use and random drug testing for persons employed in certain occupations, for example, airline pilots, and the continued prohibition for minors. *Id.*; *see supra* note 27.

Because the right to self-determination is a fundamental right, any governmental action that encroaches upon it must be justified by a "substantial" state interest and be tailored in the narrowest manner possible. *See United States* v. *O'Brien*, 391 U.S. 367, 377 (1968); *Young* v. *New York City Transit Auth.*, 903 F.2d 146, 157 (2d Cir.), *cert. denied*, 498 U.S. 984 (1990). Like governmental action encroaching on the individual's First Amendment right to free expression, governmental action encroaching on the right to self-determination faces a scale that is tipped heavily against it before the balancing analysis even begins. *See Simon & Schuster, Inc.* v. *Members of New York State Crime Victims Bd.*, 112 S. Ct. 501, 514 (1991) (Kennedy, J., concurring); *Loper* v. *New York City Police Dep't*, 802 F. Supp. 1029, 1041 (S.D.N.Y. 1992), *aff'd*, 999 F.2d 699 (2d Cir. 1993).

210. *See* Brian A. Rosborough, Note, *LSD: A Challenge to American Drug Law Philosophy*, 19 U. FLA. L. REV. 311 *passim* (1966) (written before the criminalization of LSD, it argues that LSD should be distinguished legally from other recreational drugs).

211. The envisioned limitations on drug use following the revocation of prohibition would be analogous to those governing alcohol and also similar to those that have been upheld as constitutional in limiting the exercise of free speech under the First Amendment. *See Loper*, 802 F. Supp. at 1039–41.

212. *See* 1 FEINBERG, *supra* note 141, at 45–51; 3 FEINBERG, *supra* note 141, at 21–23.

213. BERLIN, *supra* note 39, at 136–37. For discussions of the concept and kinds of legal paternalism, SEE 3 FEINBERG, *supra* note 141, at 3–26; HUSAK, *supra* note 101, at 130–41; JOHN KLEINIG, PATERNALISM (1983); Gerald Dworkin, *Paternalism*, in MORALITY AND THE LAW 107 *passim* (Richard A. Wasserstrom ed., 1971); Douglas Husak, *Recreational Drugs and Paternalism*, 8 LAW & PHIL. 353 (1989); David L. Shapiro, *Courts, Legislatures, and Paternalism*, 74 VA. L. REV. 519 (1988).

214. *Griswold* v. *Connecticut*, 381 U.S. 479, 498 (1965) (Goldberg, J., concurring); *see also*

NAACP v. Button, 371 U.S. 415, 438 (1963) ("Precision of regulation must be the touchstone in an area so closely touching our most precious freedoms.").

215. This would restore to the Food and Drug Administration its original mandate of ensuring truthful labeling.

216. *See Loper v. New York City Police Dep't.*, 802 F. Supp. 1029, 1041–47 (S.D.N.Y. 1992) (discussing "the inevitable balancing of interests") *aff'd*, 999 F.2d 699 (2d Cir. 1993); Tribe, *supra* note 142, at 137 ("most rights must, at least to some degree, be balanced against other societal and moral considerations").

217. *See supra* note 142.

218. *See* Duke & Groups, *supra* note 101, at 231–41 (discussing these and other benefits of decriminalization).

219. There are sound reasons for rejecting the terrifying mantra of the war on drugs that decriminalization would result in a substantial increase in drug consumption and a drugged-out population. *See id.*, at 241–46.

19

Principles and Proposals for Managing the Drug Problem

Eric E. Sterling[1]

INTRODUCTION

Much of the argument for "legalization" of drugs has been based on the high cost (including the effect upon civil liberties) of the current drug prohibition strategy and prohibition's lack of success in many respects. The 1994 report by the Committee on Drugs and the Law of the Association of the Bar of the City of New York, for example, devotes forty-six pages to the costs of prohibition, but only two pages on a new policy.[2] The criticism of the legalization argument is usually based primarily on a completely different ground—the presumed likelihood that drug use will increase—not countering the argument that drug prohibition is ineffective.[3]

Intense enforcement of the drug laws has been the case in the United States since the mid-1960s when the use of marijuana, heroin, methamphetamine, and other drugs began to increase dramatically. Except for a few years in the mid-1970s when marijuana decriminalization laws were adopted by about a dozen states, enforcement of drug prohibition has grown continuously and rapidly.

What can we expect the drug problem to look like five or ten years from now if we keep doing what we have been doing? Even with substantial addition of many billions in annual spending on treatment and prevention, under the regime of prohibition will the drug problem be substantially smaller? Overwhelmingly, the American people think not.[4]

No matter what strategy we follow, a very serious drug addiction problem, as well as a serious crime problem will remain. As much as prohibition aggravates these problems, it does not cause them. Eliminating prohibition will not solve all the problems associated with drugs. The repeal of alcohol prohibition eliminated many problems, but left many others we continue to struggle with.

We must have a policy that is consistent with our principles. Our society is grounded upon individual rights and responsibilities, a constitutional commitment to civil liberties, a market economy, limited government, and public safety. Prohibition, which pushed the enormous commerce in drugs outside the law and relinquished any regulatory control over it, has largely failed. By bringing drug use within the law, we can take management of drug distribution away from criminals, turning it over to law-abiding and highly respected businesspeople and government employees.

PRINCIPLES FOR MANAGING THE DRUG PROBLEM

1. Remember that drug laws and drug policy should help people, not hurt them.

People who use drugs but do not have drug "problems" and are hurting no one should be left alone. As a society, we have certainly been able to distinguish people who use the drug alcohol socially and pleasurably from uncontrolled users whom we call alcoholics, and from those who endanger others. People with drug problems are usually in some kind of physical or psychological pain. They should be offered help, not be "demonized," as were lepers under the laws of the Old Testament.[5]

In a postprohibition environment, abundant and effective treatment options can be and should be a reality. A significant percentage of the billions of dollars we squander annually in enforcement can amply fund sufficient drug treatment for those who need it.

Anyone who wants to, but cannot, quit using drugs should have access to appropriate treatment. Addicted single parents need residential treatment that won't break up their family. Many treatment programs won't accept pregnant addicts.[6] Addicts who are HIV positive should receive high priority for treatment, for their own benefit and for society, which is imperiled by spread of the virus. Yet many treatment programs won't take persons who are HIV positive. All drug-addicted prisoners should get treatment before they are released. But the most attractive route to treatment should not be prosecution or imprisonment.

MEDICAL ISSUES VERSUS "DRUG POLICIES"

An indication of how distorted our drug policy has become in the wake of overheated rhetoric is the Drug Enforcement Administration's interference with medical judgments of physicians treating gravely ill patients. Heroin, for example, can relieve relentless and unbearable pain for some terminally ill cancer patients who do not obtain adequate relief from other drugs and will kill themselves rather than continue to suffer[7]—their doctors should be able to prescribe heroin legally. In the mid-1980s, without weakening the severe penalties for the unauthorized use of heroin, the conservative Canadian government joined the United Kingdom in "legalizing" heroin for medical use only.[8] Heroin, a schedule I controlled substance, may be prescribed by an Arizona physician pursuant to Proposition 200—if a number of legal and logistical issues are resolved. Relief of physical pain is one of the oldest medical traditions and a basic human value. Our policy should be compassionate toward those who are in pain from disease or from its treatment. Marijuana, too, has well-documented medical uses.[9] Even the DEA's chief administrative law judge, Francis L. Young, after hearing evidence gathered from around the nation over a four-month period, agreed in 1988 that marijuana has medical uses.[10] Those Americans who can benefit from using marijuana medically should get it legally from their doctors. This is a perfectly respectable position, and it was endorsed by the National Association of Attorneys General on June 25, 1983.[11]

Humane medical policy should not be held hostage to drug war debates. We teach children that the medicines that doctors prescribe must be taken only according to the doctor's instructions. It doesn't glamorize a drug to know that a person dying of AIDS or cancer is using it, or that a person crippled with pain, or spasticity, is struggling to function by using a now prohibited drug. Indeed, antidrug advertising targeted to children might be enhanced by portraying a deathly ill person—hooked up with the tubes of an intensive care unit—smoking a joint with a tag line such as, "Pot smoking—isn't it glamorous?" Letting sick people use medicines that doctors prescribe can never be "the wrong message."

There is widespread concern that cancer patients do not get adequate pain relief. Some physicians and patients advocate modifying regulations and treatment protocols to provide patients with greater access to narcotic pain relief medication by expanding the use of devices that allow patients to directly control when and how much drugs they take for pain relief. This is called *PCA*, patient-controlled analgesia. Sadly, even this advocacy of greater access to narcotics for patients has become one of the burdens of those seeking drug policy reform.[12]

2. *Adopt a public health approach toward all drugs and drug users.*

The distribution of drugs is a significant economic issue that requires regulation and, inevitably, enforcement. But the use of drugs is different. Some misconduct while under the influence of drugs—such as driving, while impaired, on the public streets—is universally recognized as a criminal justice matter. On the other hand, life-threatening conduct—voluntarily engaging in high-risk sexual activity while intoxicated with alcohol or other drugs, for example—is not usually a criminal matter but, rather, an issue of public health. This is the correct model.

DRUG USER ACCESS TO SYRINGES: STERILE SYRINGES OR REUSED SYRINGES?

Very high percentages of injecting drug users are now infected with HIV, tuberculosis, hepatitis, and other highly infectious diseases. They need treatment not only out of simple compassion, but as an imperative of public health.[13]

Many of the nation's infected drug users are currently in prison or on probation and parole, and they must get medical care.[14] In 1994, 20 percent of the women prisoners in New York, 15 percent of the women prisoners in Connecticut, and 12 percent of the women prisoners in Massachusetts were HIV positive.[15] One recent study estimates that there are 10,000 HIV positive men in the California prison system. HIV positive prisoners must get medication to control the disease, including the comparatively new protease inhibitors.

To stop the spread of blood-borne disease among injecting drug addicts, clean needles should be exchanged for used ones. This is the recommendation of the National Commission on HIV and AIDS,[16] the National Research Council and the Institute of Medicine (units of the National Academy of Science),[17] and top government scientists who have studied the issue.[18] Astonishingly, distribution of hypodermic syringes is a crime in eleven states.

It is interesting to remember that until 1965 distribution of condoms to any person was a crime in some states (see *Griswold* v. *Connecticut*),[19] Thirty years ago sale of condoms in supermarkets and convenience stores was unthinkable. Now, for the widely accepted public health purpose of fighting sexually transmitted disease, condoms are widely distributed to the sexually active as one component of a public health program. When we think about drugs and disease in less judgmental terms, public health distribution of hypodermic syringes to drug injectors will no longer be shocking.

Clean needles programs can reduce the spread of HIV/AIDS, hepatitis, and other diseases. Possession of syringes is now illegal in the states with the highest incidence of AIDS among drug users.[20] Needle exchange programs have been barred from using federal funds, including funds provided to state and local governments for drug abuse or public health purposes since 1988.[21] The

National Research Council—Institute of Medicine study found that needle exchange programs increase the availability of sterile injection equipment for addicts, thus lowering the fraction of contaminated needles in circulation and the risk of HIV infection. Naturally, the "symbolism" of giving an addict a needle has been very powerful. Many people fear that this will lead to more addiction. According to the study, "There is no credible evidence to date that drug use is increased among participants as a result of programs that provide legal access to sterile equipment." The literature also reports no increase in the frequency of injection and no increase in the number of new initiates to injection drug use. The study concluded: "Needle exchange programs should be regarded as an effective component of a comprehensive strategy to prevent infectious disease." [22]

A further benefit of such programs is that dirty needles are less likely to be discarded in parks, schoolyards, alleys, and so on, and these programs were found to introduce injecting drug users to health care, drug abuse treatment, and safer sex practices.[23]

But aside from the benefits of giving sterile syringes to injecting drug users, the needle exchange effort is a more aggressive disease control strategy than current drug treatment intake and referral systems. The syringe exchange is often the first opportunity for primary health care for addicts. Addicts receive referrals to treatment of other medical conditions, nutrition counseling, advice on STD prevention, and very often referral to drug abuse treatment. Even more aggressive outreach is warranted to reduce the incidence of disease. Outreach workers with clean needles go into shooting galleries. They also need to go into crackhouses as the stems of glass crack pipes frequently break and cause cuts to the lips, increasing the risk of blood contact with others and the spread of HIV. Broken pipes need to be replaced in crackhouses.

Shifting from a penal to a public health paradigm will encourage participation by those affected. It will also change the way we educate and advise those who choose to use mood changers, both legal (alcohol, tobacco, caffeine, etc.) and illegal.

Prohibition limits the ability of the government to affect such core public health concerns as control of purity and potency, vastly increasing the user's risk of overdose and poisoning. When Tylenol was tampered with and several persons were poisoned in 1982, there was a public outcry, and tampering with consumer products became a federal crime.[24] In contrast, hundreds of drug users were poisoned in February and May 1996, when they injected what they believed was heroin or cocaine. In actuality, there was neither heroin nor cocaine in the mixture. Nonetheless, some of the news accounts described these incidents as drug overdoses.[25] A public health focus would strive to reduce the use of harmful drugs—and the harms of harmful drugs—through a comprehensive approach toward all drugs, not simply those that are now illegal. The nation's concern would move toward the drug "abuse" problem, away from the present, narrow, "illegal" drug problem.

REGULATING LEGAL AND ILLEGAL DRUGS IN AN INTEGRATED MANNER

"Illegal" drug use does not exist in legal or social isolation. Treatment professionals recognize cross-addiction and polydrug abuse. Prevention professionals describe what they call a "gateway" relationship between legal drugs and use of illegal drugs. Therefore a public health approach to the drug problem argues for heightening our concerns about alcohol and tobacco—for adults and for children—and their role in the use and abuse of other drugs.

IMPROVE PREVENTION PROGRAMS AND EFFORTS TARGETED AT YOUTH

Experimentation with drugs, alcohol, tobacco, and inhalants has increased in recent years. Yet funding for drug prevention has grown to more than $2 billion per year. The teen drug prevention program has failed in part because its has been designed primarily to accommodate political goals, not public health goals. Families, communities, and schools must focus prevention efforts on kids at high risk for serious drug use. This demands not simply an "antidrug" program, but a comprehensive effort that provides: (1) counseling around the problems from which drugs are often an escape; (2) stimulating curricula in schools; (3) peer group activities that are constructive and safe; (4) opportunities for athletics, recreation, and socializing across the wide variety of interests that kids have; (5) intervention where there is domestic violence; (6) programs that promote and support teen pregnancy prevention; and (7) nonviolent dispute resolution.

We must develop credible antidrug education. Honest comprehensive prevention programs work for adults. Cigarettes kill more than 400,000 Americans in a year and are as addictive as heroin or cocaine, according to the U.S. Surgeon General.[26] Despite the difficulties, and despite staggering amounts of tobacco industry advertising,[27] 44 million addicted cigarette smokers have quit in the past thirty years.[28] This public health campaign succeeded without jailing or testing the urine of cigarette smokers,[29] without prosecuting tobacco sellers, and without prohibition. Most policymakers reject the idea of prohibiting cigarettes almost out of hand because they recognize that it would be a disaster of corruption and crime, and wholly inconsistent with American values. Sadly, most policymakers, if they recognize these problems in the area of other drugs, are unwilling to say so publicly.

3. Insist upon drug and alcohol user accountability and responsibility.

People who hurt or endanger others must be held responsible for their actions. Drug or alcohol use is not an excuse for criminal or negligent conduct. All serious offenders must confront their wrongdoing, apologize to those they have harmed, and pay restitution to the victims. Just punishment should be imposed. Drug-addicted offenders and prisoners should get drug treatment. But in the absence of a serious crime, actual harm, or substantial risk of endangering others, offenders should not be prosecuted or imprisoned simply as a means to get treatment.

Those who commit acts of violence should forfeit the privilege of using alcohol or drugs legally. Those who commit crimes under the influence of alcohol or drugs, or in order to obtain alcohol or drugs, must be placed in drug treatment after the appropriate punishment.

Convicted predatory criminals such as robbers, rapists, assaulters, and burglars should be drug- and alcohol-abstinent while in custody and while on probation and parole.[30] This requires frequent and extensive surprise drug and alcohol testing, and a system of consistent sanctions for violations. Without testing and treatment, there will be substantial illegal traffic in drugs and the likelihood of corruption.

In critical areas of safety we should require performance tests to detect actual impairment. When we ignore impairment by sleepiness, exhaustion, illness, or use of legal over-the-counter or prescription drugs, the public safety rationale for drug testing is revealed to be a fraud. Following an accident, it is perfectly appropriate to immediately test the blood of pilots, engineers, drivers, surgeons, and nurses for evidence of alcohol and drugs. This would be appropriate not only for airplane, rail, maritime, or motor vehicle accidents, but also for medical accidents in which drugs are improperly administered or errors have been made in surgical procedures. By contrast, past use of intoxicants, identified by urine or hair tests, is irrelevant to public safety and drug user accountability.

We must encourage increased professional responsibility and peer supervision of, for example, doctors and pilots to police against on-the-job recklessness involving alcohol or drug use. Suspected misconduct that threatens public safety must be investigated and prosecuted where criminal recklessness has occurred.

Alcohol use by nonoffending adults ought to be seen as a privilege, and should be subject to a license that can be revoked for misuse.[31] Drug use by adults could be regulated, in part, in a similar manner. Persons who use drugs or alcohol might be required to get special liability insurance coverage. It need not be presumed that persons over 21 are responsible alcohol or drug users.

After the end of prohibition, we can develop social controls that set acceptable limits and standards by which drug use will be considered responsible. For example, upon meeting someone at a business dinner, most of us would think nothing if he or she ordered a cocktail. If it were a business break-fast, most of us would have an entirely different reaction. Social constraints will evolve quickly once drug prohibition is ended.

4. *Insist upon vendor accountability and responsibility.*

Just like users, vendors of alcohol and drugs need to be held responsible for their actions. The privilege to engage in such sales is subject to license. Strict regulation and enforcement will be required. Adulteration and mislabeling of legal drugs and alcohol are now subject to regulation and enforcement by the Bureau of Alcohol, Tobacco and Firearms, the Federal Drug Administration, and other agencies, and to regulation by virtue of product liability civil law remedies.[32] This body of law can be extended to drugs such as heroin, marijuana, and cocaine if the vendors are licensed and regulated. Vendors must comply with reasonable regulations and inspections, pay taxes, and resolve marketplace conflicts through the law, and no longer through violence. Violations are much more easily investigated and enforced in a regulated environment than under prohibition.

Convicted criminals cannot now be licensed to legally sell alcohol[33]—they should not be allowed to sell other drugs after the repeal of drug prohibition. The prohibition of sales to minors of tobacco, alcohol, and other drugs must be enforced more effectively. This prohibition is much easier to enforce against licensed dealers than against illegal distributors of alcohol and tobacco, which is a lesson for the control of other drugs.

There is a growing movement to enforce the prohibitions against use of tobacco and alcohol by juveniles[34]—with appropriate exceptions for supervised parental provision to their children. This is a step in the right direction. Indeed, to focus as we have, the bulk of our juvenile protection enforcement on the now illegal drugs has ignored the most important public health issue in this area.

The widespread violation of juvenile exclusion laws regarding alcohol and tobacco because of half-hearted enforcement has been twisted into an argument to maintain prohibition. The reasoning runs: since we can't (i.e., don't) keep alcohol and tobacco out of the hands of kids today, it will be impossible to prevent kids from getting the now illegal drugs if they are available to adults. Until we have a sincere attempt at effective enforcement, it would be difficult to know what effect it would have on availability. Improving regulatory enforcement techniques regarding use by juveniles will be useful lessons for postprohibition control of vendors of other drugs.

Adults who have been denied or deprived of their privilege to use alcohol or drugs should be prohibited from obtaining alcohol and drugs for some time period. Using the model of alcohol dram-shop laws,[35] over-the-counter sales of drugs to those who are already intoxicated should be barred and, if an accident results, should trigger vendor liability.

Legal theories to block or control the promotion of alcohol, tobacco, and drug use should be carefully explored. It will take a lot of work to find the approaches that do not violate the First Amendment protections of speech and the press. Advertising that either targets kids or is placed in media in which kids have legitimate interest in (e.g., professional and amateur athletics, popular music, motion pictures) should be subject to extensive counterpressure such as boycotts and picketing.

5. *Maximize the reach of law and respect for the law.*

Drug and alcohol buyers should be discouraged from patronizing criminals. For example, growing marijuana exclusively for one's own use is today still a felony,[36] and home growers risk the forfeiture of their homes or land.[37] To obtain marijuana, every marijuana user today (a number roughly between 9 and 20 million persons) either becomes a felon or has to patronize criminals. Shouldn't home cultivation for personal use be encouraged in lieu of buying marijuana, even under prohibition? We should be reducing the commercial opportunities of criminals, not expanding them. Even under prohibition, decriminalizing home marijuana cultivation would sharply reduce the $9 billion in annual profits now funding organized crime[38].

Almost no police officers or revenue agents are killed or injured enforcing the liquor laws. Marijuana, the most widely consumed illegal drug, should be taxed and sold to adults with warning messages. Very few law enforcement officers will be killed or injured enforcing a managed, regulated drug trade.

6. *Set appropriate priorities and achievable social goals.*

There are no magic solutions to problems, especially complex problems of crime, violence, and drug abuse. At the end of prohibition, while much prohibition crime will be reduced, there will continue to be crime. (And there will be violations of the regulations, which will require enforcement, just as every regulatory regime requires some enforcement.) The principal immediate goal should be to reduce the harms from drug and alcohol use and commerce to a minimum. We must realistically acknowledge that we are not aiming for the elimination of these problems, but a dramatic reduction in their severity.

7. *Be honest and self-critical.*

As we confront the challenges of the postprohibition world, we must ask ourselves if our programs are working and we must be prepared to hear the answers. We have not been good at this evaluation during the prohibition era. Repeated studies by the General Accounting Office, the RAND Corporation, and numerous scholars have pointed out serious shortcomings in our antidrug initiatives. Some shortcomings in evaluation have been revealed as the consequence of agency nonfeasance. Other shortcomings are the inevitable consequence of economic, political, or technological limitations.[39] If an agency has congressional enemies, a congressional hearing might be convened to chastise the agency. In the case of favored agencies, such as DEA, the problems are ignored. Fundamental problems in national drug control strategy have been ignored by Congress and the executive branch.

Given that teenage drug use increased between 1991 and 1996, we must rigorously evaluate drug abuse prevention programs. Mathea Falco in *The Making of a Drug-Free America* (1992) pointed out that most programs had not been evaluated. But critical research of politically favored programs is actively suppressed.[40] For many years, evaluations of DARE, America's most widespread drug abuse prevention program, found it to be ineffective. At the direction of the U.S. Department of Justice, Research Triangle Institute carefully reviewed eighteen studies in September 1994 and found DARE substantially less effective than certain other approaches in reducing drug use among the children who were exposed to the program.[41] The Justice Department declined to publish the study. When the authors took the study to the *American Journal of Public Health*, DARE America attempted to intimidate the editors into not publishing these important conclusions.[42] No member of Congress has questioned the spending of hundreds of millions of dollars on a program proved to be ineffective. Evaluations of similar teenage drug-use prevention programs in California came to similar conclusions.[43] If policymakers were actually concerned that a steadily growing percentage of teenagers is less fearful of the hazards of drug use, they would take action to correct the inadequacies of drug prevention programs that receive over $400 million in federal funds annually. But in the political realm, honest criticism is always weighed against the potential for political gain or loss.

If we are serious about prevention, we must be willing to abandon programs that don't work well, even if they are politically popular. Since cigarettes, alcohol, or marijuana can be "gateways" to use of harder drugs, prevention programs need to address all drugs truthfully.

8. Be comprehensive in addressing "root causes" of drug abuse.
Drug use is not necessarily attractive. The use of drugs requires overcoming aversion to rule breaking. The immediate effects are often unpleasant. Opiates, for example, frequently lead to nausea. Marijuana smoking is harsh to the throat and lungs, and often causes fits of coughing.

Many products are offered for sale that are not purchased, and the product disappears from the market. The fact that drugs are offered for sale does not mean that they have to be consumed. Most people who try drugs don't go on to be regular users. All of the prevalence data show that there is a substantial dropoff between those who have tried drugs in their lifetime and those who are current users (use in the past thirty days). And the daily users are a small fraction of current users for most classes of drugs.

The opportunities of drug trafficking offer enormously tempting routes to reach the American dream of prosperity. Training in the legitimate tools of entrepreneurship must be offered to our children, and economic opportunities need to be created to provide real alternatives to crime for the young. In addition to an education that prepares our youth for the workplace of the twenty-first century, youth must learn that for them opportunity truly exists.

Ending drug prohibition is the key to sharply reducing the violence and crime that make business investment in inner cities such an infrequent reality. The elimination of prohibition-related crime will draw manufacturing, research and development, retail, and housing into communities with readily available labor that are already equipped with the infrastructure of rental buildings, public utilities, and transportation.

9. *Respect other peoples, other nations, and other cultures.*

It is a sorry story when the United States blames other countries for our drug problems. Government corruption is a global epidemic that is spread by drug prohibition, and tragically such corruption exists in many places in this country. Our failed domestic drug policies aggravate the corruption problems in many other societies.

Careful economic research has shown that there is no crop eradication strategy and no military operation overseas that can substantially reduce the availability of drugs in the U.S. The notion that "it is more efficient or more economical to stop drugs at the source" has been conclusively shown to be false.[44] To deploy military or paramilitary forces against peasants who grow coca or opium not only wastes money, it politically strengthens anti-Western, antigovernment political insurgencies. To incarcerate "mules" who are at the bottom of the distribution organizations is a waste of very expensive prison space.[45]

Indians in Peru and Bolivia chew coca leaf, and professionals drink coca tea—these are harmless practices that are the business of those societies, not ours. It is ridiculous that coca leaf chewers in Peru and Bolivia became international outlaws in 1989 in violation of the Single Convention on Narcotics of 1961.[46]

In our own country, peyote (which contains the entheogenic alkaloid mescaline) is the sacrament of the Native American Church. The use of peyote by members of the church has been protected under Federal law since 1965 where federal jurisdiction applied, but until 1994 almost half the states did not protect Indian religious use of peyote. There has been no evidence of a "peyote abuse" problem, but Indians and non-Indians are prosecuted for their possession of peyote. With the passage of the American Indian Religious Freedom

Act Amendments of 1994, Native Americans are no longer subject to criminal prosecution and religious persecution by various states for possession or use of peyote for "bona fide traditional ceremonial purposes in connection with the practice of a traditional Indian religion."[47] Spiritual peyote use is no more "drug" use than sacramental wine consumed at communion is drug use, and thus religious peyote use must be protected. The Universal Declaration of Human Rights affirms that all people are free to be religious seekers.[48] Peyote use by non-Indians is not a social or public health problem. All Americans should be free to use peyote in a religious manner, without regard to their race or parentage.

9. *Recognize that drugs are a major commodity in international trade.*

Drugs have been a part of international trade since coffee, tea, and spices were introduced to Europe centuries ago.[49] By ending prohibition we will have taken control of this enormous trade away from criminals and corrupt customs officials and will be able to regulate and tax it.

The legitimate institutions in Colombia, Mexico, and at least a dozen other countries have been threatened or subverted by prohibition-financed corruption. Upon adopting a regulatory drug policy, the U.S. should offer to deploy its resources in the fight against criminal enterprises that have used their enormous profits to gain power.

Simultaneously, the U.S. should renounce increasing cigarette exports as a principal objective of U.S. trade policy. It is not criminal, but fundamentally despicable, to push an addictive and dangerous drug on others. Americans, pushing tobacco in Asia, are as contemptible as the British were when they forced China to accept Indian opium in the nineteenth century. An American cigarette brand, Marlboro, manufactured by Philip Morris, is the most popular cigarette brand in the world, and was reported as early as 1989 as selling more cigarettes outside the United States than inside.[50]

10. *Be creative and flexible to meet our goals.*

Through regulation, we can encourage means of drug administration that are less harmful and easier to control—physically, socially, culturally, and legally. A combination of educational, social, and regulatory controls is needed to discourage the more harmful means of using drugs, or the means that lead to usage patterns that are harder to control. For example, try to limit the smoking of drugs—nicotine, cocaine, heroin, marijuana—which gives intense "rushes" but is more harmful and harder to control than other forms of ingestion. On the other hand, as troubling as the smoking of drugs is in its effects on the lungs, it is probably safer than intravenous injection with its many serious risks. Education about less hazardous techniques should be a part of drug policy. It was reported in 1996, for example, that smoking heroin on aluminum foil may lead to neurological disorders. Switching to glass pipes may be safer. Less safe patterns of smoking and injecting can be discouraged. Oral ingestion is less intense, less habit-forming, and less harmful, and perhaps can be encouraged as an alternative when appropriate.

Another goal is to obtain revenue from the commerce in drugs and alcohol to cover the social costs as much as possible. Federal, state, and local alcohol taxation even at contemporary low rates raised more than $12 billion in 1989.[51] Federal and state tobacco excise taxes raised more than $11 billion in fiscal year 1992.[52] Alcohol and tobacco taxes should be substantially higher. Setting appropriate rates of taxation requires balancing discouragement of use with the profitability of bootlegging and its costs.

Excise taxes, occupational taxes, and user fees on marijuana alone could raise $10 billion to $20 billion yearly for state and federal governments. Such taxes should initially be set at low levels to draw the maximum number of buyers from the criminal markets, which will help eliminate such markets. Enforcement will be required to police the legal market. After the black market infrastructure has decayed, taxes can be raised as appropriate to discourage use.

11. *Turn down the volume on drug messages.*

In order to delay the onset of teen alcohol and tobacco use, which delays the onset of other drug use, we must reduce the promotion and availability of tobacco and alcohol to children. The Clinton administration is making a start.[53] Unfortunately, the absolute separation between legal and illegal drugs, imposed by strict prohibition, cripples any effort to convey credible cautions about the relationships between substances that fall on opposite sides of the legal divide.

Generally, drugs should neither be promoted nor hysterically attacked. We need to support strategies that prevent tobacco, alcohol, and other drug advertising from being aimed at youth. Such youth-targeting advertising includes cartoon characters such as "Spuds MacKenzie" (the dog promoting Bud Light beer), the Budweiser frogs, the Bud Bowl cartoon football battle between competing brands of beer advertised during the National Football League's Super Bowl, or Camel cigarette's "Joe Camel." A variety of constitutional mechanisms can be used to keep such advertisements from placement in youth-oriented media.

Keep antidrug messages in front of children but keep them reasonable and truthful. Subject them to tests of effectiveness, not of their political appeal to adult antidrug crusaders. The TV spot featuring a skillet and frying eggs ("This is your brain. This is your brain on drugs. Any questions?") was an example of a ludicrous antidrug message. Its dishonesty and exaggeration provoked contempt. Some young people asked friends to get stoned by saying, "Want to fry an egg?" Ironically, spokespersons for the Partnership for a

Drug-Free America sometimes introduce themselves as, "We're the fried egg people." Many of their ads are effective, and their better work is very important. But to bombard children with the message that "the most important thing in the world is that you shouldn't do drugs" has been an enticement.

TV Public service announcements that show realistic scenarios affirming kids who decline drugs offered by friends are important. Antidrug messages are a component of public health, harm reduction, pro-social programs teaching safer-sex and pregnancy prevention practices, staying in school, nonviolence, and so on. TV PSAs should be part of communitywide, integrated antidrug programs such as Project STAR, developed with National Institute on Drug Abuse (NIDA) assistance. Teenagers are more likely to listen when the messages are not clearly hypocritical or ludicrous.

12. *Recognize that drug policy, as well as being a public health and social issue, is a component of and affected by general anticrime policy.*

In addition to redesigning a national drug control strategy to more effectively fight crime and prevent drug abuse, it is critical that we recognize that drug policy is affected by the more dominant features of anticrime policy. Crime and drugs are intertwined and it is not only drug policy that must be changed. Essentially, we must concentrate on crime prevention, especially juvenile delinquency prevention, and the adoption of better policing, prosecutorial, and penological programs.

INTERVENE PREVENTIVELY

Sadly, much of the nation's anticrime effort is rhetorically driven. It is oriented toward approaches that are tough sounding.[54] "Prevention" does not sound "tough." Notwithstanding research that has identified proven crime strategies, only an infinitesimal portion of our crime fighting resources is directed to such tasks. The factors that put children at greater risk of becoming offenders, and even serious offenders, have been identified, and the means to reduce the prevalence or severity of such factors are very slowly being implemented. Research has demonstrated that juvenile justice interventions into the lives of children reduce such risks.[55]

The lessons of favorable interventions—those that improve the odds for a favorable long-term outcome for children—are that interventions have some common elements: (1) they provide a broad spectrum of services; (2) traditional professional and bureaucratic boundaries are crossed; (3) interventions are flexible and tailored to individual cases, not limited by strict protocols; (4) programs see the child in the context of the family, and the family in the context of its surroundings; (5) the staff of programs are seen by the people whom they serve as caring about them, respectful, and trustworthy; (6) the services are coherent and easy to use; (7) there is a continuity about the service and the service provider; and (8) the programs and personnel are adaptive—overcoming the constraints of bureaucracy and professional image, and responding to the immediate needs of the persons they are serving.[56]

As important as it is to focus appropriate juvenile justice resources on youth at greatest risk, based on their conduct, a comprehensive crime prevention approach must recognize the role for measures that strengthen families, improve schools, improve health, and stimulate economic opportunities.

Where we have evidence that parents are too young and untrained in the skills needed to rear their children, we can provide community-based guidance to enhance their abilities in this area. Where we have evidence that schools are failing, we know how to train and inspire principals and teachers to improve the management, the order, and the safety of schools to permit education to reach children. Where we see that children are not getting health care, where teen pregnancy is high, where treatment for drug addiction is hard to obtain, we must reform health policies and financing to assure that poor children—who are at the greatest risk—and their parents get treatment so that the children can grow with minimal physical scars and handicaps.

REFOCUS DOMESTIC LAW ENFORCEMENT

Police departments and prosecutor offices will need to be refocused and effectively managed to adapt to new priorities. All crimes of violence need to be investigated thoroughly and prosecuted. At present less than one third of the homicides in Los Angeles result in a conviction or guilty plea.[57] Special squads with plentiful resources should be devoted to the investigation of crimes of violence such as street robbery, carjacking, and house invasion in addition to homicide and rape. We will be able to afford such antiviolence measures when we stop spending disproportionately in support of the drug prohibition strategy. In addition, far greater cooperation from the community can be expected to result from a lessening of the informer-based, sting operation modality, so heavily relied upon in narcotics enforcement.

Community policing is consistent with a postprohibition environment. Consider, for example, young men "hanging" on a street corner. To a police officer driving by who doesn't know the community or the youths, they appear to be loitering for the purpose of selling drugs. But to a police officer who is part of the community, who walks up to the men and introduces himself and gets to know them, the men are members of the community. The police officers establish themselves as members of the community. The men no longer perceive the police as "outsiders"—independent of the community. The police can now tap the community's sources of authority in their work. The men "hanging" on the corner now can appreciate the police as part of the community's protection against predatory crime. However, in the strategy of "zero tolerance" prohibition, men avoid any relationship with the police, who are always looking for informants and for any scent of drugs that may lead to someone's capture and imprisonment.

When police–community relations are no longer dominated by drug enforcement and prohibition-based stereotypes of young men as dope dealers, police officers will have greater positive influence in the community and will be able to enlist residents in anticrime activities. As some scholars of the psychology of crime have demonstrated, offenders tend to rationalize their acts on the basis that they are not part of the community they are offending. As alienated youth see the police as their enemies and as disrespectful and contemptuous of their place in the neighborhood, some of those youth rationalize their crimes: "Nobody cares about us, so we don't care about nobody." The community police officer of the future can provide useful information ranging from answering questions about registering a motor vehicle or selling a car to tips on employment opportunities he may have learned of from businesses he or she visits on the beat. The officer can be trained to provide referrals for alcohol or drug treatment or for marital counseling. Without making arrests, the officer can discourage littering, flagrant alcohol consumption, or disruptive noise—the disorder that can signal to offenders that a neighborhood is safe for them, not for ordinary citizens.[58] The officer can also obtain information about criminal acts and offenders. Police officers can help create a sense of neighborhood, or they can weaken it.

An officer can improve a community's sense of security and obtain important information by giving to the neighbors his or her beeper number to call for help.[59] Instead of simply trying to reach an anonymous 911 operator, citizens can reach an officer who knows them, who will protect their confidentiality if necessary, who knows the nicknames of the suspects, and who can respond with appropriate questions. A police officer known to the community groups can help establish and expand neighborhood watch and citizen patrol efforts. These measures give the community both power and a sense of power over the forces of disorder.

James Q. Wilson and George Kelling in "Broken Windows"[60] pointed out how the rules of the street can affect the crime rate. For example, when drunks sprawl on the sidewalk it creates a climate of disorder. A community police officer can create and enforce an informal rule that advises the drunks that they can only sit, they cannot lie down. Drunks who pass out are taken to shelters, not to jail.

The replacement of open-air drug markets with carefully regulated clinics and other access systems will help make streets safer. Residents who feel safe walking in their communities will patronize local retail businesses, thus creating more local jobs. The community's capital will not go to drug dealers, but will stay in the community.

As a transition to a regulated environment regarding drugs, and the beginning of evolving norms of a post prohibition state, police might informally direct drug trafficking indoors to buildings where there are no children or residents, moving the disorder of the drug sales off the street and out of residential neighborhoods and commercial districts during business hours, and away from playgrounds, parks, and schools. In effect, crack houses and shooting galleries can begin to be regulated and policed. Community policing would work with sterile syringe exchanges, with harm reduction workers, and with street outreach teams, to provide sterile syringes, condoms, food, referrals to health care and drug treatment, training in measures to reduce the hazards of drug use, and warnings about adulterated drugs. The police could even advise drug sellers that if they believe they are being cased for a robbery, or have been robbed, they can call the police and they will be taken seriously. Of course, the more successful efforts would be institutionalized as the illegal markets are replaced by regulated channels of distribution.

REFOCUS CORRECTIONS POLICY

Corrections policy needs to be reformed. Drug sellers and drug-addicted prostitutes and thieves often crowd jails and prisons. Repeat, serious violent offenders need to be incarcerated, but they have been released in many jurisdictions because of the overcrowding caused by less serious offenders.[61] Record keeping must be improved to assure that repeat offenders are identified and not released by mistake.[62] Records and fingerprint files need to be fully automated. Prison capacity should not be used for warehousing simple drug possessors and users, or for nonviolent drug offenders. Over 20 percent of the federal prison population, for example, is now composed of nonviolent, first-time drug offenders.[63] These offenders should have their sentences modified for appropriate punishments under community supervision, which is less expensive and often more likely to prevent recidivism.

Another major corrections issue will be the question of commutation and pardon for those who are serving or have served sentences for drug trafficking offenses. A system of review of such sentences will be required to determine those who deserve commutation because the offense they were convicted of is no longer a crime. Some drug traffickers are serving terms of imprisonment for tax evasion, acts of violence, and so on. Commutation or pardon for such offenders is problematic. Hundreds of thousands of others who were convicted of simple possession offenses should have their drug offenses removed from their records. Unfortunately, this case-by-case review will be expensive and time consuming.

STRENGTHEN INTERNATIONAL LAW ENFORCEMENT

The U.S. Justice and Treasury Departments should concentrate on criminals at the highest level, including international criminals—drug cartel organizers, arms dealers, and money launderers—whose violence and corruption has undermined governments and the global financial system. The law enforcement agencies of Colombia and Mexico, to cite two examples, are simply not up to the task. The federal law enforcement objective should be to investigate and punish such crimes, not the drug possession or less important drug trafficking cases that state and local law enforcement agencies can investigate. These will be complex cases requiring the reassignment of law enforcement agents and prosecutors. Right now, the bulk of the productivity of federal law enforcement results in the imprisonment of street-level dealers, bodyguards, mules, and couriers (55.2 percent of the total drug cases); only a very small fraction are high-level dealers (11.2) or international-scope traffickers (23.7).[64]

REGULATION AND CONTROL OF DRUG USERS
AND ADDICTS

It is easier to imagine a regulatory system for the functional, employed, "recreational" drug user, but for a regulatory system to be effective, it must address the addicts—those who are functional and those who are not. We must address those adults who want (who feel compelled) to obtain drugs and who, we have seen, are often indifferent to hurting themselves. We must consider how to deal with those who will attempt to evade the regulations. We must design the system to effectively keep drugs out of the hands of children—indeed, much more effectively than prohibition does. We need to address the total environment involving the promotion of drugs, in particular the question of how drugs—including alcohol, tobacco, and over-the-counter medications—can (or cannot) be advertised. We must attune the system to address the difference between conduct that just affects the self and conduct that affects members of one's family and intimates. We must address conduct that affects others in the workplace, in parks, or otherwise in the general public.

A key consideration in the design of the postprohibition system is to recognize that the public and public health officials want to discourage drug use. At present, our culture is fundamentally pro-drug. At the level of advertising we are encouraged nightly on television to relieve pain. Almost every time we go out to eat we are asked if we would like a "drink," an alcoholic beverage. A fundamental part of American hospitality in many homes is offering an alcoholic beverage to a guest.

On college campuses, and among young adults generally, alcohol consumption to excess is widespread. At the University of Colorado, in April

1996, a foreign student asserted, during a sociology seminar I was conducting, that the students at the university were "obsessed with alcohol." The other students were asked if that was a fair claim; all twenty-five students present agreed. In some segments of the society, especially young adults, the antidrunkenness paradigm has not taken hold.

As a society, it is appropriate that we change the culture of drug use. We must get sober about using drugs. One credo of the short-lived subculture in the '60s—if it feels good, do it—has been replaced in this era of "safer sex." But it is the greater culture—of "Fast, Fast, FAST relief," of "I don't have time for the pain," of "The night belongs to Michelob," "This Bud's for you!" and "It's Miller time!"—that needs to be modified fundamentally. We need to break down the cultural paradigm that one can blithely get drunk or stoned, or mindlessly pop a pill and solve a problem.

Many in the medical profession have been moving away from this reliance on medication, and the growing holistic medical model is generally antidrug.[65] Perhaps unfortunately for the desired effect on the cultural model, in psychiatry, there is a growing trend toward pharmaceutical intervention for mental and emotional illness.

In thinking about antidrug education in the postprohibition era, it is useful to consider some of the lessons of the drug war. In the summer of 1996 it was repeatedly asserted that the recent increase in teenage marijuana use was a consequence of public discussion of legalization alternatives to drug prohibition. This assertion was never actually explained or documented by research. Public discussion of drug legalization became prominent in 1988, yet teen drug use continued to drop for the following four years.

Is it that achievement of a low level of juvenile drug use requires that public discourse about alcohol and drug policy be circumscribed? Is there any other area of public policy debate so powerful that the simple discussion of policy has a profound effect, even a measurable effect, on behavior?

The issue, fundamentally, is about behavior, and how one makes choices about behavior. The rhetoric of "sending a consistent message" is one that acknowledges the role of education, yet, ironically, those "educators" want to rely on punishment and not information or analysis. One sends a message to a donkey when one hits its flanks with a switch, but it is a reversal of centuries of Western thought to think that our children are only as bright as donkeys when it comes to teaching about matters such as drugs. It is inconsistent with serious consideration to ban discussion of alternative policies.

Drug and alcohol use ought to be carefully premeditated. Drug use ought to follow consultation with mature and experienced advisors and after consideration of appropriate cautions. These steps are consistent with notions of individual responsibility. It is fair to say that drug use is not for kids or for the foolhardy. The development of new cultural models of resistance to casual or unthinking use of tobacco and alcohol products is a part of developing socially and personally less costly ways of using drugs generally.

To a degree I suspect that I agree with conservatives (and I never thought I would say this, with Dr. William Bennett, the former drug czar), that law can and should be used to change attitudes and behavior. But in the drug area, as in most areas, the law works best by defining limits on legal behavior rather than sweeping an entire realm of behavior into prohibition.

What follows, in somewhat more specific terms, are my ideas for regulatory mechanisms and controls that could be used to transform this gangster-run business.

ADDICT MANAGEMENT

First, the typology of different stages of being an addict needs to be more fully developed for policy purposes.[66] We have to revise the popular, polar typology from addicts who are "active" in their drug use and addicts "in recovery" who are not using drugs. We need to recognize that addicts occupy a ground in a spectrum of addiction and drug use. Thinking about alcohol use and alcohol users might be useful. Some alcoholics are "winos," the alcoholic homeless, the dysfunctional; other alcoholics are sober, abstinent, and in recovery yet still define themselves as alcoholics even though they are fully functional and well adjusted. There are alcohol users (light, moderate, and heavy drinkers) along a spectrum of alcohol consumption whose functionality is not directly related to quantity consumed. We must recognize that there are drug addicts and drug users who are like moderate to heavy drinkers—their range of functioning stretches from very well to barely tolerable.

The popular typology is that drug addicts are either "junkies," "righteous drug fiends," "pipeheads," and so forth, or in abstinent recovery. But the reality is that there are addicts who are using drugs—shooting up, getting high, maybe heavily "chipping," maybe having a hard time—who are not dysfunctional. Certainly, many of them are at great risk for becoming dysfunctional, or for fully embracing criminal and deviant lifestyles, but while it is appealing for desperate family members and treatment professionals to state that a fall into complete degradation and dysfunction is inevitable, it is a false assumption. Significantly, there is a range of behaviors involved. Some stable addicts are not engaged in crime while other addicts with similar use patterns are enmeshed in criminal activity. Many dysfunctional addicts who are severely disabled are not involved in serious or extensive criminality. Along the spectrum of drug use are many addicts who are not involved in crime other than in their purchase and use of drugs (or engaging in the drug business).

The conceptual and programmatic change from prohibition thinking is to recognize and tolerate those addicts who are managing their lives: "addicts in management." But this creates a great challenge: How does society, from the perspective of family members, co-workers, employers, and teachers, address the addict "in management"?

The objective is to bring "addicts in management" more fully into the community—their families, their churches and temples, the health care system, the social services system—in the way that best serves them, their families, and society. Addicts in management, like everyone, need self-respect. They also need a greater degree of respect from the rest of us. Unfortunately, the prohibition model interferes with self-respect; reducing drug users to a monodimensional category prevents them from receiving the respect they are entitled to for the nondrug balance of their lives.

One intervention and support model might be fashioned after a program provided to some of the mentally ill who are being treated as outpatients.[67] The state of New York is supporting parents, typically mothers, who are severely mentally ill so that they can raise their children. This, it is believed, will lead to better outcomes for the mentally ill and their children, and such care will be less expensive to society. This is a win-win situation—for the patient-parent, for the children, for the taxpaying public, and for society. However, it takes a great effort to break down the mutual suspicion between the mentally ill client and the system of supporters and service providers. Similar suspicion now exists between active drug addicts and the system of health and social services, and between the homeless and government agencies. As we develop appropriate systems of intervention and support, a challenge will be to overcome countertransference—the distaste and hostility for the lifestyles of the addicts—and our suspicion of drug addicts.

Many addicts now in trouble could take care of themselves and their families *if* they did not have to spend most of their time and money trying to "cop" drugs.

To institute a regime to support addicts in management, I would experiment with a system of addict registration. An addict could register with one of a variety of agencies that he or she was comfortable with, if the agency was comfortable supervising that addict.

Registered addicts would be assured that they would get a dependable supply of the dosage of narcotics they need to avoid withdrawal syndrome, *and even enough to get high.* In exchange, the addict would have to report to a counselor on how he or she is keeping his or her life in order. They would be able to get advice on their problems. Many of them, no doubt, would be on public assistance.

ADDICTS NOT IN MANAGEMENT

In the mid-1990s, a scandal involving federal disability funds (SSI) was exposed. Addiction had been identified as a disability and addicts thus qualified for SSI. Their checks were being sent to bars, for example, and were being used to buy drugs and alcohol. This was a misuse of those funds, of course, and a breakdown in the appropriate controls. This is an example of inadequate management of a program. But in typical political fashion, instead of insisting on better management, Congress simply cut off the funds, leaving the addicts destitute.

In a climate of "welfare reform," it is easy to conclude that drug addicts and alcoholics are undeserving of support when compared with disabled children or destitute families. Upon reflection, however, providing food, housing, and medical support for addicts and alcoholics is in the interest of both society and the addicts. Properly administered, such support would reduce their disease, their dysfunctionality, and the volume of crime they tend to commit.

Consider the implications of a "no public assistance" policy for drug users at the lowest levels of functionality, the homeless. Most church-run and government-run shelters prohibit drug and alcohol use. Yet many alcoholics and drug addicts don't get sober. They too need shelter. In fact, because of their often inebriated or disoriented state they are especially vulnerable without shelter. Frankly, they need a place in which they can pass out that eliminates the likelihood that they will be robbed or hurt. This was a function of "drunk tanks" at one time. Shelters for drug addicts and alcoholics that provide refuge and meals during the day may be able to help communities as well by reducing panhandling. For addicts and alcoholics *not in management*, homeless shelters that do not require sobriety are needed. Today the homeless seek such shelter as they can in abandoned buildings and under bridges because they are unable or unwilling to be sober or straight. This is a public nuisance, of course, but it also puts them at risk. Such homeless shelters, known as "wet shelters," have been organized in some parts of the country.

Wet shelters provide a place to shoot up, but they are not run by criminals as are the shooting galleries that are unconcerned about preventing AIDS and violence. Addicts in partnership with public health outreach workers can run these places, rather than criminal drug dealers.[68]

CRACK AND COCAINE USE

Ethnographer Terry Williams studied the lives of crack users, and wrote about those who lived in a crackhouse in New York City.[69] Anthropologist Philippe Bourgois studied Puerto Rican crack users and sellers in El Barrio in New York City.[70] Crack users live in a world of shifting stability. But like all of us, they have networks of relationships and they work at various levels of jobs. Unfortunately, many of them are criminal. Crack users engage in dangerous and risky as well as criminal behavior, but in many respects they are functional.

Some middle-class crack users are struggling to reinvent a society for themselves to replace the society they are alienated from. This is the life described in *Crackhouse*. The late 40-ish leader of the crackhouse says, "I think people have to strive for the ability to handle cocaine effectively and somehow still function. Most people, the vast majority, can't do that. The drug becomes everything for them."[71] This man, formerly a very successful athlete and businessman, has abandoned middle-class life.

> I used to wear Brooks Brothers suits, button-down shirts like all my friends. And we would go to Rockefeller Center, down five martinis, eat a bunch of oysters, then go over to the Lombardy Hotel on Fifty-sixth Street and Park Avenue and have orgies.

> Do you know what? Crack is no different. I mean, really it's not. I don't see those orgies as being any different, you know, than being where we are right now and having three or four girls come up here and have us all light up. The only thing is you have less of a hangover. You don't feel as out of it on crack. Let me explain: My life was really fucked up on the martini. At least with crack I feel a little lighter and more coherent. My lungs may be fucked, but at least I'm doing what I want to do.

> But in the end it's all degenerate. In the final analysis, I think I've really exchanged one monster for another.[72]

How could cocaine or crack use be regulated? It is important to try to discourage the smoking of drugs, which is especially harmful to the lungs. Smoking allows the easy ingestion of large doses, and the rapidity of the drug's action can lead to more rapid dependence. Injection of cocaine may be less harmful to the lungs than smoking, but entails other very serious risks. Without a controlled experiment with clean sources of cocaine, clean needles, and safe injection techniques, it would be very difficult to determine whether one or the other form of use is less risky. In any event, injecting and smoking are both associated with very heavy cocaine use in which lack of control seems to be a very high risk.[73]

If powder cocaine were distributed in an effort to replace the criminal market and to create an addict management program, even though powder can easily be cooked into crack, there are reasons crack should not be distributed. First, primary availability in powder may encourage snorting in contrast to smoking—and snorting is an inefficient way of using cocaine. Second, the inconvenience of having to convert powder to crack, by slowing down the ease of use, may slightly discourage crack smoking relative to the use of powder. And third, the drug user's experience of crack use as a widespread and destructive form of cocaine abuse in the past decade makes it a highly risky choice.

(It must be acknowledged that powder cocaine is easily converted to crack by the addition of baking soda and water and the application of heat.)

It is worth noting that with regard to other drug use, the strongest forms of the drug are not always preferred. During alcohol prohibition there was a significant shift from beer consumption to whiskey consumption. This reflected the need to conceal alcoholic beverages. Since the volume of beer is mostly water, this was an inefficient way to conceal alcohol. Since the end of alcohol prohibition, beer and wine consumption has taken much greater market shares.

In the other direction from crack use is the chewing of coca leaves or, perhaps better adapted to our way of life, drinking tea made from leaves, *maté de coca*. Perhaps without the economics-of-prohibition pressure toward greater potency, many cocaine users would find a milder and subtler experience more to their liking, and easier on their dopaminergic and serotonergic systems.

HARM REDUCTION

Under appropriate controls and supervision, drugs should be made available to addicts to reduce harms. Smoking tobacco has been the most dangerous of the popular means for ingesting nicotine. Cigarettes are only crude, disposable nicotine ingestion devices. Nicotine is addicting but is not as dangerous as the tars, particulates, and gases in cigarette smoke. Since 1990 I have been urging that Nicorette chewing gum, which contains nicotine—at the time a prescription medication—be made less expensive and more freely available, arguing that many more smokers and snuff dippers would be likely to quit. The government has now agreed and the gum has been reclassified as an OTC (over-the-counter) medication.

Heroin is addicting but is not as dangerous as HIV, hepatitis, and the adulterants added by criminals who distribute street drugs. Heroin addicts who can't or won't quit should not be hunted and banished, put at risk of death, or pushed into behaviors that are even more dangerous to themselves or to society at large. Instead, they should have access to clean, affordable opiates under medical and pharmaceutical supervision, which will prevent them from spreading disease. Dr. Alfred Blumstein, one of the country's most respected criminologists and former president of the American Society of Criminology, endorses this approach to certifiable addicts.[74] (Of course, the use of heroin by addicts must not violate the principle of user accountability discussed above.)

HITTING BOTTOM

One of the fundamental axioms of a theory of drug abuse treatment is that addicts won't seek treatment until they "hit bottom." Family members, friends, and employers who tolerate the addiction are castigated as "enablers" who delay the addict from hitting bottom. Some supporters of prohibition argue that the criminal prosecution of drug users quickly "raises the bottom," forcing the drug user into treatment. Certainly there are many instances in which that has been the case. However, criminal prosecution—with loss of employment, alienation from family, the great expense of representation and bail, permanent criminal records, and incarceration and its attendant risks of violence and disease—comes at a very high price to the drug user whom society is ostensibly trying to help, and a very high price to society as well.

Is it in the interest of society to have a drug policy that is designed to put as large a number of drug users as possible on the trajectory to the "bottom"? Or does it make more sense to find the means to prevent large numbers of drug users from hitting bottom by helping them manage their lives?

INTERVENTIONS

There are, of course, many social interventions short of criminal prosecution or involuntary commitment. Such interventions are likely to be a key to reducing harm in a regime of addiction management. Just what kinds of interventions will prove most effective and appropriate will emerge from continuing research.

Libertarians will object strenuously to government interventions of whatever kind. Initially, I believe any legalization model to be accepted by the public will require controls on drug users that are believed to be likely to protect drug users from harming themselves and society. Later, cost-benefit analysis may find that such interventions are excessive. But initially there will be a political price of a reduction in freedom extracted from drug users in exchange for the creation of a "legalized" drug regimen.

For mentally ill drug users (and, of course, there are many variations of mental illness), many therapists argue that psychotherapy is pointless if the patient is actively using drugs like cocaine. It might be valuable to encourage mentally ill drug users to use drugs that are less strong as central nervous system (CNS) stimulants, but satisfy a desire to get high, drugs such as cannabis. In an environment less extreme in its stance toward drug use, psychotherapy may develop techniques for helping the mentally ill who are using drugs. Research will elucidate the interactions between drugs prescribed for psychiatric purposes and the broad class of pleasure-related drugs such as cannabis or heroin.

But for drug addicts who are not diagnosed as schizophrenic, or otherwise psychotic, there may be other dysfunctions—many the result of not having been trained to become adult, or lost through years of bad habits and indolence. Interventions or training will be required for some addicts for the same kinds of issues addressed in substance abuse programs, ranging from self-esteem to learning to read to diet. Addict counselors, responsible for being the community's intervention, could be public or private or volunteer. They could be affiliated with churches, housing agencies, schools, or even the volunteer fire department—they would not be employed solely by addiction services agencies.

The performance of the dysfunctional or marginally managing drug addicts may have to be monitored. They will live in what might be considered a "noncriminal probation" with addict counselors in lieu of probation officers, with checks on their comings and goings, their job seeking, and the meeting of family responsibilities. These counselors would be "tutors in responsible living."

For the addicts who are maintaining well with jobs and families, there would be little intervention beyond reporting. For the addicts who are struggling, there would be a higher degree of intervention and support. If an addict commits a crime, their addiction would not be an excuse.

Support groups for addicts "in management" are needed, perhaps on the twelve-step model. In Alcoholics Anonymous and Overeaters Anonymous there are participants who are in relapse. For addicts in management, the relapse is not the use of drugs per se, but the breakdown in relationships or work, and the failure to meet responsibilities.

THE PRIVILEGE OF GETTING HIGH: CAN IT BE A MOTIVATOR?

We have seen that the desire to use drugs has been a very powerful motivator to act antisocially or at least illegally. Psychologists have defined what they see as "drug-seeking behavior" on the part of drug addicts, and typically this is antisocial—prostitution, hustling, and theft, and going out on the street to cop drugs. There is no intrinsic reason that such powerful drives cannot motivate pro-social behavior.

The ability to get drugs can be made a privilege for those who obey the law. Committing crimes like robbery or burglary forfeits the privilege to use drugs; urine testing can be imposed to enforce abstinence as punishment. If drug use is important to an addict, it can be turned around to become an incentive to obey the law.

NONCOOPERATING ADDICTS

It is likely that many addicts, as well-established outlaws, will not register or participate in programs of supervision. They will be suspicious and resistant to all of the bureaucracy. Many of them are invested in the "ripping and running" lifestyle, and will be perfectly happy to continue to get drugs from criminal sources, paying with the proceeds of crime. And the organized crime syndicates that now sell drugs will be intensely anxious to keep their business.

Thus, initially, there will continue to be a criminal marketplace, and thus there will continue to be a need for drug enforcement.

POSTPROHIBITION DRUG ENFORCEMENT

Drug enforcement in the postprohibition world will be both different and similar. There will be the need to distinguish between legally and illegally distributed drugs. Drugs could be packaged in serial number-marked dosage units. Addicts would have to be responsible for not diverting or selling drugs that have been issued to them. A record of drugs distributed would be maintained to facilitate investigation of the inevitable cases of diversion. Addicts who willfully distribute would have to be sanctioned. Drug enforcement toward noncooperating users might include an option for the police to send them into addict management intake with a high level of supervision. They will have to be pressured to get drugs from the legal supply rather than to continue to patronize the criminals.

What will drive out the criminal sellers? Denial of their customer base and continued enforcement. Obviously, criminal sellers won't simply vanish. The hypothesis is: (1) community pressure will identify outlaw sellers because the community wants to eliminate the disorder and potential violence of the criminal market; (2) the authorities want to eliminate the revenues from the criminals' illegal sales; and (3) the cooperating addicts have an investment in making the system work.

LICENSED DRUG USERS

In the postprohibition world there will be new drug users. Again, we want to minimize the criminal traffic. We also want to discourage use and encourage those who use to utilize less harmful means. Perhaps with new, prospective users we will have some opportunity. A key question is whether the new regulatory approach would make drug use per se more attractive by making it more convenient.

How might we erect barriers to new use? First, we might require prospective drug users to qualify for a license to use drugs. We would establish that drug use is a privilege that can be taken away if the rules are violated or public safety is endangered. We license all kinds of behaviors, even backpacking in the National Park. Licenses typically require a minimum of knowledge of rules or fitness. Licensed drug users will have to demonstrate knowledge of the uses and hazards of the drugs they are licensed to use.

Licenses for airplane pilots require a physical examination. A license to use certain powerful drugs such as LSD or cocaine might require a person to submit to a physical and psychological examination to determine whether they have any particular risk factors for addiction or a problem in the use of drugs. Those who do not qualify will be offered counseling to encourage them not to use the drugs for which they have not qualified, and perhaps encouraged to use other drugs that entail lower risks.

NEW CULTURAL NORM: LICENSED ALCOHOL CONSUMER

Licensed drug use might help establish new cultural norms, for example, the licensed alcohol consumer. (I owe this idea to Professor Mark A. R. Kleiman at UCLA[75].) At a restaurant, bar, or even a party, a person who wants to be served a drink would have to proffer an alcohol consumption license. It is estimated that 10 percent of the alcohol-consuming public has substantial problems with their drinking—driving drunk and domestic violence and spousal abuse are at the top of the list. In a new approach, a drunk driver—in addition to other penalties and punishments—would have his or her drinking license suspended or revoked.

Obtaining a drinking license would require learning about the dangers of drinking. Motor vehicle simulators and standardized drinks would be used to impress upon prospective drivers the marked diminution in driving skills. Every prospective drinker would have to "drive" the computer auto-simulator during the consumption of common amounts of alcohol at regular intervals over the course of three or four hours. The drinker would get a videotape of the performance as well as a computer readout of the successive degradation of eye–hand coordination, problem recognition, and incident response time.

ACCESS FOR THE NEW DRUG USERS: PERSONAL CONSULTING PHARMACISTS

Another possible model to control drug use is for drug users to have confidential professional guidance in selecting and using drugs—a consulting pharmacist.

A personal consulting pharmacist might operate like a cross between a stockbroker and a psychiatrist. If you want to buy stock, you can't simply walk onto the floor of the stock exchange. You must open an account with a broker—and the broker has to follow an extensive set of rules designed to protect you, the consumer. Of the rules applying to stockbrokers, for the parallel I am trying to draw, probably the most important is the requirement that a broker has to know his or her customer's needs and risk tolerance. These facts set limitations on the riskiness of investments that a broker can lawfully recommend. A broker who recommends investments that substantially exceed the customer's risk capacity or investment objectives is subject to professional sanctions.

The newly licensed adult who wants to use drugs would contact a personal consulting pharmacist. A personal consulting pharmacist would be a variation on the profession of pharmacy, licensed to be sure, covered by malpractice and liability insurance, and subject to a battery of professional rules.

The personal consulting pharmacist would have to gather a good deal of information about the licensee before providing him or her with access to certain drugs. Prospective drug users would be encouraged to clarify their reasons for using drugs and to understand the appropriate circumstances for using them. We need to be aware of the potential for conflicts of interest if the pharmacist's revenue is based on the volume of drug consumption and sales.

The personal consulting pharmacist would provide advice on alternative, safer drugs. The clients who think they need a stimulant and want amphetamines may be encouraged to use caffeine tablets or coca chewing gum, for example.[76]

"PSYCHEDELIC TRIP LEADERS"

The state of Maine licensed canoe trip leaders in the early 1970s and probably still does so. Teenage boys and girls take "wilderness" canoe trips in northern and eastern Maine that last several weeks at a time. Every day there is a significant hazard potential of broken bones; severe lacerations from the regular use of axes, saws, and knives; a daily danger of burns from twice-daily cooking over a wood fire; and the potential for food poisoning, not to mention the risk of overturning a canoe and drowning in white water. Wilderness canoeing has great rewards: deeply experiencing nature, developing self-reliance, surmounting numerous challenges, learning teamwork, learning enormous numbers of skills, and the fun and excitement of canoeing through rapids, swimming, fishing, and fellowship. With a licensed canoe leader and proper preparation and training, a teenager can minimize risk and have a profound, life-changing learning experience.

Psychedelic drugs are very powerful in altering perceptions of self, others, and the universe. Their use therefore poses potential risks, especially to the unprepared, the unwary, or the unstable. The rewards of controlled psychedelic use, however, are profound and mightily praised by those who have used them successfully.[77] In 1995 Dr. Kary Mullis, the 1993 Nobel Prize laureate in chemistry, said, "I think I might have been stupid in some respects, if it weren't for my psychedelic experiences."[78] LSD has also been reported to be useful as an adjunct in psychotherapy.[79] Adults who want to undertake spiritual, mystical, or psychic experiences with LSD or other psychedelic drugs ought to be able to do so with competent advice and counseling, with known dosages and assured purity, and under circumstances structured to minimize fear and danger, and to maximize the potential to achieve a positive outcome.

The licensed drug user might have to be specially qualified with physical and psychiatric examinations, and required to undertake certain kinds of preparation. The user might have to buy a user's insurance policy. Trip leaders would be licensed either by the government or, more likely, by a professional association. They would have to attest to sufficient experience in the use of the drug and working with those under the drug's influence. They would be required to carry malpractice and liability insurance.

This type of psychedelic drug use is consistent with the idea of changing the cultural norms about drug use away from casual, and therefore risky, drug use. One way to reduce the acceptability to teenagers of "dosing" or dropping some "hits" and cavalierly going off to large rock and roll venues is to help define the appropriate ways in which these drugs can be used.

DRIVING UNDER THE INFLUENCE: A BASELINE PERFORMANCE APPROACH TO IMPAIRMENT

In 1994 there were 40,676 fatalities from motor vehicle crashes; 16,589 of the fatalities were alcohol-related (40.8 percent). The number of fatalities, and the alcohol-related percentage of all motor vehicle crash fatalities, has dropped steadily since at least 1982.[80] The number of drug-related motor vehicle crashes is not known. Drug use affects a person's driving ability, but accidents cannot be attributed directly to the driver's drug use, and the effects of drugs on driving performance is not well understood.[81] Stimulant drugs have particularly complex effects, such as increasing both alertness and aggression.

The offenses of driving under the influence of alcohol or drugs should be redefined to improve their effectiveness in protecting the driving public. Much of current enforcement depends on proof of blood alcohol concentrations (BAC). The BAC, however, is only a prediction or estimation of impairment. Some percentages of drivers involved in alcohol-related motor vehicle crashes have a BAC substantially below the legal standard.[82] Other drivers are not impaired at the legal threshold of .10 percent or whatever the level in a specific state. Alcohol in combination with many drugs produces impairment at low levels of drinking. Many drugs are difficult to detect, and for many drugs a great deal of research needs to be undertaken to establish the curve of impairment with the concentration in the blood or other bodily fluids. In general drugs are metabolized at rates different from those of alcohol.

A more effective means to protect the public from impaired drivers is to test for impairment. Any number of circumstances or the use of a variety of legal or illegal compounds can cause impairment of the ability to safely operate a motor vehicle, for example, over-the-counter cold or allergy medication, alcohol, or marijuana. Therefore the best technique to protect public safety is to test for actual impairment. Performance ability can be tested at the time a commercial driver, train engineer, or vessel captain or pilot takes the wheel or helm, and tested routinely throughout the shift or watch. Performance ability can be tested upon suspicion of impairment, such as a motor vehicle stop for suspicion of driving while intoxicated, and following any kind of accident or crash.

One approach to detect impairment is to set a universal standard of eye–hand coordination, problem recognition, and incident response time—a vehicle operating alertness level (VOAL).

A second approach is to set for each vehicle operator a personal benchmark for performance. For example, drivers could provide individual baseline VOALs when they obtain or renew their driver's license. To motivate people to operate at their highest levels when providing their baseline VOAL, insurance companies could be permitted or encouraged to offer lower rates to those who score at high levels. Another method would be to give immediate cash awards to those who have high VOALs. It would be logical to set an absolute floor of performance so that even a person whose sober performance is below a minimum standard would no longer be entitled to hold a license. This would create an objective standard for the revocation of the driver's licenses of the elderly whose performance has seriously eroded.

When a person is suspected of operating a vehicle while impaired, the person would be tested immediately for their VOAL.

Under the universal standard approach, the determination of whether one is impaired would be relatively simple. However, setting the standard for performance is more complicated. Assuming that there is a range of skills across the population, and assuming for the sake of argument that the reaction time of senior citizens as a class is substantially lower than the class of young people, a performance level that can regularly be achieved by most senior citizens (in order to permit them to continue to drive) may be a level reached by a partially intoxicated young person. Even though the young driver is in fact impaired in a subjective sense, by the objective standard the driver may meet the minimum standard of performance.

The second approach of individual VOAL has the advantage of testing every driver's performance at any time against their own sobriety. Impairment would be established as operating at a significant percentage below one's baseline VOAL. Determining the appropriate percentage of performance below the baseline VOAL will require research. With this approach we would maximize every driver's standard of alertness, and not use a lower common standard.

JUVENILE DRUG USE CONTROLS

Our cultural norms now tolerate a high degree of drug use by young people. Our current approach has students the number one marketing target for alcohol in televised beer and wine ads, at concerts and festivals, and at pro-

motions in vacation areas. Younger children are the prime marketing target
for tobacco with cartoon advertising. Some cigarette trademarks are now better
known to 6-year-old children than Mickey Mouse. The levels of binge drinking and inebriation by high schoolers are epidemic at a prevalence of 30 percent or more for high school seniors and college students. The 1996 Monitoring the Future survey (a survey of high school student drug use that has been
conducted annually for over twenty years) showed that more than 30 percent
of high school seniors reported drinking five or more drinks at one time in
the previous two weeks. The same survey found that almost 25 percent of tenth-
grade students reported the same type of binge drinking in the previous two
weeks. Even one in six eighth-graders reported binge drinking in the previous
two weeks. These rates of binge drinking are increases over the past five years,
most markedly for the younger students. These rates of intense alcohol use
rates have not received the same news media attention as marked increases in
self-reports of marijuana use by high school students.

Marijuana use has increased dramatically since 1991. Use at least once
in one's lifetime has increased for eighth-graders from 10.2 percent in 1991 to
23.1 percent in 1996, for tenth-graders from 23.4 percent to 39.8 percent, and
for twelfth-graders from 36.7 percent to 44.9 percent. Use at least once in the
past year has also increased markedly: for eighth-graders from 6.2 percent in
1991 to 18.3 percent in 1996, for tenth-graders from 16.5 percent to 33.6 percent, and for twelfth-graders from 23.9 percent to 35.8 percent. Use of marijuana or hashish in the past thirty days (which is generally considered the
marker of persons classified as "users," in contrast to experimenters) has also
increased markedly: for eighth-graders from 3.2 percent in 1991 to 11.3 percent in 1996, for tenth-graders from 8.7 percent to 20.4 percent, and for twelfth-
graders from 13.8 percent to 21.9 percent. Currently about one in five students in the average senior high school is a marijuana user. This has been the
result of a five-year pattern of increase that follows a twelve-year pattern of
steady decrease in marijuana use. It is important to note that current levels
are substantially lower than the levels that existed from the mid-1970s to the
mid-1980s. The use by white students is substantially higher than for black
students for all age groups. White seniors use marijuana more frequently than
Hispanic seniors, but at the eighth- and tenth-grade levels Hispanic students
use marijuana at a substantially higher rate than white or black students.

A comprehensive antidrug program for juveniles must be reconstructed.
The typical drug prevention program is a DARE class in the sixth grade.
DARE became widespread only in the mid- and late 1980s. It was earmarked
by Congress for appropriations and now receives on the order of $400 mil-
lion in federal funds and another $300 million in state, local, and private
funds. The trend in increased drug use among teenagers tracks the juvenile
cohorts that had the most intense exposure to DARE.

America's teen drug abuse prevention programs must recognize that initiation into the use of caffeine, nicotine, and alcohol is initiation into drug use. The paradigm needs to shift from associating chemicals with outlawry and rebellion to responsible use, defined as adult use only after considering the risks, and with a willingness to take responsibility for the consequences. Changing this paradigm will be very difficult because of the psychological and cultural contradictions regarding the appropriate rearing of children and between control and rule breaking that permeate this entire subject.[83]

All adults must take responsibility for keeping drugs and alcohol out of the hands of children and recognize that inconveniencing adult drug use—but not prohibiting it—is part of the price of responsible drug use. Cigarette vending machines as we know them must become "a thing of the past." New cigarette vending machines might be activated only by unique purchaser identification such as those of ATMs that distribute cash, so that only adults could access the cigarette supply.

At the same time, an important tool for teaching drug use is experiential learning in the home. Today, many children learn about using beer, wine, and whiskey, in part by what their parents let them do. Jewish children drink wine at Passover and other ritual occasions. At special events when toasts are drunk, such as weddings, children may be given small portions of wine. Drug policy should not so invade the family that appropriate training in drug use cannot take place under parental supervision.

LOCKING UP DRUGS

The culture, if not the law, might support parents who keep alcohol in locked cabinets to prevent unsupervised alcohol use. Refrigerators could be designed with compartments that lock and require keys or combinations to unlock so that chilled beer and wine can be kept from juveniles. Such refrigerators should at least be options available from manufacturers or sold as aftermarket accessories for existing refrigerators.

The prohibition for commercially distributing drugs to children should be strictly enforced, with tobacco and alcohol getting equal attention with other drugs.

Persons who hold licenses for use of heroin, cocaine, and similar drugs, if they had children, would initially have special legal responsibility to keep the drugs locked up and out the reach of their children.

Can we require that alcoholic beverages be locked up in homes to keep them away from children? Can we require as a condition of using drugs that drugs be locked up in homes to keep them away from children? These restrictions and intrusions are insignificant compared to current policies.

TOBACCO

Early, heavy tobacco use has been identified by researchers in juvenile drug experimentation as the prime marker for heavy illegal drug use. An example of this was the finding by Lloyd Johnson, Ph.D., at the University of Michigan, that a teenage cigarette smoker was fourteen times more likely to be using cocaine, heroin, or hallucinogens than a teenager who does not smoke cigarettes at all.[84] Tobacco advertising contributes to juvenile tobacco use and such advertising needs to be regulated, taxed, and otherwise restricted.

INTENSE INVESTIGATIONS OF JUVENILE DRUG USE

Unsupervised drug use by children would be an indication that the legal system of control had broken down. This would contrast with the case today in which distribution to juveniles is simply a spillover from the massive illegal trade.

Drug use by children is rarely in isolation, so intense investigation of the entire cohort of the child using drugs is probably called for as an effective means to rapidly find the source. If a juvenile is found with strong drugs like alcohol, heroin, cocaine, or psychedelics, the juvenile's parents would be alerted and questioned about the juvenile's friends and habits and opportunities to get drugs.

If the drugs had leaked from the parents' supply, the parents would be warned and offered assistance in perfecting their home control program. Further violations by parents could result in a range of sanctions, particularly if other children were getting access to the drugs. Until the adult source of the drugs is identified, the children would be shadowed by authorities.

MARIJUANA POLICY ISSUES

Marijuana policy needs to be divided into at least two areas that are completely unrelated: (1) the use of marijuana to treat medical conditions such as glaucoma, nausea, and spasticity; and (2) the recreational or pleasurable use of marijuana. These issues are no more related than the use of cocaine in eye or nose surgery by physicians, and the use of cocaine by addicts and others.

MARIJUANA AS MEDICINE

Cannabis has been used in medicine for thousands of years. It was part of the U.S. pharmacopeia until 1941.[85]

Developing a program to distribute marijuana for medical purposes that fits into American drug law requires the development of standardized sources, appropriate dosage determinations, proper labeling, and feasible distribution and preservation methods, all of which will require the issuance of regulations by the Food and Drug Administration.

The conventional wisdom has been that since "marijuana cannot be patented," there is no economic logic for a drug company to spend the money to test efficacy and safety to obtain FDA approval of a New Drug Application.

With the passage of Proposition 215 by California's voters in 1996, the economic viability of commercial development of medical quality marijuana has increased substantially. While marijuana per se cannot be patented, "new and useful" processes that are discovered that use marijuana—in the treatment of specific diseases, for example—might be patented. "New and useful" variations of marijuana, achieved through breeding or genetic manipulation, might be patented. And "new and useful" processes and inventions, such as equipment and containers, that are developed to cultivate, harvest, package, preserve, transport, and administer marijuana might also be patented.

In addition to the patent issues, the necessary investment in security around the cultivation, processing, and distribution of medicinal marijuana to comply with DEA's desire to prevent diversion to criminal distribution may be another competitive advantage for the firm that successfully undertakes the research.

Here are a few tentative thoughts about patent issues that might protect the competitive position of a company that successfully undertakes this research and marketing.

Therapeutic Processes

Because the world of science doesn't know the precise therapeutic mechanisms of action of the various cannabis compounds, learning which compounds produce specific effects could lead to a variety of patents for the processes of using compound X (or a formula of compounds X, Y, and Z) to treat epilepsy, spasticity, nausea, or any of the conditions now known and unknown that could respond to cannabis therapy.

Currently, THC is the only one of at least 60 THC-related compounds that is considered the "active ingredient" of marijuana. However, many of the other compounds may be therapeutically active. Lester Grinspoon, M.D., has suggested that it is likely that some of those other compounds may be important in treating some of the conditions that marijuana is being used for now. It is conceivable that genetic mutation of marijuana could produce new compounds with therapeutic utility. And it is also conceivable that synthetic modifications of the naturally occurring compounds may have therapeutic utility.

Manufacturing Processes

Once it is determined that a particular cannabinoid or cannabidiol (or a combination of such compounds) is optimal for treating a particular condition, it may be possible to breed a plant that has that proportion of the desired compounds. There has been a great deal of marijuana breeding and informal research to make more potent marijuana, or marijuana that has different intoxicating properties. Very little of this kind of plant breeding research has been undertaken to find plants that are more effective for the treatment of various medical conditions. Plant patents are for asexually propagated plants (i.e., those not reproduced from seeds). The Plant Variety Protection Act (P.L. 91-577, Dec. 24, 1970) sets up a system for protecting the discovery of sexually reproduced varieties of plants, within the jurisdiction of the Department of Agriculture. (I know nothing about the scope of this protection.)

There may also be patentable processes for improving on the way in which marijuana is cultivated in order to produce plants of necessary uniformity. For example, these may be related to specific processes such as absorption of nutrients, control of pests, use of certain light frequencies, and rates of growth. (It is possible, for example, that the manufacturers of penicillin have or had process patents for the manufacture of penicillin.) Some of these processes may have been patented by others but are not being used commercially now. If a company obtains the exclusive license to use such a patent (or an exclusive license for the cultivation of marijuana), that is also a potential commercial advantage.

Packaging Processes

A critical issue in using marijuana as medicine is assuring the potency of the medication at the time of use. How can marijuana be packaged so that it remains potent, free of fungi, and so on? How can it be packaged in a form that pharmaceutical wholesalers and retailers will be willing to handle? Resolving those questions may result in the development of patentable processes or inventions as well.

Marijuana Utilization Processes

An improved method or device for vaporizing marijuana, including improved pipes, might also be patentable. I suspect that a number of marijuana pipes, such as the "smokeless" variety, have been patented. If a "medically acceptable" method of inhaling marijuana were to be developed, it might be protected by means of a patent.

Limitations on the Issuance of Patents

For something to be patented, it must be "useful." It must also work—a useful idea is not patentable. For combinations of ingredients such as medicines to be patented, there must be more to the mixture than the effect of its components—it must have a new effect.

Another potential problem is that the invention must be "new." If the invention has been patented elsewhere, or was used or known in this country, or was "described in a printed publication," it is not patentable. The inventor must be careful not to describe the invention in a printed publication, or use the patent publicly, before it is patented, or else the right to a patent is lost.

Difficulty in Predicting Patentability and Patent-
Related Costs

It is very difficult to evaluate the likelihood of discovering patentable processes or inventions in the course of researching medical marijuana, and assessing how commercially valuable such patents might be. It might also be costly to pursue patent protection at the Patent and Trademark Office. A patent is the right to exclude others from "making, using or selling the invention." Thus, enforcing a patent usually requires litigation.

Starting a New Company, or Interesting an Existing
Company

Biotechnology has been a hot field for raising investment capital. But a start-up in this special field would have to be adequately financed to have a good chance of overcoming the many untested legal, regulatory, research, and marketing challenges such a venture would face. It is hard to know how much financing that would entail. Another possibility might be to encourage an existing company to undertake the medical marijuana research for commercial purposes.

International Start-Up

Would there be advantages in commencing research outside the United States? There are international treaties regarding honoring the patents issued by signatory states. Other nations might allow both research and medical use of marijuana more quickly than the United States, and at less expense to the developer. Would this body of research and clinical experience then be acceptable to the FDA?

Other Unknowns

Other questions also need to be addressed: How substantial are the medical benefits of the marijuana ingredients? How many patients would benefit? What are the comparisons between marijuana and the competing medications for the various conditions we're treating—cost, efficacy, side effects, establishment in the market?

What are the simple economics: Annual demand in number of doses, number of patients who would benefit, number of prescriptions that would be filled, cost per dose, price per dose, profit per dose? How much inventory would have to be in the pipeline? How much would a company sell each year over five or ten years?

How important is patent protection to the economic viability of the concern? Who could compete in this business? What controls would there be on a company's ability to set prices? Would illegal marijuana compete with legal, FDA-approved marijuana? What are the various ways in which drug companies operate? What would the international market be? What subsidies, write-offs, or other tax advantages might limit the risks? How long will it take to conduct the necessary safety tests and what will it realistically cost?

Physicians

A second set of issues governs the regulation of physicians who prescribe marijuana for medical purposes. Passage of the initiatives in California and Arizona in 1996 has begun to open up many questions about how physicians will use marijuana in their practice. Marijuana remains on schedule I of the Controlled Substances Act, and therefore there is no authority to write prescriptions for its use. If marijuana is moved to another schedule, then practice with marijuana will be similar to other medical practice involving controlled substances. Until rescheduling, doctors will operate in a netherworld. In any event, there is not yet a body of medical literature or tradition that tells doctors what is good medical practice for prescribing cannabis.

What needs to be written is a protocol of good medical practice that sets forth "professional medical standards" for: (1) the examination of and taking of history for patients whose diagnosis suggests that it may be appropriate for using cannabis; (2) guidance for developing an appropriate, medically sound treatment plan; (3) guidance for handling patients who request cannabis prescriptions or recommendations (including those who may not have appropriate medical conditions); (4) recommendations about dosage, side effects, follow-up; (5) appropriate cautions and warnings to give to patients; (6) practices that are inappropriate or statements that should not be made; and (7) the necessary measures to take to prevent "diversion of marijuana for nonmedical purposes."

a original draft of a document

Leading doctors in California and Arizona should develop and disseminate a draft protocol. Doctors must be given the profession's recommendations on the steps to take to demonstrate a reasonable basis for making a recommendation under the Compassionate Use Act of 1996. The effectiveness of this protocol might be enhanced if the promulgators of the protocol express their willingness to testify as expert witnesses for the prosecution of physicians who are improperly "recommending" marijuana or who are practicing in a manner leading to the diversion for nonmedical use.

Under the Arizona initiative, physicians must comply with "professional medical standards" (sec. 13-3412.01.1). This is a slightly different term than that in section 13-3412.1.2: "medical practitioners . . . while acting in the course of their professional practice, in good faith and in accordance with generally accepted medical standards." Because the Arizona initiative applies to all schedule I substances, recommendations about prescribing (or most likely *not* prescribing) schedule I substances should also be included.

Physicians also need insurance against malpractice. The recommending or prescribing of marijuana most likely is not covered by malpractice insurance policies. An insurance company ought to be willing to write an insurance binder for physicians against malpractice once a protocol is adopted by appropriate medical authorities.

It might also be necessary for physicians to obtain insurance to defend their license if DEA seeks to take their license away or indict them. A condition for issuing such a policy would be that the doctor subscribe to the insurance company's protocol for proper examination, diagnosis, and treatment. If 500 physicians purchased such a policy for $500 each per year, a $250,000 legal defense fund could be established. An insurance company might consider spending even more, if necessary, betting that a win would draw a lot of new policyholders in this area.

MARIJUANA USE FOR PLEASURE, RELAXATION, OR "INSIGHT"

In looking for a regulatory model (not a marketing or consumption model) for the pleasurable use of marijuana, much of the current regulatory approach for alcohol, based on revenue controls administered by the U.S. Bureau of Alcohol, Tobacco and Firearms, could be applied to cannabis production and distribution. Growers and distributors would be licensed, pay "special occupational taxes," and would be responsible for the collection and payment of taxes on cannabis. The cannabis would have to bear labels warning of health risks created by its ingestion. The origin and potency of the cannabis would have to be identified. Taxation could be on the basis of potency as alcohol tax is imposed on a proof gallon of distilled spirits.

Assuming that many in the public believe that many of the problems of alcohol in our society are a result of the system of marketing of alcohol, a goal for replacing marijuana prohibition would be to create a different marketing model. Reform of alcohol marketing would be an appropriate component of creating a new comprehensive alcohol policy. Marijuana distributors should not be allowed to sponsor athletic events, music events, art exhibitions, or the like. There must be full enforcement of the marijuana regulations. Distributors who sell to minors must be investigated by regulatory agencies and prosecuted. Advertising in media designed to reach young people should be restricted.

Marijuana retail prices range from $40 to $600 per ounce depending on quality, quantity, and location of the market. Marijuana sold for pleasurable use could probably be taxed in the range of $50 to $100 per ounce without creating substantial opportunities for criminal price undercutting, although enforcement would certainly be required to protect the revenues.

Today the home brewing of beer or production of wine, up to 200 gallons per year per household of two or more persons "for personal or family use," is untaxed.[86] Since marijuana is easily grown, cultivation for personal or family use should be allowed without registration or taxation.

An interim step toward regulated adult use and taxation of production might be to require licensing of adult marijuana users by the Secretary of the Treasury, or to permit the states to do so. A model of such a license and application appears in Figure 19–1.

CHALLENGES TO LEGALIZATION AND REGULATION

"LEGALIZATION" UNDEFINED

The defenders of the status quo object to "legalization" as the alternative to prohibition. But what is the "legalization" they are objecting to? They fairly protest that often those who call for legalization fail to provide a concrete proposal to replace prohibition. But they are not careful to avoid broad claims about what will result from "legalization" by failing to define what they mean when they use the term. For their convenience they assume that only the least regulated market regulation would be the form adopted.

REGULATION IS LEGALIZATION

Any form of regulation that is not prohibition is a form of legalization. It is legal to sell insurance in the state of New York, for example, but it is illegal for me to go to the corner of 5th Avenue and 44th Street and start hawking

Figure 19–1.

United States of America
MARIJUANA LICENSE
APPLICATION

Robert E. Rubin
Secretary of the Treasury

( ) License to Possess $ 100.00 per year   DATE
( ) License to Possess & Cultivate $ 200.00 per year

Name of Applicant   Date of Birth
Address
City   State   Zip

ASSUMPTION OF RESPONSIBILITY AND CONDITIONS OF LICENSE

(1) I shall never operate any vehicle, vessel, or aircraft while under the influence of marijuana.
(2) I shall never distribute marijuana commercially to any person.
(3) I shall never distribute marijuana to any person under the age of 21 years except as necessary for authorized medical purposes.
(4) I shall never distribute any marijuana that has been adulterated.
(5) I shall never commit any crime while under the influence of marijuana.
(6) I shall never cultivate marijuana in any manner that is harmful to the environment.
(7) I shall never smoke marijuana in an enclosed public space or close to unconsenting persons.
(8) I shall comply with the regulations of the Treasury Secretary regarding marijuana applying to me.

Upon issuance to me of a U.S. Treasury Department marijuana license, I hereby ACCEPT RESPONSIBILITY, AND PROMISE THE PEOPLE OF AMERICA TO BE BOUND BY these conditions.

Signature of Applicant_____ Date_____

STATEMENT OF QUALIFICATIONS

I HEREBY CERTIFY that I am at least 21 years old; and that within the past two years—
(a) I have not operated any vehicle while under the influence of marijuana, alcohol or any other drug.
(b) I have not committed any crime while under the influence of marijuana, alcohol or any other drug.
(c) I have not illegally distributed marijuana, alcohol or any other drug to a person under the age of 21.

Signature of Applicant (under penalty of perjury)_____ Date_____

UNITED STATES MARIJUANA LICENSE
[ ] POSSESSION [ ] CULTIVATION

DATE PAID____ METHOD OF PAYMENT____ TOTAL FEE PAID [ ] $200.00 [ ] $100.00

I, Robert E. Rubin, SECRETARY OF THE TREASURY, United States of America, hereby certify that _____, applicant, being qualified, having taken responsibility, and having paid the indicated fee, shall be exempt from prosecution by the United States, or any subdivision thereof, for possession, cultivation or distribution of marijuana for one year from the date of payment so long as applicant remains qualified and complies fully with the above conditions and published regulations.

FOR THE SECRETARY OF THE TREASURY   DATE

insurance policies to passersby. A traveler probably could find a vending machine for a life insurance policy at the airport, but generally, to buy insurance, one has to go to a licensed insurance seller who is subject to extensive regulation and supervision. Legalization is not a simple concept.

Everything that is legally sold is sold subject to some kind of regulatory scheme: stocks and bonds, jewelry, milk, potatoes, cars, clothing, apples, wristwatches. The only commodities that are sold now without regulation and controls are oxymoronically called "controlled substances": cocaine, heroin, and marijuana, among others.

ISSUES OTHER THAN "ILLEGAL PROFITS"

The defenders of prohibition argue that "the theory of drug legalization is that it would take the profit motive out of illegal drug dealing, eliminating the evils of drug prohibition."[87] But this "take the profits out and the problems of prohibition will be over" claim is a strawman. At a minimum, almost everyone who has thought deeply about drug policy and what a postprohibition environment might look like recognizes that there will continue to be drug abuse and drug addiction. Whether the totality of problems called drug abuse, and their many manifestations, will be a greater or lesser problem than the current problem depends on how the alternatives to prohibition are designed.

A realistic view of postprohibition policies is that they are almost certain to evolve. It is absurd to imagine that a dramatic policy change can predict perfectly all of the necessary steps that are needed. Indeed, good sense suggests that caution is warranted, and that small steps ought to be taken in advance of larger steps. The opportunity for experimentation that is built into our federal system should be taken as suggested by Daniel Benjamin and Roger Leroy Miller.[88]

It is probable that the postprohibition regulatory environment will change over time as the drug situation changes. Regulations will have to be modified as experience teaches what problems are amenable to various solutions. Many of the evils of drug prohibition, such as police corruption or gang violence, like the evils of drug use, are not going to be eliminated, but reduced.

INCREASED COMPLIANCE AND SELF-POLICING

In the drug regulation, postprohibition environment, there will be violators of the regulations, as has been true of all regulatory schemes. One feature of well-regulated markets is that when regulations are reasonable and accepted by the market participants, they join in enforcing the regulations. For example, a liquor store that does not sell liquor to minors has an interest in seeing that the competitors don't compete unfairly by selling to minors. The law-abiding liquor dealer has several interests in assuring that other liquor stores obey the regulation—economic (to maintain competitive equity), convenience (to avoid being subject to additional or onerous regulations imposed to further control the violations of others), reputational (to maintain one's reputation as a valued member of the community), as well as simply being law abiding. Infractions by violators can lead to greater restrictions on all sellers, and tarnish the reputation of all sellers. We should neither minimize nor exaggerate the power of self-policing. But we should recognize the potential important assistance that self-policing contributes to enforcement.

Customers in a regulated industry also become a part of the policing effort. In a regulated drug control system, lawful drug buyers and users have an interest in making the regulated market work since they are among the principal beneficiaries in terms of access, prices, safety, education, and so on. An objective of ending prohibition, unrelated to profits, is to increase the number of market participants—buyers as well as sellers—who ally themselves with the forces of law and order.

THE "BLACK MARKET" OF MINORS

For some prohibitionists the proof of legalizers' naivete is that ". . . prohibition of sale of . . . drugs generally to minors, would give illegal drug traffickers a continuing opportunity to exploit these markets, and thus by definition the proposal would not end the evils of drug prohibition."[89]

Frequently in a debate on "legalization" the defender of prohibition feels he has drawn blood in forcing the prohibition opponent to concede support of prohibition on sales to minors. "Aha," says the status quo defender, "you see, there will be a black market—you accomplish nothing but sending the wrong message." Undoubtedly, there will be those who will sell drugs to minors illegally. Enforcement against them will be required, as enforcement is required against the sellers of alcohol and tobacco to minors.

The variety of alcohol regulation is illustrative of the imagination, complexity, and competing objectives of a regulatory system. Beer, wine, and whiskey are regulated differently in almost every jurisdiction even though the active ingredient, ethyl alcohol (ethanol), is the same, and even though the effects of abuse of any form of alcoholic beverage produces the same physical, psychological, and social evils.

Many questions will need answers, but that should not stymie us, such as whether hashish can be consumed at a place where a license permits marijuana consumption or should low-dosage cocaine chewing gum be available by prescription the way Nicorette gum was once restricted, or sold over the counter as nicorette is now.

Market survey research might be helpful. We need to survey heroin addicts—those who are active, in recovery, and in prison—to learn what addicts' market behavior might be in a variety of regulatory systems. Can addicts be trained to respond to bureaucratic rules and regulations? They certainly accommodate many other indignities under prohibition.

There will be trade-offs. The more restrictive the access in a regulated system, the more opportunity for criminals to try to circumvent the system. For example, legal gambling has not eliminated illegal gambling. Illegal gambling competes by offering different services: A runner will come to you to take your bet. You are able to wager on credit. You might be able to bet on a number with only ten cents rather than a whole dollar. You might get better odds on payoff. Your winnings will be in cash and not reported to the IRS. A postprohibition environment will continue to respond to criminal initiatives.

WILL DRUG USE GO UP OR DOWN?

Critics of legalization say that "depenalization" of drug possession in Italy is *the cause* of a high rate of heroin addiction there. Others claim that Dutch drug policy is *the cause* of an increasing crime rate there. These claims of causation are baseless. They are based on supposition and, at best, temporal association, and not on any in-depth analysis. They are as sophisticated as an assertion that lawn mower sales are caused by increases in the number of hours of sunlight per day. Such claims ignore all other factors. It is very hard to identify a *single* cause of phenomena as complex as a change in drug use rates.

Would drug use go up if the controls were changed? A nationwide survey conducted for Richard Dennis, chairman of the advisory board of the Drug Policy Foundation, reported that 93 percent of the American people said they would not use cocaine if it were legal. Predicting behavior is very difficult. This is not dispositive, but not inconsistent with the National Household Survey of Drug Abuse for 1991, which found that among those aged 18-25 7.7 percent had used cocaine in the past year and 2.0 percent had done so in the past month. Of those aged 26 and up, 2.5 percent had used cocaine in the past year and 0.8 percent in the past month.[90]

Are the American people like small children with their noses pressed to the window of the candy store waiting for drugs to be legalized? No. And one must thank in some measure the large variety of drug use prevention messages presented through a wide variety of media. There is nothing inherent in a regulated drug market that requires advertising. Even more important, there is nothing inherent in a regulated drug market that is inconsistent with increasing the frequency and sophistication of drug abuse prevention messages in all media.

ELEMENTS OF ENDING PROHIBITION THAT
MIGHT HELP REDUCE DRUG USE

There are a couple of points to be made about the potentially increased effectiveness of prevention programs in the postprohibition environment.

1. Parents can be more honest. Under prohibition, parents have to overcome a significant hurdle to be honest with their children about their drug use experiences, positive *or* negative. The parent who admits to drug use admits to breaking the law. Postprohibition, a parent could share negative experiences without being an example of legal disobedience.

Indeed, under prohibition, parents are tempted to lie to their children about their drug-using experiences. Lying does not strengthen the trust between parents and children that is believed to be an important factor in preventing or reducing adolescent drug use.

2. As Dr. Lloyd Johnston of the University of Michigan observed at the NIDA National Conference on Marijuana in the summer of 1995, one reason for increasing teenage drug use over the three previous years was that teens were not seeing the victims of drug abuse that their older siblings saw seven and twelve years previously. One drawback of the success in reducing drug abuse is that those tempted to experiment are less likely to see the tragic victims of unsuccessful experiments. In December 1996, Johnston, the nation's leading epidemiologist of teenage drug use and principal investigator of the Monitoring the Future Survey, offered an explanation of the fourth year of increased teenage drug use: "The erosion of peer norms against drug use, and the declines in the proportions of students who see them as dangerous, undoubtedly have several explanations. Among the most likely, in my opinion, is the fact that this most recent crop of youngsters grew up in a period in which drug use rates were down substantially from what they had been 10 to 15 years earlier. This gave youngsters less opportunity to learn from others' mistakes and resulted in what I call 'generational forgetting' of the hazards of drugs, as the process of generational replacement has taken place."[91]

Young whites use crack cocaine 77 percent more frequently than young blacks. In 1994, 3.2% of the whites aged 18–25 used crack cocaine, but only 1.8% of the Blacks in the same age group. Although the difference was not as great in the 12–17 and 26–34 age groups, the same pattern held true: whites are much more likely to use crack cocaine than blacks.[92] One reason that illegal drug use is believed to be lower among African-American youth than among white youth is that the former see more crackheads in their families and neighborhoods, the fallout from the crack wave of the late 1980s.

A potential effect of ending prohibition is that victims of drug abuse may come out of the closet. It may be easier for those tempted to experiment to see the negative consequences of drug use, even if drug use rates do not increase.

3. Ending prohibition may have the effect of reducing "denial" about drug problems in many families, workplaces, and neighborhoods. This may also speed entry into drug treatment, and reduce the consumption of drugs among heavy users.

Prohibition increases society's denial around drug problems, and it increases the denial when a public official, such as Washington, D.C.'s Mayor Marion Barry, has a drug problem. Yet with alcoholism there is no equivalent degree of shame, shock, or denial. If someone seeks alcohol treatment, it is barely news. In the late 1980s U.S. Rep. Bill Emerson (R-Missouri) quietly announced that he was an alcoholic and was entering treatment. No one was scandalized. No one tracked him down. No one called for his resignation or prosecution. Until he died of cancer in 1996, Rep. Emerson was serving as vice-chairman of the House Agriculture Committee in his eighth term.[93]

REDUCTIONS IN TOBACCO AND ALCOHOL USE AS A MODEL FOR ADDICTIVE DRUGS

Prohibitionists argue that "reductions in tobacco and alcohol are not reliable guidelines [sic] for legalized drugs because the pleasure-enhancing and tolerance-producing (i.e., addictive) characteristics of cocaine, crack and heroin are far more powerful than those of tobacco and alcohol."[94] This statement is not necessarily true as far as "pleasure-enhancing" properties, which are highly subjective, go. The term *drug of choice* refers to the drug that a particular addict prefers over others. More than any other durg, tobacco is the drug of choice for addicts in this country. More important, the then surgeon general of the U.S. Public Health Service, C. Everett Koop, reported in 1988 that "cigarettes and other forms of tobacco are addicting in the same sense as are drugs such as heroin and cocaine."[95]

CONCLUSION

The proposals here for addiction management, for licensing drug users, for personal consulting pharmacies, for psychedelic trip leaders, for refrigerators with locking beer coolers, are all part of changing a culture about drug use— to get more sober about using drugs.

These ideas are not being advanced for immediate adoption but for testing—testing against principles concerning what we want to achieve, testing their practical application. These ideas, after being tested, are almost certainly going to need modification to become programs.

On December 17, 1903, the Wright brothers made their first heavier-than-air flight. In 1908 the first aviator was killed in flight. Imagine yourself in the spring of 1908 hearing Wilbur and Orville Wright describing their vision of intercity air travel. Imagine a highly visionary presentation of the potential future of aviation: flights at all times of day and in almost all weather conditions—in the rain, in clouds, and after dark—and flights across the country and across the oceans. Airplanes seating dozens or hundreds of passengers. It was simply inconceivable that the dangers could be eliminated and that air travel could become as routine as it is today.

Imagine a thoughtful fellow in the audience asking Orville Wright, "Are you going to land these aeroplanes at Union Station, Washington, where the passengers are waiting to go to New York?" With the benefit of hindsight, the question is absurd.

In fact, the new form of travel brought an entirely new culture to how we travel, and new forms of social and corporate organization. Entirely new technologies developed in addition to the refinement of the airframe. Even food preparation changed. And to protect the public, regulation continued to evolve to address the many complex components of the evolving industry. Every stage of the industry's evolution required further testing of markets, facilities, social and corporate organization, services, and regulations. Today, for example, air travelers routinely allow themselves to be searched. Submitting oneself to be searched is a cultural change that would have been hard to imagine several decades ago.

In 1908, and throughout the early years of aviation, flying was terribly dangerous. The first U.S. woman pilot, Harriet Quimby, was licensed in 1911. She was killed the following summer in a flying accident over Dorchester Bay at Boston on July 1, 1912. Aviation was dangerous, but by means of regulation and scientific advancement it has been made safe. Drugs are dangerous, but they too can be regulated and benefit from scientific advancement.

We have to be willing to use our imaginations to envision what a post-prohibition environment will look like and how it can evolve. Now is the time for more creativity in addressing the problems that drugs present to us.

ENDNOTES

1. I wish to thank Chad Thevenot for his invaluable assistance in the editing and preparation of this chapter. His suggestions and research assistance were critical to the development and completion of the work. I also want to thank Charles Adler for his very valuable contributions to many sections of the chapter. Some of the issues in this chapter were explored in my articles, "The Sentencing Boomerang: Drug Prohibition Politics and Reform," 40 Villanova Law Review 383 (1995), and "Drug Policy: A Smorgasbord of Conundrums Spiced by Emotions around Children and Violence," 31 Valparaiso University Law Review 597 (1997).

2. "A Wiser Course: Ending Drug Prohibition" by the Committee on Drugs and the Law of the Association of the Bar of the City of New York in 49 THE RECORD OF THE ASSOCIATION OF THE BAR OF THE CITY OF NEW YORK, No. 5, pp. 523–577, June 1994.

3. *Ibid* at 574. *See* DRUG LEGALIZATION: MYTHS AND MISCONCEPTIONS, A DEMAND REDUCTION

Project, Seattle Field Division, Drug Enforcement Administration, Chapter 1, Addiction Rates and Drug Legalization, January 31, 1994.

4. Forty-nine percent give the grade of F or D to the federal government for dealing with drug-related crime. Only 11 percent would give a grade of A or B for this category. Fifty percent give the grade of F or D to the federal government for dealing with drug use and addiction. Only 10 percent would give a grade of A or B for that category. Only 6 percent of Americans thought drug abuse less of a problem in 1995 than in 1990. Nationwide survey by Peter Hart Research Associates for Drug Strategies, Inc., February 1995.

5. See Leviticus 13:46, Numbers 5:2.

6. In New York a drug treatment program appealed to the state's highest court, the Court of Appeals, to resist treating pregnant addicts. But the Court ruled that pregnant addicts were entitled to treatment. Nonetheless, treatment for this population is not widely available. See *Offer Treatment, Not Fear of Prosecution*, American Medical News, Sept. 7, 1992 (Editorial), at 21 (finding that at least 165 women across the nation were criminally charged for exposing their fetuses or infants to controlled substances).

7. Arnold Trebach, The Heroin Solution, Yale University Press, 1982, at 59–84.

8. Narcotics Control Act, R.S.C. 1985, c.N-1, 65(7), Departmental Consolidation Narcotic Control Act and Regulations, June 1988, Department of National Health and Welfare (Canada).

9. Lester Grinspoon, MD & James B. Bakalar, JD, Marihuana as Medicine: A Plea for Reconsideration, 273 Journal of the American Medical Association 23, 1875, 1876 (1995) (affirming that marijuana is medically useful); see also Lester Grinspoon and James B. Bakalar, Marihuana: The Forbidden Medicine, Yale University Press, 1993; Tod H. Mikuriya, MD, Marijuana: Medical Papers 1839–1972, Medi-Comp Press, Oakland, CA 1973.

10. *In the matter of Marijuana Rescheduling Petition*, Docket No. 86-22, Francis L. Young, Administrative Law Judge, Sept. 6, 1988, in R. C. Randall, Marijuana, Medicine and the Law, Volume II, Galen Press, 1989, at 403.

11. National Association of Attorneys General, "Therapeutic Use of Marijuana," Resolution Paper, Summer Meeting, June 22–25, 1983.

12. See testimony of Arnold Trebach, PhD, in 1984 before the House Committee on Energy and Commerce Subcommittee on Health and the Environment regarding the Compassionate Pain Relief Act, H.R. 5290, (98th Congress), and 130 Congressional Record S26063-96 (daily ed. Sept. 19, 1984).

13. Dawn Day, PhD, Health Emergency: The Spread of Drug-Related AIDS Among African-Americans and Latinos (Oct. 11, 1995).

14. U.S. Department of Health and Human Services, "HIV/AIDS Education and Prevention Programs for Adults in Prisons and Jails and Juveniles in Confinement Facilities—U.S. 1994," *Morbidity and Mortality Weekly Report*, April 5, 1996, Vol. 45, No. 13, p. 268; Hammett, T., "1994 Update—HIV/AIDS and STDs in Correctional Facilities," December 1995, Washington, DC, U.S. Department of Justice, Office of Justice Programs, National Institute of Justice and U.S. Department of Health and Human Services, Public Health Service, Centers for Disease Control; U.S. Health Resources and Services Administration (HRSA), "Progress and Challenges in Linking Incarcerated Individuals with HIV/AIDS to Community Services," June 1995.

15. Peter M. Brien and Allen J. Beck, PhD, HIV in Prisons—1994, Bureau of Justice Statistics, U.S. Department of Justice, March 1996, NCJ-158020.

16. National Commission on Acquired Immune Deficiency Syndrome, "The Twin Epidemics of Substance Abuse and HIV," July 1991.

17. J. Normand, D. Vlahov, L.E. Moses, *Preventing HIV Transmission: The Role of Sterile Needles and Bleach*, National Research Council and Institute of Medicine, National Academy Press, 1995, at 4.

18. See documents released to the public, March 7, 1995 by the Drug Policy Foundation.

19. 381 U.S. 479, 85 S.Ct. 1678, 14 L.Ed 2d 510 (1965).

20. George Judson, "Study Finds AIDS Risk to Addicts Drops if Sale of Syringes is Legal," *New York Times*, Aug. 30, 1995 at A1.

21. J. Normand, D. Vlahov, L.E. Moses, *Preventing HIV Transmission: The Role of Sterile Needles and Bleach*, National Research Council and Institute of Medicine, National Academy Press, 1995, at 11.

22. J. Normand, D. Vlahov, L. E. Moses, *Preventing HIV Transmission: The Role of Sterile Needles and Bleach*, National Research Council and Institute of Medicine, National Academy Press, 1995, at 4.

23. Ibid at 232, 251.

24. 18 U.S.C. Section 1365. P.L. 98-127, October 13, 1983.

25. Yvonne Latty, "Neighbors OD on decay, Drug siege causes anger, but hope is long gone," THE PHILADELPHIA DAILY NEWS, May 11, 1996, "Yesterday police reported only three drug overdoses at Temple University Hospital, bringing the binge total to about 120. . . . The latest overdose episodes left junkies in 15 hospitals around the city. . . ."

Associated Press, "Potent Heroin Brings Chaos to Philadelphia Hospitals," LOS ANGELES TIMES, May 11, 1996, "A similar batch caused concern in February, when 43 Philadelphia-area addicts were stricken. Later that month, four people died of overdoses."

Reuters, "Powerful drug lands more than 100 in hospitals," May 10, 1996, Friday, BC cycle, "Sgt. Susan Lewis, a spokeswoman for the [Philadelphia police] department, said there were no deaths attributed to the rash of overdoses."

However, *The New York Times* treated the story as one about poisonings, not "overdoses." Christopher Wren, "Heroin Addicts Falling Prey to Tainted Drugs," *The New York Times*, May 14, 1996, p. A21.

26. U.S. Department of Health and Human Services, *The Health Consequences of Smoking: Nicotine Addiction, A Report of the Surgeon General*, vi (1988) (showing that cigarettes and other forms of tobacco are addicting in the same sense as drugs such as heroin and cocaine); see generally Erich Goode, *Drugs in American Society*, 255-62 (1993).

27. See Carl E. Bartecchi et al., "The Global Tobacco Epidemic" in Scientific American, May 1995, at 47 (finding that the United States tobacco industry spent more than $5 billion on advertising in 1992).

28. Institute for Health Policy, Brandeis University, *Substance Abuse: The Nation's Number One Health Problem*, p. 28 (1993).

29. Ibid at 28, 54. Forty-two percent of the U.S. population smoked cigarettes in 1965, which amounted to 4,345 cigarettes per adult per year. Ibid at 12. By 1992, only 26 percent of the population smoked, and per capita consumption dropped to 2,629 cigarettes per year. Ibid.

30. Dr. Mark A. R. Kleiman has been one of the strongest advocates for this proposition. *Against Excess*, 1992 at 146-147, 193-194.

31. This idea has also been developed by Dr. Kleiman, *id.* at 98-101, 249-52, and 277-79.

32. The definition of "safety" will probably require modification for various compounds that are not medicines in the current sense as regulated by FDA.

33. For example, 27 CFR sec. 194.3, referring to 27 CFR sec. 1.24(a) (4-1-90 Edition). Applicant must not have been convicted of a federal or state felony within five years of the date of the application.

34. Spencer S. Hsu, "Teenage Testers Buy Cigarettes Easily in N. Va.," The Washington Post, November 14, 1996, p. D1; Paul W. Valentine, "For Minors, Buying Cigarettes Often Easy Md. Survey Finds," The Washington Post, October 2, 1996, p. A1.

35. "Dram Shop" or Civil Liability Acts in some fourteen states impose strict liability, without proof of negligence, upon the owners of taverns who serve alcohol to inebriated patrons who then are in a motor vehicle accident.

36. In the Controlled Substances Act, 21 U.S.C. 801 *et seq.*, the term "production" includes "manufacturing, planting, cultivation, growing, or harvesting of a controlled substance" (21 U.S.C. 802(22)). "The term 'manufacture' means the production . . . of a drug" (21 U.S.C. 802(15)). The unauthorized manufacture (i.e., cultivation) of less than fifty marihuana plants is a felony subject to imprisonment of up to five years (21 U.S.C. 841(b)(1)(D)).

37. Forfeiture of real property "used, or intended to be used . . . to commit . . . a violation" of the Controlled Substances Act is provided for in sec. 511 of the Controlled Substances Act, 21 U.S.C. 881(a)(7). Other paragraphs provide for the forfeiture of conveyances used to transport controlled substances illegally (a)(4), of drug paraphernalia (a)(10), and other property related to CSA violations.

38. William Rhodes, Paul Scheiman, Tanutda Pittayathikhun, Laura Collins, Vered Tsarfaty, Abt Associates, Inc., WHAT AMERICA'S USERS SPEND ON ILLEGAL DRUGS, 1988–1993, Spring 1995, A report of the Office of National Drug Control Policy, Executive Office of the President, at 5, 39. The report stresses that there is "considerable imprecision" in the variables used to make the estimate. The report relies upon an estimate of 9.0 million marijuana users in 1993 who used at least once per month. The $9 billion total would require an average user to spend $1,000 for marijuana annually. This seems like a very high average. The report notes that "the amount of marijuana that Americans cultivate for personal use is impossible to estimate" (p. 38), but as a means for high consumption consumers to reduce their cash outlay, such cultivation may be common. It is not possible to learn from the limited data on prosecutions what percentage of the felony marijuana prisoners and arrests were essentially for personal cultivation.

39. Paul B. Stares, GLOBAL HABIT: THE DRUG PROBLEM IN A BORDERLESS WORLD, The Brookings Institution, 1996; Kevin Jack Riley, Snow Job? The War Against International Cocaine Trafficking, Transaction Publishers, 1996; Patrick L. Clawson and Rensselaer W. Lee, III, The Andean Cocaine Industry, St. Martin's Press, 1996.

40. Mathea Falco, *The Making of a Drug-Free America*, Times Books, 1992, pp. 34, 44.

41. Susan T. Evans, Nancy S. Tobler, Christopher L. Ringwalt, and Robert L. Flewelling, "How Effective is Drug Abuse Resistance Education? A Meta-Analysis of Project DARE Outcome Evaluations," *American Journal of Public Health*, September 1994, Vol. 84, No. 9, pp. 1394–1401; "Results of Justice's DARE Study Not Published," NEWSBRIEFS, September–October 1994, p. 11.

42. Dennis Cauchon, "Study Critical of DARE Rejected," USA TODAY, Oct. 4, 1994, p. 2A, "DARE tried to interfere with the publication of this [study], they tried to intimidate us," Sabine Beister of the American Journal of Public Health told USA TODAY; "Results of Justice's DARE Study Not Published," NEWSBRIEFS, National Drug Strategy Network, September–October 1994, p. 11.

43. Joel H. Brown and Marianne D'Emidio Caston, On Becoming "At Risk" Through Drug Education: How Symbolic Policies and Their Practices Affect Students, 19 EVALUATION REVIEW 451 (1995); Joel H. Brown et al., Students and Substances: Social Power in Drug Education, 19 EDUCATION EVALUATION & ANALYSIS 65 (1997); Marianne D'Emidio-Caston & Joel H. Brown, *The Other Side of the Story: Student Narratives on the California Drug, Alcohol, Tobacco Education Program.*

44. Paul B. Stares, GLOBAL HABIT: THE DRUG PROBLEM IN A BORDERLESS WORLD, The Brookings Institution, 1996; Kevin Jack Riley, SNOW JOB? THE WAR AGAINST INTERNATIONAL COCAINE TRAFFICKING, Transaction Publishers, 1996; Patrick L. Clawson and Rensselaer W. Lee, III, THE ANDEAN COCAINE INDUSTRY, St. Martin's Press, 1996.

45. C. Peter Rydell and Susan S. Everingham, CONTROLLING COCAINE: SUPPLY VERSUS DEMAND PROGRAMS, RAND Drug Policy Research Center, 1994, pp. xi-xix.

46. Article 49, Paragraph 2(e) of the Single Convention on Narcotics, 1961, relating to transitional reservations, required the abolition of coca leaf chewing within twenty-five years of the coming into force of the convention, December 12, 1989.

47. "American Indian Religious Freedom Act Amendments of 1994," P.L. 103-344 (108 Statutes at Large 3125), October 6, 1994. H.R. 4230 (103rd Congress, House Report 103-675) passed the U.S. House of Representatives on August 8, 1994, and passed the U.S. Senate on September 26, 1995.

48. "Everyone has the right to freedom of thought, conscience and religion; this right includes freedom to change his religion or belief, and freedom, either alone or in community with others and in public or private, to manifest his religion or belief in teaching, practice, worship and observance." Article 18 of the Universal Declaration of Human Rights, adopted December 10, 1948 by the General Assembly of the United Nations.

49. Oakley Ray, PhD, and Charles Ksir, PhD, DRUGS, SOCIETY & HUMAN BEHAVIOR, Times Mirror/Mosby (5th ed. 1990), pp. 215-225.

50. Erich Goode, PhD, DRUGS IN AMERICAN SOCIETY, McGraw-Hill, (4th ed. 1993), p. 257.

51. Institute for Health Policy, Brandeis University, SUBSTANCE ABUSE: THE NATION'S NUMBER ONE HEALTH PROBLEM (Prepared for the Robert Wood Johnson Foundation) at 54. (October 1993).

52. Id.

53. The Food and Drug Administration published a Final Rule of "Regulations Restricting the Sale and Distribution of Cigarettes and Smokeless Tobacco to Protect Children and Adolescents" in 61 Federal Register pp. 44395 through 44445, August 28, 1996. (Food and Drug Administration Docket No. 95N-0253). The regulations took effect August 28, 1997. "The regulations prohibit the sale of nicotine-containing cigarettes and smokeless tobacco to individuals under the age of 18; require manufacturers, distributors, and retailers to comply with certain conditions regarding the sale and distribution of these products; require retailers to verify a purchaser's age by photographic identification; prohibit all free samples and prohibit the sale of these products through vending machines and self-service displays except in facilities where individuals under the age of 18 are not present or permitted at any time; limit the advertising and labeling to which children and adolescents are exposed to a black-and-white, text-only format; prohibit the sale or distribution of brand-identified promotional non-tobacco items such as hats, and tee shirts; prohibit sponsorship of sporting and other events, teams, and entries in a brand name of a tobacco product, but permit such sponsorship in a corporate name; and require manufacturers to provide intended use information on all cigarette and smokeless tobacco product labels and in cigarette advertising."

The earlier proposed rule had been published in 60 Federal Register pp. 41313-41375 on August 11, 1995.

54. Address by Philip Heymann, Harvard Law Professor, Former Deputy U.S. Attorney General, speaking at the conference, "Crime and Politics in the 1990s—A National Leadership Conference," Dec. 2, 1993, Arlington, VA, quoted in "Anti-Crime Strategies for the 1990s: A Report Campaign for An Effective Crime Policy Conference," NewsBriefs, Dec. 1994, pp. 7-9.

55. James C. Howell, ed., GUIDE FOR IMPLEMENTING THE COMPREHENSIVE STRATEGY FOR SERIOUS, VIOLENT, AND CHRONIC JUVENILE OFFENDERS, Office of Juvenile Justice and Delinquency Prevention, U.S. Department of Justice, May 1995.

56. Lisbeth B. Schorr, WITHIN OUR REACH: BREAKING THE CYCLE OF DISADVANTAGE, Anchor Books/Doubleday, 1989, Chapter 10, The Lessons of Successful Programs, pp. 256-259.

57. Frederic N. Tulsky and Ted Rohrlich, "Only 1 in 3 Killings in County Leads to Any Punishment," The Los Angeles Times, Dec. 2, 1996, p. A1.

58. James Q. Wilson and George L. Kelling, "Broken Windows: The Police and Neighborhood Safety," The Atlantic Monthly, Vol. 249, No. 3, March 1982, pp. 29-38.

59. David M. Kennedy, "Controlling the Drug Trade in Tampa, Florida," National Institute of Justice Program Focus, April 1993, NIJ-139963, p. 8.

60. James Q. Wilson and George L. Kelling, "Broken Windows: The Police and Neighborhood Safety," The Atlantic Monthly, Vol. 249, No. 3, March 1982, pp. 29-38.

61. In 1995, sixteen states had emergency release programs to control inmate population levels. *The Corrections Yearbook, 1996*, p. 49.

62. This problem was recently examined in a series in the Los Angeles Times describing the LA County sheriff's operation that relied on often illegible handwritten instructions. Tina Daunt, "Jail Again Frees Slaying Suspect erroneously," *The Los Angeles Times*, October 12, 1996; Tina Daunt, "A Paperwork Nightmare; Jail: Woefully inadequate system for tracking inmates has troubling margin of error that leads to mistaken releases." *The Los Angeles Times*, October 19, 1996; Tina Daunt, "Paperwork Clerical Errors Cited in Release of Inmates; Jails: Sheriff's first accounting of problem blames antiquated record-keeping system, data entry mistakes." *The Los Angeles Times*, October 24, 1996.

63. An internal Department of Justice report was prepared for then-deputy attorney general Philip Heymann in 1993. It revealed that 16,300 federal prisoners at that time were "low-level" drug offenders with no record of violence, no involvement in sophisticated criminal activity, and no serious prior convictions. "These 16,300—21% of the entire federal drug prisoners—were serving an average of six years in prison." Stuart Taylor, Jr., *Courage, Cowardice on Drug Sentencing*, Legal Times, April 24, 1995, at 27.

64. U.S. Sentencing Commission, Cocaine and Federal Sentencing Policy: Special Report to Congress, February 1995, Table 18 at p. 172.

65. See, for example, *Family Guide to Natural Medicine: How to Stay Healthy the Natural Way*, Reader's Digest Association, 1993. "Not only is high-tech medicine expensive, it can also be dangerous. Its methods are potent and invasive, and it is frequently harmful. This tendency is nowhere more evident that in the amount of drug toxicity caused by modern prescribing practices. Adverse drug reactions are now so common that most patients will experience one sooner or later.... The problem is that most pharmaceutical drugs are too strong. Doctors have come to like drugs that produce very intense effects very rapidly. Certainly, there is a place for such products, particularly for the treatment of emergency conditions, where time is of the essence, but for the routine management of common illnesses, exclusive use of these strong drugs is technological overkill.... One of the complaints I hear from patients today is that doctors are too ready to hand out drugs." From the Introduction, by Andrew Weil, M.D., pp. 11–12.

66. These concepts need to be considered in light of the work on addict careers reported by Charles Faupel, Ph.D., University of Delaware, in *Shooting Dope*, University of Florida Press, 1991.

67. *The New York Times*, "Helping Parents with Mental Illness," May 18, 1994, p. B1.

68. At one time the Center for Applied Nomadology in Baltimore provided information about wet shelters and shooting galleries.

69. Terry Williams, *Crackhouse . . . Notes from the End of the Line*, Addison-Wesley, 1992, 156 pp.

70. Philippe Bourgois, *In Search of Respect: Selling Crack in El Barrio*, Cambridge University Press, 1996, 392 pp.

71. *Ibid.* at 33.

72. *Ibid.* at 34.

73. Dan Waldorf, Craig Reinarman, Sheigla Murphy, *Cocaine Changes: The Experience of Using and Quitting*, Temple University Press, 1991, 29–31, 42.

74. "Anti-Crime Strategies: Campaign for Effective Crime Policy Conference Report," NewsBriefs, December 1994, p. 11.

75. Mark A.R. Kleiman, *Against Excess: Drug Policy for Results*, Basic Books, 1992, pp. 98–99, 101, 249–252.

76. Drugs would be available in a broader array of forms than just the powder of pure chemicals that are so easy for the prohibition industry to ship clandestinely. Cocaine, for ex-

ample, almost certainly should be available as a tea as it is in Peru and Bolivia. In Peru, coca tea has been shown to have some value in helping cocaine base smokers remain abstinent from that practice. Cocaine might be available in chewing gum something like Nicorette gum or Aspergum which contains aspirin.

77. See Bernard Aaronson and Humphrey Osmond, eds., *Psychedelics: The Uses and Implications of Hallucinogenic Drugs*, Anchor/Doubleday, 1970; Terence McKenna, *Food of the Gods: The Search for the Original Tree of Knowledge*, Bantam, 1992.

78. MAPS BULLETIN, Vol. 5, Summer 1994, at 43 (reporting a telephone conversation between Dr. Mullis and Rick Doblin in the Spring of 1994).

79. See Lester Grinspoon and James B. Bakalar, "Therapeutic Uses" in *Psychedelic Drugs Reconsidered*, Basic Books, 1979, pp. 192–237. See also Martin A. Lee & Bruce Shlain, *Acid Dreams: The Complete Social History of LSD*, Grove Weidenfeld, 1985, and Stanislav Grof, *LSD Psychotherapy*, Hunter House, 1994.

80. "Fatalities in alcohol-related motor vehicle crashes," Table 3.96, *Sourcebook of Criminal Justice Statistics, 1995*, p. 303.

81. Bureau of Justice Statistics, U.S. Department of Justice, *Drugs, Crime and the Justice System: A National Report*, 1992, p. 13.

82. "Fatalities in alcohol-related motor vehicle crashes," Table 3.96, *Sourcebook of Criminal Justice Statistics, 1995*, p. 303.

83. See Eric E. Sterling, "Drug Policy: A Smorgasbord of Conundrums Spiced by Emotions around Children and Violence," 31 Valparaiso University Law Review 597, Spring 1997.

84. Testimony of Lloyd D. Johnston, Ph.D., Program Director, Institute for Social Research, University of Michigan, before the House Subcommittee on Health and the Environment, Committee on Energy and Commerce, on "Advertising of Tobacco Products," Serial No. 99-167, Aug. 1, 1986, pp. 860–868.

85. Many of the medical uses of marijuana are outlined in the book by Lester Grinspoon, MD, and James Bakalar, JD, *Marihuana, the Forbidden Medicine*, Yale University Press, 1993. Older medical references were compiled by Tod Mikuriya, MD in *Marijuana: Medical Paper 1839–1972*, Medi-Comp Press, 1983.

The Galen Press of Washington, DC, has published, in four volumes, the records of the hearings, filings, and arguments before DEA administrative law judge Francis L. Young in 1987 and 1988 regarding the scheduling of marijuana, *In the Matter of Marijuana Rescheduling Petition, Docket No. 86-22*. In his opinion, recommended ruling, findings of fact, conclusions of law and decision issued September 6, 1988, Judge Young found that marijuana had a currently accepted medical use in treatment in the United States for a number of conditions—nausea and vomiting resulting from chemotherapy treatments in some cancer patients, spasticity resulting from multiple sclerosis and other causes, pseudo pseudo hypoparathyroidism (yes, two pseudos). R. C. Randall, Editor: *Marijuana, Medicine & the Law, Volumes I and II* (1988 & 1989), *Cancer Treatment & Marijuana Therapy* (1990), *Muscle Spasm, Pain & Marijuana Therapy* (1991). Randall also wrote and compiled *Marijuana & AIDS: Pot, Politics & PWAs in America* (1991). In Jenks v. Florida, 582 So. 2d 676 (Fla. Dist. Ct. App. 1991), the First District Court of Appeal in Florida reversed a conviction for cultivation of marijuana for a couple who were using marijuana to treat the nausea associated with AIDS, finding that it was effective and that their "physician was unable to find an alternative drug that effectively eliminated or diminished his patients' nausea."

Much of the many articles in the modern medical literature regarding the potential medical benefit of marijuana is compiled by Kevin Zeese, Esquire, in "Research Findings on Medicinal Properties of Marijuana," published in NewsBriefs, the newsletter of the National Drug Strategy Network, January 1997.

86. Beer—27 CFR sec. 25.205; Wine—27 CFR 240.540.

Beer and wine produced under these regulations may be removed form the home "for personal or family use including use at organized affairs, exhibitions, or competitions, such as homemaker's contests tastings or judging" but cannot be sold or offered for sale.

87. John H. Doyle, III and Daniel Markewich, "Separate Statement to A Wiser Course: Ending Drug Prohibition," a dissent to "A Wiser Course: Ending Drug Prohibition," A Report by the Committee on Drugs and the Law in The Record of the Association of the Bar of the City of New York, June 1994, pp. 574–577. (Hereafter, "Separate Statement.")

88. Daniel K. Benjamin and Roger Leroy Miller, Undoing Drugs: Beyond Legalization, Basic Books, 1991.

89. "Separate Statement" at 575. However, the two Drug Enforcement Administration publications, Drug Legalization: Myths and Misconceptions and Speaking Out Against Drug Legalization do not directly raise this argument.

90. Ten survey years between 1972 and 1991. Everingham and Rydell, *supra* at footnote 9, at 12.

91. "The rise in drug use among American Teens continues in 1996." University of Michigan News and Information Services, Dec. 19, 1996, pp. 6–7.

92. Letter from ONDCP Director Barry McCaffrey to the Congressional Black Caucus, June 26, 1997.

93. Philip D. Duncan and Christine C. Lawrence, POLITICS IN AMERICA: 1996, The 104th Congress, 1995, at 763, "Emerson crushed [Democratic challenger Wayne] Cryts two years later [in 1988], dismissing suggestions that he might be vulnerable after his admission of alcohol dependency."

94. "Separate Statement," at 575.

95. C. Everett Koop, M.D., Sc.D., The Health consequences of Smoking: Nicotine Addiction, A Report of the Surgeon General, May 3, 1988, at vi. "The processes that determine tobacco addiction are similar to those that determine addiction to other drugs, including illegal drugs." *Id.*

20

First Steps toward Legalization

Jefferson M. Fish

Too often, the debate over legalization is stopped before it begins by a drug warrior asking combatively, "What about cocaine—especially crack cocaine? And what about heroin? Would you sell them in candy stores?"

This kind of worst-case scenario—or most-difficult-substances scenario—has proved a distraction to attempts at drug policy reform. There are a variety of proposals for a variety of ways to deal with cocaine and heroin—several of them discussed elsewhere in this book—but as far as drug policy is concerned, they are almost beside the point. Not that many people use or want to use them, and considerable progress could be made on scaling down drug prohibition without even addressing them.

We have seen that our current prohibitionist policy is counterproductive because it creates a huge crime-ridden black market, so the more we "get tough on drugs," the worse things get. For this reason it follows that the more we ease up, and the smaller the black market becomes, the better things will get. Thus any steps we can take toward de-escalating the war on drugs should improve matters.

This brief chapter consists of a list of suggestions for initial steps toward legalization without addressing heroin or cocaine. The proposals are arranged in an approximate sequence from the easiest to achieve, where we know there are few potential health and social risks, to those more likely to encounter resistance because of fears of the risks involved in comparison to the benefits of change.

In other words, this chapter offers suggestions that are pragmatic rather than programmatic, first steps toward change rather than final steps completing it. If we can implement these first steps, discover that matters improve dramatically, and that the sky does not fall, then maybe we will have the courage to tackle more controversial substances. And if only a few of these are the best we can do for now, at least we will have succeeded in making the problem somewhat smaller and more manageable.

1. *Legalize drug paraphernalia (including syringes), and release those imprisoned on drug paraphernalia charges.*

Here one can have a tremendously positive effect on public health, and a lesser one on unburdening the criminal justice system, without even addressing the controlled substances themselves. Implementing needle exchange programs and legalizing the purchase of syringes (complete with the means for proper disposal—and penalties for improper disposal) will prevent the spread of AIDS and other diseases. In this way we can save the lives of countless thousands of drug injectors, their current and future sexual partners, those partners' subsequent partners (and so on), and any children resulting from any of those unions.

Similarly, water pipes for smoking marijuana or tobacco can remove carcinogenic particulates from those substances, and if more widely used could cut down on the spread of lung cancer.

As regards other public-health-irrelevant "paraphernalia," the reason for making them legal is simply that they never should have been illegal in the first place. The state has no reason to interfere with the marketplace, or to punish those who buy, sell, or own such products. We should reserve our prisons for white collar criminals, thieves, robbers, muggers, rapists, murderers, and other violent or dangerous people.

2. *Create legal means for people to test illicit substances.*

Most drug "overdoses" result from contamination, adulteration, drug mixtures, and other kinds of false labeling of illicit substances, as well as from unpredictable variations in dosage levels. Such dangers to consumers are rampant in a black market but would become all but nonexistent in a free or regulated market. As long as the black market continues, the health of users could be protected by the creation of legal (or at least legally tolerated) laboratories that could inform people of what they have and warn them of unexpected dangers.

3. *End involuntary drug testing except where public safety is involved.*

People have a right to their private lives, and not to have their physical integrity violated by government or employers examining their breath, blood, urine, or other body products or body parts. Any consequences people suffer at work should be related to their job performance, not to private actions in their personal lives.

4. *Classification of and penalties for any prohibited substances should be scaled according to scientific data.*

Quite separately from consideration of making prohibited substances legal, the internal coherence of prohibition itself should be addressed. As Robert Gable indicated in Chapter 16, the undesirable properties of illegal substances—which presumably are why they are prohibited—are unrelated to penalties for their use. While it may be a bad idea to criminalize the use of a psychoactive substance, to the extent to which we do so we should still, in the words of Gilbert and Sullivan, "make the punishment fit the crime." Thus we need to assure that legal classifications of substances are consistent with scientific ones so that severer penalties are not imposed for less harmful substances or—as in the next suggestion—for alternative forms of the same substance.

5. *Any penalties for a prohibited substance should be equalized for all its forms (e.g., the same penalty for equal amounts of cocaine in the form of powder or crack).*

This suggestion, which flows logically from the previous one, offers an opportunity to remedy a great injustice. By making the penalties for crack cocaine (preferred by inner-city blacks) a hundred times as severe as the penalties for powdered cocaine (preferred by suburban whites), we have been packing our jails with young black men and have destroyed virtually an entire generation of minority youth. That false racist stereotypes (black men high on crack brutalizing whites; black women giving birth to crack babies) were used to secure passage of such laws only makes matters worse. "Equal justice under law" is a basic principle; if cocaine possession remains illegal, then penalties should correspond to the amount of the drug seized, regardless of the form it is in. This principle should apply to all illegal substances.

6. *Legalize the medical use of marijuana and other controlled substances.*

As indicated in Chapter 17, by Lester Grinspoon, marijuana has many medical benefits with virtually no costs; and it is unconscionable that so many people should suffer unnecessarily because it is illegal. However, many other controlled substances also have important medical uses. Perhaps the best example is the undertreatment of pain because physicians are afraid to prescribe adequate dosages of opiates for fear of losing their licenses. As the population ages, increasing numbers of people will suffer painful and/or debilitating ailments. These citizens vote, and they will not tolerate the government's denying them medication. The passage of medical marijuana initiatives in Cali-

fornia and Arizona suggests that the voters may already have lost patience
with politicians on this issue.

7. *End mandatory minimum sentences and the confiscation of property for possession
of illegal substances.*

Even during the depths of Prohibition, possession of alcohol (as opposed to manufacturing it) was never a crime. We have been filling up the
prisons with nonviolent noncriminals on mandatory minimum sentences and
releasing violent criminals to make room for them. Meanwhile, allowing law
enforcement to seize for its own use the assets of people who have illegal
drugs undermines the Bill of Rights, corrupts and delegitimizes the police
power of the state, and encourages predatory drug busts for economic gain.
Finally, the misallocation of resources required to implement this disastrous
policy has led us to build prisons instead of schools, and to destroy rather
than build the futures of large numbers of our youth.

If penalties for possession of psychoactive substances cannot be done away
with immediately, they at least should be considerably reduced—and judges
should be given great latitude to determine what punishment, if any, is appropriate—in a first step toward limiting the damage.

8. *Legalize the use of drugs in established religious and cultural practices.*

One of the wonders of America is its ability to tolerate, accept, learn
from, and assimilate huge numbers of immigrants from all over the planet.
While ethnic hatred and genocide continue elsewhere, we have managed to
cope with unprecedented diversity (if not always with good humor) by simply
recognizing that "different" doesn't necessarily mean "bad" or "dangerous."
Thus, in our drug policy, we should recognize that well-established religious
and cultural practices that differ from those of the mainstream must be legitimized in the area of substance use as in other areas. Three common examples
are the use of marijuana by Rastafarians from the British West Indies, the
chewing of coca leaves and drinking of coca tea by Bolivians, Peruvians, and
other immigrants from South America's Alteplano, and the religious use of
peyote by members of the Native American Church. Criminalizing these normal, and even sacred, practices among culturally different groups is a recipe
for ethnic strife.

9. *Legalize marijuana in a manner similar to alcohol and tobacco.*

No one has ever died from a marijuana overdose, and yet the war on
drugs is primarily a war on marijuana. Legalizing marijuana, and releasing from
prison those who are there solely for its possession, would instantly save huge
amounts of money, end the shortage of prison space, free up funds for drug
treatment, and raise the possibility that consumers seeking intoxication might
choose it in preference to the much more dangerous alcohol.

One politically feasible way to go about legalizing marijuana would be to make it subject to the limitations placed on cigarettes and alcohol—whichever is more restrictive. Thus it would be sold only to those at the older legal age for the other two substances (18 or 21), and in the more restrictive location (e.g., liquor stores). Restrictions on (1) advertising, especially advertising to children (as for both alcohol and cigarettes), (2) smoking in public places (as for cigarettes), and (3) disruptive intoxicated public behavior or driving while intoxicated (as for alcohol) would also apply. Adults should, however, be allowed to grow the plant for their own consumption.

This ninth suggestion is the first one that actually addresses legalizing a currently illegal substance. If the most workable change to our current drug policy goes only as far as implementing these nine suggestions, then the dimensions of the "drug problem" and the "drug war" will have been scaled back from a self-made catastrophe to a serious issue requiring serious changes. Nevertheless, there is room for additional changes that fall short of the more controversial legalization of cocaine and heroin.

10. Legalize minimally processed coca.

Because of the long experience of Andean cultures with chewing coca leaves and drinking coca tea, it is reasonable to assume that Americans can also learn to use minimally processed coca in a responsible manner. As Chapter 10 indicated, Prohibition pushed us from beer drinkers to whiskey drinkers, and we returned gradually to beer at the end of that era. In a similar way, it is likely that the much lower dosage levels in coca leaves, along with the possible modifying effects of other substances in the leaves, will satisfy much of the public's curiosity and demand. In other words, legal coca leaves would offer consumers a way to experience the plant's stimulant properties without the risks associated with processed cocaine—as we once did when we drank the original Coca-cola. Over time, therefore, a trend away from powdered cocaine and crack—and toward coca leaves—would be expected to develop.

11. Legalize psilocybin mushrooms.

As Robert Gable indicated in Chapter 16, psilocybin is the hallucinogen with the lowest risk. As with coca leaves, legalizing the substance in its unprocessed form should also help to hold down dosage levels. Making psilocybin mushrooms legal should reduce demand for other, less predictable, hallucinogens.

12. Legalize MDMA.

As with psilocybin mushrooms, legalizing MDMA would be another way of allowing less dangerous substances into the marketplace so that few people would be willing to take the black market risks of using those substances that remain illegal.

13. Decriminalize possession of small amounts of all substances and release those imprisoned for this reason alone.

As the last of the "first steps," this proposal would not go so far as to legalize substances like cocaine and heroin. As such, it would leave their black markets intact, with all their attendant ills. Nevertheless, by reducing the penalties for possession for personal use of any substances that remain illegal to the level of a parking ticket—or a speeding ticket—we would cease packing our prisons with noncriminals.

In implementing this proposal, we can take our guidance from medicine's guiding principle: "Do no harm." People who use psychoactive substances in the privacy of their own homes should be of no interest to the police.

I would like to make three other general proposals, also aimed at moving us in the direction of a more rational and humane drug policy.

1. Increase the supply of factual information and stop the use of scare tactics.

Much is known about the positive and negative effects of legal and illegal psychoactive substances, and that information should be made widely available to the public. The kinds of scientifically accurate warning labels on tobacco and alcohol products should be extended to caffeine products (e.g., concerning risks for ulcers, anxiety attacks, and insomnia). Any additional substances that are legalized should also have labels warning of the scientifically documented dangers they pose. In addition, because there is a limit to the amount of information that can be put on a label and to the amount that many consumers might be willing to read, it should be made extremely easy for those who are interested to obtain more extensive information. For example, stores could keep information sheets on hand, like inserts currently included with prescription drugs, for free distribution to customers who request them. In addition, the label for each substance—including tobacco, alcohol, and caffeine—could list an Internet address where one could download such information, as well as an 800 telephone number that one could call to obtain the information for free by return mail.

The discussion in Chapter 12 pointed out not only the educational benefits of clear, accurate, and personally relevant information, but also the counterproductive effects of scare tactics and false information. These include loss of respect for official sources of drug information, and the inaccurate belief that if official information about drugs is untrue, then illegal substances must be safe after all. We must put an end to propaganda (e.g., a fried egg is your brain on drugs) and misinformation (e.g., all drugs and dosage levels are the same; all use equals abuse) that undermine critical thinking. Instead, by providing factual knowledge and encouraging thoughtful debate, we can help citizens to make informed decisions about an important area of their private lives.

2. End coercive "treatment" (e.g., therapy or jail); increase the availability of therapy and medical care for substance abusers who request them.

To begin with, coercive "treatment" doesn't work; its failure has given all drug treatment a bad reputation, despite the fact that voluntary treatment often does succeed. However, even if it did work, coercive "treatment" should be ended because it undermines the institution of therapy and the honesty, trust, and confidentiality on which it is based. In coercive "treatment," clients must pretend to participate in therapy to avoid punishment; therapists must pretend to be working for their clients when they are really agents of the state; therapists must lie (and/or deceive themselves) about their clients' motivation and progress to get paid; and therapists must break confidentiality to inform on their clients. Such therapy is a sham. Mental health professionals who participate in it—because they need to earn a living and/or because they really want to help substance abusers—find themselves and their professional ideals corrupted by drug prohibition. The corrosive effects of the war on drugs pervade the mental health system as well as the criminal justice system.

In the topsy-turvy world of drug prohibition, some who are caught using proscribed substances, whether or not they are abusing them, may be forced into "treatment" even though they don't want it. Usually these are affluent white people whom the criminal justice system forces to pay a "fine" in the form of lawyers' fees and therapists' fees to avoid going to jail. On the other hand, there is a shortage of treatment available for those substance abusers who truly want to change, especially if they are poor. Such people often are in poor physical health, may have contagious diseases, and can profit from medical care as well as therapy. Treating such people promotes the public health as well as their own, and is much cheaper than incarcerating them. Even when therapy fails, society is much better off with such people in their midst than with comparable others who have learned to become criminals in prison.

3. Legalize in a way that is considerate of the feelings of those opposed to legalization.

In contrast to the behavior of drug warriors, who have prided themselves on their intolerance (as evidenced by slogans like "Zero Tolerance"), it is important to show concern for the sensibilities of others while protecting the rights of individuals to make their own decisions regarding psychoactive substances. For example, alcohol is legal but drinking in public is not. This is because such behavior offends, among others, teetotalers and parents who don't want their children to see it. In the same way, legalizing the use of currently restricted substances can be done in such a way as to minimize the affront to those who find it offensive. Limiting such use to the privacy of people's homes, or to places with restricted access, like bars, and prohibiting public intoxicated behavior from whatever substance, would protect the sensibilities of those who oppose legalization for whatever reason.

While adopting even a few of these proposals would make matters significantly better, adopting all of them—without legalizing heroin or cocaine—would leave the remaining problems so small that the social issue would largely be solved. (One might also have to legalize occasional new substances, of relatively low toxicity and abuse potential, from time to time.)

It may well be desirable to find a way to legalize heroin and cocaine (in at least some dosages, with perhaps some kind of public health supervision) so as to minimize or destroy their black markets. I would be all for it if we could do so. But there is so much that can be accomplished without legalizing these controversial substances that reformers might want to focus their efforts on other issues, at least for the time being.

21

Downsizing the Drug War and Considering "Legalization": An Economic Perspective

Mary M. Cleveland

An economic analysis of the illegal drug markets suggests that if the U.S. drug war were "downsized" (by cutting back interdiction efforts, targeting primarily large or violent dealers, and reducing severity of punishments), the following would happen:

1. Prices would fall, marijuana prices more than hard drug prices. There would be some increase in casual use, especially of marijuana, and a shift to marijuana from cocaine, heroin, and possibly alcohol.
2. The number of dealers would decrease and their age would rise. At present, probably a majority of regular illegal drug users also deal to help pay for their own use; the lower the price, the fewer would deal. Small teenage dealers would be replaced by larger, less-violent, adult dealers.
3. The *number* of hard drug abusers would probably not increase, but their *per capita consumption* might increase dramatically. Addicts who survive by petty theft would probably not steal less if drug prices declined, but simply consume more.

Downsizing the drug war alone would make the black market larger though less dangerous. It would reduce the number of juvenile dealers, but not otherwise limit children's access to drugs. Various forms of regulated "legalization" are already being tested in Europe. These could be used to shrink the size of the black market, restrict children's access to drugs and eliminate them as dealers, and get hard drug abusers out of the market and possibly into treatment.

Defenders of drug prohibition make a straightforward "supply and demand" argument: "legalization," or any lessening of aggressive enforcement, will lower the high cost of drugs in terms of price, risk of arrest, severe punishment, and social opprobrium. Consequently, drug abuse will skyrocket. According to Dr. Herbert Kleber, medical director of the Columbia Center on Addiction and Substance Abuse, and former deputy to William Bennett, drug czar under President Reagan:

> There are over 50 million nicotine addicts, 18 million alcoholics or problem drinkers, and fewer than 2 million cocaine addicts in the United States. Cocaine is a much more addictive drug than alcohol. If cocaine were legally available, as alcohol and nicotine are now, the number of cocaine abusers would probably rise to a point somewhere between the number of users of the other two agents, perhaps 20 to 25 million . . . the number of compulsive users might be nine times higher . . . than the current number. [Kleber, as cited in DEA, 1994, p. 16]

This is a tough challenge to answer. None of us can predict the future very well; fear of the unknown often makes us rather bear those ills we have than fly to others we know not of.

However, predictions derived by economic logic depend on the underlying assumptions about reality; change the assumptions and the predictions change too. Defenders of prohibition make one set of assumptions; critics, myself included, make other assumptions. Table 21–1 is a brief paraphrase of prohibitionist assumptions, contrasted with alternative assumptions.

The following section surveys some evidence supporting the alternative set of assumptions. The next section applies some basic economic principles to these assumptions. The final section examines some policy implications, including possible benefits and risks of "legalization."

THE PRESENT DRUG SITUATION IN THE UNITED STATES

PROPERTIES OF LICIT AND ILLICIT DRUGS

If both licit and illicit drugs vary greatly in danger, addictiveness, and other properties, one might expect drug control policies to depend on these properties, with stricter controls on more dangerous substances. Table 21–2 provides two rough rankings of three licit and three illicit drugs. Both rankings put al-

Table 21-1. Prohibitionist Assumptions versus Alternative Assumptions

PROHIBITIONIST ASSUMPTIONS	ALTERNATIVE ASSUMPTIONS
Illicit drugs are all extremely dangerous and addictive. Marijuana is a "gateway" to hard drugs.	Licit and illicit drugs vary greatly in danger and addictiveness. Few marijuana users go on to hard drugs.
All use of illicit drugs, or underage use of licit drugs like alcohol, is "abuse"—assumed to be individually and socially destructive. This assumption is built into official language, such as the U.S. Department of Health and Human Services' "National Household Survey on Drug Abuse."	Most use is not abuse. Durg users, like alcohol drinkers, fall naturally into three categories: a small proportion of abusers, a larger proportion of regular users, and a majority of casual users. Drug abusers are equivalent to (and often also are) alcoholics. Regular users, like regular drinkers, control the quantity and timing of use so as not to disrupt work or a normal family life.
The addictive properties of illicit drugs cause "abuse." Perfectly normal young people who try drugs are liable to become hooked. By implication, the number of abusers is proportional to the availability and addictiveness of a drug.	Drug and alcohol abuse are symptoms of underlying emotional problems—though substance abuse may make those problems harder to treat. By implication, the number of abusers is proportional to the number of troubled people.
Illicit drugs cause crime, driving users to violent behaviour, and to theft to support addiction.	While a majority of violent or property criminals use and/or deal illicit drugs, most illicit drug users do not commit any nondrug crimes.
Cost and access are major determinants of illicit drug use.	Personal tastes and social norms are in most cases more important than cost or access.

cohol near the top with heroin and cocaine, and marijuana near the bottom with caffeine. If these rankings are valid, they cast doubt on the prohibitionist assumption that illicit drugs are so much more dangerous than licit drugs as to require "zero tolerance."

PATTERNS OF LICIT AND ILLICIT DRUG USE IN THE UNITED STATES

Table 21-3 is compiled from the 1994 National Household Survey on Drug Abuse published annually by the U.S. Public Health Service. It summarizes a survey of use for alcohol, cigarettes, and five categories of illicit drugs. Respondents were polled as to whether they had ever used, used in the last year, and used in the last month. In some categories respondents were asked if they had used twelve or more days last year, or used fifty-one or more days.

Table 21-2. Two Doctors[1] Compare the Seriousness of Six Well-Known Drugs[2]

1. Henningfield Ratings (1 Worst; 6 Least Serious)

Substance	Withdrawal	Reinforcement	Tolerance	Dependence	Intoxication	Total
Heroin	2	2	1	2	2	9
Alcohol	1	3	3	4	1	12
Cocaine	4	1	4	3	3	15
Nicotine	3	4	2	1	5	15
Marijuana	6	5	6	6	4	27
Caffeine	5	6	5	5	6	27

2. Benowitz Ratings (1 Worst; 6 Least Serious)

Substance	Withdrawal	Reinforcement	Tolerance	Dependence	Intoxication	Total
Heroin	2	2	2	2	2	10
Cocaine	3	1	1	3	3	11
Alcohol	1	3	4	4	1	13
Nicotine	3	4	4	1	6	18
Caffeine	4	5	3	5	5	22
Marijuana	5	6	5	6	4	26

Source: Steven C. Markoff in consultation with Drs. Henningfield, Benowitz, and Perrine.

[1]Dr. Jack E. Henningfield (Ph.D. in Psychopharmacology), formerly of the National Institute on Drug Abuse, and Dr. Neal L. Benowitz (M.D.) of the University of San Francisco rank six common substances in five problem areas.
[2]Appendix A at the end of this chapter briefly reviews properties and health effects of major licit and illicit drugs.

These figures surely understate illicit drug use, both because respondents may be unwilling to admit illegal activity, even in total confidence, and because some of the heaviest illicit drug users are in jail or homeless. Nonetheless a few points stand out:

- *Use of alcohol and cigarettes is many times the use of illicit drugs.*
- *Use of the "soft" drug marijuana is many times the use of the "hard" drugs cocaine and heroin.* Some 65 million adults—about one third the adult population—admit having tried marijuana. Some 22 million admit having tried cocaine; some 2 million admit having tried heroin. Clearly, only a small proportion of marijuana users go on to try cocaine or heroin, let alone become addicted.

Table 21-3. National Household Survey on Drug Abuse: Population Estimates 1994 (in Thousands)

USE SUBSTANCE:	Alcohol	Cigarettes	Total illicit	Marijuana	Cocaine	Inhalants	Stimulants	Tranquilizers	Sedatives	Heroin
Ever	176,290	153,509	71,935	65,229	21,821	12,178	9,671	8,390	5,460	2,083
Percent ever *	84.2	73.3	34.4	31.1	10.4	5.8	4.6	4.0	2.6	1.0
Last year	140,121	66,475	22,663	17,813	3,664	2,213	1,419	2,405	736	281
Percent in last year	66.9	31.7	10.8	8.5	1.7	1.1	0.7	1.1	0.4	0.1
Last month	112,804	59,955	12,553	10,112	1,382	799	678	967	222	**
Percent in last month	53.9	28.6	6.0	4.8	0.7	0.4	0.3	0.5	0.1	**
12 or more days last year	84,995			8,541	1,255					
Percent 12 or more days	40.6			4.1	0.6					
51 or more days last year	45,662			5,139	734					
Percent 51 or more days	21.8			2.5	0.4					

* Percent of population 12 years and older

** too small to estimate from this sample

Substance Abuse and Mental Health Services Administration, Office of Applied Studies
U.S. Department of Health and Human Services, Public Health Service, Rockville, MD 20857

Table 21-4. Drugs in College 1994

USE SUBSTANCE:	Alcohol	Marijuana	Other hallucinogen	LSD	Amphetamines	Cocaine	Tranquilizers	Crack	Heroin	Steroids
Percent last year	84.2	23.6	4.3	4.0	3.4	2.0	2.1	0.5	0.2	0.2
Percent last month	70.4	12.5	1.2	1.1	1.2	0.6	0.7	0.2	0.1	0.1

Harvard School of Public Health Alcohol Studies Program (Wechsler et al. 1994)

- *Licit substances used illicitly constitute a major portion of "abuse."* Right after cocaine come "inhalants," that is, gasoline, glue, laughing gas, amyl nitrate, and other legal substances. (Inhalants are used primarily by children, who lack access to more serious intoxicants.) Next in magnitude are stimulants, mostly amphetamines. Then comes nonprescription use of prescription tranquilizers and sedatives.
- *Heroin use is so small overall that the survey cannot produce an acceptable estimate for the number of users in the last month.*
- *Only a small portion of those who have tried illicit drugs still use them; a much larger portion of those who have ever used alcohol and cigarettes still use them.*

Table 21-4, prepared from a survey of 17,592 college students by the Alcohol Studies Program at the Harvard School of Public Health, shows a similar pattern. It also shows how small illicit drug use is compared to alcohol use. The survey found that 44 percent of the students were "binge drinkers," defined as taking five or more drinks in a row during the two weeks prior to the survey (Wechsler et al. 1994).

Figure 21-1 shows trends in drug use by young adults over the last ten years. Marijuana use trends down and then rises slightly, cocaine use drops precipitously, alcohol and cigarette use fall very slightly.

THREE KINDS OF DRUG USERS

Users of drugs—licit or illicit—fall naturally into three rough categories: casual users, regular users, and abusers. Since the term *abuser* is so often applied to all users of illicit drugs, I will generally use the less ambiguous term "problem user" for the third category.

Casual Users or Experimenters. These include light or social drinkers and people who may try drugs when offered by a friend. These also include teenage "beginners." Casual users are largest in number, but account for only a small fraction of drug volume.

Regular Users. Regular users of alcohol drink daily after work; some may binge on weekends. Regular illegal drug users follow a similar pattern. Regulars lead normal lives, maintaining jobs, families, friends, and health. They consider drug use as a form of relaxation or recreation. Regular users of illegal–or legal–drugs enjoy their drugs, and usually share them with friends. Most regular users of illegal drugs also deal them, to pay for their own use.

Problem Users. Unlike regular users, problem users characteristically feel worthless and hopeless. Their lives may become an obsessive pursuit of hard drugs and/or alcohol, at the expense of jobs, family, friends, and health. They may try repeatedly to stop; every failure makes them feel yet more worthless

Figure 21–1. Recent Trends in Drug Use Among Young Adults

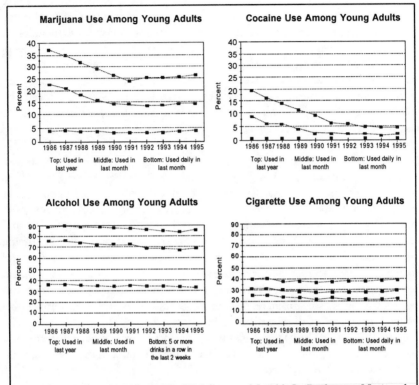

Lloyd D. Johnson, Patrick M. O'Malley, and Jerald G. Bachman, **National Survey Results on Drug Use from the Monitoring the Future Study, 1975–1995,** Vol. 2, College Students and Young Adults, U.S. Department of Health and Human Services, National Institute on Drug Abuse (Washington, DC: USGPO, 1996). Adapted from *Sourcebook of Criminal Justice Statistics 1995,* pp. 288–290, Bureau of Justice Statistics, U.S. Department of Justice.

and hopeless. Unless supported by family, extreme problem users lead a degrading, hand-to-mouth existence. They may survive by panhandling, scavenging, prostitution, odd jobs, petty theft, public assistance, or mooching on relatives and friends. Problem users of illegal drugs rarely deal; no distributor could trust them with drugs on consignment. Many are so-called "polydrug abusers," consuming whatever intoxicants are available at the moment, often in combination. Though smallest in number, problem users account for the greatest volume of alcohol or drug consumption. They are also the most likely to suffer from disease due to contaminated needles, or to die from overdoses.

These three categories do not quite match up with the five categories in Table 21–3. But the table clearly shows that the harder the drug, the fewer the users and the fewer the more frequent users as a percentage of total users. Assuming that the category "Used 12 or more times in last year" includes all regular and problem users, then regular and problem users as a percentage of "ever used" are no more than 48 percent for alcohol, 13 percent for marijuana, and 6 percent for cocaine. There are no reliable estimates of what proportion of total consumption each group accounts for. However, assuming "Zipf's Law" describing common patterns of distributions applies here, it's reasonable to assume that the top 20 percent of consumers account for some 80 percent of consumption of each drug.

As suggested by the relatively small proportion of problem users, as well as abundant sociological and psychological research (Peele 1989), drugs do not cause problem drug use. Rather, problem drug use is a symptom of the way people feel about themselves and their situation: that they are no good, unlovable, or incompetent ("worthless"), and that they have no future and no control over their lives ("hopeless"). To ill-educated poor people coming from abusive homes, or no homes, such feelings may seem to have powerful objective justification. Of course, the consequences of initially nonproblem drug use, such as rejection by family, expulsion from school, or imprisonment for drug possession, may exacerbate feelings of worthlessness and hopelessness, leading to full-blown problem drug use.

In 1995, *The New York Times* interviewed Dr. Jack Block, director of a major ongoing longitudinal study of several hundred children in Oakland, California. According to the article:

> [W]hen the teen-agers reached 18, . . . not all adolescent drug use boded a grim future. In this study, those teen-agers who had experimented with drugs like marijuana during their teen-age years—compared both to those who used them heavily and those who abstained—were the best adjusted. The teen-agers who use drugs most frequently were the most alienated, had the poorest impulse control and the most emotional distress, while those who had never tried any drugs were the most anxious, emotionally constricted and socially inept. . . . Dr. Block's conclusion was that [problem] drug use is a symptom of maladjustment, not a cause, and that it can best be understood in the context of the larger course of life. [Goleman 1995a, Shedler and Block 1990]

Problem drug use is but one form of harmful behavior associated with feelings of hopelessness and worthlessness. Other forms include "eating disorders" like anorexia, compulsive gambling, and obsession with sex. These disorders respond to good counseling, often combined with antidepressant medication, to help people feel they can control their lives (Beck 1993, Peele 1989).

DRUG DEALERS

Legal Dealers. Dealers of legal drugs, of course, are all respectable adults: liquor and tobacco industry members, pharmacists, shopkeepers, bar and restaurant owners.

Illegal Dealers. The greatest difference between legal and illegal dealers is *volume.* Retail alcohol and tobacco markets are supplied by relatively few, high-volume dealers. In the United States the retail illegal drug markets are supplied by a guerrilla army of small dealers, most of them temporary, part-time, unsophisticated, and generally unprofessional in their business conduct. There are three major categories of small dealers: user-dealers, juvenile dealers, and "mules."

1. *User-dealers.* Most illegal dealers, from "kingpins" on down, are regular users. Retail user-dealers generally do not sell much beyond what they need to pay for their own use. They sell drugs wherever they go or wherever they can: at work, at school, at parties. As a last resort, the poorest of them sell on the streets, exposed to arrest and violence from other dealers. A 1990 RAND study of drug economics in Washington, D.C., for 1985-1988, when the crack-cocaine market was just beginning, estimated that one sixth to one third of young black men (ages 18–24) in D.C., or about 24,000 men, sold drugs at street level part-time or full-time. Two thirds of these men also held low-paying jobs, averaging $7 an hour. They sold drugs primarily evenings or weekends when the market was active. The study found that few of these men made much money at this activity; they simply covered the cost of their own use and often spent some of their earned money in addition [Reuter et al. 1990].

2. *Juvenile dealers.* In the United States at least, there is another important category of low-level dealer besides the user-dealers: nonusing juveniles, teen and preteen, mostly boys, recruited to the drug trade by older siblings, relatives, friends, or neighborhood gangs. Some of these youngsters are coerced into the business; others are attracted by what seems easy money. In addition, as juveniles, they face relatively low penalties if arrested. Most of these juvenile dealers will eventually become users.

3. *Mules.* "Mules" are ordinary persons not regularly in the drug trade who are occasionally recruited to transport large quantities of drugs precisely because they do not appear suspicious. Despite their peripheral involvement, mules face the heaviest sentences when caught, since penalties depend on weight of drugs and mules have little or no information to bargain with prosecutors.

DRUGS AND CRIME

The war on drugs is often justified as a crime control measure. In fact, the war may generate more crime than it controls. The relationship between drugs and crime is well reviewed by Rasmussen and Benson in their book *The Economic Anatomy of a Drug War* (1994) and their new report, *Illicit Drugs and Crime* (1996). But in brief:

Illicit Drug Use and Crime. A large majority of those who commit violent and property crimes are also illicit drug users and small dealers. However, the converse does not hold. Most illicit drug users do not commit violent or property crimes. This is also clear from Table 21-3: some 70 million people, one third the U.S. adult population, admit to using illicit drugs at some time; 12.5 million admit using in the month prior to the survey.

Drugs and Violent Crime. Alcohol is the only drug consistently associated with violent behavior "under the influence." Most "drug-related" violence arises in turf battles between rival dealers (Goldstein 1989).

Drugs and Property Crime. Both proponents and many opponents of drug prohibition agree that drug addicts must steal to get drug money. Proponents and opponents of prohibition draw opposite policy conclusions. Proponents advocate stricter and more punitive enforcement of drug laws, on the grounds that making drugs unavailable and locking away addicts will lower property crime. Opponents argue that ending prohibition will bring down hard drug prices so that addicts would not need to steal.

If drugs do not "cause" property crime, then both policy prescriptions will fail.

First, as noted, most drug users do not steal. They buy drugs with their own money. Consequently, a general war on drug users diverts scarce criminal justice resources from the pursuit and imprisonment of property and violent offenders. Rasmussen and Benson present statistics from Florida showing how the drug war in Florida during 1984–1989 resulted in early release of nondrug offenders from overcrowded prisons and an increase in property and violent crime as police shifted their efforts toward the apprehension of drug offenders (Rasmussen and Benson 1994, 1996).

Second, sociological evidence indicates that most individuals first engage in criminal activities, including theft, as juveniles, *a year or two before they become drug users* (Reuter et al. 1990). Often, of course, these are the same juveniles who are recruited as lookouts and runners for the illegal drug trade. Through the drug trade they come into regular contact with older, confirmed property criminals. Thus, to the extent that the war on drugs creates enticing criminal opportunities for juveniles, it may draw them into lives of nondrug crime.

Finally, down-and-out hard-drug addicts steal as part of the degraded lifestyle of problem users. Too disturbed to be employable, they steal to survive and get high to make a miserable life briefly more bearable. A more punitive approach will not deter them. It will more likely confirm their degraded status. Nor will a fall in drug prices deter them either. On the contrary: lower drug prices may make theft more rewarding by allowing them to purchase more drugs for their money!

DRUGS, PERSONAL PREFERENCES, AND SOCIAL NORMS

Defenders of current drug prohibition argue that the fall in drug prices following "legalization" or even some slackening of enforcement would lead to a large increase in drug "abuse." This claim rests on the standard prohibitionist assumption that all use is abuse, and the further assumption that price is a major consideration for most users or would-be users. Prohibition defenders also argue that the drug war, besides punishing users and dealers, "sends a message" condemning drug use. By "sends a message" they presumably mean affects individual views, or "personal preferences," and shared group views, or "social norms."

I believe that the evidence shows that, as with most consumption, personal preferences and social norms influence most people more than the price of drugs. (As I will show later, price *is* important to down-and-out problem users). As for the "message" claim, the antidrug message may well have had a powerful impact on social norms—the norms of people who have little knowledge of or contact with drugs and therefore support the drug war. The "message" does not appear to have gotten through very clearly to actual drug users. Unfortunately, as so many advertisers discover to their dismay, preferences cannot be manipulated at will, and norms have a way of taking off into unexpected fads and fashions. Moreover, norms are often specific to small groups in special circumstances, hard to influence from the outside.

Here are some examples of the impact of personal preferences and social norms on drug use.

Alcohol has always been far more popular than other intoxicants in Western culture. This was true in the early twentieth century before Prohibition, when opiates and cocaine were legal and widely available. In several European countries and in Australia actual or de facto decriminalization of possession has not produced any significant increase in drug use; alcohol remains king. Miron and Zweibel estimate that while total alcohol consumption fell to 30 percent of prior levels at the beginning of Prohibition, it soon rose again to 60–70 percent, and then remained stable through the end of Prohibition and for ten years afterward, rising again in the 1940s (Miron and Zweibel 1991).

(The failure to rise immediately may have been due to the Depression.) In any case, serious alcohol drinkers quickly found their way around Prohibition.

Thousands of GI's became addicted to high-grade opium while serving in Vietnam. Despite fears of an explosion in opiate addiction, most quickly and easily kicked the habit on returning to the U.S. (Robins 1973). Why? It may have been acceptable to get stoned while sweltering in a bug-infested jungle camp, waiting for shots from an invisible enemy. But the social norms of the communities to which the GI's returned did not tolerate opiate use and the GI's themselves had better things to do.

According to a *New York Times* series (Verhovek 1995a), illegal drugs are easily and cheaply available in U.S. prisons, smuggled in by prisoners' relatives and corrupt guards. At one prison, drugs are so cheap that prisoners actually export them for sale outside. Prison is no obstacle to people who want drugs badly enough. Imprisonment without treatment does not deter problem drug users. If anything, it makes them more hopeless and prone to drug use.

The Center on Addiction and Substance Abuse at Columbia University (CASA), in its *National Survey of American Attitudes on Substance Abuse* (CASA 1995), found that 30 percent of sixth- through twelfth-graders surveyed stated that it was easy to obtain cocaine or heroin—yet 82 percent reported that none of their circle of friends used hard drugs and another 13 percent reported that "less than half" used them, leaving only 5 percent with "more than half" (p. 88). The CASA survey does not distinguish regular use from occasional experimentation, so even the 5 percent greatly overstates hard drug use. Most people with easy access to drugs don't touch them.

The CASA survey also asked teenagers what they considered the main reason "someone your age gets started on drugs." The top four responses were 31 percent—"because friends use drugs," 29 percent—"curiosity," 15 percent—"to be cool," and 9 percent—"personal problems" (p. 91). Other responses were scattered. Adding "because friends use" to "to be cool" gives us some 46 percent for peer pressure. Again, social norms overwhelmingly determine use or nonuse of drugs.

Perhaps the strongest evidence for the impotence of laws in the face of human preferences comes from the drug war itself. Since the Nixon administration declared war in the early '70s, federal, state, and local governments have thrown ever more resources against the drug menace. The Bush administration opened a massive campaign to interdict foreign sources. A 1995 survey of the Latin-American cocaine industry in *The Economist* reports that, "after the United States has spent more than $50 billion on its anti-drug fight, Latin America's illegal drug industry is still booming" (pp. 21–24). According to the Drug Enforcement Administration:

In 1993, cocaine . . . was readily available in all major U.S. metropolitan areas. Generally, the price of cocaine remained relatively low and stable at all levels of the traffic during 1993. The purity of cocaine remained relatively high and stable . . . Heroin was readily available for users in all major U.S. metropolitan areas. High retail purities and relatively stable wholesale prices per kilogram in those areas indicated continued availability, a development consistent with national trends over the past few years. . . . Marijuana remained the most commonly used illicit drug in the United States. . . . Rates of marijuana use increased among high school seniors, to 35.3 percent of respondents as reflected in the 1993 *National High School Senior Survey*, from 32.6 percent in 1992. [NNICC 1994, pp. vii–ix]

Until recently, the DEA consoled itself for failing to stem the tide of illegal drugs by claiming credit for the decline in casual use: "We have made significant progress in reducing drug use in this country. Now is not the time to abandon our efforts" (DEA 1994, p. 13, table p. 14). As will be seen below, drug enforcement surely deters casual users. Alcohol Prohibition not only deterred light drinkers, it probably changed their habits so that they did not resume drinking when Prohibition ended. But the recent upsurge in marijuana use among high school students suggests that enforcement is at best only part of the story. Possibly the long decline in casual use of drugs arose from antidrug messages, or possibly it arose from the same concern for health that led to the simultaneous decline in smoking, or both. Cigarette smoking among teenagers has recently begun to rise again, apparently as part of a backlash against the obsessive focus on health (Verhovek 1995b). The increase in marijuana experimentation may well derive from the same backlash, or even from a reaction against heavy-handed antidrug "education" and advertising.

Substance abusers suffer from feelings of worthlessness and hopelessness, which they try to escape from with intoxicants. Changes in the price of those intoxicants may affect the quantity and combination consumed, but not the underlying feelings. Effective drug treatment relies on changing abusers' attitudes: convincing them that they have worth and dignity as individuals, that their situation is not hopeless, and that they can in fact control drug use that threatens their health, their jobs, their families, or other valuable parts of their lives (Beck 1993).

To summarize: most people choose not to use illicit drugs even when they have cheap and easy access to them. Enforcement can have some effect on light users; regular and problem users will get their drugs even in prison. Drug treatment and changes in social norms have far more influence on drug use than enforcement, because they change individuals' attitudes.

ECONOMIC IMPLICATIONS OF DRUG POLICY CHANGES

In addition to their assumptions about drugs, prohibition supporters make two crucial assumptions about policy. Critics make alternative assumptions (Table 21–5).

Table 21–5. Prohibitionist Assumptions versus Alternative Assumptions

Prohibitionist Assumptions	Alternative Assumptions
"Drug-free" is a realistic political objective, to be pursued by a strategy of "zero tolerance" for drugs and drug users.	"Drug-free" is not just unrealistic, it cuts off sophisticated consideration of alternative objectives and trade-offs between those objectives. "Zero tolerance" in practice fosters ineffective deployment of resources, notably going first for the easy targets: small street-level dealers or marijuana smokers.
We have only two choices of policy: "prohibition" or "legalization."	In reality, we can choose among a huge range of policy options, along many dimensions. Policy options include not only actual laws, but enforcement strategies and—a crucial reality often ignored by noneconomists—the allocation of limited resources among those strategies.

Here are seven possible options for change in drug policy:

1. We can give up foreign drug eradication and interdiction efforts, primarily in Latin America, which studies by the RAND Institute and others have indicated to have a negligible impact on domestic prices and availability of illicit drugs.
2. We can scale back and restructure domestic enforcement to concentrate efforts on major traffickers and violent dealers, ignoring small user-dealers and ordinary users as long as they remain discreet and nonviolent. This is more or less the practice in Europe, Canada, Australia, and some U.S. localities, notably San Francisco and New Haven, Connecticut.
3. We can reduce penalties for drug possession or dealing; in particular—the long, mandatory minimum prison sentences that a 1997 RAND study has shown to be both costly and ineffective in deterring drug dealers (Caulkins et al. 1997). We can reduce or eliminate penalties for possession, and shift from prison to fines. We can eliminate property forfeitures.
4. We can provide treatment to problem users who seek it, including easy access to methadone for opiate addicts. We can provide clean needles and other health care to those who do not seek treatment.
5. We can provide better educational opportunities and counseling, in-

cluding "big brother" and "big sister" programs, to disadvantaged children who are most at risk of becoming problem users or dealers.

6. We can replace drug "education" designed to frighten children and their parents with drug education that conveys accurate information about the characteristics and risks of different legal and illegal drugs.

7. We can follow some of the European "decriminalization" and "legalization" and "medicalization" experiments, or design our own. Many Western countries, including Great Britain, Germany, and Italy, treat possession of small quantities of drugs as a minor offense or no offense at all. For over twenty years the Dutch have allowed adults to purchase small quantities of cannabis in "coffee shops." For over two years the Swiss have provided heroin to hard-core addicts under tightly controlled in-clinic programs.

The first three changes amount to a retreat from aggressive, indiscriminate prohibition enforcement. Since prohibition enforcement has steadily escalated since President Nixon declared war on drugs in the late '60s, it would mean a return toward earlier U.S. policies. I will call such a change "downsizing the drug war" with a hope that it would mean not only a smaller but a more cost-effective endeavor.

The second three changes—improved treatment, prevention, and education—simply expand on programs already sporadically implemented in some localities. A 1994 RAND study financed by the U.S. Army (!) estimated that additional spending on treatment would reduce cocaine consumption by seven times as much as additional spending on domestic enforcement (Rydell 1994a).

Only the last change—experimenting with extensive "decriminalization," "legalization," or "medicalization"—goes beyond policies with which we have direct experience in the U.S. I will refer to these as "experimental policies" to indicate that they are not well tested and encompass a wide range of possibilities.

In the discussion that follows, I will focus on the consequences of downsizing the drug war, without and with experimental policies, for two reasons. First, it is hard to imagine implementation of experimental policies in the U.S. without prior changes in criminal justice, health care, and education. Second, when prohibition defenders predict the consequences of "legalization," they seem actually to describe—inaccurately, I believe—the consequences of a large, poorly controlled black market. Prohibition critics hope that the experimental policies they advocate will actually shrink and control the black market.

All else being equal, downsizing the drug war would accelerate the long-term trend of falling black market prices and increasing purity and availability of illicit drugs. However, we cannot simply assume, as prohibition defenders do, that such downsizing would automatically produce an explosion in drug abuse. As suggested above, for most people under most circumstances price and availability of illicit drugs are at best a minor consideration. The consequences of downsizing are complex and not obvious—and can be strongly affected by simultaneous changes in other policies.

In the rest of this section I will apply basic economic principles to suggest the consequences of downsizing the drug war. In the final section I will address "experimental policies."

IMPACT OF DOWNSIZING ON DANGEROUSNESS OF DRUGS

- *Downsizing the drug war will shift consumption to less potent and dangerous drugs.* The combination of two useful economic principles explains why:

1. *High transportation and transaction costs screen out low-value goods.*
   Only the best California artichokes get shipped to New York. It doesn't pay to ship average or low quality ones. During Prohibition (1920–1933) beer and wine weren't worth smuggling. Bootleggers concentrated on hard liquor, including 120 proof, which had a high ratio of value to transportation cost. Only the finest wines made it to the tables of the rich. After Prohibition, beer and wine soon dominated the alcohol market again and high-proof hard liquor disappeared. Today the cost and risk of drug smuggling shift the mix of available drugs toward highly concentrated heroin and cocaine, or designer drugs, and away from less potent drugs, especially from bulky, odorous marijuana. Put another way, while drug prohibition raises the cost of all illegal drugs, it disproportionately raises the cost of milder drugs, especially marijuana. *Downsizing the drug war will lower the cost of marijuana more than that of hard drugs.*
2. *People constantly make trade-offs. All else being equal, people who want to get high will do so in ways that offer the least dangers and side effects.* Most drinkers choose beer and wine over hard liquor. Intravenous drug users choose clean needles if they can get them (Goleman 1995b). Opiate users sniff heroin or even eat opium if it's available. Cocaine users sniff powder rather than smoke crack. Most drug takers choose marijuana over heroin or cocaine. In fact, given the opportunity, many choose marijuana over alcohol. Combining the preference for safer highs with a fall in drug prices, especially the price of marijuana relative to hard drugs and alcohol, we get a clear economic prediction: *Downsizing the drug war will shift consumption to less potent, safer drugs.*

It will increase the use of marijuana in proportion to hard drugs and alcohol. It will also shift hard drug users toward safer practices, for example, sniffing instead of injecting heroin.

IMPACT OF DOWNSIZING ON CASUAL, REGULAR, AND PROBLEM USERS

- *Downsizing the drug war will affect casual, regular, and problem drug users quite differently: the number of casual and regular users may increase, regular users may consume about the same, but deal less, while problem users may substantially increase per-capita consumption.* Another two useful economic principles underlie these predictions:

1. *The market price of a good is often a very poor measure of its cost, which includes time, risk, inconvenience, side effects, and any number of other considerations.*

   The cost of out-of-season asparagus is high for me. Not only must I pay a high price, but I must spend time searching for a store that carries it. This cost is negligible to the greengrocer. Similarly, the black market street prices of illegal drugs may be wildly off from the true cost to users, in either direction.

2. *The effect of cost on the buyer of a good depends heavily on how important the good is in his overall budget; the larger the budget share, the greater the effect.*

   I don't watch the cost of copy paper; an office manager does. The effect of cost on drug buyers depends on the proportion of their income they spend on drugs.

From these two principles it follows that *convenience and risk matter more than price to casual users and potential experimenters.* Casual users include teenagers sampling illegal drugs for the first time. Virtually all regular and problem users start use as teenagers.

To a casual drug user, a high street price (say, $100 a gram of cocaine) is barely relevant because drugs are so small a part of his budget. Even a 14-year-old can easily come up with $10 or $20 from time to time. Casual users are strongly affected by convenience and risk. For an unconnected would-be adult drug buyer, the cost is the street price plus the time, inconvenience, and risk of cruising around to locate a dealer, and the risk of obtaining drugs of uncertain concentration, that may be cut with some toxic chemical. In short, for the casual buyer the cost is far higher than the street price. Whether a would-be experimenter buys at all depends on the availability of trusted dealers. For children too young or timid to go to town, drugs become accessible and attractive only if their circle of friends and acquaintances includes user-dealers.

Downsizing the drug war may make illegal drugs more easily and safely available to casual users, if possible. (Marijuana is now more easily available to children than alcohol.) Since marijuana appears to be coming back into fashion—in the teeth of aggressive prohibition—a downsizing might facilitate a substantial increase in casual marijuana use.

Regular user-dealers obtain drugs at very low effective cost, making them insensitive to market price. Regular users include both adults and teenagers. These individuals may consume large dollar quantities of illegal drugs. Some may be addicted to heroin or cocaine, but not to the extent that they cannot function. Most hold jobs or attend school.

Unless they earn very high incomes, or inherit money, regular users also sell drugs to cover the cost of their own use. That is, they buy drugs from a familiar wholesaler, sometimes on consignment, sell part retail and use the rest. (Even very rich users often give drugs to friends, which is still dealing in the eyes of the law.) For user-dealers with little earning power and low aversion to risk—true of most teenagers and many low-wage workers—a few hours a week selling drugs to pay for their own use may seem a negligible cost.

Regular users prove particularly hard to discourage from taking drugs. Like regular or moderately heavy drinkers, they have enough control over use that they don't consider themselves to have a problem. Since they get their drugs virtually free, a decline in drug prices will not increase their personal use of drugs. However, a decline in prices may lead some of them to spend less time dealing, or stop dealing altogether. Unfortunately, the ones least likely to be discouraged from dealing by a decline in drug prices are those with the lowest earning power: poorly educated teenagers. These are precisely the dealers it is most important to eliminate as they are the ones who recruit new users and dealers from their peers.

Down-and-out problem users are strongly affected by the street price of drugs. Down-and-out problem users are too unreliable or emotionally disturbed to deal drugs to support their habit. No drug wholesaler would trust them with a consignment.

Drugs constitute a major part of problem users' meager budgets. Although relatively few in number, they provide much of the demand that fuels the drug market. They pay the high street price, and spend their lives in search of drugs, and of cash to purchase drugs. Their drug consumption is severely limited by the amount of cash they can beg, steal, scrounge, or earn by turning tricks. Fluctuations in the street price and availability of drugs make their lives an endless rollercoaster.

Unlike experimenters and regular users, problem users will consume substantially more drugs if prices decline from current market prices. Only when the price has fallen so low that problem users can afford quantities near their physiological limit will further declines in price not lead to more consumption.

I note that the characterization of down-and-out problem users as extremely sensitive to price runs directly counter to the assumption of many prohibition supporters and critics alike: that addicts "must" get their daily fix, and if need be will steal whatever it takes. From this assumption flows the—I think vain—hope that if drug prices fall, addicts will steal less.

The 1994 RAND study of cocaine markets supports this predicted behavior of users. The study divides users into two groups: "light" and "heavy." Their "heavy" users correspond roughly to combined "regular" and "problem" users. According to their estimates, based on the 1990 National Household Survey of Drug Abuse, the 22 percent of users classified as "heavy" consumed 70 percent of cocaine (Rydell and Everingham 1994a).

Figure 21–2 (RAND figure 1.1) taken from the study shows heavy and light users for 1972 through 1992, a period of steady drug war escalation. Light users peak in about 1982, decline steadily until about 1990, and then start to rise again. Numbers of heavy users increase only slightly over the 1982-1992 period. Figure 21–3 (RAND Figure 1.2) for the same period shows consumption by light users first rising then falling, while use by heavy users increases dramatically, especially after 1980. Figure 21–4 (RAND Figure 1.3) shows expenditure cocaine for the period. While expenditure by light users rises and falls, expenditure by heavy users remains remarkably constant. Figure 21–5 (RAND Figure 1.4) shows a dramatic decline in real cocaine prices from 1977 to 1992, from about $750 per pure gram to a little over $100 per pure gram (Rydell and Everingham 1994b, pp. 2–4).

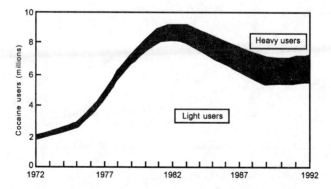

Figure 21-2. Number of Cocaine Users, by Intensity of Use

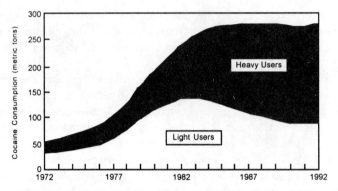

Figure 21–3. Cocaine Consumption by Type of User

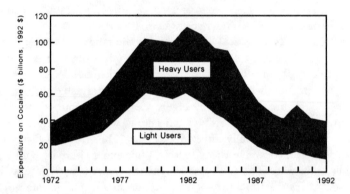

Figure 21–4. Expenditure on Cocaine, by Users

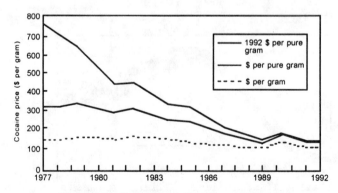

Figure 21–5. Price of Cocaine: 1977–1992

A reasonable interpretation of these data is as follows: light and heavy users of cocaine increase in number during the '70s as cocaine becomes fashionable and prices fall. In the '80s light users drop out (or never start) as the drug war makes casual use increasingly risky and inconvenient. Heavy users maintain an almost constant dollar volume of consumption over the period. During the second half of the period the number of heavy users increases only slightly, so per capita expenditure by heavy users remains nearly constant in the face of sharply declining prices. This suggests, in turn, that a large proportion of heavy users are spending everything they can get on cocaine. Price times volume remains constant: the lower the price, the more they spend. Clearly, down-and-out problem users dominate the heavy use category. They cannot scrounge enough money to consume anywhere close to the physiological limit (3–5 grams a day). Consequently, as prices fall, their per capita consumption continues to increase. If prices fall from $100 per gram to $50 a gram, their consumption might double.

In this very limited sense, prohibition defenders are correct: a fall in the price of cocaine or heroin will indeed produce a dramatic increase in per capita consumption by down-and-out problem users. But possibly not for very long. Booming illicit drug markets may eventually bring prices so low that junkies, like winos, can easily afford their physiological limit.

IMPACT OF DOWNSIZING ON DRUG MARKETS

- *Downsizing the drug war will shift the illicit drug market into the hands of fewer, older, and less violent sellers.*

Illicit drug markets in the U.S. are notorious for the presence of large numbers of ill-educated, violent juveniles. Surprisingly enough, this is not the case in European or Australian illicit drug markets, where drug dealing is not prosecuted with anything like U.S. zeal (Zimring 1992). The "principle of comparative advantage" suggests why: *People find the occupation, not that they are absolutely the best at, but that they are relatively the best at, even though they may be absolutely terrible at this occupation.*

The textbook example of comparative advantage is the lawyer and her secretary: the lawyer types much faster than her secretary, but it still pays for her to go to court, leaving the secretary at the word processor. An example closer to hand: most common criminals are astoundingly incompetent at crime, and make at best a miserable living before they are (usually quickly) caught. The explanation: if these hapless individuals were more competent at anything else, they wouldn't be criminals.

In any well-functioning competitive market, buyers and sellers develop long-term personal relationships. Sellers try to retain their customers by providing quality goods and services. Customers seek out and stick with reliable sellers. Long-term relationships are even more important in "normal" illegal markets, like numbers, or escort services, or drug suppliers to the well-to-do—where trust and discretion are at a premium. Illegal sellers work out turf arrangements quietly and without violence, lest they frighten the customers or attract the police.

Low-end drug markets are another story. Police routinely conduct "drug sweeps" of poor urban neighborhoods, arresting and searching all the occupants of a building, or all the pedestrians on a block. Persons caught with drugs are offered a deal by prosecutors: they will be charged with lesser offenses, carrying lower mandatory sentences, if they "cooperate" by turning in or entrapping other drug sellers, buyers, or even potential buyers. (A tape recording of someone agreeing to buy drugs is enough to convict, even without any evidence that the person actually could or would buy the drugs [Adler 1997].)

This kind of "search and destroy" drug enforcement drives out any marginally decent or competent sellers. It pushes drug markets from one neighborhood to the next, giving an advantage to sellers who can quickly establish new turf before the next sweep. It creates an atmosphere of suspicion and fear in which sellers and customers don't know each other, and don't want to either (Zimmer 1990). Who sells drugs in such a dangerous market? Low income user-dealers, who need to pay for their habits. And young, ill-educated, and violent teenagers, kids who will trade their very limited futures, and even their lives, for a few hundred bucks.

The characterization of low-end illicit drug markets as the opportunity of last resort runs counter to another assumption shared by many prohibition supporters and critics alike: that retail drug-dealing is immensely profitable. As the RAND study of dealers in Washington, D.C., showed, most small dealers at best merely pay for their own use (Reuter et al. 1990). Young teens may briefly make a few hundred a day. Before long, they will be arrested, or shot, or become regular user-dealers, consuming their profits. Eventually, many will become problem users. Joey Tranchina, who operates the AIDS Prevention and Action Network in San Mateo County, California, recently conducted an "unscientific survey" of drug treatment centers in four San Francisco Bay Area counties. He asked, "What percentage of your adolescent self-described drug addicts were dealers before they were regular users of drugs?" The answer: 70 to 80 percent! (Tranchina, personal communication, 1997).

Nicholas Pastore, until recently the police chief of New Haven, Connecticut, pursued a strategy of targeting violent drug gangs while ignoring discreet and nonviolent small dealers (Pastore, personal communication, 1996). "Comparative advantage" suggests that, even with no change in drug laws, such an approach allows drug markets to be reclaimed by more businesslike adults who care about serving long-term customers. A return of the markets to nonviolent adults in turn reduces opportunities for teenage dealers, and therefore teenagers' access to drugs.

POLICY IMPLICATIONS: CAN "LEGALIZATION" HELP PROBLEM USERS AND PROTECT CHILDREN?

What should be the objectives of drug policy? Fewer users? Fewer abusers? Less aggregate use of illicit drugs? Less use by abusers? Less use by children? Better health of users? Less violent illegal drug markets? Greater cost-effectiveness of enforcement?

If "drug-free" is an impossible dream, then we must settle for lesser objectives, set priorities, and accept trade-offs. I propose that we select two primary objectives: protecting children and helping problem users. Protecting children means both restricting their access to drugs as much as feasible and reducing the likelihood and seriousness of problems. (This is equivalent to discouraging children from early sex, but providing condoms for those who're "gonna do it" anyway.) Helping problem users means not only getting them into treatment, but addressing their underlying problems, including depression, disease, and lack of education. To the extent that helping problem users shrinks the black market, it also furthers the goal of protecting children.

A downsizing of the drug war contributes in a limited way to the goal of protecting children. It shifts the market toward marijuana and away from hard drugs, it makes the markets less violent, and it reduces incentives for children to deal. On the other hand, downsizing the drug war permits a larger (though safer) black market, with easier access for casual users, including nondealing children. As for problem users, assuming that substance abuse is a symptom of emotional problems, not merely a consequence of access to drugs, downsizing should not much affect the number of problem users, but it will enable them to consume more, possibly much more.

Can experimental policies of "legalization" or "medicalization" retain the benefits of downsizing while controlling the disadvantages?

According to the analysis above, here's how the illicit drug market works: regular user-dealers sell to casual users on the one hand and to problem users on the other. In addition, some retail dealers are non-users, particularly young teenage recruits to the inner-city drug business. Casual users, who include teen experimenters, are not sensitive to price, but very sensitive to risk and convenience. Down-and-out problem users are very sensitive to price. Regulars are not very sensitive to either price or risk. Problem users account for the bulk of drug consumption. Can we design policies to take advantage of these characteristics?

Since children are casual users, to keep them out of the black market, we must make the market inconvenient. That is, we must make it hard for children to find sellers. The first step is to reduce or eliminate the primary sellers to children: other children. The second step is to shrink the black market itself; the smaller the market, the harder it becomes for casual users, or would-be users, to connect with dealers.

MARIJUANA

The above logic underlies the Dutch "legalization" experiment. For twenty years the Dutch have allowed sale of small quantities of cannabis (marijuana or hashish) to adults in "coffee shops" while keeping hard drugs illegal. By making the least dangerous and most popular illegal drug legal, the Dutch have sought to simultaneously shrink the black market drastically and shift consumption further away from hard drugs and toward cannabis. By making cannabis available only to adults under carefully supervised circumstances, they also hope to minimize black market access by children. After twenty years of coffee shop legalization, estimated Dutch marijuana consumption per capita remains well below that of the U.S.—again suggesting that culture is more important than price and availability. The Dutch are satisfied the policy works; the only serious complaints have come from prohibitionist neighbors, notably France.

The Dutch approach to marijuana—a limited number of outlets selling small amounts to adults only—resembles a restrictive version of U.S. alcohol control as practiced in most localities. What might it accomplish? I think we could expect a virtual elimination of black market marijuana dealers, including juvenile dealers. However, there would probably not be a great reduction in underage access.

Absent a black market, underage marijuana control would depend on the questionable cooperation of otherwise law-abiding adults—as with alcohol. There is no significant black market in alcohol. There are no teenage alcohol dealers in the schools. Yet drinking is rampant among high school and underage college students, especially binge drinking on the weekends (Wechsler et al. 1994). Why? Because adults tolerate or facilitate it. Liquor sellers fail to check ID's. Kids just turned 21 supply younger siblings and friends. Parents don't control access to their liquor cabinet. Parents permit their children to party without proper supervision. Colleges allow fraternities to serve liquor to underage students. Why do adults wink at underage drinking? Because they also drank as teenagers! (At my high school graduation party, not only were many of my classmates drunk, but so were three sets of parent chaperones!) Nonetheless, I maintain that parents who seriously want to keep their children from drinking can usually do so until the children leave home. Elimination of black market marijuana might give parents similar control of access.

The difficulty with Dutch-style legalization of marijuana is of course that it "sends a message" of greater tolerance for marijuana. Norms already seem to be shifting toward greater tolerance. Prohibition defenders have a realistic concern that a change in laws may accelerate the shift.

HEROIN

Heroin lies at the opposite end of the illicit drug spectrum from marijuana. Users are few compared to users of cocaine or marijuana, but include a large number of problem users, many seriously ill. If we can just get the problem users out of the market, the market will shrink drastically.

We can of course get many problem users out of the market by expanding drug-free treatment—a proposal with which no one disagrees. We can get even more out by expanding methadone maintenance programs for heroin addicts who cannot go drug-free, and lifting the restrictions that make them so ineffective [Rettig and Yarmolinsky 1995]. As programs in the U.S. and Europe have demonstrated, many addicts can take methadone indefinitely and still lead reasonably normal lives.

The Swiss Experiment. After years of offering free high-quality treatment, including methadone maintenance, the Swiss recognized that some addicts simply did not respond. Three years ago they began an experimental program of providing heroin or morphine to addicts in clinics. Some points are noteworthy:

1. In the experimental protocol, the Swiss specifically excluded addicts who did not seem to have health or other problems with their habits. They selected about 1,000 long-term hard-core addicts suffering serious health and emotional problems, who had repeatedly failed other treatment programs.
2. The addicts in the program, who were allowed to choose their own daily dose level, quickly settled on a relatively low, stable dose. Their health improved. Freed of their obsessive daily search for drugs, many began to deal with underlying emotional problems; a few even found jobs.
3. The program has retained some 80 percent of its clients, even though it is very restrictive, requiring addicts to show up at the clinics two or three times a day.
4. There has been no "leakage" of heroin back into the black market, and no "incidents" to upset the public.

Similar "medicalization" programs are being planned or have been proposed in several other countries. Mayor Kurt Schmoke of Baltimore has proposed such a program, as has the Connecticut Law Revision Commission (1997).

The Swiss experiment is not large enough or old enough to determine the impact on the black market. However, it seems logical that, were such a program expanded to include most hard-core addicts, the black market might shrink substantially. At present, user-dealers sell to casual users on the one hand and to problem users on the other. Departure of problem users from the market would in turn deprive user-dealers of their best customers. They might find it difficult to locate enough casual users to finance their own use. In turn, would-be casual users might find it much harder to locate dealers.

On the other hand, the Swiss experiment suffers from serious limitations. First, the very tight controls of the program—requiring clients to visit the clinic two or three times daily, as well as give up a driver's license—make the program unattractive to less desperate heroin users, notably those with a regular job. If the controls were to be relaxed, for example, by allowing clients to take a small supply home, there are bound to be "incidents" that upset the public. Second, the program attracts and retains clients by providing them with very cheap, pure heroin. As drug war downsizing or expansion of foreign production makes black market heroin cheaper and purer, the program's constraints will appear less tolerable. Finally, the Swiss program cannot be applied to cocaine.

COCAINE

Unlike heroin, cocaine is psychologically but not physiologically addictive. A stimulant, it gives users a powerful feeling of well-being and alertness, but does not cause withdrawal symptoms. Problem users tend to binge, staying awake two or three days and then sleeping it off. This pattern seems to preclude a Swiss-style clinic approach.

What might happen if, say, cocaine were cheaply dispensed in small amounts to adult users by prescription? The prescription requirement might pose a substantial barrier of inconvenience to would-be casual users, though obviously adults with a prescription might share with friends, including underage friends. More important, a prescription approach for adults could eliminate teenage dealers, many of whom are at risk of becoming problem users.

What about Dr. Kleber's frightening predictions, quoted at the beginning, of an explosion in cocaine abuse consequent on "legalization"? His predictions are of course a guess, possible but exceedingly unlikely. Legalization by prescription might increase the overall number of users (whom Dr. Kleber conflates with abusers). But it might simultaneously decrease the number of problem users by eliminating teenage dealers.

In any case, the only way to find out for sure what would happen with "legalization" in any form is to experiment cautiously.

CONCLUSIONS

Let's assume the primary purpose of drug policy is to keep troubled young people from becoming problem substance users, and to help problem users, young or old, achieve healthier and more productive lives. Then we already know what works, imperfectly, and what probably makes things worse. Troubled young people need education and other activities to make them feel productive; they need emotional support to make them feel valuable as individuals. Problem users need treatment that helps them overcome the feelings of worthlessness and hopelessness that they seek to obliterate with alcohol or drugs. Policies that stigmatize and imprison drug users may hurt rather than help troubled young people and problem users.

The abstractions of "prohibition" or "legalization" have little to do with the behavior or needs of troubled people. There must always be some policing of illegal drug markets, just as with bootleg liquor markets. But the drug war makes the black markets very dangerous, and therefore attractive to troubled young people with limited opportunities and a high risk of becoming problem users of hard drugs. It doesn't cause the family and social problems that put young people at risk, but it does divert resources and attention from education and treatment programs that could help them. "Legalization" in any of its many possible variations cannot solve family and social problems either— any more than repeal of alcohol Prohibition solved the problems leading some individuals to become alcoholics. However, combined with a downsizing of the drug war, "legalization" can help restrict casual access to drugs while making it easier for problem users to find treatment.

APPENDIX A

Use, "Abuse," Adverse Health Effects, and Addiction

Not only is "drug abuse" often defined as all illegal use, it is also commonly equated with both adverse health effects and addiction.

In reality, patterns of use vary enormously, from drug to drug and from person to person. I distinguish "occasional," "regular," and "problem" use above, while avoiding the term *abuse*. Adverse health effects and addiction are separate issues.

ADVERSE HEALTH EFFECTS

Adverse health effects of drugs fall into three categories: (1) adverse effects of the drugs themselves, (2) adverse effects of the mode of ingestion, and (3) adverse effects of the degraded lifestyle of problem users.

1. *Adverse effects of the drugs themselves.* Prolonged heavy doses of alcohol cause liver damage and eventually brain damage as well as mental retardation of children exposed in utero. Cocaine and amphetamines can cause heart problems and even heart failure in a small minority of susceptible individuals; otherwise these stimulants have little scientifically documented ill effects on health. South American natives chew coca leaves lifelong to no ill effect. Cocaine is the local anesthetic of choice for nasal surgery–in doses higher than those taken by recreational users. Nicotine causes loss of peripheral circulation and even gangrene in susceptible individuals; women who smoke heavily during pregnancy also tend to have low-birthweight babies. Caffeine causes a variety of ill-defined problems for susceptible individuals. Opiates cause constipation but no scientifically documented lasting injury to health; however overdoses can be fatal. The active ingredients of marijuana, cannabinols, may cause some short-term memory loss after recent heavy use, but no scientifically documented lasting injury to health, and there are no recorded deaths from overdose.

2. *Adverse effects of the mode of ingestion.* Nicotine and cannabinols are ingested by smoking, causing lung damage. Injection users of opiates, cocaine, or amphetamines risk sepsis, hepatitis, and AIDS from contaminated needles.

3. *Adverse effects of the degraded lifestyle of problem users.* Poverty, unhygienic lifestyle, and desperation make problem users particularly liable to infection and disease from contaminated needles as well as poisoning by adulterants and accidental overdoses of street heroin. In 1989 a "crack baby" scare erupted, attributing low-birthweight babies to smoking of "crack" (smokable cocaine) by poor inner-city mothers. Further investigation traced the cause not to crack per se, but to the heavy-drinking, heavy-cigarette-smoking, malnourished lifestyle of problem users (Cotton 1994).

ADDICTION

Addiction is a slippery concept. The Latin root means "being led to." Addictive behaviour belongs to a continuum that includes normal behaviour like eating when hungry or falling in love. The most important component of addiction may be psychological: addicts feel a powerful urge to take some pleasurable action—light up a cigarette, drink a scotch, eat a box of chocolates, gamble, go jogging, go shopping, make love, or snort cocaine! The urge is generally triggered by certain events or situations; for example, a smoker feels the urge to light up at the end of a meal. Some drugs, including alcohol, nicotine, caffeine, and opiates, are physiologically as well as psychologically addictive for some heavy users in that they produce withdrawal symptoms—adding a stick of physical discomfort to the pleasurable carrot encouraging repetitive use.

ADDICTION AND PROBLEM USE

The relationship between problem use and addiction is complex and depends on the substances, on the individual, and on the individual's culture and situation. As a rough generalization, most but not all problem users are addicted to alcohol and/or hard drugs (opiates or stimulants). But the converse does not hold. While most alcohol addicts are problem users, many hard drug addicts are not problem users. Nicotine and caffeine addicts are rarely problem users either. The difference between nonproblems and problem addicts lies in the extent to which the addicts control or yield to urges with immediate adverse consequences.

1. *Nicotine.* Nicotine is by far the most physiologically addictive drug. Most people who try cigarettes get hooked quickly, and most smokers cannot go even a few hours without experiencing "nic fits." Though they may incur future health effects, nicotine addicts lead normal lives. They do not suffer the feelings of worthlessness, hopelessness, and obsession with a drug or drugs characteristic of problem users. (This might not always be the case were cigarettes illegal and expensive. I once read an essay by a woman who marooned herself in a country house without cigarettes in an effort to quit. Within a day she found herself walking along a highway collecting butts tossed from cars.)
2. *Alcohol.* Obviously, most alcohol drinkers are neither addicts nor problem users. Those who drink heavily and regularly enough to become physiologically addicted are also thereby impaired enough to count as problem users. Some nonphysiologically addicted binge drinkers probably qualify as problem users.
3. *Cocaine and amphetamines.* Cocaine and amphetamines are not physiologically addictive. Cocaine and amphetamines are psychologically addictive to some users, especially people with a poor self-image. These stimulants produce a sense of alertness, confidence, and well-being that such users feel a strong urge to repeat. Heavy users may binge for days, then sleep it off. Many regular cocaine or amphetamine users still lead relatively normal lives, keeping their daily intake at a level that

does not seriously impede their productivity, and/or bingeing only on weekends. My bar-hopping friends tell me this is the cocaine use pattern of many young Wall Street traders.

4. *Heroin, morphine, methadone, and other opiates.* Most users do not become addicts, and even addicts often voluntarily stop use for days or weeks. (Opiate withdrawal symptoms are less severe than those for nicotine.) Nonaddicts include occasional smokers of heroin, so-called "chippers." Pain patients may take regular large doses of opiates without becoming psychologically addicted, though they do experience withdrawal symptoms. Unlike alcohol addiction, opiate addiction does not necessarily impair normal functioning. This is obviously true of methadone, which suppresses withdrawal effects without giving a "rush." It is also true for heroin and morphine. For example, Great Britain allows physicians to prescribe heroin. While few actually do so, there are nonetheless several hundred registered heroin addicts who have received prescribed heroin for as many as forty years while leading otherwise ordinary lives. It is one of the dirty little secrets of medicine that some practicing physicians and nurses are opiate (mostly Demerol) addicts—often with little apparent detriment to themselves or their patients.

5. *Marijuana.* Marijuana is not physiologically addictive, and does not appear to hook users psychologically as does cocaine. Nonetheless, some perpetual "potheads" may rate as problem users to the extent they neglect the concerns of normal lives and try to escape feelings of worthlessness and hopelessness in a cloud of smoke.

REFERENCES

Associated Press (1994). 44% of college students are binge drinkers, poll says. *The New York Times*, December 7, p. B12.

Beck, A. T., Wright, F. D., Newman, C. F., and Liese, B. S. (1993). *Cognitive Therapy of Substance Abuse.* New York: Guilford.

CASA. (1995). *National Survey of American Attitudes on Substance Abuse.* New York: Center on Addiction and Substance Abuse at Columbia University, July.

Caulkins, J. P., Rydell, C. P., Schwabe, W. L., and Chiesa, J. (1997). *Mandatory Minimum Sentences: Throwing Away the Key or the Taxpayers' Money?* Drug Policy Research Center. Santa Monica, CA: RAND.

Committee on Drugs and the Law (1994). A wiser course: ending drug prohibition. *The Record of the Association of the Bar of the City of New York*, Vol. 49, No. 5, June.

Connecticut Law Revision Commission (1997). Drug policy in Connecticut and strategy options: report to the judiciary committee of the Connecticut general assembly. Hartford, CT.

Cotton, P. (1994). Smoking cigarettes may do developing fetus more harm than ingesting cocaine, experts say. *Journal of the American Medical Association*, February 23.

Drug Enforcement Administration (DEA) (1994). *How to Hold Your Own in a Drug Legalization Debate.* U.S. Department of Justice, August.

The Economist (1995). Columbia's drug business: the wages of prohibition. December 24, 1994– January 6, 1995, pp. 21–24.

Goldstein, P. J. (1989). Drugs and violent crime. In *Pathways to Criminal Violence*, ed. A. Weiner and M. E. Wolfgang, Newbury Park, CA: Sage.

Goleman, D. (1995a). 75 years later, study still tracking geniuses. *New York Times*, March 7, p. C1.

———— (1995b). Researcher kills a myth of syringe sharing. *New York Times*, September 20, p. B10.

Kleber, H. (1994). Our current approach to drug abuse—progress, problems, proposals. *New England Journal of Medicine*, Feb. 3, Vol. 330, No. 5, cited in DEA, p. 15.

Miron, J. A., and Zweibel, J. (1991). Alcohol consumption during prohibition. *American Economic Review* 81(2):242–247.

National Narcotics Intelligence Consumers Committee (NNICC) (1994). *The NNICC Report 1993: The Supply of Illicit Drugs to the United States*, pp. vii–ix. Drug Enforcement Administration. Arlington, VA, August.

Peele, S. (1989). *Diseasing of America: Addiction Treatment Out of Control.* Lexington, MA: Lexington Books.

Rasmussen, D., and Benson, B. (1994). *The Economic Anatomy of a Drug War.* Lanham, MD: Rowman & Littlefield.

———— (1996). *Illicit Drugs and Crime.* Oakland, CA: The Independent Institute.

Rettig, R., and Yarmolinsky, A., eds. (1995). *Federal Regulation of Methadone Treatment.* Institute of Medicine. Washington, DC: National Academy Press.

Reuter, P., MacCoun, R., and Murphy, P. (1990). *Money from Crime: A Study of the Economics of Drug Dealing in Washington, D.C.* Washington, DC: RAND.

Robins, L. N. (1973). *The Viet Nam Veteran Returns.* Washington, DC: U.S. Government Printing Office.

Rydell, C. P., and Everingham, S. S. (1994a). *Modeling the Demand for Cocaine*, Drug Policy Research Center, RAND. Data from U.S. Department of Health and Human Services, National Household Survey on Drug Abuse, Rockville, MD.

———— (1994b). *Controlling Cocaine: Supply Versus Demand Programs.* Drug Policy Research Center, RAND. Data from U.S. Department of Health and Human Services, National Household Survey on Drug Abuse, Rockville, MD.

Shedler, J., and Block, J. (1990). Adolescent drug use in psychological health, a longitudinal inquiry. *American Psychologist* 46:612–30.

U.S. Department of Health and Human Services (1995). *National Household Survey on Drug Abuse: Population Estimates 1994*, Rockville, MD.

Verhovek, S. H. (1995a). Warehouse of addiction. *New York Times*, July 2, 3, 4, p. 1.

———— (1995b). Young, carefree, and in love with cigarettes. *New York Times*, July 30, p. 1.

Wechsler, H., Davenport, A., Dowdall, G., et al. (1994). Health and behavioral consequences of binge drinking in college. *Journal of the American Medical Association* 272(21):1672–1677, December 7.

Weil, A., and Rosen, W. (1993). *From Chocolate to Morphine: Everything You Need to Know about Mind-Altering Drugs.* New York: Houghton-Mifflin.

Zimmer, L. (1990). Proactive policing against street-level drug trafficking in New York City. *American Journal of Police* 9:43–74.

Zimring, F. E., and Hawkins, G. (1992). *The Search for Rational Drug Control.* Cambridge, MA: Cambridge University Press.

22

Thinking Seriously about Alternatives to Drug Prohibition

Ethan A. Nadelmann

Four years after the notion of drug legalization reemerged into public view [Ed. note: this chapter was written in 1992], the time has come to step back and evaluate what it is all about and where it should be headed.[1] I cannot help but write as one who has become closely identified with the notion, but I also write as one who has tried to step back from the debate over drug legalization and analyze critically its contributions, missteps, and potential to beneficially redirect drug control policies. My principal interest lies not in the debate itself but in the future of psychoactive drug use and drug control policies in the United States and abroad. This article is thus not a response

I am grateful to the members of the Princeton Working Group on the Future of Drug Use and Alternatives to Drug Prohibition for their participation in the project, and to the Smart Family Foundation for its financial support of the working group. I am also indebted to the Ford Foundation and the Robert C. Linnell Foundation for their research support. I am grateful for comments on previous drafts of this paper from Michael Aldrich, Virginia Berridge, John Dilulio, Ernest Drucker, David Hawks, Sylvia Law, Stanton Peele, Craig Reinarman, Sasha Shulgin, Kenneth Warner, and Alex Wodak.

This article is reprinted by permission of *Daedalus*, Journal of the American Academy of Arts and Sciences, from the issue "Political Pharmacology: Thinking About Drugs," Summer 1992, Vol. 121, No. 3.

to the many critics of drug legalization, nor even a dispute with those who have favored the notion with somewhat different arguments and suppositions. It generally refrains from repeating the well documented costs of drug prohibition or the reasons why we need to consider alternative approaches.[2] And it pays scant attention to the political context of the debate or the political future of drug control policy. Its objective, rather, is to create and advance a more informed and sophisticated public discourse about alternatives to drug prohibition—one that breaks free from the intellectual and moralistic confines of contemporary prohibitionist norms.[3]

My specific objectives are fourfold. The first is to identify and examine the essential differences that separate those in the reasonable middle ground of the debate. The second is to offer new ways of thinking about radical alternatives to current drug prohibition policies, to identify the sorts of questions that must be asked, and to suggest how they might be addressed. The third is to provide evidence in support of the proposition that even a radical decriminalization of drug prohibition will not result in the sorts of dramatic increases in substance abuse that self-identified critics of drug legalization fear. And the fourth is to propose a drug regulatory model that eliminates many of the worst consequences of drug prohibition without reproducing the unfortunate consequences of our alcohol and tobacco control policies.

Many of the ideas and arguments presented in this paper were proposed and developed in meetings of the Princeton Working Group on the Future of Drug Use and Alternatives to Drug Prohibition. This group, composed of eighteen scholars representing more than a dozen disciplines, is currently pursuing each of these four objectives. This article should thus be read as a synopsis of a collaborative work-in-progress, the final version of which will be completed in late 1993. I anticipate that many of the ideas advanced below will be revised and refined as the working group proceeds.

THE "LEGALIZATION" LABEL

To legalize or not to legalize? That, as two pairs of drug policy skeptics have recently written, is not really the right question.[4] The appropriate question is much broader, and it is one that incorporates the "legalize or not" question with respect to particular psychoactive drug products: What, simply stated, are the best means to regulate the production, distribution, and consumption of the great variety of psychoactive substances available today and in the foreseeable future? For a variety of reasons, the efforts of myself and others to answer that highly complex question have been captured by the label of "legalization." The term itself proved immensely successful in drawing the attention of tens of millions in the United States and elsewhere to what was at once a radical sounding but quite sensible critique of American drug control policies. But it exacted a stiff price with its implication that the only alternative to current policies was something resembling current U.S. policies with respect to alcohol and tobacco. Few of those publicly associated with legalization in fact advocated such an alternative, but the misimpression has stuck in the public mind.

Legalization has always meant different things to different people. From my perspective, it has been first and foremost a critique of American drug prohibitionist policies which stresses the extent to which most of what Americans commonly identify as part and parcel of "the drug problem" are in fact the results of those policies. The failure of most Americans to perceive the extent and content of this causal relationship, and to distinguish between the problems that stem from the misuse of drugs per se and those that stem from drug prohibitionist policies, remains the single greatest obstacle to any significant change in American drug control policies. The recognition of this causal relationship does not, it should be stressed, lead automatically to a public policy recommendation that all of drug prohibition be abandoned. But it does suggest that alternative policies less dependent upon prohibitionist methods are likely to prove more effective.

Legalization also implies a set of policy objectives at odds with the government's proclaimed objectives of fighting a war against drugs and creating a drug-free society. Any drug control strategy, I and others have argued, should seek to minimize both the negative consequences of drug use and the negative consequences of the policies themselves. This is as true of public policies with respect to alcohol, tobacco, and caffeine as it is of policies directed at limiting the misuse of cannabis, cocaine, amphetamine, opiates, hallucinogens, and all other drugs. It is imperative, for instance, that any drug control policy distinguish among casual drug use that results in little or no harm to anyone, drug misuse that causes harm primarily to the consumer, and drug misuse that results in palpable harm to others, and then focus primarily on the last of these, secondarily on preventing the misuse of drugs, and little if at all on casual drug use. It is also imperative that any drug control policy be assessed not only in terms of its success in reducing drug abuse but also in terms of its direct and indirect costs.

Implicit in the legalization critique of American drug control policies are in fact two different types of arguments. At one level, it points out the ways in which drug prohibition per se is responsible for many drug-related problems. By criminalizing the production, distribution, and use of particular drugs, drug prohibition fundamentally transforms the nature of the drug markets, the ways in which people consume drugs, the lenses through which much of society views the drug problem, and the range of policies deemed appropriate for dealing with drug abuse. On another level, however, the critique advances a far more modest claim, which is that there are better and worse types of drug prohibition, with the Dutch "harm reduction" approach epitomizing the former and the American "war on drugs" the latter. Indeed, for many of those characterized as advocates of drug legalization, the Dutch model offers an alternative that is preferable not only to current U.S. policies but also to the extreme libertarian model. The ideal set of drug control policies, from this perspective, can be found somewhere between the Dutch example and the libertarian model.

The harm reduction (or harm minimization) approach emerged in the Netherlands and Great Britain during the 1970s and early 1980s. It has since become increasingly influential both in those countries and in other parts of Europe and Australia as public health and other officials have recognized the need for more innovative and less punitive policies to stem the transmission of the HIV virus by illicit drug users.[5] Harm reduction policies seek to minimize the harms that result from illicit drug use. Rather than attempt to wean all illicit drug addicts off drugs by punitive means, harm reduction policies begin with the acknowledgment that some users cannot be persuaded to quit. These policies then seek to reduce the likelihood that they will contract or spread diseases such as hepatitis and AIDS, overdose on drugs of unknown purity and potency, or otherwise harm themselves or others. Proponents of harm reduction policies typically favor an assortment of drug treatment programs including the use of methadone and other maintenance programs. They insist on the need for needle exchange programs. They recommend public health and community outreach efforts to maintain contact between health service providers and illicit drug users. And they demand that drug policies acknowledge, both in law and policy, the human rights of drug users. Also implicit in most harm reduction approaches is the notion of "normalization," which posits that the harms associated with illicit drug use are best minimized by integrating drug users into normal society rather than isolating them in separate clinics, programs, markets, and neighborhoods.[6]

The relationship between the harm reduction approach and the notion of drug legalization remains ambiguous. Some proponents of the harm reduction approach vigorously oppose any broader trend toward disassembling the drug prohibition system. They are quick to point out that much of the opposition they have encountered stems from fears and perceptions that the harm reduction approach represents no more than a stepping stone to legalization. Others insist that a harm reduction approach taken to its logical and sensible conclusion would more closely resemble a legal regulatory regime than the current prohibition system. Any harm reduction approach, they argue, must reduce not just the harms to users but also the many other negative consequences of drug prohibition: the violence that accompanies illicit drug markets; the corruption of public officials; the de facto subsidy of organized crime; the incarceration of hundreds of thousands of people; the deprivation of individual liberties; and so on. All agree, however, that modest efforts to reduce the negative consequences of status quo policies are better than no efforts whatsoever.

LEGALIZERS, PROHIBITIONISTS, AND
THE COMMON GROUND

The basic analysis advanced by most "legalizers" is remarkably similar to that advanced by those who have appeared as the most sensible, progressive, and nonideological among the prohibitionists. Both generally agree on the basic diagnosis of American drug prohibition, on the need to assess drug policy options in terms of their costs and benefits, and on the set of objectives noted above. The "progressive prohibitionists" largely acknowledge that casual drug use is not a problem in and of itself, and the legalizers grant that some policies designed to reduce overall levels of drug use may be effective in reducing the overall negative consequences of use. There is a shared recognition that many dimensions of the American war on drugs represent a form of overkill, that more modest criminal justice measures can accomplish the same objectives as successfully as the harsher measures, and that a more vigorous adherence to public health precepts and objectives will result in a superior mix of drug control policies. Both further agree that a dramatic expansion in the availability of drugs in society will likely increase the cumulative consumption of drugs. And both agree that it is important to draw distinctions among different drugs, and among different formulations of the same drugs, in designing drug control policies. Stated otherwise, few in either camp believe that marijuana, or coca tea, should be treated the same as crack cocaine.

This common ground is fundamentally at odds with the views expressed by the more conservative and reactionary prohibitionists. Articulated most vigorously by President Bush's first Drug Czar, William Bennett, this perspective has demonstrated no interest whatsoever in analyses of costs and benefits or in the need to minimize the negative consequences of drug control policies. Casual use of illicit drugs has been depicted as an immoral form of activity as well as a dangerous source of contagion requiring the treatment of users.[7] Social science research and public health precepts are of value only insofar as they conform with their ideologically based assumptions and policies. There is, in short, no room for dispassionate dialogue concerning any policy alternatives that do not appear tougher than what has been tried before.[8] Combining a penchant for punitive sanctions with a view of drug use best described as "pharmacological Calvinism,"[9] the reactionary prohibitionists have insisted that the only legitimate objective of drug control policy must be the elimination of illicit drug use.

The common ground is also at odds, albeit not quite so fundamentally, with the conservative libertarian perspective on drug control.[10] For those libertarians who believe as an absolute matter of principle in the sanctity of individual sovereignty over property and the freedom of contract, no governmental controls on the commerce in drugs are acceptable no matter what the consequences. Other libertarians are more utilitarian in their thinking, placing their faith in the free market and assuming that the dual policy objectives would best be accomplished in the absence of governmental interventions. Less committed libertarians start from the same assumptions about the magic of the free market but acknowledge that modest governmental controls, particularly truth-in advertising and labeling requirements, may be necessary to correct for the excesses and abuses that the free market invites. All of these libertarians tend to support the more civil libertarian commitments to individual privacy and freedom in the choice of one's lifestyle—although they insist that freedom of contract includes the freedom of employers to insist upon drug testing as a condition of employment. Civil libertarians, by contrast, tend to regard the freedom of contract with less deference than the right to privacy. They are more apt to speak of a right to consume drugs,[11] and are more likely to integrate considerations of social justice and public health into their principles and policy calculations.

Putting aside the perspectives of the reactionary prohibitionists and the hardcore libertarians, there are two principal differences among the progressive legalizers and the progressive prohibitionists. The first reflects disagreements as to the weight that should be accorded to such values as individual liberty, privacy, and tolerance in calculating the costs and benefits of different drug control policies.[12] Most legalizers weigh these values heavily, with the more committed civil libertarians regarding them as absolutes that cannot be compromised and other progressive legalizers perceiving them as highly important but not inherently immune to some restraints. At the very least, most legalizers insist, the possession of modest amounts of drugs for personal consumption should not be the subject of criminal laws. The progressive prohibitionists are sympathetic to such values but accord them much less weight, both because they perceive them as undermining efforts to reduce drug abuse and because they are more willing to defer to majoritarian opinion in defining and weighting them. Confronted with potential trade-offs between levels of drug abuse and levels of coercion directed at drug users and sellers, most legalizers are willing to concede modest increases in drug abuse levels in return for reductions in the numbers of those punished for using and selling drugs. Progressive prohibitionists, by contrast, are far more willing to limit individual liberty to the extent they perceive a potential gain in public health.

The second major difference of opinion involves the assessment of the vulnerability of the American population to the substantial increases in drug availability that would follow from any of the more far reaching drug legalization schemes. Where most prohibitionists can envision the possibility of a fiftyfold increase in the number of people dependent upon cocaine, and conclude that the future of the nation might well be at stake if cocaine were made as available as alcohol, most legalizers regard such estimates and predictions as the unsubstantiated folly of doomsayers.[13] Both agree that substantial research is required to better estimate this vulnerability, but the wide disparities are primarily a reflection of visceral fears, beliefs, and instincts regarding individual and collective human nature in the context of American society. Whereas most legalizers perceive, both instinctually and intellectually, ample evidence of a fundamental societal resilience, most progressive prohibitionists share with their more reactionary allies a fundamental pessimism regarding the susceptibility of American society to a dramatic liberalization of drug availability.

The roots of this viscerally based debate can be found in a related difference of opinions regarding the balance of power between psychoactive drugs and the human will. Prohibitionists typically see the balance favoring the former, with its potential to disrupt and destroy the lives of consumers. Legalizers, by contrast, emphasize the latter, with its assumption that the balance of basic human desires in most people effectively limits the destructive potential of drugs. For most prohibitionists, the relevant evidence includes the worst case examples of drug addiction and other abuse, the experiments on captive rats, monkeys, and other nonhuman animals to determine the addictive liability of different drugs, and the biological evidence of withdrawal symptoms in human beings following sustained consumption of particular drugs. Most legalizers, by contrast, focus on the less dramatic but more abundant evidence of casual and controlled drug use, insist that the "set and setting" of drug use are at least as important as the drug itself in determining whether a person becomes a drug abuser, and see the animal studies and biological evidence as less significant than the abundant historical, cross-cultural, and contemporaneous evidence of individual and societal resilience vis-à-vis all psychoactive drugs. ("Set is a person's expectations of what a drug will do to him, considered in the context of his whole personality. Setting is the environment, both physical and social, in which a drug is taken.")[14] Many prohibitionists seem to see some psychoactive drugs as possessed of powers akin to those of the Sirens whose alluring voices no man could resist. Most legalizers, by contrast, perceive such a notion as absurd. They find more persuasive the substantial evidence that most people (including children), given sufficient information, are unlikely to use a drug in the first place, that most of those who do try a particular drug tend either to stop shortly thereafter or to use it in moderation, and that even most of those who become addicted to a drug or otherwise misuse it ultimately moderate or stop their use.

These differences, however, still leave abundant room for common ground on how drug control policies can be reformed in the short term. For even though the progressive prohibitionists share with their more reactionary allies a deep seated fear of greater drug availability, they lack the reactionaries' political and moral commitments to repressive policies. And even though most legalizers feel substantial revulsion for the more punitive prohibitionist measures, they recognize both the inevitability of, and the need for, some criminal justice accompaniments to any regulatory regime. The public health model, with its emphasis on reducing morbidity and mortality, appears to provide something of an ideologically neutral set of guidelines and parameters for working out a preferable set of drug policies—although legalizers are wary of the totalitarian potential of a public health model taken to its logical extreme. Both legalizers and most progressive prohibitionists also perceive merit in the harm reduction policies developed by the Dutch as well as local authorities in England and Australia—even if they differ as to the extent to which those policies could be adapted to the American environment.

There is also a shared assumption, from which only the most libertarian of the legalizers dissent, that government does have an important role to play in shaping and improving the lives of its citizens. Where all sides differ is in their view of the appropriate means by which government should pursue this, with the progressive prohibitionists viewing criminal justice and other coercive mechanisms as perfectly acceptable and often efficient means and the progressive legalizers favoring less coercive measures ranging from education and voluntary treatment programs to broader provision of social services. There also is something of a consensus that the top priority of drug control programs should be to minimize the harm that drug users do to others, with the secondary priority involving the more traditional public health objectives of minimizing the harm that drug users, and especially children, do to themselves. But underlying even this consensus are differing assumptions regarding the appropriate reach of social control measures designed to detect and curtail the illicit use of drugs. Thus even among those who identify themselves as proponents of a "public health" approach to the drug problem, there are some who sympathize deeply with the legalizers but prefer to keep their more ideological, liberty-based, values out of their analyses, and others who see criminal justice sanctions and civil commitment laws as useful means with which to coerce drug users into treatment programs.[15]

The fact that legalizers and progressive prohibitionists have so much in common is significant for a number of reasons. First, it suggests that there is a basic framework of analysis, predicated upon systematic assessment of costs and benefits, that is regarded as intellectually legitimate by all serious analysts of drug control policy. The fact that the evaluation of the costs and benefits varies greatly depending upon one's ethical values and ideological assumptions does not negate this. Second, it suggests that the current framework and direction of drug prohibition policies in the United States are fundamentally at odds with any conceivable policy predicated upon either public health precepts or notions of harm reduction. Indeed, the only way to explain and justify many current policies is by reference to the fears, prejudices, and primitive moralisms of those who have transformed drug control policy into a modern version of an authoritarian crusade. Third, it suggests that the debates *among* the legalizers over the design and evaluation of alternative drug control policies may well be of interest to many who share neither all of the legalizers' values nor their visceral confidences.

THE DRUG POLICY SPECTRUM

It should be clear by this point that drug legalization and drug prohibition do not represent simply radical alternatives to one another and that there is no single version of either one. Virtually all drug control policies incorporate elements of both prohibition and legal availability. Alcohol, for instance, is regarded as a legal drug but it is illegal to sell it to anyone under the age of twenty-one, illegal to drive while under its influence, and illegal, in many states and localities, to consume in public or to sell or buy except from government controlled or government-licensed outlets. Many of the same prohibitions increasingly apply to cigarettes and other tobacco products. Nicotine gum, which is substantially less harmful than smokeable tobacco, cannot even be purchased over-the-counter. Cocaine and most opiates are typically regarded as illegal drugs, but both are prescribed by doctors, the former for nasal and dental surgery as well as (in a few cases) treatment of pain, the latter as a prescribed treatment for pain or, in the case of methadone, as an authorized alternative to illicit heroin. The distinction between legal regulatory policies and prohibitionist policies becomes even more obscure when one surveys the broad spectrum of alcohol control policies that have been employed around the world during the past century; the same is true of opiate control policies and, to a lesser extent, public policies directed at the control of most other psychoactive drugs.

Nonetheless, one can distinguish between prohibition and legalization in at least two significant respects. The sharper distinction concerns whether or not a drug can be purchased over-the-counter, which is to say that it can be purchased legally by adults without first obtaining permission from a government agency or government-licensed agent such as a doctor. The more ambiguous, but equally important, distinction is between those policies that rely primarily on criminal sanctions to control the misuse of drugs and those that rely primarily on the informed choices of citizens as shaped by public health policies, regulatory structures, and honest drug education.

It can be useful to think about alternative drug control policies as arrayed along a spectrum, with the strictly prohibitionist and highly punitive at one end, the unregulated free market at the other end, and a wide array of regulatory policies in the middle. It requires minimal insight, moreover, to recognize that any drug control policy driven principally by public health considerations and stripped of the moralistic and authoritarian impulses that motivate contemporary policy would have little use for many of the more punitive measures in evidence today. The hard questions begin when values such as privacy, tolerance, and a presumption against imprisonment for most nonviolent drug-related activities are factored into the analysis of costs and benefits. They become even tougher to answer the further we venture along the policy spectrum into the relatively unknown territory of untested regulatory mechanisms and over-the-counter availability of drugs that currently can be purchased, if at all, only with a doctor's prescription.

Why venture into the unknown terrain of a truly nonprohibitionist drug policy given both the difficulties of evaluating the consequences of such a policy and the unlikelihood of it being favored by a majority of Americans within the foreseeable future? There are four reasons, each of which are developed below. First, only such a policy can dramatically reduce the many negative consequences of drug prohibition. Second, it helps us to address fundamental questions about the basic need for a drug prohibition system—in particular long unexamined assumptions about the differences between psychoactive substances and other consumer items as well as the vulnerability of the population to a broader availability of psychoactive drugs. Third, drug policy is one area in which libertarian assumptions regarding the magic of the free market may be more right than wrong. And fourth, the future may bring both new drugs as well as new ways of altering our states of consciousness that are not readily susceptible to governmental controls and that transform the ways in which Americans think about drugs and consciousness alteration.[16]

Thinking seriously and systematically about radical alternatives to current drug prohibition policies requires a degree of intellectual "stretching" that is relatively unusual in policy analysis generally and virtually unknown in the specific case of drug control policy analysis. This stretch is best accomplished by asking two complementary questions: How do we best maximize the benefits of the free market model and minimize its risks? And how do we best retain the advantages of drug prohibition while minimizing its direct and indirect costs? This stretch can be visualized by focusing on the extremes of the drug policy spectrum, with the free market at one end and contemporary American drug prohibition near the other end, and then trying to stretch each toward the other by applying notions of harm minimization to each.

The stretch from contemporary prohibition is, of course, the easier and more familiar one. It begins with a known quantity, the status quo, which is far easier to evaluate than theoretical alternatives—even if many causal relationships resist precise identification. The tendency of policy analysts and policymakers to focus on options that fall within or close to the realm of politically acceptable options means that far more thought and discussion have been devoted to the more modest revisions of current prohibition policies. Many of the initial steps that one can envision already have been taken in the Netherlands, England, Australia, and elsewhere. And even many of the steps that might be taken beyond what is currently happening abroad still require no radical changes in either the structure or the mechanisms of prohibition.

The further one stretches from the contemporary prohibition model, however, in terms of reducing criminal justice and other coercive controls on the distribution of drugs, the more difficult it becomes to evaluate the consequences. It is, for instance, not that difficult to estimate the consequences of making marijuana, heroin, and other strictly prohibited drugs available by prescription, or of legalizing the sale and possession of syringes and other drug paraphernalia, or of extending the limited decriminalization of marijuana possession enacted by eleven states during the 1970s to the entire country. There are powerful reasons to believe that each of these policy changes would substantially reduce the undesirable consequences of drug prohibition and present only modest risks in terms of public health. But it is quite another thing to estimate the consequences of making cocaine, amphetamine, morphine, or heroin more readily available to registered addicts, and surely an even greater intellectual challenge to evaluate the consequences of making these drugs legally available over-the-counter. That challenge cannot be met, I suspect, by taking contemporary prohibition, and the patterns of drug use that have emerged under it, as the starting reference points.

EVALUATING THE "SUPERMARKET" MODEL

Starting from the alternative extreme of the policy spectrum, the free market, obliges us to focus on the question that lies at the heart of the debate between legalizers and prohibitionists of all stripes: What would be the consequences for American society of having virtually no drug control policy whatsoever? Imagine, for instance, that Congress passed a law granting the freedom of drug consumption and even production and distribution the same legal protections as the rights of freedom of speech, press, religion, and assembly. And imagine that "supermarkets" existed all around the country in which drugs of every variety could be purchased at prices reflecting nothing more than retailers' costs plus reasonable profit margins and sales taxes. This is, of course, the nightmare scenario portrayed by the opponents of legalization—even if it is not the policy favored by virtually any of those identified as proponents of legalization apart from the most hardcore libertarians.[17] But it also bears a close resemblance to the relatively free market in drugs found in late nineteenth-century America—a period characterized by a fairly high rate of opiate and other drug consumption but dramatically fewer drug-related problems than we see today.[18]

The great advantage of this model is that it eliminates virtually all of the direct and indirect costs of drug prohibition: the many billions of dollars spent each year on arresting, prosecuting, and incarcerating hundreds of thousands of Americans, the diversion of scarce governmental resources from dealing with other, more immediately harmful, criminal activities, the tens of billions of dollars earned each year by organized and unorganized criminals, much of the violence, corruption and other criminal activity associated with the illicit drug markets, the distortion of economic incentives for inner-city residents, the severe problems posed by adulterated and otherwise unregulated drugs, the inadequate prescription of drugs for the treatment of pain, the abundant infringements on Americans' civil liberties, and all the other costs detailed in the extant literature on drug prohibition and legalization.

The great disadvantage of the supermarket model is its invitation to substantial increases in both the amount and the diversity of psychoactive drug consumption. What needs to be determined as best as possible are the magnitude and nature of that increase and its consequences. Among the more explicit assumptions of the legalization analysis is that the vast majority of Americans do not need drug prohibition laws to prevent them from becoming drug abusers. By contrast, prohibitionists typically assume that most Americans, and at the very least a substantial minority, do in fact need such laws—that but for drug prohibition, tens of millions more Americans would surely become drug abusers. The supermarket model provides no immediate insights into which perspective is closer to the truth, but it does suggest two important approaches on analyzing the implications of a free market.

First, it is imperative that analysts broaden their horizons to examine not just potential changes in the consumption of drugs that are currently illicit but changes in the cumulative consumption of all psychoactive substances. Virtually all human beings consume psychoactive substances. Alcohol and caffeine are certainly the two most common in the United States today, followed by nicotine, marijuana, and a variety of the more popular prescription drugs used to alleviate feelings of depression and anxiety. With the notable exception of alcohol, which has retained its preeminent position throughout the history of American psychoactive drug consumption, all other drugs have witnessed substantial changes in their levels of consumption.

Some of these changes have been a result of changes in drug laws. Others have reflected the emergence of new drugs, or new formulations of familiar drugs, as well as changes in medical prescription practices, new marketing techniques, changing fads and fashions in recreational drug usage, and broader changes in popular culture as well as particular subcultures. The notion of a truly free market in drugs obliges us to consider what would happen if alcohol, nicotine, and caffeine no longer were artificially favored over other drugs by virtue of their legal status. One strong possibility is that other drugs—including some that are common in other societies, some that were once more popular in America than they are today, and some that have yet to be designed or discovered—would compete with and substitute for those drugs that are most familiar to Americans today.

Indeed, one of the silver linings on the black cloud of greater drug use under different legalization regimes is the prospect that less dangerous drugs would drive out the more dangerous ones. By most accounts, alcohol and tobacco represent two of the most dangerous drugs that have ever entered into common usage in human society. Between them, they present a high proportion of all of the harms associated with other drugs that have experienced widespread usage at one time or another. Tobacco, especially when consumed in the form of cigarettes, is both highly addictive and readily identified as a cause of cancers, cardiovascular diseases, and other ills. Alcohol can be highly addictive for some users; consumed in abundance, it can cause death by overdose in the short term and cirrhosis of the liver and other diseases in the long term. It also is strongly associated with violent behavior and accidental injuries in a great variety of societies. There is no reason to assume that their predominant position in the hierarchy of favored psychoactive substances will persist forever, and good reason to believe that the desirable functions they serve can be replaced by other substances that pose far fewer dangers to the health of consumers in both the short and long term. The same may well be true of relatively less dangerous drugs, such as caffeine, which might well lose out in the competition to other psychoactive substances, such as low potency coca and amphetamine products, that may improve performance more effectively with even fewer negative side effects.

The possibility of dramatic substitution effects under a free market regime suggests that the most important issue in evaluating the consequences of such a model is neither the overall magnitude of drug consumption nor the number of drug users under such conditions, but rather the magnitude of the negative consequences that would result: the immediate effects of drug misuse on the health and behavior of the user; the debilitating effects of sustained misuse; and the deadly effects of sustained consumption. Each of these effects may also be of consequence for nonusers ranging from those who love or live with drug abusers to those who depend upon them in the workplace to those who encounter them on the roads. The evaluation of these consequences, and the assessment of which are more or less serious, inevitably involve ethical judgments. But it is important to recognize that public policy can seek to shift patterns of drug use and even abuse in safer directions by favoring drugs, sets, and settings that cause less harm to users and others. It is, in short, possible for the undesirable effects of drug use to decrease significantly even as the amount and diversity of drug consumption increase substantially.

Indeed, if we really seek to be truly objective in our assessments, what needs to be calculated are not just the cumulative negative consequences but the positive ones as well.[19] Proponents of the public health perspective as well as substantial segments of the American population are reluctant to speak of the positive benefits of psychoactive drug use except to the extent they conform with conventional notions of physical health and medical treatment. Alcohol's benefits, for instance, are defined primarily in terms of their potential to reduce heart disease, and those of prescription drugs entirely in terms of their capacity to alleviate pain, depression, anxiety, and feelings that disrupt normal functioning. Yet most people use drugs because they enjoy the effects and many perceive a variety of personal benefits that are rarely measured by physical, medical, or social scientists. Some of these resemble the effects approved by medical and public health criteria, but they typically are not interpreted as such either because they involve an informal form of self-medication or because they confront the common value judgment that one should not have to use psychoactive drugs to be or feel a certain way. The moderate consumption of alcohol as a social lubricant, and of coffee and other caffeinated beverages as a mild stimulant to increase alertness, are probably the most easily accepted and widely acknowledged nonmedical benefits associated with nonprescribed psychoactive drug consumption. But it is also the case that millions of Americans justify their past use and/or explain their current use of marijuana, cocaine, hallucinogens, and a variety of other drugs in terms of the benefits that they have derived from their consumption of those substances. Such claims are easily belittled in a society that adopts the notion of "drug-free" as its motto, and are often dismissed by scientists who find such benefits particularly difficult to measure. Nonetheless, it seems inherently unreasonable to dismiss entirely the perceptions of consumers, especially when the negative consequences of their consumption are not apparent. We thus have no choice but to calculate the consequences of changes in drug consumption not just in negative terms but as a net calculation that incorporates both positive and negative consequences.

The second perspective suggested by the supermarket model is that the potential negative health consequences of a free market, or of any other substantial change in policy, are best assessed by considering the respective susceptibilities of different sectors of the population to such changes. I proceed from two assumptions: that it is possible to distinguish among sectors based upon their susceptibility to drug abuse and hence their vulnerability to changes in drug policy; and that close examination of both current and historical patterns of drug use and abuse, as well as other patterns of human behavior, provide important clues into the nature and degree of susceptibility under alternative regimes. Implicit in the second assumption is the recognition that Americans, and most other people, already live in a society in which powerful psychoactive substances are widely available to both adults and children. One need only consider the easy availability of alcohol, tobacco, and caffeine virtually throughout the country; the continued ease of obtaining marijuana and other illicit drugs in much of the country; the extensive presence of powerful psychoactive substances, generally prescribed by medical practitioners, in the medicine closets of American homes; and the entirely uncontrolled availability throughout the United States of many other psychoactive substances, ranging from gasoline and glue to the wide array of drugs available over-the-counter in pharmacies.

What conclusions can be drawn from an analysis of the cumulative consumption of psychoactive drugs in this country? First, virtually all Americans consume psychoactive substances—and even the small minority who appear to abstain entirely, such as the Mormons, seem to compensate by consuming substances that are not traditionally viewed as psychoactive, such as sugar and caffeinated soft drinks. Second, a substantial majority of Americans consume these substances only in moderation, suffering little or no harm as a result. Third, the drugs that prove most addictive to most Americans are those, such as cigarettes and caffeinated beverages, that can be easily integrated into everyday life with minimal hassle or disruption. Fourth, virtually all drugs, even heroin, cocaine, and other drugs most associated with destructive patterns of consumption, are consumed in moderation by most of those who use them.[20] Fifth, a substantial majority of those who enter into destructive patterns of drug consumption eventually pass on to either abstinence or moderate patterns of consumption.[21]

When we focus on those who appear most susceptible to destructive patterns of drug consumption, further conclusions are apparent. First, while certain types of drugs are more difficult to use in moderation than others, the principal determinants of destructive drug use patterns involve not the pharmacology of the drug but the set and setting in which the drug is consumed. That is why alcohol consumption among conquered aboriginal groups and cocaine consumption among some inner-city populations have more in common with one another than either does with patterns of alcohol or cocaine consumption among less vulnerable sectors of the population. Indeed, no set and setting is more conducive to extensive and severe drug abuse than the combination of poverty and maladjustment to a mainstream society. Second, those who engage in destructive patterns of consumption with one drug are the most likely to repeat that pattern with other drugs; conversely, those who demonstrate an ability to consume alcohol and common prescription drugs responsibly, or who have succeeded in either stopping or dramatically curtailing their consumption of tobacco, are much less likely to engage in destructive patterns of consumption with other drugs.

Consider the results of recent polls on drug use in the United States. Approximately one-third of Americans over the age of twelve claim that they have not used alcohol in the past year, and close to half report that they have not consumed any alcohol in the past month.[22] In a December 1990 Gallup poll, 43 percent of those polled described themselves as abstainers from alcohol—up from 29 percent in the years 1976–1978.[23] Among African-Americans, the proportion who claim to abstain from alcohol is 58 percent.[24] Of those Americans who did drink within the past month, only one in ten (or about 5 percent of the household population) reported that they had drunk heavily during that time.[25] Approximately 75 percent of all Americans over the age of twelve have smoked at least one cigarette; slightly less than 30 percent report that they smoked within the past month, of which half consume about a pack or more a day.[26] With respect to marijuana, about 33 percent of Americans have used it at least once, 11 percent in the past year, 6 percent in the past month, and about 1 percent on something resembling a daily basis.[27] There is reason to believe that there is substantial overlap not only between those who drink heavily and those who smoke heavily, but also between those two groups and those who use illicit drugs heavily—although detailed cross-tabulations of available surveys are required to reach more exact estimates. Indeed, one also finds substantial overlap with those who engage in compulsive gambling and other harmful activities. The principal exception to this substantial overlap may involve the misuse of tranquilizers and other prescription drugs, especially among women. Even if we assume that self-reports of alcohol and tobacco consumption tend to underreport actual consumption by 30–50 percent, we still must conclude that at least 70 percent of Americans are resistant to the sorts of temptations and risks posed by the easy availability of cigarettes, and that more than 90 percent either refrain from powerful drugs altogether or else consume them responsibly and in moderation. This conclusion strongly suggests that a very substantial majority of Americans are immune to any far reaching liberalizations in drug availability for the simple reason that they do not really need drug laws to prevent them from entering into destructive relationships with drugs.

The important question is thus not whether or not millions of Americans would change their patterns of drug consumption under a radically different drug control regime—since there is good reason to assume they would—but rather whether those patterns would be more (or less) destructive than their current patterns of drug consumption. Among the tens of millions of Americans who abstain from alcohol consumption, it seems reasonable to assume that they would have little interest in, and perhaps substantial moral reservations against, consuming other powerful psychoactive drugs. Among the even larger number of Americans who consume alcohol in moderation, despite the great potential for that drug to be consumed in a destructive fashion, it is also reasonable to assume that the same individual and societal restraints that protect them against alcohol's seductive powers would control their consumption of other substances. For the vast majority of Americans, therefore, the principal danger posed by a free market in drugs has little to do with drugs like crack cocaine, since so few Americans would be likely either to try it in the first place or, if they did try it, to continue to use it. (Public opinion polls consistently reveal that few Americans believe they would consume cocaine, heroin, or even marijuana if those drugs were legally available.)[28]

The greatest danger of a free market in drugs, I suspect, is the possibility that a drug, assumed at first to be relatively safe, becomes popular among millions of Americans and then is revealed to be far more harmful than initially believed. This danger is one that has proven commonplace in the annals of pharmaceutical innovation, medical prescription practice, and inebriation, from morphine and cocaine during the nineteenth century to cigarettes, barbiturates, amphetamines, tranquilizers, and many nonpsychoactive drugs, including steroids, during the twentieth. It is one that has continued to frustrate the regulatory efforts of the Food and Drug Administration in recent decades, and that promises to persist into the future regardless of whether or not the drug laws change substantially. But it is fair to assume that the dangers would be greater if far more products were to become legally available.

The most common fear of legalization, however, is usually of a different sort, and it must be taken seriously. It is that there are millions of Americans for whom the drug prohibition system represents the principal bulwark between an abstemious relationship with drugs and a destructive one. Under a free market regime, it is feared, many of those who currently abstain from, or consume in moderation, alcohol and other powerful intoxicants would become drug abusers, and many of those who already have demonstrated either a potential for, or a pattern of, drug abuse would engage in even more destructive patterns of drug use. Underlying this fear are a variety of assumptions: that the only things which prevent many current users of illicit drugs from engaging in far more destructive patterns of drug use are the high price and lower availability of those drugs under the current prohibition regime; that at least some of the illicit drugs are more seductive than those that are currently legal and/or available; that a free market regime would inevitably invite greater levels of drug experimentation, which in turn would lead to higher levels of use and abuse; that many people would be more likely to complement their current drug use with newly available drugs than to substitute those for their current preferences; and that the heightened societal tolerance for more varied psychoactive drug use that would likely accompany a free market regime would lend itself to higher levels of drug misuse.

Even if we assume that the vast majority of those who now consume psychoactive drugs safely would continue to do so under a free market regime, and further assume that a substantial proportion of those who currently misuse illicit drugs would be no worse and quite likely better off under a free market regime, the fact remains that there is a relatively small, but indeterminate, proportion of Americans for whom the drug prohibition system provides not just the image but the reality of security. Figuring out, with some measure of confidence, the magnitude and composition of this vulnerable population is among the most important intellectual challenges confronting those who take seriously the need to estimate the consequences of alternative regimes. And designing policies that minimize the magnitude of this at-risk group without resorting to criminal justice and other coercive measures is surely an even greater challenge.

Most of those who would suffer from the absence of the current drug prohibition regime can be found among those who currently smoke cigarettes and/or abuse alcohol. The first group includes both those adolescents and adults who have demonstrated a willingness or ability to disregard the well known consequences of cigarette smoking, as well as those adults who have demonstrated an inability to abandon a dangerous habit. The second group, which overlaps substantially with the first, includes those adolescents and adults who have demonstrated an inability to control a powerful psychoactive substance, i.e., alcohol, despite the existence of increasingly strong social controls. There are certainly others who neither smoke cigarettes nor abuse alcohol who would enter into destructive relationships with other drugs if they were more readily available, but there is (as I already have suggested) good reason to doubt that their numbers would prove substantial.

In trying to predict which drugs will prove most popular in the future, who will use them responsibly and who will do so destructively, it is important to keep in mind why people use drugs and why they use the drugs they do. The choice of drugs for most members of most societies can barely be described as a choice at all. Dominant cultures strongly favor some drugs over others, hence the preferred position of alcohol throughout much of the world, with different societies evidencing a preference for beer, wine, or distilled liquors, or of coffee in most Islamic societies and quat in some, of kava in some South Pacific islands and coca in the Andes. Alcohol's dominant position no doubt stems as well from the fact that its simple means of production was easily discovered millennia ago by a wide diversity of societies, so that it was not merely readily available in most societies but also provided with substantial opportunity to entrench itself.[29] Tobacco's secondary position somewhat similarly can be attributed to its great success in sweeping the globe and becoming entrenched in a great variety of societies before the emergence of any international capacity for its suppression—although its powerful addictive qualities must also be given credit for ensuring that markets once penetrated remained markets thereafter. As for substances such as kava, betel nut, coca, cannabis, opium, and various hallucinogens, each has benefited, not unlike alcohol, from being an indigenous product.

To the extent that drug consumption patterns and preferences can really be described as a choice, it is fair to say that people choose those drugs that give them what they want. Most people can in fact be described as rational consumers even in their choice of psychoactive drugs. They use drugs because they seek or like their effects, whether those involve relief from pain, reduction of stress and anxiety, release from inhibitions, stimulation of the senses and the intellect, enhancement of physical or mental performance, or any of the many other psychoactive effects of drugs. Most people, moreover, tend to limit their consumption in order to minimize the negative consequences, whether those involve hangovers, heart disease, or cancer. The evidence from a broad variety of cultures suggests that the single most important determinant of a drug's popularity is its capacity to be integrated into ordinary lives with minimal disruption.

It is important to recognize that the same notion of rational drug consumption applies to some extent even to those who are engaged in highly destructive patterns of consumption. For many hardcore drug users in the inner cities and among aboriginal populations, their intensive involvement with powerful drugs provides a powerful source of relief from emotional and other psychological pain, some excuse for isolating themselves both from mainstream society and difficult personal responsibilities, and (particularly for those most engaged in the day to day hustling for the means to procure their expensive drugs) a source of self-esteem and motivation to keep getting out of bed in the mornings despite the absence of any promising prospects in their lives. This is not to say, of course, that the destructive drug use patterns of those living on the edge of despair can be described as entirely rational. But it is to say that even hardcore drug abusers tend to prefer drug consumption options that minimize the risks of death in both the long and the short term; the growing evidence about the willingness of intravenous drug addicts to take modest steps to reduce the likelihood of contracting the HIV virus attests to this.[30] Relatively few hardcore drug addicts can be described as truly committed to an early death. It is thus reasonable to assume that even most current and potential hardcore drug users will, if given the choice, opt for drugs that are, at the very least, no more dangerous than those consumed today.

One can supplement the notion of rational drug consumption, which focuses on the individuals' preferences, with another notion also drawn from libertarian philosophy. It is that societies, like individuals, generate nonlegal social norms in the absence of governmental prohibitions and other restrictive laws. Societies, simply stated, are not entirely at the mercy of free markets, but retain the potential to create self-protective mechanisms designed to minimize the risks presented by such markets. Indeed, some libertarians argue, one of the more significant costs imposed by governmental prohibitions is the withering of societal norms that often operate more powerfully and effectively than governmental interventions. Evidence in support of this argument can be found in anthropological and sociological studies of traditional and modern cultures alike, wherever patterns of human intercourse are allowed to evolve in the absence of significant governmental prohibitions. Particularly reassuring in this regard are the many decriminalizations that one can point to throughout civilized human history that were opposed by those who feared for the civility and even the survival of society but that turned out to be far less destabilizing than was feared. Such fears impeded efforts to do away with restrictions on speech, press, religion and assembly, on relations between people of different classes and races, on sexual and familial relations, and on the availability of psychoactive drugs that are now integrated into modern society.[31] The same sorts of unjustified fears now stand in the way of efforts to do away with current drug prohibitions.

The arguments of the libertarians are both powerful and, at least with respect to the majority of society, quite convincing. They confront, however, three counterarguments that most Americans currently find compelling. The first is simply that drugs and drug consumption are fundamentally different [from] all other commodities and activities—so different that ordinary libertarian assumptions do not apply. The second, like the notion of rational drug consumption, derives from economic reasoning. It is the evidence that suggests that levels of consumption of desirable consumer items tend to increase as their availability increases and their price decreases. And the third is the epidemiological evidence suggesting that the negative consequences associated with the use of any drug in a society are a direct function of the overall level of use of that drug. Of these three arguments, the first represents the weakest in terms of logical analysis but the most powerful from an emotional and political viewpoint. It can be repudiated by reference to the many ways in which other commodities and activities generate the same sorts of behavior as do the consumption of drugs, be it the alteration of consciousness, the transformation of social behavior, or the creation of dependent relationships.[32] But the belief in the unique power of psychoactive drugs is so entrenched in our society that even highly prominent liberal theorists, including those with strong libertarian inclinations, either avoid the subject altogether or else carve out awkward exceptions to their otherwise more coherent philosophies. The second and third arguments, by contrast, present far more powerful reasons to refrain from placing one's faith entirely in libertarian assumptions.

There are other reasons as well to put the purist libertarian assumptions and the supermarket model to the side. The more one speculates about the consequences of such a model, the more one realizes that all sorts of additional assumptions have to be made about the type of society that would favor such a model—and that these assumptions are even more speculative than anything we assume about the vulnerability of today's population to such a model. At the very least, the sets and settings that so powerfully shape the nature and consequences of drug use would inevitably differ dramatically from their contemporary formulations. Furthermore, as soon as one engages in the process of trying to think through the consequences of such a model, one encounters the inevitable tendency to begin framing restrictions on the supermarket. Whether one analogizes to alcohol and tobacco, or to the nineteenth-century model of widespread drug availability, one confronts the tendency both in the United States and elsewhere to impose restrictions on the distribution of psychoactive drugs.

THE "RIGHT OF ACCESS" MODEL

We thus return to the question: How can the risks and harms of the free market model be reduced without undermining the many benefits that such a model offers? And how far can the free market model be stretched without giving up its essential feature? That essential feature, it must be stressed, is the legal availability of drugs in the absence of any requirement that the permission of a government-sanctioned gatekeeper be obtained beforehand. It is that feature that distinguishes the legal status of alcohol, tobacco, caffeine, and aspirin from that of marijuana, cocaine, morphine, and Valium—and that accounts for the generally greater and easier availability of the legal drugs compared to the illegal drugs. Legal drugs are almost always available over-the-counter; illegal drugs are not. Government-sanctioned medical authorities and pharmacists, and sometimes additional barriers as well, stand between the illegal drug and the person who wishes to obtain it.

It is important to recognize that legal availability does not always connote easy availability, and that the restricted legal status of a drug does not always make it that difficult to obtain. Legal drugs may, for instance, be so expensive—either because of high costs of production or high taxes—that they are for all intents and purposes unavailable to many potential consumers. Distribution channels may be relatively undeveloped or otherwise circumscribed. And efforts by government to restrict severely the availability of a legal drug without depriving consumers entirely of the right to purchase it legally may prove successful. Powerful evidence in support of these propositions can be found in the alcohol control efforts of the United States, Australia, and much of Europe during the 1920s and 1930s. Whereas the former initially favored Prohibition, the latter opted instead for tough, but nonprohibitionist, regulatory regimes. The results were more substantial, and more lasting, declines in alcohol consumption and alcohol-related ills in Europe and Australia than in the United States.[33]

Illegal drugs, by contrast, can occasionally prove to be highly available. Medical practitioners often write prescriptions for mild tranquilizers, sedatives, and other psychoactive drugs in response to their clients' plaints. They may do so because they believe that such drugs are a proper and effective way of medicating their clients, or because they believe that a client's satisfaction with a visit to her doctor depends in part upon the doctor's willingness to end the visit by writing a prescription. And even apart from such channels, illegal drugs can prove readily available wherever substantial markets generate high levels of supply—as was the case with marijuana in much of the country during the 1970s and 1980s. The same holds true of more localized markets, in particular the inner-city markets for cocaine since the mid-1980s as well as for other drugs that have attained high levels of popularity in particular neighborhoods or cities. In cases such as these, illegal drugs may prove more available than many legal drugs, such as alcohol, for which the hours of sale are often restricted by government. In many highly restricted environments, moreover, such as prisons, jails, and mental institutions, illegal drugs are often more available than alcohol because their smaller bulk makes them easier to smuggle past guards and other barriers.

The foregoing analysis suggests that it is possible to construct legal drug control regimes in which certain drugs may be less available than is the case under prohibition regimes. When we stretch as far as possible from the free market extreme of the drug policy continuum, but seek at the same time to retain the basic feature of nongatekeeper accessibility, the model that emerges is one that might be called the "right of access" or "mail-order" model. It is based on the notion that adults should be entitled not merely to the right to possess small amounts of any drug for personal consumption but also to the right to obtain any drug from a reliable, legally regulated source responsible (and liable) for the quality of its products. In identifying such a right, I must stress, I do not mean to suggest that it is on a par with the more privacy-based right of possession and/or consumption, but merely that it provides a useful parameter—both ethically and conceptually—for designing alternative drug control policies. Unlike the supermarket model, the right of access model is one that can be superimposed on the current drug prohibition system.

If such a right of access were legally acknowledged by Congress or the Supreme Court—a prospect, I recognize, with scant political or jurisprudential potential in the foreseeable future—those desirous of minimizing the potential threat to public health might well advocate the notion of a mail-order system. In order to ensure a right of access to all residents of the United States no matter where they might live, at least one mail-order source would have to be available in the United States from which any adult could order a modest amount of any drug at a reasonable price reflecting production costs and taxes.

Most states, cities, and other communities might well continue to prohibit the sale and public consumption of most drugs within their jurisdictions as they do now, but would be obliged to acknowledge the basic right of access by mail order as well as the basic right of possession and consumption. Some localities might also adopt, if they had not already done so, the various sorts of harm reduction policies that are advisable under any regime. One might also imagine many other local variations by different states and municipalities to accommodate the particular health, criminal justice, and moral concerns of each. But the option of ordering one's drugs by mail would allow any adult to opt out, in effect, of the local control system insofar as private consumption was concerned.

The right of access notion offers us, I think, a more valuable, modest, and realistic alternative extreme than the supermarket model from which to stretch toward the optimal policy. As a model, it retains in skeletal form the essence of a legalization regime, which is the elimination of any sort of gatekeeper—policeman, doctor, pharmacist, etc.—between the seller and consumer of drugs with the power to deny the latter access. It thus strikes at the heart of much of what is wrong with drug prohibition, in particular the creation of violent and powerful black market entrepreneurs, the harms that result from unregulated production of psychoactive drugs, and the many infringements on individual freedoms. But it also provides a skeletal framework that can be filled out with many of the sorts of antidrug abuse measures that we associate with both harm reduction approaches to illicit drug control policy and public health approaches to alcohol and tobacco control. It has the advantage of resembling actual models in other domains of public policy both today and in recent history, including the alcohol distribution system in Canada and Sweden during the early decades of this century as well in pre- and post-Prohibition United States, and the modification of FDA policy in recent years to allow individuals to import by mail small amounts of drugs that are legally available outside the United States but that have yet to be approved by the FDA for the treatment of AIDS or cancer.[34] Given the preference among critics of drug prohibition for a fairly high degree of "local option," it addresses the inevitable tensions among different state and local drug control policies, between those policies and federal policies, and even (albeit to a lesser extent) between domestic policies and international requirements. At the same time, it offers a paradigm for addressing and reconciling the tensions between individual rights and communitarian interests that lie at the heart of so many struggles over public policy in democratic societies.

This model is not, I must stress, a panacea, nor should it be misconstrued as a final proposal for an alternative drug control regime. It raises numerous questions such as how such a mail-order system would be established and maintained, who would run it and profit from it, who would oversee it, who would have access to its mailing lists and other information about consumers, how consumer privacy would be protected, how minors would be prevented from taking advantage of it, how new drugs would be made available, and so on. Most of these questions strike me as susceptible to fairly precise answers, in good part because there are so many close analogies to a mail-order system. More difficult to assess are the same sorts of questions raised by the supermarket model and all other alternative models, in particular those that focus on assessing changes in psychoactive drug consumption—although I assume that they are easier to answer with respect to a mail-order model since such a system is more readily integrated with the current prohibition model than is the case with the supermarket model.

One prominent difference between the right of access or mail-order model and the supermarket model is that the former fails to eliminate the black market. Just as some gun control laws rely on waiting periods between the time a person orders a firearm and the time he obtains possession, so a mail-order system imposes a sort of waiting period—presumably a minimum of one day. It is highly reasonable to assume that black markets would persist not only to supply minors—which is presently the case with most psychoactive substances, including alcohol and tobacco—but also to supply those who will not or cannot wait to obtain their drugs from the mail-order system, as well as those who want to obtain more at any one time than is allowed by law.

We typically assume that an important objective of legalizing drugs is to undercut the black markets and place them in the hands of either government or goverment-licensed and regulated distributors. This objective is tempered by the recognition that there are better and worse features of illicit markets, and that a preferable drug policy ideally would focus on eliminating the worst while tolerating the better features. It would, for instance, attempt to undermine the accumulation of power by organized criminals, reduce the violence that attends such markets and generally push large-scale production into the hands of regulated, tax paying, and collecting producers and distributors. But at the same time, it might well choose to ignore smaller scale illicit markets— what are often referred to less disparagingly as informal or unregulated markets—which are of value not just because they often prove more innovative and enterprising in designing and offering new products but also because they provide an important source of income for many people who face substantial disadvantages in their efforts to penetrate and succeed in the more established legitimate markets. This holds true, for instance, of both rural producers of marijuana and inner-city entrepreneurs engaged in the low-level distribution of crack and other drugs. Two probable advantages of the right of access model are that it would effectively undercut efforts by organized criminals to create highly profitable national distribution systems, since any adult could purchase the drugs by mail. At the same time, it would not eliminate many illicit small scale, localized production and distribution systems that meet local demands for immediate availability, rapid delivery, and specialized products. Local authorities could choose, in effect, either to suppress such black markets vigorously or to manage them through conventional vice control methods. But the scale of such markets would probably bear a closer resemblance to illicit prostitution rings in cities that sanction regulated prostitution than to contemporary illicit drug markets.

TRANSITION ISSUES

Few drug control regimes are static. Prohibitions, regulations, and decriminalizations tend to evolve as new drugs emerge, as drug use patterns shift, as other drug-related norms change, and as popular and elite perceptions of various drugs, drug consumers, and drug problems shift. In contemplating alternatives to the current drug prohibition regime, we need to distinguish between transition phases, longer term consequences, and equilibria, keeping in mind that there is no drug control regime that will suffice forever. The distinction is important with respect to issues of both drug consumption and black markets. It is safe to assume that illicit markets do not just shrivel up and die when confronted with competition from licit markets. Rather, illicit entrepreneurs may continue to compete with licit markets during the initial phase when licit producers and distributors are still gearing up, having the advantage of their previous investments in production and/or distribution as well as their expertise. The share of the market that is captured by legal producers and distributors in the long term, however, probably would depend more on price, availability, competition, the intensity of continued law enforcement efforts to suppress the remaining black market, and changing tastes and fads among consumers. There are also important policy questions regarding the extent to which those involved in the illicit markets during prohibition should be allowed or encouraged to play a role in legal markets after prohibition.

Close examination of the aftermath of Prohibition in the United States, other postprohibition periods elsewhere, and other decriminalizations, such as of gambling, prostitution, pornography as well as of nonvice markets in countries experiencing significant deregulations (such as the former Soviet bloc countries) can provide important insights into how drug markets are likely to evolve.[35] The impact of decriminalization on those involved in illicit drug dealing, as well as on those who would have become involved in drug dealing but for decriminalization, is especially important when we focus on African-American and Latino youth in the urban ghettos. Clearly the dramatic drop in the price of currently illicit drugs following decriminalization would greatly reduce one of the most powerful incentives for engaging in drug dealing and other criminal activities. According to a recent report by the Justice Department's

Bureau of Justice Statistics, 13 percent of all convicted jail inmates, and 19 percent of those convicted of drug trafficking offenses, said they had committed their offense to obtain money to buy illicit drugs.[36] Dramatic reductions in the size and profitability of the illicit markets would also remove the powerful financial and social incentives that have lured so many urban youth into drug dealing activities even before they began to consume illicit drugs.

Further insights into this question can be derived both from analyzing the response of bootleggers to the repeal of Prohibition and from observing how illicit drug dealers adapt when illicit drug markets decline, as seems to be the case today.[37] Illicit vice entrepreneurs seem to respond to decriminalizations and shrinkages in illicit markets in any of four ways. Some succeed in making the transition to legal entrepreneurship in the same line of work. Some seek to remain in the business illegally, whether by supplying products and services in competition with the legal market or by employing criminal means to take advantage of the legal markets. For instance, following Prohibition, some bootleggers continued to market their products by forging liquor tax stamps, by strongarming bartenders into continuing to carry their moonshine and illegally imported liquors, and by muscling their way into the distribution of legal alcohol. Some also fought to retain their markets among those who had developed a taste for corn whiskey before and during Prohibition. The third response of bootleggers and drug dealers is to abandon their pursuits and branch out instead into other criminal activities involving both vice opportunities and other sorts of crime. Indeed, one potential negative consequence of decriminalization is that many committed criminals would adapt to the loss of drug dealing revenues by switching their energies to crimes of theft, thereby negating to some extent the reductions in such crimes that would result from drug addicts no longer needing to raise substantial amounts of money to pay the inflated prices of illicit drugs. The fourth response—one that has been and would be attractive to many past, current, and potential drug dealers—is to forgo criminal activities altogether. Relatively few criminal pursuits can compare in terms of paying so well, requiring so few skills, remaining fairly accessible to newcomers, and presenting attractive capitalist opportunities to poorly educated and integrated inner-city youth. During Prohibition, tens if not hundreds of thousands of Americans with no particular interest in leading lives of crime were drawn into the business of illegally producing and distributing alcohol; following its repeal, many if not most of them abandoned their criminal pursuits altogether. There is every reason to believe that drug decriminalization would have the same impact on many involved in the drug dealing business who would not have been tempted into criminal pursuits but for the peculiar attractions of that business. The challenge for researchers, of course, is to estimate the relative proportions of current and potential drug dealers who would respond in any of these four ways. The even broader challenge is to determine the sorts of public policies that would maximize the proportion that forgo criminal activities altogether.

The need to distinguish between transition phases and longer term consequences and equilibria also applies to the impact of decriminalization on potential and current illicit drug users. The initial liberalization of availability is likely to spark high levels of curiosity, stimulated both by the media and by the mere fact of legal access, and substantial experimentation with different drugs—but it is reasonable to assume that this would moderate over the long term. At the same time, the initial reluctance of many Americans to try newly available drugs to which they are unaccustomed may fade over time. Those who have grown up under a prohibition system, moreover, and have thus been influenced to one degree or another by the many assumptions that prohibition conveys about drug use, are likely to experience a legal regime differently than succeeding generations for whom it will represent the norm.

GATEKEEPERS, NORMS, AND INFORMATION SYSTEMS

There is also the question of how a liberalization of legal availability will affect both the doctor–patient relationship and the role of pharmacists. It would be useful to know, for example, what proportion of visits to doctors are motivated principally by the desire or need to obtain a prescription for a controlled substance. Between one-half and two-thirds of all consultations with doctors result in the writing of a prescription.[38] A legal drug regime would negate the need for visits motivated solely by the need to obtain a prescription, with mixed results. Some people would suffer as a result of not being obliged to consult with a doctor, but many others who now must waste time and money on unnecessary doctor visits would surely benefit. The problem of undermedication, and particularly undertreatment of pain, would almost surely be less of a problem than it is now. But some people would surely be more likely to use inappropriate drugs and to develop unhealthy dependencies on drugs that are now available only by nonrenewable prescription. Better insights into these issues can be gained by analyzing the available evidence about why people go to doctors as well as patterns of self-medication and doctor visitation in other times and places in which there have been fewer controls on the availability of drugs.[39]

The role of doctors and pharmacists as gatekeepers for prescription drugs is of course part and parcel of a broader question about the basic need for creating and maintaining a distinction between over-the-counter and prescription drugs. This question has been addressed most sharply by economists, although the literature on the broader implications of the distinction remains quite limited.[40] The notion of requiring prescriptions for drugs other than cocaine and opiates is, as Peter Temin wrote in his historical study of drug regulation in the United States, a relatively recent notion—one that was not consonant with the 1938 Federal Food, Drug, and Cosmetic Act but that emerged in spite of a legislative intent to the contrary.[41] Implicit in the notion was the belief that many Americans would not act rationally in their choice and use of drugs and thus needed to be shielded from their own irresponsibility by governmental controls. One result was a significant constriction in the provision of information about drugs to consumers. The supposition that a mandatory drug prescription system plays an essential role in protecting the health of consumers has yet to be systematically tested. One study that employed a cross-national comparative perspective concluded that the prescription requirement did not yield a net benefit in health effects.[42] Another, by Peter Temin, suggested certain criteria that could be used to determine when a drug should be restricted or made available over-the-counter.[43] These studies provide valuable insights, but they represent only a small step in the direction of determining the likely consequences of severely restricting or eliminating the mandatory prescription system.

I should stress that these issues are at least as important with respect to the urban ghettos as they are in thinking about middle class drug usage. Much illicit drug abuse in urban ghettos can fairly be described as a form of self-medication for depression and other psychological pain among people who tend not to seek out psychiatrists and other doctors for such ills. The drugs they use to hide and forget their pain—alcohol, illegal heroin and cocaine, and other "street" drugs—are often more dangerous but no more effective than those prescribed to middle class patients by their doctors. At the same time, urban ghettos are full of poor people who might well benefit from access to the same sorts of antidepressants and other drugs that middle class Americans obtain from their doctors but who fail to obtain them both because they eschew the illicit markets and because financial and cultural limitations preclude visits to doctors. Here it is worth pointing out the patent absurdity of the claim that drug legalization would devastate inner-city populations. Both legal and illegal drugs are already so widely available in inner cities that virtually any resident can obtain them far more quickly than in suburban neighborhoods. But a liberalization of drug availability would make more easily available drugs that are safer than those now sold in urban liquor stores, crack houses, and street markets. At the same time, it would substantially reduce the negative consequences of prohibition—all of which are felt most severely in the urban ghettos.

More broadly, there is good reason to think that a regime of legal availability would substantially, even radically, transform the ways in which Ameri-

cans relate to psychoactive drugs. One might well imagine that pharmacological experts, certified perhaps by either government or professional agencies, would play an increasingly important role not so much as gatekeepers
but as educators and consultants on the preferred uses of drugs for medicinal, psychotherapeutic, recreational, and other purposes. But even more importantly, nonlegal norms would undoubtedly emerge in the absence of current prohibitionist norms to shape the way people relate to drugs, the ways
in which they use them, and the cautions they exercise. Here again, there is
the question of determining which people are likely to prefer the least potent and least risky drugs and which are more likely to opt for the most
potent, quickest acting, and so on. There is also the possibility that a world
of widespread drug availability might be more likely to generate self-protective norms against all forms of drug taking. And it is fair to assume that far
more people would assume greater responsibility for their relationship to drugs
than is currently the case, since the gatekeeper role of doctors effectively
transforms consumers into far more passive actors.

This in turn leads to the question of how information about psychoactive
drugs could be better distributed to a population so that it is readily available
and intelligible to typical consumers. The challenges here are fourfold. The
first is to design an effective means of distinguishing among categories of drugs
so that those who purchase either by mail or at retail outlets are properly informed of the risks and appropriate uses. This task could be performed by either
a Food and Drug Administration or a nongovernmental agency such as *Consumer Reports*, or both. The second is to design an information system separate from the distribution systems whereby consumers can obtain necessary
information on their own at little or no cost. This might involve information
distribution systems accessible by telephone or other easily accessed computer
hookups. Current efforts by the FDA, and by consumer organizations such
as those promoted by Ralph Nader, to ensure that consumers are provided
with both more accurate and more accessible information may well provide
something of a model in thinking about issues such as these. The third challenge is to create honest drug education programs that tell children the truth
about drugs without stimulating premature desires to try them.[44] And the fourth
is to design public health campaigns that effectively discourage drug misuse
without resorting to lies, scare tactics, and the demonization of people who
use drugs. The public service advertisements directed at discouraging tobacco
consumption and drunken driving provide far better models in this respect
than the "Fried Egg" ads, caricatures, and untruths promoted by the Partnership for a Drug-Free America.[45]

Most of what people know about drugs they have never used comes from
the commercial media. It has repeatedly played a central role in transforming
local fads and fashions into national and even international phenomena.[46] We

can safely assume that it will play a crucial role in the distribution of information and the shaping of public perceptions about drugs, particularly those that are relatively unfamiliar to most Americans. One need only imagine what impact the news magazines' cover stories in late 1989 and early 1990 on the new antidepressant, Prozac, would have had if Prozac were available over-the-counter or by mail; indeed, it would be interesting to know what impact those stories actually did have on potential consumers.[47] How many people, for instance, visited doctors thereafter with the intention of obtaining prescriptions for Prozac, how many succeeded, and—even more difficult to say—how many benefited or suffered as a consequence? Conversely, how many people who might benefit from Prozac have not yet tried it solely because they are unaccustomed to visiting a doctor to obtain assistance in alleviating depression? Certainly there is good reason to fear the media's impact on drug consumption preferences under a legal regime given its historic and persistent incapacity to provide accurate and balanced information about psychoactive drugs.[48] On the other hand, the media occasionally has demonstrated its capacity to shape preferences in healthier and otherwise better directions. It is certainly a loose cannon insofar as our efforts to evaluate the future direction of drug use are concerned. But there is good reason to devote at least some effort to considering how the media has shaped drug consumption patterns in the past.

The issue of advertising is a difficult one. In 1986, the Supreme Court ruled in *Posadas de Puerto Rico Associates* vs. *Tourism Company of Puerto Rico* that strict restrictions on advertising casino gambling were constitutionally permissible.[49] There seems to be little question that comparable restrictions on advertising psychoactive drugs would also be regarded as legal.[50] The difficult issues thus involve balancing the costs and benefits of both specific types of advertising as well as the advertising of psychoactive products generally. There is good reason to fear, and to curtail, the mass promotion of psychoactive drugs that present the sorts of harm associated with alcohol and cigarettes.[51] There are also substantial incentives to avoid a revival of medical quackery and the mass marketing of patent medicines that once tricked millions of Americans into buying products that did them little good and occasionally much harm. On the other hand, advertising can play a valuable role in informing people of new and beneficial products, in luring consumers to switch from more dangerous to less dangerous drugs, and in promoting competition that saves consumers money.[52] This is true of both psychoactive and nonpsychoactive drugs as well as those used for both recreational and more traditional therapeutic purposes. The solution to the advertising dilemma—to the extent we are willing to put aside First Amendment concerns—may well lie in a combination of restrictions on the promotion of more harmful products with vigorous educational campaigns to discourage their consumption.

CONCLUSION

Predicting human behavior remains, and shall always remain, an imprecise art. Social science can provide modest insights into the consequences of incremental changes in regulatory structures on human behavior. But when we try to envision the consequences of more far reaching changes in such structures, our confidence in social science insights falters. The variables are too numerous, the changes in individual and societal consciousness too unpredictable, and the tools too paltry to pretend that we can really know the future. Here history offers a more powerful guide—with its potential to shed light on both the accretion of incremental changes and the suddenness of revolutionary change. But even its lessons are limited by unanswerable questions regarding the potential of the future to evolve in unprecedented ways. Ultimately our predictions are bounded by theories of human behavior, and particularly of human and societal vulnerability and resilience, that have more to do with our visceral fears and confidences than any objective readings of the evidence.

When we switch from predicting the future to trying to plan it, our preferences are determined not only by our calculations of their consequences but also by our choices among competing ethical values. Such choices may be made implicitly, as when we accept without question conventional ethical values, or explicitly. They establish the parameters beyond which policy options will not be considered. They influence our calculations of the costs and benefits of various options. And they guide us in deciding who should benefit and who may be harmed by choosing one option over another. There are no objective standards by which to choose among ethical values. One can only appeal to conscience, principle, and empathy.

The challenges of evaluating radical alternatives to our current drug prohibition system are formidable. But so are the challenges of predicting the consequences of persisting with our current policies. In 1960, few Americans had ever heard of LSD, and the notion that sixty million Americans would smoke marijuana during the next three decades would have seemed bizarre to most Americans. In 1970, few Americans gave much thought to cocaine, and most would not have believed that twenty-five million Americans would try it during the next two decades. By the late 1970s, many Americans believed that marijuana would be sold legally within a few years. In 1980, no one had ever heard of "crack" cocaine; the notion of an AIDS epidemic among injecting drug users seemed inconceivable; and the prospect of a quarter-million Americans in jail or prison by 1990 for violating drug prohibition laws seemed preposterous. Clearly, retention of our drug prohibition system provides no guarantees about future patterns of drug use or the scale of future drug problems. Legalization may present a wider array of possibilities, but its uncertainties are not dramatically greater than those of persisting with prohibition.

There are powerful reasons for taking seriously the alternatives to drug prohibition. The first is simply that drug prohibition has proven relatively ineffective, increasingly costly, and highly counterproductive in all sorts of ways that many Americans are only beginning to appreciate. Nowhere is this more true than in the urban ghettos, where the war on drugs has failed to reduce the availability of illicit drugs or the incidence of drug abuse and offers no prospect of doing so in the future. At the same time, these neighborhoods and their residents have suffered the negative consequences of drug prohibition more severely than any others. Not unlike Chicago under Al Capone, they must live with the violence and corruption generated by prohibition, the diversion of law enforcement resources, the distortion of economic and social incentives for their youth, the overdoses that result from unregulated drugs, the AIDS that spreads more rapidly because clean syringes are not legally or readily available, and the incarceration of unprecedented numbers of young men and women. Those who contend that legalization would mean writing off impoverished inner-city neighborhoods ignore the remarkable extent to which drug prohibition has both failed and devastated the urban ghettos. Drug legalization offers no panacea, particularly if it is not accompanied by more fundamental changes in the norms and leadership of urban societies. But there is no question that it can alleviate many urban ills at relatively little risk.

Second, there are good reasons to believe that a nonprohibitionist regime would not result in dramatic increases in drug abuse. Public opinion polls reveal that few Americans believe they would use drugs that are now illicit if they were legally available. Important implications, moreover, can be derived from the observation that we already live in a society in which all sorts of psychoactive substances are cheaply and readily available to both adults and children. Legalization would make more drugs more available than they are today, but it would not present a situation dramatically different from that which currently exists. The same sorts of norms and interests that prevent most Americans from misusing drugs today would persist. And even many of those who do misuse illicit drugs would be no worse off, and in many ways better off, under an alternative regime. Some Americans would suffer from the abolition of drug prohibition, but all the evidence suggests that their numbers would be modest. We possess, in short, substantial evidence of a fundamental societal resilience in the face of widespread drug availability.

Third, there are also good reasons to anticipate positive shifts in drug consumption patterns if we move in the direction of nonprohibitionist controls. The current drug control regime favors certain legal and illegal drugs over others that may well present fewer dangers to both consumers and society generally. Under a legalization regime, alcohol and tobacco would no longer be artificially favored by their legal status. Crack cocaine would no longer benefit from the perverse dynamics of the illicit market. And traffickers and consumers would no longer be obliged to favor more compact and potent drugs over bulkier but more benign substances simply because the former were less detectable. Both illicit drug abusers and responsible consumers, particularly among the poor, would have better access to drugs that are safer than those that are most available now. Drug legalization might thus result in more consumption of a wider array of substances than is currently the case but with dramatically fewer negative consequences.

Fourth, those who take seriously such values as tolerance, privacy, individual freedom, and individual responsibility have little choice but to seek out alternatives to the current system. These values are fundamentally at odds with a prohibition regime that criminalizes the possession of small amounts of any drug for personal consumption. They are seriously threatened, moreover, by a war on drugs that promotes notions of zero tolerance toward drug users, that pursues its objective of a drug-free society with few restraints, that encourages neighbors and family members to inform on one another, and that incarcerates hundreds of thousands of Americans for engaging in vice activities that were entirely legal less than a century ago.

In proposing a mail-order distribution system based on a right of access, I have tried to offer a model that strikes at the heart of what is most problematic about drug prohibition. I realize that such a model is easily mocked by those with little interest in thinking seriously about alternatives to drug prohibition. My intended audience are the progressive prohibitionists and legalizers of all stripes interested in developing the discourse about alternatives to drug prohibition. I believe the model offers an effective means of eliminating or reducing the worst consequences of drug prohibition. It represents the best compromise I can envision between individual rights and communitarian interests. It provides for both a skeletal framework at the federal level and substantial flexibility for local option at the state and local level. It allows for substantial latitude in implementing public health measures and campaigns designed to reduce drug abuse. And it offers a system that can be fairly easily superimposed on the current prohibition system.

The model does not, to be sure, represent a panacea. It raises as many questions as it answers. Like any other model, it has its vulnerabilities and it is susceptible to abuse by those determined to take advantage of it. Its potential effectiveness depends, moreover, on the extent to which it is filled out with sensible and humane drug control policies at state and local levels of government. But it does compare favorably, I believe, with both the American prohibition system and the supermarket model preferred by extreme libertarians. It presents greater risks than the conventional, prohibition-bound harm reduction model one finds in parts of Europe and Australia, but it also offers far more potential to transform drug consumption patterns in both the urban ghettos and the population at large in safer directions.

Intellectual ruminations about supermarket models, mail-order distribution systems, and a right of access to psychoactive drugs seem far removed from current political debates over drug control policy in the United States. There are, nonetheless, good reasons to develop the intellectual capital associated with the analysis of alternative drug control regimes. First, scholars are obliged to pursue their intellectual inquiries unencumbered by the blinders imposed by current prejudices and political realities. To limit the questions that one asks and the answers that one ventures to those sanctioned by officialdom is to forsake our moral and intellectual obligations to both our profession and our society. Future generations are ill served if today's scholars uniformly submit to the intellectual conservatism that so dominates social science and public policy analysis. Second, many of the assumptions that underlie both the current war on drugs and the prohibition system itself have not been systematically examined for a long time. Even those who desire no substantial revisions in drug control policies can benefit from such an appraisal. Third, no one knows what the future will bring. New drugs and new ways of altering one's state of consciousness will surely emerge. The challenges of regulating psychoactive drugs are certain to increase. And the pharmacological Calvinism that dominates contemporary American public opinion and policy analysis can only persist for so long.

Cost-benefit analysis can, and should, play an important role in the debate over the future of drug control policy, if only because it provides us with the closest thing to an objective framework of analysis for clarifying our objectives and assessing our options. Ultimately, however, the debate over drug policy is really a debate over competing moral visions of society. I see no merit, and much evil, in calls for zero tolerance and a drug-free society. I also see nothing immoral, I must admit, about the consumption of psychoactive drugs by those who do no harm to others and who fulfill the obligations they have assumed to others. The challenge, from my perspective, is one of designing and promoting a drug control policy that combines a healthy respect for individual freedom and responsibility with a strong sense of compassion. These values do not trump all others all of the time. But it is important that they be not forgotten or pushed to the side whenever the fearful specter of DRUGS is uttered.

ENDNOTES

1. The relationship between the current debate over drug legalization and prior debates is analyzed in Ronald Bayer, "Introduction: The Great Policy Debate—What Means This Thing Called Decriminalization?," *Milbank Quarterly* 69(3)(1991):341–63.

2. See the following articles by Ethan A. Nadelmann, "Drug Prohibition in the United States: Costs, Consequences and Alternatives," *Science* 245 (1 September 1989):939–47; "U.S. Drug Policy: A Bad Export," *Foreign Policy* 70 (Spring 1988):1–139; and "The Case for Legalization," *The Public Interest* 92 (Summer 1988):3–31. Also see James Ostrowski, "The Moral and Practical Case for Drug Legalization," *Hofstra Law Review* 18(3) (Spring 1990):607–702; Richard Lawrence Miller, *The Case for Legalizing Drugs* (New York: Praeger, 1991); Arnold S. Trebach, *The Great Drug War* (New York: Macmillan, 1987); Steven Wisotsky, *Breaking the Impasse in the War on Drugs* (Westport, Conn.: Greenwood Press, 1986); and the collections of articles in Melvyn B. Krauss and Edward P. Lazear, eds., *Searching for Alternatives: Drug-Control Policy in the United States* (Stanford, Calif.: Hoover Institution Press, 1991); in David Boaz, ed., *The Crisis in Drug Prohibition* (Washington, D.C.: CATO Institute, 1990); in Ronald Hamowy, ed., *Dealing with Drugs: Consequences of Government Control* (Lexington, Mass.: Lexington Books, 1987); in Arnold S. Trebach and Kevin B. Zeese, eds., the three-volume *Drug Prohibition and the Conscience of Nations* (Washington, D.C.: Drug Policy Foundation, 1990), *The Great Issues of Drug Policy* (1990), and *New Frontiers in Drug Policy* (1991); and in Bruce K. Alexander, *Peaceful Measures: Canada's Way Out of the 'War on Drugs'* (University of Toronto Press, 1990).

3. Recent efforts to analyze nonprohibitionist drug policy options include Doug Bandow, "Dealing with Legalization," *The American Prospect* 8 (Winter 1992):82–91; and Chester Nelson Mitchell, *The Drug Solution* (Ottawa: Carleton University Press, 1990). A proposed research agenda can be found in Ethan Nadelmann, "Beyond Drug Prohibition: Evaluating the Alternatives," in Krauss and Lazear, eds., 241–50.

4. See Franklin E. Zimring and Gordon Hawkins, *The Search for Rational Drug Control* (New York: Cambridge University Press, 1992), 82–110; and Mark A. R. Kleiman and Aaron J. Saiger, "Drug Legalization: The Importance of Asking the Right Question," *Hofstra Law Review* 18(3) (Spring 1990):527–66.

5. See, generally, Pat O'Hare, Russell Newcombe, Alan Matthews, Ernst C. Buning, and Ernest Drucker, eds., *The Reduction of Drug Related Harm* (London: Routledge, 1991); Peter McDermott and Pat O'Hare, eds., *Reducing Drug-Related Harm: New Developments in Theory and Practice* (London: Whurr Publishers, 1992); and Nick Heather, Alex Wodak, Ethan Nadelmann, and Pat O'Hare, eds., *Psychoactive Drugs and Harm Reduction: From Faith to Science* (London: Whurr Publishers, 1993). Also see John Strang and Gerry V. Stimson, eds., *AIDS and Drug Misuse: The Challenge for Policy and Practice in the 1990s* (New York: Routledge, 1990).

6. See Govert Frank van de Wijngaart, "A Social History of Drug Use in the Netherlands: Policy Outcomes and Implications," *Journal of Drug Issues* 18(1988):481–95.

7. See the first *National Drug Control Strategy* issued by the Office of National Drug Control Policy, Executive Office of the President, in September 1989 (Washington, D.C.: US Government Printing Office, 1989), 11.

8. See Zimring and Hawkins, *The Search for Rational Drug Control*, 4–21, for a fine analysis of the report and its ideological assumptions.

9. See Gerald L. Klerman, "Psychotropic Hedonism vs. Pharmacological Calvinism," *Hastings Center Report* 2(4) (September 1972):1–3.

10. See Thomas Szasz, *Our Right to Drugs: The Case for a Free Market* (Greenwood Press, 1992); David Boaz, "The Consequences of Prohibition," in Boaz, ed., *The Crisis in Drug Prohibition*; and the speech delivered by Milton Friedman to the Fifth International Conference on Drug Policy Reform, Washington, D.C., 16 November 1991.

11. See David A. J. Richards, *Sex, Drugs, Death, and the Law: An Essay on Human Rights and Overcriminalization* (Totowa, N.J.: Rowman and Littlefield, 1982), 157–214.

12. See, generally, the collection of articles in Thomas H. Murray, Willard Gaylin, and Ruth Macklin, eds., *Feeling Good and Doing Better: Ethics and Nontherapeutic Drug Use* (Clifton, N.J.: Humana Press, 1984), in particular the concluding article by Ruth Macklin, "Drugs, Mod-

els, and Moral Principles," 187–213. Also see James B. Bakalar and Lester Grinspoon, *Drug Control in a Free Society* (New York: Cambridge University Press, 1984), and Douglas Husak, *Drugs and Rights* (New York: Cambridge University Press, 1992).

13. As John Kaplan wrote in 1988, "It is true that if the number of those dependent upon cocaine merely doubled, we would arguably be well ahead of the game, considering the large costs imposed by treating those users as criminals. But what if there were a fiftyfold increase in the number of those dependent on cocaine? We simply cannot guarantee that such a situation would not come to pass; since we cannot do so, it is the height of irresponsibility to advocate risking the future of the nation." See John Kaplan, "Taking Drugs Seriously," *The Public Interest* 92 (Summer 1988):32–50. Avram Goldstein and Harold Kalant assert more confidently: "There is no reason to doubt that the increased costs to society [of drug legalization] would rival those now attributable to alcohol." See Avram Goldstein and Harold Kalant, "Drug Policy: Striking the Right Balance," *Science* 249 (28 September 1990):1513–21.

14. See Andrew Weil, *The Natural Mind: An Investigation of Drugs and the Higher Consciousness* (Boston: Houghton Mifflin, 1972, revised edition 1986), 29. Weil credits Timothy Leary and Richard Alpert with first recognizing the importance of these two variables. The significance of "set and setting" is examined at length in Norman E. Zinberg, *Drug Set and Setting: The Basis for Controlled Intoxicant Use* (New Haven, Conn.: Yale University Press, 1984).

15. See, for instance, Lawrence O. Gostin, "Compulsory Treatment for Drug-Dependent Persons: Justifications for a Public Health Approach to Drug Dependency," *Milbank Quarterly* 69(4)(1991):561–93.

16. See Nathan S. Kline, "The Future of Drugs and Drugs of the Future," *Journal of Social Issues* 27(3)(1971):73–87; Wayne O. Evans and Nathan S. Kline, eds., *Psychotropic Drugs in the Year 2000* (Springfield, Ill.: Charles C. Thomas, 1971); Alexander Shulgin and Ann Shulgin, *PIHKAL: A Chemical Love Story* (Berkeley, Calif.: Transform Press, 1991); Ronald K. Siegel, *Intoxication Life in Pursuit of Artificial Paradise* (New York: E. P. Dutton, 1989), 298–317; and Henry B. Clark, *Altering Behavior: The Ethics of Controlled Experience* (Newbury Park, Calif.: Sage Publications, 1987). A particularly bleak and pessimistic perspective is provided in Morton A. Kaplan, "2042: A Choice of Futures—A Nightmare," *The World & I* (January 1992):108–115.

17. Note that the "needle park" experiment in Zurich, Switzerland, from 1990 to 1992 shared little in common with the sort of "supermarket" model developed here. Production and distribution of drugs remained illegal, the place of sale was strictly limited to one small park, and the entire scheme was developed within a fairly strict prohibitionist context. Much the same is true of the "open air" illicit drug markets in many urban ghettos. See Arnold S. Trebach, "Lessons from Needle Park," *The Washington Post*, 17 March 1992.

18. See David T. Courtwright, *Dark Paradise: Opiate Addiction in America before 1940* (Cambridge, Mass.: Harvard University Press, 1982); and see Ethan A. Nadelmann, "Historical Perspectives on Drug Prohibition and its Alternatives," *American Heritage* (forthcoming).

19. See, for instance, Michael R. Aldrich, "Legalize the Lesser to Minimize the Greater: Modern Applications of Ancient Wisdom," *Journal of Drug Issues* 20(1990):543–53.

20. Controlled consumption of heroin is examined in Zinberg, *Drug, Set and Setting*. Controlled consumption of cocaine is examined in Dan Waldorf, Craig Reinarman, and Sheila Murphy, *Cocaine Changes: the Experience of Using and Quitting* (Philadelphia: Temple University Press, 1991), and in Peter Cohen, *Cocaine Use in Amsterdam in Non Deviant Subcultures* (Amsterdam: Instituut voor Sociale Geografie, Universiteit van Amsterdam, 1989).

21. See Stanton Peele, *Diseasing of America: Addiction Treatment Out of Control* (Lexington, Mass.: Lexington Books, 1989), who further observes that most drug abusers eventually quit or curtail their destructive behavior without resort to conventional treatment programs. Also see Charles E. Faupel, *Shooting Dope: Career Patterns of Hard-Core Heroin Users* (Gainesville: University of Florida Press, 1991).

22. US Department of Justice, Bureau of Justice Statistics, *Sourcebook of Criminal Justice Statistics—1990* (Washington, D.C.: US Government Printing Office, 1991), 347; and US National Institute on Drug Abuse, *National Household Survey on Drug Abuse: Highlights 1988* (Washington, D.C.: Department of Health and Human Services, Alcohol, Drug Abuse and Mental Health Administration, 1990), 8.

23. *The Gallup Poll Monthly*, Nos. 288 and 303, reprinted in *Sourcebook of Criminal Justice Statistics—1990*, 347.

24. Ibid.

25. *National Household Survey on Drug Abuse: Highlights 1988*, 44.

26. Ibid., 8, 45–50.

27. Ibid., 17–22.

28. In a nationwide poll commissioned by Richard Dennis and the Drug Policy Foundation, 4 percent of the 1401 respondents said that they would be "very likely" to try marijuana if it were legal, 6 percent said they would be "somewhat likely," 8 percent said "not very likely," and 81 percent said "not at all likely." Asked the same question about the legalization of cocaine, 2 percent said they would be "very likely" or "somewhat likely," 4 percent said "not very likely," and 93 percent said "not at all likely." Similarly, in the annual survey of American high school students conducted by the Monitoring the Future Project at the University of Michigan, 73 percent of respondents said they would not use marijuana even if it were legal, 11 percent said they would use it about as often as they do now, or less, 7 percent said they might try it, and only 3 percent said they would use it more often than at present. See Lloyd D. Johnston, Patrick O'Malley, and Jerald G. Bachman, *Drug Use Among American High School Seniors, College Students and Young Adults, 1975–1990* (Rockville, Md.: National Institute on Drug Abuse, 1991), 141–42.

29. See Richard H. Blum & Associates, *Society and Drugs* (San Francisco: Jossey-Bass, 1969), 25–44.

30. See National Research Council, National Academy of Sciences, *Evaluating AIDS Prevention Programs* (Washington, D.C.: National Academy Press, 1988); and the report by the National Commission on AIDS, *The Twin Epidemics of Substance Abuse and HIV* (Washington, D.C., 1991).

31. See Thomas Szasz, *Ceremonial Chemistry: The Ritual Persecution of Drugs, Addicts, and Pushers* (Anchor Books, 1975).

32. See Stanton Peele, *The Meaning of Addiction: Compulsive Experience and Its Interpretation* (Lexington, Mass.: Lexington Books, 1985); and John Booth Davies, *The Myth of Addiction* (Philadelphia, Pa.: Harwood Academic Publishers, 1992).

33. The Australian policy is analyzed in Robin Room, "The Dialectic of Drinking in Australian Life: From the Rum Corps to the Wine Column," *Australian Drug and Alcohol Review* 7(1988)413–37. The British policy is assessed in Arthus Shadwell, *Drink in 1914–1922: A Lesson in Control* (London: Longmans, Green & Co. 1923). The impact of Prohibition on alcohol consumption and alcohol-related ills in the United States is assessed in John P. Morgan, "Prohibition is Perverse Policy: What Was True in 1933 Is True Now," in Krauss and Lazear, eds., *Searching for Alternatives*, 405–23; Mark Thornton, *The Economics of Prohibition* (Salt Lake City: University of Utah Press, 1992); and Jeffrey A. Miron and Jeffrey Zweibel, "Alcohol Consumption during Prohibition," *American Economic Review* 81(2)(1991):242–47. More generally, see Ethan A. Nadelmann, "Response to Letters," *Science* 246(1989):1109–1103; and Harry G. Levine and Craig Reinarman, "From Prohibition to Regulation: Lessons from Alcohol Policy for Drug Policy," *Milbank Quarterly* 69(3)(1991):461–94.

34. Early twentieth-century models of alcohol control, many of which allowed adults to import alcoholic beverages into "dry" locales, are analyzed in Raymond B. Fosdick and Albert L. Scott, *Toward Liquor Control* (New York: Harper & Brothers, 1933); Leonard V. Harrison and Elizabeth Laine, *After Repeal: A Study of Liquor Control Administration* (New York: Harper

& Brothers, 1936); and Reginald E. Hose, *Prohibition or Control? Canada's Experience with the Liquor Problem, 1921–1927* (New York: Longmans, Green & Co., 1928). The modification in F.D.A. policy is discussed in James H. Johnson, *How to Buy Almost Any Drug Legally Without a Prescription* (New York: Avon Books, 1990).

35. See, for instance, David Dixon, *From Prohibition to Regulation: Bookmaking, Anti-Gambling, and the Law* (Oxford: Clarendon Press, 1991).

36. US Department of Justice, Bureau of Justice Statistics, "Drugs and Jail Inmates, 1989" (August 1991), 1, 9.

37. See Mark H. Haller, "Bootleggers as Businessmen: From City Slums to City Builders," in David E. Kyvig, ed., *Law, Alcohol, and Order: Perspectives on National Prohibition* (Westport, Conn.: Greenwood Press, 1985), 139–57.

38. See D. M. Warburton, "Internal Pollution," *Journal of Biosocial Science* 10(1978):309–19; and Ruth Cooperstock, "Current Trends in Prescribed Psychotropic Drug Use," in *Research Advances in Alcohol and Drug Problems* 3(1976):297–316.

39. Some of these issues are considered in John P. Morgan and Doreen V. Kagan, eds., *Society and Medication: Conflicting Signals for Prescribers and Patients* (Lexington, Mass.: Lexington Books, 1983).

40. But also see Chester N. Mitchell, "Deregulating Mandatory Medical Prescription," *American Journal of Law and Medicine* 12(2)(1986):207–39.

41. See Peter Temin, *Taking Your Medicine: Drug Regulation in the United States* (Cambridge, Mass.: Harvard University Press, 1980), and Peter Temin, "The Origin of Compulsory Drug Prescriptions," *Journal of Law and Economics* 22 (April 1979):91–105.

42. See Sam Peltzman, "The Health Effects of Mandatory Prescriptions," *Journal of Law and Economics* 30 (October 1987):207–38, and Sam Peltzman, "By Prescription Only . . . or Occasionally?" *AEI Journal on Government and Society* (3/4)(1987):23–28.

43. Peter Temin, "Costs and Benefits in Switching Drugs from Rx to OTC," *Journal of Health Economics* 2(1983):187–205.

44. See the excellent drug education text by Andrew Weil and Winifred Rosen, *Chocolate to Morphine: Understanding Mind-Active Drugs* (Boston: Houghton Mifflin, 1983). Also see David F. Duncan, "Drug Abuse Prevention in Post-Legalization America: What Could It Be Like?" *The Journal of Primary Prevention* 12(4):317–22; I. Clemenst, J. Cohen, and J. Kay, *Taking Drugs Seriously: A Manual of Harm Reduction Education on Drugs* (Liverpool: Healthwise, 1990); David F. Duncan and Robert S. Gold, *Drugs and the Whole Person* (New York: Macmillan, 1985); and Ruth C. Engs, *Responsible Drug and Alcohol Use* (New York: Macmillan, 1979).

45. The efficacy of antismoking campaigns is discussed in Kenneth E. Warner, "The Effects of the Anti-Smoking Campaign On Cigarette Consumption," *American Journal of Public Health* 67(1977):645–50; and, by the same author, "Effects of the Anti-Smoking Campaign: An Update," *American Journal of Public Health* 79(1989):144–51. Also see Martin Raw, Patti White, and Ann McNeill, *Clearing the Air: A Guide for Action on Tobacco* (London: British Medical Association, 1990). The Partnership's advertisements are evaluated favorably in the Committee on the Value of Advertising, *What We've Learned About Advertising from The Media-Advertising Partnership for A Drug-Free America* (New York: American Association of Advertising Agencies, 1990). More critical analysis is provided in Richard Blow, "How to Decode the Hidden Agenda of the Partnership's Madison Avenue Propagandists," *Washington City Paper* 11(49)(6–12 December 1991):29–35; Cynthia Cotts, "Hard Sell in the Drug War," *The Nation* 254(9)(9 March 1992):300–302; and Lynn Zimmer, "The Partnership for a Drug-Free America and the Politics of Fear," paper delivered to the Fifth International Conference on Drug Policy Reform, Washington, D.C., 15 November 1991.

46. See "How to Launch a Nationwide Drug Menace," in Edward M. Brecher and the Editors of Consumer Reports, *Licit and Illicit Drugs* (Boston: Little, Brown and Co., 1972).

47. See "The Promise of Prozac," *Newsweek*, 26 March 1990; Fran Schumer, "Bye-Bye, Blues: A New Wonder Drug for Depression," *New York*, 18 December 1989; and the more balanced "Beating Depression," *U.S. News & World Report*, 5 March 1990.

48. See F. Earle Barcus and Susan M. Jankowski, "Drugs and the Mass Media," *Annals of the American Academy of Political and Social Science* 417(1975):86–100; Patrick T. MacDonald and Rhoda Estep, "Prime Time Drug Depictions," *Contemporary Drug Problems* 12(1985):419–37; William Braden, "LSD and the Press," in B. Aaronson and H. Osmond, eds., *Psychedelics* (New York: Doubleday, 1970); Jock Young, "Drugs and the Mass Media," *Drugs and Society* 1(November 1971):14–18; and Craig Reinarman and Harry G. Levine, "Crack in Context: Politics and Media in the Making of a Drug Scare," *Contemporary Drug Problems* 16(1989):535–77.

49. 478 U.S. 328, 92 L. Ed. 266, 106 S. Ct. 2968 (1986).

50. See Sylvia A. Law, "Addiction, Autonomy and Advertising," *Iowa Law Review* 54 (1992); and Peter Hirsch, "Advertising and the First Amendment," in Trebach and Zeese, eds., *New Frontiers in Drug Policy*, 404–407.

51. See Joe B. Tye, Kenneth E. Warner, and Stanton A. Glantz, "Tobacco Advertising and Consumption: Evidence of a Causal Relationship," *Journal of Public Health Policy* 8(1987):492–508. The debate over tobacco advertising is aired in *Advertising of Tobacco Products: Hearings before the Subcommittee on Health and the Environment of the Committee on Energy and Commerce*, House of Representatives, 99th Cong., 2nd Sess. (1986) (Serial No. 99-167). The debate over alcohol advertising is aired in *Alcohol Advertising: Hearing Before The Subcommittee on Children, Family, Drugs and Alcoholism of the Committee on Labor and Human Resources*, United States Senate, 99th Cong., 1st Sess. (1985) (S. Hrg. 99-16), and *Beer and Wine Advertising: Impact of Electronic Media: Hearing Before the Subcommittee on Telecommunications, Consumer Protection, and Finance of the Committee on Energy and Commerce*, House of Representatives, 99th Cong., 1st Sess. (1985) (Serial No. 99-16).

52. See Alison Masson and Paul H. Rubin, "Plugs for Drugs," *Regulation* (September/October 1986), 37–53, which argues for fewer restrictions on prescription drug advertising.

23

Forms of Legalization

Steven B. Duke, Albert C. Gross

A comprehensive drug legalization proposal should answer at least these important questions:

1. Which drugs will be legalized?
2. Where will drug use be permitted?
3. What will we do about juvenile access?
4. How will the drug market be regulated?
5. What form will licensing and distribution take?
6. What will become of our Pure Food and Drug regulations?
7. Will drug advertising be permitted or restricted?
8. How will we cope with drug abuse in the workplace?
9. What residual law enforcement demands will remain?

WHICH DRUGS TO LEGALIZE

One option would be to legalize selectively. We might sate the public appetite for intoxicants by legalizing some illicit drugs while we attempt to hold the line on more dangerous drugs. We might distinguish between marijuana, which is relatively benign, and cocaine, which is more hazardous. It seems likely that when legalization arrives it will do so incrementally, and that marijuana is almost certainly the first important recreational drug that will be converted from contraband to legal status. But legalizing marijuana will not remove the evils of prohibition, or even greatly ameliorate them. Because marijuana is so easily home grown, its price per dose can never get very high for very long and the profits in it cannot support major black market organizations.

The chief evils of prohibition are related to cocaine and heroin. We should legalize those drugs as well, in either the first or the second stage of legalization. Should we stop there? Some argue that we should not legalize drugs whose prohibition does not create serious social problems. Thus, since there appears to be no huge problem associated with the consumption of and trafficking in PCP, LSD, amphetamines, or methadone, we should perhaps not legalize them, even though we can expect a significant black market to continue with those drugs, as with tranquilizers, barbiturates, codeine, other opiates, and numerous designer drugs.

Such a halfway move toward legalization would not be advisable, other than as a cautionary step in the legalization process. The line remaining between legal and illegal drugs under such a scheme would make no more sense than the present dichotomy. There is little basis for distinguishing legally between amphetamines and cocaine, for example, other than the current consumer preference for cocaine, a preference that is almost certainly transitory. And it would be ludicrous to legalize the most potent, addictive, and dangerous natural opiate, heroin, while continuing to criminalize trafficking in all the lesser opiates. Since one of the advantages of legalization is removal of the black market incentives toward more powerful forms of drugs, thus encouraging drug consumers to use less potent, safer, less addictive forms, we should legalize all opiates and virtually all stimulants. We should certainly legalize coca when, if not before, we legalize cocaine.

It might be tempting to draw the legal line at crack and "ice" (smokable methamphetamine) because these drugs seem to be so addictive. This temptation should be resisted. Crack is easily manufactured by anyone who possesses cocaine, and ice can be manufactured in the basement or garage of anyone with elementary chemistry knowledge who can read a recipe book.[1] If there is a strong market for these drugs, prohibiting them is certain to fail. Market forces, however, are likely to take care of the problem. If the price of cocaine is greatly reduced, as it would be under legalization, the incentives for manufacturing and using crack or ice would also be greatly reduced. If crack is more addictive than cocaine in powder form, then consumers will eventually become aware of that (if they are not already) and will opt for the less addictive form of the drug. According to Dartmouth College neuroscientist Michael S. Gazzaniga:

This is so because if cocaine were reduced to the same price as crack, the abuser, acknowledging the higher rate of addiction, might forgo the more intensive high of crack, opting for the slower high of cocaine. . . . [O]n another front—we know that 120-proof alcohol doesn't sell as readily as the 86 proof, not by a long shot, even though the higher the proof, the faster the psychological effect that alcohol users are seeking.[2]

Thus market forces under legalization should largely eliminate crack and ice.

It is arguable that some psychoactive drugs should remain in the controlled category. Some synthetic opiates, for example, are so powerful and dangerous that they are analogous to grenades or other highly dangerous weapons that are effectively prohibited. If the most popular plant drugs are legalized, it is doubtful that any serious, lucrative market is likely to develop for a synthetic drug such as fentanyl that can be so deadly to its users. Hence, we would recommend that such drugs remain controlled at least until it is demonstrated that their prohibition creates worse problems than it prevents.

Many other drugs would remain available only on prescription and only through pharmacies. Any proprietary drug manufactured by a pharmaceutical company that maintains patent or other legal protection of its proprietary rights in the drug would not lose its privilege and responsibility for controlling the distribution of the drug. Such patent protection is a quid pro quo for holding the manufacturers of such drugs liable for the damage they inflict on users. We cannot hold the manufacturer of a drug liable for birth defects, sterility, or other serious damage unless we permit the manufacturer to retain substantial control over its distribution. We also have to protect the proprietary rights of the drug manufacturer in order to provide an incentive for research and development of new drugs.

Some black market activity will remain regarding any psychoactive drug that is available only on prescription. But such activities, which are rampant now, will be greatly diminished when many other psychoactive drugs are available on the open market. Minor black markets are manageable costs of necessary protection of the consumer and the manufacturer.

WHERE DRUG USE SHOULD BE PERMITTED

Between 1987 and 1992 Zurich, Switzerland, explicitly tolerated the unrestrained use of heroin and other drugs in Platzspitz Park.[3] Meanwhile, the possession and sale of drugs were ferociously suppressed elsewhere in Switzerland and throughout much of Europe. When the Zurich experiment began, the park served as an open-air shooting gallery for just a few hundred regular habitués. However, the park's drug clientele eventually swelled to 20,000 junkies, one fourth of whom came from countries other than Switzerland. Once a beautiful family park, Platzspitz became dangerous, unhealthful, and unsightly. By 1992 the disorder, the nonstop toxic drug reactions, the crime, the discarded syringes and other litter strewn about, the use of the grounds as a public toilet, and the general degeneracy that characterized Platzspitz Park led the Zurich City Council to rescind its permissive policy. The experiment's physical impact on the park was so severe that more than a year's labor was necessary to restore the property to normal park uses.

Drug regulations after legalization should avoid restricting use to a few outdoor venues. The regulations should permit use in the privacy of one's own home. Public use, however, should either be forbidden or allowed in a sufficient number of locations to prevent problems of concentrated impact. Otherwise the problems of drug immigration that destroyed Platzspitz Park will recur.

Drug consumption should be prohibited in those places where alcohol cannot now be lawfully consumed (generally, in motor vehicles and in public places). Arguably, that should be extended to semipublic places as well. There should be no "drug saloons" or the modern equivalents of opium dens. We see little reason why the consumption of newly legalized drugs should be permitted in restaurants, in public transportation facilities, or in other public facilities. Denying public uses would discourage consumption of pleasure drugs without the exorbitant costs of general prohibition.

Drug use in the workplace presents special problems. There is much to be said for prohibiting drug use in the workplace, especially if the work is hazardous. But much work is not hazardous to anyone and drug use would not actually injure co-workers as cigarette smoke does. Heroin addicts, moreover, cannot be expected to go all day without a drug dose. To prohibit heroin addicts from taking heroin anywhere but in their own homes is to require them to work at home or not at all. Perhaps the matter would best be decided by agreement between employer and employees, with employers allowed to designate semiprivate places where drugs in addition to tobacco can be consumed during break times.

An alternative is to prohibit conventional drug use in the workplace but to permit heroin addicts or other drug addicts to take their drugs through transdermal patches (that could hardly be effectively prevented, in any event, without strip searches). The delivery of heroin through such a patch is probably practicable. Such patches are not now available because the technology for patch delivery of drugs is complex and is controlled by a few high-tech companies; the street doesn't yet know how to package heroin that way, and it is illegal for pharmaceutical companies to do so, since heroin is a schedule I drug and cannot be prescribed for any legitimate purpose. Delivery of heroin through a patch would eliminate or reduce the rush produced by intravenous injection and would probably provide even less kick than the snorting of heroin powder would. Transdermal delivery may therefore be an inferior means of delivery for many addicts. If necessary to keep a good job, most addicts would probably be willing to accept the inferior form of delivery, especially since it is far safer than the others.

Restrictions on where drugs can be consumed are enforceable, as we have seen with alcohol- and tobacco-use regulations. Violations of place restrictions, unlike the acquisition and private consumption of drugs, have witnesses and victims who are willing to complain and to pressure officials to prosecute. Many Americans are repulsed by the public consumption of marijuana, cocaine, or heroin, just as many are repulsed by public sexual activities. A society can legitimately protect us against such aesthetic assaults, and we think that it should do so. More important, those who are trying to quit or resist using drugs are shielded from temptation if such consumption does not occur in public or semipublic places. The government should provide such a shield.

Such regulations of newly legalized drug use—essentially confining it to the home or semiprivate places—would involve substantial enforcement costs and would also be inconsistent with our more permissive stances on the consumption of tobacco and alcohol. While the United States is becoming much more restrictive about where tobacco can be smoked and somewhat more restrictive about alcohol consumption, we are not close to confining the use of those drugs to the home. Such a policy with respect to those drugs would neither be feasible nor just. With 50 million of our residents addicted to cigarettes, it would be impossible to prohibit them from smoking on the street. It imposes suffering on cigarette addicts to prohibit their smoking in the workplace, and that can be justified only on the ground that smoking physically harms co-workers or others.

The consumption of alcohol has been so socialized and accepted by our culture for so long that to prohibit drinking in restaurants or in bars, where customers gather to watch sports events and otherwise to socialize, would be both politically impossible and inadvisable. Our culture even proselytizes against "solitary drinking" and thus encourages "social drinking" as healthier and less problematic. As long as such attitudes prevail, we must go slow in restricting the places where alcohol can be consumed.

But more restrictive regulations of newly legalized drugs is another matter. Users of such drugs are already accustomed to consuming their drugs in private to avoid arrest. There would be nothing revolutionary in a system that required them to continue to so confine their consumption. The semipublic use of tobacco and alcohol is the norm in American society, whereas such use of marijuana, cocaine, and heroin is the exception. We should try to keep it so, at least until our inability to do is clearly established.

PREVENTING JUVENILE ACCESS

Most proponents of drug legalization propose to severely limit juvenile access to drugs. As things are now, children have varying degrees of access to each of the legal and illegal drugs. Unfortunately, some of our youngsters will probably always be initiated into drug use before they are mature enough to handle the attendant risks.

If they do not obtain it directly from their parents or siblings, children can obtain alcohol by raiding the home liquor cabinet, by coaxing an older friend to purchase it for them, or occasionally by purchasing alcohol directly from retailers. A retailer risks loss of a lucrative license by selling alcohol to a minor, however. Alcohol licensing regulations, if enforced, could represent a powerful model for restricting children's access to drugs. Recent experiments demonstrating the ease with which underage minors can purchase alcohol from retailers are one of many recent steps to pressure officials to enforce the laws against the sale of alcohol to minors.[4] Lax enforcement reflects, among other things, our preoccupation with illicit drugs. Acquiescence in underage drinking also reflects an implicit preference for one kind of illegal activity—underage drinking—over another one—illicit drug use. Law enforcement officers, parents, and other interested citizens feel ambivalent about enforcing the alcohol control laws because of their fear of even worse temptations. The licensing laws, however, are a potent tool that could be effective if all recreational drugs were treated equally.

Access to cigarettes by children is virtually unlimited, in spite of laws that prohibit sales to minors. Law enforcement agencies—in part because they are overwhelmed by drug prohibition duties and ideology—ignore the statutes against selling tobacco to children.

A serious trend toward prevention of early smoking is underway, and if this effort accelerates it could attain a level of effectiveness at least as great as the partially enforced ban on drinking by children. Cigarette vending machines have been outlawed by approximately twenty Minnesota communities,[5] by a few California jurisdictions,[6] and, surprisingly, by Raleigh, North Carolina.[7] Because children also buy or shoplift tobacco products from live retailers, Chanhassen, Minnesota, has even banned all self-service tobacco sales and requires stores to limit their stocks to closely guarded cigarettes at the cashier's counter.[8]

The tobacco industry fights back, mounting sometimes effective lawsuits and legislative lobbying campaigns against such restrictions. Often the tobacco industry creates "citizens" groups as front organizations or funds the efforts of merchants' associations in this struggle against regulation.

The tobacco industry also aggressively recruits juvenile smokers. The future of the nicotine business in America is absolutely dependent on finding children to replace adult Americans who defect from the ranks of smokers or die from the habit.[9] Ninety percent of all new American smokers are in their teens or younger.[10] Aware of the public relations implications of pandering lethal drugs to children, R. J. Reynolds cynically publishes materials that purport to fight against teen smoking. Meanwhile, its erstwhile "Joe Camel" advertising campaign radically improved the juvenile market share of Camel cigarettes—previously a largely adult brand. In the first three years of the campaign the proportion of smokers under 18 who chose Camel cigarettes zoomed from 0.5 percent to 32.8 percent. The illegal sale of Camels to minors increased the earnings of R. J. Reynolds from that source nearly eighty times, from $6 million to $476 million,[11] as a consequence of omnipresent posters, billboards, and adolescent promotions, that depicted the urbane, "smooth character" Joe Camel, an anthropomorphic caricature of a dromedary.[12] The *Journal of the American Medical Association* (JAMA) published several studies on the Joe Camel campaign[13] that cumulatively suggested that R. J. Reynolds was intentionally recruiting toddlers as customers. In addition to many other disturbing findings in the JAMA articles, one of the studies indicated that 91.3 percent of 6-year-olds could identify the cigarette's cartoon logo.[14] The study presented symbols of twelve miscellaneous products, including both "adult" and "children's" brands, and only Mickey Mouse— the logo for the Disney Channel—achieved recognition comparable to that of Joe Camel.

Under a comprehensive program of drug legalization, government could effectively reduce the access by children to all drugs. The program could maintain the present bans on alcohol sales to minors and stiffen penalties for others who provide alcohol to children. Drug legalization could incorporate major improvements over the present situation by:

1. Banning the sale of cigarettes and all other drugs through vending machines
2. Enforcing existing bans on the sale or transfer of cigarettes to children
3. Genuinely banning sale of the currently illegal drugs to children

The sale of cigarettes, alcohol, and newly legalized drugs to children could be made a serious felony. As with sex crimes against children, the seriousness of the felony could vary with the ages of the perpetrator and the victim. Noncommercial distribution to children could be made a lesser offense or, to avoid undue complexity, treated the same as a sale.

We would not stop at punishing the willful distribution of tobacco, alcohol, and other drugs to children. We would encourage courts to impose civil and criminal liability for negligently providing access to such drugs by children. The liquor cabinet, and the drug cabinet, if there is one, should be locked if there are small children in the house. Since such drugs are dangerous to young children's lives and health, it would not be a great stretch of legal principle to hold the possessors of such drugs to a duty to prevent children from obtaining them. One who leaves poison in the presence of an infant would hardly be surprised to learn that he was liable for the damage done to a child who took the poison. The same principles should be applied to pleasure drugs, with infant consumption itself regarded as an actionable or punishable harm.

Many states currently exempt parents from prohibitions against giving or selling alcohol to minors, especially if it is consumed at home in the presence of the parents.[15] This exemption not only accommodates religious use of alcohol by minors, it also allows parents to introduce their children to responsible use of alcohol rather than delegating that training to the uncertainties and excesses of illicit use by teenage peers. We can think of no reason why this approach should be retained for alcohol but not extended to other drugs. Responsible recreational use of any drug is preferable to illicit, irresponsible use. If parents believe they should train their children in how to use marijuana, they should not be made felons for doing so. If they allow their children to overdose on any drug and become emergency room cases, or permit them to operate machinery under the influence, however, legal sanctions should be imposed.

MODES OF REGULATION

Because the repeal of the prohibition amendment to the Constitution restored most of the control over alcohol regulation to the states, we have many different models for drug regulation. We should examine these models in our search for the best way to repeal drug prohibition.

Let us first consider the proposal of Daniel Benjamin and Roger Miller. In *Undoing Drugs: Beyond Legalization*,[16] they recommend that federal drug prohibition statutes be repealed, leaving each state free to decide how it wants to deal with drugs: free availability, stringent prohibition, or somewhere between those extremes. There are two major advantages to this proposal. First, since it does not itself result in either legalization or prohibition but just gives each voter in each state a greater voice in the drug policy that immediately concerns that voter, it may be politically feasible. The Benjamin and Miller proposal permits each state to have the kind of drug laws that it wants. Second, the proposal permits us to try many different approaches to the illicit drug problem, to experiment, to discover and evaluate new ways of dealing with drugs. We already know much about how to deal with drugs, since we have experimented endlessly with alcohol regulation, but there are differences among drugs and there is always more to be learned. A single federal approach to the problem cuts off experimentation and creative competition in fashioning reactions to problems.

There is, however, a potential major problem with this approach. As we learned with alcohol drinking age disparities, major differences between states concerning the legal availability of drugs create ugly state-line industries that cater to persons coming to buy and consume the drugs from states in which they are not legally available. Such differences encourage interstate travel under the influence of the sought-after drug. This dangerous condition, as it applies to drinking ages, was changed by recent federal legislation that effectively raised the minimum drinking age in all states to 21.

Highway safety considerations that warranted the change of drinking ages would almost certainly be less powerful considerations where other drugs were concerned. As we explained elsewhere, none of the three major illicit drugs is likely to impair driving capacity as greatly as does alcohol.[17] Alcohol is also a more popular recreational drug among teenagers than all the illicit drugs combined—by far. It is all but inconceivable that this basic order of consumer preference would be reversed under legalization. Thus the problem of state-line drug industries and impaired driving home from source states would almost certainly be less substantial than it was with respect to alcohol.

The likely outcome of the Benjamin and Miller scheme, if enacted, would be the gradual adoption of legalization, state by state. A few states would try it, if only for the revenue. Adjoining states would find their prohibition laws even less enforceable than are now and, lustful for the loot, would align themselves with their more prescient neighbors. As the states who legalized experienced not only revenue enhancement but less crime, safer streets, increased property values, and general improvements in the quality of life, the remaining states would fall in line like dominoes. Arguably, the federal government should skip that step and not only legalize most of the drugs it now treats as "controlled," but at the same time deny the states the power to prohibit them. Some room could still be left for state regulations, as is now the case with most products, where the federal government and the states share regulatory responsibilities.

LICENSING PRODUCTION?

Should we try to license the production of plant-based drugs? It is possible to produce not only marijuana but coca and its derivatives and opium and its derivatives in the territorial confines of the United States. If we were to ban the importation of such drugs, we could give a boost to domestic farmers and exclude the Columbian narcotrafficantes at the same time. That does not seem feasible, at least in the short run. Subtropical climates have natural advantages in the growing of coca and opium, and our farmers lack experience producing either crop. The harvesting of coca and, especially, opium is also very labor intensive. It is unlikely that American farmers could compete effectively with South American coca producers or with Indian, Pakistani, or Southeast Asian opium producers, at least in the short to intermediate term. We would still have smuggling and still have major black markets if we tried to close our drug markets to importation. (We probably *could* effectively prohibit importation of marijuana, since we can grow it cheaper and better than any country in the world, but there would be no need to do so. The market itself would produce that result.)

A more feasible possibility is the licensing of later stages of drug production, say from the coca or opium stages to refined production of cocaine or opium derivatives. While we could not effectively prevent the importation of coca, opium, and all their derivatives from abroad, we might try to confine some refining activities to licensed American manufacturers. We could thus hope to better control the purity of the drugs and to reduce the risk of contaminated products. Health and safety could thus be promoted. We do not do this with other drugs or food products, however, and it is hard to see why we should treat pleasure drugs differently. If foreign pharmaceutical companies can produce cheaper drugs than our manufacturers, and can satisfy Customs and the FDA that they have produced uncontaminated drugs, we see no reason—other than economic protectionism—why they should be prohibited from doing so.

REGULATION OF DOMESTIC DISTRIBUTION

The domestic distribution of pleasure drugs, like the distribution of pharmaceuticals, foods, alcohol, tobacco, and every other product, should be subject to regulation by American law. The question is what kind of regulation. Several options are available:

Unfettered distribution. Few but the most doctrinaire libertarians would favor this system for drug distribution, which threatens to replicate one of the worst problems that we now have with the largely unregulated distribution of cigarettes. Children would have easy access to drugs.

Under the present regime of drug prohibition, we have a de facto unregulated drug market. When buying from drug pushers, it is caveat emptor. Thus the unfettered option also would possess many of the disadvantages of the present regime, in which the consumer has no protection against mislabeled drugs or products tainted by toxic adulterants. There is nothing wrong with—and much to be gained by—drug regulation short of prohibition.

Unrestrained drug trade also would lead to aggressive marketing to attract young customers, new-product development, and creation of market niches for extrapotent forms (just as there now is a market niche for extrapotent beers—so-called malt liquors). Those aggressive marketing ploys would occur no matter how much tax the government put on the product. Paradoxically, many of the evils of prohibition would remain.

Government as sole distributor. One possible distribution system might be an exclusive federal government dispensary system. By having the dispensaries run by the federal government as opposed to the state governments, the problems of competition between neighboring states would be avoided. There would be one price and distribution system across the United States, and no interstate travel induced by the drug business. The effort to keep drugs out of the hands of juveniles would be greatly facilitated. Advertising could also be eliminated without any First Amendment problems. While private organizations may have constitutional rights to advertise their products, nothing *requires* the government to advertise.

There are, however, major disadvantages to government drug dispensaries. As we have learned from the Eastern Bloc countries, when government is the sole legal distributor of a commodity, competition and self-interest are not available to promote the efficient workings of the market. Thus the Soviet Union and Eastern Europe experienced shortages, hoarding, and black market distribution, which greatly contributed to the collapse of their economies and ultimately their governments. The temptation of government to increase profits by raising prices on a controversial product would also exacerbate the problems. Black markets that legalization was designed to prevent would develop parallel to the government drug-distribution system, just as illegal gambling organizations compete with state-run lotteries.

Finally, when the government has a financial interest in promoting vice, as it does in those states that have lotteries, states frequently engage in shameless promotions, even fraud, to induce their citizens to part with their money.[18] There is little of that in state-controlled alcohol dispensary systems, but the lottery example is another reason to worry about turning the drug business over to government-run monopolies.

A prescription system. Another option for distribution would be a "medical system," in which prescriptions would be filled at pharmacies. This could provide a modicum of state regulation and some protection against consumption by minors and drug abusers, but in black market consequences far more regulation and cost than is desirable. People who can afford to pay doctor's fees can already get a potpourri of drugs from unethical physicians who are at present a gray market distribution system that competes with black marketers. Legalizing the gray market would not solve prohibition's problems. It would merely make drug dealers out of our health professionals. Drug distribution as an adjunct to medical treatment or to maintain addicts as a stage of rehabili-

tation can be legitimate medical practice, but retailing recreational drugs manifestly is not. To impose that function on the medical profession would impose
intolerable pressures on the profession.

Licensed suppliers. A third possible distribution system would be to license
and regulate distributors and retailers who would sell psychoactive drugs as
commercial products. The late New York State Senator Joseph L. Galiber's
proposed legalization bill would have implemented essentially this system, while
funding treatment and education programs from taxes on retail sales.[19]

Alcohol distribution, which is already licensed, and tobacco trade, which
is largely unfettered, could be brought under this regulatory umbrella, too.

The main advantage of this system of distribution would be that it would
be far more likely than government dispensaries or a prescription system to
destroy the black market. A troubling disadvantage is that it would undermine the system by which psychotropic prescription drugs are distributed only
by licensed pharmacists on written authorization of a medical doctor. But people
who are reluctant to experiment or self-medicate with over-the-counter drugs
will—if they can afford it—still seek the advice and guidance of a physician, so
that the prescription system, although weakened, would not be destroyed.
Doctors today prescribe medication that can be bought without prescription.
They would continue to do so under a legalized drug regime. Also, as noted
earlier, there would in any event be a large number of psychoactive proprietary drugs that could legally be bought only on prescription. Nor would the
legalization of psychoactives be inconsistent with the prescription-only system
for medicinal drugs such as antibiotics. Many of these are proprietary drugs
and there is no significant black market problem.

Distribution licenses could be conditioned on good character and proof
of insurance or financial responsibility. Since a substantial benefit of legalization is that it would permit us to require drug distributors to sell uncontaminated and properly labeled products, distributors would have to establish their
financial responsibility for defaulting on their obligations. This would be a major
function of a licensing system. No monopolies or oligopolies should be created. Any person or organization meeting minimum requirements should get
a license.

A commercial licensing system should also include mandatory warning
labels, generic packaging (no brand names, slogans, or touting), and detailed
description of contents and purities. It might also be advisable to limit the quantities of drugs that any individual could purchase, to require records of sales,
and to forbid quantity price discounts. If those regulations—and others dealing with purity, potency, and so forth—are complied with, the manufacturers
and distributors of the drugs should receive immunity for the damage done
by their drug. Alcohol and tobacco distributors now have the same immunity
for the damage done by their products.[20] Otherwise the price of drugs would

have to reflect highly uncertain liability risks and would therefore be very high relative to production costs. A powerful black market would result.

A *practical choice.* Given drug prohibition's counterproductivity and the drawbacks of the other options we have described, the most practical alternative would be commercial licensing. While government regulation is not risk free, there is ample, successful precedent for regulating dangerous products and services. The government would regulate the drug marketplace in the public interest just as it regulates power companies, telecommunication companies, liquor sales, and gambling.

THE ROLE OF THE FOOD AND DRUG ADMINISTRATION

For the most part, the food and drug regulatory system accomplishes the goals that were set for it when it was first enacted in 1906. Prior to that, quackery was far more common than it is today and the purveyors of patent medicines foisted on an unwary public myriad potions and medicines for ailments real and imagined. Often these remedies did more harm than the diseases they purported to treat. At best, many were harmless but ineffective.

At present, a new drug must go through years of testing—often ten years or more—before it is approved for sale to the public. The Food and Drug Administration (FDA) supervises testing to determine that the proposed drug product is both efficacious and safe; that it will do what it claims to do and will do no unacceptable harm to the patient if used as directed.

In recent years the medical and pharmaceutical communities' authorized monopoly over medicinal drugs has been controversial. The FDA also has come under attack. During the 1960s and 1970s the alleged cancer cure, laetrile, acquired a cult of advocates who warred against the FDA's refusal to approve that drug. In the late 1980s there was controversy over scandals regarding the testing and regulation of generic drugs as substitutes for brand-name drugs. More recently the drug L-tryptophan has been restricted and advocates of its use claim the restrictions were unwarranted. Advocates for AIDS victims also frequently complain about FDA delays in approving AIDS drugs. Nonetheless, the agency does much good by protecting the public from tainted food and unsafe drugs. The FDA also provides powerful protection to desperate sufferers against medical fraud. It ensures that those who have a disease for which there is effective treatment will not be sidetracked by worthless remedies.

No rational legalization proposal would subject well-established recreational drugs to the new drug approval process of the FDA, for such drugs probably never could receive approval. Rather, the common recreational drugs that we would legalize should be "grandfathered" as were alcohol, tobacco, and aspirin, none of which was ever subjected to that process. Newly discovered plant drugs or synthetics, however, would be subject to FDA scrutiny, as they now are, before they could be sold. They too would receive a patent monopoly and could be sold only on terms fixed by the proprietor of the drug. This would reward the drug companies for the research and the lengthy process of testing necessary to get FDA approval.

The major difference between our scheme and the present scheme, insofar as newly discovered drugs are concerned, is that the FDA should approve drugs developed to provide intoxication as well as those having "medicinal" value. This would provide substantial incentives to the pharmaceutical companies to develop safer and less addictive pleasure drugs than most of those now on the market. What should happen when the manufacturer's exclusive rights in such a drug expire? If the drug is a popular recreational drug, and no more dangerous than the drugs already available, such drugs should enter the over-the-counter market.

BANNING ADVERTISING: A PESKY CONSTITUTIONAL QUESTION

An important dilemma for drug legalization advocates has been expressed by Milton Friedman:

> With respect to restrictions on advertising, I feel uneasy about either position. I shudder at the thought of a TV ad with a pretty woman saying, "My brand will give you a high such as you've never experienced." On the other hand, I have always been very hesitant about restrictions of freedom of advertising for general free speech reasons. But whatever my own hesitations, I have very little doubt that legalization would be impossible without substantial restrictions on advertising.[21]

A ban on all drug advertising, including cigarette and alcohol advertising, might be a worthwhile trade-off for the benefits of drug legalization. We already have a ban on broadcast advertising of cigarettes, the American Medical Association has endorsed extending that ban to print advertising,[22] and American distillers voluntarily keep their hard-liquor advertising off the air.[23] Certainly the powerful alcohol and tobacco lobbies would fight legislation that would produce such radical restrictions on their advertising. Those lobbies would be joined by some civil liberties organizations as well. Whether the bans if enacted would then be upheld by courts is unclear. Despite earlier Supreme Court decisions suggesting that "purely commercial advertising" is not protected by the First Amendment,[24] the Court has several times rejected that theory. Plain and simple advertising is entitled to protection by the First Amendment.

Drug advertising should perhaps be an exception, and there is precedent for that position. As recently as 1986 the Supreme Court held that Puerto Rico, although permitting gambling, could forbid advertising of gambling aimed at Puerto Ricans. Said Justice Rehnquist for a five-justice majority, "The greater power to completely ban casino gambling necessarily includes the lesser power to ban advertising of casino gambling."[25] He added that it would be "a strange constitutional doctrine which would concede to the legislature the authority to totally ban a product or activity, but deny to the legislature the authority to forbid the stimulation of demand for the product or activity through advertising on behalf of those who would profit from such increased demand."[26] The Court also suggested that all advertising of cigarettes and alcoholic beverages could be banned in all media, on the same theory.[27]

The Puerto Rico case was an aberration, and the Court has repudiated the greater-includes-the-lesser theory of the First Amendment. In *Virginia Board of Pharmacy* v. *Virginia Consumer Council,*[28] for example, the Court held that a licensed pharmacist had a First Amendment right to advertise truthfully the prices of prescription drugs. More recently, bans on truthful advertising of liquor have been struck down.[29] The Court has also invalidated restrictions on lawyer advertising[30] and on the posting of "for sale" signs on property.[31]

We are troubled by the free speech implications of a ban on drug advertising. Even if the Court would uphold such a ban, we would oppose it, especially if it did not include tobacco and alcohol, and probably even if it did so.

It is important under any drug regime—a legalized one as we propose or a dichotomous one as we have now—that there be free and open debate not only on the merits of legalization or prohibition but on the merits, risks, and evils of drugs themselves, either on their own footing or in comparison to other drugs. No one should worry about legal repercussions for advocating the use or nonuse of any drug. People should be encouraged to discuss, debate, and explain the safe use of drugs and the dangers of combining particular drugs as well as the joys or evils of same. An all-media prohibition on drug advertising would have a chilling effect on such debate, because the line between advertising and advocacy is murky.

The reason why we have had little difficulty to date in distinguishing between advertising and advocacy is that in television and radio, where we have discouraged or banned alcohol and tobacco advertising, the costs of advertising are so high that it seldom makes sense for anyone to advertise who is not hawking a particular brand name in a thirty-second spot. In such an expensive medium there is little doubt about what is and is not advertising. Very little private benefit accrues for advocating generic drugs.

Nonetheless, enterprising tobacco and liquor companies find ways of encouraging the audience to use tobacco and alcohol that escape bans on advertising. For example, the Partnership for a Drug-Free America campaign, which urges television, radio, and print audiences to avoid "drugs," makes clear that the "drugs" they are crusading against do *not* include tobacco or alcohol. The reason: tobacco and alcohol companies are major financial contributors to the campaign.[32] They realize that currently illegal drugs are in competition with their own products and that the clearer a line is drawn between those products and theirs, the more beneficial it is to them. Hence, ironically, our largest drug manufacturers support campaigns against "drugs." We also see messages on public television, which eschews "advertising," that are difficult to distinguish from advertising. Programs are "sponsored" or "underwritten" by oil companies or other giant manufacturers or distributors of products and the viewers are so informed. This is apparently "public relations," not "advertising."

If there is a lot of money to be made from advertising, a ban on advertising will encourage the creation of forms and modes of communication that come as close in function to advertising as is legally possible. The way to eliminate or greatly to curb advertising is not to ban it, but to make it unprofitable. If we prohibit the use of brand names on packaging or any other claims about the desirable effects of using a drug, confining descriptions to generic, chemical contents and explicit warnings about adverse consequences, we would eliminate most of the commercial incentive for advertising or its functional equivalent. Withholding trademark protection from newly legalized drugs would be the near-equivalent of such a prohibition and such a move is surely constitutional.

Manufacturers or distributors of marijuana might pool their resources and try to persuade potential customers to switch to marijuana from alcohol, and they might use sexual or other imagery in which to conduct that persuasion, but that would make economic sense only if most of the producers of marijuana could be induced to make a pro rata contribution to the "public relations fund." Otherwise, free riders could enjoy the benefits of the campaign without sharing any of the costs. We have some such campaigns by the tobacco industry or the beer industry because a small group of producers account for a large share of the total market, a state of affairs produced largely by brand-name advertising. If we make sure that there are no oligopolies in the marijuana business, there will be little pooling of resources for advertising. In a market where competition is mainly based upon price, there is little incentive for advertising anything *but* price. We should so structure the drug market that there are no excess funds to be spent on advertising. An alternative way to assure that there is little commercially motivated advocacy of particular generic drugs would be to require that any such advocacy by or on behalf of a manufacturer, distributor, or retailer of a drug, or any organization of such persons, be accompanied by specified warnings. If the mode of advertising were print, the warnings could be required to be in no smaller type than the largest type in the ad (or one half of that size, if we want to be generous to the merchants). If the spoken word is the medium, the warnings would have to be repeated every thirty seconds, and so on. No one has a constitutional right to commit fraud or to purvey falsehood, and claims about the desirability of any product are arguably fraudulent if not offset by disclosure of effects, side effects, and risks.

It is reasonably clear that we *can* legally prohibit advertising of drugs on radio and television, which are by far the most powerful advertising media for influencing children. There may be no First Amendment right to advertise on the airways because they are owned by the public. Just as none have the right to advertise their wares in the Supreme Court Building, neither do they have such rights on the public airways. That is not an entirely persuasive theory, but it appears to be well established in the courts.[33]

RESIDUAL LAW ENFORCEMENT

When drugs are legal, there still will be many important law-enforcement functions. First and foremost, police can revive their neglected tasks of trying to solve and deter murder, rape, robbery, burglary, theft, and other serious crimes. Police still will need to enforce the laws against intoxicated driving. However, drug legalization will offer a substantial advantage over prohibition. The police resources that are now wasted on unsuccessful interdiction and suppression will be available for policing impaired driving and impaired operation of other dangerous machinery.

Police still will be required to enforce regulated conditions of drug use, just as we now must enforce rules on where and when drugs like alcohol and tobacco may be used, and, most important, to enforce laws against access by juveniles.

As with alcohol now, under drug legalization the state still will need to enforce the laws against nuisances. Just as it is not desirable to live next door to a rowdy bar, it may not be desirable to live next door to a drug dispensary. A person offended by a drug retailer's mode of operation can make complaints to authorities and can seek nuisance abatement in the courts, just as now can be done with obnoxious alcohol establishments. Zoning of neighborhoods and licensing of drug retailers can restrict placement of retail drug establishments. State laws now specify how far liquor stores and bars must be from schools, houses of worship, and residential neighborhoods. Officers of the state also will be called upon to enforce similar regulations regarding the location and operation of drug businesses.

COPING WITH DRUG ABUSE IN THE WORKPLACE

Patricia Saiki, administrator of the Small Business Administration, reported that substance abuse costs the economy "more than $100 billion annually in lost productivity and wages."[34] Estimates of the cost to American business of drug and alcohol abuse vary, but some measures support Saiki's claim, putting the amount in the ballpark of 100 billion per year.[35] Consequently, during the late 1970s and early 1980s, federal government experts on workplace substance abuse developed a comprehensive system, called "employee assistance program" (EAP), that employers could use to deal with employee drug and alcohol problems if they affect an individual's job performance.

Many EAPs concentrate only on substance abuse problems, while other so-called "broad-brush" EAPs also tackle other off-duty difficulties, such as compulsive gambling, family or marital strife, the stress of life, and mismanagement of personal finances.

At its optimum, an EAP is a resource that an employee can tap for confidential help when substance abuse or other problems have gotten out of hand. Ideally, the employee makes a self-referral to the program, although supervisors generally also can refer a "problem" employee to the program. In return for self-referral or cooperation after supervisorial referral, the EAP is supposed to give the employee a measure of job protection. That is, so long as the employee carries out the program's reasonable recommendations for obtaining professional help and therapy, the employee usually will be able to retain his or her job. Such programs do not operate as a means for identifying and firing a problem person, but as a positive means to use the employee's drive for job survival to encourage that person to come to grips with important problems, including drug abuse problems. When EAPs operate properly, they are humane, legally defensible, and fair. Employers like the programs because they protect legitimate interests of the employer, such as workplace safety and worker efficiency. Employees and unions like properly operating EAPs because they respect the workers' right to be left alone regarding off-the-job behavior as long as it does not affect on-the-job performance or safety. Under EAPs, law enforcement is left to the state rather than usurped by corporations.

EAPs encourage troubled workers to get outside help in a relatively nonpaternalistic manner that involves no more coercion than is justified by the employer's legitimate interests. Under an EAP, loss of a job is not punishment; it is an inevitable consequence of an employee's uncorrected performance deficits.

Professor Dale A. Masi of the University of Maryland was a pioneer in the development of such programs. From 1979 to 1984 he directed the model federal employee assistance program for the U.S. Department of Health and Human Resources. As Dr. Masi testified to the 1988 Congressional committee hearings on drug legalization, "a majority of drug abusers (of both legal and illicit drugs) are in the workplace."[36] EAPs therefore could help reduce drug abuse by focusing attention where drug abusers are most likely to be found: on the job. EAPs succeed because holding on to productive and meaningful employment is a powerful incentive for a person troubled by substance abuse to become and remain sober.

According to general principles of behavioral psychology, the *inevitable* prospect of losing a good job as a result of a return to drug abuse is likely to promote sober behavior, while threat of punishment would probably only promote guile in continuing the drug-abusing behavior. If they are nothing else, successful EAPs are evidence that positive incentives can promote sobriety even though the entire coercive apparatus of the state has failed to keep contraband drugs off the market.

EAPs are likely to be more effective in a system in which acknowledging drug use, or abuse, is not a confession of crime and one can seek help without accepting the stigma of criminality. The goal in a legalized system will also be more reasonable and realistic: promoting not merely abstinence but the alternative of responsible use; reducing drug abuse, not drug use.

Under a legalized regime we would be compelled to rethink our present attitudes toward compulsory drug testing, both within and outside the workplace. Much of the support for routine testing today rests on the assumption that users of illicit drugs are criminals, likely to steal or otherwise engage in illegal behavior. When drug use is lawful, justifications for drug testing will have to be closely tailored to specific job performance requirements.

PUTTING DRUG CONTROL MONEY WHERE IT WOULD DO SOME GOOD

During the past decade and a half, America has undergone a shocking amount of economic and social decay. An American merchant seaman who visited Calcutta in the 1930s recently reminisced that he was astonished to observe people sleeping on the streets in that city. In that respect Calcutta of the 1930s is the United States of the 1990s. We have people sleeping on the streets, and it no longer shocks most of us. The gap between the wealthiest and the poorest in this country is growing, partly because middle-class blue-collar workers have lost jobs to foreign competition, partly because minority participation in the middle class declined as a result of cutbacks in government employment and white resistance to affirmative action, and partly because our educational systems have failed in their mission.

The surest way to deal with the problem of drug abuse in this country is to do something about the hopelessness felt by large portions of the American population. Instead of wasting its resources on futile drug prohibition, the country needs to invest in economic development of its urban communities and in rebuilding our educational infrastructure. Every dime spent on Head Start is worth 5 spent on drug prohibition. Any young person who sees hope for advancement and for a rewarding and useful life will have something better to do than obsessive pursuit of intoxication. One of the most important steps in a comprehensive drug control program under legalization is to reestablish opportunities for America's underclass.

ENDNOTES

1. See for example Uncle Fester, *Secrets of Methamphetamine Manufacture*, 2d ed. (Port Townsend, WA: Loompanics Unlimited, 1989 and 1991); Michael V. Smith, *Psychedelic Chemistry* (Port Townsend, WA: Loompanics Unlimited, 1981).

2. Michael S. Gazzaniga, "Opium of the People," *National Review*, 5 February 1990, 34.

3. Roger Cohen, "Amid Growing Crime, Zurich Closes A Park It Reserved for Drug Addicts," *New York Times*, 11 February 1991.

4. Michele L. Norris, "D.C. The Most Lax on Issue, Study Says: Washington College one of the Few Places Where Youths Can Legally Buy Alcohol," *Washington Post*, 3 March 1993.

5. "Minnesota Is Talking . . ." *Newsweek*, 6 November 1989, 7; Associated Press, "Town Delivers Health Kick to Cigarette Vending Machines," *Los Angeles Times*, 12 October 1989.

6. Myron Levin, "Fighting Laws On Smoking With Proxies: Retailing: Tobacco Companies Quietly Fund The Battle Against Restrictions, Opponents Say," *Los Angeles Times*, 5 August 1991.

7. "The Nation," *USA Today*, 1 April 1992.

8. Kevin Duchschere, "Chanhassen Orders Cigarettes Be Sold From Behind Counter," *Star Tribune*, October 17, 1991.

9. See Joseph R. DiFranza, John W. Richards, Jr., Paul M. Paulman, Nancy Wolf-Gillespie, Christopher Fletcher, Robert D. Jaffe, and David Murray, "RJR Nabisco's Cartoon Camel Promotes Cigarettes to Children," *Journal of the American Medical Association*, 266 (11 December 1991), 3149–53; citing John P. Pierce, Michael C. Fiore, Thomas E. Novotny, et al., "Trends In Cigarette Smoking In The United States—Projections To The Year 2000," *Journal of the American Medical Association*, 261, no. 1 (6 January 1989), 61–65.

10. DiFranza, Richards, Jr., Paulman, et al., "RJR Nabisco's Cartoon Camel," 3149–53.

11. Ibid., 3151.

12. Ibid., 3149–53; Geoffrey Cowley, "I'd Toddle a Mile For a Camel: New Studies Suggest Cigarette Ads Target Children," *Newsweek*, 23 December 1991, 70.

13. Paul M. Fisher, Myer P. Schwartz, John W. Richards, Jr., Adam O. Goldstein, and Tina H. Rojas, "Brand Logo Recognition by Children Aged 3 to 6 Years; Mickey Mouse and Old Joe the Camel," *Journal of the American Medical Association*, 266 (11 December 1991), 3145–48; DiFranza, Richards, Jr., Paulman, et al., "RJR Nabisco's Cartoon Camel," 3149–53; and John P. Pierce, Elizabeth Gilpin, David M. Burns, Elizabeth Whalen, Bradley Rosbrook, Donald Shopland, and Michael Johnson, "Does Tobacco Advertising Target Young People to Start Smoking?: Evidence From California," *Journal of the American Medical Association*, 266 (11 December 1991), 3154–58. See also Henry Waxman, "Tobacco Marketing; Profiteering From Children," *Journal of the American Medical Association*, 266 (11 December 1991), 3185–86.

14. Fisher, Schwartz, Richards, Jr., et al., "Brand Logo Recognition by Children," 3145–48.

15. See 45 Am. Jur. 2d § 274 (1995); 48A C.J.S. §259; *Bell v. Alpha Tan Omega Fraternity*, 98 Nev. 109, 642 P. 2d 161 (1982); *Craves v. Inman*, 223 Ill. App. 3d 1059, 586 N.E. 2d 367 (1991).

16. Daniel K. Benjamin and Roger Leroy Miller, *Undoing Drugs: Beyond Legalization* (New York: Basic Books, 1991).

17. See Steven B. Duke and Albert C. Gross, *America's Longest War: Rethinking Our Tragic Crusade Against Drugs* (1993), Chapter 4.

18. See Valerie C. Lorenz, "It's Time to Take Action to Halt Addiction That Knows No Bounds," *USA Today*, 26 March 1991.

19. Introduced, as New York State Senate Bill S-1918, 6 February 1989. Reintroduced, as New York State Senate Bill 4094-A, 21 March 1991.

20. They may, of course, be liable for fraudulent advertising. See *Cipollone* v. *Liggett Group, Inc.*, 60 U.S.L.W. 4703 (24 June 1992). Litigation is currently underway seeking to pierce the tobacco industry immunity and *some* success in that regard seems likely. See "Florida Gives Go-Ahead for a Cigarette Liability Suit," *New York Times*, June 27, 1996.

21. Milton Friedman, in *Reason*, October 1988.

22. "Media Advertising for Tobacco Products," *Board of Trustees Report, Journal of the American Medical Association*, 255 (28 February 1986), 1033.

23. See Peter Grier, "Coalition Asks FTC to Prohibit Liquor Ads Aimed at Young People," *Christian Science Monitor*, 23 November 1983. Recently the liquor industry announced its intention to terminate its voluntary ban on liquor advertising on television. The announcement produced a flurry of protests and demands for reconsideration. See Rick Badie, "Critics Say Liquor Ads Neither Hip Nor Cool," *Orlando Sentinel*, 1 December 1996; "FTC Launches Review of TV Liquor Ads," *Los Angeles Times*, 28 November 1996.

24. *Valentine* v. *Chrestensen*, 316 U.S. 52 (1942).

25. *Posadas de Puerto Rico Associates* v. *Tourism Company*, 478 U.S. 328 52 (1986).

26. Ibid., 346.

27. Ibid.

28. 425 U.S. 748 (1976).

29. See 44 *Liquormart, Inc.* v. *Rhode Island*, 64 USLW 4313 (1996).

30. *Bates* v. *State Bar of Arizona*, 429 U.S. 813 (1976).

31. *Linmark Associates, Inc.* v. *Willingboro*, 431 U.S. 85 (1977).

32. Cynthia Cotts, "Condoning the Legal Stuff: Hard Sell in The Drug War," *Nation*, 9 March 1992, 300.

33. See *Capital Broadcasting Co.* v. *Mitchell*, 333 F. Supp. 582 (D.C. 1971), affd. sub nom. *Capital Broadcasting Co.* v. *Acting Attorney General Kleindienst*, 405 U.S. 1000 (1972).

34. PR Newswire Association, "U.S. Small Business Administration Named As Member of Federal Drug-Fighting Team," *PR Newswire*, 29 January 1992.

35. The United States Chamber of Commerce claims that drugs cost American business $160 billion per year. (Eric Reguly, "Drug Abuse Still a Problem For U.S. Firms," *Financial Post*, 25 October 1991). A University of California San Francisco study, commissioned by National Institute on Drug Abuse, estimates that in 1988 drug and alcohol abuse cost the United States economy a total of $144.1 billion, including medical expenses and other costs in addition to business-productivity losses. (Dorothy P. Rice, Sander Kelman, Leonard S. Miller, and Sarah Dunmeyer, *The Economic Costs of Alcohol and Drug Abuse and Mental Illness, 1985*. Report submitted to the Office of Financing and Coverage Policy of the Alcohol, Drug Abuse, and Mental Health Administration, U.S. Department of Health and Human Services, San Francisco, CA: Institute for Health & Aging, University of California, 1990, 2.)

36. Dale A. Masi, Testimony before the House Select Committee on Narcotics and Drug Control, September 29, 1989.

24

Perfect Drug Legalization

Mark Thornton

INTRODUCTION

A growing number of academic and independent investigators have found narcotics prohibition to be a failure; yet those who oppose the war on drugs have made little progress in policy reform. In fact, the war on drugs continues to escalate and is expanding to the alcoholic beverage and tobacco products industries. This chapter presents a radical alternative to prohibitionism called *perfect legalization* and provides an explanation for the failure of advocates of "legalization" to achieve reform.[1]

Perfect legalization involves the complete elimination of government intervention from the drug market. *Perfect* refers to a policy that is complete or unadulterated and does not imply that legalization would solve all problems. Utopia is not an option.[2] In terms of implementation, whenever the question arises, "Should the government do X?" the answer should always be No unless it reduces the role of government and prohibition. Reform should always proceed by extracting government at all levels from involvement in the drug market. In the limit, minors would be allowed to buy heroin, as far as the government is concerned.[3] Basically, the government would not discriminate for or against drugs. They would be treated just like any other product and subject to the same taxes and liability laws as any other product. This policy is based on my study of real-world markets, from free to prohibited, and has wide and growing empirical and historical support.[4]

This policy is shocking, if not completely unacceptable, to most people. Nearly all drug policy experts, including those who oppose the war on drugs, reject this option. However, I will argue that perfect legalization is the *only* policy option that can effectively oppose prohibitionism and reduce the problems of drug abuse, and that advancing the case for perfect drug legalization is the best, if not the only, approach to achieve real reform.[5]

Most opponents of the war on drugs argue against prohibition based on some notion of costs outweighing another notion of the benefits. Faced with such "evidence," prohibitionists simply say that the benefits of prohibition are worth any cost to them.[6] Even if everyone had the same notions about costs and benefits, such arguments would not suffice without some viable alternative to prohibition. The lack of clear and viable policy alternative is the major strength of prohibitionism.

Most legalizers offer "politically acceptable" reform proposals, such as government drugstores and addiction treatment centers. The real-world results of such government-based "politically acceptable" proposals by opponents of prohibition have been mediocre at best and not highly acclaimed.[7] Therefore, the public has been highly skeptical of trusting bureaucracy with difficult tasks such as drug abuse and addiction treatment.

There are a great variety of reform proposals. The wide diversity of policy views among those who oppose prohibition helps create the political conditions for irrational policies like prohibition to persist. Some reformers provide further support for prohibitionism by advocating policies that share the basic ideology of prohibition that the government must provide people with their moral compass for the common good. In fact, I will argue below that many reforms supported by advocates of "legalization" are actually prohibitionist policies.

THE ALTERNATIVE TO PROHIBITION

The most common reform proposals include taxation, regulation, and government provision. For example, taxation is combined with regulation and age prohibition to generate the traditional policy on alcohol and tobacco. The British medicalization model used both regulation (by doctor's prescription from the 1920s to the 1960s) and government provision (registered addicts at government clinics beginning in the 1960s). Most "legalization" schemes involve a combination of harsh government interventions and elements of direct prohibition, such as prohibition of sales to minors.

It is also possible to find quite complex policy proposals dealing with drugs that call for a different policy to deal with each separate drug. This hodge-podge approach to public policy fails on several crucial grounds. However, it is very popular politically because it provides politicians with a justification for new spending and allows them to better maximize their political support. It leads to an expansion in both the scale and scope of policies that I categorize as prohibitionist.[8]

There is also a plethora of suggestions for reforming prohibition. Most of these suggestions are concerned with changes in enforcement personnel management, bureaucratic organization, enforcement techniques, the structure of penalties, and the funding of prohibition. The first defense of prohibition has always been that we just need to get the right people, more money, stricter penalties, or better technology. Each type of reform has been tried and has failed many times; a variety of reasons have been given for these failures.[9]

One prominent reform of prohibition known as the *harm reduction model* is popular among many legalizers. This policy model calls for a shifting of resources to reduce the cost of prohibition on drug users and society. The direct enforcement of prohibition is reduced, while other forms of government intervention—such as demand reduction and drug substitution policies—are increased.[10] Advocates of harm reduction are correct: this does reduce the social cost of prohibition in the short run, but such policy shifting will be shown to be crucial for the long-term stability of the prohibitionist regime.[11]

At the heart of this long-term stability is the ideology of prohibitionism, an ideology that originated with Puritanism and other "heretical" religious groups. Prohibitionism is based on the notion that certain objects or goods are the source of sin, not the individual sinner. Accordingly, these goods should be greatly reduced, strictly regulated, or eliminated entirely to purify society and prepare for the second coming of God. This powerful ideology has become increasingly secularized, but the basic policy goals have remained intact.[12]

Prohibitionists promote prohibition of "sinful" goods, but they have also supported alternative consumption-control policies from the earliest days of Colonial America. In fact, American history is replete with various Puritan-inspired social control measures, such as anti-alcohol policies. Sometimes prohibition was called for and established. At other times less restrictive measures—such as local option (to prohibit), government stores, licensure, blue laws, and sin taxes—were established, depending on the political clout of prohibitionists and whether they sought moderation, temperance, or abstinence. A representative cross-section of the variety of alcohol policies emerged in the wake of the 21st Amendment when alcohol was returned to state control.[13]

When remedial measures fail to achieve the prohibitionists' goals, the policy response is to strengthen them or to adopt intermediate restrictions, depending on the political power of prohibitionists. Indeed, there is a cyclical nature to prohibitionist policies in which restrictive measures are intensified until prohibition is established. Once prohibition fails politically, the restrictions are reduced but not eliminated. This cycle of progressive interventionism is not unique to prohibitionism.[14]

The most common fallback position for prohibitionists is called *modified prohibition*, a policy designed to control and limit the consumption of a good via a network of government interventions. It involves a combination of raising the price, regulating the production, and restricting the distribution of the product.[15] Ironically, this policy is what many legalizers now advocate for narcotic drugs.

Increasing the cost of consumption is achieved with a combination of taxes, restrictions on output, and higher transaction costs (i.e., reduced hours and days of operation, longer average travel distance to the "drugstore"). Regulation of production can involve limitations on the number of producers, the size and potency of the product, and product attributes. Restrictions on distribution would include the number of and qualification of sellers, age prohibitions, location prohibitions, unreasonable seller liability laws, quantity limitations, and restrictions on advertising.

Some of these government interventions seem like reasonable constraints on behavior when it comes to dangerous drugs. I would be hard-pressed to argue separately against the practicality of each and every one of them, especially age prohibitions, because they are similar in intent to private prohibitions and regulations.[16] However, government intervention fails even in cases where it is deemed necessary or morally essential. Most government interventions, such as regulation, are in fact some form of prohibition. The Food and Drug Administration's regulation of drug safety, for example, prohibits the sale of newly discovered drugs. The federal government's regulation and allocation of human organs for transplant is actually a prohibition on the sale of human organs. In these two well-documented cases, government intervention has been found to be more costly and a deterrent to public health, and to significantly increase the number of deaths over free market conditions.[17]

Modified prohibition is a package deal and the real-world results of modified prohibition are disappointing at best. For one thing, modified prohibition does not eliminate the presence of the black market. Alcohol and tobacco are both sold on the black market; more important, much of the illegal alcohol is produced in the black market.[18] Modified prohibition does tend to reduce the overall quantity purchased from free market levels, but some reduced expenditures are diverted to more dangerous products.[19] Even the manner in which the product is consumed is often negatively affected.[20]

Modified prohibition can also reduce the overall harmful and socially disruptive effects of prohibition, but it does not reduce them to free market levels and has little positive impact on the problems with drug abuse. Modified prohibition concentrates and highlights the social problems of drug abuse and makes them subject to political reactions rather than social resolutions. The alcohol prohibition movement that resulted in the 18th Amendment and the Volstead Act is a good example of how modified prohibition politicizes a problem and makes it worse. This movement was led by the Anti-Saloon League, a political pressure group organized during an era of intense modified prohibition (late 1800s-World War I) in reaction to the problems associated with government-licensed saloons.[21]

Two different types of prohibitionists dominate policy advocacy during different phases of the cycle of prohibitionist policy change. When intervention fails, extremists emerge to advocate stronger measures and direct prohibition. Extremists even oppose sin taxes that would put their government in league with the devil. When prohibition and other harsh measures fail, the pragmatists emerge as dominant. The pragmatist admits that effective prohibition is beyond the scope of the government's ability and that high sin taxes, for example, should be imposed to control behavior and to make sinners pay for their sins against society and the social costs they impose on taxpayers.[22]

Tax revenue, not ideology or truth, is the most important factor in generating this cycle of policy reform. Politicians rarely look for truth, and true ideologues are rarely elected (or reelected) to public office as stable, cohesive majorities. Politicians seek reelection by producing legislation that will result in a winning number of votes. Taxes are an important ingredient in the production of legislation and achieving reelection because revenue must be obtained to spend on special-interest legislation and higher tax rates can lose votes for incumbents.[23]

Politicians benefit from the tax revenue produced by modified prohibition. It produces revenue via an excise tax, government-monopoly drugstore, or both. Most goods targeted by prohibitionists, such as alcohol, Freon, gambling, narcotics, and tobacco, are "habit forming" or "addictive," which suggests that sin taxes and government-monopoly stores will produce substantial amounts of revenue.[24] Reducing the number of sales outlets also reduces the costs of monitoring sales and collecting revenue.[25] In fact, we could say that politicians attempt to maximize the tax revenue from sin taxes (subject to voter sensitivity) and that sin taxes are a lucrative source of revenue that comes at a low political cost.

In terms of public finance, prohibition is an expenditure rather than a revenue source.[26] However, politically it is highly popular among two important groups, prohibitionists and black marketeers, who form a strange coalition that Bruce Yandle has dubbed "Baptists and Bootleggers."[27] Prohibition also requires an enforcement bureaucracy and additional expenditures on courts and prisons. Several federal, state, and local agencies are charged with enforcing narcotics prohibition and these bureaucracies normally covet this responsibility as a source of publicity, power, and justification for larger budgets.[28] Many bureaucracies owe their entire existence to the war on drugs so that once prohibition is enacted, the coalition expands to "Baptists, Bootleggers, and Bureaucrats" and becomes much stronger politically.

The role of economic incentives facing politicians can be best seen during times of crisis and significant political change. The adoption of the 18th Amendment was a dramatic event in public finance history as alcohol taxes represented a major source of revenue for the federal and local governments. Federal politicians were willing to forgo this revenue and placate the ideological preferences of prohibitionists because the 16th Amendment had established an income tax, a new and highly remunerative source of revenue for the federal government. Only in the depths of the Great Depression, when income tax revenue was falling dramatically, was Prohibition recognized as a failure and repealed.[29]

One recent example of this cycle of prohibitionist policy reform has been the legalization of gambling because "legalized gambling" represents modified prohibition, not perfect legalization.[30] Politicians in certain states wanted the revenue more than they needed the votes of extreme prohibitionists, so they switched prohibitionist policy regimes supposedly to make the sinners pay for the social problems they create.[31] Legalized gambling and state lotteries clearly fit the model of modified prohibition because they involve a multitude of taxes, licenses, regulations, and age and location prohibitions.[32]

Reform measures like modified prohibition and harm reduction are at best the lull within the cycle of failed prohibitionist policies. The "middle path" between perfect legalization and direct prohibition has been the path to expanding the prohibitionist agenda in two ways. First, it acts as a buffer between legalization and prohibition when prohibition fails politically. Second, these reform measures are the seedbed of new prohibitions. No reformer's plan is ever enacted into legislation as first proposed, and few pieces of legislation are put into effect as written. The two major drug prohibitions, narcotics and marijuana, were established legislatively as regulatory taxes (the Harrison Narcotics Act of 1917 and the Marijuana Tax Act of 1937). Both laws were explicitly regulation via taxation measures that were quickly turned into outright prohibitions by the administering bureaucracy.[33]

It is highly unlikely that politicians and bureaucrats will take the lead in a true reform of prohibition. Real reform will require an intellectual and ideological conversion of the general population and the political self-interest necessary to overthrow the prohibitionist establishment. In the following section, perfect legalization will be shown to be the best way of solving the problems of drug prohibition and the best policy for dealing with the problems of drug abuse. It will also be shown that the best means of achieving real policy reform—legalization—is to advocate perfect legalization.

LEGALIZATION, PROHIBITION, AND DRUG ABUSE

The effects of prohibition are well known and widely recognized. The black market is the manifestation of most of these effects, such as a much higher price for the product because of higher production costs and the risk involved with black market production and distribution. The product tends to be of lower quality and higher potency, making the product much more dangerous to consume. Consumers do not have access to free market protections, such as product liability laws, legal protections against fraud and torts, regulation by insurance, consumer sovereignty, and market competition.

Prohibition is a significant factor in raising the crime rate.[34] Black market distribution and consumption is itself criminal. Crimes such as drive-by shootings are committed in support of sales territories and black market contracts. Property crimes committed to support the habits of drug addicts can be attributed to prohibition. Prohibition also increases crime by diverting police resources away from property crimes and by increasing the returns to criminal employment.[35] We have found that prohibition can cause courts and prisons to become so overcrowded that effective penalties are reduced on criminals and crime proliferates.[36] Prohibition is a major cause of political corruption both domestically and in foreign countries that supply and transport illegal drugs.[37]

Alterations in the policy of prohibition will have diverse, yet predictable effects. As discussed above, changing to modified prohibition will tend to reduce the social costs of prohibition (i.e., "harm reduction") but does not eliminate the black market, crime, or corruption associated with prohibition.

The perennial question remains. How can we completely rid ourselves of illegal drugs and black market crime? The Cinderella answer is that perfect legalization eliminates all prohibition-related problems. The beauty of perfect legalization is that there would no black market or prohibition-related crime and corruption. Like Cinderella, perfect legalization is an unrecognized beauty forced to drudge and suffer in undeserved obscurity and neglect. And yet, is it only a fantasy to think that such an effective policy might not some day be lifted from obscurity and given a place of honor and significance?

The reason many "legalizers" oppose perfect legalization is that they feel it would make the problems of drug abuse much worse. Many legalizers share the prohibitionist view that drugs are incompatible with freedom or they have a general anticapitalistic view that the market economy actually causes or stimulates a host of problems like drug abuse. The premise of harm reduction strategies is therefore a trade-off between the costs of prohibition and the costs of drug abuse. Contrary to this view, it will be argued below that perfect legalization is actually the best policy to address the problems of drug abuse.

People would still abuse drugs and commit crimes while using drugs under perfect legalization, but there are many reasons to reject the view that legalization leads to social chaos or even an increase in drug-related crime.[38] First and foremost is the highly questionable hypothesis that drug use causes crime.[39] Second, there are already laws against the crimes that drug addicts might commit so that removing drug laws would not prevent the police from dealing with real criminals. Third, crimes due to drug intoxication are much smaller in number and severity than prohibition-related crimes. Fourth, our system of criminal justice is overburdened with the war on drugs and suffering from the "tragedy of the commons."[40] Fifth, perfect legalization would allow the criminal justice system to concentrate its limited resources on violent and property crimes, and, as crime statistics suggest, intoxicated criminals are easier on average to catch. Refocusing the criminal justice system on crime, rather than on a supposed catalyst (drugs), will cause a dramatic drop in crime.[41]

The conclusion that a free market in drugs caused the problems of drug abuse and addiction and that legalization will make the problems worse suggests a misunderstanding of how markets and the profit motive work. Most illegal drug experts are not trained in market analysis and have less than average experience in real-world markets.[42] In fact, most modern economists are not highly trained in the finer aspects of the market process and lack even an average level of experience in real-world markets. Most economists receive their training in mathematics and statistics. Their only training in market analysis is based on the model of perfect price competition, a highly informative model but one that abstracts away from the multifaceted competition that takes place in the real world and substitutes a simpler model in which competition is boiled down to price. This is a perfectly reasonable model for examining normal aspects of the economy or basic changes in markets, but it is inappropriate for examining major changes in an economy, such as the downfall of communism or the legalization of drugs.[43]

The myopia of price competition results in legalization misinterpreted solely as a lowering of price and increase in consumption, abuse, addiction, overdoses, and social problems. Reinforced by the lack of any direct experience with legal narcotic drug markets, this interpretation creates a horrific portrait of legalization. The fear is understandable, but in the move from prohibition to perfect legalization, the change in price is one of the least important features of change.

Some government interventions have few significant effects on the market. Raising the gas tax by three cents, for example, would cause the price of gasoline to go up two or three pennies per gallon and it might cause total gas consumption to decline a small amount from what it would have been without the tax. Few people would switch to different grades of gasoline and it would not change the gas itself, how it is made, or distributed. The tax would not cause a black market in gasoline to develop or cause crime or corruption. So if government repealed the tax it would not have any significant effects either.

If the government banned gasoline-powered cars or raised the gasoline tax by $3 per gallon, we would experience many changes besides the amount of gasoline legally consumed. Prohibition changes everything to a black market, and adopting perfect legalization would change everything back to the market. Besides completely removing the deleterious effects of prohibition, the return to a free market process in narcotic drugs has three primary, although often neglected, beneficial effects, as is discussed in detail below. First, it reestablishes all the market mechanisms that would help reduce the social costs of drug abuse. Second, it would free up and therefore stimulate the role that private prohibitions play in controlling drug use and abuse. Finally, the free market has a discovery procedure that finds solutions to problems in a cost-effective manner.

The market mechanisms of free enterprise and free competition raise the best suppliers to the top, remove the least effective suppliers from the market, and push suppliers to price their products close to minimal cost. These are the institutions of capitalism that actually drive the price lower, but they also ensure that suppliers meet the demands of consumers and drive suppliers of the worst products from the market. This is why consumer sovereignty exists in a true market economy: consumers are king when it comes to the products produced.

The market also provides levels of product heterogeneity and homogeneity that are consistent with consumer choice, cost, technology, and the extent of the market. For example, there are a variety of light bulb companies that sell a finite variety of competing products and most light bulbs fit into categories (e.g., 60, 75, 100 watts) and into most sockets. Market-based products also have a constancy in that one pack of Marlboro Lights is basically the same as another pack. A box of Tide is the same across the country and stays the same until it reads "new and improved." This would imply that narcotics would be sold in known, set doses. This alone would greatly reduce or eliminate accidental overdoses of such drugs as heroin, a leading cause of drug-related deaths.

Consumers have better information about products in the free market than in black or regulated markets. Products are packaged and labeled. They are advertised. Information is given and certain claims are made that can be verified by consumers and other sources, such as *Consumer Reports* and Underwriters Laboratories.[44] Many products have directions and warnings posted on them and are backed up with warranties or guarantees. Advertising claims also act as a formal extension of producer liability so that narcotics advertised as "safe and effective" must be so when used as directed. Consumers, therefore, are much better informed about the products they consume from the free market than from black or regulated markets and are harmed less as a result.

The case of PowerMaster beer is instructive on this point. Heilman Brewery tried to introduce a new high-potency beer. The government, however, had established a prohibitionist-style regulation that breweries could not advertise or even list the potency on their products. To give some indication of the product's primary feature, Heilman decided to call the beer PowerMaster. The federal government balked and vetoed the use of the name because it would properly inform consumers. Later the surgeon general called for the establishment of a new regulation that would require all brewers to list the alcohol content of their products. Neither advertising regulation is optimal, of course, because the prohibition leads to not enough information and the requirement leads to too much. In a free market, companies advertise only the special or unique features of their products and do their best to bring that information to the attention of their potential customers.[45]

Most goods and services we buy in the market are backed by both the retailer and producer, creating a double fire wall between the consumer and unsafe products. Wal-Mart, for example, must be concerned with the value and safety of all the products it sells for fear that one bad product might hurt overall business and the reputation of the firm. Likewise, Proctor and Gamble must be concerned with every one of the products it sells and even who is retailing its products. McDonalds must be concerned with quality and service at each of its locations for fear of how safety and quality problems can reflect badly on each franchise of the whole corporation. For example, the reporting of a few overcharges and unnecessary repairs at some Sears automotive repair centers in California reduced business not only at the repair centers; it also adversely affected sales in the main stores and in stores throughout the region and nation.[46] This double level of risk aversion, especially among large corporations and franchise organizations, would ensure that dangerous narcotic products would not be readily available and would provide a strong signal for customers about safety and risk.[47]

The consumer is king in the free market and consumer sovereignty drives producers to meet consumer demands. Where entrepreneurs are free to do so, we find a stock and flow of product improvements that enhance safety. For example, cigarettes are now filtered and ultra-low tar brands are available at no extra cost.[48] In terms of alcohol, the market has responded with low alcohol, no alcohol, and light brands that have gained an increasing share of the market. Even with caffeine, the market has moved in the direction of reduced caffeine and caffeine-free products and caffeine substitutes. In black markets the tendency is toward more dangerous products and there is very little tendency toward product safety. Interventionist policies make matters worse. Heavy sin taxes encourage the consumption of higher potency and more dangerous brands, such as unfiltered cigarettes, fortified wines, and products from the black market. Perfect legalization would stimulate innovation in the direction of safety, such as low-dose and time-released brands of narcotics for those seeking maintenance treatment and gradual withdrawal treatments for addiction and abuse prevention.

Customers in the market also have legal remedies for their problems because suppliers can be held liable for the safety of their products. Wrongful death lawsuits can be brought against producers who sell unsafe products that result in death or debilitating injury. Fraud is a common occurrence in illegal drug markets but is relatively rare in free markets where producers can be successfully prosecuted for fraud. Customers can also sue for damages done willfully or negligently by the seller or under circumstances when strict liability applies. If the supplier breaches the contract in some other way, the customer can bring a civil suit. These legal protections work less effectively or not at all in government-regulated markets because firms are more immune from legal charges due to government grants of limited liability or their status as a government entity or for being in compliance with government regulations.[49] The important point is that the market encourages suppliers to reduce product risk, but in the black market consumer liability risk for sellers is low and the bulk of incentives drives suppliers toward more dangerous products.[50] Therefore, in a legalized market, producers would be producing and retailers would be selling products that were significantly safer and more reliable to use than those produced and sold in black markets.[51]

Legalization would also stimulate private prohibition and regulation. In contrast to government measures, which are very general and universally applicable, private controls target the tangible social problems with drugs, are effective in establishing control, provide the control in a cost-effective manner, and are flexible for changing conditions. Some firms even discovered that it was important to prohibit customers from entering their stores when, for example, they were not wearing shoes.[52] This rule could be for the aesthetic comfort of customers and employees, but it also recognizes the potential human danger and economic risk from broken glass.

A plethora of private prohibitions already exist and could easily and immediately be extended to cover narcotic drugs where necessary. Customers are prevented from smoking in certain restaurants and at most gasoline stations; they could also be prevented from smoking marijuana. Commercial drivers and pilots are restricted from consuming alcohol (long before government regulations); they could be prevented from consuming cocaine and other drugs. Families, churches, schools, civic groups, clubs, and employers all set and enforce certain rules and regulations on their members and provide incentives for good behavior. Such rules are targeted at social problems associated with drug abuse and many of these groups have programs to help individuals to deal with problems of drug abuse and addiction. Perfect legalization would allow these rules and programs to be fully extended to narcotics and would no doubt have beneficial effects for the drug abusers themselves. The greater the freedom, the more likely that entrepreneurs will discover new, private prohibitions and regulations that are uniquely suited for the problems associated with narcotics.

Drug testing and lie detector tests have greatly enhanced the role of private prohibitions in targeting the social problems of drug abuse. These monitoring devices bring a substantial economic cost to drug users and abusers because the surety of detection and punishment has been found to play a key role in deterrence. Employers can monitor the behavior of their employees—especially pilots, drivers, and machine operators—more effectively and at a low cost. Such monitoring can be made a condition of the labor contract and is therefore voluntary. However, because of the costs and potential unintended consequences of such monitoring, the government should neither encourage nor discourage such testing, but allow the market to decide where and how to use it.[53]

Regulation by insurance plays a major role in reducing risk in the market. Naturally, firms want to reduce their risks due to fire, employee injury, and product liability. They can make the workplace and product safer, obtain insurance, or risk losing everything. Insurance is costly, and to maximize their profits many firms will work to reduce risks for employees and customers to the economic minimum. Insurance providers are willing to work with firms to reduce such risks (and cut their rates) because they are in the business to pay as few claims as possible. This provides companies who specialize in the production of goods and services with direct access to companies who specialize in methods and techniques of risk reduction.

The experience of Chamberlain Contractors demonstrates the power of economic incentives to deal with drug abuse on the job. President Harold Green claimed that the company was paying $250,000 per year in insurance premiums before setting up a drug-testing program. The program cut the company's insurance cost by more than half, to $120,000, while the drug screening and counseling for his sixty employees cost about $10,000 per year. He considers it money well spent, stating, "That doesn't include the increased productivity, quality-control issues and all the other areas that aren't measurable. All it takes is one driver who is high to hit a school bus carrying 15 kids and I'm out of business for good."[54]

Understanding the power of these market mechanisms and private prohibitions eradicates the fantasy image of perfect legalization as a world lost in addiction and chaos. Those who suffer under prohibition would be helped, the overwhelming majority would benefit from reduced crime and better living standards, and a small number who profit politically and economically from prohibition would suffer a loss. For most people the establishment of perfect legalization would produce little noticeable change in their day-to-day life. Your city and stores would look the same. Your mortgage payment would not change, and you would have the same number of weeds in your yard.

The main effects would be quite localized and isolated. Inner-city ghettoes and public schools would be helped. Gangs would dissipate or have to find other prohibitions to finance their organizations. Products such as marijuana cigarettes and cocaine tonics would appear for sale. Heroin addicts could get their narcotics and clean needles at their local pharmacy, and over-the-counter products using marijuana, cocaine, and heroin would become available. The demand for alcohol would probably fall and specialized firms would develop for the consumption of drugs and for treatment and rehabilitation of addiction.

Although it is no panacea, legalization would be a boost for the economy. It would free up many improperly allocated resources from the prohibition bureaucracy, black market economy, and the nonviolent drug-law prisoners, thereby increasing the economic pie by the equivalent of adding over one million people to the labor force. Without any changes in the Tax Code, government revenue would increase and expenditures would decrease by tens of billions of dollars each.

The primary prohibited drugs have important "legitimate" uses that government prohibition generally prevents. Perfect legalization would ensure that all such uses were available and that new uses would be found. Heroin is a legitimate painkiller and medical product. In fact, before prohibition, heroin pills from Bayer were available and prescribed for babies. Cocaine is an important anesthetic and painkiller and was sold as a medicinal tonic by the Coca-Cola Company prior to prohibition.

Marijuana is one of the earliest known cultivated plants and can be used in a variety of product applications. The marijuana plant (hemp) has been grown for fiber that can be made into clothing, rope, and canvas. It has been grown for seed used as bird food, an oil used in paint and chemical products, and converted into a protein substitute. It can be grown for the psychoactive substance used to treat the pain and nausea caused by cancer and AIDS treatments. It is also an effective treatment for glaucoma and, before prohibition, was listed in medical texts as a component of a variety of medical treatments and preparations such as liniment. The ability to grow it in a wide variety of climates and soils without special fertilization and pesticides makes it an ideal product for underdeveloped economies and marginal farmland.

The most important and least understood reason for perfect legalization is the market's discovery process. This feature of the market involves the procedures for the discovery of new goods, improvements in existing goods, and new mechanisms to deal with existing problems via the profit motive. We often take this process for granted, but it is vital for improving our standard of living and it exists only in a market economy. Prohibition completely suppresses the market's discovery process and stimulates the black market's discovery process. Harm reduction, modified prohibition, and decriminalization all suppress the market's discovery process and stimulate the negative effects of the black market's discovery process.

Perfect legalization would result in many new, beneficial discoveries, some of which we have already speculated about, such as time-released narcotic pills, regulation by insurance, and new treatment methodologies for drug addiction. We cannot even imagine the full range of beneficial discoveries any more than someone at the beginning of this century could imagine computer technology and its full implications. Modified prohibition, including most current proposals for drug legalization, would severely hamper the market's discovery process and thereby stifle progress on the problems of drug addiction and drug abuse and increase the likelihood of a return to prohibition.

Entrepreneurs are at the heart of the market's discovery process. They have the incentive to solve our problems because it can result in profits for them. The entrepreneur searches for ways to provide the consumer with value at the lowest possible cost to himself. Profits (and losses) are the market's way of signaling the entrepreneur about consumers' demands concerning such things as new products, managerial techniques, and advertising strategies. Therefore, the market has a mechanism of generating new solutions and identifying the solutions that consumers actually value by a process of incentives and price signals. On the other hand, bureaucrats do not have the incentive to innovate and do not have a mechanism for separating good (i.e., socially efficient) discoveries from bad ones. In fact, it is not in the economic interest of bureaucrats to make discoveries that solve problems that would put them out of a job.[55]

THE PATH TO REAL REFORM

The only effective alternative to prohibition is perfect legalization. All other suggestions for reform retain extensive governmental authority and do not eliminate the problems of prohibition, nor do they effectively address the problems of drug abuse and addiction. The result is a prohibitionist regime that has remained intact and is stable from a long-term perspective.

The superiority of legal markets is supported by both theory and historical evidence. Even when applied to markets involving dangerous products and drugs, markets are superior to government control. And yet, even when this finding is conceded or acknowledged, it is often dismissed as politically impossible. Critics can argue persuasively that perfect legalization has no chance of being enacted. The bureaucrats will fight for their jobs, politicians would never give up this authority, the majority of voters would simply not permit it, and the overwhelming number of citizens just would not stand for such a drastic and radical change in public policy. Opinion polling can also be used to support this contention.

True. The general population does suffer from the inability to imagine a world of legal drugs as anything more than a chaotic nightmare. Given this ignorance, reformers argue for "legalization" or harm reduction policies that displace direct prohibition with something highly tangible, recognizable, and authoritative, such as government drugstores, clinics, heavy taxation, and prohibitions on selling to minors. If reformers can describe the tangible controls that will replace prohibition, their proposals might have a better chance of being accepted.

However, there are fundamental problems with any approach to constructing public policy and policy reform proposals based on a criterion of political acceptability rather than effectiveness. Drug policy experts are not experts on political acceptability and should probably not spend time trying to predict the future of politics. To the extent that political acceptability and effectiveness are incompatible, political success may result in professional and social failure. Many "reforms" that are politically feasible are counterproductive. Minimum wage laws and protectionist trade policies attest to the political popularity of irrational and counterproductive public policies.

The biggest stumbling block to the so-called moderate approach to public policy reform is that it is *not* truly politically acceptable. Citizens don't have much confidence in the ability of the post office to deliver the mail, and opinion polls indicate that the majority of Americans feel that government does the wrong thing most of the time. They surely cannot have much confidence in the ability of the government to dispense dangerous drugs or cure drug addiction. Americans have plenty of evidence that government prohibitions on sales to minors (as part of modified prohibition) are either ineffective or counterproductive. In other words, modified prohibition is politically feasible, but it is not viewed as a clear answer to the problems of prohibition and drug abuse.

To maximize their effectiveness, illegal drug experts should confine their recommendations to their own findings and areas of expertise. When experts do have policy-relevant training and expertise, then their policy recommendations should be made irrespective of political feasibility. Once an argument has been accepted or accepted with stipulations about short-term political feasibility, intermediate and transitional reforms that are both politically feasible and drive policy reform in the direction of the reform ultimately sought can begin to be examined.[56] For example, if perfect legalization of all drugs is not politically acceptable, then the suggestion might be that one drug be completely legalized while the others are made available by prescription and for "legitimate" purposes and that perfect legalization of the remaining drugs be undertaken in a period X number of months from now. These negotiations should come only after an extensive education process has led the public to accept the general recommendations for reform.

Advocating perfect drug legalization is an educational process in which new generations are immunized against the irrational ideology of prohibition. This process is a long and arduous one, but one that will work and might be hastened by real-world events and experience. All other approaches to reform will produce only fleeting victories, but will never win ultimate victory against prohibition.

THE POSSIBILITY OF PERFECT LEGALIZATION

The free market is the alternative to government control. This general proposition is more apparent and better understood around the world with the downfall of communism and the collapse of government economic planning, but is not yet understood when applied to dangerous drugs. The failure of advocates of legalization to advocate true or perfect legalization is a major barrier to reform. Substituting one form of government intervention for another does little to achieve public policy goals or to educate the public about ineffectiveness of prohibition. Therefore, we find the ironic circumstance that despite a growing volume of evidence against prohibition, the war on drugs is growing stronger and prohibition is gaining ground in other markets, such as alcohol and tobacco.

Perfect legalization will require a better understanding of its beneficial properties and the costs of prohibition. A crisis in prohibition is all but inevitable and the prospects for the spread of understanding of perfect legalization have improved. The drug legalization movement is composed increasingly of people who better understand the superiority of free markets over government allocation of resources. Milton Friedman, Gary Becker, and George Schultz are all prominent economists and advocates of legalization. William Buckley advocates legalization and has a better than average understanding of how markets work. The new illegal drug experts have a much better understanding of how black markets work and the most serious students of prohibition are vitally rewriting the case against the war on drugs.[57]

Once the movement toward perfect legalization has been achieved and is working for the good of society, the possibility of extending free market reform is greatly increased. The extended free market solution to drug abuse would involve restoring the status of property rights above those of "civil rights" and "entitlements." This solution would greatly enhance the market's ability to control problems of drug abuse because it would greatly increase the cost of drug abuse to drug abusers, thereby reducing the social cost and level of drug abuse.[58]

Perfect legalization is one part Cinderella and one part Scrooge and some readers are probably convinced that the author is writing from a drug-induced fantasy world. Others will no doubt recognize the shortcomings of the drug legalization movement and the fact that perfect legalization simply implies a different method of control that works better because it is based on individual self-interest and enforced by the profit motive. The truth is that successful reform does involve the willingness to be both cold-hearted and open-minded in the search for scientific knowledge. I am optimistic that a direct confrontation with the pragmatic ideals of perfect legalization will topple the ideology of prohibition and the policy regime of prohibition.

ENDNOTES

1. See Thornton 1995a for a review of alternative policies, the "free-market solution," the "extended free-market solution," and my "moral case for legalization."

2. Reformers and advocates tend to exaggerate the potential of their policy recommendations. I have often heard, for example, people advocating the legalization and taxation of marijuana to balance the federal budget. Economist Irving Fisher, a strong advocate of alcohol prohibition, claimed that the prosperity of the 1920s was due to alcohol prohibition, a fact he was at pains to explain after the stock market crash of 1929 and the ensuing economic depression.

3. Reformers are correct to suggest that minors are a key to the drug problem and its resolution. Unfortunately, the prohibitionist approach is highly counterproductive. See Note 16 for a discussion of minors and perfect legalization.

4. It is not the purpose of this volume or this chapter to marshal the evidence against prohibition and for legalization. In fact, my general methodology is based on the Austrian school of economics, which places empirical evidence in a separate and inferior category of knowledge compared to economic theory. For a more complete discussion see Thornton 1991a, Chapters 1, 3.

5. This chapter therefore answers both "how to" questions by providing an answer to the question of how do we get to drug policy reform and how to implement reform.

6. Although social scientists use cost-benefit analysis all the time, we must remember that costs and benefits are inherently individual and subjective concepts, and it is invalid to make interpersonal utility comparisons. You might even want to consider the costs and benefits as even more "subjective" (or more difficult to calculate) when analyzing concepts like addiction, death, and one's soul.

7. The decriminalization of marijuana is a clear case where reform made society better off, but opponents have been able to distort the results and stifle further reform. Marijuana decriminalization in the Netherlands has been successful but controversial, especially when the government has taken an activist approach rather than proceeding toward perfect legalization (see Jenifer Chao, "City Hall reluctantly gives drug dealers some competition," *Daily News* (Associated Press), September 4, 1996, p. 7b).

8. See Thornton 1994 for my review and critique of Mark Kleiman's *Against Excess: Drug Policy for Results*. Kleiman's proposals, which I dub the "Harvard Plan," are a hodgepodge of self-contradictory policies that are often based on faulty economic logic. While ostensively against excess, Kleiman calls for an intensification of policy efforts and increased budgets.

9. The latest piece of evidence of these failures has been changes in technology, including long-range radar and sophisticated X-ray machines. See "Heroin use rising, drug czar warns," *Montgomery Advertiser* (Gannett News Service), June 15, 1996, p. 6a.

10. It is important to note that not all forms of government intervention are necessarily "prohibitionist." For example, government-sponsored advertising of the scientific effects of drugs would not necessarily be classified as "prohibitionist" unless it was part of an antidrug propaganda program.

11. Achieving a harm reduction policy is like winning the battle but losing the war. It is a short-term victory that neither addresses the underlying problems nor progresses to true legalization. Usually the prohibition returns.

12. See Thornton 1996a, in which I show where the prohibitionist ideology comes from and how it has developed in America over time. I also show how the policy positions of prohibition have developed over time, and how their policy of opportunity has strengthened prohibition in America over time. In terms of the strength and secularization of modern prohibition Philip Jenkins (1994) has noted that "future historians will certainly regard Neo-Puritanism as a hallmark of the times in which we are presently living. However, they will also be struck by the paradox of this particular outbreak in public righteousness, which differs from its predecessors in its conspicuous lack of overtly moral or religious foundation—which is not to say that the underlying agenda may not reflect religious assumptions" (p. 40).

13. See Harrison 1936 for more details about the diversity of policies that existed after the repeal of alcohol prohibition and the problems with many of those policies.

14. See Thornton 1996b in which this political choice model is developed in greater detail. For a more general description of this process of progressive, or increasing, government intervention see Thornton 1991a, Chapter 3, and McKie 1970.

15. For a good description of "modified prohibition" see Ely 1888. Ely was an economist and a big advocate of prohibitionism—modified prohibition in particular, and big government in general.

16. Perfect legalization would have no prohibition or government regulation of the sale to minors. Of course, such sales to minors would not be binding on the minors, and would impose extra liability and risk on the sellers, who would therefore have to self-regulate their own sales. Parents would be the legal guardians of their children and be responsible for their behavior. Many countries, such as France, do not have prohibitions on the sale of alcohol to minors but do not have substantial social problems with alcohol abuse by youth. Without commenting on the exact nature of the cause and effect, it does appear that countries with the age prohibitions actually have much worse problems with alcohol abuse among minors. Even if cultural differences explain this result, it would be hard to argue against the notion that such cultural differences are in large part the result of the parental and proprietor responsibility under perfect legalization.

17. There is an extensive literature on the problems of the FDA's regulation of new drugs. After reviewing this literature in light of economic analysis, Robert Higgs concluded:

> Banning a product can never improve the well-being of consumers properly understood, that is, understood as individual consumers' prospective and subjective utility. This proposition remains valid even when risk is incorporated into the analysis. Risk of inefficacy or adverse side effects is simply another dimension of each good, like taste, size, or location, about which the consumer has preferences. Government restrictions have the same effect on consumer welfare regardless of the dimension of the good that is restricted; in this regard there is nothing special about risk. [1994, pp. 17–18]

With regard to organ transplants and government provision of kidney dialysis services see Barnett et al. 1993, 1996, Barnett and Kaserman 1991, 1993, and Barnett et al. 1992.

18. Production in the black market is not constrained by market forces and tends to be much more dangerous to consume (see Thornton 1991a, Chapter 4a,b). On the smuggling of cigarettes into Canada in reaction to higher excise taxes, see "Smuggled smokes," *Forbes*, December 7, 1992 pp. 47, 48, and "Canada getting tough on cigarette smuggling," *Washington Post*, February 2, 1994, A, 14:5. To see the same progressive effects from the new sin tax on freon, see "A black market in coolants," *New York Times*, October 26, 1994, A, 22:4; "Freon smugglers find big market," *New York Times*, April 3, 1995, 1:5; "Rising illegal imports of CFCs slow effort to protect ozone layer," *Washington Post*, January 26, 1996, D, 1:1; and "Black market is thriving in CFCs," *Boston Globe*, January 1, 1996, 48:2.

19. The history of prohibitions is replete with such counterproductive substitutions. Teenagers have turned to dropping LSD and inhaling chemical aerosols because of reduced access to alcohol and marijuana. On the effects of one of the more recent such substitutions, see Riedel 1995 for the case of inhaling of aerosol paint propellants to get high.

20. See Wilkinson 1987 and Asch and Levy 1990 on the ineffectiveness of minimum-age drinking laws that can be interpreted not just as ineffective but as counterproductive because they tend to reduce or delay teenage drinking experience. See Thornton 1991a, Chapter 4, for how excise taxes promote higher-potency beer and nonfiltered cigarettes. Modified prohibition tends to promote binge drinking and to discourage controlled and moderate consumption patterns.

21. See Odegard 1966 and Thornton 1996a, 1997.

22. See Thornton 1996a.

23. See Thornton 1997. This general approach to politicians seeking reelection is based on the economic approach to politics or public choice perspective.

24. In economics, the market demand for these products is price inelastic. We expect the tax revenue-maximizing politician to raise the excise tax to a level that maximizes tax revenues. In a lecture at Auburn University, a member of Alabama's Alcohol Beverage Control Board stated that its purpose was to reduce consumption, but upon further questioning admitted that the tax rate was designed to maximize revenue, not to minimize alcohol sales.

25. The sale of draft beer was illegal in Lee County, Alabama, while the sale of bottles and cans was legal. One justification for the ban was that the sale of draft beer was more difficult to monitor and tax than the sale of bottles and cans because of cheating and the spillage factor with kegs. However, when kegs began to be imported illegally (due both to their lack of local availability and a lower beer tax in surrounding tax jurisdictions), the county legalized keg sales in 1983 in order to capture some of the revenue that was "spilling" over into other tax jurisdictions.

26. The important exception to this is the confiscation of property associated with illegal drug sales via a loose asset forfeiture law such as the Comprehensive Crime Act of 1984. The revenue incentive of confiscating property has resulted in large revenue increases and higher property crime rates in the jurisdiction that actively pursues this revenue source (see Benson et al. 1995).

27. See Yandle 1983, 1989.

28. See, for example, Rasmussen and Benson 1994, Chapters 6 and 7.

29. See Boudreaux and Pritchard 1994 for a demonstration of how tax revenues influenced these decisions. Also see Weise 1998, who shows that the property tax revolts in several major cities were quickly quelled after Prohibition was repealed in 1933 as the cities could again rely on alcohol tax and license revenues rather than on just property taxes.

30. Between 1976 and 1996 the number of states with casino gambling increased from two to twenty-four (1100% ↑) and the number of states with lotteries increased from thirteen to thirty-seven (185% ↑). "As gambling fever spreads, industry deserves a look," *USA Today*, June 18, 1996, p. 12a.

31. Jackson et al. (1994) show the rational economic process that led state legislators to the benefits of adopting state-run lotteries.

32. See "The Potential Economic Impact of Casino Gambling and a State Lottery in Alabama," prepared by the University of Alabama at Birmingham Research Foundation, for a detailed example of all of the typical government interventions.

33. I strongly suspect that the Food and Drug Administration is trying to establish a prohibition of tobacco by establishing new regulatory authority (see Thornton 1995b).

34. See Thornton (1991a, Chapter 5, and 1991b), in which the crime wave of the 1920s and the crime wave beginning in the 1960s is attributed to prohibition policies.

35. See Sollars et al. 1994.

36. See, for example, Rasmussen and Benson 1994.

37. See Thornton 1991a, Chapter 5, and Nadelmann 1988 on corruption.

38. We must also recognize that individuals might might make and consume some highly dangerous products that are not available on the market. This behavior, however, would be a highly isolated phenomenon.

39. The notion of many social scientists that drugs cause crime is derived from the Puritan notion that alcohol and other products cause sin. While cause and effect are sometimes difficult to disentangle, the evidence does not support the Puritanical approach (see Chaiken and Chaiken 1990 and Fagen 1990). In terms of drug use and social problem like crime, James Q. Wilson (1990, p. 521) concludes that "there is no reason to believe that vigorously enforcing the drug laws will achieve any of these goals and many reasons to think that they may make matters worse."

40. Rasmussen and Benson (1994) model our criminal justice system as a common property resource that anyone can use at a low additional cost. The tregedy of the commons occurs because such resources get so overused that their value to society falls to practically zero. Rasmussen and Benson show that the war on drugs is such a catalyst for the overuse of the criminal justice system.

41. Again, see Thornton 1991a and b for the dramatic fall in crime associated with the repeal of alcohol prohibition. Also see Levitt 1996; Levitt estimates that an additional burglary arrest will deter two additional burglaries. Combining the elimination of prohibition-related crime with the reduction in crime resulting from reallocating law enforcement and the resulting deterrence, we could conservatively estimate a 75 percent reduction in the number of crimes committed.

42. Many of course have a very well-developed knowledge of how illegal markets operate, but this actually seems to cloud their understanding of how legal markets would work after reform.

43. Jeffrey Sacks, a leading mainstream economist from Harvard University, was hired as one of the leading advisors for the former Soviet Union. His advice was to free up prices and let the price system work out all the problems without first providing for private property rights, stable money, and a system of adjudicating disputes that are so necessary for a properly functioning market economy.

44. See Thornton 1996c.

45. See Thornton 1991c.

46. See Denise Gellene, "Sears car repair shops come under fire in N.J.," Los Angeles Times, June 16, 1992, p. d2, 3, and Yin Tung, "Sears is accused of billing fraud at auto centers," Wall Street Journal, June 12, 1992, p. b1, 6.

47. See Ault and Ekelund 1991 and Boudreaux and Ekelund 1988 on market-based methods of how producers and wholesalers organize to provide for the maintenance of product quality.

48. The market has also produced nicotine substitutes to help people quit smoking altogether and has produced a smokefree cigarette that the government prevented the sale of. It should be pointed out that, in countries with high excise taxes or bans on advertising, we have not seen the switch to filtered, low tar, and ultra-low tar brands.

49. For example, the federal government limits the liability of firms such as airlines and nuclear power plant operators so that there is a limit on damages from a plane crash or a nuclear power plant disaster. This leads to a suboptimal amount of resources devoted to safety and more accidents.

50. As the lawsuits against tobacco companies illustrate, those who deal in dangerous goods face risk themselves and that risk is expensive even when they win the lawsuits.

51. It is true that suicidal drug abusers still might seek out or make dangerous concoctions, but these products could not compete successfully against products that are inexpensive, readily available, and relatively safe.

52. Other firms prohibit customers who are too young, too old, too short, pregnant, intoxicated, or smoking cigarettes or who have a heart condition.

53. Government-mandated tests can crowd out testing for certain drugs because an employer might be unwilling to pay the cost of two complete sets of drug tests (the mandated set and the desired set). Government prohibitions or restrictions on testing would also be detrimental to the effectiveness of these devices.

54. "Perspective: just say no," *Investor's Business Daily*, August 30, 1996, p. 1b.

55. This is a slight variation on the well-known lack of bureaucratic incentives to economize on their budgets. Bureaucrats (i.e., people who work in government) are generally modeled as budget maximizers and we might extend this to model them as problem maximizers.

56. This approach is recommended by W. H. Hutt (1971).

57. Ethan Nadelmann, John Morgan, and Sam Staley would be examples of the "new illegal drug law experts."

58. This extended free market solution has many applications; one important example will suffice to show the "cold-hearted" superiority of a property rights approach over the civil rights approach in dealing with drug abuse. A property rights regime would end government health care subsidies and mandates to treat everyone at public expense. This approach would end government welfare for drug addicts so that addicts and abusers would have to become more self-reliant or dependent on private charity. The combination of self-responsibility and increased opportunity in a property rights regime would be a great disincentive to drug abuse and would greatly reduce the social problems associated with it.

REFERENCES

Asch, P., and Levy, D. T. (1990). Young driver fatalities: the roles of drinking age and drinking experience. *Southern Economic Journal*, vol. 57, No. 2 (October), pp. 512–520.

Ault, R. W., and Ekelund Jr., R. B. (1991). *The economic consequences of transshipping, quantity discounts, and "mix and match" strategies in Indiana beer marketing.* Unpublished manuscript.

Barnett, A. H., Beard, T. R., and Kaserman, D. L. (1993). Inefficient pricing can kill: the case of regulation in the dialysis industry. *Southern Economic Journal* (October), pp. 393–404.

——— (1996). Scope, learning, and cross-subsidy: organ transplants in a multi-division hospital—an Extension. *Southern Economic Journal* (January), pp. 760–767.

Barnett, A. H., Blair, R. D., and Kaserman, D. (1992). Improving organ donation: compensation versus markets. *Inquiry* (Fall), pp. 372–378.

Barnett, A. H., and Kaserman, D. (1991). An economic analysis of transplant organs: a comment and extension. *Atlantic Economic Journal* (June), pp. 57–63.

——— (1993). The shortage of organs for transplantation: exploring the alternatives. *Issues in Law & Medicine* (Fall), pp. 117–137.

Benson, B. L., Rasmussen, D. W., and Sollars, D. L. (1995). Police bureaucracies, their incentives, and the war on drugs. *Public Choice*, vol. 83, No. 1–2 (April), pp. 21–45.

Boudreaux, D. J., and Ekelund Jr., R. B. (1988). Inframarginal consumers and the per se legality of vertical restraints. *Hofstra Law Review* (Fall), pp. 137–158.

Boudreaux, D. J., and Pritchard, A. C. (1994). The price of prohibition. *Arizona Law Review*, vol. 36, No. 1 (Spring), pp. 1–10.

Chaiken, J. M., and Chaiken, M. R. (1990). Drugs and predatory crime. In *Drugs and Crime*, ed. M. Tonry and J. Q. Wilson, pp. 203–240. Chicago: University of Chicago Press.

Ely, R. T. (1888). *Taxation in American States and Cities.* New York: Crowell.

Fagan, J. (1990). Intoxication and aggression. In *Drugs and Crime*, ed. M. Tonry and J. Q. Wilson, pp. 241–320. Chicago: University of Chicago Press.

Harrison, L. V. (1936). *After Repeal: A Study of Liquor Control Administration.* New York: Harper.

Higgs, R. (1994). Banning a risky product cannot improve any consumer's welfare (properly understood), with applications to FDA testing requirements. *Review of Austrian Economics*, vol. 7, No. 2, pp. 3–20.

Hutt, W. H. (1971). *Politically Impossible . . . ?* London: Institute of Economic Affairs.

Jackson, J. D., Saurman, D. S., and Shughart, W. F. (1994). Instant winners: legal change in transition and the diffusion of state lotteries. *Public Choice*, vol. 80, pp. 245–263.

Jenkins, P. (1994). The Puritanism that dare not speak its name. *Chronicles*, vol. 18, No. 7 (July), pp. 20–23.

Levitt, S. D. (1996). Why do increased arrest rates appear to reduce crime: deterrence, incapacitation, or measurement error? Working Paper 5268, National Bureau of Economic Research.

McKie, J. W. (1970). Regulation and the free market: the problem of boundaries. *Bell Journal of Economics and Management Science*, vol. 1, No. 1 (Spring), pp. 6–26.

Nadelmann, E. A. (1988). U.S. drug policy: a bad export. *Foreign Policy*, No. 70 (Spring), pp. 83–108.

Odegard, P. H. (1928). *Pressure Politics: The Story of the Anti-Saloon League.* New York: Octagon, 1966.

Rasmussen, D. W., and Benson, B. L. (1994). *The Economic Anatomy of a Drug War: Criminal Justice in the Commons.* Lanham, MD: Rowman and Littlefield.

Riedel, S. (1995). Inhalants: a growing health concern. *Behavioral Health Management*, vol. 15 (May/June), pp. 28–30.

Sollars, D. L., Benson, B. L., and Rasmussen, D. W. (1994). Drug enforcement and deterrence of property crime among local jurisdictions. *Public Finance Quarterly*, vol. 22 (1994), pp. 22–45.

Thornton, M. (1991a). *The Economics of Prohibition.* Salt Lake City, UT: University of Utah Press.

———— (1991b). *Alcohol Prohibition Was a Failure.* Washington, DC: Cato Institute Policy Analysis.

———— (1991c). What's brewing with powermaster. *Free Market*, vol. 9, No. 8 (August), pp. 7–8.

———— (1994). The Harvard plan for drugs. (A review of *Against Excess: Drug Policy for Results*, by M. A. R. Kleiman, New York: Basic Books, 1992.) *Review of Austrian Economics*, vol. 7, No. 1 pp. 147–150.

———— (1995a). The repeal of prohibitionism. In *Liberty for the 21st Century: Contemporary Libertarian Thought*, ed. T. R. Machan and D. R. Rasmussen, pp. 187–204. Lanham, MD: Rowman & Littlefield.

———— (1995b). Are cigarettes doomed? *Free Market*, vol. 13, No. 10 (October), pp. 1, 7–8.

———— (1996a). The fall and rise of puritanical policy in America. *Journal of Libertarian Studies*, vol. 12, No. 1 (Spring), pp. 143–160.

———— (1996b). The market for safety. *Free Market*, vol. 14, No. 3 (March), pp. 1–7.

———— (1997). Prohibition: the ultimate tax. In *Taxing Choice: The Political Economy of Fiscal*

Discrimination, ed. W. F. Shughart II, pp. 171–195. New Brunswick, NJ: Transaction Publishers.

Weise, C. (1998). Prohibition, public choice, and propaganda. Master's thesis in progress. Auburn University, Auburn, AL.

Wilkinson, J. T. (1987). Reducing drunken driving: which policies are most effective? *Southern Economic Journal*, vol. 54, No. 2 (October), pp. 322–334.

Wilson, J. Q. (1990). Drugs and crime. In *Drugs and Crime*, ed. M. Tonry and J. Q. Wilson, pp. 521–545. Chicago: University of Chicago Press.

Yandle, B. (1983). Bootleggers and baptists: the education of a regulatory economist. *Regulation*, vol. 7, pp. 12–16.

———— (1989). *The Political Limits of Environmental Regulation*. New York: Quorum Books.

Credits

Where chapter authors have made use of their previous work, they so indicated in a footnote or otherwise. The following three chapters merit special mention, and permission to use them is gratefully acknowledged.

Chapter 4, "Discontinous Change and the War on Drugs," by Jefferson M. Fish, appeared in a slightly different form in *The Humanist*, 1994, (54)5:14–17.

Chapter 10, "The Transition from Prohibition to Regulation: Lessons from Alcohol Policy for Drug Policy," by Harry G. Levine and Craig Reinarman, is a revised and updated form of their article "From Prohibition to Regulation: Lessons from Alcohol Policy for Drug Policy," which appeared in the *Milbank Quarterly*, 1991, 69(3):461–494.

Chapter 24, "Thinking Seriously about Alternatives to Drug Prohibition," by Ethan A. Nadelmann, appeared originally in *Daedalus*, 1992, 121(3):85–132.

Index